Financial Remedies Handbook

Thirteenth Edition

Roger Bird
Former District Judge

Sophie Harrison
District Judge, Reading County Court and Family Court Hearing Centre

LexisNexis® UK & Worldwide

United Kingdom	RELX (UK) Limited trading as LexisNexis®, 1–3 Strand, London WC2N 5JR
LNUK Global Partners	LexisNexis® encompasses authoritative legal publishing brands dating back to the 19th century including: Butterworths® in the United Kingdom, Canada and the Asia-Pacific region; Les Editions du Juris Classeur in France; and Matthew Bender® worldwide. Details of LexisNexis® locations worldwide can be found at www.lexisnexis.com

© 2021 RELX (UK) Ltd.
Published by LexisNexis®

ISBN 978-1-7847-3479-4

9 781784 734794

ISBN for this volume: 9781784734794

Printed and bound by Hobbs the Printers, Hampshire SO40 3WX

Visit LexisNexis at http://www.lexisnexis.co.uk

Foreword to First Edition

Within the wider field of family law the comparative importance of ancillary relief is not always recognised. I am in no doubt that there is a ready market for a practitioners' handbook, and who better to write one than Roger Bird. There can be few, if any, district judges who have greater experience of the work in court. Furthermore, he has been an invaluable member of the Lord Chancellor's Ancillary Relief Advisory Group almost since its inception. He is, thus, extremely well informed on policy issues and the perceived weaknesses in the existing law and practice. His concluding chapter, 'A Summing Up', well illustrates Roger's virtues. It is so succinct that it challenges the reader to detect some deficiency. But he will search in vain. It is refreshingly practical and it is the product of original and reflective writing.

I am confident that significant changes in law and practice are imminent. So it is easy to predict that the ancillary relief handbook will be for Roger a demanding creation.

The Rt Hon Lord Justice Thorpe
October 1998

Preface to the Thirteenth Edition

Over the last year the lives of everyone have been overshadowed by the Coronavirus and its malign effects, and family lawyers have not escaped these misfortunes. Readers will not need reminding of the difficulties involved in interviewing clients and dealing with other parties while working from home, still less of presenting a case to the court by way of the Cloud Video Platform or other digital methods. The burden on judges and the courts has been equally exacting and one can only hope that some degree of normality will return in the foreseeable future.

In the meantime the higher courts have produced their usual series of interesting points which must be noted and which we have tried to record here. The Financial Remedies Court is now up and running nationwide but Government initiatives have been noted by their absence which is not surprising given the pandemic and the Parliamentary paralysis caused by the Brexit legislation; in a related field the Domestic Abuse Bill, which was confidently predicted to be on the statute book, received Royal Assent only two days ago.

As always, the comments of readers will be welcomed. The law is as at the date given below.

Roger Bird
1 May 2021

Contents

Foreword to First Edition   v

Preface to the Thirteenth Edition   vi

Table of Abbreviations   xxiii

Table of Statutes   xxv

Table of Statutory Instruments   xxix

Table of European Material   xxxiii

Table of Cases   xxxv

Chapter 1   Introduction to Financial Remedies

Scope of this chapter   1.1

Definitions   1.5

The principles governing the exercise of the court's discretion   1.8

Equality and fairness   1.13

    White v White   1.17

    Miller and *McFarlane*   1.21

        White v White re-affirmed   1.22

        Legitimate expectations and standard of living   1.25

        Application to smaller money cases   1.27

    Charman v Charman   1.32

    Case law since *Charman*   1.34

        Equality and periodical payments   1.43

Compensation   1.44

All the circumstances of the case   1.48

First consideration the welfare of children   1.52

No one factor more important than others   1.55

Financial resources   1.61

    The duty of full disclosure   1.67

Contents

Income and earning capacity	1.71
Earning potential	1.73
Property	1.74
Dissipated assets	1.88
Expectations	1.90
Financial needs, obligations and responsibilities	1.98
Standard of living during marriage	1.104
Ages of parties and duration of marriage	1.108
Duration of marriage: short marriage	1.110
Pre-*Miller/McFarlane* cases	1.113
Miller/McFarlane guidance	1.123
Disability	1.131
Contributions	1.132
Financial contributions	1.133
Exceptional contributions	1.141
Non-marital contributions	1.148
Post-separation accruals	1.157
Non-financial contributions	1.166
Future contributions	1.173
Conduct	1.175
Financial conduct	1.176
Non-financial conduct	1.181
Conduct in the course of the proceedings	1.187
Lost benefits	1.193
Agreements	1.199
Radmacher v Granatino	1.202
The general approach to agreements	1.207
Vitiating factors	1.209
The foreign element	1.211
Fairness	1.212
Case law since *Radmacher*	1.216
Agreements to compromise litigation	1.236
Self-sufficiency	1.241

Guidelines in children orders cases   **1.244**

When may orders be made?   **1.245**

    Jurisdiction   **1.247**

Chapter 2   Periodical Payments

Introduction   **2.1**

Definitions   **2.3**

Who may apply?   **2.5**

Procedure   **2.6**

General principles   **2.7**

How does the court make its orders?   **2.9**

    Should there be an order at all?   **2.10**

       Earning capacity/potential   **2.12**

       Cohabitation   **2.13**

       Conduct   **2.19**

       Length of marriage   **2.20**

    What should be the amount of the order?   **2.21**

       Periodical payments after *Miller/McFarlane*   **2.34**

    Should the order be limited in duration?   **2.53**

Maintenance pending suit   **2.55**

Legal services orders   **2.61**

Form of order   **2.67**

Tax considerations   **2.69**

The clean break

    Introduction   **2.70**

    Statutory provisions   **2.72**

    Summary of statutory provisions   **2.76**

    Judicial guidance as to when a clean break is appropriate   **2.77**

    Should there be an immediate clean break?   **2.79**

    Summary   **2.93**

    The clean break on variation   **2.99**

    Direction under the Inheritance (Provision for Family and Dependants) Act 1975   **2.100**

    Extension of terms   **2.103**

Contents

Chapter 3   Secured Periodical Payments

Introduction   3.1

Statutory provisions   3.3

Nature of the order   3.5

    Secure   3.6

    The term   3.7

    The amount to be secured   3.9

    The security   3.10

When will such an order be made?   3.15

Variation and amendment   3.18

Chapter 4   Lump Sum Orders

Introduction   4.1

Statutory provision   4.4

Number of lump sums   4.5

How are lump sum orders calculated?   4.14

    Cases where assets do not exceed needs   4.18

Big money cases   4.19

    The millionaire's defence   4.22

    The *Duxbury* fund   4.24

Business cases   4.31

Tax considerations   4.53

Chapter 5   Transfer of Property Orders and Housing Needs

Introduction   5.1

Statutory provision   5.5

Rules   5.10

The basis on which orders are made   5.11

Types of transfer of property orders   5.17

    Outright transfer   5.19

    Transfer subject to charge   5.25

    Mesher orders   5.29

    Martin orders   5.37

    Other orders   5.39

Transfer of tenancy   5.41

Chapter 6   Settlement of Property Orders and Variation of Settlements

Introduction   **6.1**

Statutory provision   **6.2**

What is a settlement?   **6.4**

Variation of settlement   **6.7**

Chapter 7   Orders for Sale

Introduction   **7.1**

Order for sale under section 24A of MCA 1973   **7.2**

    How is jurisdiction exercised?   **7.12**

    Interim orders   **7.13**

    FPR 2010, rule 9.24   **7.14**

The Trusts of Land and Appointment of Trustees Act 1996   **7.16**

Chapter 8   Avoidance of Disposition and Other Injunctions

Introduction   **8.1**

Applications under section 37 of MCA 1973 for an avoidance of disposition order   **8.4**

    Two types of remedy   **8.7**

    The requirement for an application for a financial remedy **8.9**

    Only the applicant can apply   **8.12**

    What is a 'disposition'?   **8.13**

    'With the intention of defeating the claim for financial relief'   **8.14**

    Special considerations in applications to set aside dispositions **8.19**

    Reviewable dispositions   **8.20**

    Presumption of intention to defeat claim in some cases   **8.23**

    Consequential directions   **8.25**

    How will the court exercise its discretion?   **8.26**

    Foreign property   **8.30**

    Procedure   **8.31**

    Forms   **8.36**

Applications for avoidance of disposition under the inherent jurisdiction of the court   **8.37**

Freezing injunctions   **8.42**

Search orders   **8.48**

Contents

Chapter 9   Consent Orders

Introduction   9.1

The duty of the court   9.4

Information required by the court   9.9

Exceptions to the general rule   9.13

Notes on drafting consent orders   9.16

   The distinction between matters which may be ordered and
   those which may not   9.17

       Recitals of fact   9.20

       Recitals of agreement   9.21

       Undertakings   9.24

   Dismissal of claims and clean break orders   9.31

   Some common faults   9.32

Forms   9.34

Chapter 10   Pensions

Introduction   10.1

   What is a pension: income or capital?   10.5

How did we get to where we are now? A short history of
pensions on divorce   10.6

The orders available to the court   10.11

Types of pension   10.12

   State pensions   10.17

Valuation   10.21

What are you trying to achieve?   10.26

Expert evidence   10.31

   When should an expert be instructed?   10.32

   What type of expert should be instructed?   10.36

   How to instruct the expert   10.38

Pension sharing in detail   10.41

   Sharing state pension rights   10.44

   Restrictions on pension sharing   10.47

   Potential disadvantages of pension sharing   10.48

   Making and implementing the pension sharing order   10.52

   'Reverse' pension sharing   10.59

Pension attachment in detail   **10.61**

    Disadvantages of pension attachment   **10.64**

    When might pension attachment still be useful?   **10.66**

    Restrictions on pension attachment   **10.68**

    Making and implementing the pension attachment order   **10.69**

Pension offsetting   **10.70**

The section 25 exercise   **10.81**

    Discounting for pre-marital pension contributions?   **10.82**

    Discounting for post-marital pension contributions?   **10.83**

    Health issues   **10.84**

The Pension Protection Fund   **10.86**

International issues   **10.91**

    Pension orders against pensions in other jurisdictions   **10.92**

    Pension orders following an overseas divorce   **10.93**

Variation   **10.94**

Enforcement and pension orders   **10.96**

Same sex relationships   **10.98**

Bankrupt spouses and pensions   **10.99**

Chapter 11   Children

Introduction   **11.1**

The Child Support Act 1991   **11.3**

    Basic principles of the formula   **11.6**

When may applications be made to the court?   **11.17**

    (a) Cases where the Secretary of State does not have jurisdiction   **11.18**

    (b) Applications to the court permitted by the Act   **11.19**

    (c) Certain consent orders   **11.20**

    (d) Capital orders   **11.21**

    (e) Applications under 'transitional provisions'   **11.22**

    (f) Variation and duration of orders   **11.23**

Applications to the court   **11.24**

    Jurisdiction   **11.26**

    Age limits   **11.27**

    Principles on which the court exercises its jurisdiction   **11.32**

Contents

Periodic orders for children	11.34
Capital provision for children	11.40
School fees	11.46
Interim applications	11.48

Chapter 12   Insolvency and Rights of Creditors

Introduction	12.1
The Insolvency Act 1986 and sale of the matrimonial home	12.2
Effect of bankruptcy on order for financial relief	12.13
Property adjustment orders	12.16
Lump sum orders	12.24
Periodical payments orders	12.32
The rights of third-party creditors	12.35

Chapter 13   Variation

Introduction	13.1
Statutory provisions	
What orders can be varied?	13.3
Capital orders	13.7
Maintenance pending suit and periodical payments	13.9
Secured periodical payments	13.14
Lump sum payable by instalments	13.15
Provision in respect of pension rights	13.16
Settlement of property or variation of settlement	13.19
'Variation' of undertakings	13.21
The principles on which the court exercises its discretion	13.22
The clean break on variation applications	13.26
Changes in circumstances	13.28
Procedure	13.35
Forms of order	13.36
Variation subject to conditions	13.37

Chapter 14   Miscellaneous Applications

Introduction	14.1
Applications under MCA 1973, section 27	14.2
Applications under MCA 1973, section 10(2)	14.10

Orders for alteration of agreements during lifetimes of parties   **14.19**

Chapter 15   Financial Relief after Overseas Divorce

Introduction   **15.1**

Jurisdiction   **15.2**

Applications for permission   **15.6**

Orders which may be made   **15.14**

Chapter 16   Procedure

Introduction   **16.1**

Issue of proceedings   **16.4**

The overriding objective   **16.7**

Issuing the application

     Mediation Information and Assessment Meetings   **16.8**

     Where to issue Form A   **16.9**

     Delay in making the application   **16.10**

Service and parties   **16.13**

     Service on third parties   **16.14**

     Joinder of parties   **16.15**

Special rules relating to pensions   **16.18**

Filing of evidence   **16.19**

Other documents to be served   **16.22**

The statement of apparent issues   **16.23**

Questionnaires and requests for documents   **16.25**

The first appointment   **16.27**

Expert evidence   **16.32**

The financial dispute resolution hearing   **16.36**

The final hearing   **16.44**

Procedure on drafting and submitting the order   **16.46**

Transparency in final hearings   **16.49**

Disclosure orders against third parties   **16.50**

Interim orders

     Interim income orders   **16.53**

     Interim capital orders   **16.54**

     Other interim orders   **16.55**

Contents

The 'fast-track' procedure   16.56

The PD9A protocol   16.58

Court bundles   16.59

Litigants in person   16.60

Communicating with the court   16.61

Relief from sanctions   16.62

Chapter 17   Costs and Funding

Introduction   17.1

Costs: the starting point   17.5

Costs: the 'general rule' and the 'clean sheet'   17.6

    The general rule   17.7

    The clean sheet   17.17

Costs: practical issues

    Informing the client about costs   17.21

    How to make a claim for costs   17.24

    Quantifying costs   17.26

    Paying costs   17.29

Costs: protecting the client's position   17.31

Costs: future developments   17.34

Costs: orders against non-parties and lawyers   17.38

Costs on appeal   17.41

Funding   17.43

Chapter 18   Appeals and Setting Aside

Introduction   18.1

Permission required   18.3

Time limits   18.10

Routes of appeal   18.13

Contents of notice   18.14

Powers of appellate court   18.15

Material omissions   18.21

Procedure   18.23

Applications to set aside consent orders   18.24

    Non-disclosure, fraud and misrepresentation   18.29

New or supervening circumstances   18.44

   (1) Disputes as to the value of an asset   18.47

   (2) Remarriage or cohabitation   18.53

   (3) Death   18.56

   (4) Other matters   18.61

Appeal or setting aside?   18.67

Procedure on rehearing   18.70

Chapter 19   Enforcement

Introduction   19.1

Applications for enforcement by 'such means as the court may
consider appropriate'   19.3

Applications for particular enforcement remedies for the payment of money   19.7

   Attachment of earnings   19.8

   Third party debt orders   19.14

   Charging orders   19.17

   Warrants of control   19.21

   Orders to obtain information from judgment debtors   19.24

Judgment summons   19.25

Orders for sale of property and obtaining vacant possession of
land   19.32

Other useful enforcement options

   Execution of documents by a third party such as a judge   19.37

   Committal for contempt of court   19.39

   Surrender of passport   19.41

   '*Hadkinson*' orders   19.42

   Adjourning an aspect of financial provision and adjusting
   subsequent provision in the event of non-compliance with
   another part of the order   19.45

   Means of payment order   19.46

   Undertakings   19.47

   Bankruptcy   19.48

   Receivership and freezing injunctions   19.50

   Registering a maintenance order in the magistrates' court   19.52

Inter-relationship of enforcement and variation   19.53

Contents

Reciprocal enforcement of cross-border orders 19.56

Enforcement against crypto-assets 19.57

Future reform? 19.58

Chapter 20 The Impact of the Human Rights Act 1998

Introduction 20.1

A very brief overview of the HRA 1998 20.3

The effect of the HRA 1998 in practice: some highlights 20.7

Chapter 21 The Proceeds of Crime Act 2002, Money Laundering and Criminal Property

Introduction 21.1

Anti-money laundering regulations 21.3

Criminal offences under POCA 2002 and reporting to the National Crime Agency and HMRC 21.6

Tax fraud and disclosure to HMRC 21.7

Criminal offences under POCA 2002 21.9

Criminal property 21.12

Chapter 22 Non-Court Dispute Resolution, Arbitration and 'Private FDRs'

Introduction 22.1

Mediation 22.2

Collaborative law 22.7

Arbitration 22.8

Applying for an order to reflect the award, by consent 22.12

Challenge to the arbitrator's award 22.13

Private FDRs 22.19

Chapter 23 Future Developments

Introduction 23.1

Reform of MCA 1973, section 25 23.2

Enforcement 23.12

The Family Justice Review 23.15

The European element 23.16

Procedure 23.17

Chapter 24 A Summing Up

Introduction 24.1

The primacy of the statute 24.3

The importance of finding the facts   24.5

No mathematical starting point   24.7

Reasonable needs and ability to provide   24.8

The importance of housing   24.9

No redistribution for its own sake   24.10

The yardstick of equality   24.11

Self-sufficiency   24.12

Pensions not a separate regime   24.13

Some practical hints on preparing a case   24.14

Appendix   **Legislation**   A1.1

Index   525

Table of Abbreviations

CCA 1984	County Courts Act 1984
CE	cash equivalent
CMOPA 2008	Child Maintenance and Other Payments Act 2008
the Convention/ ECHR	European Convention for the Protection of Human Rights and Fundamental Freedoms 1950
CPR	Civil Procedure Rules 1998
CSA 1991	Child Support Act 1991
CSPSSA 2000	Child Support, Pensions and Social Security Act 2000
ECtHR	European Court of Human Rights
FDR	financial dispute resolution
FLA 1996	Family Law Act 1996
FPR 1991	Family Proceedings Rules 1991
FPR	Family Procedure Rules 2010
HRA 1998	Human Rights Act 1998
IA 1986	Insolvency Act 1986
LPA 1925	Law of Property Act 1925
MCA 1973	Matrimonial Causes Act 1973
MFPA 1984	Matrimonial and Family Proceedings Act 1984
NRP	non-resident parent
POCA 2002	Proceeds of Crime Act 2002
PPF	Pension Protection Fund
PWC	parent with care
RSC	Rules of the Supreme Court 1965, SI 1965/1776
SCA 1981	Senior Courts Act 1981

Table of Abbreviations

SERPS	State Earnings Related Pensions Scheme
SJE	single joint expert
TOLATA 1996	Trusts of Land and Appointment of Trustees Act 1996
WRPA 1999	Welfare Reform and Pensions Act 1999

Table of Statutes

A

Administration of Justice Act 1970
Sch 8 .... 19.25
Armed Forces Act 2006
.... 19.12
Army Act 1955 .... 1.94
Attachment of Earnings Act 1971
.... 19.12
s 3(4) 19.31
14(1) 19.11
23(1A) 19.11
(2)(c) 19.11
24 .... 19.8
25(2) 19.8
Sch 1 .... 19.8

B

Bankers' Books Evidence Act 1879
s 7 .... 16.50

C

Charging Orders Act 1979
.... 19.17
Child Maintenance and Other Payments
Act 2008
Sch 4
para 3 .... 11.7
(3) 11.13
Child Support Act 1991
..... 1.102, 1.174, 2.86, 11.2–11.4,
11.6, 11.17, 11.20, 11.21, 11.35,
11.37, 11.38, 11.40, 11.48, 14.21
s 3 .... 11.10
4 .... 11.23, 11.48
(10) 11.23
8(3) 11.3
(5) 9.22, 11.20
(6)–(9) 11.19
9(2) 11.20
Sch 1
para 2 .... 11.7, 11.13
3 .... 11.15
10(1) 11.14
(2) 11.14
10C(2) 11.11
Child Support, Pensions and Social Security
Act 2000 .... 11.23
Children Act 1989
s 31(1)(a) 11.25
105 .... 11.28
Sch 1 .. 1.6, 1.117–1.119, 1.234, 11.24,
11.42, 16.1, 16.56
Children and Families Act 2014
s 10(1) 16.8

Civil Jurisdiction and Judgments Act 1982
.... 15.5
Civil Partnership Act 2004
.... 10.98, 16.1
Pt 3 .... 7.14
Sch 5 .... 1.7
6 .... 10.92
7
para 9(4) 7.14
Civil Procedure Act 1997
s 7 .... 8.48–8.50
County Courts Act 1984
s 38 .... 3.14, 8.44
110(2) 19.28

D

Debtors Act 1869 .... 19.28
s 5 .... 19.25, 19.48
(2) 19.29
Debtors Act 1969 .... 20.10
Divorce Reform Act 1969
s 2 .... 14.10
Domestic Proceedings and Magistrates' Courts Act 1978
s 63(1) 14.8
Domicile and Matrimonial Proceedings Act
1973
Sch 1
para 8 .... 1.252
11 .... 1.252

E

Equality Act 2010 .... 10.98

F

Family Law Act 1996
.... 14.3, 16.1, 19.44, 23.2
Pt IV 5.4, 7.3
s 30 .... 12.11
33 .... 16.54
(3)(e) 7.3
(5) 12.11
Sch 7 .... 5.47, 5.49
8
para 7 .... 13.10
Family Law (Scotland) Act 1985
.... 23.2
Finance Act 1988 ...... 2.69, 11.46

H

Housing Act 1980 .... 5.43, 5.45
Housing Act 1985
s 79 .... 5.47

Housing Act 1988
  Pt I (ss 1–45) 5.47
Human Rights Act 1998
  .... 20.1, 20.10
  s 1 .... 20.3
  2 .... 20.4
  3 .... 20.4
  4 .... 20.4
  6 .... 20.5
  7(1)(a) 20.5
  7(1)(b) 20.5
  8 .... 20.5

I

Inheritance (Provision for Family and
  Dependants) Act 1975
  .... 2.102, 16.1
  s 1(1)(b) 2.100
  15(1) 2.101
Insolvency Act 1986
  .. 10.99, 12.2, 12.12, 12.13, 12.25,
                                  12.26
  s 280(2)(c) 12.32
  282(1)(a) 12.13
  283(1)(b) 12.32, 12.34
  284(1) 12.23
  306 .... 12.2
  307(1) 12.32
  310(1) 12.32, 12.34
  (2) 12.32, 12.33
  (5) 12.32
  335A(3) 12.22
  336(3) 12.11
  (4) 12.3
  (5) 12.4
  337(2) 12.12
  (5), (6) 12.12
  339 .... 12.16, 12.20
  (3)(a) 12.20
  (c) 12.20
  340(1), (2) 12.25
  (6) 12.25
  341 .... 12.18
  342A 10.99
  382(1) 12.32, 12.34
  385(1) 12.32, 12.33
  423 .... 12.25

L

Legal Aid, Sentencing and Punishment of
  Offenders Act 2012
  .... 17.43
Law of Property Act1925
  s 30 .... 7.16, 7.17, 12.3, 12.38
Limitation Act1980
  s 20(1) 12.3
  24 .... 19.2

M

Maintenance Enforcement Act 1991
  s 1 .... 19.46
Maintenance Orders Act 1958
  .... 19.52
Marriage (Same Sex Couples) Act 2013
  .... 10.98
Married Women's Property Act 1882
  .... 16.1, 16.54
Matrimonial and Family Proceedings Act
  1984 ..... 1.73, 1.89, 1.104, 1.106,
                            2.70, 2.72
  Pt III 1.6, 10.92, 10.93, 16.1
  s 4 .... 14.8
  12(1) 15.2
  (2) 15.2
  13 .... 15.6
  14 .... 15.14
  15 .... 10.93, 15.4
  16 .. 15.6, 15.19, 15.21, 15.22, 15.23
  (1) 15.6
  (2) 15.6
  (a)–(i) 15.7
  17 .... 15.14, 15.21, 15.23
  (2) 7.14
  18 .... 15.14, 15.21, 15.22, 15.24
  19 .... 15.14
  20 .... 15.14
  21 .... 15.14
  22 .... 15.14
  23 .... 15.14
  24 .... 15.14
  25 .... 15.14
  26 .... 15.14
  31E 19.41
  (1)(a) 9.17
  31F(6) 18.25
  31J 16.50
  32 .... 8.44
Matrimonial Causes Act 1973
  ...... 1.15, 1.22, 1.23, 1.76, 1.153,
    2.13, 2.72, 4.14, 4.50, 8.40, 9.7,
    11.24, 13.1, 15.21, 15.22, 21.12,
            21.15, 22.16, 23.3
  Pt II (ss 21–40A) 2.5, 9.17, 9.18
  s 1 .... 14.12
  (2)(d) 14.10, 14.12
  (e) 14.10, 14.12
  9(2) 14.17
  10(2) 14.1, 14.11, 14.12, 14.17,
                            14.18, 16.11
  (3) 14.11, 14.13, 14.14, 14.16
  (4) 14.14, 14.16
  21(1) 1.7, 2.3
  (a) 2.4
  (c) 4.4
  (2)(a) 5.5
  21A 10.8, 10.11, 10.41
  (1)(b) 10.22, 10.42
  21B 10.88

Matrimonial Causes Act 1973 – *cont.*
s 22 .... 1.223, 1.245, 2.55, 2.57, 2.59,
2.63, 8.5
22ZA 2.64, 16.56, 17.19, 17.47,
19.33, 20.12
22ZB 2.64
ss 22A–24A 2.73
s 23 . 1.9, 1.48, 1.50, 1.245, 2.47, 4.11,
7.2, 8.5, 9.17, 10.61, 16.54
(1) 16.10
(a) 2.47, 2.75
(b) 2.75, 3.3
(c) 4.4, 13.4
(3)(a) 4.11
(c) 13.4
(6) 4.5
24 . 1.9, 1.48, 1.50, 1.82, 1.83, 1.245,
5.47, 6.2, 7.2, 8.5, 9.17, 16.54
(1) 6.2, 10.92
(a) 5.6, 5.43, 5.44, 11.27
(b) 13.4
(c) .. 6.13, 6.16, 6.19, 6.23, 13.4
(d) 13.4
24A 1.9, 1.48, 1.50, 7.2, 7.3, 7.6,
7.7, 7.11–7.14, 8.40, 16.54, 19.33,
19.35
(1) 7.2, 13.4
(2) 7.7
(3) 7.4
(6) 7.10
24B 8.5, 13.4
ss 24B–24D 10.8, 10.11, 10.41
s 24B(4), (5) 10.47
ss 24E–24G 10.88
s 25 .. 1.9, 1.10, 1.11, 1.13, 1.26, 1.33,
1.34–1.39, 1.56, 1.63, 1.66, 1.89,
1.108, 1.114, 1.117, 1.119, 1.121,
1.124, 1.125, 1.134, 1.136, 1.149,
1.169, 1.199, 1.222, 1.237, 2.7, 2.9,
2.22, 2.24, 2.27, 2.34, 2.42, 2.56,
2.57, 2.76, 2.90, 2.93, 3.12, 4.14,
4.15, 4.19, 4.38, 4.40, 5.11, 5.12,
5.41, 6.8, 6.22, 7.12, 8.26, 9.5–9.7,
10.4, 10.11, 10.71, 10.81, 10.82,
10.83, 12.19, 12.35, 13.28, 14.6,
14.19, 15.14, 16.19, 16.29, 16.41,
16.48, 16.60, 18.20, 18.35, 18.54,
22.15, 23.2, 23.4, 24.3, 24.4, 24.7,
24.10, 24.11, 24.13, 24.14
(1) 1.48, 1.50–1.52, 2.47, 5.14,
7.10, 11.1
(2) 1.8, 1.44, 1.47, 1.55, 1.60,
1.73, 1.195, 1.196, 2.34, 2.38,
2.47, 4.1, 14.6, 16.53
(a) 1.56, 1.62, 1.66, 1.149,
1.196, 2.12, 2.70, 2.72, 2.76,
4.31, 5.14, 6.8, 10.4, 10.88,
11.32, 15.23, 24.5
(b) 1.98, 2.22, 5.13, 11.32,
12.35, 15.23
(c) ... 1.93, 1.104, 1.106, 11.32,
15.23

Matrimonial Causes Act 1973 – *cont.*
s 25(2)(d) 1.108, 15.23
(e) 1.131, 11.32, 15.23
(f) 1.132, 1.137, 15.23
(g) 1.89, 1.175, 15.23, 17.13
(h) ... 1.193, 1.194, 1.196, 10.4,
10.88, 15.23
(3) 1.244, 11.32, 11.38
(a)–(e) 11.32
(4) 11.33, 11.38, 14.19
(a)–(c) 11.33
25A ... 1.9, 1.10, 1.73, 1.108, 1.242,
2.53, 2.70, 2.73, 9.6, 9.7
(1) .. 2.53, 2.73, 2.76, 2.80, 2.88,
2.90, 2.93
(2) .. 2.53, 2.74, 2.76, 2.80, 2.88,
2.89, 2.93, 10.95
(3) 2.75, 2.76
25B 1.75, 1.79, 1.86, 1.87, 1.94,
1.194, 1.195, 10.7, 10.11
ss 25B–25D 10.7, 10.11, 10.61
s 25B(1) 1.196
(a) 10.4
(b) 10.4
(2) 1.198
(4) 13.4, 13.16
(7) 10.63
25C 13.4, 13.16
(2) 10.67
(a) 10.63
(b) 10.63
25D 6.2
25E(1) 10.88
25G 10.88
27 ..... 1.2, 1.6, 8.5, 14.1–14.3, 14.7,
14.9, 15.1
(1) 14.4
(2) 14.4
(3) 14.6
(5) 14.5
(6) 1.7, 14.5
(7) 14.5
(b) 13.4
28(1)(a) 2.90
(b) 3.7
(1A) .. 2.54, 2.77, 2.78, 2.83, 2.86,
2.90, 2.103, 13.5
(3) 2.5, 16.4, 16.5, 16.11
29(1) 11.27
(2) 11.27
(3) 11.28–11.30
30 .... 3.13
31 ...... 2.10, 2.63, 3.18, 8.5, 10.47,
10.94, 13.2–13.4, 13.18, 13.19,
16.56, 19.53
(1) 13.5
(2) 13.3, 13.7, 13.8, 13.15
(b) 10.94
(dd) 13.17
(e) 10.94
(2A) 13.9
(2B) 13.15, 13.18

Matrimonial Causes Act 1973 – *cont.*
s 31(4) 13.19
(6) 13.14
(7) 2.96, 9.20, 13.20, 13.21,
13.22, 13.23
(a) 2.90, 13.24
(b) 13.25
(7A) 13.10
(7B) 10.95, 13.10
(ba) 10.9
(10) 13.13
32(1) 19.2
33A 9.9
(1) 9.9
(3) 9.2
34 .... 1.221, 9.23, 9.27, 14.20
35 .... 8.5, 14.19, 14.22, 14.23
(1) 14.19
(2) 14.19, 14.21
(3) 14.22
37 ...... 8.2, 8.4–8.7, 8.9, 8.10, 8.12,
8.13, 8.18, 8.22, 8.26, 8.30, 8.31,
8.33, 8.37, 8.38, 10.10, 10.56, 10.65,
12.25, 12.31
(1) 8.4, 8.5, 8.11, 8.15, 8.24
(2) 8.4, 8.5, 8.9, 8.12
(a) 8.23, 8.27
(b),(c) 8.20, 8.23, 8.31, 8.33
(4) 8.20, 8.22
(5) 8.23
(6) 8.13
39 .... 12.16
40A(5) 18.9
40B(2) 18.9
52(1) 1.52, 11.26

P

Pensions Act 1995 ...... 1.194, 10.7
Pensions Act 2004 .... 10.86
Proceeds of Crime Act 2002
...... 1.70, 21.1, 21.2, 21.6, 21.12
s 10 .... 21.16
10A 21.20
50 .... 21.17
51(8) 21.17, 21.20
58 .... 21.20
77 .... 21.2
328 .... 21.9, 21.10

Proceeds of Crime Act 2002 – *cont.*
s 330 .... 21.9
(6) 21.11
333 .... 21.9

R

Recognition of Divorces and Legal Separations Act 1971
s 2 .... 15.3
3 .... 15.3
4 .... 15.3
5 .... 15.3
6 .... 15.3
Rent (Agriculture) Act 1976
.... 5.47

S

Senior Courts Act 1981
s 34(2) 16.50
37 .... 8.44, 10.63, 10.64
(1) 19.50
(3) 19.51
39 .... 3.14, 17.36
51 .... 17.5
(6) 17.40
Solicitors Act 1974
s 73 .... 17.45

T

Taxation of Pensions Act 2014
.... 10.1, 10.9, 10.27, 10.56, 10.65
Trusts of Land and Appointment of Trustees Act 1996 ...... 4.10, 5.18, 7.19,
12.41, 12.42, 16.1, 16.3,
16.54, 19.34
s 14 .... 7.16–7.18, 12.3
15 .... 7.17, 12.42

W

Welfare Reform and Pensions Act 1999
.... 6.11, 10.8
s 29 .... 10.42
(7) 10.55
34 .... 10.55

Table of Statutory Instruments

A

Armed Forces (Forfeitures and Deductions)
Regulations 2009, SI 2009/1109
.... 11.11

C

Child Maintenance and Other Payments Act
2008 (Commencement No 10 and
Transitional Provisions) Order 2012,
SI 2012/3042 .... 11.7
Child Maintenance (Written Agreements)
Order 1993, SI 1993/620
.... 9.22
Child Support Maintenance Calculation
Regulations 2012, SI 2012/2677
.... 11.7
Child Support (Miscellaneous Amendments)
Regulations 2018, SI 2018/1279
.... 11.7
Civil Procedure Rules 1998, SI 1998/3132
.... 16.2, 16.13, 16.58, 19.1
Pt 8 .... 19.34
r 28.3(2) 17.15
    (3) 17.15
    (4)(b) 17.19
33.8 .... 21.22
40.17 .... 19.35
Pt 44 .... 2.64
Pts 44–47 .... 17.5
r 44.2(3) 17.41
    (4) 17.18
    (5) 17.18
    (6) 17.15
    (7) 17.15
    (8) 17.30
44.3(1)–(3) 17.28
44.7 .... 17.29
PD 44
para 9.5 .... 17.26
    9.6 .... 17.26
    9.10 .... 17.26
r 46.8 .... 17.40
PD 46
para 5 .... 17.40
Pt 47 .... 17.27
r 52.3(7) 18.18
52.19 .... 17.37
70.2(2)(b) 19.2
Pt 71 .... 19.24
r 71.6 .... 19.5
71.7 .... 19.5
Pt 72 .... 19.14
r 72.5 .... 19.15
72.7 .... 19.16
72.8(1) 19.16

Civil Procedure Rules 1998, SI 1998/3132 –
cont.
r 72.8(6) 19.16
73.10C 19.34
Pt 83 .... 19.21
84 .... 19.21
89 .... 19.8
Sch 1
RSC Ord 15, r 6(2)(b)
.... 16.22
        31, r 1 .... 4.8, 7.15

D

Divorce etc (Pensions) Regulations 2000,
SI 2000/1123
reg 3 .... 10.21
4 .... 10.65
5 .... 10.65

F

Family Court (Composition and
Distribution of Business) Rules 2014,
SI 2014/840 .... 16.9
r 17(5) 19.27
Family Procedure Rules 2010, SI 2010/2955
..... 1.3, 2.3, 5.10, 16.2, 16.7, 16.41,
23.14
Pt 1 .... 16.2, 16.7, 16.13
r 1.1 .... 2.65, 16.15
    (2)(c) 20.12
1.4(1) 16.15
2.3 ... 8.6, 13.35, 14.9, 14.18, 14.23,
16.1
    (1) 1.5, 1.7, 17.7
3.3 .... 22.1
3.8 .... 16.8, 22.2
3.9 .... 22.3
3.10 .... 22.3
    (1) 18.14
    (2) 18.14
PD 3A
para 13 .... 22.2
    (1) 16.8
20 .... 16.8
37 .... 16.8
Pt 4 .... 16.2, 16.29, 16.43
r 4.1 .... 16.15
4.4 .... 16.10, 17.19
4.5 .... 16.62
4.6 .... 16.62, 17.19
5.4 .... 16.9
5.7 .... 16.61
PD 5A 16.11
Pt 6 .... 15.8, 16.13
r 6.23 .... 19.9

Family Procedure Rules 2010, SI 2010/2955
  – *cont.*
PD 6B 16.13
Pt 8, Ch 7 .... 5.49
   9 .... 16.1–16.3
   , Ch31 .... 11.25
r 9.1 .... 14.9
   9.3 .... 8.6
   9.4 .... 16.4
   9.5(2) 14.9
   9.6(1) 8.31
      (2) 8.31
   9.7 .... 2.64
      (1) 16.53
         (e) 17.19
      (3) 16.56
      (4) 16.56
   9.9A 17.19, 18.9, 18.25
   9.9B 16.56
      (4) 16.57
   9.11 .... 6.21
   9.12 .... 16.12
      (1) 16.20
         (a) 16.19
         (b) 16.19
   9.13 .... 6.21, 16.14
   9.14(1) 16.19
      (2) 16.20
      (3) 16.19
      (4) 16.25
      (5) 16.22, 16.26
   9.15(1) 16.29
      (2) 16.29
      (3) 16.29
      (4) 16.30
      (5) 16.51
      (7) 16.30
         (b) 16.30
         (c) 16.18
      (8) 16.27
   9.16(1) 16.26
   9.17 .... 16.37
      (2) 16.37
   9.18 .... 16.56
   9.18A 16.57
   9.20 .... 16.56
   9.24 .... 19.35
      (1) 7.14
   9.26 .... 9.9, 15.8
      (1)(b) 9.14
      (5) 9.13
   9.26B 16.15
   9.27 .... 16.27, 17.21
   9.27A 16.41, 16.44, 17.32, 17.33
   9.28 .... 16.44, 17.32
   9.30 .... 16.18
   9.31 .... 16.14
   9.33 .... 10.69
   9.34 .... 10.69
   9.37 .... 10.87
rr 9.37–9.45 .... 16.18
r 9.39 .... 10.87

Family Procedure Rules 2010, SI 2010/2955
  – *cont.*
r 9.40–9.45 .... 10.88
PD 9A 16.58
para 4.1 .... 16.28
   13.5 .... 18.26, 18.27
r 12.42B 18.9
   12.52A 18.9
   16.24 .... 11.25
Pt 17 .... 8.33, 16.2
   18 ...... 10.38, 13.39, 15.9, 16.15,
                     16.34, 16.51, 16.53
r 18.2 .... 8.33
rr 18.4–18.12 .... 8.33
r 18.8 .... 2.64
Pt 20 .... 8.46
r 20.2(1) 16.55
      (c)(v) 7.3, 16.54
PD 20A 8.46
r 21.2 .... 16.50, 20.15
      (6) 16.52
Pts 22–24 .... 16.2
r 22.1 .... 20.14
   22.10 .... 16.62
PD 22A 16.41
Pt 25 .. 4.41, 10.38, 10.39, 16.2, 16.32
r 25.3 .... 16.32
   25.4(2) 16.32
      (3) 10.32, 16.32
   25.5 .... 10.39
      (2) 16.32, 16.34
   25.6 .... 10.38
   25.7 .... 10.38
   25.9(2) 16.35
   25.10 .... 16.35
   25.19 .... 16.49
PD 25B 16.32
para 9.1 .... 16.35
PD 25C 16.32
   25D 10.38
para 2.1 .... 16.33
Pt 27 .... 16.2
r 27.10 .... 20.11
   27.11(2)(f) 20.11
PD 27A 16.3, 16.59
Pt 28 .... 16.2
r 28.1 .... 17.5
   28.3(4) 17.41
      (5) 17.6, 17.7
      (6) 17.8, 17.11
      (7) 17.9, 17.11
      (8) 17.10, 17.34, 17.42
      (9) 17.19
PD 28A 17.11, 17.33
para 4.2(a) 17.7
   4.4 .... 17.11, 17.25, 17.32
   4.5 .... 17.24
r 29.12 .... 21.7
   29.15 .... 1.245, 1.246
   29.16 .... 18.17, 18.18
   29.17 .... 16.9
      (3) 19.23

Family Procedure Rules 2010, SI 2010/2955
– *cont.*
r 29.17(4) 19.23
  29.18 .... 16.9
  29.19 .... 16.9
Pt 30 .... 18.2
r 30.1 .... 18.2
  30.3 .... 18.3
    (6) 18.5
  30.4 .... 18.5
    (2) 18.10
    (4) 18.10
  30.5 .... 18.5
    (4) 18.11
    (5) 18.11
  30.6 .... 18.14
  30.7 .... 18.6
    (1) 18.12
    (2) 18.12
  30.8 .... 18.7
  30.9 .... 18.14
  30.11 .... 18.15
    (2) 18.15
    (3) 18.15
  30.12 .... 18.16
    (1)(b) 22.17
    (2) 22.17
  33.2 .... 19.2
  33.3(1) 19.3
    (2)(b) 19.3, 19.5, 19.7
  33.4(3) 19.23
  33.9 .... 19.25
rr 33.9–33.17 .... 10.30
r 33.10(1) 19.27
    (2) 19.27
  33.20 .... 19.22
  33.23 .... 19.24
  33.24(1A) 19.15
PD 30A 18.2
para 2.1 .... 18.13
    4.1B 18.9
paras 4.6–4.9 .... 18.21
para 5 .... 18.23
Pt 33 .... 8.44, 19.1
r 33.1 .... 8.44
    (2) 19.21
  33.3(1) 19.9
  33.11(3)–(6) 19.28
  33.14 .... 19.29
    (1) 19.28
    (3) 19.28
  33.16(1), (2) 19.31
  33.24 .... 19.14
  33.25 .... 19.17
PD 33A 9.27

Family Procedure Rules 2010, SI 2010/2955
– *cont.*
para 2.1 .... 19.47
    2.2 .... 19.47
PD 36J 16.49
Pt 37 .... 19.39, 19.40
  39 .... 19.8
r 39.1(1) 19.8
    (2) 19.8
  39.6(1) 19.9
  39.7 .... 19.9
  39.9(1) 19.11
  39.11 .... 19.11
  39.20 .... 19.9, 19.13
  39.21 .... 19.9
Pt 40 .... 19.17
r 40.5(2)(a) 19.18
  40.6(3)(e) 19.18
    (f) 19.18
  40.8(2) 19.19
    (4) 19.19
PD 40A 19.17
para 1.4 .... 19.17
    4.1 .... 19.20
r 46.1(2), (3) 16.51

I

Insolvency (England and Wales) Rules
  2016, SI 2016/1024
r 14.2(2)(c) 12.27, 12.34

M

Money Laundering and Terrorist Financing
  (Amendment) Regulations 2019, SI
  2019/1511 .... 21.4
Money Laundering, Terrorist Financing and
  Transfer of Funds (Information on the
  Payer) Regulations 2017, SI 2017/692
  .... 21.2, 21.3, 21.5
reg 11 .... 21.4
  12 .... 21.4

P

Pensions on Divorce etc (Charging)
  Regulations 2000, SI 2000/1049
reg 3 .... 10.23
Pensions on Divorce etc (Provision of
  Information) Regulations 2000,
  SI 2000/1048
reg 3 .... 10.21

Table of European Material

E

EU Council Regulation (EC) 1347/2000 on
Jurisdiction and the Recognition and
Enforcement of Judgments in
Matrimonial Matters and in Matters of
Parental Responsibility for Joint
Children ('Brussels IIA')
.... 1.248, 1.249

European Convention for the Protection of
Human Rights and Fundamental
Freedoms 20.1, 20.4, 20.6
Art 6 .... 19.40, 20.7, 20.8, 20.12
  (1) 11.17
  8 . 20.9, 20.11, 20.13, 20.15, 20.16
  10 .... 20.11
Seventh Protocol
Art 5 .... 20.7

Table of Cases

A

A v A (A Minor: Financial Provision) [1994] 1 FLR 657, [1994] Fam Law 368, FD
.... 11.42
A v A (Elderly Applicant: Lump Sum) [1999] 2 FLR 969, [1999] Fam Law 752, FD
.... 1.134, 4.27
A v A (Financial Provision) [1998] 2 FLR 180, [1998] Fam Law 393, FD 1.71, 4.15
A v A (Financial Provision: Conduct) [1995] 1 FLR 345, [1995] Fam Law 242, FD
.... 1.181
A v A (Maintenance Pending Suit: Provision for Legal Fees) [2001] 1 FLR 377, [2001]
Fam Law 96, FD 2.61, 2.62
A v A [2007] EWHC 99 (Fam), [2007] 2 FLR 467, [2009] WTLR 1 .... 1.74
A v A [2018] EWHC 340 (Fam), [2018] 4 WLR 66, [2018] 2 FLR 342, [2018] Fam Law
658, [2018] All ER (D) 160 (Feb) 13.21
A v A, B v B [2000] 1 FLR 701, [2000] Fam Law 470, FD 1.69, 21.7
A v B [2018] EWFC 4, [2018] 4 WLR 100, [2019] 1 FLR 1, [2018] Fam Law 798,
[2018] All ER (D) 98 (May) 16.10
A v B (No 2) [2018] EWFC 45, [2019] 1 FLR 17, [2018] Fam Law 1114, [2018] All ER
(D) 152 (Jun) 16.10
A v L (Departure from Equality: Needs) [2011] EWHC 3150 (Fam), [2012] 1 FLR 985,
[2012] Fam Law 395 .... 1.38
A v S (Financial Relief After Overseas US Divorce and Financial Proceedings) [2002]
EWHC 1157 (Fam), [2003] 1 FLR 431, FD 15.15
A v T (Ancillary Relief: Cultural Factors), sub nom A v T (Divorce: Ancillary Relief)
[2004] EWHC 471, [2004] 1 FLR 977, [2004] Fam Law 404, FD 1.49
AB v CB (Financial Remedy: Variation of Trust) [2014] EWHC 2998 (Fam), [2014] Fam
Law 1670, [2015] WTLR 1 .... 2.18, 6.15
AB v CD (Financial Remedy: Consent Order: Non-Disclosure) [2016] EWHC 10
(Fam) 18.42
AB v CD [2017] EWHC 3164 (Fam), [2018] 2 FLR 150, [2018] Fam Law 270,
[2017] All ER (D) 50 (Dec) 11.50
AB v FC (Short Marriage: Needs: Stockpiling) [2016] EWHC 3285 (Fam) 1.129
ABCDEF (Fact Finding: Honour Based Violence), Re [2019] EWHC 406 (Fam) 17.39
ABX v SBX (DX intervening) [2018] EWFC 81, [2019] 1 Costs LO 7 .... 17.34
AD v BD [2020] EWHC 857 (Fam), [2020] 2 FLR 662, [2020] All ER (D) 51 (May)
.... 1.219
AF v SF [2019] EWHC 1224 (Fam), [2020] 1 FLR 121, [2019] Fam Law 1279,
[2019] All ER (D) 175 (Mar) 1.186
AG v VD [2021] EWFC 9 .... 16.44, 16.59, 17.2
AH v PH [2013] EWHC 873 (Fam), [2014] 2 FLR 251 .... 1.231–1.233
AM v SS (Legal Services Order) [2014] EWHC 4380 (Fam) 2.65
AR v AR (Treatment of Inherited Wealth) [2011] EWHC 2717 (Fam), [2012] 2 FLR 1,
[2012] WTLR 373, [2012] Fam Law 15, (2011) 109 (44) LSG 19 .... 1.152
AW v AH [2020] EWFC 22, [2020] 2 FLR 519, [2020] All ER (D) 152 (Apr) .. 2.92, 17.2,
17.12
Agbaje v Agbaje [2010] UKSC 13, [2010] 1 AC 628, [2010] 1 FLR 1813, SC 15.12,
15.18, 15.20–15.22
Aggett v Aggett [1962] 1 WLR 183, [1962] 1 All ER 190, CA 3.17
Al Khatib v Masry [2002] EWHC 108 (Fam), [2002] 1 FLR 1053, FD 1.181, 1.189
Allen v Allen [1986] 2 FLR 265, [1986] Fam Law 268, CA 1.98, 1.99, 5.31
Amey v Amey [1992] 2 FLR 89, FD 18.57
Amin v Amin [2017] EWCA Civ 1114, [2017] 4 WLR 138, [2018] 1 FLR 1083, [2017]
Fam Law 1077, 167 NLJ 7757, [2017] All ER (D) 197 (Jul) 10.97, 13.7, 19.45
Ansari v Ansari [2008] EWCA Civ 1456, [2009] Fam Law 279, [2009] NPC 2 ...... 8.22
Arbili v Arbili [2015] EWCA Civ 542, [2016] 1 FLR 473, [2015] Fam Law 882,
[2015] All ER (D) 228 (May) 20.14
Armstrong v Armstrong (1974) 118 SJ 579, (1974) Fam Law 156, CA 1.181

Ashley v Blackman [1988] Fam 85, [1988] 3 WLR 222, [1988] 2 FLR 278, FD 2.84, 13.26

Askew-Page v Page [2001] Fam Law 794, Bath Cty Ct 4.13

Assoun v Assoun (No 1) [2017] EWCA Civ 21, [2017] 2 FLR 1137, [2017] Fam Law 595, [2017] All ER (D) 193 (Mar) 13.39

Atkinson v Atkinson [1988] Ch 93, [1988] 2 WLR 204, [1988] 2 FLR 353, CA . 2.13, 2.16

Atkinson v Atkinson [1995] 2 FLR 356, [1995] Fam Law 604, FD 2.13, 2.16

Attar v Attar (No 2) [1985] FLR 653, [1984] Fam Law 252, FD 1.113

Austin-Fell v Austin-Fell and Midland Bank [1990] Fam 172, [1990] 3 WLR 33, [1989] 2 FLR 497, FD 12.40

Avis v Turner and Avis [2009] 1 FLR 74, [2008] BPIR 1143, [2008] Fam Law 1185 .... 12.22

B

B (Child: Property Transfer), Re [1999] 2 FLR 418, [1999] Fam Law 535, CA 11.42

B (confiscation order), Re [2008] EWHC 690 (Admin), [2008] 2 FLR 1, [2008] Fam Law 635 .... 21.21

B v B (Ancillary Relief) [2009] EWHC 3422 (Fam), [2010] 2 FLR 887, [2010] Fam Law 903 .... 1.75

B v B (Ancillary Relief: Consent Order: Appeal Out of Time) [2007] EWHC 2472 (Fam), [2008] 1 FLR 1279, [2008] Fam Law 111 .... 18.52

B v B (Discovery: Financial Provision) [1990] 2 FLR 180, [1990] Fam Law 335, FD 4.23

B v B (Financial Provision) (1982) 3 FLR 298, (1982) Fam Law 92, CA 1.79

B v B (Financial Provision) [1990] 1 FLR 20, [1989] Fam Law 432, (1990) 154 JPN 106, FD 2.72, 4.25

B v B (Financial Provision: Leave to Appeal) [1994] 1 FLR 219, [1994] Fam Law 187, FD 18.50, 18.53

B v B (Mesher Order) [2002] EWHC 3106 (Fam), [2003] 2 FLR 285, [2003] Fam Law 462, FD 1.120, 2.86, 5.33

B v B [2010] EWHC 193 (Fam), [2010] 2 FLR 1214, [2010] Fam Law 905 ..... 1.37, 1.86

B v B [2012] EWHC 314 (Fam), [2012] 2 FLR 22 .... 10.94

B v B (No 2) [2008] EWCA Civ 483, [2008] 2 FLR 1645, [2008] Fam Law 717 ...... 1.34

B v B (P Ltd Intervening) (No 2) [1995] 1 FLR 374, [1995] Fam Law 244, CA 8.21

B v B (Real Property: Assessment of Interests) [1988] 2 FLR 490, [1988] Fam Law 435, FD 1.67, 1.187

B v IB (Order to set aside disposition under Insolvency Act) [2013] EWHC 3755 (Fam) 12.25

B v United Kingdom (Application Nos 36337/97, 35974/97) (2001) 11 BHRC 667, 34 EHRR 529, [2001] 2 FLR 261, [2001] 2 FCR 221, [2001] Fam Law 506, (2001) Times, 15 May, [2001] ECHR 36337/97, [2001] All ER (D) 241 (Apr), EctHR 20.11

BD v FD [2014] EWHC 4443 (Fam), [2016] 1 FLR 390, [2014] All ER (D) 368 (Oct) 2.59, 2.60

BG v BA (Deceased) [2015] EWHC 3947 (Fam) 9.33

BR v VT [2015] EWHC 2727 (Fam), [2016] 2 FLR 519, [2015] Fam Law 1458, [2015] All ER (D) 13 (Oct) 7.3, 16.54

B-T v B-T (Divorce: Procedure) [1990] 2 FLR 1, [1990] Fam Law 294, FD 18.28

Bacon v Bacon [1947] P 151, [1948] LJR 530, [1947] 2 All ER 327 .... 6.20

Bailey (A Bankrupt) (No 25 of 1975), Re, Bailey v Trustee of the Property of the Bankrupt [1977] 1 WLR 278, [1977] 2 All ER 26, DC 12.6

Bank of Ireland Home Mortgages Ltd v Bell [2001] 2 FLR 809, [2001] 2 All ER (Comm) 920, [2001] Fam Law 805, CA 12.42

Barca v Mears [2004] EWHC 2170 (Ch), [2005] 2 FLR 1, [2005] BPIR 15, ChD 12.5

Barder v Barder (Caluori intervening), sub nom Barder v Caluori [1988] AC 20, [1987] 2 WLR 1350, [1987] 2 FLR 480, HL 18.43, 18.45, 18.46, 18.49, 18.52, 18.56, 18.58– 18.60, 18.65, 18.66, 18.68

Barker v Barker [1952] P 184, [1952] 1 All ER 1128, 96 SJ 358, CA 3.6, 3.11

Barnes (RM) v Barnes (GW) [1972] 1 WLR 1381, [1972] 3 All ER 872, 116 SJ 801, CA 1.72

Barnett v Barnett [2014] EWHC 2678 (Fam), [2014] Fam Law 1518, [2014] All ER (D) 36 (Aug) 10.93

Barrister, a (wasted costs order No 1 of 1991), Re [1993] QB 293, [1992] 3 All ER 429, [1992] 3 WLR 662, 95 Cr App Rep 288, [1992] 24 LS Gaz R 31, [1992] NLJR 636, 136 Sol Jo LB 147 .... 17.40
Barry v Barry [1992] Fam 140, [1992] 2 WLR 799, [1992] 2 FLR 233, FD 4.8, 4.9
Bateman v Bateman [1979] Fam 25, [1979] 2 WLR 377, (1978) Fam Law 86, FD
   .... 1.181, 5.37
Beach v Beach [1995] 2 FLR 160, [1995] Fam Law 545, FD 1.176
Behbehani v Behbehani [2019] EWCA Civ 2301, [2020] All ER (D) 20 (Jan) 16.17
Ben Hashem v Al Shayif [2008] EWHC 2380 (Fam), [2009] 1 FLR 115, [2008] Fam Law 1179 .... 4.47, 4.50, 6.23
Besharova v Berezovsky [2016] EWCA Civ 161 .... 9.33
Besterman dec'd, Re, Besterman v Grusin [1984] Ch 458, [1984] 3 WLR 280, [1984] 2 All ER 656, CA 4.15
Birch v Birch [2015] EWCA Civ 833, [2015] 3 FCR 249, [2015] Fam Law 1327 .... 1.207
Birch v Birch [2017] UKSC 53, [2018] 1 All ER 108, [2017] 1 WLR 2959, [2017] 2 FLR 1031, [2017] Fam Law 1078, (2017) Times, 07 August, [2017] All ER (D) 165 (Jul), SC 13.21
Blight v Brewster [2012] EWHC 165 (Ch), [2012] 1 WLR 2841, (2012) Times, 10 April, [2012] BPIR 476, [2012] All ER (D) 190 (Feb) 10.63, 10.96, 10.99, 19.50
Bloom v Bloom (Kontipaylova intervening) (2018) 168 NLJ 7787, [2018] Lexis Citation 16, [2018] All ER (D) 122 (Mar) 21.7
Bowman v Fels [2005] EWCA Civ 226, [2005] 1 WLR 3083, [2005] 2 FLR 247, CA
   .... 21.2, 21.10
Boylan v Boylan [1988] 1 FLR 282, [1988] Fam Law 62, (1988) 152 JPN 770 ...... 13.29
Brack v Brack [2018] EWCA Civ 2862, [2019] Fam Law 258 .... 1.235
Bradley-Hole (A Bankrupt), Re [1995] 2 FLR 838, [1995] Fam Law 673 .... 12.27
Bremner (A Bankrupt), Re [1999] 1 FLR 912, [1999] BPIR 185, [1999] Fam Law 293, ChD 12.8
Brisset v Brisset [2009] EWCA Civ 679, [2009] 4 Costs LR 641, [2009] 2 FLR 1451
   .... 18.19
Brooks v Brooks [1996] 1 AC 375, [1995] 3 WLR 141, [1995] 2 FLR 13, HL ... 6.7, 6.11, 6.16
Brown v Brown [1959] P 86, [1959] 2 WLR 776, [1959] 2 All ER 266, CA 6.12
Burgess v Burgess [1996] 2 FLR 34, [1996] Fam Law 465, CA 8.50
Burrow v Burrow [1999] 1 FLR 508 .... 10.70
Butler v Butler (Nos 1 and 2) [1997] 2 All ER 822, [1997] 2 FLR 311, [1997] Fam Law 603, CA 1.252, 1.253
Byford (Deceased), Re, sub nom Byford v Butler [2003] EWHC 1267, [2004] 1 FLR 56, [2004] 2 FCR 454, ChD 12.11

C

C v C (Financial Provision: Personal Damages) [1995] 2 FLR 171, [1995] Fam Law 605, FD 1.95
C v C (Financial Relief: Short Marriage) [1997] 2 FLR 26, [1997] 3 FCR 360, [1997] Fam Law 472 .... 1.114, 2.90, 2.91
C v C (Divorce: Stay of English Proceedings) [2001] 1 FLR 624, [2001] Fam Law 181, FD 1.252, 1.253
C v C (12 December 2001, unreported) 1.181
C v C (Variation of Post-Nuptial Settlement: Company Shares) [2003] 2 FLR 493, FD
   .... 5.40
C v C [2008] EWHC 2033 (Fam), [2009] 1 FLR 8, [2008] Fam Law 1181 .... 1.36
C v C (Appeal: Hadkinson Order) [2010] EWHC 1656 (Fam), [2011] 1 FLR 434, [2010] Fam Law 1257 .... 18.7, 19.44
C v C (Financial Orders: Non-Disclosure: Set-Aside) [2013] Fam Law 953 .... 18.36
C v C (Freezing Orders: Jurisdiction) [2015] EWHC 2795 (Fam), [2016] Fam Law 20
   .... 8.47
C v C (Post-Separation Accrual: Approach to Quantification of Sharing Claim where Non-Matrimonial Property) [2018] EWHC 3186 (Fam), [2019] Fam Law 129 .... 1.34
CB v KB [2019] EWFC 78, [2020] 1 FLR 795, [2020] All ER (D) 90 (Jan) ... 11.37, 18.27
CH v WH [2017] EWHC 2379 (Fam), [2017] 4 WLR 178, [2018] 1 FLR 495, [2017] Fam Law 1299, [2018] 1 P & CR D12, [2017] All ER (D) 25 (Oct) 9.17

CM v CM [2019] EWFC 16 .... 16.33, 22.17
CO v CO [2004] EWHC 287 (Fam), [2004] 1 FLR 1095, [2004] Fam Law 406 ..... 1.127
CR v CR [2007] EWHC 3334 (Fam), [2008] 1 FLR 323, [2008] 1 FCR 642 ... 1.34, 2.83, 4.6
CS v ACS [2015] EWHC 1005 (Fam) 18.69
Calderbank v Calderbank [1976] Fam 93, [1975] 3 All ER 333, [1975] 3 WLR 586, [1976] Fam Law 93, 119 Sol Jo 490 .... 17.34, 17.35, 17.36, 17.42
Campbell v Campbell [1976] Fam 347, [1976] 3 WLR 572, [1977] 1 All ER 1 .... 2.25
Campbell v Campbell [1998] 1 FLR 828, [1998] Fam Law 394, CA 1.101, 2.27
Carson v Carson [1983] 1 WLR 285, [1983] 1 All ER 478, (1981) 2 FLR 352, CA
.... 5.29, 5.32
Cartwright v Cartwright (No 2) [2002] EWCA Civ 931, [2002] 2 FLR 610, CA 12.27
Chamberlain v Chamberlain [1973] 1 WLR 1557, [1974] 1 All ER 33, 117 SJ 893, CA 5.37
Chapelgate Credit Opportunity Master Fund Ltd v Money [2020] EWCA Civ 246
.... 17.39
Charamalous v Charamalous (Financial Provision: Post Nuptial Settlements), sub nom C v C (Ancillary Relief: Nuptial Settlement), C v C (Variation of Post Nuptial Settlement), [2004] EWCA Civ 1030, [2004] 2 FLR 1093, [2004] 2 FCR 721, CA
.... 6.13
Charman v Charman [2007] EWCA Civ 503, [2007] 1 FLR 1246, [2007] 2 FCR 217, CA, [2006] EWHC 1879 (Fam), [2007] 1 FLR 593, [2007] 1 FCR 33, FD 1.16, 1.32, 1.34, 1.44, 1.58, 1.61, 1.74, 1.86, 1.141, 1.144–1.146, 1.163, 1.170, 23.3, 24.7
Chaterjee v Chaterjee [1976] Fam 199, [1976] 2 WLR 397, [1976] 1 All ER 719, CA
.... 16.8
Citro (Domenico) (A Bankrupt), Re, Citro (Carmine) (A Bankrupt), Re [1991] Ch 142, [1990] 3 WLR 880, [1991] 1 FLR 71, CA 12.5, 12.9
Clark v Clark [1999] 2 FLR 498, [1999] Fam Law 533, CA 1.183, 1.184
Clutton v Clutton [1991] 1 WLR 359, [1991] 1 All ER 340, [1991] 1 FLR 242, CA
.... 2.86, 5.37
Coleman v Coleman [1973] Fam 10, [1972] 3 WLR 681, [1972] 3 All ER 886 .... 4.5
Compton (Marquis of Northampton) v Compton (Marchioness of Northampton) and Hussey [1960] P 201, [1960] 3 WLR 476, [1960] 2 All ER 70 .... 6.21, 6.22
Conran v Conran [1997] 2 FLR 615, [1997] Fam Law 724, [1997] TLR 383, CA ... 1.166, 1.172
Cook v Cook [1988] 1 FLR 521, [1988] Fam Law 163, CA 18.53
Cooper-Hohn v Hohn [2014] EWHC 4122 (Fam), [2015] 1 FLR 745, [2015] Fam Law 124 .... 1.155, 1.158–1.165
Corbett v Corbett [2003] EWCA Civ 559, [2003] 2 FLR 385, CA 13.37
Cordle v Cordle [2001] EWCA Civ 1791, [2002] 1 FLR 207, [2002] Fam Law 174, CA 2.44, 2.48–2.51
Cornick v Cornick [1994] 2 FLR 530, [1994] Fam Law 617, FD 18.47, 18.65
Cornick v Cornick (No 3) [2001] 2 FLR 1240, [2001] Fam Law 871, (2002) 99(9) LSG 27, FD 13.10, 13.31
Couvaras v Wolf [2002] 2 FLR 107, FD 12.31
Cowan v Cowan [2001] EWCA Civ 679, [2002] Fam 97, [2001] 2 FLR 192, CA 23.3
Crake v Supplementary Benefits Commission [1982] 1 All ER 498, (1981) 2 FLR 264, DC 2.14
Crittenden v Crittenden [1990] 2 FLR 361, [1990] Fam Law 432, [1990] TLR 305, CA 8.13
Crossley v Crossley [2007] EWCA Civ 1491, [2008] 1 FLR 1467, [2008] 1 FCR 323
.... 16.30
Crowther v Crowther [2020] EWHC 3555 (Fam), [2021] 1 WLR 2705, [2021] Fam Law 344, [2020] Costs LR 1859, [2021] All ER (D) 38 (Jan) 17.20
Crozier v Crozier [1994] Fam 114, [1994] 2 WLR 444, [1994] 1 FLR 126, FD 18.61
Cumbers v Cumbers [1974] 1 WLR 1331, [1975] 1 All ER 1, 118 SJ 598, CA 14.17
Currey v Currey [2006] EWCA Civ 1338, [2007] 1 FLR 946, CA 2.63

D

D v D (Production Appointment) [1995] 2 FLR 497, [1995] Fam Law 670, FD 16.52

D v D (Lump Sum: Adjournment of Application) [2001] 1 FLR 633, [2001] Fam Law
    254, FD 1.96, 4.20
D v D and B Ltd [2007] EWHC 278 (Fam), [2007] 2 FLR 653, [2007] 1 FCR 603
    .... 4.37
DB v PB (Pre-Nuptial Agreement: Jurisdiction) [2016] EWHC 3431 (Fam) 1.234
DL v SL [2015] EWHC 2621 (Fam) 16.49
DN v UD (Sch 1 Children Act: capital provision) [2020] EWHC 627 (Fam), [2021] 1
    WLR 595, [2021] 1 FLR 497, [2020] All ER (D) 153 (Jan) 11.28
DS v HR (Hadkinson Order) [2019] EWHC 2425 (Fam), [2020] 1 FLR 945 .... 19.44
Daga v Bangur [2018] EWFC 91, [2019] 1 FLR 1340, [2019] Fam Law 356, [2019]
    WTLR 455, [2019] All ER (D) 155 (Jan) 1.77, 17.14
Daubney v Daubney [1976] Fam 267, [1976] 2 WLR 959, [1976] 2 All ER 453, CA
    .... 1.95
Dart v Dart [1996] 2 FLR 286, [1997] 1 FCR 21, [1996] Fam Law 607, [1995] Lexis
    Citation 1675, CA 16.5
Dean v Stout (the Trustee in Bankruptcy of Dean) [2005] EWHC 3315 (Ch), [2006] 1
    FLR 725, [2006] Fam Law 11, ChD 12.6
Debtor, Re A, JP v A Debtor [1999] 1 FLR 926, [1999] Fam Law 293, ChD 12.27
de Dampierre v de Dampierre [1988] AC 92, [1987] 2 WLR 1006, [1987] 2 FLR 300,
    HL 1.252, 1.253
de Gafforj v de Gafforj [2018] EWCA Civ 2070, 168 NLJ 7812, [2018] All ER (D) 01
    (Oct) 19.43
Derhalli v Derhalli [2021] EWCA Civ 112, [2021] Fam Law 492 .... 19.36
Delaney v Delaney [1990] 2 FLR 457, [1991] Fam Law 22, (1990) 154 JPN 693, CA
    .... 11.34
Dietz v Lennig Chemicals Ltd [1969] 1 AC 170; [1967] 3 WLR 165; [1967] 2 All ER
    282 .... 18.39
Dinch v Dinch [1987] 1 WLR 252, [1987] 1 All ER 818, [1987] 2 FLR 162, HL 13.7
Dipper v Dipper [1981] Fam 31, [1980] 3 WLR 626, [1980] 2 All ER 722, CA 2.70
Dixon v Marchant [2008] EWCA Civ 11, [2008] 1 FLR 655, [2008] 1 FCR 209 .... 18.55
Donaldson v Donaldson [1958] 1 WLR 827, [1958] 2 All ER 660, 102 SJ 548 .... 1.79
Donohoe v Ingram (Trustee in Bankruptcy of Kirkup) [2006] 2 FLR 1084, [2006] Fam
    Law 733, ChD 12.9
Dorney-Kingdom v Dorney-Kingdom [2000] 2 FLR 855, [2000] Fam Law 794, (2000)
    97 (30) LSG 39, CA : 11.49
Duxbury v Duxbury [1987] 1 FLR 7, [1987] Fam Law 13, CA 4.25–4.30
Dymocks Franchise Systems (NSW) Pty Ltd v Todd [2004] UKPC 39, [2005] 4 All ER
    195, [2004] 1 WLR 2807, [2005] 3 LRC 719, [2004] NLJR 1325, 148 Sol Jo LB 971,
    [2005] 1 Costs LR 52, [2004] All ER (D) 420 (Jul), PC 17.38

E

E v C (Child Maintenance) [1996] 1 FLR 472, [1996] Fam Law 205, FD 11.35
E v E (Financial Provision) [1990] 2 FLR 233, [1990] Fam Law 297, (1989) 153 JPN
    722, FD 6.20–6.22
Edgar v Edgar [1980] 1 WLR 1410, [1980] 3 All ER 887, (1980) Fam Law 20, CA
    .... 1.237
Egerton v Egerton [1949] 2 All ER 238, [1949] LJR 1683, 93 SJ 551, CA 6.22
Emanuel v Emanuel [1982] 1 WLR 669, [1982] 2 All ER 342, FD 8.48
Estrada v Al-Juffali (Secretary of State for Foreign and Commonwealth Affairs
    Intervening) [2016] EWCA Civ 176 .... 1.250
Evans v Evans [1989] 1 FLR 351, (1989) 153 JP 78, (1989) 153 JPN 169, CA 1.181,
                                                                                    1.182
Evans v Evans [1990] 1 WLR 575, [1990] 2 All ER 147, [1990] 1 FLR 319, FD 4.35,
                                                                                    16.59
Evans v Evans [2013] EWHC 506 (Fam), [2013] 2 FLR 999, [2013] Fam Law 958
    .... 1.155
Ezair v Ezair [2012] EWCA Civ 893, [2013] 1 FLR 281 .... 17.13

F

F v F (Divorce: Insolvency: Annulment of Bankruptcy Order) [1994] 1 FLR 359, [1994] Fam Law 253, FD 12.31

F v F (Ancillary Relief: Substantial Assets) [1995] 2 FLR 45, [1995] Fam Law 546, FD 1.107, 4.8, 4.23

F v F (Duxbury Calculation: Rate of Return) [1996] 1 FLR 833, [1996] Fam Law 467, FD 2.82, 4.26, 4.27

F v F [1996] 2 FCR 397, [1995] 2 FLR 45, [1995] Fam Law 54 .... 2.59

F v F (Clean Break: Balance of Fairness) [2003] 1 FLR 847, [2003] Fam Law 311 .... 2.85, 2.86

F v F (Financial Remedies: Premarital Wealth) [2012] EWHC 438 (Fam), [2012] 2 FLR 1212, [2012] WTLR 1079, [2012] Fam Law 1198 .... 1.221

F v G (Child: Financial Provisions) [2004] EWHC 1848 (Fam), [2005] 1 FLR 261, FD 11.44

FRB v DCA (No 2) [2020] EWHC 754 (Fam), [2020] All ER (D) 204 (Mar) 1.186

FZ v SZ (Ancillary Relief: Conduct: Valuations) [2010] EWHC 1630 (Fam), [2011] 1 FLR 64, [2010] Fam Law 1259 .... 1.185

Fallon v Fallon [2008] EWCA Civ 1653 .... 18.19

Fields v Fields [2015] EWHC 1670 (Fam), [2016] 1 FLR 1186, [2015] Fam Law 883 .... 16.49

Finch v Baker [2021] EWCA Civ 72, [2021] Fam Law 491, [2021] All ER (D) 10 (Feb) 10.22, 10.29, 10.42, 10.81

Fisher Meredith v JH and PH (Financial Remedy: Appeal: Wasted Costs) [2012] EWHC 408 (Fam), [2012] 2 FLR 536, [2012] 2 FCR 241, [2012] PNLR 22, [2012] Fam Law 650 .... 16.17, 17.40

Fisher-Aziz v Aziz [2010] EWCA Civ 673, [2010] 2 FLR 1053, [2010] Fam Law 908 .... 5.21

Flavell v Flavell [1997] 1 FLR 353, [1997] Fam Law 237, CA 2.89

Fleming v Fleming [2003] EWCA Civ 1841, [2004] 1 FLR 667, [2004] Fam Law 174, CA 2.16, 2.17, 2.99, 13.27

Fletcher v Fletcher [1985] Fam 92, [1985] FLR 851, FD 1.72

Foley v Foley [1981] Fam 160, [1981] 3 WLR 284, [1981] 2 All ER 857 .... 1.127

Foster v Foster [2003] EWCA Civ 565, [2003] 2 FLR 299, [2005] 3 FCR 26 .... 1.119, 1.123–1.125, 1.139

Fournier v Fournier [1998] 2 FLR 990, [1998] Fam Law 662, CA 2.87, 4.27

Frary v Frary [1993] 2 FLR 696, [1993] Fam Law 628, CA 16.52

Freeman v Swatridge [1984] FLR 762, [1984] Fam Law 215, CA 1.98, 1.100

G

G v G (Periodical Payments: Jurisdiction to Vary) [1997] 2 WLR 614, [1997] 1 All ER 272, [1997] 1 FLR 368, CA 2.103

G v G (Financial Provision: Separation Agreement) [2000] 2 FLR 18, [2000] Fam Law 472, FD 1.117, 4.27

G v G (Maintenance Pending Suit: Costs) [2002] EWHC 306 (Fam), [2003] 2 FLR 71, [2003] Fam Law 393, FD 2.62

G v G (Financial Provision: Equal Division) [2002] EWHC 1339 (Fam), [2002] 2 FLR 1143, FD 1.19

G (Financial Provision: Liberty to Restore Application for Lump Sum), Re [2004] EWHC 88 (Fam), [2004] 1 FLR 997, [2004] 2 FCR 184, FD 1.97, 1.122

G v G (Matrimonial Property: Rights of Extended Family) [2005] EWHC 1560 (Admin), [2006] 1 FLR 62, FD 1.49

G v T [2020] EWHC 1613 (Fam), [2021] 1 FLR 57, [2020] All ER (D) 197 (Apr) 4.48

GS v L (Financial Remedies: Pre-Acquired Assets, Needs) [2011] EWHC 1759 (Fam), [2013] 1 FLR 300, [2012] Fam Law 800 .... 1.152, 1.218

GW v RW (Financial Provision: Departure from Equality) [2003] EWHC 611 (Fam), [2003] 2 FLR 108, [2003] 2 FCR 289, FD 1.128, 1.136, 10.39, 11.36, 11.37

Garcia v Garcia [1992] Fam 83, [1992] 2 WLR 347, [1992] 1 FLR 256, CA 14.17

Gavin Edmondson Solicitors Ltd v Haven Insurance Company Ltd [2018] UKSC 21, [2018] 3 All ER 273, [2018] 1 WLR 2052, [2018] RTR 339, (2018) Times, 25 April, [2018] 2 Costs LR 347, [2018] All ER (D) 63 (Apr), SC 17.45

Gibson v Revenue and Customs Prosecution Office [2008] EWCA Civ 645, [2009] QB 348, [2009] 2 WLR 471, [2008] 2 FLR 1672, [2008] Fam Law 847, (2008) Times, 14 July, [2008] All ER (D) 157 (Jun) 21.18
Gladwell v Gladwell [2019] EWFC 32, [2019] 2 FLR 443, [2019] Fam Law 889, [2019] All ER (D) 109 (May) 19.23
Goddard-Watts v Goddard-Watts [2016] EWHC 3000 (Fam) 18.70
Goddard-Watts v Goddard-Watts [2019] EWHC 3367 (Fam), [2020] 4 WLR 51, [2020] 1 FLR 885, [2019] All ER (D) 202 (Nov) 18.71
Gohil v Gohil (No 2) [2014] EWCA Civ 274; [2015] UKSC 61 .... 18.37, 18.41
Gojkovic v Gojkovic [1990] 2 All ER 84, [1990] 1 FLR 140, [1990] Fam Law 100, CA 2.82
Gojkovic v Gojkovic (No 2) [1992] Fam 40, [1991] 3 WLR 621, [1991] 2 FLR 233, CA 4.26, 4.40, 17.17
Goodinson v Goodinson [1954] 2 QB 118, [1954] 2 WLR 1121, [1954] 2 All ER 255 .... 1.239
Gorman (A Bankrupt), Re, ex parte Trustees of The Bankrupt v The Bankrupt [1990] 1 WLR 616, [1990] 1 All ER 717, [1990] 2 FLR 284, ChD 12.2
Gotham v Doodes [2006] EWCA Civ 1080, [2007] 1 WLR 86, [2007] 1 FLR 373, CA 12.3
Gould v Gould [1970] 1 QB 275, [1969] 3 WLR 490, [1969] 3 All ER 728 .... 1.239
Gowers v Gowers [2011] EWHC 3485 (Fam), [2012] 1 FLR 1040, [2012] Fam Law 517 .... 1.80
Goyal v Goyal [2016] EWFC 50 .... 10.92
Gray v Gray [1976] Fam 324, [1976] 3 WLR 181, [1976] 3 All ER 225 .... 14.8
Green v Green [1993] 1 FLR 326, [1993] Fam Law 119, FD 4.8
Grey v Grey [2009] EWCA Civ 1424, [2010] 1 FLR 1764, [2010] 1 FCR 394 .... 2.17
Grigson v Grigson [1974] 1 WLR 288, [1974] 1 All ER 478, (1973) 118 SJ 116, CA 14.17

H

H v H (Family Provision: Remarriage) [1975] Fam 9, [1975] 2 WLR 124, sub nom H v H (Financial Provision: Remarriage) [1975] 1 All ER 367 .... 1.48
H v H (Financial Provision: Capital Allowance) [1993] 2 FLR 335, [1993] Fam Law 520, FD 1.63, 4.15, 6.22, 10.10
H v H (Financial Provision: Conduct) [1994] 2 FLR 801, [1994] Fam Law 672, FD 1.181
H v H (Financial Relief: Conduct) [1998] 1 FLR 971, [1998] Fam Law 395, FD 1.178
H v H (Financial Provision: Special Contribution) [2002] 2 FLR 1021, FD 1.136
H v H (Financial Relief: Attempted Murder as Conduct) [2005] EWHC 2911 (Fam), [2006] 1 FLR 990, [2006] Fam Law 264, FD 1.181
H v H [2007] EWHC 459 (Fam), [2007] 2 FLR 548, [2008] 2 FCR 714 .... 1.36, 2.52
H v H [2008] EWHC 935 (Fam), [2008] 2 FLR 2092, [2008] Fam Law 718 .... 1.36, 4.51
H v H (Financial Provision) [2009] EWHC 494 (Fam), [2009] 2 FLR 795, [2009] Fam Law 787 .... 2.17
H v H [2009] EWHC 3739 (Fam), [2010] 2 FLR 173, [2010] Fam Law 575 .. 10.22, 10.42
H v H [2014] EWCA Civ 1523, [2015] Fam Law 127 .... 1.45
H v W (Cap on Wife's Share of Bonus Payments) [2013] EWHC 4105 (Fam), [2015] 1 FLR 75, [2014] Fam Law 445 .... 2.30–2.33
H-J v H-J (Financial Provision: Equality) [2002] 1 FLR 415, [2002] Fam Law 176, FD 1.19, 1.102
H-L (a child) (care proceedings: 'necessary' expert evidence), Re [2013] EWCA Civ 655, [2014] 1 WLR 1160, [2013] 2 FLR 1434, [2013] Fam Law 1252, [2013] NLJR 29, [2013] All ER (D) 112 (Jun) 10.32, 16.32
Hadkinson v Hadkinson [1952] P 285, [1952] 2 All ER 567, (1952) FLR Rep 287, CA 13.37, 19.42
Hale v Hale [1975] 1 WLR 931, [1975] 2 All ER 1090, 30 P&CR 98, CA 5.43, 5.44
Haley v Haley [2020] EWCA Civ 1369, [2021] 2 WLR 357, [2021] 1 FLR 1429, [2020] All ER (D) 110 (Oct) 22.9, 22.10, 22.14, 22.15, 22.16
Hall v Hall [1984] FLR 631, [1984] Fam Law 54 .... 1.181, 1.182
Hall v Hall [2008] EWCA Civ 350, [2008] 2 FLR 575 .... 1.191

Hamilton v Hamilton [2013] EWCA Civ 13, [2013] Fam Law 539, (2013) 157(4) SJLB 43 .... 4.7, 13.8
Hamlin v Hamlin [1986] Fam 11, [1985] 3 WLR 629, [1986] 1 FLR 61, CA 8.30
Hanlon v Hanlon [1978] 1 WLR 592, [1978] 2 All ER 889, (1977) 122 SJ 62, CA 5.19
Happe v Happe [1990] 1 WLR 1282, [1991] 4 All ER 527, [1990] 2 FLR 212, CA 1.94
Hardy v Hardy (1981) 2 FLR 321, (1981) 125 SJ 463, (1981) The Times, June 11, CA 1.71
Hargood (formerly Jenkins) v Jenkins [1978] Fam 148, [1978] 2 WLR 969, sub nom Jenkins v Hargood (formerly Jenkins) [1978] 3 All ER 1001, 122 Sol Jo 296 .... 16.5
Harman v Glencross [1984] Fam 49, [1984] 3 WLR 759, [1984] FLR 652, FD 12.38
Harris v Manahan [1996] 4 All ER 454, [1997] 1 FLR 205, [1997] 2 FCR 607, [1997] Fam Law 238 .... 18.67
Hart v Hart [2016] EWCA Civ 497 .... 2.18
Harvey v Harvey [1982] Fam 83, [1982] 2 WLR 283, [1982] 1 All ER 643, CA . 5.30, 5.37
Heard v Heard [1995] 1 FLR 970, [1995] Fam Law 477, CA 18.50
Hector v Hector [1973] 1 WLR 1122, [1973] 3 All ER 1070, 117 SJ 485, CA 5.25
Hedges v Hedges [1991] 1 FLR 196, [1990] FCR 952, [1991] Fam Law 267, CA ... 1.115, 10.9
Hellyer v Hellyer [1996] 2 FLR 579, [1997] BPIR 85, [1996] Fam Law 702, CA 12.29
Hepburn v Hepburn [1989] 1 FLR 373, [1989] Fam Law 271, (1989) 153 JPN 465, CA 2.13
Hewitson v Hewitson [1995] Fam 100, [1995] 2 WLR 287, [1995] 1 FLR 241, CA 1.127, 15.11
Hildebrand v Hildebrand [1992] 1 FLR 244, [1992] Fam Law 235 .... 16.25, 16.44, 20.13
Hill v Haines [2007] EWCA Civ 1284, [2008] Ch 412, [2008] 1 FLR 1192, CA, [2007] EWHC 1012 (Ch), [2007] 2 FLR 983, [2007] 2 FCR 513, ChD 12.20
Hill v Hill [1998] 1 FLR 198, [1997] Fam Law 657, CA, [1997] 1 FLR 730, [1997] Fam Law 394, FD 1.127, 13.7
Hobhouse v Hobhouse [1999] 1 FLR 961, [1999] Fam Law 212, CA 1.116, 4.14
Holliday (A Bankrupt), Re, ex parte Trustee of the Bankrupt v The Bankrupt [1981] Ch 405, [1981] 2 WLR 996, [1981] 3 All ER 353, CA 12.6, 12.9
Holmes v Holmes [1989] Fam 47, [1989] 3 WLR 302, [1989] 2 FLR 364, CA 15.10
Hope-Smith v Hope-Smith [1989] 2 FLR 56, [1989] Fam Law 268, (1989) 139 NLJ 111, CA 18.50
Horton (as Trustee in Bankruptcy of Michael Gerard Henry) v Henry [2016] EWCA Civ 989 .... 10.99
Howard v Howard [1945] P 1, [1945] 1 All ER 91, 61 TLR 189, CA 1.79
Hvorostovsky v Horostovsky [2009] EWCA Civ 791, [2009] 2 FLR 1574, [2009] 3 FCR 650 .... 13.31
Hyman v Hyman [1929] AC 602 .... 1.199

I

IC v RC [2020] EWHC 2997 (Fam), [2020] All ER (D) 74 (Nov) 18.17
Imerman v Imerman [2010] EWCA Civ 908, [2011] 2 WLR 592, [2010] 2 FLR 814, [2009] EWHC 3486 (Fam), [2010] 2 FLR 752, [2010] 3 FCR 371 ..... 8.50, 16.25, 16.44, 20.13
Ipekçi v McConnell [2019] EWFC 19, [2019] 2 FLR 667, [2019] Fam Law 743, 169 NLJ 7837, [2019] All ER (D) 51 (Apr) 1.77, 1.219
IX v IY (Financial Remedies: Unmatched Contributions) [2018] EWHC 3053 (Fam), [2019] Fam Law 127 .... 1.148

J

J (Income Support: Cohabitation), Re [1995] 1 FLR 660, [1995] Fam Law 300, SSC 2.14
J v C (Child: Financial Provision) [1999] 1 FLR 152, [1999] Fam Law 78, FD 11.42
J v J (Financial Orders: Wife's Long-Term Needs) [2011] EWHC 1010 (Fam), [2011] 2 FLR 1280, [2011] Fam Law 684 .... 1.152
J v J [2014] EWHC 3654 (Fam), [2015] Fam Law 372 .... 16.20, 16.33, 17.21, 17.37

JK v MK (E-Negotiation Ltd (trading as "amicable") and another intervening) [2020] EWFC 2, [2020] 1 WLR 5091, [2020] 1 FLR 1234, [2020] All ER (D) 76 (Jan) 17.49

JL v SL (No 2) (Financial Remedies: Rehearing: Non-Matrimonial Property) [2015] EWHC 360 (Fam), [2015] Fam Law 519 .... 1.165, 10.83

JP v NP (Financial Remedies: Costs) [2014] EWHC 1101 (Fam), [2015] 1 FLR 659, [2014] Fam Law 1101 .... 1.245

JS v RS [2015] EWHC 2921 (Fam) 1.212, 10.79

Jackson v Jackson [1973] Fam 99, [1973] 2 WLR 735, [1973] 2 All ER 395 .... 1.48

Jenkins v Livesey (formerly Jenkins) [1985] AC 424; [1985] 2 WLR 47; [1985] 1 All ER 106; [1985] 1 FLR 813, HL 18.39

Jones (MA) v Jones (W) [1976] Fam 8, [1975] 2 WLR 606, [1975] 2 All ER 12, CA 1.181

Jones v Jones [1997] Fam 29, [1997] 2 WLR 373, [1997] 1 FLR 27, CA .. 5.16, 5.43, 5.45

Jones v Jones [2000] 3 WLR 1505, [2000] 2 FLR 307, [2000] Fam Law 607, CA 2.53, 2.54, 2.103, 13.26

Jones v Jones [2011] EWCA Civ 41, [2011] 1 FCR 242, [2011] Fam Law 455 . 1.66, 1.149

Jordan v Jordan [1999] 2 FLR 1069, [1999] Fam Law 695, (1999) 143 SJLB 211, CA 15.11

Joy v Joy [2014] EWCA Civ 520 .... 8.29

Joy v Joy-Morancho (No 3) [2015] EWHC 2507 (Fam) 6.18, 17.10

Judd v Brown (Bankrupts No 9587 and 9588 of 1994, Re) [1998] 2 FLR 360, [1997] BPIR 470, ChD 12.7

Judge v Judge [2009] EWCA Civ 1458, [2009] 1 FLR 1287, [2009] 2 FCR 158 ..... 18.46

Jump v Jump (1883) 8 PD 159, 52 LJP 71, 31 WR 956 .... 6.20

K

K v K (Avoidance of Reviewable Disposition) (1983) 4 FLR 31, (1982) 12 Fam Law 143, CA 8.14

K v K [1990] 2 FLR 225, [1990] Fam Law 19, (1990) 154 JPN 312 .... 1.181, 1.182

K v K (Ancillary Relief: Pre-nuptial Agreement) [2003] 1 FLR 120, [2002] Fam Law 877, FD 1.118, 11.43

K v K (Periodical Payments: Cohabitation) [2005] EWHC 2886 (Fam), [2006] 2 FLR 468, FD 2.15

K v K (Ancillary Relief: Deed of Appointment) [2007] EWHC 3485 (Fam) 6.18

K v K [2007] EWHC 3485 (Fam), [2008] 3 FCR 773, [2009] Fam Law 921 .... 6.13, 6.14

K v K (financial remedy final order prior to decree nisi) [2016] EWFC 23, [2017] 1 FLR 541, [2016] Fam Law 804 .... 1.245, 16.39

K v L (Ancillary Relief: Inherited Wealth) [2011] EWCA Civ 550, [2011] 3 All ER 733, [2012] 1 WLR 306, [2011] 2 FLR 980 affirming [2010] EWHC 1234 (Fam), [2010] 2 FLR 1467, [2010] Fam Law 909 .... 1.149, 1.150

KM v CV [2020] Lexis Citation 245, [2020] All ER (D) 202 (Feb) 10.3, 10.83

KSO v MJO [2008] EWHC 3031 (Fam), [2009] 1 FLR 1036, [2009] Fam Law 185 .... 17.21

Kaur v Matharu [2010] EWCA Civ 930, [2010] 3 FCR 164, [2010] Fam Law 1165 .... 18.19

Kaur (previously known as Minda Singh) v Randhawa [2015] EWHC 1592 (Fam), [2015] All ER (D) 116 (Jun) 19.5

Kean v Kean [2002] 2 FLR 28, [2002] Fam Law 508, FD 18.51

Kepa v Kepa (1983) 4 FLR 515, FD 8.48

Kiely v Kiely [1988] 1 FLR 248, [1988] Fam Law 51, CA 11.40

Kimber v Kimber [2000] 1 FLR 383, [2000] Fam Law 317, FD 2.14

Kingdon v Kingdon [2010] EWCA Civ 1251, [2011] 1 FLR 1409, [2011] 1 FCR 179, CA 18.35

Knibb v Knibb [1987] 2 FLR 396, [1987] Fam Law 346, (1987) 131 SJ 692, CA 5.25

Kokosinski v Kokosinski [1980] Fam 72, [1980] 3 WLR 55, (1980) 1 FLR 205, FD 1.48

Kremen v Agrest (Financial Remedy: Non-Disclosure: Post Nuptial Agreement) [2011] EWHC 1759 (Fam), [2013] 1 FLR 300, [2012] Fam Law 800 .... 1.218

Kyte v Kyte [1988] Fam 145, [1987] 3 WLR 1114, [1987] 3 All ER 1041, CA 1.181

L

L v L [2006] EWHC 956 (Fam), [2008] 1 FLR 26, [2008] Fam Law 306 .... 18.24
L v L (Financial Remedies: Deferred Clean Break) [2011] EWHC 2207 (Fam), [2012] 1
FLR 1283, [2012] Fam Law 518 .... 2.91
LKH v TQA AL Z (Interim Maintenance and Costs Funding) [2018] EWHC 1214
(Fam), [2018] 3 Costs LR 519, HC 2.65
Ladd v Marshall [1954] 1 WLR 1489, [1954] 3 All ER 745, (1954) 98 SJ 870 ...... 18.19,
18.41
Laing v Laing [2005] EWHC 3152 (Fam), [2007] 2 FLR 199 .... 13.38, 19.44
Lambert v Lambert [2002] EWCA Civ 1685, [2003] 2 WLR 631, [2003] 1 FLR 139,
CA 1.19, 1.33, 1.136, 1.144, 1.168, 1.169, 5.33, 23.3
Lauder v Lauder [2007] EWHC 1227 (Fam), [2007] 2 FLR 802, [2008] 3 FCR 468
.... 13.30
Lawrence v Bertram (Preliminary Issue) [2004] Fam Law 323, CC (Croydon) 5.22
Le Foe v Le Foe and Woolwich plc, Woolwich plc v Le Foeand Le Foe [2001] 2 FLR 970,
FD 1.176
Levy v Legal Services Commission [2001] 1 FLR 435, [2001] Fam Law 92, CA 12.32,
12.34
Lewis v Lewis [1977] 1 WLR 409, [1977] 3 All ER 992, (1976) 121 SJ 271, CA 13.28
Lifely v Lifely [2008] EWCA Civ 904, (2008) Times, 27 August, [2008] All ER (D) 396
(Jul) 20.14
Lilford (Lord) v Glynn [1979] 1 WLR 78, [1979] 1 All ER 441, (1978) 9 Fam Law 81
.... 1.53, 11.40
Livesey (formerly Jenkins) v Jenkins [1985] AC 424, [1985] 2 WLR 47, [1985] 1 All ER
106, HL 1.51, 1.67, 9.5, 9.8, 9.9, 9.17, 9.25, 18.29, 18.31, 18.53
Lowrie, Re, ex parte The Trustee of the Bankrupt v The Bankrupt [1981] 3 All ER 353,
DC 12.5
Lowsley v Forbes (t/a LE Design Services) [1999] 1 AC 329, [1998] 3 All ER 897, [1998]
3 WLR 501, [1998] 2 Lloyd's Rep 577, [1998] NLJR 1268, (1998) Times, 24 August,
142 Sol Jo LB 247, [1998] All ER (D) 382, HL 19.2
Luckwell v Limata [2014] EWHC 502 (Fam), [2014] 2 FLR 168, [2014] Fam Law
792 .... 1.225, 16.49
Lumsden v Lumsden (unreported), 11 November 1998, CA 19.13
Lykiardopulo v Lykiardopulo [2010] EWCA Civ 1315, [2011] 1 FLR 1427, [2011] 1
FCR 61, [2011] Fam Law 237, 154 Sol Jo (no 46) 30, [2010] 47 LS Gaz R 17, [2010]
NLJR 1686, [2010] All ER (D) 225 (Nov) 20.11
Lyons v Lyons [2010] EWCA Civ 177 .... 18.19

M

M v B (Ancillary Proceedings: Lump Sum) [1998] 1 FLR 53, [1998] Fam Law 75, CA
.... 1.102, 1.134, 5.12
M v L (Financial Relief After Overseas Divorce) [2003] EWHC 328 (Fam), [2003] 2 FLR
425, [2003] Fam Law 541, FD 15.17
M v M (Financial Provision) [1987] 2 FLR 1, [1987] 195, FD 1.106, 2.77
M v M (Financial Provision after Foreign Divorce) [1994] 1 FLR 399, FD 15.11
M v M (Maintenance Pending Suit) [2002] EWHC 317 (Fam), [2002] 2 FLR 123, [2002]
Fam Law 510, FD 2.57, 2.59
M v M (Financial Provision: Valuation of Assets) [2002] Fam Law 509, HC (NI) 1.136
M v M (Financial Relief: Substantial Earning Capacity) [2004] EWHC 688 (Fam),
[2004] 2 FLR 236, [2004] Fam Law 496 .... 11.39
M v M (Ancillary Relief: Conduct: Disclosure) [2006] Fam Law 923 .... 1.190, 16.52
M v M (Third Party: Subpoena: Financial Conduct) [2006] EWHC 2250 (Fam) 20.15
M v M [2015] EWFC B 63 .... 10.82, 10.84, 10.97
MA v SK: S Investments v MA (Financial Relief after Overseas Divorce) [2015] EWHC
887 (Fam) 15.22
MAP v MFP [2015] EWHC 627 (Fam), [2016] 1 FLR 70, [2015] Fam Law 522,
[2015] All ER (D) 251 (Mar) 17.33
MB v EB (No.2) [2019] EWHC 3676 (Fam), [2020] 1 FLR 1086, [2019] All ER (D) 124
(Dec) 17.2, 17.11, 17.47
MAP v RAP (Consent Order: Appeal: Incapacity) [2013] EWHC 4784 (Fam), [2014]
Fam Law 1671 .... 1.235, 18.68

MET v HAT (Interim Maintenance) [2013] EWHC 4247 (Fam), [2015] 1 FCR 296,
[2014] 2 FLR 692 .... 15.2
MET v HAT (Interim Maintenance) (No 2) [2014] EWHC 717 (Fam), [2015] 1 FLR
576, [2014] Fam Law 1110 .... 15.2
MH v MH (1982) 3 FLR 429, M v M (1982) The Times, January 9, FD 2.13
MT v MT (Financial Provision: Lump Sum) [1992] 1 FLR 362, [1992] Fam Law 99,
FD 1.92
McCann v United Kingdom (application 19009/04) (2008) 47 EHRR 913, [2008] LGR
474, [2008] 2 FLR 899, [2009] 1 FCR 390, [2008] Fam Law 729, [2008] 2 EGLR 45,
(2008) Times, 23 May, [2008] ECHR 19009/04, [2008] All ER (D) 146 (May),
EctHR 20.16
McCartney v Mills McCartney [2008] EWHC 401 (Fam), [2008] 1 FLR 1508, [2008] 1
FCR 707 .... 1.126, 1.175, 11.39
McDonnell v McDonnell [1977] 1 WLR 34, [1977] 1 All ER 766, (1976) 120 SJ 87,
CA 5.25
McFarlane v McFarlane [2009] EWHC 891 (Fam), [2009] 2 FLR 1322, [2009] Fam Law
1020 .... 13.34
McFarlane v McFarlane, Parlour v Parlour [2004] EWCA Civ 872, [2004] 3 WLR 1480,
[2004] 2 FLR 893, CA 2.34, 2.39–2.51, 2.93, 4.23
McGladdery v McGladdery [1999] 2 FLR 1102, [2000] BPIR 1078, [2000] Fam Law
160, CA 9.16, 12.16, 18.46
MacLeod v MacLeod [2008] UKPC 64, [2010] 1 AC 298, [2009] 1 FLR 641 . 1.202, 1.206
Mann v Mann [2014] EWCA Civ 1674 .... 2.10
Mansfield v Mansfield [2011] EWCA Civ 1056, [2012] 1 FLR 117, [2011] 3 FCR 167,
[2012] Fam Law 17 .... 5.35
Mareva Compania Naviera SA v International Bulk carriers SA, The Mareva [1980]
1 All ER 213n, [1975] 2 Lloyd's Rep 509, CA 8.42
Martin v Martin [1976] Fam 335, [1976] 3 WLR 580, [1976] 3 All ER 625, CA 1.88,
1.176, 2.48–2.51, 6.5, 6.6, 12.22
Martin (BH) v Martin (D) [1978] Fam 12, [1977] 3 WLR 101, [1977] 3 All ER 762,
CA 5.37, 5.38
Martin-Dye v Martin-Dye [2006] EWCA Civ 681, [2006] 4 All ER 779, [2006] 1 WLR
3448, [2006] 2 FLR 901, [2006] 2 FCR 325, [2006] Fam Law 731, [2006] NLJR 917,
(2006) Times, 5 June, [2006] All ER (D) 369 (May) 10.5, 10.39, 10.73, 10.76
Maskell v Maskell [2001] EWCA Civ 858, [2001] 3 FCR 296, [2003] 1 FLR 1138
.... 10.76
Matthews v Matthews [2013] EWCA Civ 1874, [2014] 2 FLR 129, [2014] Fam Law
962 .... 2.93–2.95
Maughan v Wilmot [2014] EWHC 1288 (Fam) 19.50
Mawson v Mawson [1994] 2 FLR 985, [1995] Fam Law 9, FD 2.86
Mekarska v Ruiz and Bowden (Trustee in Bankruptcy) [2011] EWHC 913 (Fam), [2011]
2 FLR 1351, [2011] 2 FCR 608, [2011] BPIR 1139, [2011] Fam Law 802 .... 12.10
Mesher v Mesher and Hall (Note) (1973) [1980] 1 All ER 126, CA .. 5.29, 5.31–5.36, 6.1,
6.5, 6.6, 12.22
Michael v Michael [1986] 2 FLR 389, [1986] Fam Law 334, (1986) 130 SJ 713, CA
.... 1.92
Middleton v Middleton [1998] 2 FLR 821, [1998] Fam Law 589, CA 18.49
Miller v Miller [2005] EWCA Civ 984, [2006] 1 FLR 151, [2005] 2 FCR 713, CA
.... 1.25, 1.26, 1.93
Miller v Miller [2006] UKHL 24, [2006] 2 AC 618, [2006] 1 FLR 1186, HL ... 1.15, 1.16,
1.19–1.33, 1.58, 1.104, 1.112, 1.123–1.126, 1.137, 1.141, 1.144, 1.146, 1.148, 1.150, 1.153,
1.214, 2.7, 2.8, 2.34, 2.93, 4.14–4.16, 4.19, 4.51, 6.22, 13.28, 23.3, 24.4, 24.7
Miller-Smith v Miller-Smith [2009] EWCA Civ 1297, [2010] 1 FLR 1402, [2010] Fam
Law 142, CA 7.19
Mills v Mills [2018] UKSC 38, [2018] 4 All ER 612, [2018] 1 WLR 3945, [2018] 2 FLR
1388, [2018] Fam Law 1272, 168 NLJ 7803, [2018] All ER (D) 107 (Jul), SC . 2.98, 13.12,
13.32
Milne v Milne (1981) 2 FLR 286 .... 10.10, 10.11
Minkin v Landsberg (Practising as Barnet Family law) [2015] EWCA Civ 1152, [2016]
1 WLR 1489, [2016] 2 FLR 948, [2016] 1 FCR 584, [2016] Fam Law 167, [2015]
6 Costs LR 1025, [2015] All ER (D) 153 (Nov) 17.48
Minton v Minton [1979] AC 593 .... 2.10

Minwalla v Minwalla and DM Investments SA, Midfield Management SA and CI Law
  Trustees Ltd [2004] EWHC 2823 (Fam), [2005] 1 FLR 771, FD 1.67, 2.62
Mohan v Mohan [2013] EWCA Civ 586 .... 19.30
Moher v Moher [2019] EWCA Civ 1482, [2020] Fam 160, [2020] 2 WLR 89, [2020] 1
  FLR 225, [2019] Fam Law 1282, 169 NLJ 7855, [2019] All ER (D) 99 (Aug) 1.67
Morris v Morris [1985] FLR 1176, [1986] Fam Law 24, (1986) 150 JP 7, CA 13.26
Mortgage Corporation v Shaire [2000] 1 FLR 973, [2000] BPIR 483, (2000) 80 P&CR
  280, ChD 12.41
Mortimer v Mortimer-Griffin [1986] 2 FLR 315, [1986] 305, CA 5.22, 5.32
Moses-Taiga v Moses-Taiga [2005] EWCA Civ 1013, [2006] 1 FLR 1074, [2006] Fam
  Law 266, CA 2.63
Mountney v Treharne [2002] EWCA Civ 1174, [2002] 2 FLR 930, [2002] Fam Law
  809, CA 12.17
Mubarak v Mubarak (No 1) [2001] 1 FLR 698, [2001] 178, CA 9.26, 20.10
Mubarak v Mubarik [2004] EWHC 1158 (Fam), [2004] 2 FLR 932, [2005] Fam Law
  355, FD 13.37
Mubarak v Mubarik [2007] EWHC 220 (Fam), [2007] 2 FLR 364, [2007] Fam Law
  793 .... 8.18
Musa v Karim [2012] EWCA Civ 1332, [2013] Fam Law 16 .... 18.67
Mutch v Mutch [2016] EWCA Civ 370 .... 2.53, 2.54
Myerson v Myerson [2008] EWCA Civ 1376, [2009] 1 FLR 826, [2009] Fam Law 101,
  CA 16.37
Myerson v Myerson [2009] EWCA Civ 282, [2010] 1 WLR 114, [2009] 2 FLR 147,
  CA 13.8, 18.63

N

N v C (Property Adjustment Order: Surveyor's Negligence) [1998] 1 FLR 63, [1998]
  Fam Law 19, CA 16.59
N v F (Financial Orders: Pre-Acquired Wealth) [2011] EWHC 586 (Fam), [2011] 2 FLR
  533, [2012] 1 FCR 139, [2011] Fam Law 686 .... 1.151, 10.82
N v N (Consent Order: Variation) [1993] 2 FLR 868, [1993] Fam Law 676, (1993) The
  Times, July 29, CA 2.86
N v N (Financial Order: Appellate Role) [2011] EWCA Civ 940, [2012] 1 FLR 622,
  [2011] Fam Law 1069 .... 18.19
N v N (Foreign Divorce: Financial Relief) [1997] 1 FLR 900, [1997] Fam Law 396,
  FD 15.11
N v N (Financial Provision: Sale of Company) [2001] 2 FLR 69, [2001] Fam Law 347
  .... 4.36
N v N (Periodical Payments: Non-Disclosure) [2014] EWCA Civ 314 .... 18.43
N v N and F Trust [2005] EWHC 2908 (Fam) 6.19
ND v KP (ex parte application) [2011] EWHC 457 (Fam), [2011] 2 FLR 662, [2011]
  Fam Law 677, (2011) 161 NLJ 702 .... 8.32
NN v AS [2018] EWHC 2973 (Fam), [2019] Fam Law 25 .... 15.23, 17.14
NG v SG [2011] EWHC 3270 (Fam), [2012] 1 FLR 1211, [2012] Fam Law 394 ...... 1.67
NR v AB [2016] EWHC 277 (Fam) 6.19
Naish v Naish (1916) 32 TLR 487, CA 3.17
Neil v Neil (also known as Henderson) [2019] EWHC 3330 (Fam), [2020] 1 FLR 1095,
  [2020] Fam Law 305, [2019] All ER (D) 97 (Dec) 1.180
Newlon Housing Trust v Alsulaimen [1999] 1 AC 313, [1998] 3 WLR 451, [1998] 2
  FLR 690, HL, [1997] 1 FLR 914, (1997) 29 IILR 767, [1997] Fam Law 397, CA
  .... 5.43, 5.44, 8.13
Newmarch v Newmarch [1978] Fam 79, [1977] 3 WLR 832, [1978] 1 All ER 1, FD
  .... 14.8
Norman v Norman [1983] 1 WLR 295, [1983] 1 All ER 486, (1983) 4 FLR 446, FD
  .... 5.29, 5.32
Norris v Norris [2002] EWHC 2996 (Fam), [2003] 1 FLR 1142, [2003] Fam Law 301,
  FD 1.88, 1.102, 1.135, 1.136
North v North [2007] EWCA Civ 760, [2008] 1 FLR 158, [2007] 2 FCR 601 .... 13.32
Northrop v Northrop [1968] P 74, [1967] 3 WLR 907, [1967] 2 All ER 961, CA 14.7
Nunn (Bankruptcy: Divorce: Pension Rights), Re, sub nom Roberts v Nunn [2004] 1
  FLR 1123, [2004] BPIR 623, [2004] Fam Law 324, ChD 12.28

O

OG v AG [2020] EWFC 52, [2021] 1 FLR 1105, [2020] All ER (D) 170 (Jul) 1.175, 17.11

OS v DS (Oral Disclosure: Preliminary Hearing) [2004] EWHC 2376 (Fam), [2005] 1 FLR 675, FD 16.43

O'Dwyer v O'Dwyer [2019] EWHC 1838 (Fam), [2019] 2 FLR 1020, [2019] Fam Law 1281, [2019] All ER (D) 89 (Jul) 1.35

Olu-Williams v Olu-Williams [2018] EWHC 2464 (Fam) 19.39

Owens v Owens [2018] UKSC 41, [2018] AC 899, [2018] 4 All ER 721, [2018] 3 WLR 634, [2018] 2 FLR 1067, [2018] Fam Law 1111, 168 NLJ 7804, [2018] All ER (D) 144 (Jul), SC 1.18

P

P (Child: Financial Provision), Re [2003] EWCA Civ 837, [2003] 2 WLR 865, [2003] 2 FLR 865, CA 1.118, 11.44

P (children) (adoption: parental consent), Re [2008] EWCA Civ 535, [2009] PTSR 150, [2008] 2 FLR 625, [2008] 2 FCR 185, [2008] Fam Law 830, [2008] All ER (D) 265 (May), sub nom SB v X County Council (2008) Times, 29 May 10.32, 16.32

P v P (Financial Provision) [1989] 2 FLR 241, [1989] Fam Law 313, (1989) The Times, February 3, FD 4.34, 16.59

P v P (Financial Relief: Non-disclosure) [1994] 2 FLR 381, [1994] Fam Law 498, FD 1.67, 1.106, 1.187

P v P (Inherited Property) [2004] EWHC 1364 (Fam), [2005] 1 FLR 576, FD 1.136

P v P [2007] EWHC 2877 (Fam), [2008] 2 FLR 1135, [2008] Fam Law 614 .... 1.36

P v P (Variation of Post-Nuptial Settlement) [2015] EWCA Civ 447 [2016] 1 FLR 437, [2015] Fam Law 773 .... 6.17

Page v Page (1981) 2 FLR 198, CA 1.56

Parlour v Parlour, sub nom J v J (Ancillary Relief: Periodical Payments) [2004] EWHC 53 (Fam), [2004] 1 FCR 489, [2004] Fam Law 408, FD 2.34, 2.36–2.38, 2.44

Parra v Parra [2002] EWCA Civ 1886, [2003] 1 FLR 942, [2003] Fam Law 314, CA 1.64, 2.48–2.51

Paulin v Paulin [2009] EWCA Civ 221, [2010] 1 WLR 1057, [2009] 2 FLR 354 ..... 12.31

Peacock v Peacock [1991] 1 FLR 324, [1991] Fam Law 324, FD 13.7

Pearce v Pearce (1980) 1 FLR 261 .... 1.157

Pearce v Pearce [2003] EWCA Civ 1054, [2004] 1 WLR 68, [2003] 2 FLR 1144, CA 13.11

Petrodel Resources v Prest [2012] EWCA Civ 1395, [2013] WLR 557, [2013] 1 All ER 795, [2013] 2 Costs LO 249, [2012] 3 FCR 588, [2013] Fam Law 150, [2013] UKSC 34, (2013) 163(7565) NLJ 27, The Times, January 2, 2013 .... 1.81–1.83

Phillips v Peace [1996] 2 FLR 230, [1996] Fam Law 603, FD 11.42

Phillips v Peace [2004] EWHC 3180 (Fam), [2005] 2 FLR 1212, FD 11.42

Piglowska v Piglowski [1999] 1 WLR 1360, [1999] 3 All ER 632, [1999] 2 FLR 763, HL 1.55, 5.13

Piller (Anton) KG v Manufacturing Processes Ltd [1976] Ch 55, [1976] 2 WLR 162, [1976] 1 All ER 779, CA 8.48, 8.50

Potanina v Potanin [2021] EWCA Civ 702 .... 15.13

Poon v Poon [1994] 2 FLR 857, [1994] Fam Law 673, FD 8.39

Potter v Potter [1982] 1 WLR 1255, [1982] 3 All ER 321, (1983) 4 FLR 331, CA 4.14, 4.33

Pounds v Pounds [1994] 1 WLR 1535, [1994] 4 All ER 777, [1994] 1 FLR 775, CA 1.212, 9.4, 9.6, 9.7

Practice Direction: President's Direction of 5 June 1992 (Family Division: Distribution of Business) [1992] 1 WLR 586, [1992] 3 All ER 151, [1992] FLR 87 .... 8.44

Prescott (formerly Fellowes) v Fellowes [1958] P 260, [1958] 3 WLR 288, [1958] 3 All ER 55, CA 6.10

Prest v Prest (Judgment Summons: Appeal) [2015] EWCA Civ 714 .... 19.30

Preston v Preston [1982] Fam 17, [1981] 3 WLR 619, [1982] 1 All ER 41, CA 4.25

Priest v Priest (1980) 1 FLR 189, (1979) Fam Law 252, CA 1.94

Primavera v Primavera [1992] 1 FLR 16, [1991] Fam Law 471, CA 1.177, 13.33

Q

Quan v Bray [2018] EWHC 3558 (Fam), [2019] Fam Law 254, 169 NLJ 7824 . 2.54, 2.78
Quan v Bray [2019] EWFC 46 .... 19.5, 19.26

R

R v B [2017] EWFC 33, [2017] Fam Law 952, [2017] All ER (D) 224 (Mar) . 1.188, 17.25
R v R (Disclosure to Revenue) [1998] 1 FLR 922, sub nom R v R (Inland Revenue: Tax
Evasion) [1998] Fam Law 321, FD 1.68
R v R (Financial Relief: Company Valuation) [2005] 2 FLR 365, [2005] Fam Law 608,
FD 4.36
R v R (Lump Sum Repayments) [2003] EWHC 3197 (Fam), [2004] 1 FLR 928, [2004]
Fam Law 333, FD 4.5
R v R [1988] 1 FLR 89, Roots v Roots [1987] Fam Law 387, (1988) 152 JPN 254,
CA 1.54, 11.34
R (Kehoe) v Secretary of State for Work and Pensions, sub nom Secretary of State for
Work and Pensions v Kehoe, Kehoe v Secretary of State for Work and Pensions [2005]
UKHL 48, [2006] 1 AC 42, [2005] 2 FLR 1249, HL, [2004] EWCA Civ 225,
[2004] QB 1378, [2004] 1 FLR 1132, CA 11.17
RH v RH [2008] EWHC 347 (Fam), [2008] 2 FLR 2142, [2008] Fam Law 841 ..... 17.25
RH v SV (Pension Apportionment: Reasons) [2020] EWFC B23 .... 10.3, 10.82
RM v TM [2020] EWFC 41, [2020] 2 FLR 1048, [2020] All ER (D) 43 (Jun) . 17.2, 17.16
RP v RP [2006] EWHC 3409 (Fam), [2007] 1 FLR 2105, [2008] 2 FCR 613 .... 1.34
RR v CDS [2020] EWCA Civ 1215, [2021] 1 FLR 996, [2020] All ER (D) 40 (Sep)
.... 1.188, 17.13
Radmacher v Granatino [2010] UKSC 42, [2011] 1 AC 534, [2010] 2 FLR 1900, SC,
[2009] EWCA Civ 649, [2009] 2 FLR 1181, [2009] 2 FCR 645, CA . 1.199, 1.200, 1.203–
1.215, 1.220, 1.227, 1.230, 6.22, 18.7, 18.16, 18.18
Ram v Ram (No 2) [2004] EWCA Civ 1684, [2005] 2 FLR 75, [2005] Fam Law 348,
CA 7.11
Ram v Ram [2004] EWCA Civ 1452, [2005] 2 FLR 63, [2005] 2 BCLC 476, CA ... 12.41
Ramnarine v Ramnarine [2013] UKPC 27, 83 WIR 481, [2014] 1 FLR 594, [2014] Fam
Law 14, [2013] All ER (D) 132 (Aug), PC 1.11
Rattan v Kuwad [2021] EWCA Civ 1, [2021] Fam Law 486, [2021] All ER (D) 23
(Jan) 2.60
Raval (A Bankrupt), Re [1998] 2 FLR 718, [1998] BPIR 389, [1998] Fam Law 590,
ChD 12.7
Redmond v Redmond [1986] 2 FLR 173, [1986] Fam Law 260, Liverpool Cty Ct
.... 18.34
Regan v Regan [1977] 1 WLR 84, [1977] 1 All ER 428, (1976) Fam Law 17, FD 5.43,
5.44
Reid v Reid [2003] EWHC 2878, [2004] 1 FLR 736, [2004] Fam Law 95, FD 18.59
Revenue and Customs Comrs v Charman [2012] EWHC 1448 (Fam), [2012] STC 2076,
[2012] 2 FLR 1119, [2012] 3 FCR 389, [2012] 24 LS Gaz R 23, [2012] NLJR 781,
(2012) Times, 22 August, [2012] SWTI 1838, [2012] 6 Costs LO 818, [2012] All ER
(D) 256 (May) 21.7
Richardson v Richardson [1994] 2 WLR 241, [1993] 4 All ER 673, [1994] 1 FLR 286,
FD 2.103
Richardson v Richardson (No 2) [1994] 2 FLR 1051, [1995] Fam Law 14, FD 13.26
Richardson v Richardson [2011] EWCA Civ 79, [2011] 1 FCR 301, [2011] Fam Law
456 .... 18.46
Ridehalgh v Horsefield [1994] Ch 205, [1994] 3 All ER 848, [1994] 3 WLR 462, [1994]
2 FLR 194, [1994] Fam Law 560, [1994] BCC 390, (1994) Times, 28 January,
[1994] Costs LR (Core) 268 .... 17.40
Roberts v Roberts [1986] 1 WLR 437, [1986] 2 All ER 483, [1986] 2 FLR 152, FD
.... 1.94
Robertson v Robertson [2016] EWHC 613 (Fam) 1.144
Robin v Robin (1983) 4 FLR 632, 13 Fam Law 147, CA 16.5
Robinson v Robinson (Disclosure) [1982] 2 All ER 699, (1983) 4 FLR 102, (1982) 126
SJ 360, CA 18.30
Robson v Robson [2010] EWCA Civ 1171, [2011] 1 FLR 751, [2011] 3 FCR 625,
[2011] Fam Law 224, (2010) 107(43) LSG 20, (2010) 160 NLJ 1530 .... 1.149

Roche v Roche (1981) Fam Law 243, CA 1.95, 8.38
Rogan v Rogan [2019] EWHC 814 (Fam) 19.31
Roocroft v Ball (Personal Representative of the Estate of Ainscow (Dec'd)) [2016]
EWCA Civ 1009, [2017] 1 WLR 1137, [2017] 2 FLR 810, [2017] Fam Law 44,
(2016) Times, 13 December, [2016] All ER (D) 91 (Oct) 16.10
Rose v Rose [2002] EWCA Civ 208, [2002] 1 FLR 978, [2002] 1 FCR 639 .. 1.238, 16.40
Rose v Rose [2003] EWHC 505 (Fam), [2003] 2 FLR 197, FD 18.33
Rossi v Rossi [2006] EWHC 1482 (Fam), [2007] 1 FLR 790, FD 1.246
Rubin v Rubin [2014] EWHC 611 (Fam), [2014] 2 FLR 1018, [2014] Fam Law 797
.... 2.64
Russell v Russell [1998] 1 FLR 936, [1998] BPIR 259, [1998] Fam Law 313, ChD
.... 12.27

S

S v AG (Financial Orders: Lottery Prize) [2011] EWHC 2637 (Fam), [2012] 1 FLR 651,
[2011] 3 FCR 523, [2012] Fam Law 18, The Times, November 22, 2011 .... 1.152
S v E [2018] EWFC 30, [2018] 3 All ER 938, [2018] 1 WLR 3757, [2018] 2 FLR 1213,
[2018] Fam Law 965, 168 NLJ 7796, [2018] All ER (D) 91 (May) 8.44, 19.20, 19.34
S v P (Settlement by Collaborative Law Process) [2008] 2 FLR 2040, [2008] Fam Law
1177 .... 9.15
S v S [1982] Fam Law 183 .... 1.181
S v S [1986] Fam 189, [1986] 3 WLR 518, [1987] 1 FLR 71, FD 13.10
S v S (Financial Provision) (Post-Divorce Cohabitation) [1994] 2 FLR 228, [1994] 2 FCR
1225, [1994] Fam Law 438 .... 1.128
S v S (Judgment in Chambers: Disclosure) [1997] 1 WLR 1621, TC Leaflet No 3518, sub
nom S v S (Inland Revenue: Tax Evasion) [1997] 2 FLR 774, FD 1.68, 21.7
S v S (Matrimonial Proceedings: Appropriate Forum) [1997] 1 WLR 1200, sub nom S v
S (Divorce: Staying Proceedings) [1997] 2 FLR 100, [1997] Fam Law 541, FD 1.252,
1.253
S v S (Ancillary Relief: Consent Order) [2002] EWHC 223 (Fam), [2002] 1 FLR 992,
[2002] Fam Law 422, FD 18.62
S v S (Ancillary Relief: Importance of FDR) [2007] EWHC 1975 (Fam), [2008] 1 FLR
944, [2008] Fam Law 397 .... 1.154
S v S [2006] EWHC 2793 (Fam), [2007] 1 FLR 1496 .... 1.181
S v S (financial remedies: arbitral award) [2014] EWHC 7 (Fam), [2014] 1 WLR 2299,
[2014] 1 FLR 1257, [2014] 2 FCR 484, [2014] Fam Law 448, [2014] All ER (D) 63
(Jan) 22.10
SA v PA (Pre-Marital Agreement: Compensation) [2014] EWHC 392 (Fam), [2014] 2
FLR 1028, [2014] Fam Law 799 .... 1.46, 1.230
SJ v RA [2014] EWHC 4054 (Fam) 10.27, 10.33, 10.77, 10.95
SR v CR (Ancillary Relief: Family Trusts) [2008] EWHC 2329 (Fam), [2009] 2 FLR
1083, [2009] 2 FCR 69, ... 1.75
SR v HR (SC (as Trustee in Bankruptcy of SR) intervening) [2018] EWHC 606 (Fam),
[2018] 4 WLR 68, [2018] 2 FLR 843, 168 NLJ 7790, [2018] BPIR 1188,
[2018] All ER (D) 176 (Mar) 13.7
SRJ v DWJ (Financial Provision) [1999] 2 FLR 176, [1999] Fam Law 448, CA 2.86
SS v NS [2014] EWHC 4183 (Fam), [2015] Fam Law 267 .... 2.23
Sandford v Sandford [1986] 1 FLR 412, [1985] Fam Law 104, CA 13.26
Saunders v Saunders (1980) 1 FLR 121, (1980) Fam Law 58, CA 2.21
Scatliffe v Scatliffe [2016] UKPC 36 .... 1.156
Scheeres v Scheeres [1999] 1 FLR 241, [1999] Fam Law 18, CA 1.11, 2.25, 4.1
Schofield v Schofield [2011] EWCA Civ 174 .... 10.93
Seagrove v Sullivan [2014] EWHC 4110 (Fam), [2015] 2 FLR 602, [2015] Fam Law
141, [2014] All ER (D) 61 (Dec) 16.59
Sears Tooth (A Firm) v Payne Hicks Beach (A Firm) [1997] 2 FLR 116, [1997] Fam Law
392, (1997) 94(5) LSG 32, FD 2.61, 17.44
Segal v Pasram [2008] EWHC 3448 (Ch), [2008] 1 FLR 271, [2007] BPIR 881 ...... 12.13
Sharland v Sharland [2015] UKSC 60, [2016] AC 871, [2015] 3 FCR 481, [2015] 2 FLR
1367 reversing [2014] EWCA Civ 95, [2014] 2 FLR 89 .... 18.36–18.39, 18.69, 18.71
Sharpe v Sharpe (1981) Fam Law 121, (1981) The Times, February 7, CA 1.9, 2.7

Shaw v Shaw [2002] EWCA Civ 1298, [2002] 2 FLR 1204, [2002] Fam Law 886, CA
.... 18.33
Shearn v Shearn [1931] P 1, [1930] All ER Rep 310, 100 LJP 41 .... 3.12, 3.17
Shield v Shield [2014] EWHC 23 (Fam), [2014] 2 FLR 1422, [2014] Fam Law 801,
[2014] All ER (D) 27 (Feb) 16.17
Shipman v Shipman [1991] FLR 250, [1991] Fam Law 145, FD 8.38
Shokrollah-Babee v Shokrollah-Babee [2019] EWHC 2135 (Fam), [2019] 1 WLR 6517,
[2019] All ER (D) 43 (Aug) 16.37
Sibley v Sibley (1981) 2 FLR 121, (1980) Fam Law 49, FD 2.21
Slater v Slater (1982) 3 FLR 364, (1982) Fam Law 153, (1982) The Times, March 26,
CA 1.101
Smallman v Smallman [1972] Fam 25, [1971] 3 WLR 588, [1971] 3 All ER 717 .... 1.239
Smith v Kay (1859) VII HLC 749 .... 18.39
Smith v Smith [1974] 1 WLR 247, (1974) Fam Law 80, (1973) 117 SJ 525, CA 8.17
Smith v Smith (Smith and Others intervening) [1992] Fam 69, [1991] 3 WLR 646,
[1991] 2 FLR 432, CA 1.56, 18.58
Smith v Smith and Graves (1887) 12 PD 102 .... 6.22
Solomon v Solomon [2013] EWCA Civ 1095, [2013] All ER (D) 233 (Sep) 17.17
Sorrell v Sorrell [2005] EWHC 1717 (Fam), [2006] 1 FLR 497, [2006] Fam Law 12,
FD 1.141
Soulsbury v Soulsbury [2007] EWCA Civ 969, [2008] 2 WLR 834, [2008] 1 FLR 90
.... 1.239
Stockford v Stockford (1982) 3 FLR 58, (1982) Fam Law 30, (1981) The Times,
November 5, CA 1.72, 1.101, 2.25, 2.27
Stodgell v Stodgell [2009] EWCA Civ 243, [2009] 2 FLR 244, [2009] Fam Law 566
.... 21.19
Suter v Suter and Jones [1987] Fam 111, [1987] 3 WLR 9, [1987] 2 FLR 232, CA
.... 1.54, 2.13, 2.77
Symmons v Symmons [1993] 1 FLR 317, [1993] Fam Law 135, FD 9.26
Symphony Group plc v Hodgson [1994] QB 179, [1993] 4 All ER 143, [1993] 3 WLR
830, [1993] 23 LS Gaz R 39, [1993] NLJR 725, (1993) Times, 4 May, 137 Sol Jo LB
134, [1993] Costs LR (Core) 319 .... 17.38

T

T v R (Maintenance after Remarriage: Agreement) [2016] EWFC 26 .... 9.23, 14.20
T v S (Financial Provision for Children) [1994] 2 FLR 883, [1995] Fam Law 11, FD
.... 11.42
T v T (Interception of Documents) [1994] 2 FLR 1083, [1995] Fam Law 15, [1994] TLR
458, FD 1.187
T v T (Financial Relief: Pensions) [1998] 1 FLR 1072 .... 10.69
T v T (Agreement not embodied in Consent Order) [2013] EWHC B3 (Fam) 1.222
TF v FF [2013] EWHC 390 (Fam) 17.37
TJB v RJB (Financial Order: Declaration) [2016] EWHC 1171 (Fam) 7.6
TL v ML (Ancillary Relief: Claim against Assets of Extended Family) [2005] EWHC
2860 (Fam), [2006] 1 FLR 1263, [2006] 1 FCR 465 .... 2.58, 2.59, 2.64, 2.68, 16.16
TM v TM (Minors)(Child Maintenance: Jurisdiction and Departure from Formula)
[2016] Fan Law 15 .... 11.37
Tattersall v Tattersall [2018] EWCA Civ 1978, [2019] 1 FLR 470, [2018] Fam Law
1383, [2018] All ER (D) 139 (Aug) 19.13, 19.55
Tavoulareas v Tavoulareas [1998] 2 FLR 418, [1998] 521, CA 1.187, 6.6, 11.40
Teeling v Teeling [1984] FLR 808, [1981] CAT 389, CA 1.52
Thiry v Thiry [2014] EWHC 4046 (Fam) 1.60
Thomas v Thomas [1995] 2 FLR 668, [1996] 2 FCR 544, [1995] Fam Law 672, CA
.... 1.75
Thompson v Thompson [1976] Fam 25, [1975] 2 WLR 868, [1975] 2 All ER 208,
CA 5.43, 5.44
Thompson v Thompson [1986] Fam 38, [1985] 3 WLR 17, [1985] FLR 863, CA 5.32
Thompson v Thompson [1991] 2 FLR 530, [1992] Fam Law 18, [1991] NPC 95, CA
.... 18.32
Thyssen-Bornemisza v Thyssen-Bornemisza (No 2) [1985] FLR 1069, [1985] Fam Law
283, CA 4.22

l

Tomney v Tomney [1983] Fam 15, [1982] 3 WLR 909, (1983) 4 FLR 159 .... 18.24
Tracey v Tracey [2006] EWCA Civ 734, [2007] 1 FLR 196, sub nom T V T (Financial
  Provision: Private Education) [2005] EWHC 2119 (Fam), [2006] 1 FLR 903, [2006]
  182, FD 11.47
Traversa v Freddi [2009] EWHC 2101 (Fam), [2010] 1 FLR 324, [2009] Fam Law
  1022 .... 15.13, 15.20
Trippas v Trippas [1973] Fam 134, [1973] 2 WLR 585, [1973] 2 All ER 1, CA . 1.48, 4.14
Trowbridge v Trowbridge [2003] 2 FLR 231, [2003] Fam Law 476, ChD 12.25

U

UL v BK (Freezing orders: Safeguards: Standard Examples) [2013] EWHC 1735 (Fam)
  .... 8.45, 20.13
Ulrich v Ulrich and Felton [1968] 1 WLR 180, [1968] 1 All ER 67, 19 P&CR 699,
  CA 6.22

V

V v V (Child Maintenance) [2001] 2 FLR 799, [2001] Fam Law 649, FD 11.41
V v V (Prenuptial Agreement) [2011] EWHC 3230 (Fam), [2012] 1 FLR 1315, [2012] 2
  FCR 98, [2012] Fam Law 274, (2012) 109(4) LSG 17 .... 1.216, 18.20
VB v JP [2008] EWHC 112 (Fam), [2008] 1 FLR 742, [2008] FCR 682 .... 13.30
Vasilyeva v Shemyakin [2019] EWHC 932 (Fam), [2019] 2 FLR 948, [2019] Fam Law
  882, [2019] All ER (D) 08 (May) 15.24
Vaughan v Vaughan [2007] EWCA Civ 1085, [2008] 1 FLR 1108, [2007] 3 FCR 533,
  CA 2.83, 10.78
Vaughan v Vaughan [2008] EWCA Civ 248, [2008] 1 FLR 1721, [2008] Fam Law
  608 .... 1.88, 1.89
Vaughan v Vaughan [2010] EWCA Civ 349, [2010] 3 WLR 1209, [2010] 2 FLR 242
  .... 2.83
Versteegh v Versteegh [2018] EWCA Civ 1050, [2019] Fam 518, [2019] 2 WLR 399,
  [2018] 2 FLR 1417, [2018] Fam Law 966, [2018] All ER (D) 64 (May) 1.219
Vicary v Vicary [1992] 2 FLR 271, [1992] Fam Law 428, CA 1.166, 4.26, 18.32
Vilinova v Vilinov [2019] EWHC 1107 (Fam), [2019] 2 FLR 972, [2019] Fam Law
  884 .... 15.16
Vince v Wyatt [2015] UKSC 14, [2015] 1 FLR 972, [2015] 2 All ER 755, [2015] 1 WLR
  1228 .... 1.51, 1.157, 9.5, 16.16

W

W v H (divorce financial remedies) [2020] EWFC B10 .... 10.3, 10.29, 10.73
W v J (Child: Variation of Financial Provision) [2003] EWHC 2657 (Fam), [2004] 2 FLR
  300, [2004] Fam Law 568, FD 11.45
W v W (Financial Provision: Lump Sum) [1976] Fam 107, [1975] 3 WLR 752, [1975]
  3 All ER 970 .... 1.182
W v W (Judicial Separation: Ancillary Relief) [1995] 2 FLR 259, [1995] Fam Law 548,
  FD 1.166
W v W (Financial Relief: Appropriate Forum) [1997] 1 FLR 257, [1997] Fam Law 240,
  FD 1.252, 1.253
W v W [2001] Fam Law 656 .... 1.179
WA v The Estate of HA deceased [2015] EWHC 2233 (Fam) 18.60
WS v HS [2018] EWFC 11, [2018] 4 WLR 111, [2018] 2 FLR 528, [2018] Fam Law
  663, 168 NLJ 7785, [2018] All ER (D) 158 (Feb) 7.3, 16.54
WS v WS [2015] EWHC 3941 (Fam) 10.33, 10.78, 10.79
WX v HX (Treatment of Matrimonial and Non-Matrimonial Property [2021] EWHC
  241 (Fam), [2021] Fam Law 640 .... 1.153
Wachtel v Wachtel [1973] Fam 72, [1973] 2 WLR 366, [1973] 1 All ER 829, CA 1.48,
  1.139, 1.166, 1.182
Waggott v Waggott [2018] EWCA Civ 727, [2019] 2 WLR 297, [2018] 2 FLR 406,
  [2018] Fam Law 659, 168 NLJ 7790, [2018] All ER (D) 44 (Apr) 1.34, 2.83
Wagstaff v Wagstaff [1992] 1 WLR 320, [1992] 1 All ER 275, [1992] 1 FLR 333, CA
  .... 1.95

Walkden v Walkden [2009] EWCA Civ 627, [2010] 1 FLR 174, [2009] 3 FCR 25 .... 18.46
Walker v Innospec Ltd [2017] UKSC 47, [2017] 4 All ER 1004, [2018] 1 LRC 310, [2018] 1 CMLR 707, [2017] IRLR 928, [2017] ICR 1077, (2017) Times, 25 July, [2017] All ER (D) 77 (Jul), SC 10.98
Walker v Walker (Army Gratuity) (1983) 4 FLR 455, (1983) Fam Law 181, (1983) The Times, May 5, FD 8.38
Ward v Ward and Greene [1980] 1 All ER 176, (1980) 1 FLR 368, sub nom Ward v Ward (1980) Fam Law 22, CA 2.21
Waterman v Waterman [1989] 1 FLR 380, [1989] Fam Law 227, CA 2.77
Webber v Webber (CPS intervening) [2006] EWHC 2893 (Fam), [2007] 1 WLR 1052, [2007] 2 FLR 116 .... 21.15
Wehmeyer v Wehmeyer [2001] 2 FLR 84, [2001] Fam Law 493, ChD 12.32, 12.34
Whaley v Whaley [2011] EWCA Civ 617, [2012] 1 FLR 735, [2011] 2 FCR 323, [2011] WTLR 1267, 14 ITELR 1, [2011] Fam Law 804, [2011] NPC 53 .... 1.76
Wheatley v Wheatley [1999] 2 FLR 205, [1999] BPIR 431, [1999] Fam Law 375, QBD 12.27
Whig v Whig [2007] EWHC 1856 (Fam), [2008] 1 FLR 453, [2007] BPIR 1418 ..... 12.13
White v White [2001] 1 AC 596, [2000] 3 WLR 1571, [2000] FLR 981, HL, [1999] 2 WLR 1213, [1998] 4 All ER 659, [1998] 2 FLR 310, CA 1.10, 1.15–1.19, 1.21, 1.22, 1.28, 1.50, 1.56, 1.57, 1.63, 1.64, 1.103, 1.123, 1.124, 1.134, 1.135, 1.137, 1.166, 1.167, 1.214, 2.34, 2.48–2.51, 4.14–4.16, 4.19, 4.27, 4.30, 4.36, 4.40, 4.51, 5.33, 6.22, 18.62, 23.3, 24.4
Whitehouse-Piper v Stokes [2008] EWCA Civ 1049, [2009] 1 FLR 983, [2009] Fam Law 184, [2008] Fam Law 948, [2008] All ER (D) 194 (Jul) 16.5
Whiting v Whiting [1988] 1 WLR 565, [1988] 2 All ER 275, [1988] 2 FLR 189, CA 2.77
Whittingham v Whittingham [1979] Fam 19, [1978] 2 WLR 936, [1978] 3 All ER 805, CA 8.13, 8.21
Wickler v Wickler [1998] FLR 326, [1998] Fam Law 457, FD 14.17
Wicks v Wicks [1999] Fam 15, [1998] 3 WLR 277, [1998] 1 FLR 470, CA . 4.9, 7.15, 8.40, 16.54
Williams v Lindley [2005] EWCA Civ 103, [2005] 2 FLR 710, CA 18.35, 18.54
Wodehouse v Wodehouse [2018] EWCA Civ 3009, [2019] Fam Law 623 .... 1.76
Woodley v Woodley (No 2) [1994] 1 WLR 1167, [1993] 4 All ER 1010, [1993] 2 FLR 477, CA 12.27, 12.29, 19.48
Work v Gray [2017] EWCA Civ 270 affirming Gray v Work [2015] EWHC 834 (Fam), [2015] Fam Law 104 .... 1.144–1.147, 1.220
Wright v Wright [2015] EWCA Civ 201, [2015] Fam Law 523 .... 2.96
Wyatt v Vince [2015] UKSC 14, [2015] 2 All ER 755, [2015] 1 WLR 1228, [2015] 1 FLR 972, [2015] 1 FCR 566, [2015] Fam Law 525, 165 NLJ 7645, (2015) Times, 25 March, [2015] All ER (D) 116 (Mar), SC 10.10, 16.10

X

XW v XH [2019] EWCA Civ 2262, [2020] 4 WLR 22, [2020] 1 FLR 1015, [2020] Fam Law 309, [2019] All ER (D) 118 (Dec) 1.18, 1.39, 1.147, 23.6
Xydhias v Xydhias [1999] 1 FLR 683, [1999] 2 All ER 386, [1999] 1 FCR 289 ..... 1.236, 1.237, 1.239, 1.240, 9.7, 16.39

Y

Y v Y (Financial Orders: Inherited Wealth) [2012] EWHC 2063 (Fam), [2013] Fam Law 535 .... 1.152
Young v Young [1962] P 27, [1961] 3 WLR 1109, [1961] 3 All ER 695, CA 6.10
Young v Young [2012] EWHC 138 (Fam), [2012] Fam 198, [2012] 3 WLR 266, [2012] 2 FLR 470, [2012] 2 FCR 83, [2012] All ER (D) 36 (Feb) 19.41
Young v Young [2013] EWHC 3637 (Fam), [2014] 2 FLR 786, [2014] Fam Law 291 .... 12.30

Z

Z v A (Financial Remedy after Overseas Divorce) [2012] EWHC 1434 (Fam), [2013]
Fam Law 393 .... 15.21
Z v Z (Financial Position: Overseas Divorce) [1992] 2 FLR 291, FD 15.10
Z v Z (Financial Remedies: Marriage Contract) [2011] EWHC 2878 (Fam), [2012] 1
FLR 1100, [2012] Fam Law 136 .... 1.216
Zimina v Zimin [2017] EWCA Civ 1429, [2018] Fam Law 27, [2017] All ER (D) 57
(Oct) 15.23

Chapter 1

INTRODUCTION TO FINANCIAL REMEDIES

SCOPE OF THIS CHAPTER

1.1 Financial remedies comprise those orders of a financial nature which the court may make in proceedings for divorce, judicial separation or nullity of marriage. In this chapter, the range of possible orders is set out and the general principles on which orders are made are considered. In later chapters, each type of order (eg periodical payments orders) is examined in detail; in this chapter, certain matters common to all such orders are considered, although where any individual factor merits more detailed examination it is the subject of a chapter in its own right.

1.2 This book also deals with one type of remedy which does not depend on the issue of proceedings for divorce etc, namely, applications for neglect to maintain under s 27 of the Matrimonial Causes Act 1973 (MCA 1973). The principles applicable to such applications are considered in CHAPTER 14.

1.3 Many older readers may have been more familiar with the term 'ancillary relief' than 'financial remedy'. The change in nomenclature was brought about by the Family Procedure Rules 2010 (hereafter FPR) which came into force on 6 April 2011.

1.4 It would be unusual for the court to consider making one type of order only. That might in fact be the result of a particular case, but the court must have regard to the overall position, and the result of most applications is that a combination of orders is made. The court must take an overview of the whole case.

DEFINITIONS

1.5 'Financial remedy' is defined by the FPR[1] as:

'(a)   a financial order;'

[1]   FPR 2.3(1).

1.6 This is the class of remedies with which this book will principally be concerned. However, the term encompasses a number of other remedies such as:

1

- an order under Sch 1 to the Children Act 1989 (orders for children);
- an order under Part III of the Matrimonial and Family Proceedings 1984 (relief after overseas divorce);
- an order under s 27 of the MCA 1973 (failure to maintain).

A complete list will be found in the rules printed in the Appendix to this book.

1.7 'Financial order' is defined as:

'(a) an avoidance of disposition order;
(b) an order for maintenance pending suit;
(c) an order for maintenance pending outcome of proceedings;
(d) an order for periodical payments or lump sum provision as mentioned in section 21(1) of the 1973 Act, except an order under section 27(6) of that Act;
(e) an order for periodical payments or lump sum provision as mentioned in paragraph 2(1) of Schedule 5 to the 2004 Act, made under Part 1 of Schedule 5 to that Act;
(f) a property adjustment order;
(g) a variation order;
(h) a pension sharing order; or
(i) a pension compensation sharing order;

("variation order", "pension compensation sharing order" and "pension sharing order" are defined in rule 9.3.)'[1]

[1] Pension compensation sharing order and pension sharing order are considered in more detail in CHAPTER 10.

THE PRINCIPLES GOVERNING THE EXERCISE OF THE COURT'S DISCRETION

1.8 Before embarking on a detailed consideration of the individual factors in s 25(2), the court's overall approach will be considered. This must involve consideration of the issues of equality and fairness, which have assumed greater significance over recent years.

1.9 Section 25 of MCA 1973 contains the matters to which the court is to have regard in deciding how to exercise its powers under ss 23, 24 and 24A. It has frequently been said[1] that the statutory 'guidelines' must be the principal determining factors for the court; decided cases showing how the court's discretion has been exercised on other occasions are of limited relevance although, clearly, guidance from appellate courts as to occasions on which courts have misdirected themselves are valuable.

[1] Notably, first in *Sharpe v Sharpe* (1981) Fam Law 121, (1981) Times, 7 February.

1.10 In a leading case[1], Butler–Sloss LJ, as she then was, stated the position as follows:

'There is a danger that practitioners in the field of family law attempt to apply too rigidly the decisions of this court and of the Family Division, without sufficiently recognising that each case involving a family has to be decided upon broad principles adapted to the facts of the individual case. Ancillary relief applications are governed by the statutory framework set out in the Matrimonial Causes Act 1973 as amended in 1984. Sections 25 and 25A provide the guidelines and require the court to have regard to all the circumstances of the individual case and to exercise the discretion of the court to do justice between the parties.'

1   *White v White* [1998] 2 FLR 310, CA.

1.11 In *Scheeres v Scheeres*[1], Thorpe LJ said, at p 243 G/H:

'It is very important in these ancillary relief cases, where the court exercises a very broad discretion, that the judge should carry out the s.25 exercise rigorously, in an attempt to inject some sort of clear rationality and principle to what otherwise could be said to be palm tree adjudication.'

This decision, and specifically the need for the exercise to be conducted rigorously, was cited with approval by the Privy Council in *Ramnarine v Ramnarine*[2].

1   [1999] 1 FLR 241.
2   [2014] 1 FLR 594 at [10].

1.12 Each case will turn on its own facts, and reference to the statutory criteria is therefore always essential. However, this point needs reinforcing in view of the attention given to leading cases which have reached the House of Lords and Supreme Court in recent years and which must be analysed in some detail. The point which will be made, and which perhaps needs to be made now so that it may be borne in mind when the reader considers decisions of any of the highest courts, is that, notwithstanding the valuable guidance given in the speeches or judgments, authority for any proposition must ultimately be derived from the statute and not from any judicial gloss thereon.

EQUALITY AND FAIRNESS

1.13 Although s 25 prescribes the matters to which the court must have regard, it does not suggest or recommend any starting point, tariff or formula for deciding what proportion of the assets of the parties each should receive. This is in contrast to other jurisdictions, many of which contain prescriptions as to percentages to be awarded to each party, often depending on the length of the marriage. It is frequently argued by practitioners and academic commentators that the law of England and Wales should be amended to contain such guidelines. However, judges have continued to emphasise that such prescription is not possible within the terms of the statute, and that each case must be considered on its own merits against the background of consideration of the s 25 factors. What has been described as 'the search for principle' continues.

1.14 Having said that, guidance was given in the two decisions of the House of Lords which are about to be considered, and it will be seen that, save in one important area (as to which see **1.137**), there was general agreement as to certain important principles.

1.15 Neither the words 'fairness' nor 'equality' appear in the MCA 1973. However, in *White v White*, Lord Nicholls, after recording the self-evident proposition that the court must act in a just and non-discriminatory way, set out the important principle that the court must be fair, and that fairness implies equality. The 6 years which elapsed between the decision of their Lordships'

House in *White v White (White)* and *Miller v Miller* and *McFarlane v McFarlane (Miller/McFarlane)* saw much discussion on the part of practitioners and judges as to what this meant in various classes of case.

1.16 Before analysing the statutory factors therefore, we will consider the following:

(1)   the significance of *White v White*;
(2)   *Miller/McFarlane*; and
(3)   developments post *Miller/McFarlane*, in particular *Charman v Charman*.

White v White

1.17 Very few cases relating to financial remedies reached the House of Lords or now reach the Supreme Court. Family cases which get that far usually relate to children, particularly public law issues. When the financial dispute between Mr and Mrs White reached their Lordships in 2000[1] it was thought that this would be the final word on these matters for some considerable time. *White* set out guidelines for the determination of such cases which may be summarised as follows:

• The court must be fair. There can be no discrimination between husband and wife in their respective roles. Whatever the division of labour, fairness dictates that this should not prejudice either party when considering the statutory factors. There should be no bias in favour of the breadwinner as against the homemaker and child-carer.
• When carrying out the statutory exercise, the judge should always check his tentative views against the 'yardstick of equality of division'. Equality should only be departed from if, and to the extent that, there is good reason for doing so. This does not mean that there is a starting point or presumption of equality.
• The concept of reasonable requirements is erroneous. The statute refers to 'needs' but this is only one of the statutory factors.

[1]   *White v White* [2001] 1 AC 596.

1.18 These principles and the philosophy behind them were referred to in the recent important case of *XW v XH (Financial Remedies: Business Assets*[1] Moylan LJ made the following observation:

'I would emphasise that the important principles enunciated in *White* reflect, what was referred to in *Owens v Owens* [2018] 2 FLR 1067 as, "the relevant social norm which has changed most obviously during the last 40 years", Lord Wilson at [34]. This "related to society's insistence upon equality between the sexes; to its recognition that marriage is a partnership of equals". In *White* this "insistence" can be found in the speech of Lord Nicholls when he powerfully emphasised "one principle of universal application", namely that: "In seeking to achieve a fair outcome, there is no place for discrimination between the husband and the wife and their respective roles".'

[1]   [2019] EWCA Civ 2262.

1.19 However, the guidance in *White v White* was not to be the last word and certain issues remained to trouble the courts, including the Court of Appeal. These issues may be summarised as essentially the search for fairness, and what fairness means. Given that the court must be fair, and given that the yardstick of equality is overriding but does not amount to a rigid regime of equality, what are the circumstances in which the court may be fair and at the same time depart from equal shares? Would this be appropriate where, for example, the marriage was short; if so, what constitutes a short marriage? Would it be appropriate where one party had created the wealth enjoyed by the couple by his or her exceptional contributions? If so, how exceptional would the contributions have to be? It would be inappropriate to recite here the cases in which these issues were discussed and sometimes contradictory answers given[1]. Running parallel with all this was academic criticism of the whole approach of the law of England and Wales[2]. This law is based on a discretionary approach, and even in recent times judges in the Court of Appeal have gone out of their way to emphasise that there is no formula which will apply to all cases; these matters have to be considered on a case-by-case basis[3]. The criticism made is that even on that basis, analysis of the cases reveals no rational pattern, and further, that this unpredictable case-by-case approach is unfair, since parties who wish to settle their disputes are given uncertain guidance and often have to risk large sums of money to achieve a result.

[1] For a detailed analysis see R Bird 'Dividing Marital Assets after Lambert' [2003] Fam Law 534. However, two decisions of Coleridge J require careful reading, namely *H-J v H-J (Financial Provision: Equality)* [2002] 1 FLR 415, and *G v G (Financial Provision: Equal Division)* [2002] EWHC 1339 (Fam), [2002] 2 FLR 1143. In *Lambert v Lambert* [2002] EWCA Civ 1685, [2003] 1 FLR 139, CA Thorpe LJ said that Coleridge J was not wrong (ie he was right!) to find that '50/50 resonates with fairness' para [38].
[2] Among many others see in particular R Bailey-Harris [2003] Fam Law 386, J Eekelar [2003] Fam Law 828 and Jens M Scherpe in 'Fifty years in Family Law, Essays for Stephen Cretney (Intersentia 2012,) p 133.
[3] See eg Wall LJ in *Miller v Miller* at para [88].

1.20 The combined appeals of *Miller v Miller* and *McFarlane v McFarlane* which were decided by the House in May 2006 therefore attracted widespread interest, both among family lawyers and in the popular press.

Miller and McFarlane

1.21 The House of Lords heard the appeals in *Miller v Miller* and *McFarlane v Macfarlane (Miller/McFarlane)* together because they clearly raised similar issues. Both were 'big money' cases, and both dealt with the issues arising out of *White* which are briefly outlined above. The facts in both cases need not be described here[1]; rather, the principles established or affirmed will be considered.

[1] For more detail see R Bird *Miller and McFarlane: The Implications for Family Lawyers* (Family Law, 2006).

White v White re-affirmed

1.22 The two most important speeches were those of Lord Nicholls and Baroness Hale, who tried to set out a clear list of principles to be followed. They began with some fairly obvious but nonetheless important points; the court must be fair, and the statutory first consideration of the welfare of the children must be observed. The principles of *White v White*, such as fairness, non-discrimination and the yardstick of equality, were repeated and remain of primary importance.

THREE PRINCIPLES: MEETING NEEDS, COMPENSATION AND SHARING

1.23 The House underlined the fact that financial relief is not a matter of taking from one party to give to the other, but is rather a matter of a proper and fair sharing of assets which both of them, in their interdependent and joint lives, have acquired. The three principles which this case established and/or confirmed as being the rationale for financial provision contained in the 1973 Act may be summarised as follows:

(a) *Meeting the needs of the parties*: Lord Nicholls said that mutual dependence begets mutual obligations of support. Fairness requires that the assets of the parties should be divided so as to meet their housing and financial needs. Baroness Hale said that the most common rationale for redistribution is that the relationship has generated needs which it is right that the other party should meet. Needs may arise as a result of one party having been a homemaker and childcarer, and needs generated by such a choice are 'a perfectly sound rationale for adjusting the parties respective resources in compensation'.

(b) *Compensation*: Lord Nicholls said that compensation is aimed at redressing any significant prospective disparity between the parties arising from the way they conducted their marriage. Baroness Hale described this as compensation for relationship-generated disadvantage, which goes beyond need.

(c) *Sharing*: Lord Nicholls saw sharing as derived from the basic concept of equality permeating a marriage. Husband and wife are equal partners in marriage. Baroness Hale described this as the sharing of the fruits of the matrimonial partnership.

1.24 These three principles may be taken as the foundation for any intellectual approach to the task of awarding financial provision. However, both Lord Nicholls and Baroness Hale made it clear that these are general principles and that they must be adapted to suit the requirements of a particular case. In particular, Lord Nicholls emphasised that equality applies 'unless there is good reason to the contrary. The yardstick of equality is to be applied as an aid, not a rule'.

Legitimate expectations and standard of living

1.25 The judge at first instance, and the Court of Appeal, had approved the concept of 'legitimate expectations'. The House of Lords strongly disapproved this concept; this could play no part in the decision-making process.

1.26 However, the importance of the standard of living of the parties during the marriage was affirmed, and this was one of the statutory factors used by Lord Nicholls to justify the *Miller* award. For obvious reasons, it will only be important in cases where assets exceed needs, but this is an important reminder of the need to consider all the s 25 factors.

Application to smaller money cases

1.27 One of the problems with discussing decisions of the higher courts is that they normally involve very large amounts of money and rich parties. Many practitioners will be more interested in whether or not they apply to the normal run of cases.

1.28 It must first be said that the *White v White* principles of fairness, non-discrimination and the yardstick of equality apply to all cases, big or small and regardless of the length of the marriage. However, Lord Nicholls makes it clear that while the approach has to be the same, the result will be different in cases where the needs exceed the assets because the funds are not available to take the matter further. It is worth repeating his words:

> 'When the marriage ends fairness requires that the assets of the parties should be divided primarily so as to make provision for the parties' housing and financial needs, taking into account a wide range of matters such as the parties' ages, their future earning capacity, the family's standard of living, and any disability of either party. Most of these needs will have been generated by the marriage, but not all of them. Needs arising from age or disability are instances of the latter.
>
> In most cases the search for fairness largely begins and ends at this stage. In most cases the available assets are insufficient to provide adequately for the needs of two homes. The court seeks to stretch modest finite resources so far as possible to meet the parties' needs. Especially where children are involved it may be necessary to augment the available assets by having recourse to the future earnings of the money-earner, by way of an order for periodical payments.'

1.29 Baroness Hale expressed similar views. An equal partnership does not always dictate equal sharing of the assets. (One could interject there the view that, in lower value cases, it almost never does.) As Baroness Hale, said, equal division may have to give way to the needs of one party or the children.

1.30 Baroness Hale adds that recognising this is one reason why English law has been successful in retaining a home for the children.

> 'Too strict an adherence to equal sharing and the clean break can lead to a rapid decrease in the primary carer's standard of living and a rapid increase in the breadwinner's. The breadwinner's unimpaired and unimpeded earning capacity is a powerful resource which can frequently repair any loss of capital after an unequal distribution.'

1.31 Other issues were discussed in this case, but they will be considered under their separate subject-matter headings, see:

- 'Duration of marriage' at **1.108**;
- 'Contributions' at **1.132** et seq; and
- 'Conduct' at **1.175**.

Charman v Charman

1.32 After the decision of the House of Lords in *Miller/McFarlane*, the courts were not idle. The first significant development was the decision of the Court of Appeal in *Charman v Charman* to which reference must now be made. In its judgment in *Charman*, the court dealt with several issues of considerable importance[1].

[1] It is worth noting that this was a particularly strong court, consisting of the President, and Thorpe and Wilson LJJ. It would be difficult to conceive a greater concentration of expertise in this field. Moreover, the judgment was the judgment of the court, so there are no differences of opinion to be analysed.

1.33 The first of these issues was how the yardstick of equality should be approached. In the course of argument, there had been debate as to whether a judge should begin with some notion of equality and then, as it were, depart from it where appropriate, or whether the various s 25 factors should be considered with no preconceptions and then the provisional result compared with the yardstick of equality. The court dealt with this by reference to the new concept of 'sharing' introduced in *Miller*, and it is worth quoting the passage from the judgment of the court in full. This begins at para [64] where it is said that:

> '"The yardstick of equality of division", first identified by Lord Nicholls in *White* at p 605G, filled the vacuum which resulted from the abandonment in that decision of the criterion of "reasonable requirements". The origins of the yardstick lay in s 25(2) of the Act, specifically in s 25(2)(f), which refers to the parties' contributions: see the preceding argument of Lord Nicholls at p 605D–E. The yardstick reflected a modern, non-discriminatory conclusion that the proper evaluation under s 5(2)(f) of the parties' different contributions to the welfare of the family should generally lead to an equal division of their property unless there was good reason for the division to be unequal. It also tallied with the overarching objective: a fair result.
>
> [65] Although in *White* the majority of the House agreed with the speech of Lord Nicholls and thus with his description of equality as a "yardstick" against which tentative views should be "checked", Lord Cooke, at p 615D, doubted whether use of the words "yardstick" or "check" would produce a result different from that of the words "guideline" or "starting point". In *Miller* the House clearly moved towards the position of Lord Cooke. Thus Lord Nicholls, at [20] and [29], referred to the "equal sharing principle" and to the "sharing entitlement"; those phrases describe more than a yardstick for use as a check. Baroness Hale put the matter beyond doubt when, referring to remarks by Lord Nicholls at [29], she said, at [144],
>
>> "I agree that there cannot be a hard and fast rule about whether one starts with equal sharing and departs if need or compensation supply a reason to do so, or whether one starts with need and compensation and shares the balance."
>
> It is clear that the court's consideration of the sharing principle is no longer required to be postponed until the end of the statutory exercise. We should add that, since we take the "the sharing principle" to mean that property should be shared in equal proportions unless there is good reason to depart from such proportions, departure is not from the principle but takes place within the principle.'

It might seem from this, therefore, that sharing, which means equality and equal shares, is now more of a starting point than a yardstick, a point which is reinforced by the judgments in *XW v XH* (see **1.39**).

Case law since *Charman*

1.34 Since the decisions in these leading cases have been handed down there has been a natural tendency on the part of practitioners to refer to them as if they and not the statute were the primary source of authority. The High Court has been at pains to try to refute this view as will be seen by the comments in a few leading decisions.

- In *RP v RP*[1] Coleridge J said that care must be taken not to elevate passages from the speeches to some kind of quasi-statutory amendment. In particular, it was not possible or desirable to break up ancillary relief claims into separate 'heads of claim' like a personal injury matter. His Lordship also doubted whether 'compensation' added anything to 'financial obligations and responsibilities'.
- In *CR v CR*[2] Bodey J repeated these points; it was important that the terms 'sharing', 'compensation' and 'need' were not elevated into separate 'heads of claim' or 'loss' independent of the words of the statute. Otherwise, there could be a danger of double counting.
- In *B v B (No 2)*[3] it was said that the reported authorities did not establish the proposition that equal division was the starting point in all cases. The starting point remains the financial position of the parties and s 25 of the MCA 1973. In all cases the objective was fairness and avoidance of discrimination. The outcome of the s 25 exercise must always be tested against the yardstick of equality, which should be departed from only if and to the extent that there was some good reason for doing so.

In *Waggott v Waggott*[4] the wife had argued that the judge at first instance should have awarded her a greater share of the capital assets because of the husband's greatly superior earning potential; this disregarded the sharing principle and also the issue of compensation. Further, the wife was disadvantaged because she had to use part of her capital to produce an income, whereas the husband had his earned income. In respect of whether an earning capacity is capable of being a matrimonial asset to which the sharing principle applies Moylan LJ held that there were a number of reasons why the clear answer was that it was not. These included the fact that any extension of the sharing principle to post-separation earnings would fundamentally undermine the court's ability to effect a clean break. The principle would apply to every case in which one party had earnings which were greater than the other's, regardless of need and would inevitably require the court to assess the extent to which the earning capacity had accrued during the marriage. Where would the court start and by reference to what factors would the court determine this issue? The sharing principle applied to marital assets, being 'the property of the parties generated during the marriage otherwise than by external donation' (*Charman v Charman (No 4)*, para 66). An earning capacity was not property and, in the context of this case, it resulted in the generation of property after the marriage. The court did not accept the argument that the wife's capital should be protected and should not be used to meet her income needs. This again would conflict with the clean break principle to such a significant extent as to undermine the statutory 'steer' because, absent other resources, the applicant spouse would always have a claim for an additional award to meet his or her income needs. As a matter of principle 'the court applies the need principle when determining whether the sharing award is sufficient to meet that party's future needs'. In respect of the compensation principle the court did not accept the wife's argument; it was clear from Miller 'that compensation is for the disadvantage sustained by the party who has given up a career.' The Supreme Court has refused permission to appeal this decision.

In *C v C (Post-Separation Accrual: Approach to Quantification of sharing Claim where Non-Matrimonial Property)*[5] Roberts J followed the approach in Waggott and said that assets derived from income earned and invested since the separation should only be 'invaded' and shared if there was a sound and principled reason for doing so, such as meeting the needs of the other spouse. This was not such a case.

[1]   [2007] 1 FLR 2105.
[2]   [2008] 1 FLR 323.
[3]   [2008] EWCA Civ 483.
[4]   [2018] EWCA Civ 727.
[5]   [2018] EWIIC 3186 (Fam).

1.35 In *O'Dwyer v O'Dwyer*[1] Francis J held that the judge below had been plainly wrong to identify the income stream of a business as matrimonial property. Any remaining doubts as to whether an income stream is an asset which can be shared, save for the purposes of paying needs or compensation, were clearly and unequivocally dispelled by the decision in *Waggott*. It is now settled law that income cannot be shared.

[1]   [2019] EWHC 1838 (Fam).

1.36 Similar points are made in *P v P*[1], *H v H*[2] (Charles J), *H v H*[3] (Moylan J), and *C v C*[4], in which it was said that a formulaic approach should be resisted; the proper approach was to consider the s 25 factors and then to consider the principles of needs and sharing (and also compensation where appropriate, which was not the case here). In this case the judge added that, after a long marriage, factors of substance had to justify a departure from an equal division of assets.

[1]   [2008] 2 FLR 1135.
[2]   [2007] 2 FLR 548.
[3]   [2008] EWHC 935 (Fam), [2008] 2 FLR 2092.
[4]   [2008] EWHC 2033 (Fam), [2009] 1 FLR 8.

1.37 One issue which remains difficult is that of wealth acquired by one party after separation. In *B v B*[1] Moylan J held that to award the wife half of the wealth existing at the date of trial would give insufficient weight to the fact that a substantial part of the husband's wealth had accrued directly as a result of his efforts since separation. Nor could such an award be justified on the basis of the wife's needs. As a general proposition, absent needs or compensation, the sharing principle should end at the end of the marital partnership.

[1]   [2010] EWHC 193 (Fam), [2010] 2 FLR 1214.

1.38 For a recent case where departure from equality was justified on the ground of the parties' modest means, see *A v L (Departure from Equality: Needs)*[1]. For further discussion of the proper treatment of inherited wealth, see the section on 'Contributions' at **1.132** et seq. *Sharp v Sharp* was, according to the Court of Appeal, 'one of the very small number of cases' in which several factors justified departure from the equal sharing principle. Those factors were the fact that there were no children, the cohabitation and marriage taken together were relatively short (6 years), both parties had their own careers and organised their own separate finances, and the husband was not privy to details of the wife's bonuses (which were considerable and the central area of dispute). The majority opinion in *Miller v Miller* should be followed.

1   [2011] EWHC 3150 (Fam).

1.39 The most recent important decision to be considered is *XW v XH (Financial Remedies: Business Assets)*. This was a case involving exceptional wealth (the total assets exceeded £530m) and was concerned with the way the court should treat business assets (this is considered in more detail in CHAPTER 4 at **4.31**). However, Moylan LJ, with whose judgment the court agreed, dealt with several issues of general importance.

1.40 At first instance, Baker J had placed great weight on the fact that the assets which had grown so substantially during the marriage were the husband's business assets, and had awarded the wife about 29% of the combined assets. Moylan LJ said that insofar as they were the product of endeavour during the marriage they were marital assets which should be shared equally between the parties absent other factors.

1.41 The husband had argued that his 'special contribution' entitled him to a greater share, which Baker J had accepted , but on this issue Moylan LJ held that Baker J had failed to undertake the required assessment, namely to consider whether there was such a disparity in the parties' respective contributions to the welfare of the family that it would be inequitable to disregard, and his finding on this must therefore be set aside. Baker J did refer to W's contributions in the course of his judgment, but in his critical assessment he referred only to H's financial contribution. He did not focus on the extent of any disparity in the parties' respective contributions. There was no balancing of the parties' contributions. Baker J had referred to W's contributions as 'incalculable' but this was in the context of an overall assessment of fairness, not in the specific context of special contribution.

1.42 The court therefore set aside Baker J's order and considered the matter anew. It concluded that it was fair to treat 60% of the wealth derived from the shares as matrimonial property (£293 million) and 40% as non-matrimonial (£195 million). The court could not see how a proper application of the legal principles could lead other than to a determination that there was not such a disparity in the parties' respective contributions that it would be inequitable to disregard them when deciding what award to make. Although the husband's contributions had clearly been very significant, the necessary disparity was not present in this case and there were no other relevant factors which might lead to the conclusion that an equal sharing of the marital wealth would not be fair. Accordingly the assets and home were divided equally.

This case seems to represent a further movement towards equality being a starting point rather than a yardstick.

Equality and periodical payments

1.43 The impact of the cases cited above on periodical payments will be considered in more detail in CHAPTER 2.

COMPENSATION

1.44 Mention was made in *Charman*, above, of the relevance of compensation and there has been some debate and dissension about the part which this should play. Compensation is not one of the factors to which the court is directed to have regard by s 25(2). However, there is authority for saying that it can be one of the matters which play a part in the court's decision.

1.45 In *H v H*[1] Coleridge J, at first instance, had expressly treated compensation as a relevant factor and also treated capital available to the wife as having a rate of return of 3.75%. The Court of Appeal allowed the husband's appeal and remitted the case for re-hearing. The compensation element was recognised but Coleridge J was criticised for choosing the rate of 3.75% and for failing to undertake a more sophisticated exercise.

[1]   [2014] EWCA Civ 1523.

1.46 Compensation was one of the matters which Mostyn J had to consider in *SA v PA (Pre-Marital Agreement: Compensation)*[1] since it was the wife's case that she had given up a very high-powered career to allow the husband's career to flourish while she cared for the four children. At the conclusion of Mostyn J's review and consideration of the authorities as to the compensation principle, he concluded that it was hard to identify any case where compensation had been separately reflected as a premium or additional element. He said that there were now four principles concerning a compensation claim in light of the authorities:

'(i)   It will only be in a very rare and exceptional case where the principle will be capable of being successfully invoked.

(ii)   Such a case will be one where the court can say without any speculation, ie with almost near certainty, that the claimant gave up a very high earning career which had it not been foregone would have led to earnings at least equivalent to that presently enjoyed by the respondent.

(iii)   Such a high earning career will have been practised by the claimant over an appreciable period during the marriage. Proof of this track-record is key.

(iv)   Once these findings have been made compensation will be reflected by fixing the periodical payments award (or the multiplicand if this aspect is being capitalised by Duxbury) towards the top end of the discretionary bracket applicable for a needs assessment on the facts of the case.

Compensation ought not to be reflected by a premium or additional element on top of the needs based award.'

[1]   [2104] EWHC 392 (Fam).

1.47 It was Mostyn J's firm belief that, save in highly exceptional cases, an award for periodical payments should be assessed by reference to the principle of need alone. A perhaps more nuanced view was expressed by Moylan J in *BD v FD (Maintenance Pending Suit)*[1] (see **2.59** below).

[1]   [2014] EWHC 4443 (Fam).

ALL THE CIRCUMSTANCES OF THE CASE

1.48 In deciding whether to exercise its powers under ss 23–24A, and, if so, in what manner, it is the duty of the court to 'have regard to all the circumstances of the case'[1]. The section goes on to set out particular factors, but the term 'all the circumstances' must be taken to mean what it says. It is in wide terms, and it has been held that the court must not confine itself to the specified factors[2]. It is necessary to consider all other circumstances, whether past, present or future. For example, the remarriage of one of the parties is not specifically referred to as one of the statutory factors, but it has been held that it is one of the circumstances into which the court may properly enquire[3]. Another circumstance which is not specifically set out in the statute but which is nonetheless important is the existence of an agreement between the parties. This is considered in more detail below.

[1]   MCA 1973, s 25(1).
[2]   See eg *Kokosinski v Kokosinski* [1980] Fam 72 at 183; *Trippas v Trippas* [1973] Fam 134 at 144.
[3]   *H v H* [1975] Fam 9; *Jackson v Jackson* [1973] Fam 99 at 104. However, prospects of remarriage are not a 'guessing game' and findings must be supported by some reasonable evidence: *Wachtel v Wachtel* [1973] Fam 72 at 86. A spouse is under a duty to be frank and give complete disclosure.

1.49 In *A v T (Ancillary Relief: Cultural Factors)*[1], a case where the cultural values of both parties were not those of this country, it was held that where the parties had only a secondary attachment to the English jurisdiction, the court should give due weight to the primary cultural factors and not ignore the differential between what one party might anticipate from determination here as opposed to another jurisdiction[2].

[1]   [2004] 1 FLR 977.
[2]   For another example see *G v G (Matrimonial Property: Rights of Extended Family)* [2005] EWHC 1560 (Admin), [2006] 1 FLR 62.

1.50 As has been seen when considering the decisions of the House of Lords in *White v White*[1] and succeeding cases above two further extra-statutory principles, 'the yardstick of equality' and 'fairness', must now be borne in mind at all times.

[1]   [2000] 2 FLR 981, HL.

1.51 The need to consider all the circumstances of the case was emphasised in the unusual case of *Vince v Wyatt* which is discussed in more detail under Procedure in CHAPTER **16**. One of the reasons why the Supreme Court allowed the wife's appeal and referred the case for re-hearing was that her claim had been struck out before it could be heard on the basis of a (non-existent) power to grant summary judgment. Lord Wilson put the matter as follows:

'The objection to a grant of summary judgment upon an application by an ex-spouse for a financial order in favour of herself is not just that its determination is discretionary but that, by virtue of section 25(1) of the 1973 Act, it is the duty of the court in determining it to have regard to all the circumstances and, in particular, to the eight matters set out in subsection (2). The determination of an application by a court which has failed to have regard to them is unlawful: *Livesey (formerly Jenkins) v Livesey* [1985] AC 424 at p 437, Lord Brandon of Oakbrook. The meticulous duty cast upon family courts by section 25(2) is inconsistent with any summary power to determine either that an ex-wife has no real prospect of successfully prosecuting her claim or that an ex-husband has no real prospect of successfully defending it.'

FIRST CONSIDERATION THE WELFARE OF CHILDREN

1.52 It is provided that 'the first consideration' of the court must be given to '. . . the welfare while a minor of any child of the family who has not attained the age of eighteen'[1]. This requirement is therefore limited to children of the family, 'child of the family' being defined as any child who has been treated by both of the parties to the marriage as a child of their family[2]. It includes stepchildren and, where the parties have lived together with a child, it is difficult to imagine circumstances in which a stepchild would not be a child of the family[3].

[1]   MCA 1973, s 25(1).
[2]   MCA 1973, s 52(1).
[3]   See eg *Teeling v Teeling* [1984] FLR 808, CA.

1.53 The child must be under 18 years of age, and the scope of the court's duty under this provision is limited to the period ending with the child's eighteenth birthday. This is not to say that the court may or should not have regard to dependent children who are over 18[1], but such consideration would arise from one of the other factors such as the financial obligations or responsibilities of the parties, or as one of the circumstances of the case, and would not be the first consideration of the court.

[1]   *Lilford (Lord) v Glyn* [1979] 1 WLR 78.

1.54 As to the meaning of 'the first consideration', it has been held that this is not the same as the paramount consideration[1]. The welfare of a child is not to be regarded as taking precedence over all other matters but is the first matter to which the court should direct itself (see below).

[1]   *Suter v Suter and Jones* [1987] Fam 111, CA. In that case, it was held that the judge had been wrong to elevate the children's interests so as to control the outcome of the case. However, see also *R v R* [1988] 1 FLR 89, CA, where it was said that, broadly speaking, a person having an obligation to maintain his children has an obligation to order his financial affairs with due regard to his responsibility to pay reasonable maintenance for them and to meet his reasonable financial obligations.

NO ONE FACTOR MORE IMPORTANT THAN OTHERS

1.55 The statute sets out a list of matters to be considered, first when making orders as between the parties to the marriage and secondly when making orders in relation to children. The court is directed to have regard to all the matters contained in s 25(2), and there is nothing in the Act to indicate that any one factor shall be more important than any other. Clearly, in some cases, consideration of one factor (eg discrepancies in age, or the length of the marriage) will occupy more of the time of the court than the others, and it may be that, in the circumstances of a particular case, one factor will prove to be more important than the others. In principle, however, there is no intrinsic reason why one factor should outweigh the importance of the others[1].

[1] It used to be argued, for example, that if significant conduct were proved, this might be the major determining factor in the case. This is not, and never has been, so. See also *Piglowska v Piglowski* [1999] 2 FLR 763, HL.

1.56 In one case[1], Thorpe LJ, after considering the historical evolution of s 25, and the deletion in 1984 of the statutory duty to attempt to place the parties in the financial position in which they would have been had the marriage not broken down, observed that even prior to that amendment the Court of Appeal[2] had defined the judge's ultimate aim as being to do that which is fair, just and reasonable between the parties, and that had continued to be the judicial interpretation of the objective of the section. Parliament had not chosen to lay any emphasis on any one of the eight specific factors above any other[3]. He continued:

> 'Although there is no ranking of the criteria to be found in the statute, there is as it were a magnetism that draws the individual case to attach to one, two, or several factors as having a decisive influence on its determination . . . That said there is, if not a priority, certainly a particular importance attaching to s 25(2)(a).'

[1] *White v White* [1998] 2 FLR 310, CA.
[2] In *Page v Page* (1981) 2 FLR 198, CA, at 206.
[3] See also *Smith v Smith* [1991] 2 FLR 432, CA, per Butler-Sloss LJ.

1.57 The reasons for that priority will be considered further below. Thorpe LJ concluded this part of his judgment as follows:

> 'It has often been said, and cannot be too often repeated, that each case depends on its own unique facts and those facts must determine which of the eight factors is to be given particular prominence in determination.'

1.58 In *Charman v Charman*[1] the Court of Appeal gave guidance on a further difficult question, namely how to resolve any irreconcilable conflict between the result suggested by one principle and that suggested by another. At para [73] of the judgment of the court, Sir Mark Potter P said:

> 'Often conflict can be reconciled by recourse to an order for periodical payments: as for example in *McFarlane*, per Baroness Hale at [154]. Ultimately, however, in cases in which it is irreconcilable, the criterion of fairness must supply the answer. It is clear that, when the result suggested by the needs principle is an award of property greater than the result suggested by the sharing principle, the former result should in principle prevail: per Baroness Hale in *Miller* at [142] and [144]. At least in applying the needs principle the court will have focussed upon the needs of both parties; analogous focus on the respondent is not present in the compensation principle and we leave for another occasion the proper treatment of irreconcilable conflict between that principle and one of the others. It is also clear that, when the result suggested by the needs principle is an award of property less than the result suggested by the sharing principle, the latter result should in principle prevail.'

[1] [2007] EWCA Civ 503, [2007] All ER (D) 425 (May).

1.59 The developing law as to pre-nuptial and other agreements provides a good example of how one issue (in these cases, the significance of an agreement) should be considered. These cases are considered in more detail at **1.199**.

1.60 In *Thiry v Thiry*[1] Sir Peter Singer observed that the court must have regard to all the circumstances of the case but not all of them apply in every case and in many cases there is a 'magnetic factor' which dominates. There is no reason in principle why a factor not listed in s 25(2) could not qualify as magnetic. In this case restorative justice was the dominating factor.

[1]   [2014] EWHC 4046 (Fam).

FINANCIAL RESOURCES

1.61 The financial resources of the parties are crucial to any application for a financial order. It is only when the court has all the evidence as to the resources of the parties that it can decide whether, and if so, how, to redistribute them. As Coleridge J put it in *Charman v Charman* at first instance[1], 'the obvious starting point for all these applications is the financial position of the parties now'.

[1]   Approved by the CA at para [59] of its judgment.

1.62 The court must have regard to[1]:

'(a)   the income, earning capacity, property and other financial resources which each of the parties to the marriage has or is likely to have in the foreseeable future, including in the case of earning capacity any increase in that capacity which it would in the opinion of the court be reasonable to expect a party to the marriage to take steps to acquire.'

[1]   MCA 1973, s 25(2)(a).

1.63 In *White v White*, referred to above, in the Court of Appeal, Thorpe LJ underlined the importance of this factor by saying that, in almost every case, it is logically necessary to determine what is available before considering how it should be allocated, and repeated his opinion, first expressed in *H v H (Financial Provision: Capital Allowance)*[1], that the discretionary powers of the court to adjust capital shares between spouses should not be exercised unless there was a manifest need for intervention upon the application of the s 25 criteria.

[1]   [1993] 2 FLR 335 at 347.

1.64 It has to be said that the second part of that statement cannot survive unscathed the decisions of the House of Lords in *White v White* and of the Court of Appeal in *Lambert v Lambert*. It is certainly still the case that the court has to fulfil a fact-finding role but even then some caution must be exercised. In *Parra v Parra*[1] Thorpe LJ was concerned that the judge had examined the financial position of the parties at very great length and in extraordinary detail and gave the following guidance:

'The outcome of ancillary relief cases depends upon the exercise of a singularly broad judgment that obviates the need for the investigation of minute detail and equally the need to make findings on minor issues in dispute.'

[1]   [2003] 1 FLR 942, CA.

1.65 The task of the judge in ancillary relief litigation was different from that of the judge in the civil justice system; on the one hand, his quasi-inquisitorial role gave him a certain independence from the arguments of the parties but, on the other, he had an obligation to eschew over-elaboration and to: ' . . . endeavour to paint the canvas of his judgment with a broad brush rather than with a fine sable. Judgments in this field need to be simple in structure and simply explained'.

1.66 The issue of what are 'matrimonial assets' and 'non-matrimonial assets' was raised in *Jones v Jones*[1]. Here, the Court of Appeal held that for the purpose of the sharing principle it was appropriate to divide assets into non-matrimonial and matrimonial. The matrimonial assets were £16m and the non-matrimonial £9m. It was held that there was no reason to depart from an equal division of the matrimonial assets. However, it was also held that the trial judge had erred in ascribing a capital value to the earning capacity of the husband and treating it as a non-matrimonial asset. For further comment on this case and on the issue of marital assets generally see **1.75** and **1.149** below.

[1]   [2011] EWCA Civ 41.

The duty of full disclosure

1.67 The exercise by the court of its statutory powers will be frustrated if either party is less than frank. Both sides are therefore under an obligation to make full and frank disclosure of all relevant circumstances[1]. It is not appropriate to give partial disclosure, nor to wait for the other party to demand certain information. The information must be given voluntarily and completely. Failure to give full disclosure may result in the court exercising its powers to make interlocutory orders, for example for disclosure and production of documents[2], will probably lead to the offender being condemned in costs, and, in extreme cases, may be regarded as conduct of a financial nature which it would be inequitable to disregard[3]. Readers are referred to the protocol that is discussed in CHAPTER **16**. For a recent detailed summary of the case law on non-disclosure see the judgment of Mostyn J in *NG v SG*[4].

[1]   [2011] EWCA Civ 41.
[2]   See FPR 9.15(2)(b).
[3]   *P v P (Financial Relief: Non-disclosure)* [1994] 2 FLR 381; *B v B (Real Property: Assessment of Interests)* [1988] 2 FLR 490. See also *Minwalla v Minwalla* [2004] EWHC 2823 (Fam), [2005] 1 FLR 771; where the court finds that a party has set out to conceal resources and to obstruct proper investigation it may draw adverse inferences and reflect such conduct in costs.
[4]   [2011] EWHC 3270 (Fam) – but note that in *Moher v Moher* [2019] EWCA Civ 1482 Moylan J disapproved Mostyn J's dicta that the court was obliged to come up with some broad bracket or figure for the scale of the assets in a case of non-disclosure.

1.68 A related issue is the extent to which disclosure of potentially incriminating documents or evidence is privileged. In *S v S (Inland Revenue: Tax Evasion)*[1] Wilson J dismissed an application by the Revenue to keep a transcript which had irregularly come into its possession and to inspect affidavits and documents, on the ground that the public interest in encouraging full and frank disclosure in ancillary relief proceedings outweighed the interest in countering tax evasion. However, in *R v R (Disclosure to Revenue)*[2], he permitted the Revenue to retain a transcript because it contained explicit findings as to evasion which had already resulted in action by the Revenue.

1   [1997] 2 FLR 774.
2   [1998] 1 FLR 922.

1.69 In *A v A; B v B*[1], Charles J went further. A party to financial remedy proceedings should be aware that if he or she does not claim protection against self-incrimination, the court may make or authorise disclosure in the overall public interest to a prosecuting or other public authority. The risk of serious harm being done to the administration of justice does not outweigh the public interest in the payment of all sums lawfully due to the Revenue. Where a court is satisfied that there has been illegal or unlawful conduct it should generally report the relevant material to the relevant authority. Advisers and courts should be alert to warning parties of their privilege against self-incrimination, but the fact that such a party may have assumptions made against him or her that result in a high award is not something that founds a public interest that disclosure should not be made.

1   [2000] 1 FLR 701.

1.70 Since those decisions the position has become yet more difficult for practitioners with the coming into force of the Proceeds of Crime Act 2002 (as to which, see CHAPTER 21).

Income and earning capacity

1.71 Further consideration will be given to this matter in the section on periodical payments at **2.12**. Here it may be noted that the court will make an order on the basis of what the parties may reasonably be expected to receive if their opportunities are fully exploited. A party who chooses not to work when he or she could do so, or who chooses not to take advantage of opportunities to earn or to receive funds which are available to him or her, will find that the court draws adverse inferences from such unwillingness[1]. This is referred to as earning capacity, as opposed to earning potential.

1   See eg *Hardy v Hardy* (1981) 2 FLR 321. But, for a contrary decision in a 'big money' case, see *A v A (Financial Provision)* [1998] 2 FLR 180.

1.72 The income to be taken into account does not normally include welfare benefits, so that it would be unusual, to say the least, to make a periodical payments order against a person whose only income was income support[1]. Nevertheless, the availability of welfare benefits to one party may be a source of comfort to a court which feels unable to make an order in favour of that party.

1   *Barnes v Barnes* [1972] 3 All ER 872; *Stockford v Stockford* (1982) 3 FLR 58, CA; *Fletcher v Fletcher* [1985] Fam 92 at 100.

Earning potential

1.73 Slightly different considerations arise when the court considers any increase in earning capacity which it might be reasonable to expect a party to take steps to acquire, and s 25(2) recognises this by making it a separate matter. This wording was added to the statute by the Matrimonial and Family Proceedings Act 1984 (MFPA 1984), and must be read together with s 25A which is considered at **2.53** et seq.

Property

1.74 Property includes all real and personal property owned by a party or in which he or she has an interest. It therefore may include beneficial interests under trusts[1]. The law relating to trusts was considered at length by Munby J in *A v A* and *St Georges Trustees and others*[2]. It was held that a spouse who seeks to extend an ancillary relief claim to assets which appear to be in the hands of a third party has to identify, by reference to some established principle, some proper basis for doing so. The determination of a dispute as to ownership between a spouse and a third party is completely different from the usual discretionary exercise between spouses and must be approached on exactly the same legal basis as if it were being determined in the Chancery Division.

[1]   For the position as to a discretionary trust, see eg *Charman v Charman* (above); the husband had appealed against the decision of Coleridge J to the effect that the assets which were in a Bermudan discretionary trust (a very sizeable proportion of the total) were to be regarded as assets over which he had control. The CA rejected the appeal.
[2]   [2007] EWHC 99 (Fam).

1.75 Where one party argues that certain property is 'non-matrimonial' and so should be excluded from consideration, the burden lies on that party to establish that fact.

Guidance was given by Moylan J in *B v B (Ancillary Relief)*[1]. A two-stage process is required. First, it is necessary to determine whether trust assets are resources in which a spouse has any present or potential interest. Secondly, if he had, it is necessary to determine what (if any) legitimate expectation he has and, accordingly, the extent of resources likely to be available to him in the foreseeable future[2]. See also **1.149** et seq below for further consideration of material and non-marital contributions.

[1]   [2009] EWHC 3422 (Fam), [2010] 2 FLR 887.
[2]   For other examples see *Thomas v Thomas* [1995] 2 FLR 668, CA and *SR v CR (Ancillary Relief: Family Trusts)* [2008] EWHC 2329 (Fam), [2009] 2 FLR 1083 (Singer J).

1.76 The court has no jurisdiction under the MCA 1973 to order lump sum payments against a third party[1].

However, in *Whaley v Whaley*[2] the trial judge had found that although £7m of the total assets of £10m were held in a Jersey trust, the trustees of that trust would do whatever the husband asked, and accordingly those resources were available to him. The Court of Appeal dismissed an appeal against the judge's order.

[1]   *Wodehouse v Wodehouse* [2018] EWCA Civ 3009.
[2]   [2011] EWCA Civ 617.

1.77 In *Daga v Bangur*[1] it was held that while *Thomas v Thomas* established that a court can, in appropriate cases, make a financial remedy order in reliance on funds in a trust and give the trustees 'judicious encouragement' to provide the funds with which to pay it, the court must not put undue pressure on them. Moreover, in *Ipekci v McConnell*[2] Mostyn J said 'I agree with the Chief Justice of Hong Kong that the concept of judicious encouragement in cases of this type should be abandoned'.

[1] [2018] EWFC 91.
[2] [2019] EWFC 19.

1.78 For a detailed review of the Family Division's various approaches to trusts in the exercise of its jurisdiction see the judgment of Mostyn J in *BJ v MJ (Financial Orders: Overseas Trust)*[1].

[1] [2011] EWHC 2708 (Fam).

1.79 Property also includes land, shares in public or private companies, partnership assets, business stock, choses in action, money, jewellery, chattels, and so on. Nothing of value which is within the control of the party concerned should be excluded[1].

[1] See *Donaldson v Donaldson* [1958] 2 All ER 660 (husband derived his living, food and accommodation from running a farm, and his only other source of income was a pension. He was ordered to pay an equivalent sum to the whole of the pension to his wife and children). However, where a spouse receives income under a discretionary trust over which he or she genuinely has no control, the court should only take account of the actual income received (this would not apply where the spouse had de facto control): *Howard v Howard* [1945] P 1; see also *B v B (Financial Provision)* (1982) 3 FLR 298, CA.

1.80 However, care must be taken not to breach the principle that a person and a company in which that person may have an interest are separate legal entities. In *Gowers v Gowers*[1] a district judge had found that the husband 'was the company' in the sense that he appeared able to deal with the company finances and ordered that £500,000 which had been paid into court but which was in fact company money should be paid to the wife. On appeal Holman J said that the court had no jurisdiction to make such an order; the company was not a party to the marriage and the court could not pierce the corporate veil.

[1] [2011] EWHC 3485 (Fam).

1.81 This issue has now received some guidance from the highest level in the decision of the Supreme Court in *Prest v Petrodel Resources Ltd*[1]. In this case the husband had placed certain assets in the names of various companies (the respondents to the appeal). The judge at first instance ordered the husband to procure the transfer of the seven UK properties legally owned by the companies to the wife in partial satisfaction of a lump sum order. He also directed the companies to execute such documents as might be necessary to give effect to the transfer of the matrimonial home and seven properties. In addition he awarded costs to the wife, and directed that the companies should be jointly and severally liable with the husband for 10% of those costs. The husband had been less than frank in his disclosure and appeared to be trying to mislead the court.

[1] [2013] UKSC 34.

1.82 The judge concluded that there was no general principle of law that entitled him to reach the companies' assets by piercing the corporate veil. This was because the authorities showed that the separate legal personality of the company could not be disregarded unless it was being abused for a purpose that was in some relevant respect improper. He held that there was no relevant impropriety. He nevertheless concluded that in applications for financial relief ancillary to a divorce, a wider jurisdiction to pierce the corporate veil was available under s 24 of the MCA 1973. The companies appealed and the Court of Appeal allowed the appeal (Thorpe LJ dissenting). The wife appealed to the Supreme Court.

1.83 Giving the lead judgment of the court, Lord Sumption said that there were three possible legal bases on which the assets of the companies might be available to satisfy the lump sum order against the husband, namely:

(1)   It might be said that this was a case in which, exceptionally, a court was at liberty to disregard the corporate veil in order to give effective relief.

(2)   Section 24 of the MCA 1973 might be regarded as conferring a distinct power to disregard the corporate veil in matrimonial cases.

(3)   The companies might be regarded as holding the properties on trust for the husband, not by virtue of his status as their sole shareholder and controller, but in the particular circumstances of the case.

1.84 After lengthy analysis he concluded that the first two bases did not exist and that the only basis on which the companies can be ordered to convey the seven disputed properties to the wife would be the third, namely that they belonged beneficially to the husband, by virtue of the particular circumstances in which the properties came to be vested in them (namely that the companies held the properties on resulting trusts for the husband). Only then would they constitute property to which the husband was 'entitled, either in possession or reversion'. His conclusion, with which the court unanimously agreed, was that this was such a case and that the order of the judge should be restored (albeit on different grounds).

1.85 The sanctity of the corporate veil has therefore been preserved, but, in cases where the evidence shows that a party has provided all the funds for the acquisition of properties that are then vested in a company, the court may regard those properties as beneficially owned by that party and therefore available for distribution.

1.86 The position as to property acquired after the separation remains in doubt. In *Charman v Charman* the Court of Appeal[1] considered that a bonus generated by work done 14 months after separation was clearly an asset of the husband, but that the way the court should treat such an asset (eg by applying different percentages for 'sharing') was a 'grey area which this court may need to survey upon a suitable appeal'. However, in *B v B*[2] Moylan J sought to bring some clarity to this (see **1.34**). See also **1.132** as to contributions.

[1]   [2007] EWCA Civ 503, [2007] All ER (D) 425 (May) at [104].
[2]   [2010] EWHC 193 (Fam), [2010] 2 FLR 1214.

1.87 An entitlement under a pension scheme is frequently a valuable asset and, were it not for s 25B, would have to be considered in detail here. However, that section makes separate provision for pensions, and so pensions will be considered in detail in CHAPTER 10.

Dissipated assets

1.88 A party who recklessly or irresponsibly wastes or dissipates assets will not escape unscathed, because it has been held that it is a proper exercise of the court's discretion to 'add back' or notionally attribute such wasted assets to the party responsible for the dissipation when considering the overall position as to the means of the parties. In *Norris v Norris*[1] Bennett J said that it is only fair to add back into a spouse's assets the amount by which he or she has recklessly depleted the assets and thus potentially disadvantaged the other spouse[2]. Reckless behaviour may well amount to conduct which the court cannot disregard; see further at **1.175**.

[1] [2003] 1 FLR 1142.
[2] For further authority see *Martin v Martin* [1976] Fam 335, and *Vaughan v Vaughan* [2008] 1 FLR 1721, CA.

1.89 However, this is not a principle to be applied rigidly. In another case[1] Wilson LJ said that a notional re-attribution has to be conducted very cautiously by reference only to clear evidence of dissipation (in which there is a wanton element). This approach was upheld by Moylan J in *BD v FD (Financial Remedies: Needs)*[2] who explained the position as follows:

> '69. How does reattribution fit within the statutory framework? It is clearly an example of the application of section 25(2)(g), namely it is based on the conduct of a party being such 'that it would in the opinion of the court be inequitable to disregard if'. This sub-section was added when section 25 was amended by the Matrimonial and Family Proceedings Act 1984 in order to clarify the circumstances in which conduct could be taken into account. Previously the section had referred to conduct but without any additional formulation to assist with its interpretation.

> 70. In my view the terminology used by Wilson LJ, as referred to above, is designed to reflect this statutory test and the court's approach to its application. The threshold is high as reflected by the court's approach to the issue, more generally, of whether it would be inequitable to disregard conduct.'

[1] *Vaughan v Vaughan* [2008] 1 FLR 1721, CA.
[2] [2016] EWHC 594 (Fam).

Expectations

1.90 The court must have regard to income, property etc which a party has or is likely to have in the foreseeable future. This does not include pensions, which are dealt with separately.

1.91 The most common example of a financial expectation is where one party is, or is likely to be, a beneficiary under a will or an intestacy. However, here the court must recognise that wills may be changed and that testators may outlive beneficiaries. The court also has problems of evidence, since it cannot compel a potential benefactor to disclose his or her intentions nor can it always accurately estimate the size of the potential inheritance.

1.92 What is the foreseeable future may also be debatable. In one case, it was held that the prospects of a 64-year-old woman inheriting from her mother who was in poor health should be disregarded[1]. In another, where the husband was indefeasibly entitled under German law to a substantial inheritance from his father, and the parties had always made their financial arrangements on that basis, the wife's application was adjourned until the death of the father[2].

1   *Michael v Michael* [1986] 2 FLR 389.
2   *MT v MT (Financial Provision: Lump Sum)* [1992] 1 FLR 362.

1.93 When *Miller v Miller* was decided by the Court of Appeal[1], it was held that when she married a rich man the wife had a 'legitimate expectation' to be maintained thereafter as the wife of a rich man. As has been seen (see **1.32**), the House of Lords rejected this finding (while re-emphasising the importance of s 25(2)(c) (standard of living) – see **1.104**).

1   [2005] EWCA Civ 984, [2006] 1 FLR 151.

1.94 Before the coming into force of s 25B of MCA 1973 in 1996, there were authorities to the effect that the entitlement of a serviceman to a lump sum on retirement cannot be taken into account because of the provisions of the Army Act 1955 and similar statutes. It was also held that expectations which were more than a few years away were to be disregarded[1]. These decisions have been reversed by s 25B, which is considered in CHAPTER 10.

1   *Roberts v Roberts* [1986] 2 FLR 152; see also *Priest v Priest* (1980) 1 FLR 189 and *Happe v Happe* [1991] 4 All ER 527.

1.95 Another common example of a financial expectation is a claim for personal injuries[1]. For this to be relevant, the court would have to be satisfied as to the likelihood of success, and the amount likely to be recovered. It should also be said that since, in serious cases, the award of damages would be intended to compensate a party for past and future loss, the damages would fall into a different category than, say, investments acquired during the marriage or a windfall inheritance.

1   *Daubney v Daubney* [1976] Fam 267; *Roche v Roche* (1981) Fam Law 243, CA; *Wagstaff v Wagstaff* [1992] 1 All ER 275, CA; *C v C (Financial Provision: Personal Damages)* [1995] 2 FLR 171, FD.

1.96 In *D v D (Lump Sum Order: Adjournment of Application)*[1], it was held that a court which decides to adjourn a lump sum application is doing no more than exercising the discretion vested in it, albeit that this step should be taken only rarely, where justice to the parties could not otherwise be done. One such circumstance was the real possibility of capital from a specific source becoming available in the near future.

1   [2001] 1 FLR 633, Connell J.

1.97 In another somewhat unusual case[1] after a short marriage which ended 21 years ago a claim for a lump sum had been adjourned generally to allow the wife to apply again when the husband received an inheritance and the judge made the order for a lump sum many years later. The needs of the children were said to be the most important factor.

1   *Re G (Financial Provision: Liberty to Restore Application for Lump Sum)* [2004] EWHC 88 (Fam), [2004] 1 FLR 997, Wilson J.

Financial needs, obligations and responsibilities

1.98 The court is directed to have regard to[1]:

'(b)   the financial needs, obligations and responsibilities which each of the parties to the marriage has or is likely to have in the foreseeable future.'

¹   MCA 1973, s 25(2)(b).

1.99 In most cases, the task of the court will be to calculate the reasonable needs of the parties, in particular the needs of a parent who is caring for the children of the family, and to make a decision as to whether there should be a transfer between the parties of assets or income to meet those needs. In such a case, it is also necessary to ensure that the 'paying party' is left with sufficient to meet his or her reasonable needs¹.

¹   *Allen v Allen* [1986] 2 FLR 265, CA.

1.100 In low to average income cases, the subsistence level indicated by benefit rates, together with the cost of housing is frequently regarded as a minimum figure for needs¹.

¹   *Allen v Allen* [1986] 2 FLR 265, CA; but see *Freeman v Swatridge* [1984] FLR 762.

1.101 What constitutes obligations and responsibilities may be more debatable. Legal obligations assumed by one party from which it would be impossible to withdraw will normally be accepted¹. The cost of maintaining a second family is clearly frequently contentious, particularly where the result is that that party is rendered unable to afford to maintain the first family. However, the court must be realistic, and must recognise that a second family which is being maintained by a person of average income will not have access to State benefits, whereas the first family might. There is nothing which the court can do to stop someone from establishing a second union and assuming the responsibility for children.

¹   See eg *Stockford v Stockford* (1982) 3 FLR 58, CA, where a husband had left his wife and first family in the former matrimonial home and bought a new house for his own occupation with the aid of a large mortgage. The court decided not to make an order against him since to do so would mean that he could not service the mortgage. Contrast *Slater v Slater and Another* (1982) 3 FLR 364 where the court thought that the husband had been extravagant in deciding to live in a country house with heavy expenses, and took no account of the unreasonable expenses. See also *Campbell v Campbell* [1998] 1 FLR 828, CA.

1.102 Where assets are surplus to needs it may be that a different approach will be adopted¹. Where there are children, the liability of either party under the Child Support Act 1991 (CSA 1991) is an obligation to be taken into account. It has been held that the court should make a distinction between 'hard debts' such as debts to banks, and 'soft debts' such as money borrowed from relatives².

¹   For two different approaches in relatively big money cases see *Norris v Norris* [2002] EWHC 2996 (Fam), [2003] 1 FLR 1142 (new children ignored) and *H-J v H-J (Financial Provision: Equality)* [2002] 1 FLR 415 (account taken of new responsibilities).
²   *M v B (Ancillary Proceedings: Lump Sum)* [1998] 1 FLR 53, CA, at 56 and 60.

1.103 It was once the case that different considerations were applied to 'big money cases' where the parties enjoyed considerable affluence. This is the subject of a separate section in CHAPTER 4, where it will be seen that, until the decision of the House of Lords in *White v White*, the concept of 'reasonable requirements' was used in place of that of needs. It has now been established that reasonable requirements were an unwarranted judicial gloss on the words of the statute and that consideration of the needs of the parties is all that the statute permits (although an award will not necessarily be limited to a party's needs).

STANDARD OF LIVING DURING MARRIAGE

1.104 Before the changes introduced by the 1984 Act, the court was directed to put the parties in the position in which they would have been if the marriage had not broken down. That was frequently impossible, and is no longer one of the concerns of the court. However, the court is still directed to have regard to 'the standard of living enjoyed by the family before the breakdown of the marriage'[1]. This was upheld by the House of Lords in the conjoined appeals of *Miller v Miller* and *McFarlane v McFarlane*[2] (see **1.32**).

1   MCA 1973, s 25(2)(c).
2   [2006] 1 FLR 1186, HL.

1.105 It is perhaps important to note that the subsection refers to 'the family' and not to the parties; taken with the 'first consideration', this might entitle the court to take steps to ensure that the children of the family suffered as little as possible, even at the expense of one of the parents.

1.106 In most cases, the concern of the court will be to ensure that the standard of life of one party does not deteriorate to a greater extent than that of the other[1]. For a comment on the relevance of previous standard of living in applications for maintenance pending suit, see *BD v FD (Maintenance Pending Suit)*[2] per Moylan J.

1   See generally *M v M (Financial Provision)* [1987] 2 FLR 1; *Leadbeater v Leadbeater* [1985] FLR 789; *P v P (Financial Relief: Non-disclosure)* [1994] 2 FLR 381.
2   [2014] EWHC 4443 (Fam).

1.107 Separate considerations may arise in cases of a short marriage and in big money cases. These are considered in more detail at **1.149** and CHAPTER **4**, respectively. However, it may be helpful to note here that it has been held that, where there has been a high degree of affluence in the marriage, it is not necessary to ensure that the same high degree of affluence is maintained for both parties[1].

1   See eg *F v F (Ancillary Relief: Substantial Assets)* [1995] 2 FLR 45.

Ages of parties and duration of marriage

1.108 The next factor in the s 25 checklist is 'the age of each party to the marriage and the duration of the marriage'[1]. The age of the parties is normally relevant in relation to their earning capacity. Subject to the needs of young children, a young wife will normally be taken to have an earning potential, and the provisions of s 25A will apply (see CHAPTER **2**).

1   MCA 1973, s 25(2)(d).

1.109 Very different considerations apply to a woman aged over 50 who has not worked for many years. The court will take the age of such a person into account when deciding whether she has an earning potential[1].

[1] See the cases cited in CHAPTER 2 on 'Periodical payments', in particular 'The clean break' at 2.70 et seq.

Duration of marriage: short marriage

1.110 When a marriage has subsisted for more than the average number of years, the significance of its duration is not normally an important factor; the usual guidelines apply and there is no separate point to be made about the length of the marriage. Duration is really only significant in the case of a short marriage, which is a topic which must now be considered.

1.111 The duration of a short marriage is not, of course, an isolated factor; associated with a short marriage are normally such other important factors as the length of any prior cohabitation, contributions (or lack of contributions), children, and earning potential. For example, when all the capital contributions have come from one party, and the marriage ends after a short period, in the absence of other factors the non-contributing party could not expect a substantial redistribution of assets.

1.112 The proper approach to a short marriage was considered by the House of Lords in the conjoined appeals of *Miller v Miller* and *McFarlane v McFarlane*[1]. It may be helpful first to summarise the leading pre-*Miller/McFarlane* cases and then to contrast these with the House of Lords guidance.

[1] [2006] 1 FLR 1186, HL.

Pre-Miller/McFarlane cases

1.113 In *Attar v Attar (No 2)*[1], the marriage had lasted for only 6 months and the actual cohabitation only 7 weeks. It was held that because of those facts it was impossible to have regard to all the usual s 25 factors; the only proper approach was to have regard to the effect on the parties of the marriage and its dissolution. There were no children, the husband was very wealthy, and the order was for a limited term of periodical payments to enable the wife to readjust.

[1] [1985] FLR 653.

1.114 In *C v C (Financial Relief: Short Marriage)*[1], the facts of the case were described as 'highly unusual' with features that made it 'unique'. There was, however, a child of the marriage. The judge had ordered periodical payments with no term, and this was upheld by the Court of Appeal. Ward LJ said that the appropriateness of a term order depended on all the s 25 checklist criteria, including the welfare of any child; it was not appropriate simply to presume the imposition of a term whenever there was a short-term marriage.

[1] [1997] 2 FLR 26, CA.

1.115 In *Hedges v Hedges*[1], the marriage had lasted 4½ years; there were no children, and the wife had continued to work. She was awarded half the husband's liquid assets to help deal with her housing needs, and periodical payments for 18 months to help her to readjust. This was upheld by the Court of Appeal.

1   [1991] 1 FLR 196, CA.

1.116 In *Hobhouse v Hobhouse*[1], the parties divorced after 4 years of marriage; there were no children. The wife had inherited £0.5m and expected to inherit a further £1.5m on her mother's death. The husband's wealth was indicated by the fact that he pleaded the 'millionaire's defence'[2]. The wife was likely to return to Australia and her family home there within 3 to 5 years. The judge awarded her a lump sum of £175,000. The wife's appeal was dismissed. The marriage was childless and brief; the wife had not sacrificed any financial advantage; she had been allowed 3 to 5 years to rebuild her life. There was no obvious bracket, and the award was well within the judge's discretion.

1   [1999] 1 FLR 961, CA.
2   See **4.22**.

1.117 In *G v G (Financial Provision: Separation Agreement)*[1], the marriage lasted 4½ years. The wife brought into the marriage her two children from a previous marriage and they enjoyed a luxurious lifestyle. It was held that the short duration of the marriage was only one factor; both parties had made significant contributions to the welfare of the family and were likely to continue to do so. The husband's total wealth exceeded £4.5m; the wife earned £11,500 per annum and had a house (purchased for her by the husband) worth £250,000. She was awarded a lump sum of £240,000.

1   [2000] 2 FLR 18, Connell J.

1.118 For an example of a more recent decision involving substantial assets see *K v K (Ancillary Relief: Pre-nuptial Agreement)*. The most interesting point to emerge from that case in this context is that, after dealing with the capital claims of the wife, the judge dealt with the needs of the child of the family almost as a discrete issue and as if it were an application under Sch 1 to the Children Act 1989. The husband was ordered to provide a home and furnishings for the child at a cost of £1.2m, to revert to him eventually[1].

1   For an even more generous order in favour of a child made under Sch 1 see *Re P (Child: Financial Provision)* [2003] EWCA Civ 837, [2003] 2 FLR 865.

1.119 In *Foster v Foster*[1] the Court of Appeal allowed an appeal from a circuit judge and restored the order of a district judge awarding a wife 61% of the assets after a very short marriage where she had introduced the bulk of the capital. The district judge had sought to give the parties back what they had brought into the marriage at the value it held at that date, and that was not unfair. That was the only possible reason to depart from equality in this case. As will be seen below, this case is probably the most important of the pre-2006 cases.

1   [2003] 2 FLR 299.

1.120 In *B v B (Mesher Order)*[1] the marriage had lasted 10 months and there was one child. The district judge found the wife needed £220,000 to rehouse herself and awarded her a lump sum of £175,000 and periodical payments. The husband appealed and argued, inter alia, that there should have been a

Mesher order. This was rejected on the ground that, given the wife's continuing contributions to bringing up the child, her prospects of being able to generate capital were small whereas the husband's were good. A *Mesher* order would therefore produce inequality of outcome. It was also held that a term order for periodical payments for the wife was not appropriate in view of the uncertainty and that the proper approach was to impose no term and to leave it to the payee to seek variation.

¹   [2003] 2 FLR 285, [2003] Fam Law 462.

1.121 Perhaps the best way to summarise these decisions would be to reaffirm the importance of considering all the s 25 factors without preconceptions, while recognising that many of those factors will have little relevance in many cases of a short marriage. It was important to consider what had been the effect of the marriage on the parties, and, perhaps, to ask what they had lost in financial terms.

1.122 Where there is a child, it cannot be denied that this will have a significant effect on the parent caring for the child, and this would seem to make it prima facie inappropriate to impose a term on periodical payments¹.

¹   See also *Re G (Financial Provision: Liberty to Restore Application for Lump Sum)* [2004] EWHC 88 (Fam), [2004] 1 FLR 997, where after a short marriage a claim for a lump sum was adjourned generally with liberty to restore to enable the wife to apply in the event of the husband's inheritance; it was said that the interests of the children changed the perception of fairness.

Miller/McFarlane guidance

1.123 The House of Lords held that, if it were not clear before *Foster v Foster*, it must now be clear that the old law relating to short marriages was swept away by *White v White*. The old principle of trying to restore one party, normally the wife, to her position before the marriage, was no longer applicable.

1.124 The principles of *White*, particularly the yardstick of equality and the concept of sharing, apply as much to short as to long marriages. *Foster v Foster* had made clear that all the s 25 guidelines must be applied in such a case. Having said that, in his speech Lord Nicholls also made clear that the application of these principles will not necessarily result in equal division. When he said that the length of the marriage 'will affect the quantum of the financial fruits of the partnership' he can only mean that the court must look at what the partnership produced during the term of the relationship, and that will be one of the factors to be considered.

1.125 Unsurprisingly, Baroness Hale agreed with the approval of her judgment in *Foster*. Referring to *Foster*, she said that:

> ' . . . [a]lthough one party had earned more and thus contributed more in purely financial terms to the acquisition of those assets, both contributed what they could, and the fair result was to divide the product of their joint endeavours equally.'

1.126 A post-*Miller/McFarlane* case dealing with a short marriage but where the assets were large was *McCartney v Mills McCartney*¹. This case attracted enormous public interest out of proportion to its legal significance because of the notoriety of the parties, but it does provide a useful example of how the courts may approach such a case. The marriage was a short one, but there was one child. The husband's assets exceeded £400m, but had almost entirely been earned by his exceptional talents many years before the marriage. The wife's assets were £8m. The wife was awarded £16.5m, and provision for the child.

1   [2008] 1 FLR 1508, Bennett J.

1.127 An issue associated with the length of the marriage may be the significance which the court should give to cohabitation outside marriage. As to pre-marital cohabitation, the law once seemed reasonably clear; the court may have regard only to the period between the marriage and the breakdown when considering the length of the marriage[1]. The same applies to post-marital cohabitation[2].

1   *Foley v Foley* [1981] Fam 160; *Campbell v Campbell* [1976] Fam 347.
2   *Hill v Hill* [1997] 1 FLR 730, an unusual case which turned on other issues, eg whether an order made in 1969 could be set aside on the ground of 25 years' cohabitation after dissolution. 'Under English law, a relationship of cohabitation no matter how long nor how great the dependence does not give the wife any right to claim nor power in the court to order either maintenance or discretionary capital provision', per Holman J. See also *Hewitson v Hewitson* [1995] 1 FLR 241, CA. See also *CO v CO* [2004] EWHC 287 (Fam), [2004] 1 FLR 1095, where Coleridge J held that committed settled relationships which endure for years outside marriage must be regarded as every bit as valid as marriage; where such an arrangement existed and seamlessly preceded the marriage it is as capable of being as important a non-financial circumstance as any other.

1.128 However, perhaps a more contemporary approach can be derived from *GW v RW (Financial Provision: Departure from Equality)*[1] where it was held that where a marriage moved seamlessly from cohabitation to marriage it was unrealistic and artificial to treat the periods differently. However, it was equally unrealistic to treat the period of estrangement conducted under the umbrella of a divorce petition as part of the duration of the marriage.

1   *GW v RW (Financial Provision: Departure from Equality)* [2003] EWHC 611 (Fam), [2003] 2 FLR 108, Nicholas Mostyn QC. See also *S v S (Financial Provision) (Post-Divorce Cohabitation)* [1994] 2 FLR 228; another unusual case, involving cohabitation of 6 years before, 8 years during and 15 years after marriage. Douglas Brown J held that it was necessary to have regard to all the circumstances and awarded the wife a lump sum of £185,000 out of the husband's free capital of £400,000 plus £100,000 in respect of her interest in the home. However, caution is required; in *Hewitson* (above), 'grave reservations' were expressed as to this decision.

1.129 In *AB v FC (Short Marriage: Needs: Stockpiling)*[1] the marriage had lasted 19 months, there was a child of 22 months and the husband was a footballer earning nearly £1m pa capital was no more than £500,000. It was agreed that this was a 'needs' case. Roberts J awarded the wife £270,000 for a deposit and stamp duty, £80,000 pa to 'stockpile' funds for a repayment mortgage and £200,000 overall for income needs of wife and child.

1   [2016] EWHC 3285 (Fam).

1.130 Cohabitation of the party who applies for financial relief after divorce will be considered in more detail at **2.13**.

DISABILITY

1.131 The court must have regard to 'any physical or mental disability of either of the parties to the marriage'[1]. This is another factor which overlaps with earning capacity or potential, and the position of disabled parties would be no different if this provision did not exist. There seems to be no other way in which disability has ever been regarded as a factor in itself.

[1] MCA 1973, s 25(2)(e).

CONTRIBUTIONS

1.132 The next s 25 factor is: ' . . . the contributions which each of the parties has made or is likely in the foreseeable future to make to the welfare of the family, including any contribution by looking after the home or caring for the family'[1]. The purpose of this subsection is, clearly, to try to reflect the value of each of the parties to the whole marriage, which is not an easy task. This factor may be subdivided into several categories.

[1] MCA 1973, s 25(2)(f).

Financial contributions

1.133 Contributions of a financial nature will include the earnings of both parties over the course of the marriage, any capital sums provided by them, for example for the acquisition of a house, and any inheritances which they have received from which the family has benefited. It also includes the value of a discounted purchase price for a former council house under the 'right to buy' scheme.

1.134 The court has a duty to make findings of fact where there is a dispute as to any financial contributions made by either party; any decision as to how available capital is to be divided to give effect to the s 25 criteria must start from an accurate assessment of what the parties' respective proprietary interests are[1]. As to 'negative contributions', see **1.179**.

[1] *M v B (Ancillary Proceedings: Lump Sum)* [1998] 1 FLR 53, CA, per Thorpe J at 58. See also *White v White* [1998] 2 FLR 310, and *A v A (Elderly Applicant: Lump Sum)* [1999] 2 FLR 969.

1.135 In *White v White* the relevance of inherited wealth as a contribution was mentioned and for a time it was thought by some that this class of asset might fall outside the ambit of the normal division of assets. However, in *Norris v Norris*[1] Bennett J held that Lord Nicholls had not enunciated a guideline that inherited contributions should not be included in the pool of assets for division. In theory, a spouse could claim more than half for this reason, but only in very limited and quite exceptional circumstances. Inherited property represented a contribution by one of the parties and was a factor to be taken into account.

[1] [2002] EWHC 2996 (Fam), [2003] 1 FLR 1142.

1.136 This case was of some significance since it post-dated *Lambert v Lambert*[1] and clearly reflects the thinking as to 'special contributions' in that case. A similar conclusion was reached by Nicholas Mostyn QC in *GW v RW (Financial Provision: Departure from Equality)*[2]. Nevertheless, the fact that there might be room for more than one point of view on this issue was demonstrated by the decision of Munby J in *P v P (Inherited Property)*[3]. This was a case involving a family farm which had been in the husband's family for several generations. His Lordship held that fairness might demand a different approach if the inheritance were a pecuniary legacy which accrued during the marriage than if it were a landed estate which had been in one spouse's family for generations and had been brought into the marriage with an expectation that it would be retained in specie for future generations. In the instant case, the proper approach was to make an award based on the wife's reasonable needs for accommodation and income; to do more would be to tip the balance unfairly in her favour and unfairly against the husband.

[1]   [2002] EWCA Civ 1685, [2003] 1 FLR 139, CA. Cases such as *M v M (Financial Provision: Valuation of Assets)* [2002] Fam Law 509 and *H v H (Financial Contributions: Special Contribution)* [2002] 2 FLR 1021 which arrive at the opposite conclusion may be distinguished and doubted for that reason.

[2]   [2003] EWHC 611 (Fam), [2003] 2 FLR 108.

[3]   [2004] EWHC 1364 (Fam), [2005] 1 FLR 576.

1.137 The potential differences in judicial opinion at the highest level were revealed in the speeches of Lord Nicholls and Baroness Hale in *Miller/McFarlane*. *White v White* had already established that the contributions of the breadwinner are not to be favoured over those of the homemaker and childcarer. Both Lord Nicholls and Baroness Hale sought to deal with the vexed issue of the evaluation of special or exceptional contributions, such as, for example, those of an exceptionally gifted sportsman, musician or entrepreneur (these are the author's examples, not those of the court).

1.138 The difference in opinion between Lord Nicholls and Baroness Hale related to the relevance of 'non-matrimonial property'. Lord Nicholls' approach was that non-matrimonial property should be viewed as all property which the parties bring with them into the marriage or acquire by inheritance or gift during the marriage (plus perhaps the income or fruits of that property), while matrimonial property should be viewed as all other property. The yardstick of equality should apply generally to matrimonial property (although the shorter the marriage, the smaller the matrimonial property is in the nature of things likely to be). But the yardstick is not so readily applicable to non-matrimonial property, especially after a short marriage, but in some circumstances even after a long marriage.

1.139 Baroness Hale's approach took a more limited concept of matrimonial property, as embracing 'family assets' (cf *Wachtel v Wachtel*[1]) and family businesses or joint ventures in which both parties work (cf *Foster v Foster*[2]). In relation to such property she agreed that the yardstick of equality may readily be applied. However, she identified other 'non-business-partnership, non-family assets', to which that yardstick may not apply with the same force particularly in the case of short marriages; these included not merely (a) property which the parties bring with them into the marriage or acquire by inheritance or gift during the marriage (plus perhaps its income or fruits), but also (b) business or investment assets generated solely or mainly by the efforts of one party during the marriage.

1 [1973] Fam 72 at 90, per Lord Denning MR.
2 [2003] EWCA Civ 565, [2003] 2 FLR 299, 305 at para 19, per Hale LJ.

1.140 Baroness Hale's view was that the source of assets may be taken into account but that this would become less important with the passage of time; she points out that the court is directed to take account of the length of the marriage. She continued:

'If the assets are not "family assets", or not generated by the joint efforts of the parties, then the duration of the marriage may justify a departure from the yardstick of equality of division. As we are talking here of a departure from that yardstick, I would prefer to put this in terms of a reduction to reflect the period of time over which the domestic contribution has or will continue rather than in terms of accrual over time.'

Exceptional contributions

1.141 The matter was considered in some detail when *Charman* reached the Court of Appeal for obvious reasons; this was a case involving very considerable assets (£138m) which it was common ground had almost entirely been generated by the exceptional and in every way 'special' efforts and ingenuity of the husband[1]. Giving the judgment of the court, Sir Mark Potter P said:

'It was inevitable, so it seems to us, that the notion of a special contribution should have "survived" the decision in *Miller* [as to which, see below]. The statutory requirement in every case to consider the contributions which each party has made to the welfare of the family, as well as those which each is likely to make to it, would be inconsistent with a blanket rule that their past contributions to its welfare must be afforded equal weight. Nevertheless the difficulty attendant upon a comparison of their different contributions and the danger of its infection by discrimination against the home-maker led the House in *Miller* heavily to circumscribe the situations in which it would be appropriate to find that one party had made a special contribution, in the sense of a contribution by one unmatched by the other, which, for the purpose of the sharing principle, should lead to departure from equality. In this regard the House was unanimous.'

1 For a similar case with a similar result see *Sorrell v Sorrell* [2005] EWHC 1717 (Fam), [2006] 1 FLR 497.

1.142 The court declined the invitation to identify a figure as a 'threshold' beyond which a special contribution would be appropriate, considering it dangerous to do so. Nevertheless, it was prepared to give guidance (at para [90]) as to 'the appropriate range of percentage adjustment to be made in cases in which the court is satisfied that the principle requires departure from equality'. Even there, however, it was said that 'it is necessary however to bear in mind that fair despatch of some cases may require departure even from the range which we propose'.

1.143 The guidance offered was as follows:

(1)   The adjustment should be significant as opposed to token. The court found it hard to conceive that where such a special contribution was established the percentages should be nearer equality than 55%–45%.

(2)   Equally, it should not be too great. The court approved Coleridge J's comment that 'I think you need to be careful, after a very long marriage, to give a wife half of what you give the husband'. The judgment of the Court of Appeal continued:

> 'Arbitrary though it is, our instinct is the same, namely that, even in an extreme case and in the absence of some further dramatic feature unrelated to it, fair allowance for special contribution within the sharing principle would be most unlikely to give rise to percentages of division of matrimonial property further from equality than 66.6%–33.3%.'

1.144 These issues were considered by Holman J in *Gray v Work*[1]. He summarised the requirements for special contribution, derived from *Miller* and *Charman*, as follows:

(1)   The characteristics or circumstances which would result in a departure from equality have to be of a wholly exceptional nature such that it would very obviously be inconsistent with the objective of achieving fairness for them to be ignored: per Bodey J in *Lambert* but quoted with obvious approbation by Lord Nicholls of Birkenhead in *Miller* at para 68.

(2)   Exceptional earnings are to be regarded as a factor pointing away from equality of division when, but only when, it would be inequitable to proceed otherwise (Lord Nicholls of Birkenhead in *Miller* at para 68).

(3)   Only if there is such a disparity in their respective contributions to the welfare of the family that it would be inequitable to disregard it should this be taken into account in determining their shares (Baroness Hale of Richmond, in *Miller* at para 146).

(4)   It is extremely important to avoid discrimination against the home-maker (the Court of Appeal in *Charman* at paras 79 and 80).

(5)   A special contribution requires a contribution by one unmatched by the other (the Court of Appeal in *Charman* at para 79).

(6)   The amount of the wealth alone may be so extraordinary as to make it easy for the party who generated it to claim an exceptional and individual quality which deserves special treatment. Often, however, he or she will need independently to establish such a quality, whether by genius in business or some other field (the Court of Appeal in *Charman* at para 80). A windfall is not enough.

(7)   There is no identified threshold for such a claim to succeed (the Court of Appeal in *Charman* at para 88)[2].

[1]   [2105] EWHC 834 (Fam) at para 140.
[2]   See also *Robertson v Robertson* [2016] EWHC 613 (Fam) where Holman J said that it is fundamental to a successful claim for special contribution that it be unmatched.

1.145 The husband appealed. In the judgment of the court[1], the Court of Appeal indicated that this appeal provided an opportunity for the court to review the issue of special contribution and its proper scope, if any, in applications for financial relief. The issues included what was the proper approach of the court in determining whether one party had made a special contribution which, in the application of the sharing principle, justified an unequal division of marital wealth. Although the issue of a special contribution was likely to be relevant in only a very small number of cases, the court attached particular importance to the public interest in the promotion of clarity and consistency.

[1] *Work v Gray* [2017] EWCA Civ 270.

1.146 The court considered in detail the judgments in *Miller v Miller* and *Charman v Charman* (referred to above) and concluded that nothing had occurred in the years since those judgments to show that the principles elucidated in the those cases were erroneous or had caused unfairness. The wife had argued that the concept of a special contribution was potentially discriminatory but it was not open to the court to substitute any personal concepts as to fairness for those reflected in the principles on special contribution set out in *Miller* and *Charman*.

1.147 The court concluded that Holman J had correctly identified the principles which he should apply and had applied those principles correctly. Accordingly the appeal was dismissed.

Reference has already been made to the decision of the Court of Appeal in *XW v XH* (see **1.39** above) which to modify further the court's approach to exceptional contributions and to reinforce the presumption of equality.

Non-marital contributions

1.148 A separate (though often overlapping) issue from 'special contributions' is that of 'non-marital property', that is property that has been acquired or brought in by one party before the marriage or eg by a lottery win. How the court should treat such assets has been the cause of considerable litigation and it cannot be said that there is one clear answer at present. Clearly the views of Lord Nicholls and Baroness Hale in *Miller/McFarlane* (see above) provide the starting point for discussion but since that date the law has been refined in various ways.

In *IX v IY (Financial Remedies: Unmatched Contributions)*[1] Williams J said that the sharing principle is now firmly embedded and where the parties have substantial wealth the court starts from the position that the matrimonial assets will be divided. However, in applying the sharing principle a distinction is drawn between matrimonial and non-matrimonial assets. This exercise is ultimately fact specific and recent decisions of the Court of Appeal support a more flexible and common-sense approach.

[1] [2018] EWHC 3053 (Fam).

1.149 Two leading authorities at Court of Appeal lever are *Robson v Robson*[1] and *Jones v Jones*[2]. In *Robson* Ward LJ set out guidance for dealing with big money cases involving inherited wealth, and stated the following principles:

- The words of the statute are the first source of authority, and judicial glosses should be avoided.

- Inherited wealth forms part of the property and resources of the parties and so must be taken into account under s 25(2)(a). It must not be quarantined.
- Inherited wealth that has not been earned can be treated differently from wealth accrued by joint efforts. The nature of the inheritance may be relevant.
- Relevant s 25 factors to be taken into account are the duration of the marriage, the time during which the wealth has been enjoyed by the parties, the standard of living and the extent to which that has been afforded by drawing on the wealth.
- The more and longer the wealth has been enjoyed by the marriage the less fair it is that it should be ring-fenced and excluded from distribution.

In *Jones v Jones* Wilson LJ adopted a slightly different approach involving two stages. First, the scale of the matrimonial property to be excluded should be identified and then the resulting matrimonial property should be divided in accordance with the equal sharing principle.

1 [2010] EWCA Civ 1171.
2 [2011] EWCA Civ 41.

1.150 Wilson LJ considered the issue further in *K v L (Non-Matrimonial Property: Special Contribution)*[1] where the Court of Appeal had to consider the significance of the wife's inherited wealth, which had grown enormously in value during the marriage and which had been ring-fenced and allowed to grow. He held that the importance of the source of the assets may, rather than will, diminish over time and preferred the dictum of Lord Nicholls in *Miller/McFarlane* to that of Baroness Hale. (The appeal against the order of Bodey J (reported as *K v L (Ancillary Relief: Inherited Wealth)*[2]) which had made an award in favour of the husband based on need was dismissed.)

1 [2011] EWCA Civ 550.
2 [2010] EWHC 1234 (Fam).

1.151 There have been a number of decisions at first instance that have sought to apply the guidance given from above. In *N v F (Financial Orders: Pre-Acquired Wealth)*[1] Mostyn J set out the principles to be followed in such cases, adding that these cases are fact-specific and very discretionary. The longer a marriage went on, the easier it was to say that by virtue of the mingling of the pre-acquired wealth with the fruits of the marriage, the supplier had in effect agreed to share it. Where the court considered that the existence of pre-acquired wealth should be reflected in an order, a two-stage approach (as set out in *Jones v Jones*) should follow. The court should do the following:

- determine whether the existence of the marital property should be reflected in the order at all; that depended on questions of duration and mingling;
- if it was fair to do so, decide how much of the pre-marital assets should be excluded;
- divide the remaining property equally;
- test the fairness of the approach by the overall percentage technique;

- finally, consider the question of need.

[1]   [2011] EWHC 586 (Fam).

1.152 However, Mostyn J's approach was specifically disapproved by the Court of Appeal in *Hart v Hart* where the court upheld a judge's decision to employ a 'multi-faceted approach' to such cases. It was held that the court was not required to adopt a formulaic approach in determining whether the parties' wealth comprises any non-matrimonial property or in deciding what order to make when it does. When the existence of non-matrimonial property is being asserted a case management conference should be held to determine whether, and if so, what, proportionate factual investigation is required. In *XW v XH* Baker J shared Moylan LJ's view that it is preferable not to adopt a formulaic approach in such matters.

However, this approach has not been universally followed. Given that, as Mostyn J reminds us, many of these cases are fact-specific, it is unnecessary to analyse the leading all reported cases on this topic. Some of the most significant are as follows:

- In *J v J (Financial Orders: Wife's Long-Term Needs)*[1] Moylan J said the correct approach was to start with the principle of need and then to consider the sharing principle. Where the result suggested by the needs principle was greater than that suggested by the sharing principle, the former should prevail.
- In *AR v AR (Treatment of Inherited Wealth)*[2] Moylan J held that the sharing principle can apply to non-matrimonial property if justified by the circumstances of the case. Nothing had happened to the non-matrimonial property to change it into matrimonial property. The principle best guiding the court was need; this could encompass the length of the marriage, the wife's contributions and the standard of living. The court's objective is fairness, not certainty.
- In *S v AG (Financial Orders: Lottery Prize)*[3] Mostyn J had to consider the best approach to money derived from a share of £500,000 in a lottery prize that the wife had won in 2000. She had invested the money in a home in which she and her new husband lived and that was now worth £495,000 subject to a mortgage of £305,000. In an apparent effort to defeat the husband's claims, the wife had transferred £250,000 to a third party. Both parties were otherwise of modest means. The husband sought, and was granted, a lump sum of £85,000 to assist him in his retirement. Mostyn J said that it would be a rare case where the sharing principle would lead to a distribution to a claimant of non-matrimonial property. However, an award to meet needs was commonplace. The husband was not entitled to anything like an equal share but 15–20% would be fair.
- In *GS v L (Financial Remedies: Pre-Acquired Assets; Needs)*[4] Eleanor King J found that the husband had come into the marriage with substantial assets. However, those assets (except the husband's pension) were required to satisfy the immediate and long-term needs of the wife and children. With minor adjustments, the assets were divided equally.
- In *Y v Y (Financial Orders: Inherited Wealth)*[5] Baron J said that the wife's needs were to be interpreted fairly, on application of the statute, in the context of the factor that the wealth was inherited. The wealth

was derived from the husband's family, which made it prima facie non-matrimonial property and placed it in a special category. As such, the court should be slow to invade it without good reason, but the fact that property is inherited will carry little if any weight where the claimant's financial needs cannot be met without recourse to it. The wife was awarded a lump sum of £8,738,000 (32.5% of the total assets). The award was needs based and did involve sharing assets that would be invaded to cover the award. In this case needs, and the right to sharing, were the same thing.

In *HW v FW* it was accepted that the parties' wealth (estimated at £40m) had been entirely acquired or inherited by the husband before the marriage. However, the wife had exceptional medical needs arising out of her medical condition and the court had the duty to reach an outcome which was as fair as possible in all the circumstances. The wife was awarded £15,251,098.00.

1   [2011] EWHC 1010 (Fam).
2   [2011] EWHC 2717 (Fam).
3   [2011] EWHC 2637 (Fam).
4   [2011] EWHC 1759 (Fam).
5   [2012] EWHC 2063 (Fam).

1.153 A very recent case in which the law as to the treatment of marital and non-marital property was summarised in *WX v HX (Treatment of Matrimonial and Non-Matrimonial Property*[1] where Roberts J stated the principles as follows:

(1)   The fact that property or assets owned by a party derive from a source outside the marriage (such as inheritance or pre-acquired wealth) does not per se lead to its exclusion altogether from the court's consideration of a fair outcome to both parties. Insofar as it represents a contribution by one of the parties to the welfare of the family, it is a factor which the judge should take into account: per Lord Nicholls in *White v White* (above).

(2)   The overarching principle which supports fairness to both parties is that of 'non-discrimination'. The court will treat the contributions made by each of the parties to the marriage as having a broadly equivalent value even though they be different in kind: *Miller v Miller*; *McFarlane v McFarlane*[1].

(3)   Each case has to be considered on its own facts and the court's assessment of fairness in that particular case. The judge must consider whether the existence of such property should be reflected in outcome at all. This will depend on the extent to which it has been 'mingled' with matrimonial property and the length of time over which that 'mingling' has taken place. In other words, the way in which such property has been used over the course of the marriage has the potential to affect whether it remain 'separate' property.

(4)   Assets or property which are matrimonial in character will be captured by the 'sharing principle' and divided equally between the parties. Matrimonial property is now recognised as being property which is the product of, or reflective of, marital endeavour or 'generated during the marriage otherwise then by external donation'.

(5)   The application of the sharing principle impacts, in practice, only on the division of marital property and not on non-marital property.

(6)   The application of the sharing principle will not always lead to an arithmetically equal division of the marital wealth. In appropriate circumstances factors such as risk and liquidity may impact the means by which sharing is achieved: *XW v XH* (above) at para [136].

[1]   [2021] EWHC 241 (Fam).
[1]   [2006] UKHL 24, [2006] 2 AC 618, [2006] 1 FLR 1186.

1.154 In *S v S (Ancillary Relief: Importance of FDR)*[1] the judge at first instance had 'ring-fenced' certain assets of the wife because they had emanated from her family in 1996 and always treated by her as her separate property. That decision was overturned on appeal and the properties brought into the general 'pot'; this was a needs case and the money was needed to fund homes and lifestyle.

[1]   [2008] 1 FLR 944, Baron J.

1.155 In *Evans v Evans*[1] the husband's claim that he had made a special contribution was rejected; for a contribution to be classed as special and to influence the court's division of capital it had to be of a wholly exceptional nature such that it would very obviously be inconsistent with fairness for it to be ignored. Special contributions are considered further below at **1.158** in the judgment of Roberts J in *Cooper-Hohn v Cooper-Hohn*. In *WM v HM* where the husband already had a successful business at the date of the marriage which went on to greater success during the marriage, Mostyn J treated the value of the business as at the date of marriage as non-matrimonial property and excluded it from the sharing calculation. However, he rejected the husband's claim that his contribution was exceptional and so should justify further unequal division; such cases were 'as rare as a white leopard'.

[1]   [2013] EWHC 506 (Fam).

1.156 Finally, guidance was given by Lord Wilson in the Privy Council case of *Scatliffe v Scatliffe*[1]. His Lordship's advice may be summarised as follows:

> 'In an ordinary case the proper approach is to apply the sharing principle to the matrimonial property and then to ask whether, in the light of all the matters specified in [the statute] and of its concluding words, the result of so doing represents an appropriate overall disposal. In particular it should ask whether the principles of need and/or of compensation, best explained in the speech of Lady Hale in the Miller case at paras 137 to 144, require additional adjustment in the form of transfer to one party of further property, even of non-matrimonial property, held by the other.'

[1]   [2016] UKPC 36. It should be noted that although the statute governing the law in this case was that of the British Virgin Islands, that statute is sufficiently similar to the MCA 1973 to make this guidance of general interest.

Post-separation accruals

1.157 The unusual facts and decision of the Supreme Court in *Vince v Wyatt* are discussed in more detail under the heading of Procedure in CHAPTER **16**. When the parties separated their means were modest and they agreed a consent order in accordance with those limited means. Post-separation, the husband flourished financially and some years later the former wife applied for variation. One of the reasons why the Supreme Court allowed the appeal and referred the matter for re-hearing was that proper consideration had not been given to the wife's contributions, principally after the breakdown of the marriage. The wife claimed that she had cared for the child of the marriage for 16 years and another child treated as a child of the family for 10 years and then into her adult years, with little or no help, financial or otherwise, from the husband. Lord Wilson referred to and relied on the judgment of Ormrod LJ in *Pearce v Pearce*[1].

[1]   (1980) 1 FLR 261.

1.158 Several of these issues were brought into sharp focus in the judgment of Roberts J in *Cooper-Hohn v Hohn*[1], a case noteworthy for the vast sums of money involved if for no other reason. Roberts J described the principal issues as:

'i.   What is the extent of the assets available for distribution as between the husband and the wife (the computation issue)?

ii.   To what extent do those assets fall to be considered as part of the marital acquest or, alternatively, to what extent have they been generated (or added to) in the period between separation and the date of trial (the marital acquest or post-separation accrual issue)?

iii.   What percentage of the overall available wealth should each party receive at the end of the marriage? In particular, is a departure from equality justified on the facts by either or both of (i) post-separation accrual and/or (ii) special contribution on the part of the husband (the distribution issue)?

iv.   In either event, should there be a Wells sharing of any or each of the various categories of assets, to include any goodwill value which I find to exist in the TCI entities over and above the value of the assets they currently hold?'

The judge held that the total gross assets available for distribution were worth US$1.484 billion (£869 million).

[1]   [2014] EWHC 4122 (Fam).

1.159 At the time of the parties' separation in March 2012, the marital assets were in the region of US$700 million to US$750 million and their value had increased significantly post-separation (to the tune of 93%, on the husband's figures).

1.160 The judge noted that the law required her to value the assets as they stood at the date of trial and held:

'[183] Thus what I have to decide is whether and to what extent the new work and new investments created by the husband in the period after the parties separated falls to be considered in the character of matrimonial property in which the wife should be entitled to a share or whether some or all of it falls at a point too distant from the essential character of the matrimonial partnership to qualify.'

1.161 She held that a fair outcome in the case had to reflect some departure from equality of division in order to reflect the contributions made by the husband in the two or more years since separation and whilst she would value the assets at the time of trial, it would not be fair to treat the wealth creation after the breakdown of the marriage as simply part and parcel of the marital acquest in which the wife was entitled to an equal share.

1.162 Roberts J summarised her approach to post-separation accruals as follows:

' . . . [I]t is not my intention that this wife should receive no share of the assets which fall outside the marital acquest in this case. She will receive a share and that share and that share will form part and parcel of the overall award which I will make on the basis of fairness to both parties. There is no question of her entitlement to any element of post-separation accrual being triggered by a "needs" argument but I take the view that, notwithstanding the exponential increase in the growth of the Fund post-separation, its genesis as a matrimonial asset is a factor of considerable significance. That factor must, in my view, find its reflection in the overall quantum of the financial award she will receive at the conclusion of these proceedings. It goes to the heart of what I consider to be fair in the overall context of the case.'

1.163 The husband sought a departure from equality on the basis of his special contribution to the matrimonial assets. Roberts J discussed the applicable legal principles to this area and in particular the Court of Appeal decision in *Charman (No 4)*. She noted that, first, she needed to determine whether there was a special contribution made by the husband and secondly the extent to which this should affect the wife's award.

1.164 Roberts J held that the wife had made a 'full' contribution to the marriage and noted that for a period she was caring for four children under the age of 5 whilst also in employment. The question for her to determine, however, was whether the husband had made 'some further contribution, over and above that made by the wife, and unmatched by her in terms of their joint endeavours within the partnership which was their marriage' (see para [278]). She did not seek to define what could be classified as a special contribution, but identified the following specific questions to answer in this case (at para [282]):

'i.   Can it properly be said that [the husband] is the generating force behind the fortune rather than the product itself?

ii.   Does the scale of the wealth depend upon his innovative vision as well as on his ability to develop those visions?

iii.   Has he generated truly vast wealth such that his business success can properly be viewed as exceptional?

iv.   Does he have a special skill and effort which is special to him and which survives as a material consideration despite the partnership or pooling aspect of the marriage?

v.   Would it, in all the circumstances, be inequitable for me to disregard that contribution?'

1.165 Roberts J answered all of the above questions in the affirmative. She then set out the extent to which she took into account the special contribution of the husband at paras [288]–[294]. She noted that she had to be conscious that the wife's financial position would crystallise as a result of the award she would make, but the husband would, on the basis of the returns he had proved he was able to generate through his investment fund (on his evidence in the region of 24%) he would within a relatively short period earn back any sums he had to pay the wife. Roberts J concluded that the wife's award should be

US$530 million, which on current exchange rates converted to £330 million. The sum reflected 36% of the global resources[1].

1   For further analysis of the principles relating to what is and what is not matrimonial property, see the judgment of Mostyn J in *JL v SL (No 2) (Financial Remedies: Rehearing: Non-Matrimonial Property)* [2015] EWHC 360 (Fam) in which Mostyn J refers approvingly to the 'monumental judgment' of Roberts J above.

Non-financial contributions

1.166 If the only contributions which the court could consider were financial, a wife and mother who had stayed at home to look after children would be at a distinct disadvantage. Thus it is that the court is directed to have regard to the value to the family of a non-working party. It may be that before the decision of the House of Lords in *White v White*[1] the guidance which was given as to how, if at all, such contributions should be weighed in the balance against financial contributions was not entirely clear. For example, it was held that it was wrong to make a distinction between cases where a wife makes actual financial contributions to the assets of the family and those in which her contribution is indirect[2]. However, in another, admittedly unusual, case[3], it was held that, where there were ample assets and the wife had made a full contribution to the welfare of the family but had not contributed directly to the build-up of the family assets, the remarks in *Wachtel v Wachtel*[4], to the effect that there should be a starting point of equality, should be confined to division of the family home and not to division of the family assets as a whole.

1   [2001] 1 AC 596, [2000] 2 FLR 981.
2   *Vicary v Vicary* [1992] 2 FLR 271, CA, cited with approval in *Conran v Conran* [1997] 2 FLR 615 by Wilson J.
3   *W v W (Judicial Separation: Ancillary Relief)* [1995] 2 FLR 259 (husband was 87, wife 78; wife's reasonable needs were limited).
4   [1973] Fam 72.

1.167 In *White v White*[1], it was held that it is a principle 'of universal application' that there can be no discrimination between husband and wife in their respective roles. Different roles are assumed for many different reasons. Whatever the division of labour, fairness dictates that this should not prejudice either party when considering the statutory factors. There should be no bias in favour of the money-earner and against the homemaker and childcarer.

1   See **1.17**.

1.168 This principle was developed in *Lambert v Lambert*[1]. Here, judges were given clear guidance as to how to deal with issues of contributions. Any bias in favour of a breadwinner is an example of gender discrimination and therefore to be disapproved[2]:

'The danger of gender discrimination resulting from a finding of special financial contribution is plain.'

1   [2002] EWCA Civ 1685, [2003] 1 FLR 139.
2   [2002] EWCA Civ 1685, [2003] 1 FLR 139, per Thorpe LJ at para 45.

1.169 The statutory requirement to consider all the s 25 factors does not require a detailed critical appraisal of the performance of each of the parties during the marriage[1]:

'Couples who cannot agree division are entitled to seek a judicial decision without exposing themselves to intrusion, indignity, and possible embarrassment of such an appraisal.'

¹   [2002] EWCA Civ 1685, [2003] 1 FLR 139, per Thorpe LJ at para 38.

1.170 Special financial contributions are dealt with above. However, it should not be forgotten that not all special contributions are financial. In *Charman v Charman*, above, it was pointed out at para [80] that:

'The notion of a special contribution to the welfare of the family will not successfully have been purged of inherent gender discrimination unless it is accepted that such a contribution can, in principle, take a number of forms; that it can be non-financial as well as financial; and that it can thus be made by a party whose role has been exclusively that of a home-maker.'

1.171 It is, perhaps, necessary to say again that no one factor is to be regarded as intrinsically more important than the others; the court must take an overall view.

1.172 In another unusual case¹, it was said that the proper approach is to survey the wife's reasonable requirements and then place her contributions and all other factors in the balance, taking into account the nexus between the contributions and the creation of the resources.

¹   *Conran v Conran* [1997] 2 FLR 615; unusual because of the size of the parties' wealth if for no other reason.

Future contributions

1.173 The court must take account of the future as much as of the past. This will normally be relevant when one party is to care for the children of the family, and the longer the dependency the greater the significance of this factor. If one party is unable, for financial reasons, to make any significant contribution to the future welfare of the family, so that the burden will inevitably fall on the other party, this might well be a significant factor.

1.174 Since the advent of CSA 1991, and the virtual impossibility of contracting out of child support in most cases, the considerable sums which many 'non-resident parents' will have to pay is a future contribution which cannot be ignored.

CONDUCT

1.175 The court is directed to have regard to¹:

'(g)   the conduct of each of the parties, if that conduct is such that it would in the opinion of the court be inequitable to disregard it.'

As has been emphasised before, no one factor is normally the sole determining factor in any application, and there are few examples of cases where conduct has been a major let alone the sole determining matter². In *OG v AG (Financial Remedies: Conduct)*³ Mostyn J listed four scenarios in which conduct would be relevant in financial remedy proceedings. These were personal misconduct (which he described as being rare); add-back cases; litigation misconduct (which is addressed in costs); and failure to provide full and frank disclosure which will lead to adverse inferences being drawn.

1   MCA 1973, s 25(2)(g).
2   In *McCartney v Mills McCartney* [2008] 1 FLR 1508, Bennett J declined to hear evidence or argument about conduct on the ground that it would make little or no difference to the final result.
3   [2020] EWFC 52.

Financial conduct

1.176 Cases where it can be demonstrated that the behaviour of one party has had a clear (and, impliedly, detrimental) effect on the fortunes of the parties are the most usual examples of conduct having a real significance. In one case, the husband had dissipated the family capital, and the court held that he could not be allowed to fritter away assets and then claim as much of what was left as if he had behaved reasonably[1]. In another case, the husband, a farmer, had brought about financial disaster and his own bankruptcy; in the words of the judge he had 'obstinately, unrealistically and selfishly trailed on to eventual disaster, dissipating in the process not only his own money but his family's money, his friends' money, the money of commercial creditors unsecured and eventually his wife's money'[2]. Even so, he was not deprived of all entitlement but was restricted to the minimum sum needed to rehouse himself.

1   *Martin v Martin* [1976] Fam 335.
2   *Beach v Beach* [1995] 2 FLR 160, per Thorpe J. See also *Le Foe v Le Foe and Woolwich plc* [2001] 2 FLR 970.

1.177 These decisions may perhaps be contrasted with another[1], in which a wife had inherited her mother's estate and then sold part to her daughter at an undervalue, thereby depleting her own assets. The argument that this was 'financial conduct' was rejected, but the actions of the wife were held to be clearly relevant as one of the circumstances.

1   *Primavera v Primavera* [1992] 1 FLR 16, CA.

1.178 In another case, it was held that although the husband's conduct in relation to certain financial transfers was such that it would be inequitable to ignore it, the approach should be not to fix a sum as a penalty, but rather an evaluation based on all the relevant factors taken in the round[1].

1   *H v H (Financial Relief: Conduct)* [1998] 1 FLR 971.

1.179 An unusual situation arose in *W v W*[1]. Both parties had agreed not to pursue allegations of conduct but the husband then sought to argue that, because of the wife's drinking, her contributions were 'negative'. Wilson J said that 'negative contributions' was an unhelpful oxymoron. Where a nil contribution or conduct were alleged, the allegations should be put in those terms. More comment on dissipated assets will be found at **1.88**.

1   [2001] Fam Law 656, Wilson J.

1.180 In *Neil v Neil*[1] the judge found that the conduct of the wife had been thoroughly dishonest and that she had been guilty of fraud affecting the husband. He set aside the consent order for periodical payments which had been obtained by the fraud, dismissed her claim for periodical payments and ordered her to pay the costs.

[1] [2019] EWHC 3330 (Fam).

Non-financial conduct

1.181 The task of summarising some of the leading cases on what might be regarded as relevant conduct was made easier and more authoritative by the judgment of Stanley Burton J in *S v S*[1]. His Lordship had to consider whether or not the alleged conduct in that case should be taken into account. He was at pains to point out that he did not normally sit in the Family Division and so relied on the two expert counsel[2] appearing before him. He dealt with the position as follows:

'I have been told by Counsel that there are only rare cases in the reports where this has occurred. I have been taken to what I believe must be all of them. The examples given include:

(i)   *Armstrong v Armstrong* [1974] SJ 579: wife shoots husband with his shotgun with intent to endanger life.

(ii)   *Jones v Jones* [1976] Fam 8: husband attacks wife with a razor and inflicts serious injuries: there are financial consequences (wife rendered incapable of working).

(iii) *Bateman v Bateman* [1979] 2 WLR 377: wife twice inflicts stab wounds on her husband with a knife.

(iv)   *S v S* [1982] Fam Law 183: husband commits incest with children of the family.

(v)   *Hall v Hall* [1984] FLR 631: wife stabs husband in the abdomen with a knife.

(vi)   *Kyte v Kyte* [1987] 3 AER 1041: wife facilitates the husband's attempted suicide.

(vii) *Evans v Evans* [1989] 1 FLR 351: wife incites others to murder the husband.

(viii) *K v K* [1990] 2 FLR 225: husband's serious drink problem and "disagreeable" behaviour led to the forced sale of the matrimonial home and serious financial consequences to the wife.

(ix)   *H v H* [1994] 2 FLR 801: serious assault and an attempted rape of wife by husband: and financial consequences because the consequent imprisonment of husband destroyed his ability to support her.

(x)   *A v A* [1995] 1 FLR 345: husband assaults the wife with a knife.

(xi)   *C v C* (Bennett J 12 December 2001 unreported): wife deliberately drugged husband to make him very sleepy and then while he was in a somnolent state placed a bag over his head, which she held in such a way that the husband could not breathe. Although it was found that the wife did not have an intent to kill, Bennett J concluded that the husband did believe that she was trying to kill him, and that her aim was to make him so believe.

(xii) *Al-Khatib v Masry* [2002] 1 FLR 1053: husband guilty of "very grave" misconduct in abducting the children of the marriage in contempt of court.

(xiii) *H v H* [2006] 1 FLR 990: very serious assault by husband on wife with knife, leading to 12 years' imprisonment for attempted murder and with financial consequences, namely destroying her Police career.'

[1] [2006] EWHC 2793 (Fam).
[2] Mr Nicholas Mostyn QC and Mr Philip Moor QC.

1.182 His Lordship's comments on these cases were as follows:

'As will be seen, it is not suggested that there were any financial consequences from the conduct of which the Applicant complains in this case, which factor may have exacerbated, in the judgment of Scott Baker J, the facts in *K v K* referred to at (viii) above. However, that case apart, all of the conduct found in those cases appears of manifest seriousness. Apart from the statutory provision, and the words of Ormrod J in *Wachtel* quoted by Baroness Hale above, there is a certain amount of recurrent phraseology: "If the courts were in these circumstances not to discharge the order, the public might think that we had taken leave of our senses" (per Balcombe LJ at 355 in *Evans* at (vii) above): Sir Roger Ormrod in *Hall* at (v) above describes (at 632) the conduct as "gross and obvious" which has "nothing to do with the ordinary run of fighting and quarrelling in an unhappy marriage" and which the judge's "sense of justice required to be taken into account": Bennett J in *C* at (xi) above, asks whether "it would be repugnant to any sense of justice for the wife to receive any award at all". Mr Mostyn QC pointed to the words of Sir George Baker P in *W v W* [1976] Fam 107 at 110D when he referred to the sort of conduct which would cause the ordinary mortal to throw up his hands and say " . . . surely that woman is not going to get a full award": and, in the course of submissions, he suggested a test of applying what he called the "gasp factor".'

1.183 One case which was, perhaps surprisingly omitted from this pantheon of wrongdoing was *Clark v Clark*[1] which was described by Thorpe LJ as 'one of the most extraordinary marital histories that I have ever encountered' and 'as baleful as any to be found in the family law reports'. The wife was 36 years younger than the husband. At the date of the marriage, he was rich while her liabilities exceeded her assets. The marriage was never consummated. Over the 5-year marriage, she persuaded him to purchase a number of properties, most of which were vested in her sole name. In addition, she acquired shares, a racehorse, a Bentley and a boat. The husband was coerced into transferring a large house into the wife's name, and he was then forced to live as a virtual prisoner in part of the house while she occupied the larger part with her lover. He attempted suicide, and when he returned home he was again confined as a virtual prisoner, the wife removing his telephone and gate buzzer. He was eventually rescued by relatives. The judge found that the wife had exercised undue influence over the husband, that this was a short marriage, that the husband's contributions had been enormous while hers were negligible and that her marital and litigation conduct must be condemned in the strongest terms. Nevertheless, he awarded her a lump sum of £552,500. Both parties appealed.

[1]   [1999] 2 FLR 498, CA.

1.184 The wife's appeal was dismissed and the husband's appeal allowed. The judge had fallen into manifest error in allowing the wife £552,500. He had failed to reflect his findings on the wife's misconduct in his award; it would be hard to conceive of a case of graver marital misconduct. This was a rare case in which litigation misconduct should be reflected in the substantive award. However, to leave the wife with nothing was impracticable since that would have required her to make substantial repayments to the husband, and the lump sum was reduced to £125,000.

1.185 For a case where the conduct of both parties was equally reprehensible and so cancelled each other out and had no effect on the award see the judgment of Mostyn J in *FZ v SZ (Ancillary Relief: Conduct: Valuations)*[1].

In *R v B and Capita Trustees* the husband was guilty of fraud in hiding two loans totalling £7m from the wife, never declaring income to HMRC, taking money to which he was not entitled, the pursuit of ruinous litigation and repeatedly lying to the court. His behaviour had brought financial catastrophe on the family. The judge found that this was conduct which he should take into account.

[1] [2010] EWHC 1630 (Fam), [2011] 1 FLR 64.

1.186 In *FRB v DCA (No 2)*[1] the wife had allowed the husband to bring up a child in the belief that he was the natural father, and he only found that he was not the biological father after divorce. The judge found that this was conduct so egregious that it would be inequitable to disregard it. Fortunately, perhaps, this was a case where the parties were extremely wealthy and the husband's disclosure had been seriously deficient. The judge sought to reflect the emotional damage caused to the husband by not trying to put a figure on the undisclosed assets while not reducing the wife's award.

In *AF v SF*[2], over the course of the proceedings the husband (who lacked capacity to litigate) sent numerous highly offensive messages to the wife, her advisers and the press. The judge found that this had been very distressing for the wife but decided, by the narrowness of margins, not to take this conduct into account since it was difficult to see how it had affected her needs.

[1] [2020] EWHC 754 (Fam).
[2] [2019] EWHC 1224 (Fam).

Conduct in the course of the proceedings

1.187 The conduct of the parties during and in relation to the proceedings may be a relevant factor. In *B v B (Real Property: Assessment of Interests)*[1], it was held that a wife whose conduct in relation to discovery and dishonest statements had amounted to contempt as well as conduct which it was inequitable to disregard should have the award which she would otherwise have received reduced to take account of the conduct. However, this may be a decision which will rarely be followed. In another case[2], where a wife had knowingly misrepresented her true financial position and failed in her duty to give full disclosure, Thorpe J held that, while accepting that such behaviour was conduct which it would be inequitable to disregard, this should be reflected in an order for costs rather than a reduction of the share of the assets[3].

[1] [1988] 2 FLR 490.
[2] *P v P (Financial Relief: Non-disclosure)* [1994] 2 FLR 381.
[3] A similar result occurred in *T v T (Interception of Documents)* [1994] 2 FLR 1083 where a wife had obtained documents belonging to the husband by reprehensible means. See also *Tavoulareas v Tavoulareas* [1998] 2 FLR 418, CA.

1.188 Litigation misconduct is frequently reflected in an order for costs, but in *Rothschild v De Sousa*[1] Moylan LJ pointed out that an order for costs does not remedy the effect of there being less wealth to be distributed. There are cases in which the conduct is such that it should be taken into account in determining the award. In *R v B and Others*[2] Moor J said that the court must be entitled to prioritise the needs of the party who has not been guilty of the misconduct.

1   [2020] EWCA Civ 1215.
2   [2017] EWFC 33.

1.189 In *Al Khatib v Masry*[1] the husband had been highly obstructive and unco-operative in the wife's application for ancillary relief and the court observed that it would be difficult to imagine a worse case of litigation misconduct. The husband had also abducted the children to Saudi Arabia. It was thought that the husband's assets were at least £50m. The wife was awarded a lump sum of £10m, a *Duxbury* award of £5.5m and a 'fighting fund' for legal costs of £2.5m to assist her to recover the children.

1   [2002] EWHC 108 (Fam), [2002] 1 FLR 1053.

1.190 In *M v M (Ancillary Relief: Conduct)* it was held that the husband's conduct both in respect of gambling and his disregard of court orders should not be disregarded. Such conduct should be taken into account in a broad way and not with mathematical precision and affected the order and not just the costs.

1.191 Finally, mention should be made of *Hall v Hall*[1]. Here, a wife had steadfastly refused to take part in the husband's application for ancillary relief and, clearly in desperation, the district judge had transferred all the assets to the husband. The Court of Appeal held that this was the wrong approach; the husband's counsel should have dissuaded the judge from making an order which went beyond the husband's own case, and the denial of the wife's entitlement to equality was a wholly disproportionate response to her 'tardy engagement' in the proceedings.

1   [2008] EWCA Civ 350, [2008] 2 FLR 575.

1.192 For discussion of the position where the court has preferred to penalise litigation misconduct by an order for costs and has deprecated the practice of reflecting its displeasure in an increased financial award, see CHAPTER 17.

LOST BENEFITS

1.193 The court is directed to have regard to[1]:

'(h)   in the case of proceedings for divorce or nullity of marriage, the value to each of the parties to the marriage of any benefit which, by reason of the dissolution or annulment of the marriage, that party will lose the chance of acquiring.'

This is the factor most frequently relied on when loss of pension benefits is an issue, and its significance is clear.

1   MCA 1973, s 25(2)(h).

1.194 The Pensions Act 1995 amended the MCA 1973 to introduce a new s 25B which is concerned entirely with pensions. The original reference to pensions in s 25(2)(h) has been deleted, and the court is now directed to have regard to the value to each of the parties of any benefit which, by reason of the dissolution or annulment of the marriage, that party will lose the chance of acquiring. Since pensions are now adequately covered elsewhere, it would seem that this is now to be a 'catch-all' provision, and it is difficult to think of circumstances which would be applicable to this subsection only and which would not be covered by some other provision.

1.195 As was seen above, pensions have been removed from the s 25(2) factors and given their own place in s 25B. Pensions is a very important subject which is considered in some detail in CHAPTER 10.

1.196 Here, it is only necessary to consider the requirement on the court to consider the subject; s 25B(1) in effect adds further s 25(2) factors to be considered in every case. It is provided that the matters to which the court is to have regard under s 25(2) include:

(a)   in the case of subs (2)(a) (ie when considering the income, means, etc of the parties) any benefits under a pension scheme which a party to a marriage has or is likely to have; and

(b)   in the case of subs (2)(h) (ie loss of benefits) any benefits under a pension scheme which, by reason of the dissolution or annulment of the marriage, a party to the marriage will lose the chance of acquiring.

It is also provided that, in relation to benefits under a pension scheme, the words 'in the foreseeable future' should be regarded as being deleted from s 25(2)(a).

1.197 The result of this is that, in every case, it is necessary to consider the benefits which either party may receive from a pension scheme, no matter how remote that event may seem. In the same way, the effect on the other party of the loss of any such pension benefits must be calculated.

1.198 Section 25B(2) goes on to direct the court as to how it should consider dealing with loss of pension benefits. This is best considered in CHAPTER 10 on pensions.

AGREEMENTS

1.199 There is no specific mention of agreements in s 25 but they are generally agreed at least to be one of the 'circumstances' which the court must take into account. The traditional attitude of the courts to agreements was the somewhat paternalistic statement in *Hyman v Hyman*[1] that 'the wife cannot by her own covenant preclude herself from invoking the jurisdiction of the court or preclude the court from the exercise of that jurisdiction'. Previous editions of this book contained detailed examinations of the way in which the courts have sought to qualify that doctrine and bring it into line with the wishes of divorcing couples and their advisers. Most of this is now of historical interest only due to the decision of the Supreme Court in *Radmacher (formerly Granatino) v Granatino*[2].

[1]   [1929] AC 602.
[2]   [2010] UKSC 42, [2010] 2 FLR 1900.

1.200 The issue in *Radmacher v Granatino* was how far the terms of a pre-nuptial contract should dictate the result of a husband's application for a financial remedy; the wife, who was extremely wealthy, sought to rely on the agreement to limit the husband's claim. However, the decision of the Supreme Court goes far beyond that issue and gives guidance as to the manner in which the court should deal with all agreements, whether made pre- or post-marriage.

1.201 The most common kinds of agreement which need to be considered are:

* post-nuptial agreements made (normally) on separation to compromise claims;
* pre-nuptial agreements; and
* agreements to settle litigation.

The first two will be considered together, since the same principles now apply. First, however, a short account of the reasoning of the Supreme Court in arriving at its decision may be helpful.

Radmacher v Granatino

1.202 The most recent previous occasion on which the issue of pre-nuptial contracts had been determined at the highest level was the decision of the Privy Council (on appeal from the courts of the Isle of Man) in *MacLeod v MacLeod*[1]. In that case, it was said that:

> 'Post-nuptial agreements . . . are very different from pre-nuptial agreements. The couple are now married. They have undertaken towards one another the obligations and responsibilities of the married state. A pre-nuptial agreement is no longer the price which one party may extract for his or her willingness to marry.' (para 36)

[1]   [2008] UKPC 64.

1.203 In *Radmacher v Granatino* the Supreme Court disapproved this statement:

> '60.   . . . we do not see why different principles must apply to an agreement concluded in anticipation of the married state and one concluded after entry into the married state.
>
> 61.   This is not to say that there are no circumstances where it is right to distinguish between an ante-nuptial and a post-nuptial agreement. The circumstances surrounding the agreement may be very different dependent on the stage of the couple's life together at which it is concluded, but it is not right to proceed on the premise that there will always be a significant difference between an ante- and a post-nuptial agreement. Some couples do not get married until they have lived together and had children.'

1.204 At para 63, the judgment continues:

> 'In summary, we consider that the Board in *MacLeod* was wrong to hold that post-nuptial agreements were contracts but that ante-nuptial agreements were not. That question did not arise for decision in that case any more than in this and does not matter anyway. It is a red herring. Regardless of whether one or both are contracts, the ancillary relief court should apply the same principles when considering ante-nuptial agreements as it applies to post-nuptial agreements.'

It seems therefore conclusively to be the case that, when considering whether or not an agreement should be adhered to or departed from, the same principles will be applied irrespective of whether the agreement is pre-nuptial or post-nuptial.

1.205 The Supreme Court also dealt with the question of whether the usual rules as to validity of a contract applied. At para 62 the question was asked:

> 'Is it important whether or not post-nuptial or ante-nuptial agreements have contractual status? The value of a contract is that the court will enforce it. But in ancillary relief proceedings the court is not bound to give effect to nuptial agreements, and is bound to have regard to them, whether or not they are contracts. Should they be given greater weight because in some other context they would be enforceable? Or is the question of whether or not they are contracts an irrelevance?'

1.206 In *MacLeod*, the Privy Council had been concerned with whether the agreement in that case was a contract properly so-called. The view of the Supreme Court in *Radmacher* was that this was not important but that there were clearly factors which would justify the court in departing from the terms of a contract. These will be considered below.

The general approach to agreements

1.207 At the end of para [75] of the majority judgment, the Supreme Court advanced the following general proposition to govern the correct approach to pre- or post-nuptial agreements:

> 'The court should give effect to a nuptial agreement that is freely entered into by each party with a full appreciation of its implications unless in the circumstances prevailing it would not be fair to hold the parties to their agreement.'

This is now, therefore, the general rule to be applied in all cases. The court has no jurisdiction to revisit a final order whether by consent or otherwise for capital adjustments in the absence of vitiating factors such as fraud, misrepresentation or material non-disclosure[1].

[1]   *Birch v Birch* [2015] EWCA Civ 833.

1.208 Two areas of discussion are therefore suggested and must be considered. They are, first, the factors which might lead a court to consider that the agreement was not freely entered into (for the sake of convenience these are here described as 'vitiating factors'), and secondly, the circumstances in which a court might consider it was not fair to hold the parties to the agreement. These two sets of issues might overlap in some cases but they are in fact distinct.

Vitiating factors

1.209 The Supreme Court considers these factors in detail in paras [71]–[73]. Here, they may be summarised as follows:

(1)   Material lack of disclosure or information, and lack of sound legal advice. However, this is subject to the qualification that:

> ' . . . if it is clear that a party is fully aware of the implications of an ante-nuptial agreement and indifferent to detailed particulars of the other

party's assets, there is no need to accord the agreement reduced weight because he or she is unaware of those particulars. What is important is that each party should have all the information that is material to his or her decision, and that each party should intend that the agreement should govern the financial consequences of the marriage coming to an end.'

(2)   The parties must have intended that the agreement should be effective. This cannot always be inferred from the mere existence of the agreement.

(3)   Any of the standard vitiating factors in contract such as duress, fraud, illegality or misrepresentation.

(4)   Unconscionable conduct such as undue pressure (falling short of duress) would be likely to reduce the weight to be placed on an agreement.

(5)   Unworthy behaviour such as exploitation of a dominant position to secure an advantage would reduce or eliminate the value of an agreement.

1.210 The Supreme Court added the following important observations.

'The circumstances of the parties at the time of the agreement will be relevant. Those will include such matters as their age and maturity, whether either or both had been married or been in long-term relationships before. For such couples their experience of previous relationships may explain the terms of the agreement, and may also show what they foresaw when they entered into the agreement. What may not be easily foreseeable for less mature couples may well be in contemplation of more mature couples. Another important factor may be whether the marriage would have gone ahead without an agreement, or without the terms which had been agreed. This may cut either way.'

The foreign element

1.211 The Supreme Court then considered the factors which might enhance the weight to be placed on an agreement, the most important of which is a foreign element. This was dealt with succinctly as follows:

'When dealing with agreements concluded in the past, and the agreement in this case was concluded in 1998, foreign elements such as those in this case may bear on the important question of whether or not the parties intended their agreement to be effective. In the case of agreements made in recent times and, a fortiori, any agreement made after this judgment, the question of whether the parties intended their agreement to take effect is unlikely to be in issue, so foreign law will not need to be considered in relation to that question.'

Fairness

1.212 Having, as it were, cleared the decks by dealing with such of the above factors as may be relevant, the court must then deal with what the Supreme Court described as the difficult question of the circumstances in which it might not be fair to hold the parties to an agreement. It began with the observation that the reason why the court should give weight to a nuptial agreement is that there should be respect for individual autonomy. The court should accord respect to the decision of a married couple as to the manner in which their financial affairs should be regulated. It would be paternalistic and patronising to override their agreement simply on the basis that the court knows best. This is particularly true where the parties' agreement addresses existing circumstances and not merely the contingencies of an uncertain future[1].

[1] In *JS v RS* [2015] EWHC 2921 (Fam) Sir Peter Singer held that, where one party puts forward a coherent case for an outcome which appears less advantageous than that which the court might have adopted, the court is under no obligation to make a higher order in line with what it regards as that individual's entitlement. See also *Pounds v Pounds* [1994] 1 FLR 775 at 779; the court is entitled to assume that parties who are sui juris and legally represented know what they want.

1.213 The factors which might lead to argument over whether an agreement was unfair were summarised as follows:

(1)   *Children of the family.* A nuptial agreement cannot be allowed to prejudice the reasonable requirements of any children of the family.
(2)   *Non-matrimonial property.* Where one or both parties own property at the date of the marriage or anticipate receiving such property, and wish to make provision for that property in the event of the dissolution of the marriage, there is nothing inherently unfair in such an arrangement and there may be a good objective reason for it such as obligations to other family members.
(3)   *Future circumstances.* Where a pre-nuptial agreement attempts to address the unknown, and often unforeseen, contingencies of the couple's future relationship there is more scope for future events to make it unfair to hold them to their agreement. The circumstances of parties often change over time in ways or to an extent which either cannot be, or was not, envisaged. The longer the marriage has lasted, the more likely it is that this will be the case.

1.214 The Supreme Court considered the hypothetical case of a pre-nuptial agreement providing for no recovery by each spouse from the other in the event of divorce, where the marriage had seen the formation of a fortune which each spouse had played an equal role in their different ways in creating, but the fortune was in the hands for the most part of one spouse rather than the other. It asked whether it would be right to give the same weight to their early agreement as in another perhaps very different example. It concluded that the answer was likely to be 'no'. Of the three strands identified in *White v White* and *Miller/McFarlane*, it was the first two, needs and compensation, which could most readily render it unfair to hold the parties to a pre-nuptial agreement. The parties were unlikely to have intended that their agreement should result, in the event of the marriage breaking up, in one partner being left in a predicament of real need, while the other enjoyed a sufficiency or more, and such a result was likely to render it unfair to hold the parties to their agreement. If the devotion of one partner to looking after the family and the home had left the other free to accumulate wealth, it was likely to be unfair to hold the parties to an agreement that entitled the latter to retain all that he or she had earned.

1.215 However, where these considerations did not apply and each party was in a position to meet his or her needs, fairness might well not require a departure from their agreement as to the regulation of their financial affairs in the circumstances that had come to pass. It was in relation to the third strand, sharing, that the court would be most likely to make an order in the terms of the nuptial agreement in place of the order that it would otherwise have made.

Case law since *Radmacher*

1.216 As is always the case, this decision of the Supreme Court was not the last word on the subject and there have been a number of cases where the proper approach to an agreement has been in issue. The first reported case following was *Z v Z (Financial Remedies: Marriage Contract)*[1]. The parties, who were French, had made a marriage contract in France in 1994. The marriage broke down in 2008 by which time the parties were living in London. In his judgment Moor J said that, had it not been for the agreement, this would have been a case for equal division of assets. However, the burden on someone arguing that a marital agreement had been varied was a heavy one, and there had to be clearest evidence before a court would contemplate using this as a reason for not enforcing the agreement. Further, even where the parties have made an agreement as to capital, there can still be a substantial liability for the provision of ongoing support for a spouse and children. In *V v V (Prenuptial Agreement)*[2] an award at first instance was set aside on the ground that the judge had failed to give proper weight to a 'marriage settlement'. This settlement provided a good and powerful reason for departing from an equal division of assets and was capable of founding an award that differed from the one that would have been made had it not been entered into.

[1]   [2011] EWHC 2878 (Fam).
[2]   [2011] EWHC 3230 (Fam).

1.217 These decisions therefore reflect the changed emphasis on the weight to be placed on an agreement. However, other decisions demonstrate the need for an agreement to be freely agreed and fair in all respects.

1.218 In *Kremen v Agrest (Financial Remedy: Non-Disclosure: Post-Nuptial Agreement)*[1] Mostyn J said that it only be in would be an unusual case that, without legal advice and full disclosure, a party could be taken to have freely entered into a marital agreement with full appreciation of its implications. In *GS v L (Financial Remedies; Pre-acquired Assets: Need)*[2] the parties had signed a post-marriage agreement in Spain. The judge held that neither party had a full appreciation of what the agreement meant and there was no common understanding. It was therefore ignored.

[1]   [2012] EWHC 45 (Fam).
[2]   [2011] EWHC 1759 (Fam).

1.219 In *D v D (Financial Remedies: Pre-marital agreement and Unequal shares)*[1] Cohen J found that the pre-marital agreement should not be accorded any weight. The wife had had no understanding of it and had given no thought to its implications[2].

For a rare case where the court decided to accord no weight to a prenuptial agreement see *Ipekci v McConnell*[3].

[1]   [2020] EWHC 857 (Fam).
[2]   But see also *Versteegh v Versteeg* [2018] EWCA Civ 1050.
[3]   [2019] EWFC 19.

1.220 The principles set out in *Radmacher v Granatino* were applied by Holman J in *Gray v Work*[1] but the judge held that the post-nuptial agreements had no effect on the exercise of the court's discretion since they expressly preserved the wife's right to seek relief from the court.

[1]   [2015] EWHC 834 (Fam).

1.221 The agreement also has to be intended as an agreement that might bind the parties in the event of separation. In *F v F (Financial Remedies: Pre-marital Wealth)*[1] the parties during the marriage had made a shareholders agreement reclassifying and assigning shares in a family company between the parties and providing for salaries etc. In the financial proceedings following divorce the issue of whether this agreement was a maintenance agreement under s 34 MCA 1973 arose. It was held that it was not; the definition of financial agreements covered only agreements made with the expressed or clearly implied purpose of governing the parties' financial affairs including in the event of separation.

[1]   [2012] EWHC 438 (Fam).

1.222 In *T v T (Agreement not embodied in Consent Order)*[1] the parties had made a separation agreement negotiated by solicitors in 1991 settling all matters between them; the agreement was fully implemented. They were divorced in 1995 but no consent order was ever applied for or granted. In 2012 the wife applied for financial relief and the husband applied for the agreement to be made a consent order. Parker J acknowledged that the court must make its own assessment of any application and carry out the s 25 exercise, but also relied on the principle that formal agreements made with legal advice should not be displaced in the absence of good and substantial grounds for concluding that injustice would be caused by holding the parties to their agreement. The wife's delay was of great importance and she had not shown cause that the agreement should not be made an order of the court.

[1]   [2013] EWHC B3 (Fam).

1.223 The decision in *BN v MA (Maintenance Pending Suit: Pre-Nuptial Agreement)*[1] related to the wife's application, for, inter alia, maintenance pending suit under s 22 of the MCA 1973 and involved detailed consideration of an English prenuptial agreement which the parties had entered into prior to their marriage.

[1]   [2013] EWHC 4250 (Fam).

1.224 After considering the law on prenuptial agreements and how it applied to the present agreement, the court found that[1]:

' . . . when adjudicating the question of interim maintenance, where there has been a prenuptial agreement, the court should seek to apply the terms of the prenuptial agreement as closely and practically as it can, unless the evidence of the wife in support of her application demonstrates, to a convincing standard, that she has a prospect of satisfying a court that the agreement should not be upheld.'

[1]   At para 33.

1.225 In *Luckwell v Limata*[1] shortly before the marriage, in 2005, the parties signed a pre-marital agreement (PMA) setting out that they intended to retain separate property and would not make claims against each other's property.

The PMA specifically considered gifts given to the wife by her family. Later the parties signed two supplemental agreements when the wife's family were intending to give her substantial gifts, including a property in Connaught Square. Without the original PMA there would have been no marriage. Without the supplement agreements there would have been no gifts.

¹ [2014] EWHC 502 (Fam).

1.226 The parties had three children. The total assets in the case, taking liabilities into account, amounted to the equity in the Connaught Square property of £6.74m, held in the wife's sole name, with net debts of £226,000 on the husband's side. The core issue for Holman J to decide was how much weight if any should be given to the agreements.

1.227 His Lordship adopted the propositions of law to be drawn from *Granatino v Radmacher*, and added at [132] that the court must be 'scrupulous to avoid gender discrimination or gender bias . . . there must be no discrimination of bias based on gender alone, nor any stereo-typical view that a wife may be dependent upon her husband but not vice versa'. In light of these propositions of law, he held at [133] that very great weight should be given to the agreements, in the absence of any vitiating factors. If the court were to make an order, then the wife would face a substantial reduction in her income and would no longer have the children's school fees paid. The weakness or unfairness of the agreements in this case was from the start that they provided nothing at all for the husband no matter how long the marriage or how great his need upon breakdown, although the present circumstances are the only circumstances to be dealt with by the court at this stage. The husband was now in a 'predicament of real need' while the wife enjoyed a 'sufficiency or more', adding that if the facts were the same but the genders reversed it would be inconceivable that the wife would be held to the agreements.

1.228 Although any order would, on these facts, require the wife and the children to move, this upheaval would be less damaging than providing the husband with nothing at all which would result in the children seeing the wife living in relative luxury and the husband living in relative penury.

1.229 The judge therefore held that he must make some capital provision for the husband on the basis of his needs and in conjunction with his role as father. Given his age (compared to Mr Granatino) and his capacity to make provision for his old age is in doubt, the judge ordered a stepped approach, the terms of which included orders that the house in Connaught Square should be sold to release £6.74m of equity to the wife, and for the wife to provide up to £900,000 for the purchase of a three-bedroomed property for the husband's use but not owned by him.

1.230 In *SA v PA (Pre-Marital Agreement: Compensation)*¹ Mostyn J made a number of findings in respect of a pre-marital agreement, including that the wife was fully aware of the contents of the agreement, that (despite her assertion to the contrary) she had attended a notary's firm in The Hague and that the notary had witnessed and executed the deed putting the agreement into effect. The agreement did not provide for maintenance. In a detailed analysis of the guidance given by the Supreme Court in *Granatino v*

Radmacher, Mostyn J arrived at the conclusion that the wife knew precisely what she was signing up to, that she had seen all of the drafts of the agreement and that it was therefore clear that the parties had intended to enter into a binding agreement. The agreement as to capital division would therefore be implemented as the parties had intended.

¹   [2014] EWHC 392 (Fam).

1.231 In *AH v PH*[1] the wife was aged 30 and the husband aged 33. They were from a Scandinavian country. The marriage lasted for 4 years with approximately 1½ years' cohabitation beforehand. There were two children, aged 5 and 4.

¹   [2014] EWHC 392 (Fam).

1.232 All the assets, amounting to some £76m, were 'non-matrimonial' as they were inherited by the husband prior to the marriage. The parties had made a marriage settlement before marriage restricting the wife's claims. The expert evidence in respect of the applicable foreign law suggested that the document would not be upheld in the country of origin.

1.233 The judge concluded that where a party was not fully aware of the implications of a marriage settlement, because he or she lacked all the material information, it would depend upon the circumstances of the case as to how much weight the agreement should nevertheless be afforded. He decided that, in most respects, the marriage settlement should be disregarded as it did not provide for English housing for the wife and it did not prevent a claim for maintenance. However, the agreement was a relevant factor as 'one of the circumstances of the case' in so far as it protected the husband's inherited wealth. Therefore he determined that the husband's inherited wealth should be invaded to meet the wife's housing needs and her need for capitalised maintenance only. He accepted that in the absence of the marriage settlement he would have reached the same conclusions by virtue of the short marriage, the age of the parties and the origin of the husband's wealth.

1.234 In *DB v PB (Pre-Nuptial Agreement: Jurisdiction)*[1], while upholding a pre-nuptial agreement on the ground that it was not vitiated by any of the usual factors and that the wife had received independent legal advice which she had ignored, Francis J nevertheless concluded that it could not be fair after a marriage of 14 years with two children for the wife to be left with almost nothing. It was the court's duty to step in and alleviate the unfairness which could be partially achieved by a capital order under Sch 1 to the Children Act 1989.

¹   [2016] EWHC 3431 (Fam).

1.235 For an example of a case where permission to appeal was given to a wife who applied to set aside a consent order on the ground of lack of capacity to consent to the order because of bipolar disorder see *MAP v RAP (Consent Order: Appeal: Incapacity)*[1].

In *Brack v Brack*[2] the Court of Appeal set aside part of an order where the judge had concluded that because the effective pre-nuptial agreement did not meet the wife's needs he was therefore constrained to make an order limited to providing for those needs. This was incorrect. The court is bound to take into account all the s 25(2) factors. However, there is nothing which prevents a party from contracting out of 'sharing' and the court may in the exercise of its discretion interfere with the terms of the agreement only to the extent necessary to provide for the needs of the wife and children.

1   [2013] EWHC 4784 (Fam).
2   [2018] EWCA Civ 2862.

Agreements to compromise litigation

1.236 Whether or not an agreement to compromise litigation has been made and, if so, in what terms, may be in dispute. In *Xydhias v Xydhias*[1], there were prolonged negotiations shortly before trial, which led to the wife asking for the trial to be vacated and for a short directions appointment. The wife applied successfully for an order in the terms of an agreement made between the parties, the husband failing in his purported withdrawal of all previous offers. The husband appealed, unsuccessfully, to the circuit judge and thence to the Court of Appeal. His appeal was dismissed.

1   [1999] 1 FLR 683, CA.

1.237 It was held that it was a fundamental principle that an agreement for the compromise of an ancillary relief application did not give rise to an agreement enforceable in law; ordinary contractual principles did not apply. The award of ancillary relief was always fixed by the court. The court had a discretion in determining whether an accord had been reached, but if the court decided that agreement had been reached it might have to consider whether the terms of the agreement were vitiated by, for example, non-disclosure or one of the *Edgar v Edgar*[1] factors. In every case, the court must carry out its independent discretionary review under s 25. In this case, it was held that an agreement had been reached.

1   [1980] 1 WLR 1410.

1.238 This development was extended in *Rose v Rose*[1] where, at the end of a financial dispute resolution (FDR) appointment, the judge was told that the parties had come to terms and it was left to counsel to draw up an agreed order. This draft order was agreed but the husband then sought to resile from it. On reference back to the judge, the judge refused to convert the agreement to an order. On appeal, an order was made in the terms of the agreement; it mattered not that the hearing had been an FDR appointment.

1   [2002] EWCA Civ 208, [2002] 1 FLR 978.

1.239 However, in *Soulsbury v Soulsbury*[1] the view was expressed, per curiam, that the conclusion expressed by Thorpe LJ in *Xydhias* that an agreement to compromise a claim was not enforceable until converted into a court order was too wide. If there were negotiations leading to agreement there was a duty to seek the court's approval. However, even an agreement subject to the approval of the court was binding on the parties to the extent that neither could resile from it[2]. The position is therefore that two differently composed Courts of Appeal have expressed different views on this topic, both per curiam. It remains to be seen what will come of this.

1   [2008] 1 FLR 90, CA.
2   The court relied on *Goodinson v Goodinson* [1954] 2 QB 118; *Gould v Gould* [1970] 1 QB 275 and *Smallman v Smallman* [1972] Fam 25.

1.240 Clearly, however, in the light of these decisions, when parties are negotiating at court and an agreement is reached, it is wise for the advocates to agree between themselves and record when a *Xydhias* agreement has been made.

SELF-SUFFICIENCY

1.241 So far, we have considered the factors which the court is directed to have in its mind when deciding whether, and if so, in what manner, to make an order for a financial remedy. No one factor is more important than any other; the court must weigh them all in its mind, and make a balanced judgment.

1.242 However, there is a further factor to which the court is directed to have regard, and that is the possibility of the parties achieving self-sufficiency. It has already been seen that, when considering the financial means of the parties, the court must consider what increase in the earning capacity of the parties it would be reasonable to expect them to acquire. This is reinforced by s 25A, which directs the court, when making a periodical payments order or secured periodical payments order, to consider whether the financial obligations of the parties to each other should be terminated as soon as the court considers it just and reasonable. In such circumstances, the court must also consider whether it should direct that no further application may be made.

1.243 There is therefore a positive obligation on the court to consider imposing a clean break in every case. Whether or not this will be the result depends on the circumstances of the case, and the position is, perhaps, not as clear as it might be. This is considered further in CHAPTER 2.

GUIDELINES IN CHILDREN ORDERS CASES

1.244 So far, the factors for the consideration of the court have been exclusively confined to orders between the parties to the marriage. When the court makes an order for a child, different criteria apply, and these are contained in s 25(3). These are considered further in CHAPTER 11.

WHEN MAY ORDERS BE MADE?

1.245 An order for maintenance pending suit may be made at any time after the filing of the petition. Other orders, such as orders for periodical payments, a lump sum or property adjustment, may only be made on or after the grant of a decree[1]. By FPR 29.15 the court may direct that an order take effect from such later date as the court may specify. See *JP v NP (Financial Remedies: Costs)*[2] where a financial relief order was made before decree nisi to take effect as from decree nisi. However, in *K v K (Financial Remedy: Final Order prior to Decree Nisi)*[3] it was held that an order made prior to decree nisi purporting to take immediate effect was a nullity. Interim capital provision is discussed further in CHAPTER 4.

1   MCA 1973, ss 22–24.
2   [2014] EWHC 1101 (Fam).
3   [2016] EWFC 23.

1.246 Mr Nicholas Mostyn QC, sitting as a deputy High Court judge in *Rossi v Rossi*, expressed certain views as to whether there is a time-limit on applications for ancillary relief. These statements have authority in the sense that they are from the High Court, but there may be room for doubt about whether they are universally shared.

Jurisdiction

1.247 Jurisdiction to make orders for financial relief (except for those after a foreign decree – see CHAPTER 14) depends on the grant of a decree of divorce, nullity or judicial separation. Whether or not the court may make an order for financial relief is therefore the same question as whether it has jurisdiction to entertain the proceedings leading to the decree.

1.248 This is now governed by the EU Council Regulation on Jurisdiction and the Recognition and Enforcement of Judgments in Matrimonial Matters and in Matters of Parental Responsibility for Joint Children (known as 'Brussels IIA'). This is binding on all EU Member States except Denmark and applies to all proceedings filed after 1 March 2001.

1.249 The Regulation deals with the jurisdiction of the court in matrimonial cases and in 'civil proceedings relating to parental responsibility for the children of both spouses'. As to matrimonial cases (eg divorce), Art 3 sets out a multiple choice of jurisdictional factors which do not have a hierarchy; ie no one factor is more important than any other. The factors are:

- both spouses' habitual residence;
- the last habitual residence of both spouses, one spouse still being habitually resident there;
- the respondent spouse's habitual residence;
- in cases of a joint application, either spouse's habitual residence;
- the applicant's habitual residence based on 12 months' residence immediately before the application;
- the applicant's habitual residence based on 6 months' residence immediately before the application coupled with nationality or (in the case of the UK or Ireland) domicile; and
- the nationality of both the spouses or (in the case of the UK and Ireland) their domicile.

Where no Member State has jurisdiction under the above factors, jurisdiction is determined according to the laws of each State.

1.250 For a detailed analysis of the principles for establishing permanent residence see the judgment of the Court of Appeal in *Estrada v Al-Juffali (Secretary of State for Foreign and Commonwealth Affairs Intervening)*[1].

[1] [2016] EWCA Civ 176.

1.251 Where courts have concurrent jurisdiction, a court must defer to the court first seised of the case unless it needs to take protective measures in urgent cases. A court is seised of a case when the documents instituting the proceedings 'or other equivalent document' is lodged with the court, provided that steps are taken to serve it or, when it has to be served before issue, when it is received by the authority responsible for service.

1.252 Schedule 1 to the Domicile and Matrimonial Proceedings Act 1973 makes provision for a stay of proceedings where there are proceedings affecting the marriage in another jurisdiction. Such a stay may be obligatory (Sch 1, para 8) or discretionary (Sch 1, para 11).

1.253 Questions of jurisdiction can assume some importance in cases of ample means where it is thought that the approach of the courts of England and Wales may be more, or less, generous than that to be found elsewhere[1].

[1] See eg *de Dampierre v de Dampierre* [1987] 2 FLR 300, HL; *W v W (Financial Relief: Appropriate Forum)* [1997] 1 FLR 257; *S v S (Divorce: Staying Proceedings)* [1997] 2 FLR 100; *Butler v Butler (Nos 1 and 2)* [1997] 2 FLR 311, CA; *C v C (Divorce: Stay of English Proceedings)* [2001] 1 FLR 624.

Chapter 2

PERIODICAL PAYMENTS

INTRODUCTION

2.1 Periodical payments can be distinguished from other forms of financial orders by the fact that they constitute a continuing obligation, normally an obligation to pay a weekly or monthly sum, as opposed to a once and for all payment such as a lump sum or a transfer of property. A further distinction is that they can be varied, whereas, with certain exceptions, the general principle is that there can be only one order for payment of a lump sum or transfer of property. This type of relief is what was once called, and which the layperson may still call, 'maintenance'.

2.2 Periodical payments ordered to be paid before final decree of divorce or decree of judicial separation are called maintenance pending suit.

DEFINITIONS

2.3 Periodical payments are not defined by FPR. This is because they are a type of financial order, which is defined as any of the orders mentioned in s 21(1) of MCA 1973. It is therefore to the statute that reference must be made.

2.4 One of the types of financial provision order contained in s 21(1)(a) is an order that a party must make, in favour of another person, such periodical payments, for such term, as may be specified (a 'periodical payments order')[1]. This is the statutory authority for this type of order.

[1] MCA 1973, s 21(1)(a).

WHO MAY APPLY?

2.5 Only a party to the marriage or a child of the family may apply for periodical payments[1]. A party who has remarried cannot apply for periodical payments, even if the application is made before remarriage[2]. Orders for children are dealt with in CHAPTER 11.

[1] Heading to Pt II of MCA 1973.
[2] MCA 1973, s 28(3).

PROCEDURE

2.6 The procedure for applying for periodical payments is the same as for any other form of financial remedy. Reference should therefore be made to CHAPTER **16**.

GENERAL PRINCIPLES

2.7 As with any other form of financial order, orders for periodical payments are rarely made in isolation; they are usually part of a combination of the various forms of remedies, including lump sum, property adjustment and provision for children (whether made by the Statutory Child maintenance authorities or the court). When the court comes to decide whether or not an order for periodical payments should be made and, if so, in what sum, it must have regard to the needs of the parties and the ability of the paying party to meet the needs of the other party by these means. Such an exercise will normally be carried out after the court, at least notionally, has allocated the available capital. In particular, the court must have regard to the factors set out in s 25 of MCA 1973; these are considered in general terms in CHAPTER **1**. Case law is perhaps of even more uncertain value in this field than when considering other forms of financial relief[1].

[1] See eg *Sharpe v Sharpe* (1981) Fam Law 121, (1981) Times, 7 February.

2.8 However, one important principle has been established by the case of *McFarlane v McFarlane*;[1] for a detailed discussion see **2.34** et seq. The principle established was that periodical payments are not limited to maintenance, but can include provision for compensation and to reflect any capital imbalance between the parties.

[1] [2006] 1 FLR 1186, HL.

HOW DOES THE COURT MAKE ITS ORDERS?

2.9 Orders are made after consideration of the evidence and in the light of the factors in s 25. However, it would be logical to divide the reasoning process as follows:

•   whether an order for periodical payments should be made at all;
•   consideration of the amount of the order;
•   whether any order should be limited in time.

These will be considered in turn.

Should there be an order at all?

2.10 Provided the party applying for periodical payments has not remarried[1], there is no absolute bar to an order being made. If the means of the parties are such that either the applicant does not need support or the respondent is unable to provide any support, an order would not normally be made. It may also be that, on consideration of all the factors, the court will decide that in the case before it the obligations of the parties to each other should be terminated and that there should be a clean break[2].

[1] And provided no order has been made that the claim for periodical payments be dismissed. See *Mann v Mann* [2014] EWCA Civ 1674 where the Court of Appeal relied upon the dictum of Lord Scarman in *Minton v Minton* [1979] AC 593: 'Once an application [for periodical payments] has been dealt with upon its merits, the court has no future jurisdiction save where there is a continuing order capable of variation or discharge under s 31 of the Act'. For the further difficulties of non-payment and enforcement endured by these parties, see *Mann v Mann* [2016] EWHC 314 (Fam).

[2] For a detailed consideration of the clean break, see 2.70 et seq.

2.11 However, provided both need and ability to pay can be demonstrated, the following matters may be relevant in making an initial decision as to whether an order should be made.

Earning capacity/potential

2.12 The court is required to have regard to the financial means of the parties at the time or in the foreseeable future[1] ' . . . including in the case of earning capacity any increase in that capacity which it would in the opinion of the court be reasonable to expect a party to the marriage to take steps to acquire'. The court may not, therefore, consider only the means of the parties at the time of the hearing. It is required to inquire into whether or not a party, particularly the applicant, could take reasonable steps to improve her position and even render herself self-sufficient.

[1] MCA 1973, s 25(2)(a).

Cohabitation

2.13 A party who is cohabiting is not thereby precluded from applying for periodical payments. His or her financial position will clearly have to be considered in the light of the cohabitation, which will be one of the circumstances which the court is directed to consider. In some circumstances, cohabitation may be a source of considerable financial advantage; in others, quite the contrary. The principles have been lucidly set out as follows[1]:

> 'First, cohabitation is not to be equated with marriage. In performing its functions under the Matrimonial Causes Act 1973 (as amended) . . . cohabitation is not to be given decisive weight. Secondly, cohabitation is, however, a relevant factor in that it bears upon the financial circumstances, particularly upon the assessment of the wife's financial needs. But to me it seems above all that the court should strive to discern the realities in determining what weight to give to the factor of cohabitation, particularly since the subjective presentation of the parties often seeks to disguise or distort the realities.'

[1] *Atkinson v Atkinson* [1995] 2 FLR 356 per Thorpe J. See also *Hepburn v Hepburn* [1989] 1 FLR 373; *MH v MH* (1982) 3 FLR 429; *Suter v Suter and Jones* [1987] Fam 111, and *Atkinson v Atkinson* [1988] 2 FLR 353 at 356 per Waterhouse J.

2.14 As to what constitutes cohabitation, it has been held[1] that, whilst it is impossible to produce a comprehensive list of criteria to determine the existence of cohabitation, relevant factors were living together in the same household; a sharing of daily life; stability and a degree of permanence;

finances; a sexual relationship; children; intention and motivation; and the opinion of the reasonable person with normal perceptions.

[1]   In *Kimber v Kimber* [2000] 1 FLR 383. See also *Crake v Supplementary Benefits Commission* [1982] 1 All ER 498; *Re J (Income Support: Cohabitation)* [1995] 1 FLR 660.

2.15 The traditional statement of the law as set out above has been the subject of some judicial attack and it might seem that there has been a divergence of judicial view. In *K v K (Periodical Payments: Cohabitation)*[1] Coleridge J referred to the 'social revolution' which has occurred and said that this should be recognised by the law. In the instant case he found that the cohabitation of the wife could not be ignored as a circumstance of the case and that the husband should be expected to support the wife for a shorter period than that envisaged by a previous consent order. However, he felt constrained by Court of Appeal authority from going further.

[1]   [2005] EWHC 2886 (Fam), [2006] 2 FLR 468.

2.16 However, In *Fleming v Fleming*[1] the Court of Appeal had held that *Atkinson* did not require revisiting. The principle that cohabitation was not to be equated with remarriage was as sound as ever.

' . . . we do not consider that the right approach to a case of this kind is to seek to apply the so-called one-third rule. The right approach is rather to consider the disposable income of each party apart from any order and then to see what order will produce a redistribution of the disposable incomes which is fair and just in all circumstances.'

[1]   [2003] EWCA Civ 1841, [2004] 1 FLR 667.

2.17 In *H v H (Financial Provision)*[1] Singer J made no findings as to the wife's cohabitation, even though she was pregnant and admitted she was in a permanent relationship. The appeal is reported as *Grey v Grey*[2]. The appeal was allowed and the issue of spousal maintenance remitted to the judge. It was held that post-separation cohabitation is a relevant factor for the court to take into account when considering the appropriate level of spousal maintenance. The judge should have attached significant weight to the wife's new relationship and investigated and assessed its financial consequences. The approach set out in *Fleming* was sound and sufficiently flexible to enable courts to do justice.

[1]   [2009] EWHC 494 (Fam), [2009] 2 FLR 795.
[2]   [2009] EWCA Civ 1424, [2010] 1 FLR 1764.

2.18 Finally, in *Hart v Hart*[1] Sir James Munby P said that the judgment of Mostyn J in *AB v CB*[2] did not lay down any principle of law. In his judgment, these matters were quintessentially matters of fact where the trial judge had to have regard to the totality of the evidence, including the nuance of that evidence, before coming to a conclusion as to whether the prospects of remarriage, or indeed the future prospects of the relationship, should or should not, and if they should to what extent they should, be taken into account.

[1]   [2016] EWCA Civ 497 at para 6.
[2]   [2014] EWHC 2998 (Fam).

Conduct

2.19 Conduct of the parties is dealt with in more detail in CHAPTER 1. Here it may suffice to say that, although it is unusual for conduct to play a major part in the award of financial remedies, there may be rare cases in which the conduct of one party has been such as to disentitle him or her from any relief.

Length of marriage

2.20 Special considerations arising from short marriages are considered in CHAPTER 1.

What should be the amount of the order?

2.21 It would be misleading to think that there is a conventional starting point for the quantification of a periodical payments order. Some older cases contain references to, for example, the 'one-third starting point'[1]. However, this is not now regarded as a proper approach[2].

[1] For a comparatively recent example, see *Sibley v Sibley* (1981) 2 FLR 121, in which the principle did not seem to be challenged. See also, however, *Ward v Ward and Greene* (1980) 1 FLR 368: 'the one-third rule is only a starting point'.
[2] See eg *Saunders v Saunders* (1980) 1 FLR 121, per Brandon LJ.

2.22 The only proper starting point is s 25. The particular factor which is normally important as an initial figure is the 'financial needs, obligations and responsibilities'[1] of the applicant party; these must be reduced to a figure which the court considers necessary to enable the applicant to live at a standard which is appropriate in the light of the other s 25 factors such as the standard of living during the marriage, the contributions of the parties and the length of the marriage. From this figure must be deducted the actual or potential income of that party; this will include non-means related State benefits such as retirement pension or child benefit, but not lone parent benefit. However, the ability of a party to increase his/her income by the proper use of state benefits cannot be overlooked. For example, working tax credit and child tax credit are clearly appropriate benefits for many working mothers on low incomes and should be applied for.

[1] MCA 1973, s 25(2)(b).

2.23 Helpful guidance on the principles applicable to spousal maintenance has recently been given in *SS v NS*[1] Mostyn J summarised the principles which govern the award of spousal maintenance in the following passage:

'46. Pulling the threads together it seems to me that the relevant principles in play on an application for spousal maintenance are as follows:
i) A spousal maintenance award is properly made where the evidence shows that choices made during the marriage have generated hard future needs on the part of the claimant. Here the duration of the marriage and the presence of children are pivotal factors.
ii) An award should only be made by reference to needs, save in a most exceptional case where it can be said that the sharing or compensation principle applies.
iii) Where the needs in question are not causally connected to the marriage the award should generally be aimed at alleviating significant hardship.

iv)   In every case the court must consider a termination of spousal maintenance with a transition to independence as soon as it is just and reasonable. A term should be considered unless the payee would be unable to adjust without undue hardship to the ending of payments. A degree of (not undue) hardship in making the transition to independence is acceptable.

v)   If the choice between an extendable term and a joint lives order is finely balanced the statutory steer should militate in favour of the former.

vi)   The marital standard of living is relevant to the quantum of spousal maintenance but is not decisive. That standard should be carefully weighed against the desired objective of eventual independence.

vii)   The essential task of the judge is not merely to examine the individual items in the claimant's income budget but also to stand back and to look at the global total and to ask if it represents a fair proportion of the respondent's available income that should go to the support of the claimant.

viii)   Where the respondent's income comprises a base salary and a discretionary bonus the claimant's award may be equivalently partitioned, with needs of strict necessity being met from the base salary and additional, discretionary, items being met from the bonus on a capped percentage basis.

ix)   There is no criterion of exceptionality on an application to extend a term order. On such an application an examination should to be made of whether the implicit premise of the original order of the ability of the payee to achieve independence had been impossible to achieve and, if so, why.

x)   On an application to discharge a joint lives order an examination should be made of the original assumption that it was just too difficult to predict eventual independence.

xi)   If the choice between an extendable and a non-extendable term is finely balanced the decision should normally be in favour of the economically weaker party.'

[1]   [2014] EWHC 4183 (Fam) at para 46.

2.24 Having ascertained the needs of the applicant party, the court must then assess the ability of the other party to meet those needs. This will involve consideration of that party's needs, obligations and responsibilities and all the other s 25 factors. It will also involve assessment of that party's financial means.

2.25 Clearly, one party cannot be ordered to pay money which he does not have. Nor should he normally be required to pay such sums as will reduce him to below subsistence level[1]. However, this is not inflexible, particularly where the court considers that the paying party has assumed obligations recklessly and without proper regard to his liability to the applicant and/or the children of the family, or even where they have been assumed voluntarily[2]. In one case[3], where the parties were comparatively affluent, Thorpe LJ observed that a 'conventional adjudication' would be to say that half the husband's net available income should be earmarked for the support of the wife and (two) children. This resulted in a figure of £20,000 from which it was necessary to deduct a Child Support Agency assessment of £7,500, the final sum being rounded down to £12,000 pa. However, this should not be taken as a 'rule' and perhaps is more akin to a maximum amount or even a starting point.

[1]   *Stockford v Stockford* (1982) 3 FLR 58, CA.
[2]   See *Campbell v Campbell* [1998] 1 FLR 828, CA.
[3]   *Scheeres v Scheeres* [1999] 1 FLR 241, CA.

2.26 When calculating the incomes of the parties, the net figures (after income tax and national insurance contributions) are taken. Periodical payments are not taxable income in the hands of the recipient, nor is tax relief available on periodical payments orders[1].

1 See **2.69**.

2.27 It is at this final stage that the court may wish to consider the proportion of the paying party's income which it is proposing to pay to the applicant and to consider the justice of the case in the round. Because of the essentially practical nature of this exercise, there are few reported cases on the appropriate proportion. It has been observed[1] that 'it has never been the custom in ancillary relief litigation to look with scrupulous care at the budget items of the prospective payer. Of course it is incumbent on the judge to cross-check to ensure that the adjudication that meets the applicant's needs is an adjudication which the respondent can afford'. It is difficult to improve on the reported words of Ormrod LJ in what is now a comparatively old case[2]:

> ' . . . the court, in all cases, must apply the provisions of s 25 of the Matrimonial Causes Act 1973 . . . without superimposed judicial glosses . . . it becomes necessary to assess the actual impact of any order for periodical payments on the parties' respective financial means . . . The court must, therefore, look broadly at the overall position rather than enter upon a detailed investigation of household budgets . . . In essence, it involves, working out . . . on the basis of [a] hypothetical order [the position of the parties] . . . The two figures [payer's and payee's positions as a result of the hypothetical order] can then be compared and related to the respective needs, and the hypothetical order adjusted accordingly. This is the "net effect" method . . . '

1 By Thorpe LJ in *Campbell v Campbell* (above).
2 *Stockford v Stockford* (above).

2.28 In all but the simplest cases, therefore, it is essential to prepare a 'net effect schedule' to demonstrate what will be the result of the order which is being proposed for each of the parties. This would involve starting with the net incomes from all sources for each party, making allowance for any tax changes which may occur as a result of the proposed order (though these are unlikely to be many), and deducting (or adding, as the case may be) the amount of the proposed order. This will show the total income of each party if the order is made, and this figure can then be compared with each party's reasonable needs or requirements.

2.29 Once again, it should be noted that periodical payments are not limited to the maintenance of the receiving party though one has to say that the practical effect of this will only be felt in cases where the means of the parties are considerable.

2.30 The position where the income of the paying party is made up partly by regular salary and partly by bonus was considered by Eleanor King J in *H v W (Cap on Wife's Share of Bonus Payments)*[1].

1 [2013] EWHC 4105 (Fam).

2.31 Her Ladyship said at para 38:

'In my judgment, where the family income is routinely made up of salary and bonus and the bonus represents such a significant proportion of the total that the Judge is driven to making a convention monthly order for a sum less than that which he would otherwise feel to be appropriate... he may well provide for a part of the W's maintenance to be paid from the bonus. Such payment, given the intrinsic uncertainty of bonuses, can only be expressed in percentage terms.'

2.32 The proper approach was to calculate two figures, one for ordinary expenditure and another for 'additional, discretionary items which will vary from year to year and are not reflected in [the] annual budget'. A monthly order could then be made for a fair sum to be paid from salary and the balance to be expressed as a percentage of bonus.

2.33 Her Ladyship, however, added that:

'The inherent uncertainty of bonus payments provides, in part, the reason why the setting of a cap is essential in order to avoid the unintentional unfairness that which may arise as a consequence of a wholly unanticipated substantial bonus paid to the Husband.'

Periodical payments after Miller/McFarlane

2.34 The question of whether, and if so to what extent, equality should apply to periodical payments as opposed to capital has been debated since *White* and was the subject of the combined appeals of *McFarlane v McFarlane* and *Parlour v Parlour*[1]. The general principles enunciated by the House of Lords in *Miller/McFarlane* are discussed in detail in CHAPTER 1. Here, the discussion is limited to equality and periodical payments, where the general thrust of the Court of Appeal's judgment was not disturbed, save in the important respect that the 5-year term imposed on Mrs McFarlane's order was removed.

[1]   [2004] EWCA Civ 872.

2.35 Thorpe LJ put it like this:

'If the decision in *White v White* introduces the yardstick of equality for measuring a fair division of capital why should the same yardstick not be applied as the measure for the division of income?'

2.36 In the *Parlour* case, before Bennett J, the judge at first instance, the wife argued that she should receive the same proportion of the husband's income as that which had been agreed in respect of his capital, namely 37%. This would give her £444,000 pa for herself and the three children. The husband contended for a global figure of £120,000 pa.

2.37 The wife's argument, in a nutshell, was that an earning capacity developed during marriage was a resource or thing of value which should be equitably shared, and that an award of periodical payments should not be confined to the wife's maintenance needs. The husband argued for restriction to reasonable needs.

2.38 Bennett J said that to confine periodical payments to needs or reasonable requirements would be a faulty exercise of discretion. That would apply only one matter in s 25(2) and ignore the rest. To award only 10% of the husband's income 'is thoroughly mean and would be unfair'. However, to award her £444,000 would be 'an unprincipled and unfair award'. The court 'must seek a way that does justice to the parties and which does not, so far as is possible, impose a glass ceiling on the one hand but which does not hand out capital on the other'.

2.39 In the *McFarlane* case, the first hearing was before District Judge Redgrave who found that the parties' contributions to this long marriage had been different but of equal value. The wife's contributions had enabled the husband to create a working environment which had produced greater rewards, in respect of which she should have her fair share. It was unreasonable to expect the wife to take steps to improve her earning capacity in the foreseeable future.

2.40 The order made was for £250,000 pa, ie 33.18% of the husband's net income, to be index-linked. In the Court of Appeal Thorpe LJ commented at para [23] that 'implicit within the district judge's reasoning is first the conclusion that the wife should have the same opportunity as the husband to make provision for the years of retirement and second the conclusion that she should have the means with which to insure herself and the children against the risk of premature cessation of the husband's high professional earnings'.

2.41 The husband appealed on several grounds and the first appeal was heard by Bennett J who said:

'. . . it is my judgment, with all due respect to the district judge, that, having given the wife an award from which she is likely to be able to save large sums of money and thereby accumulate capital, it is no answer to say, as she did, that it is a matter for the wife whether she chooses to make provision for pension and other matters.'

2.42 He therefore chose to exercise his discretion afresh. He asked the question 'what figure should then be substituted for £250,000?' and answered:

'. . . the quantification of periodical payments is more an art than a science. The parameters of s 25 are so wide that it might be said that it is almost impossible to be "scientific". In my judgment, I would be doing justice to both parties if I award the wife £180,000 per annum by way of periodical payments.'

2.43 In the Court of Appeal, Thorpe LJ observed that:

'. . . the skeleton arguments prepared for the appeals . . . address the very general question: what should be the principles governing an award of periodical payments during joint lives or until remarriage in any case where the net income of the payer significantly exceeds what both parties need in order to meet their outgoings at the standard of living which the court has found to be appropriate.'

2.44 As far as *McFarlane* was concerned, the court decided that Bennett J had erred in interfering with the district judge's order which was therefore restored (applying *Cordle v Cordle*) subject only to the imposition of a 5-year term (subsequently removed by the House of Lords) and removal of the index-linking provision. In *Parlour*, Thorpe LJ observed that Mr Parlour, a professional footballer, might be nearing the end of his playing career and continued:

'These considerations only underline the obvious need for a substantial proportion of the income in the present fat years to be stored up against the future famine. Again I conclude that it would be wrong in principle to leave the responsibility and opportunity to the husband alone. The wife's and the children's needs were put at £150,000 by the judge. To award her the global figure of £444,000 per annum sought by Mr Mostyn allows her and obliges her to lay-up £294,000 per annum as a reserve against the discharge of her periodical payments order. I would in this case order a four-year extendable term. Hopefully a clean break will be achievable then on an assessment of the husband's earning capacity at thirty-five years of age and the wife's independent fortune derived from the original capital settlement augmented by the substantial annual surplus built into her periodical payments order in the interim.'

2.45 The Court of Appeal was at pains to emphasise that the two cases before it were exceptional and outside the normal run of financial relief applications which come before the court. The exceptional factors were the very large incomes of the parties coupled with the fact that there was insufficient capital to provide a clean break now. One might also add the fact that the wives in both cases had no immediate prospect of improving their earning capacity and had to care for young children. The predominating factor therefore became how best to prepare for a clean break in years to come.

2.46 However, even if the effect of the judgment were limited to that class of case, it might still have a significant effect. As Thorpe LJ pointed out, there must be many high-earning professional couples who will find themselves in a similar financial situation.

2.47 One important lesson from the Court of Appeal's judgment is that periodical payments cannot be limited to the needs of the receiving party. To do so would be to concentrate on one s 25(2) factor to the exclusion of the others. This was upheld by the House of Lords decision. In his speech at para [31] Lord Nicholls said:

'There is nothing in the statutory ancillary relief provisions to suggest Parliament intended periodical payments orders to be limited to payments needed for mainte-nance. Section 23(1)(a) empowers the court, in quite general language, to order one party to the marriage to make to the other "such periodical payments, for such term, as may be specified in the order". In deciding whether, and how, to exercise this power the statute requires the court to have regard to all the circumstances of the case: s 25(1). The court is required to have particular regard to the familiar wide-ranging checklist set out in s 25(2). These provisions, far from suggesting an intention to restrict periodical payments to the one particular purpose of mainte-nance, suggest that the financial provision orders in s 23 were intended to be flexible in their application.

[32] In particular, I consider a periodical payments order may be made for the purpose of affording compensation to the other party as well as meeting financial needs. It would be extraordinary if this were not so. If one party's earning capacity has been advantaged at the expense of the other party during the marriage it would be extraordinary if, where necessary, the court could not order the advantaged party to pay compensation to the other out of his enhanced earnings when he receives them. It would be most unfair if absence of capital assets were regarded as cancelling his obligation to pay compensation in respect of a continuing economic advantage he has obtained from the marriage.'

2.48 It has to be said that the judgments do not assist in deciding what proportion of the payer's income should be taken. In *Parlour's* case, the wife's submission was that the division of income should be in the same proportions as the division of capital and that submission succeeded. The wife had conceded that a departure from equality of capital was appropriate. One has to ask whether, if that concession had not been made and if the court had divided capital equally, the division of income would also have been equal.

2.49 Little help is derived from the *McFarlane* case because the Court of Appeal merely restored the district judge's order, on *Cordle* principles, and the district judge had not stated any particular principle in arriving at her figure of £250,000 pa. Needs had been put at £128,000 and the eventual award was about one-third of the husband's net income. Bennett J was similarly imprecise when he reduced the figure to £180,000 merely saying that he thought this would do justice to both parties. The imposition of a term is of course important.

2.50 In the Court of Appeal, Wall LJ was clearly unsure as to what, if any, principle, should replace the emphasis on needs. He felt it necessary to fall back on the words of Ormrod LJ in *Martin v Martin* 26 years ago:

' . . . the court should preserve, so far as it can, the utmost elasticity to deal with each case on its own facts. Therefore it is a matter of trial and error and imagination on the part of those advising clients.'

2.51 This of course, was echoed by Thorpe LJ in *White v White* and *Parra v Parra*. Practitioners may therefore find it difficult to draw any more general lessons from this case than others in the past. Some useful guidance may be derived from the treatment of the *McFarlane* case on the subsequent variation application made by the wife. This is considered in detail in CHAPTER 13.

2.52 Words of caution have been expressed by Charles J in *H v H*[1]. His Lordship said that the fact that both parties are free to terminate a marital relationship means that by reference to the rationale of compensation the lower earner is not entitled to long-term economic parity. The aim is self-sufficiency. Nevertheless, in this case, fairness required that the wife receive an extra award to reflect her contribution over the years of partnership which had led to the husband's increased earning capacity.

[1] [2007] 2 FLR 548.

Should the order be limited in duration?

2.53 Section 25A of the MCA 1973 contains the statutory authority for the 'clean break'. This is considered as a topic in its own right at **2.70**. Here, it should merely be noted that, in addition to s 25A(1) which requires the court to consider whether the financial obligations of the parties to each other should be terminated, s 25A(2) requires the court in every case where it makes a periodical payments order to consider whether it would be appropriate to require those payments to be made only for such term as would in the opinion of the court be sufficient to enable the party in whose favour the order is made to adjust without undue hardship to the termination of his or her financial dependence on the other party.

2.54 Only an express direction made under s 28(1A) MCA excludes an application to extend the term of a periodical payments order. The fact that an application made before the end of the term is heard after the end of the term does not affect the court's power to extend it[1].

In *Quan v Bray and Others*[2] Mostyn J said that ss 2A and 28(1A) had been 'strangely neglected since they were enacted'. He emphasised that in every case where an award of periodical payments is made the court must consider whether the award should be term limited and, if so, whether that term should be extendable or not. A limited term should be imposed unless the court is satisfied that the claimant would not be able to adjust to a cut-off without undue hardship. Generally speaking, there would have to be shown good reasons why a term maintenance order should not be made. Usually where a term maintenance order is made there would have to be shown good reasons as to why it should not be non-extendable.

1 *Mutch v Mutch* [2016] EWCA Civ 370; *Jones v Jones* [2000] 2 FLR 307.
2 [2018] EWHC 3558 (Fam).

MAINTENANCE PENDING SUIT

2.55 The jurisdiction to make an order for periodical payments depends on the grant of a decree. Any order for periodic maintenance before that time is called maintenance pending suit. Once a petition has been filed[1]:

' . . . the court may make an order for maintenance pending suit, that is to say, an order requiring either party to the marriage to make to the other such periodical payments for his or her maintenance and for such term, being a term beginning not earlier than the date of the presentation of the petition and ending with the date of the determination of the suit, as the court thinks reasonable.'

1 MCA 1973, s 22.

2.56 There is no special law relating to this form of relief and such applications invariably turn on their own facts. The court must use the usual s 25 factors, the only difference being that the application will be normally to deal with a short-term position rather than the permanent situation.

2.57 *M v M (Maintenance Pending Suit)*[1] was a case where the parties were very rich. The judge awarded the wife maintenance pending suit of £330,000 pa, holding that in the instant case the court must have regard to the standards of the very rich and not to middle-class standards. He also held that a decision as to maintenance pending suit should not be taken as a pointer to the future.

1 [2002] EWHC 317 (Fam), [2002] 2 FLR 123.

2.58 In *TL v ML*[1] it was held that the sole criterion for determining an application for maintenance pending suit is 'reasonableness', ie fairness. It was emphasised that there should always be before the court a specific budget for the application for maintenance pending suit.

1 [2005] EWHC 2680 (Fam), [2006] 1 FLR 1263.

2.59 This case was followed by Moylan J in *BD v FD (Maintenance Pending Suit)*[1]. Applying *TL v ML* Moylan J held that the purpose of the section was to give the court the power to address income needs which cannot await the final resolution of the substantive claims either by agreement or court determination.

- The sole criterion to be applied in determining the application is 'reasonableness' (s 22 MCA 1973), which, to Moylan J's mind, was synonymous with 'fairness'.
- A very important factor in determining fairness is the marital standard of living (*F v F*). This is not to say that the exercise is merely to replicate that standard (*M v M*).
- In every maintenance pending suit application there should be a specific maintenance pending suit budget which excludes capital or long term expenditure more aptly to be considered on a final hearing (*F v F*). That budget should be examined critically in every case to exclude forensic exaggeration (*F v F*).
- Where the affidavit or Form E disclosure by the payer is obviously deficient the court should not hesitate to make robust assumptions about his ability to pay. The court is not confined to the mere say-so of the payer as to the extent of his income or resources. In such a situation the court should err in favour of the payee.

[1] [2014] EWHC 4443 (Fam).

2.60 In *Rattan v Kuwad*[1] Moylan LJ distinguished the facts in that case from those in *BD v FD* as follows: in *BD v FD* 'The wife had cash and investments of approximately £1.4 million and was living in a house purchased, following the breakdown of the marriage, for £2.9 million with funds provided by the husband. The husband was paying, and proposed to continue to pay, maintenance pending suit at the rate of just over £200,000 per year. The wife was seeking an additional sum of between £70,000 and £190,000. It was in that context that I made comments about when the court's jurisdiction should be invoked. The comments I made have no relevance to the present appeal'. The means of the parties were considerably more modest in this case. Referring to the decision of the deputy district judge (which a circuit judge had set aside), Moylan LJ said:

> 'She clearly accepted, as she was entitled to do, the wife's budget as representing her reasonable income needs. It was not an extensive budget of the type which was considered in *F v F*. It was the type of budget which will be very familiar to judges determining financial claims and which they are well placed to decide, on a broad assessment, whether they are or are not reasonable for the purposes of determining an application for maintenance pending suit. The court is not required to undertake any greater "critical" analysis of a schedule of income needs than is required of any other aspect of the case. The court is required to undertake such analysis as is sufficient to be satisfied that the ultimate award is "reasonable". In some cases this might require a detailed examination of a budget, in others, such as the present case, it will be immediately apparent whether the listed items represent a fair guide to the applicant's income needs.'

Moylan LJ also said that it is not necessary for an applicant for maintenance pending suit to provide a list of income needs distinct from that set out in the Form E. He added that school fees and mortgage payments could be reflected in the order for maintenance pending suit. The order of the deputy district judge was restored.

¹ [2021] EWCA Civ 1.

LEGAL SERVICES ORDERS

2.61 One of the problems of parties to matrimonial proceedings, particularly wives, is that they may be (and now, of course, invariably are) ineligible for public funding because of some modest accumulation of capital but have insufficient resources to pursue their rights against their spouse. This is made more acute when the spouse is wealthy, litigious or obstructive[1]. To some extent, this difficulty was overcome by the decision of Holman J in *A v A (Maintenance Pending Suit: Provision for Legal Fees)*[2]. Holman J ordered maintenance pending suit to include £4,000 per month towards legal costs, backdated to the discharge of the wife's certificate of public funding. He said that the costs of the matrimonial proceedings were not in a different category from other expenses; in fact, they were the wife's most urgent and pressing need. There was no authority excluding such an element as a matter of law. Holman J emphasised that the court should be cautious in including such a costs element in an order, and it may be noted that in this case the husband was of great wealth and the combined costs exceeded £350,000.

¹ See *Sears Tooth v Payne Hicks Beach and Others* [1997] 2 FLR 116 at 118H–119A per Wilson J.
² [2001] 1 FLR 377.

2.62 In *G v G (Maintenance Pending Suit: Costs)*[1] it was held that *A v A* was correctly decided and that maintenance pending suit could include an element for costs. The principle was further reinforced in *Minwalla v Minwalla*[2].

¹ [2003] Fam Law 393.
² [2004] EWHC 2823 (Fam), [2005] 1 FLR 771.

2.63 In *Moses-Taiga v Moses-Taiga*[1] it was held that a costs element would only be included in an order for maintenance pending suit in an exceptional case. However, a more positive approach was given by the Court of Appeal in *Currey v Currey*[2]. Here, it was held that the principles applicable to determining whether support to meet legal costs should be given are no different whether under s 22 or under s 31 (variation applications). The initial overarching enquiry is into whether the applicant for a costs allowance can demonstrate that she cannot reasonably procure legal advice and representation by any other means. Thus, to the extent that she has assets, the applicant must demonstrate that they cannot reasonably be deployed whether directly or as means of raising a loan. She also has to demonstrate that she cannot reasonably procure legal services by offering a charge on ultimate capital recovery.

¹ [2005] EWCA Civ 1013, [2006] 1 FLR 1074.
² [2006] EWCA Civ 1338, [2007] 1 FLR 946.

2.64 In *Rubin v Rubin*[1] Mostyn J established the principles applicable to applications for a legal services order as follows:

'13. I have recently had to deal with a flurry of such applications and there is no reason to suppose that courts up and down the country are not doing likewise. Therefore it may be helpful and convenient if I were to set out my attempt to summarise the applicable principles both substantive and procedural.

i)   When considering the overall merits of the application for a LSPO the court is required to have regard to all the matters mentioned in s 22ZB(1)–(3).

ii)   Without derogating from that requirement, the ability of the respondent to pay should be judged by reference to the principles summarised in *TL v ML* [2005] EWHC 2860 (Fam) [2006] 1 FCR 465 [2006] 1 FLR 1263 at para 124 (iv) and (v), where it was stated

"iv)   Where the affidavit or Form E disclosure by the payer is obviously deficient the court should not hesitate to make robust assumptions about his ability to pay. The court is not confined to the mere say-so of the payer as to the extent of his income or resources. In such a situation the court should err in favour of the payee.

v)   Where the paying party has historically been supported through the bounty of an outsider, and where the payer is asserting that the bounty had been curtailed but where the position of the outsider is ambiguous or unclear, then the court is justified in assuming that the third party will continue to supply the bounty, at least until final trial."

iii)   Where the claim for substantive relief appears doubtful, whether by virtue of a challenge to the jurisdiction, or otherwise having regard to its subject matter, the court should judge the application with caution. The more doubtful it is, the more cautious it should be.

iv)   The court cannot make an order unless it is satisfied that without the payment the applicant would not reasonably be able to obtain appropriate legal services for the proceedings. Therefore, the exercise essentially looks to the future. It is important that the jurisdiction is not used to outflank or supplant the powers and principles governing an award of costs in CPR Part 44. It is not a surrogate inter partes costs jurisdiction. Thus a LSPO should only be awarded to cover historic unpaid costs where the court is satisfied that without such a payment the applicant will not reasonably be able to obtain in the future appropriate legal services for the proceedings.

v)   In determining whether the applicant can reasonably obtain funding from another source the court would be unlikely to expect her to sell or charge her home or to deplete a modest fund of savings. This aspect is however highly fact-specific. If the home is of such a value that it appears likely that it will be sold at the conclusion of the proceedings then it may well be reasonable to expect the applicant to charge her interest in it.

vi)   Evidence of refusals by two commercial lenders of repute will normally dispose of any issue under s 22ZA(4)(a) whether a litigation loan is or is not available.

vii)   In determining under s 22ZA(4)(b) whether a Sears Tooth arrangement can be entered into a statement of refusal by the applicant's solicitors should normally answer the question.

viii)   If a litigation loan is offered at a very high rate of interest it would be unlikely to be reasonable to expect the applicant to take it unless the respondent offered an undertaking to meet that interest, if the court later considered it just so to order.

ix)   The order should normally contain an undertaking by the applicant that she will repay to the respondent such part of the amount ordered if, and to the extent that, the court is of the opinion, when considering costs at the conclusion of the proceedings, that she ought to do so. If such an undertaking is refused the court will want to think twice before making the order.

x) The court should make clear in its ruling or judgment which of the legal services mentioned in s 22ZA(10) the payment is for; it is not however necessary to spell this out in the order. A LSPO may be made for the purposes, in particular, of advice and assistance in the form of representation and any form of dispute resolution, including mediation. Thus the power may be exercised before any financial remedy proceedings have been commenced in order to finance any form of alternative dispute resolution, which plainly would include arbitration proceedings.

xi) Generally speaking, the court should not fund the applicant beyond the FDR, but the court should readily grant a hearing date for further funding to be fixed shortly after the FDR. This is a better course than ordering a sum for the whole proceedings of which part is deferred under s 22ZA(7). The court will be better placed to assess accurately the true costs of taking the matter to trial after a failed FDR when the final hearing is relatively imminent, and the issues to be tried are more clearly defined.

xii) When ordering costs funding for a specified period, monthly instalments are to be preferred to a single lump sum payment. It is true that a single payment avoids anxiety on the part of the applicant as to whether the monthly sums will actually be paid as well as the annoyance inflicted on the respondent in having to make monthly payments. However, monthly payments more accurately reflects what would happen if the applicant were paying her lawyers from her own resources, and very likely will mirror the position of the respondent. If both sets of lawyers are having their fees met monthly this puts them on an equal footing both in the conduct of the case and in any dialogue about settlement. Further, monthly payments are more readily susceptible to variation under s 22ZA(8) should circumstances change.

xiii) If the application for a LSPO seeks an award including the costs of that very application the court should bear in mind s 22ZA(9) whereby a party's bill of costs in assessment proceedings is treated as reduced by the amount of any LSPO made in his or her favour. Thus, if an LSPO is made in an amount which includes the anticipated costs of that very application for the LSPO, then an order for the costs of that application will not bite save to the extent that the actual costs of the application may exceed such part of the LSPO as is referable thereto.

xiv) A LSPO is designated as an interim order and is to be made under the Part 18 procedure (see FPR rule 9.7(1)(da) and (2)). 14 days' notice must be given (see FPR rule 18.8(b)(i) and PD9A para 12.1). The application must be supported by written evidence (see FPR rule 18.8(2) and PD9A para 12.2). That evidence must not only address the matters in s 22ZB(1)-(3) but must include a detailed estimate of the costs both incurred and to be incurred. If the application seeks a hearing sooner than 14 days from the date of issue of the application pursuant to FPR rule 18.8(4) then the written evidence in support must explain why it is fair and just that the time should be abridged.'

[1] [2014] EWHC 611 (Fam) at para 13.

2.65 For further authority see *AM v SS (Legal Services Order)*[1] Moylan J held that in determining whether to make an order under s 22ZA the court should, in addition to s 22ZB, also have regard to the overriding objective in r 1.1 of FPR. In *LKH v TQALZ*[2] Holman J declined to make any order regarding past costs incurred by a wife, where solicitors were saying that they could not proceed without payment, but made an order regarding future costs. He directed that that there must be a suitable formula for the solicitors to regularly account to the husband as to how the monthly amount was being spent and if there was a surplus at the end of the proceedings it must be credited back to the husband.

1   [2014] EWHC 4380 (Fam).
2   [2018] EWHC 1214 (Fam).

2.66 In summary, the applicant must demonstrate that she cannot reasonably procure legal advice and representation by any other means, but the court should also consider the subject matter of proceedings, the reasonableness of the applicant's stance and, where the payer's evidence is obviously deficient the court should not hesitate to make 'robust assumptions about his ability to pay'. The judge awarded a charge over the respondent's property rather than the usual monetary award. For the form of order, see below. For the general principles of costs see CHAPTER 17.

FORM OF ORDER

2.67 Any order for periodical payments is for the joint lives of the parties, and is therefore discharged on the death of either.

2.68 The form of an order for maintenance pending suit including a costs element was considered in *TL v ML and Others*[1] where it was held that the order should be expressed as including a legal expenses component of, eg £50,000 payable at the rate of, eg £2,000 per month, upon the applicant undertaking to pay such legal expenses to her solicitors to be credited against any costs order which she may ultimately recover against the respondent.

1   [2005] EWHC 2680 (Fam), [2006] 1 FLR 1263.

TAX CONSIDERATIONS

2.69 Before the budget of 1988, tax relief was available on orders for periodical payments, and the computation of the fiscal benefits to be derived from various orders occupied much of the time of family lawyers. That fiscal regime was abolished by the Finance Act 1988, and the position until April 2000 was that recipients of periodical payments were no longer taxed on their receipts, and paying parties were allowed a flat rate annual sum by way of tax relief, or the actual sum paid, whichever was the lesser. From 6 April 2000, the position is different again. Tax relief on maintenance is largely abolished as from this date. Relief is retained only where one or both of the parties was aged 65 or over as at 5 April 2000. Relief under 'old orders' (ie those made before 30 June 1988) has also ended.

THE CLEAN BREAK

Introduction

2.70 When periodical payments were considered at **2.1**, it was noted that the difference between that form of financial remedy and the others is that periodical payments are a continuing form of relief whereas relief of a capital nature can normally be given only once. The standard form of order for periodical payments provides for payments during the joint lives of the parties and until the payee shall remarry. Periodical payments may therefore continue during the lifetime of the payer and may be varied at any time. Until the passage into law of MFPA 1984, it was possible to terminate the right of one party to apply for periodical payments only by consent[1]. However, as a result of that statute, the provisions of which are now contained in s 25(2)(a) and s 25A of MCA 1973, it is now possible for the court to terminate the right to periodical payments without consent; this provision is generally known as the 'clean break'.

[1] See eg *Dipper v Dipper* [1981] Fam 31.

2.71 The meaning of the term 'clean break' is clear: once the break has occurred, neither party has any continuing financial claim on the other. When this change in the law occurred in 1984, it was generally considered to be an enlightened measure, and the desirability of a clean break in most cases has come to be regarded as axiomatic. During the period since then, judicial dicta have varied but it has seemed that the legal profession and the public generally have accepted, perhaps uncritically, the need for a clean break wherever possible. However, as will be seen, it may be that this has come about because of a failure to consider carefully the provisions of the statute.

Statutory provisions

2.72 The clean break provisions in MCA 1973 fall under four categories. The first of the changes effected in 1984 was that s 25(2)(a) was amended. This contains the statutory factors to which the court must have regard in respect of the means, including income, of the parties. The change by the 1984 Act was to add, after the reference to the income, etc of the parties, the words[1]:

'(a)   . . . including in the case of earning capacity any increase in that capacity which it would in the opinion of the court be reasonable to expect a party to the marriage to take steps to acquire.'

This may be taken, therefore, to represent the presumption of the desirability of self-sufficiency[2].

[1] MCA 1973, s 25(2)(a).
[2] Supported by some judicial dicta, eg Ward J in *B v B (Financial Provision)* [1990] 1 FLR 20.

2.73 Section 25A is more detailed. The second clean break provision is s 25A(1) which provides that whenever the court exercises any of its powers under ss 22A–24A, (except when making an interim order):

' . . . it shall be the duty of the court to consider whether it would be appropriate so to exercise those powers that the financial obligations of each party towards the other will be terminated as soon after the grant of the decree as the court considers just and reasonable.'

2.74 Thirdly, s 25A(2) provides that where the court decides to make an order for periodical payments or secured periodical payments in 'favour' of a party to the marriage:

' . . . the court shall, in particular, consider whether it would be appropriate to require those payments to be made or secured only for such term as would in the opinion of the court be sufficient to enable the party in whose favour the order is made to adjust without undue hardship to the termination of his or her financial dependence on the other party.'

2.75 The fourth provision is s 25A(3), which contains the power to dismiss and prevent further applications. When the court exercises its powers under MCA 1973 to make an order for financial provision in favour of a party and considers that no continuing obligation should be imposed on either party to make or secure periodical payments in favour of the other, it may ' . . . dismiss the application with a direction that the applicant shall not be entitled to make any future application in relation to that marriage for an order under s 23(1)(a) or (b) above'.

Summary of statutory provisions

2.76 The position may therefore be summarised as follows:

(1) When considering the earning capacity of either party, the court must consider whether it would be reasonable to expect that party to take steps to increase such capacity[1].

(2) When making any order for financial relief (except an interim order), the court must consider whether the obligations of the parties to each other should be terminated[2]. If the court does come to that conclusion, the next paragraph is unnecessary.

(3) When it does decide to make an order for periodical payments or secured periodical payments the court must consider whether such order should be for a limited term only, such term being that which is sufficient to enable the receiving party to adjust without undue hardship to termination[3].

(4) The above provisions are positive duties for the court. These matters must be considered in every case.

(5) The duty of the court must be exercised after consideration of all the factors contained in s 25. It is only after proper consideration of all those factors, that the court can come to an informed decision.

(6) When the court decides that there should be termination, it must effect this by the orders set out in s 25A(3)[4].

(7) These provisions apply only to divorce and nullity cases. They do not apply to judicial separation.

[1]   MCA 1973, s 25(2)(a).
[2]   MCA 1973, s 25A(1).
[3]   MCA 1973, s 25A(2).
[4]   MCA 1973, s 25A(3).

Judicial guidance as to when a clean break is appropriate

2.77 As might have been expected, there have been many decided cases in which the court has given guidance on when a clean break is appropriate[1]. However, as will have been seen above, the decision which the court must make is not always one single issue. In many cases, the court will have to make two decisions:

(1)   whether the obligations of the parties towards each other should be terminated (the immediate clean break); and, if not,

(2)   whether they should be terminated at some future time (the delayed clean break).

These two possibilities are the subject of different, though sometimes overlapping, case law.

¹   See, eg *Waterman v Waterman* [1989] 1 FLR 380 (term order for 5 years when child would be 10, wife working as secretary, short marriage); *Suter v Suter and Jones* [1987] 2 FLR 232, CA (nominal order where wife with young children and uncertainties as to her future); *M v M (Financial Provision)* [1987] 2 FLR 1 (47-year-old wife, no prospect of self-sufficiency, no clean break); *Whiting v Whiting* [1988] 2 FLR 189 (wife self-sufficient, husband unemployed, no clean break; this is generally accepted to be an untypical decision).

2.78 When a delayed clean break is adopted, the separate question arises of whether a direction under s 28(1A) should be given and, if not, whether the term for periodical payments may be extended. These possibilities must be considered separately. The observations of Mostyn J in *Quan v Bray and Others* (see **2.54** above) are helpful guidance.

Should there be an immediate clean break?

2.79 Dicta from two cases will be considered shortly. Like all fields of law, this is an evolving and constantly changing area and these cases contain the guidance which is most likely to predict accurately the approach of the higher courts. Accordingly, it may be that some of the earlier examples of the way in which the court has exercised its discretion will be of less importance than might previously have been the case, and those cases will, therefore, be summarised rather than set out in detail.

2.80 It is striking that s 25A(1) gives no guidance to the court as to how its discretion should be exercised. This is in contrast to s 25A(2) which seems to suggest that periodical payments should only be for a fixed term if, at the end of that term, the payee has adjusted without undue hardship to the loss of dependency. It might be thought that that test is also appropriate to s 25A(1), but that is not what the statute says.

2.81 Cases in which the principle of an immediate clean break has been approved by the court may be categorised as 'big money cases' and 'no money cases', 'intermediate cases' providing more of a problem.

2.82 Examples of the former are *Gojkovic v Gojkovic*¹, and *F v F (Duxbury Calculation: Rate of Return)*². These cases will be considered in more detail in CHAPTER 4 (big money cases) but it will be seen that the important factor was that it was possible to provide sufficient funds from ample capital resources to secure a fund from which the wife's income needs could be met for her lifetime. Accordingly, the rationale for the dismissal of all continuing claims in such cases seems to have been that true self-sufficiency could be achieved by an order for redistribution of capital.

¹   [1990] 1 FLR 140, CA.
²   [1996] 1 FLR 833.

2.83 This trend has continued in two recent reported cases. In *Vaughan v Vaughan*[1] inequality of division of capital in favour of a wife was justified by the need for a clean break, though on appeal[2] it was held that the judge had erred in his appraisal of the husband's income and effectively given priority to the hypothetical claims of a second wife. In *CR v CR*[3] the court ordered a lump sum to be paid by instalments, as the husband was unable to pay it in one sum, to avoid the need for a continuing periodical payments order and to ensure a lump sum.

In *Waggot v Waggot*[4] the husband had appealed against the first instance judge's decision to make a joint lives maintenance order, and the court allowed this appeal. It held that the judge had determined whether to impose a term maintenance order by reference only to whether the wife would be able to earn the shortfall between her income needs and the amount generated by her free capital, and as such she could not adjust without undue hardship. This was too narrow an approach and the issue should have been addressed more broadly including by considering whether it would be fair for the wife to deploy part of her capital to meet her income needs. This broader consideration was required both so as properly to address the question of undue hardship and also so as to give proper weight to the clean break principle. As such the court imposed a term order with a s 28(1A) bar. The Supreme Court refused permission to appeal on the ground that the application did not raise an arguable point of law.

1   [2008] 1 FLR 1108, CA.
2   [2010] EWCA Civ 349.
3   [2008] 1 FLR 323.
4   [2018] EWCA Civ 727.

2.84 In the 'no money' cases, such as *Ashley v Blackman*[1], the rationale for the immediate clean break has been that there never was and never would be any prospect of the husband paying periodical payments and so, for the achievement of certainty and the avoidance of further unnecessary litigation, an immediate clean break was the only sensible answer.

1   [1988] 2 FLR 278.

2.85 *F v F (Clean Break: Balance of Fairness)*[1] was a case involving assets of £3.48m which included shares in a family company worth £2.8m. The husband argued that the illiquidity of his company justified a departure from equality. After making orders to secure the wife's housing, Singer J ordered the husband to pay periodical payments of £75,000 pa. Here a clean break was neither feasible nor just. Where assets exceeded needs good reason must be found for departing from equality. The order for periodical payments would enable both parties to share in the results of the company's performance until a clean break was feasible.

1   [2003] 1 FLR 847.

2.86 It is, perhaps, in the intermediate cases that the courts have been placed in the most difficult position. In many such cases, it is clear that the income of the paying party (normally the husband) is such that a periodical payments order would cause hardship, while, at the same time, the income of the other party is not such as to entitle the court to find her to be self-supporting. There may have been a tendency, at least until the advent of CSA 1991, to make clean break orders where a matrimonial home was transferred to a mother so that children continued to live in the family home[1]. Nevertheless, there is clear authority that a direction under s 28(1A) prohibiting further applications should not be made where there are young children[2]. In *SRJ v DWJ (Financial Provision)*[3], it was held that there is no presumption in favour of a clean break; in this case, there was a young child, and it was observed that it is difficult to achieve a financial clean break when there cannot be a personal clean break between the parties.

1   See eg *Clutton v Clutton* [1991] 1 FLR 242 at 245 per Lloyd LJ.
2   See *N v N (Consent Order: Variation)* [1993] 2 FLR 868 at 883 per Roch LJ for a clear statement of this principle. See also *Mawson v Mawson* [1994] 2 FLR 985 for a more mixed message (wife with young child, Thorpe J ordered term of 9 months but no s 28(1A) direction as this would not be appropriate where young child involved, complication because previous agreement to which the parties should be held). See also *B v B (Mesher Order)* [2002] EWHC 3106 (Fam), [2003] 2 FLR 285 (no presumption of term order in short marriage).
3   [1999] 2 FLR 176, CA.

2.87 In another case[1], where the husband had been ordered to pay periodical payments but had obstinately failed to do so, it was held that these developments demonstrated that the order made was not appropriate or practical, and that a clean break should be imposed to put an end to the expensive process of enforcement. It should, however, be noted that there were sufficient capital assets to enable the court to award a lump sum of the wife's capitalised maintenance requirements.

1   *Fournier v Fournier* [1998] 2 FLR 990, CA.

2.88 If the 'no money cases' are put to one side, it seems that the courts look to the test contained in s 25A(2) in order to make a decision under s 25A(1), an approach which is wholly reasonable even though it might seem not to be dictated by the words of the statute. This is not an insignificant point, since the two cases about to be considered were concerned with s 25A(2) and not s 25A(1). Nevertheless, the principles set out in the judgments of Ward LJ in these cases seem to establish authoritative guidelines for both subsections.

2.89 In *Flavell v Flavell*[1], the court was concerned with a wife aged 54 who had a very limited earning capacity and no pension. The judge at first instance observed that it was not usually appropriate to provide for the termination of periodical payments in the case of a woman in her mid-50s, an opinion which Ward LJ endorsed with his approval. Ward LJ continued:

> 'The words of [s 25A(2)] do not impose more than an aspiration that the parties should achieve self-sufficiency. The power of the court to terminate dependency can, however, be exercised only in the event that adjustment can be made without undue hardship. There is, in my judgment, often a tendency for these orders to be made more in hope than in serious expectation. Especially in judging the case of ladies in their middle years the judicial looking into a crystal ball very rarely finds enough of substance to justify a finding that adjustment can be made without undue hardship. All too often, these orders are made without evidence to support them.'

1   [1997] 1 FLR 353, CA.

2.90 Ward LJ gave further guidance in *C v C (Financial Relief: Short Marriage)*[1]. The facts of this case are unimportant save that it may be noted that, as its name suggests, it was concerned with a short marriage where the husband was comparatively wealthy. The judge at first instance had awarded the wife a lump sum and periodical payments of a level which, on appeal, was described as being 'at the top of the bracket' but which was nevertheless upheld. Ward LJ summarised the proper approach of the court as follows:

(4) The statutory test is this: is it appropriate to order periodical payments only for such a term as in the opinion of the court would be sufficient to enable the payee to adjust without undue hardship to the termination of financial dependence on the paying party?

(5) What is appropriate must of necessity depend on all the circumstances of the case including the welfare of any minor child and the s 25 checklist factors, one of which is the duration of the marriage. It is, however, not appropriate simply to say, "this is a short marriage therefore a term must be imposed".

(6) Financial dependence being evident from the very making of an order for periodical payments, the question is whether, in the light of all the circumstances of the case, the payee can adjust – and adjust without undue hardship – to the termination of financial dependence and if so when. The question is, can she adjust, not should she adjust. In answering that question, the court will pay attention not only to the duration of the marriage but to the effect the marriage and its breakdown and the need to care for any minor children has had and will continue to have on the earning capacity of the payee and the extent to which she is no longer in the position she would have been in but for the marriage, its consequences and its breakdown. It is highly material to consider any difficulties the payee may have in entering or re-entering the labour market, resuming a fractured career and making up any lost ground.

(7) The court cannot form its opinion that a term is appropriate without evidence to support its conclusion. Facts supported by evidence must, therefore, justify a reasonable expectation that the payee can and will become self-sufficient. Gazing into the crystal ball does not give rise to such a reasonable expectation. Hope, with or without pious exhortations to end dependency, is not enough.

(8) It is necessary for the court to form an opinion not only that the payee will adjust, but also that the payee will have adjusted within the time that is fixed. The court may be in a position of such certainty that it can impose a deferred clean break by prohibiting an extension of the term pursuant to s 28(1A). If, however, there is any doubt about when self-sufficiency will be attained, it is wrong to require the payee to apply to extend the term. If there is uncertainty about the appropriate length of the term, the proper course is to impose no term but to leave the payer to seek the variation and if necessary go through the same exercise, this time pursuant to s 31(7)(a).'

[1]   [1997] 2 FLR 26, CA.

2.91 In *L v L (Financial Remedies: Deferred Clean Break)*[1] a district judge had made a periodical payments order in favour of the wife for joint lives. On appeal, Eleanor King J substituted a term order for 2 years 5 months with a bar on further applications. There was evidence that the wife could soon become self-sufficient, and the husband had undertaken responsibility for school fees, which the district judge had failed to consider. The proper approach was summarised by Ward LJ in *C v C (Financial Relief: Short Marriage)*[2].

[1]   [2011] EWHC 2207 (Fam).
[2]   [1997] 2 FLR 26, CA.

2.92 While the court must strive to achieve finality and an end to litigation between the parties, in some cases it not possible to do justice at the time of the hearing but this may be possible in the foreseeable future. For an example of such a case see *AW v AH and Others*[1] where it was held that, despite the imperative to achieve a clean break, this was not a case where a fair outcome could be achieved other than by adjourning the wife's application for lump sum and property adjustment orders.

[1]   [2020] EWFC 22.

Summary

2.93 An important gloss was added by the dicta of the House of Lords in *Miller/McFarlane* (see **1.21** et seq). As previously discussed, the House held that periodical payments are not to be limited to maintenance but may include an element of compensation. Lord Nicholls put it in this way (paras [37]–[39]):

> '[37] This statutory statement of principle raises a question of a similar nature to that affecting the whole of s 25. By s 25A(1) and (2) duties are imposed on the court but the court is left with a discretion. The court is required to "consider" whether it would be "appropriate" to exercise its powers in a particular way. But the section gives no express guidance on the type of circumstance which would render it inappropriate for the court to bring about a clean break.

> [38] In one respect the object of s 25A(1) is abundantly clear. The subsection is expressed in general terms. It is apt to refer as much to a periodical payments order made to provide compensation as it is to an order made to meet financial needs. But, expressly, s 25A(1) is not intended to bring about an unfair result. Under s 25A(1) the goal the court is required to have in mind is that the parties' mutual financial obligations should end as soon as the court considers just and reasonable.

> [39] Section 25A(2) is focused more specifically. It is concerned with the termination of one party's "financial dependence" on the other "without undue hardship". These references to financial dependence and hardship are apt when applied to a periodical payments order making provision for the payee's financial needs. They are hardly apt when applied to a periodical payments order whose object is to furnish compensation in respect of future economic disparity arising from the division of functions adopted by the parties during their marriage. If the claimant is owed compensation, and capital assets are not available, it is difficult to see why the social desirability of a clean break should be sufficient reason for depriving the claimant of that compensation.'

2.94 In *Matthews v Matthews*[1] the first instance judge found that there should be a clean break as the wife had a higher earning capacity than the husband and the husband would be making periodical payments to her for the children. The wife appealed on the grounds that the judge was wrong in principle, highlighting that the judge had failed to take into account that the wife might struggle to obtain full-time work and that she was exposed to the risk that she might be without work for substantial periods of time as she needed to work only in the insurance sector, as opposed to the banking sector.

[1]   [2013] EWCA Civ 1874.

2.95 The Court of Appeal upheld the judge's decision on the basis that it was 'impossible' to suggest that the judge's order was wrong in principle. Making a clean break was an exercise of discretion and that as the court is mandated to initially consider making a clean break, Parliament had indicated that there should be a clear presumption in favour of a clean break.

2.96 In *Wright v Wright*[1] a case which attracted considerable attention in the popular press, an order was made in 2008 for substantial spousal periodical payments on a joint lives basis, as well as payments for the children and school fees. In 2012 the husband, who was 59 and had been unable to save for his retirement, applied to vary the spousal order. The judge found that it had been made plain to the wife in 2008 that she would be expected to make a contribution to her own support. The district judge then had said that there was a general expectation that once a child is in year 2, most mothers can consider part time work consistent with their obligation to their children. By September 2009/2010, the wife should be able to work. She would be 46 or 47 years old. The district judge did not anticipate her having a significant earning capacity nor would it be reasonable to expect her to muck out stables for the minimum wage. However, she should make some financial contribution.

[1]   [2015] EWCA Civ 20.

2.97 The judge in 2014 concluded that the wife had taken no steps to retrain or seek work. The time had come to recognise that by the time of his retirement, the husband should no longer be paying spousal maintenance. She considered s 31(7) MCA 1973 and found that it would not be an undue hardship for the respondent to adjust to a variation in the order to achieve that result. She therefore ordered that the spousal order should be varied and that the husband should pay on a reducing basis, starting at £2,617 per month from November 2013 and ceasing altogether in 2019.

2.98 The wife sought permission to appeal. The principal ground of the application was that the judge had failed to pay adequate regard to the fact that the original order was a joint lives order. Pitchforth LJ refused permission to appeal and said, in effect, that there was nothing of substance to criticise in the judge's order.

The power of the court to make unlimited periodical payments orders is sometimes described by its critics as a 'meal ticket for life'. In *Mills v Mills*[1] Lord Wilson pointed out that the potential for an open-ended periodical payments order to be ended at any time demonstrates that there is no such thing as 'a meal ticket for life'.

[1]   [2018] UKSC 38.

The clean break on variation

2.99 It should be noted that the duty of the court to consider terminating financial dependency applies as much on a variation application as on an application for periodical payments[1].

[1]   *Fleming v Fleming* [2003] EWCA Civ 1841, [2004] 1 FLR 667. For variation generally see CHAPTER 13.

Direction under the Inheritance (Provision for Family and Dependants) Act 1975

2.100 Since a clean break order, whether immediate or deferred, is designed to terminate all continuing financial obligations between the parties, it would be illogical if this were to change on the death of one of the parties. Nevertheless, this could be the case in the absence of provision to the contrary, since a former spouse is among the class of persons on whom s 1(1)(b) of the Inheritance (Provision for Family and Dependants) Act 1975 confers the right to apply for financial relief from the estate of a deceased person.

2.101 Thus s 15(1) of the 1975 Act provides that, on the grant of an order for divorce or separation or of a decree of nullity, or at any time thereafter, the court may, if it considers it just to do so and on the application of either party to the marriage, order that the other party shall not be entitled on the death of the applicant to apply for an order under the 1975 Act.

2.102 This is now a standard order which is made whenever a clean break order is made, and, normally, it would be justified. Nevertheless, it clearly requires separate consideration by the court and a separate decision that the order is just must be made. There might be circumstances, such as the no money cases, in which an immediate clean break could be justified for pragmatic reasons but it would not necessarily follow that the right to apply under the 1975 Act should be prohibited. Further, such an order could be made only if one of the parties asked the court to do so.

Extension of terms

2.103 Where a direction is given under s 28(1A) of MCA 1973 that no further applications may be made, that is final and the court may not entertain an application for the term of a periodical payments order to be extended. This is not the case when a fixed-term order is made without such a direction. Arguably this should never happen, but it is possible for such orders to be made and the court has had to adjudicate on the position. The position is, in fact, quite simple. Provided the application to vary is made before the expiration of the term, the court has jurisdiction to entertain it[1]. However, if the term has expired, or the event on which the periodical payments were to cease has passed, the right to apply to vary is lost[2].

[1]   *Richardson v Richardson* [1994] 1 FLR 286.
[2]   Once the application is made, the hearing, and the order, can take place after the term has expired. See *Jones v Jones* [2000] 2 FLR 307, CA, disapproving *G v G (Periodical Payments: Jurisdiction)* [1997] 1 FLR 368, CA.

Chapter 3

SECURED PERIODICAL PAYMENTS

INTRODUCTION

3.1 Secured periodical payments are in some ways a curious hybrid, and are probably comparatively rare. The order incorporates an assessment of the amount of periodical payments which should be paid, with an order that they be secured, ie that security be provided for them, by some capital deposit.

3.2 The general principles on which orders for financial relief are made have already been considered, as have the detailed principles for assessment of the quantum of periodical payments. It is unnecessary to consider either here. Instead, it is proposed to consider the special circumstances which might give rise to an order for secured periodical payments and the practical consequences of such an order.

STATUTORY PROVISIONS

3.3 It is provided that[1]:

'(1) On granting a decree of divorce, a decree of nullity of marriage or a decree of judicial separation, or at any time thereafter (whether, in the case of a decree of divorce or nullity of marriage, before or after the decree is made absolute), the court may make . . .

(b) an order that either party to the marriage shall secure to the other to the satisfaction of the court, such periodical payments, for such term, as may be so specified.'

It will be noted that this is one of the types of orders which can be made only after decree.

1   MCA 1973, s 23(1)(b).

3.4 There are other statutory provisions concerning the procedure for making an order which will be considered below.

NATURE OF THE ORDER

3.5 The order requires the paying party to secure to the payee, for a specified term, the annual sum of periodical payments upon such security as may satisfy the court. The various elements of such an order are therefore as follows.

Secure

3.6 The order does not require the payer to make payments to the payee; it merely requires him to provide the fund out of which the payments may be made. In a leading case it was said that the order was 'an order to secure and nothing else. Under it the only obligation of the husband is to provide the security; having done that, he is under no liability. He enters into no covenant to pay and never becomes a debtor in respect of the payments'[1].

[1] *Barker v Barker* [1952] P 184.

The term

3.7 The court must specify the term, which may be for any term the court thinks fit, subject to certain statutory restrictions. It is provided that[1]:

'(b)   in the case of a secured periodical payments order, the term shall begin not earlier than the date of the making of an application for the order, and shall be so defined as not to extend beyond the death or, where the order is made on or after the grant of such a decree [ie a decree of divorce or nullity], the remarriage of the party in whose favour the order is made.'

[1]   MCA 1973, s 28(1)(b).

3.8 The term must therefore be expressed to end on the death or remarriage of the payee. However, it may survive the death of the paying party. If the court considers a limited term order with a 'clean break' direction appropriate, this can be incorporated into the order.

The amount to be secured

3.9 The quantum of the periodical payments will be assessed in the usual way.

The security

3.10 The fund to be provided is in the discretion of the court. The order will either specify the asset or order 'security to be agreed or referred to the district judge in default of agreement'. The asset provided will either be an income-producing asset such as a portfolio of securities or a non-income-producing asset. In the latter case, and sometimes in the former also, it is necessary to provide for sale to provide income.

3.11 An order imposing a general charge on all the husband's assets has been expressly disapproved by the Court of Appeal as 'sweeping and indiscriminate'[1]. It must be specific.

[1]   *Barker v Barker* (above).

3.12 Although it has been said[1] that where there is ample free capital the whole of the order should be secured, it is necessary to have regard to all the circumstances of the case, including, in particular, the s 25 factors, and the order must be reasonable.

¹ In *Shearn v Shearn* [1931] P 1.

3.13 It is almost invariably necessary to require a deed to be lodged by the paying party as well as the asset itself, to give effect to the order. This would be necessary to ensure that the asset, which would remain vested in the name of the paying party, provides the payments to the payee. Where problems arise, the court may refer the matter to one of the conveyancing counsel of the court for settlement of a proper instrument to be executed by all parties¹. Further, where the paying party refuses or neglects to execute the document, an order may be made for the district judge or some other person to sign on his behalf².

¹ MCA 1973, s 30.
² MCA 1973, s 30.

3.14 The court also has power to order one party to lodge documents which are necessary for the preparation of the deed¹.

¹ Senior Courts Act 1981, s 39 and County Courts Act 1984, s 38.

WHEN WILL SUCH AN ORDER BE MADE?

3.15 The circumstances in which it might be appropriate to make an order for secured periodical payments can best be seen by considering the advantages to the payee of such an order. The principal advantage is that the payments are secure; the fund is there to make them safe and the payments will survive the death of the paying party or his bankruptcy or disappearance.

3.16 In order to be persuaded that this order is appropriate therefore, the court would normally have to come to the conclusion that there were dangers against which the payee needed protection and also, of course, that a capital fund was available for this purpose.

3.17 The nature of the problem was well illustrated by *Aggett v Aggett*¹. The judge pointed out that the court was always reluctant to burden with security something which was the sole or main asset of the respondent, but on the other hand the court was loath to leave a wife in circumstances in which it seemed clear that the husband might well leave her penniless. One had to consider whether the fears expressed on the wife's behalf were sufficiently cogent to justify making an order for security which would not be made if there was no reality in those fears².

¹ [1962] 1 All ER 190, CA.
² See also *Shearn v Shearn* [1931] P 1; *Naish v Naish* (1916) 32 TLR 487.

VARIATION AND AMENDMENT

3.18 The security may be varied or changed at any time; where this cannot be agreed the court may order a variation. Likewise, an order for secured provision may be varied by increasing or reducing the amount payable or by discharging it¹. The order survives the death of the paying party, but can be varied after death in the light of the circumstances at the time. The fact that a wife has the benefit of a secured order does not prevent her from applying for provision from her former husband's estate.

1   See MCA 1973, s 31, and CHAPTER **13**.

Chapter 4

LUMP SUM ORDERS

INTRODUCTION

4.1 A lump sum order is an order that one party pay to the other a sum of money. It is therefore to be contrasted with a property adjustment order, which requires the transfer of some specified real or personal property, and a periodical payments order which requires the payment of regular periodic (weekly, monthly or annual) sums by way of maintenance. An order for a lump sum is normally, therefore, a means of adjusting the capital resources of the parties on the dissolution of the marriage. The reasons for such an order might be various, but of course could only be based on the normal s 25(2) factors. Although in this chapter it is not intended to deal with housing needs and the matrimonial home[1], it should be noted that in many cases the housing needs of one or both of the parties are the principal needs which the order is intended to meet. Where a wife's capital claims have been fully resolved by a property adjustment order, the application for a lump sum should be dismissed so that both parties know that capital claims are not thereafter live between them[2]. Unlike a periodical payments order, a lump sum order is intended to be a final order and, with certain limited exceptions, may be made only once.

[1] See CHAPTER 5.
[2] *Scheeres v Scheeres* [1999] 1 FLR 241.

4.2 As with most classes of relief, it would be unusual for only a lump sum order to be made. Most financial remedy orders contain a variety of types of order such as lump sum, periodical payments, property adjustment and so on. The exception to this might be where there are ample funds, and the purpose of the order is to fund continuing periodical payments for life; this would be known as a *Duxbury* order and this is considered below at **4.24**.

4.3 Because of this factor, it has been thought appropriate to include in this chapter a short section on so-called 'big money' cases. As will be seen, some of the principles to be observed in such cases are not confined to big money but have significance across the board. By a process of logical extension, there will then follow a section of the special features which arise when one of the assets of the parties is a business.

STATUTORY PROVISION

4.4 A lump sum order is a financial provision order[1]. On granting a decree of divorce, nullity or judicial separation or at any time thereafter the court may make an order 'that either party to the marriage shall pay to the other such lump sum as may be so specified'[2]. The powers of the court in this respect are exercisable only after the grant of a decree. They are therefore classed as final orders.

[1] MCA 1973, s 21(1)(c).
[2] MCA 1973, s 23(1)(c).

NUMBER OF LUMP SUMS

4.5 The statute refers to 'lump sum or sums'. This does not mean that more than one lump sum order may be made, but rather that only one order may be made, which order may provide for the payment of one or more lump sums[1]. The order may also provide for payment by instalments, or for payment to be deferred, and, in that event, for the payment of interest[2].

[1] *Coleman v Coleman* [1973] Fam 10.
[2] MCA 1973, s 23(6). For an interesting example of an order to pay a lump sum by instalments see *R v R (Lump Sum Repayments)* [2003] EWHC 3197 (Fam), [2004] 1 FLR 928 where Wilson J ordered a husband to pay lump sums equivalent to the wife's obligations under a 20-year repayment mortgage, ie £30,000 forthwith and then 240 payments to cover the instalments.

4.6 In *CR v CR*[1], where there was inadequate capital at the time of the order to meet all the wife's needs, a lump sum by instalments was ordered to avoid the need for a continuing periodical payments order and to ensure a clean break.

[1] [2008] 1 FLR 323.

4.7 An order for the payment of lump sums over time is not necessarily an order for payment by instalments, but may be merely an order for the payment of several lump sums on different dates. This difference may be of practical importance since an order for a series of lump sums cannot be varied save as to timing whereas an order for payment by instalments can be varied as to quantum and not merely as to timing[1]. A lump sum payable by instalments can be varied; for further details see Chapter 13.

[1] *Hamilton v Hamilton* [2013] EWCA Civ 13.

4.8 With the limited exception mentioned below, there is at present no provision for interim lump sums. After the decision of Waite J in *Barry v Barry*[1], it was thought that the court had the power to appropriate capital of the parties to one or other of them on an interim basis, on the understanding that the asset thereby acquired would be brought into account on the eventual distribution of assets at the final hearing. This supposed power was developed in other cases on the basis of the inherent jurisdiction of the court[2] and also the court's powers to order sale under the Rules of the Supreme Court 1965 (RSC), Ord 31, r 1, as applied by FPR 1991, r 2.64[3], which then applied.

[1] [1992] Fam 140.
[2] *F v F (Ancillary Relief: Substantial Assets)* [1995] 2 FLR 45.
[3] *Green v Green* [1993] 1 FLR 326.

4.9 This line of cases was comprehensively demolished by the Court of Appeal; in *Wicks v Wicks*[1], each of the supposed bases of jurisdiction was considered and, with regret, found wanting, and the law is therefore as it was before *Barry v Barry* was decided. There is no way in which the court may order an interim lump sum.

[1]   [1998] 1 FLR 470, per Ward LJ.

4.10 For the limited circumstances in which the court might order a sale of a property under TLATA before determining any application for a financial remedy see **7.16**.

4.11 The court does, however, have limited powers to provide for payments of sums of money on an interim basis for immediate needs. It is provided that[1]:

> '(a)   an order under this section [s 23] that a party to a marriage shall pay a lump sum to the other party may be made for the purpose of enabling that other party to meet any liabilities or expenses reasonably incurred by him or her in maintaining himself or herself or any child of the family before making an application for an order under this section in his or her favour.'

[1]   MCA 1973, s 23(3)(a).

4.12 This is a little used provision, but its utility is clear. It could be used where for some reason a periodic order was inappropriate, but the applicant had some pressing need, for example some school fees, a council tax bill, or a major car repair which could not be met out of income. It would seem that the purpose for which the lump sum would be required must be limited to the maintenance of the applicant or a child, and so the subsection could not be used for major housing requirements; perhaps, however, it could be used to require the payment of a deposit on rented accommodation.

4.13 For an example (not an authority) of an order made under this subsection, see *Askew-Page v Page*[1].

[1]   [2001] Fam Law 794, Bath County Court, HHJ Meston QC.

HOW ARE LUMP SUM ORDERS CALCULATED?

4.14 As always, it must be said that the only starting point for the court is the s 25 factors. There is no justification for taking any proportion of the assets as any kind of 'rule of thumb' baseline[1]. The power to award a lump sum was, in fact, only introduced in 1970 and then incorporated into the MCA 1973. It may fairly be regarded as one of the most important developments in modern family law. In one of the early cases, it was emphasised that a lump sum was not simply another way of quantifying maintenance; the court might take into account all the factors laid down in the Act. It was essential that the court should retain complete flexibility of approach in the light of the circumstances of the case, present, past, and insofar as one could make a reliable estimate, future[2]. This, of course, has been overtaken by the comprehensive rationales contained in the speeches in *White v White* and *Miller/McFarlane* (as to which see **1.21** et seq).

[1]   See eg *Potter v Potter* (1983) 4 FLR 331, CA.
[2]   *Trippas v Trippas* [1973] Fam 134, CA. See also *Hobhouse v Hobhouse* [1999] 1 FLR 961, CA.

4.15 In another case[1], Thorpe J held that the discretionary power of the court to adjust capital shares between the parties should not be exercised unless there is a manifest need for intervention upon the application of the s 25 criteria. In particular, the idea that an applicant was entitled to a 'nest egg' against a 'rainy day' was expressly disapproved; any specific award of capital must have an evidential justification[2].

[1] *H v H (Financial Provision: Capital Allowance)* [1993] 2 FLR 335.
[2] Disapproving *Re Besterman dec'd* [1984] Ch 458. But see *A v A (Financial Provision)* [1998] 2 FLR 180, where Singer J 'rounded up' the appropriate provision.

4.16 The conventional wisdom set out above is now subject to several qualifications arising out of the decisions of the House of Lords in *White v White*[1] and *Miller/McFarlane*[2]. Both these cases, and the legal position arising from them, are considered in detail at **1.21** et seq and reference should be made to that section of this book. However, some further comments can be added in the context of lump sums and will now be set out.

[1] [2000] 2 FLR 981.
[2] [2006] 1 FLR 1186, HL.

4.17 First, it is necessary to bear in mind the fundamental distinction between those cases where assets do not exceed needs and those where they do. For the sake of clarity, the latter can be referred to as 'big money cases'.

Cases where assets do not exceed needs

4.18 In this class of case, the function of the court, with the help of the practitioner, is to manage scarce funds so that the most pressing needs of the parties are met. By definition, there is not enough money to go round and so the court has to apply a 'hierarchy of needs'. Where there is a child, the first consideration will normally be to try to provide a home for the parent with care and the child. Where there are sufficient funds, the court will then try to make such order as enables the non-resident parent to rehouse himself or herself. This will normally take up most of the parties' funds, but if any money is left over the court will then consider any item for which a need is proved.

BIG MONEY CASES

4.19 Cases involving assets surplus to needs are fundamentally different from the cases considered above. It is still necessary to be guided by the s 25 factors but with the addition of the 'yardstick of equality'. By definition, there are sufficient funds to meet the needs of the parties. The role of the court is therefore now to achieve a just result in the light of s 25 and reference should be made to the section on the post-*White* and *Miller/McFarlane* position in CHAPTER 1.

4.20 As to what constitutes a 'big money' case, it is interesting (and, perhaps surprising) that in *D v D (Lump Sum: Adjournment of Application)*[1] Connell J considered that a case where the total assets were £700,000 and the husband earned £230,000 pa net was such a case on the ground that the available assets clearly exceeded the parties' needs for housing and income.

1   [2001] 1 FLR 633.

4.21 There will now be considered two particular aspects of this class of case, namely the 'millionaire's defence' and *Duxbury* funds.

The millionaire's defence

4.22 The fact that an approach based on a mathematical proportion is even less appropriate in big money cases than is normally the case is underlined by a number of decisions establishing what was known as 'the millionaire's defence'. This so-called defence, or argument, was to the effect that since the means of the paying party are such as to enable the payer to meet any award which the court could conceivably make based on the payee's reasonable requirements, it is unnecessary to give detailed and possibly costly disclosure of the full extent of the payer's means. This was also known as the '*Thyssen* defence', after the parties in the leading case on the point[1]. There, the husband deposed in his affidavit to very substantial and complicated assets worth over £400m, and concluded by saying, 'I would meet any order the court decides to make in relation to the financial dispute between the petitioner and myself'. The wife applied for detailed discovery, designed to support her assertion that the husband's wealth was, in reality, in excess of £1,000m. It was held that, since there was more than ample wealth to make a very substantial financial order to support the wife in luxury for the rest of her life, and the largest award which could be made would not be significantly increased by proof of a larger fortune, the limited discovery which had been offered was all that was reasonably necessary.

1   *Thyssen-Bornemisza v Thyssen-Bornemisza (No 2)* [1985] FLR 1069.

4.23 This decision was followed in another case in which the assets of the husband were 'only' £8m[1]. However, it is not to be taken as carte blanche for a less than careful or conscientious approach. In another case[2] in which the assets of the husband were between £150m and £200m, it was held that, while a restrictive approach to the wife's questionnaire was justified, this did not entitle the husband to refuse reasonably framed questions designed to establish the broad realities of the case and to illuminate issues as to past dealings. The death blow to the millionaires' defence might seem to have been delivered by the dicta of Thorpe LJ in *Parlour v Parlour* and *Mcfarlane v Mcfarlane* (as to which see **2.34** et seq); his Lordship said:

> 'We were told by the Bar that a practice has grown up for substantial earners to decline any statement of their needs on the grounds that they can afford any order that the court is likely to make. These appeals must put an end to that practice.'

1   *B v B (Discovery: Financial Provision)* [1990] 2 FLR 180.
2   *F v F (Ancillary Relief: Substantial Assets)* [1995] 2 FLR 45.

The *Duxbury* fund

4.24 As was mentioned above, one of the characteristics of big money cases is that there is normally sufficient liquid capital to provide a fund of money from which one party's income for life can be derived. A well-settled practice was established by which, once a payee's reasonable income needs have been established, a calculation could be made to quantify the capital sum required to fund that income for life on an inflation-proof basis. This was based on a computer program into which it was necessary to feed such information as the age of the recipient, and certain assumptions as to tax bands, inflation and so on were made.

4.25 Until very recently the best guidance as to the weight to be placed on such calculations was to be found not in the case from which the calculation derives its name[1] but in the words of Ward J in *B v B (Financial Provision)*[2]. Here it was pointed out that, as a result of the observations made in *Preston v Preston*[3], accountants had devised a computer program which could calculate the lump sum which, if invested on the assumptions as to life expectancy, rates of inflation, return on investment, growth of capital, incidence of income tax, will produce enough to meet the recipient's needs for her life. Ward J concluded that, if their calculation were accepted as no more than a tool for the judge's use, it was a very valuable help to him in many cases[4].

[1] *Duxbury v Duxbury* [1987] 1 FLR 7.
[2] [1990] 1 FLR 20.
[3] [1982] Fam 17, [1981] 3 WLR 619, CA.
[4] For background information on the origins of the computer program, see also the article by its originator Mr Timothy Lawrence at [1990] Fam Law 12.

4.26 In other cases[1] it has been emphasised that a *Duxbury* calculation cannot by itself provide the answer as to the sum to which a wife is entitled, and that there is a danger that it might be regarded as having achieved a status far beyond that which it had in the original case. There are also obvious uncertainties in trying to calculate the rate of return for any investment over a long period.

[1] See *F v F (Duxbury Calculation: Rate of Return)* [1996] 1 FLR 833; *Gojkovic v Gojkovic* [1992] Fam 40 at 48E; *Vicary v Vicary* [1992] 2 FLR 271 at 278B.

4.27 It has been said that '*Duxbury* is a tool and not a rule', and that 'the utility of the *Duxbury* methodology depends in part upon the skill of the user. It must be applied with flexibility, with a due recognition of its limitations and with intelligent perception of special features which are capable of being incorporated within the computer program'[1]. It was held in one case[2] that a *Duxbury* calculation was not appropriate because the wife had a life expectancy in excess of 40 years.

[1] Per Thorpe LJ in *White v White* [1998] 2 FLR 310. See also *A v A (Elderly Applicant: Lump Sum)* [1999] 2 FLR 969 and *G v G (Financial Provision: Separation Agreement)* [2000] 2 FLR 18, Connell J.
[2] *Fournier v Fournier* [1998] 2 FLR 990, CA.

4.28 It would therefore always have been wrong to treat the result of a *Duxbury* calculation as being anything other than the probable best guess as to the sum which needs to be provided. There was room for argument over the method used and whether the whole basis of the *Duxbury* calculation should be changed[1]. However, the court was greatly assisted by such calculations and they should be regarded as indispensable in appropriate cases[2].

[1] See 'Is Duxbury misleading? Yes, it is' at [2001] Fam Law 747.
[2] While expert advice may be needed in complicated cases, an indispensable source of information, giving helpful tables, etc is the publication *At a Glance*, published and annually updated by the Family Law Bar Association.

4.29 As readers will know all too well, we live in unusual economic times and what has been said about *Duxbury* calculations may seem to some a relic of the past today. Quite how a sensible prediction of interest and growth rates can be made when interest rates are less than 0.5% is difficult to see. It may be that the status quo ante will be resumed at some stage in the future but, for the moment, one can only say that there are severe difficulties in the way of making any reliable calculation.

4.30 For some time the courts were troubled by the so-called '*Duxbury* paradox', arising from the fact that, when a *Duxbury* calculation was appropriate, the older (and possibly more deserving) spouse recovered a lower amount than a younger spouse, because the calculation is based, in part, on life expectancy. This paradox was to some extent made easier by the comments of Lord Nicholls in *White v White*[1], where it was said that the proper application of the 'yardstick of equality' would resolve the problem in any event.

[1] [2000] 2 FLR 981, HL. See also **4.19**.

BUSINESS CASES

4.31 Many cases involving lump sums and, a fortiori, substantial amounts of money, are cases where one of the assets is a business owned by one or both of the parties. Where the business is a 'private' business, ie one in which the parties themselves have a controlling interest and which provides the source of the family's prosperity, particular considerations arise. The court has two essential functions in such cases. The first is to establish a value for the parties' interests in the business, as part of its duty under s 25(2)(a). The second is to decide how that value should be reflected in the final distribution.

4.32 As to the issue of valuation, it should be remembered that, until very recently, the conventional wisdom was that the court will avoid making any final order, the effect of which would be that the business would have to be sold against the will of the party wishing to continue in the business; in most cases, the business would be regarded as the provider of income, now and in the future, and not as a source of liquid capital. It follows that any valuation should not be in the same detail as would be employed by someone wishing to buy the company but rather to establish a reasonably accurate figure for the income which the business could generate, and its eventual value as, for example, the source of a pension annuity.

4.33 There was a wealth of authority to establish this point. In *Potter v Potter*[1] there had been extensive and costly accountancy evidence to establish a precise value of a small business; the judge then awarded the wife one-third of the value of the assets. On appeal it was pointed out that the valuation of a business in these circumstances was a 'necessarily hypothetical exercise because the only way that it can be done is for those valuing it to assume that the business would be sold and that, of course, is the one thing which is not going to happen and very rarely does happen'. Such a valuation was 'an almost wholly irrelevant consideration', and the proper approach was to take the wife's reasonable needs and balance them against the husband's ability to pay.

[1]   (1983) 4 FLR 331, CA.

4.34 In another case[1], where there was a family company with a value of £1.2m to £1.5m, it was said that all that was required was 'the broadest evaluation of the company's worth to enable the court to decide the wife's reasonable requirements'. If there was liquidity in the company which could be realised to meet her requirements then the final order would take that liquidity into account; if there was none, in the sense that the company (the source of the breadwinner's income) would be damaged, then the court should look elsewhere.

[1]   *P v P (Financial Provision)* [1989] 2 FLR 241.

4.35 This decision was cited in *Evans v Evans*[1] in support of one of the propositions laid down for the guidance of the profession in these cases. It was emphasised that, while it may be necessary to obtain a broad assessment of the value of a shareholding in a private company, it is inappropriate to undertake an expensive and meaningless exercise to achieve a precise valuation of a private company which will not be sold.

[1]   [1990] 1 FLR 319.

4.36 It must be said that it is now necessary to approach these cases with a degree of caution. *White v White* has introduced a new set of principles, particularly in cases of substantial assets, and in *N v N (Financial Provision: Sale of Company)*[1], it was said that the older authorities disapproving the sale of the golden goose might no longer apply. The same judge (Coleridge J) held, in *R v R (Financial Relief: Company Valuation)*[2] that the valuation of companies was more of an art than a science[3].

[1]   [2001] 2 FLR 69, Coleridge J.
[2]   [2005] 2 FLR 365.
[3]   For an interesting example of valuation of a minority interest in a company, see the decision of Charles J in *A v A* [2004] EWHC 2818 (Fam), [2006] 2 FLR 115.

4.37 In *D v D and B Ltd*[1] it was held that in cases involving private companies a commercial/company law solution might be preferable to a clean break based on valuations. Practitioners should not confine their approach to valuations and liquidity but should consider commercially realistic alternatives and periodical payments. If they do not have such expertise they should consult others.

[1]   [2007] 2 FLR 653, Charles J.

4.38 These warnings must, however, still be borne in mind, as must the point that the value of one of the assets is only one (even if the most important) factor which the court will take into account in the s 25 exercise. Nevertheless, the court does still have the duty to place some value on a business, and the following comments are designed to offer some guidance as to how that might be approached.

4.39 Businesses can of course take a variety of forms. What is to follow is not concerned with shares in publicly quoted companies, since their value is a matter of public record and should cause no difficulty. Here, we are concerned with sole traders, partnerships and limited companies.

4.40 The only exceptions to the principle that a detailed and precise valuation is inappropriate would be where one party was likely in the near future to convert his or her interest in the business into a liquid form, for example by sale, retirement or takeover, or where the wife had acquired a quantifiable interest in the business, for example by a direct financial contribution or by working in the business[1]. Perhaps the best test as to the latter point would be to ask whether the wife would be able to prove some beneficial interest in the business if she were a stranger and not involved in matrimonial proceedings; if this were the case, she would be entitled to an interest in the business in her own right, and not only as part of the s 25 exercise, and a more detailed examination might be appropriate[2].

[1]   See eg *Gojkovic v Gojkovic* [1990] 1 FLR 140, CA.
[2]   See *White v White* [1998] 2 FLR 310, CA.

4.41 If any valuation of the business is to be carried out with a view to relying on it in court proceedings or advice to a client, it will at some stage become necessary to instruct an accountant. A lawyer who relied on his or her own expertise for such a purpose would be in grave danger of an action for negligence. Nevertheless, there are several reasons why the family lawyer should be familiar with methods of valuation. First and foremost, such knowledge enables the lawyer to scrutinise the evidence of experts, to understand the terms which are used, and, if necessary, to challenge it. It is the court which makes the final decision as to such issues, and lawyers must be able to make intelligent and informed submissions to the court, based on an understanding of what the experts have been saying. Secondly, when a case is at an early stage, the lawyer should be able to make a provisional estimate of what a business is likely to be worth, with a view to advising the client and deciding how to conduct the application.

Needless to say, any attempt to introduce an expert valuation into evidence will be subject to the rules as to expert evidence contained in FPR Pt 25. Where there is any serious dispute as to valuation the court's preference will be for a single joint expert but this may not always be possible. For the detailed rules regarding expert evidence see CHAPTER 16 at 16.32 et seq.

4.42 The value of any business is normally what a willing purchaser would pay for it on an arm's length basis. There are three bases of valuation which an interested purchaser would normally use; these are the asset basis, the dividend yield basis, and the earnings basis. Frequently, a calculation is done on each of these bases and then the results compared to obtain a cross-checked final result.

4.43 The asset basis produces the figure which would be obtained if the assets were sold and the business closed down. The problem for the family lawyer with this basis is that the book value of the assets as shown in the balance sheet is almost invariably wrong and of no assistance in calculating the market value of the assets. Expert valuation of the assets is therefore essential, but it would also be necessary to take account of the legal and other costs involved in closing down a business. For the reasons given above, businesses are rarely closed down to provide a lump sum, so, in addition to being the most difficult, this basis of valuation is unlikely to be the one finally relied on by the court.

4.44 The dividend yield basis is equally unlikely to provide a final answer. It gives the value to a potential purchaser who is principally interested in the dividend income from the company. It involves dividing the gross dividend by the required rate of return to give a value per share. It is therefore necessary to select the rate of return required. This method is usually employed as a cross-check on the result of a calculation on the earnings basis.

4.45 The earnings basis of valuation is therefore likely to be the most useful starting point. It involves first establishing the maintainable earnings of the business. This figure will be derived from one or more sources; one would be the most recent year's gross profits. Another would be the average of the last 3 years' gross profits. These could then be compared to obtain the final figure. This figure must then be adjusted to take account of such matters as inappropriate payments of various kinds (eg adding back excessive remuneration or pension contributions) and tax at the current rate must then be deducted.

4.46 The figure for maintainable earnings must then be multiplied by the P/E (profits: earnings) ratio appropriate for that type of business. This ratio can be obtained from the FT Actuaries Share Index, published daily, which should be rounded down to the nearest whole number. The resulting figure may then have to be discounted to take account of the size of the business.

4.47 To be able to carry out the calculations as above, or to instruct an expert, certain documents are necessary, and should be obtained at an early date. At the very least the last 3 years' accounts must be obtained; these will enable a preliminary valuation to be done. If an expert is to be instructed he will say what he wants, but this will include the Memorandum and Articles of Association of a company, shareholders' agreements and internal documents relating to business plans and forecasts, board minutes and cash flow projections.

4.48 The problems of valuing a private company where there are no plans to sell were extensively analysed in *G v T*[1]. The judge set out all recent authorities and said that all such valuations are difficult and fragile. The weight to be placed on a valuation is not a mathematical exercise but a broad evaluative exercise, all about weight and balance.

[1]   [2020] EWHC 1613.

4.49 Once again, it should be emphasised that the family lawyer should not try to be his or her own expert witness nor to rely on what has been said above as anything other than a guide to help find a way through the thickets of a complicated field. Nevertheless, if it succeeds in giving that limited amount of help, it should prove useful.

4.50 Where one spouse is involved in a company, the other frequently thinks that he or she must have some interest not immediately apparent on the face of the accounts and, of course, that may be true; identifying such benefits is one of the tasks of the expert. However, it is important to retain a sense of reality. The judgment in *Ben Hashem v Al Shayif*[1] contains a comprehensive analysis of the principle to be applied; in order to pierce the corporate veil it is necessary to demonstrate not only control of a company but also impropriety linked to the company structure, ie (mis)use of the company as a device to conceal a wrongdoing entirely outside the company. The question is whether the company is being used as a facade.

[1]   [2008] EWHC 2380 (Fam), Munby J.

4.51 Having obtained all the evidence regarding the value of the parties' interests in a business the court must then decide what to do with such evidence. The court's task (and sometimes dilemma) was well summarized by Moylan J in *H v H*[1] in the following terms:

> 'The experts agree that the exercise they are engaged in is an art and not a science. As Lord Nicholls said in *Miller v Miller; McFarlane v McFarlane* [2006] UKHL 24; [2006] 2 AC 618 [26]: "valuations are often a matter of opinion on which experts differ. A thorough investigation into these differences can be extremely expensive and of doubtful utility". I understand, of course, that the application of the sharing principle can be said to raise powerful forces in support of detailed accounting. Why, a party might ask, should my "share" be fixed by reference other than to the real values of the assets? However, this is to misinterpret the exercise in which the court is engaged. The court is engaged in a broad analysis in the application of its jurisdiction under the Matrimonial Causes Act, not a detailed accounting exercise. As Lord Nicholls said, detailed accounting is expensive, often of doubtful utility and, certainly in respect of business valuations, will often result in divergent opinions each of which may be based on sound reasoning. The purpose of valuations, when required, is to assist the court in testing the fairness of the proposed outcome. It is not to ensure mathematical/accounting accuracy, which is invariably no more than a chimera. Further, to seek to construct the whole edifice of an award on a business valuation which is no more than a broad, or even very broad, guide is to risk creating an edifice which is unsound and hence likely to be unfair. In my experience, valuations of shares in private companies are among the most fragile valuations which can be obtained.'

[1]   [2008] EWHC 935 (Fam).

4.52 The court must then exercise its powers in accordance with the requirements of the statute bearing in mind in particular the guidance as to fairness, equality and sharing set out by case law.

TAX CONSIDERATIONS

4.53 Since this is not a textbook on revenue law, only the briefest mention is to be made of this subject; however, it is important that family lawyers be aware of the tax implications of any proposed order. This will normally involve taking expert advice.

4.54 The simplest explanation of this topic is that the sale or transfer of any asset, other than the sole or principal residence of a person, may attract capital gains tax. The tax is on the gain between acquisition and disposal, subject to 'indexation'. When spouses are separated, and assets are sold by one of them to provide a lump sum, tax is, in principle, payable on the gain achieved by the sale. When a matrimonial home, in which both parties have continued to live, is transferred to one of them, the private residence exemption should apply. This also applies even where the transferor has left the home, provided the transferee has continued to live in it.

4.55 Before the court can decide whether to order a lump sum payment which is to be funded by the sale of assets, therefore, the tax implications of any sale must be ascertained, and the net effect of these incorporated in the calculations leading to the order.

Chapter 5

TRANSFER OF PROPERTY ORDERS AND HOUSING NEEDS

INTRODUCTION

5.1 Transfer of property orders and housing needs are both topics which, clearly, have to be considered. It has been thought appropriate to combine them in one chapter because of the obvious overlapping nature of the subjects. Nevertheless, it should be remembered that the meeting of housing needs is not the sole purpose of a transfer of property order.

5.2 A transfer of property order is an order that one party transfer to the other some property. In most cases this will be real property, such as land or a dwelling-house. However, personal property such as shares, chattels, or even the matrimonial dog may also be the subject of a transfer of property order. The essential nature of the order is that an identifiable and specific item of property is ordered to be transferred; it therefore differs from a lump sum order, which provides for the payment of a sum of money.

5.3 The housing needs of the parties are, almost invariably, a high priority in any financial remedy application. In many cases, particularly in the lower financial range, the matrimonial home is the sole or principal asset, and the whole case revolves around the housing needs of the parties and their children. The significance of this will be explored in more detail at **5.12** et seq.

5.4 The subject of transfers of tenancy will be considered at **5.41** et seq. A tenancy may be the subject of a transfer of property order, but there may also be an application pursuant to Pt IV of the Family Law Act 1996 (FLA 1996). The wording of transfer of property orders may be particularly important, and is considered in some detail at **5.17** et seq.

STATUTORY PROVISION

5.5 A transfer of property order is a type of property adjustment order[1], the other two types being settlement of property orders and variation of settlement; the latter two are dealt with elsewhere. This is the most common form of property adjustment order.

[1] MCA 1973, s 21(2)(a).

5.6 It is provided that[1]:

'(1)   on granting a decree of divorce, a decree of nullity of marriage or a decree of judicial separation or at any time thereafter (whether, in the case of a decree of divorce or of nullity of marriage, before or after the decree is made absolute) the court may make . . .

(a)   an order that a party to the marriage shall transfer to the other party, to any child of the family or to such person as may be specified in the order for the benefit of such a child such property as may be so specified, being property to which the first-mentioned party is entitled, either in possession or reversion.'

[1]   MCA 1973, s 24(1)(a).

5.7 It will be noted that the order may be made only on or after the grant of a decree; there is no provision for interim orders. It will also be seen that the court may make 'an order'; the court may not make more than one order, although it may, of course, provide for the transfer of more than one item of property in the same order.

5.8 Clearly, the person ordered to transfer may only transfer property which he is entitled to transfer, ie that which he owns. However, this may include property in which he has a joint interest (eg with the applicant) or a reversionary interest.

5.9 The provisions as to children are considered in more detail in Chapter **11**.

RULES

5.10 There are certain requirements in the Family Procedure Rules 2010 (FPR) which are specific to transfer of property orders; these are considered in more detail in Chapter **16**.

THE BASIS ON WHICH ORDERS ARE MADE

5.11 As always, it must be said that the only basis on which the court makes any financial order is the consideration and balancing of the factors in MCA 1973, s 25, and the position is no different in relation to transfer of property orders. The proper approach to financial remedies is dealt with in more detail in Chapter **1** and need not be considered in such detail here. Nevertheless, the question of housing needs is usually important, and it is therefore appropriate to consider that as a preliminary matter.

5.12 In one leading case[1], Thorpe LJ said that it was one of the paramount considerations in applying the s 25 criteria to endeavour to stretch what was available to cover the need of each party for a home, particularly where there were young children involved. Obviously the primary carer needed whatever was available to make a main home for the children, but it was of importance, albeit of lesser importance, that the other party should have a home of his own where the children could enjoy their contact time with him. In any case, where there was, by stretch and a degree of risk-taking, the possibility of a division to enable both parties to rehouse themselves, that was an exceptionally important consideration and one which would almost invariably have a decisive impact on the outcome. In the instant case, the resources were available to make a division which would, just about, enable each to rehouse and the judge's order, which had awarded the husband a lump sum of an insufficient size, was set aside and a larger sum awarded.

[1]   *M v B (Ancillary Proceedings: Lump Sum)* [1998] 1 FLR 53, CA.

5.13 This is an important restatement of, and compelling authority for, a general principle which the courts have normally striven to observe. That the need for a roof over one's head is one of the most basic human needs is a principle which hardly needs restating, and housing must, therefore, be one of the most important financial needs to be met pursuant to s 25(2)(b). However, it has also been emphasised[1] that the statement of the desirability of the non-caring parent having his or her accommodation should not be elevated into a rigid rule of law; there was no rule of law that each party must be able to purchase a property, and each case depends on its own facts.

[1]   In *Piglowska v Piglowski* [1999] 2 FLR 763, HL.

5.14 Sometimes, when assets are severely limited, the needs of one party have to give way to the needs of the family as a whole and the requirement to treat the welfare of the children as the first consideration pursuant to s 25(1). A home for the minor children is normally the principal requirement. However, that does not always mean that they should continue to occupy the former matrimonial home; that may be a desirable objective in many cases, but where they could be satisfactorily rehoused in cheaper accommodation, thereby releasing capital for the rehousing of the non-carer, that is an option which should be adopted. Each case will, of course, turn on its own facts. Ability to borrow is an important feature of such cases, and is regarded as a resource under s 25(2)(a).

5.15 The fact that one party (and the children) have to occupy a particular property does not always mean that that party is entitled to the sole ownership of that property. In the following section the various options for the court are considered, and clearly an outright transfer is not always appropriate. Where a property could be sold after the children had ceased to need it as their residence and some capital released for the non-carer, this is an option which the court should consider. This might be attractive where the non-carer was going to be under a continuing obligation to pay periodical payments as well as sacrificing all his capital. However, the factors which might persuade a court to the contrary view are:

- the desire of most parties for finality;
- the undesirability in some cases of maintaining a link between the non-carer and the carer;
- uncertainty as to the future ability of the carer to rehouse himself or herself once the children had gone;
- the value of the property in question;
- the length of time which was likely to elapse before the property could be sold; and
- the fact that ownership of a property, particularly one of modest value, is not always a markedly superior position to that of someone entitled to reasonably secure rented accommodation.

5.16 When assessing housing needs, the court must take account of the effect of its proposed order on those directly affected by its decision; in one case[1], that was described as 'the court's primary if not exclusive concern'. In that case the judge had held that he should not make an order which might be regarded as usurping the role of the local housing authority, but on appeal this was held to be an incorrect approach. Phillips LJ said that he did not see how the court could perform its duty without taking into account what would happen to those deprived of the right to live in the matrimonial home. However, he went on to say that this necessarily involved having regard to the effect of the local authority housing policy, and he did not think it correct to describe the effect of such an approach as being to manipulate housing lists or to usurp the function of the council. The fact that one party may be eligible for local authority housing is therefore a valid consideration, although, once again, each case will turn on its own facts.

[1] *Jones v Jones* [1997] 1 FLR 27, CA.

TYPES OF TRANSFER OF PROPERTY ORDERS

5.17 Once the court has decided the overall scheme of its disposition this must be incorporated into an order, and in many cases the order might take a variety of forms. In this section it is intended to set out the various types of order which may be made. Some of these orders, while being property adjustment orders, would properly fall under the heading of settlement of property or variation of settlement orders; however, for convenience, they are all set out here.

5.18 Although it may seem simplistic to make this point, it is extremely important for the practitioners to have seen the deeds or land certificate to the property well before the application is heard. The information which lay clients give about ownership of property is not always accurate and it is important to be aware of the exact nature of the title and any incumbrances. As a final preliminary point, it should be noted that there are many references in the text and elsewhere to trusts for sale of land. As a result of the Trusts of Land and Appointment of Trustees Act 1996 (TOLATA 1996), trusts for sale have been replaced by trusts of land. The wording of any orders now made will therefore have to reflect that change.

Outright transfer

5.19 The simplest form of order which can be made is for one party to transfer to the other his or her estate or interest (whether sole or joint) in a property[1]. When the property to be transferred is mortgaged, the order would have to provide either for the simultaneous redemption of the mortgage (eg by a separate order for payment of a lump sum for this purpose), or for the transfer to be subject to the existing charge (this would be the case even if the order did not provide for it). A mortgagee cannot prevent a transfer, but if the property were merely transferred subject to the charge, the property would be at risk if the terms of the mortgage were not observed and the transferor would continue to be liable under the mortgage covenants.

1   As was done in *Hanlon v Hanlon* [1978] 1 WLR 592, CA. If the house were to be sold, neither party could rehouse themselves on 50% of the proceeds. The husband was earning significantly more and it was better that the parties knew where they stood.

5.20 This frequently has to be the position. However, an order in these circumstances should normally also contain an undertaking by the transferee to perform the obligations of the mortgage and to indemnify the transferor against liability under the mortgage.

5.21 In *Fisher-Aziz v Aziz*[1] it was said that, as a matter of general principle, if a wife in occupation of a former matrimonial home (having primary regard to the needs of any children) sought the transfer of the property in preference to the proceeds of sale of the property, she should normally succeed, provided she can secure the release of the co-owner from the mortgage. It should perhaps be noted that in this case there was no available equity so the issue of any payment to the husband did not arise.

1   [2010] EWCA Civ 673.

5.22 A possible variation of this type of outright transfer order would be to transfer in return for some consideration. This consideration could take the form of a cash payment, or the discharge of the transferor's obligation to pay periodical payments by a clean break order[1]. The latter order might be appropriate where the value of the property transferred was roughly equivalent to the value of the lost benefits. It might also be appropriate where it was clear that the transferor would be unable to make any significant contribution to the support of the transferee, and it was important for the transferee (and any children) to have settled accommodation. In *Lawrence v Bertram (Judgment on Preliminary Issue)*[2] it was held that the court had jurisdiction to order a transfer of property on condition that the transferee pay the transferor a fixed sum.

1   As in *Mortimer v Mortimer-Griffin* [1986] 2 FLR 315, CA.
2   Croydon County Court [2004] Fam Law 323. This is a decision of a circuit judge in a county court and is therefore only a persuasive authority but there seems no reason to doubt it.

5.23 In the absence of other factors, it would not be appropriate where the value of the interest transferred was significantly less than the lost benefits. The desire of the transferee for certainty should not obscure the need for her advisers to have regard to the circumstances in which a clean break order is inappropriate[1].

1   See generally **2.70** et seq.

5.24 Similarly, a potential transferor should be aware that, even if the transferee's right to periodical payments can be extinguished, the same does not apply to the children, and even if a mother undertook not to claim for the children this would not be binding on the Child Maintenance Service.

Transfer subject to charge

5.25 An order may provide for the transfer to one party of a property, subject to a charge in favour of the transferor for payment of a sum of money. Such a payment would be required either on a fixed date[1] or on the occurrence of a certain event or the first of certain events, such as the death or remarriage of the transferee, the children attaining their majority or ceasing full-time education or some other event[2]. The payment to be made could be expressed as a fixed monetary amount, but it is more common, and normally preferable, for it to be a percentage of the gross or net proceeds of sale[3].

[1] *Knibb v Knibb* [1987] 2 FLR 396.
[2] As in *Hector v Hector* [1973] 1 WLR 1122, CA.
[3] See *McDonnell v McDonnell* (1976) 120 SJ 87, CA.

5.26 Orders frequently provide for the enforcement of the charge on the remarriage or cohabitation of the transferee. Where there are dependent children, this should be subject to the proviso that any enforcement on this ground should be subject to the leave of the court. In any event, the provision as to cohabitation is liable to raise problems, since cohabitation may be difficult to define and, even if proved, may not endure. Perhaps a better form of words would be: 'if any adult person other than the [transferee] and the children of the family occupies the property as his or her home for a period, whether continuous or cumulative, in excess of six months save with the written consent of the [transferor]'.

5.27 An order that the property 'stand charged' with payment of a certain sum on terms is valid and will be recognised by the Land Registry. However, this may be a less desirable form of order than the alternative which is to order the transfer in return for the delivery to the transferor of a charge duly executed by the transferee, such charge to be in a form agreed between the solicitors for the parties and, in default of agreement, to be settled by the district judge. The parties and, in default, the court, then retain some control over the terms on which the transferee occupies the property.

5.28 A brief but not exhaustive list of the possible problems which should be eliminated by a properly drawn charge is as follows:

(a) The right to redeem. In the absence of this, a mortgagee entitled to eg 30% of the net proceeds of sale could insist on a sale of the property.

(b) Provision for determination of the value of the property in the event of dispute, eg by a chartered surveyor.

(c) A bare charge for moneys on demand entitles the chargee to possession of the property without proof of breach of any term. Even where this does not apply, a chargee is entitled to take possession on breach, eg if the charge is not redeemed on the fixed date. The charge should be so drawn as to prevent either of these possibilities.

(d) Where there is no prior mortgage, or that mortgage is redeemed, the chargee is entitled to hold the deeds. This might not be desirable in many post-matrimonial situations.

(e) Unless there is express power to tack, the chargor cannot raise any further money on the security of the property. The power to lease should also be restricted.

(f)   The right to move house and transfer the charge to another property, eg during the minority of the children should be considered.

Mesher orders

5.29 A *Mesher* order, so called after the eponymous case[1], is essentially a postponement of the exercise of a trust for sale until a named event occurs; this is normally connected with the children of the family. In the case itself, the order was for the matrimonial home to be held on trust for sale for the parties in equal shares, and that the house be not sold for so long as the child of the family was under the age of 17 or until further order[2]. The wife was to live there rent-free but had to pay the outgoings, and capital repayments of the mortgage were to be shared equally. Strictly speaking, it is a settlement order rather than a transfer of property order.

[1]   *Mesher v Mesher and Hall* [1980] 1 All ER 126, CA.
[2]   'Until further order' entitles the court to make an order for earlier sale, if appropriate, but not to postpone the sale; see *Carson v Carson* [1983] 1 WLR 285, CA, and *Norman v Norman* (1983) 4 FLR 446.

5.30 Such an order may be amended to take account of the circumstances of a particular case. For example, the 'trigger event' for sale of the house could be expressed as the first of various occurrences including the death or remarriage of the carer spouse, the children continuing in full-time education, or further order; the division of the proceeds of sale could be other than equal; and the occupying party could be required to pay an occupation rent[1].

[1]   As in *Harvey v Harvey* [1982] Fam 83, CA.

5.31 Some of the comments on orders for transfer subject to charge back set out at **5.25** apply equally to *Mesher* orders. The orders can also be refined to provide for the exclusive occupation of the home by the occupying party[1]. However, there are more fundamental objections to *Mesher* orders which cannot always be met by different wordings, and whether the court's objectives could be met by other means should always be considered.

[1]   See *Allen v Allen* [1986] 2 FLR 265, CA.

5.32 One reason why a *Mesher* order might be unsuitable would be the undesirability in a particular case of the parties remaining joined together in property ownership. However, the principal objection to these orders is the state of uncertainty in which the parties might be left. When these orders were more fashionable, there were many cases in which 'the chickens came home to roost' a number of years later, and it was found that one or even both parties were unable to rehouse themselves from the available funds[1].

[1]   See *Mortimer v Mortimer-Griffin* [1986] 2 FLR 315, CA; *Carson v Carson* (above); *Norman v Norman* (above); *Thompson v Thompson* [1985] FLR 863, CA.

5.33 In *B v B (Mesher Order)*[1] it was held that a *Mesher* order was inappropriate where there was a young child, and the commitment of the mother to child rearing would mean that her ability to generate capital would be much less than that of her husband. The result would be inequality of outcome which was discriminatory and unacceptable. This is an interesting gloss on the meaning of equality in the post-*White* and *Lambert* world.

[1]   [2002] EWHC 3106 (Fam), [2003] 2 FLR 285.

5.34 With that in mind, and in the light of the requirement for the court to strive to make such order as will enable both parties to rehouse themselves, it can be said that it would now be unusual for the court to make a *Mesher* order unless it were satisfied, by credible evidence, either that the eventual net proceeds of sale would be sufficient to provide for both parties, or that, for some reason, this was not necessary or desirable.

5.35 For a recent example of a *Mesher* order see *Mansfield v Mansfield*[1]. The husband had received damages for personal injuries of £500,000, which he invested in a property in which he and the wife lived before the breakdown of the marriage. The wife left with the children and the district judge awarded her £285,000 for the purchase of a property. The circuit judge rejected the husband's appeal, which was, however, allowed by the Court of Appeal, which substituted a *Mesher* order, under which the husband would recover one-third of the value of the property on the children's majority. This would recognise the origin of the family capital and the special purpose for which it had been provided.

[1]   [2011] EWCA Civ 1056.

5.36 In summary, therefore, there may well be cases in which a *Mesher* order would be suitable, but in most cases an alternative form of order will probably be preferable.

Martin orders

5.37 A *Martin* order[1] is, in effect, a refinement of a *Mesher* order. It provides for the postponement of the trust for sale and for the division of the net proceeds when sold, but also provides for the property to be settled on the occupying party for life or until remarriage or voluntary removal. Such orders have been further refined to provide for the occupying party to pay an occupation rent[2], or for the right of occupation to terminate on the wife's co-habitation. A more sophisticated form of order was that in *Chamberlain v Chamberlain*[3] where it was ordered that the property should not be sold until every child of the family had ceased to receive full-time education or thereafter without leave of the court or with the consent of the parties.

[1]   Named after *Martin v Martin* [1978] Fam 12, CA. See also *Bateman v Bateman* [1979] Fam 25; *Clutton v Clutton* [1991] 1 FLR 242, CA.
[2]   *Harvey v Harvey* (above).
[3]   [1973] 1 WLR 1557, CA.

5.38 *Martin* orders are clearly appropriate where the justice of the case demands that one party be entitled to occupy a property for as long as he or she wishes, but it is not intended to deprive the other party of his or her capital entitlement forever and even in the event of the other party's death.

Other orders

5.39 The orders set out above are the principal types of orders made for transfer of property and/or settlement of property. It should not be forgotten that the court may also order the immediate sale of a property and the division of the net proceeds of sale in whatever proportions appear appropriate in suitable cases.

5.40 An interesting case involving transfer of shares in a company is *C v C (Company Shares)*[1] where Coleridge J held that, where a wife had played a part, and wished to continue to play a part in the future of a company, there had to be a compelling reason why she should not be entitled to do so. Where the wife had made out a sensible case for holding shares, the court should, in fairness, accede to it.

[1]   [2003] 2 FLR 493.

TRANSFER OF TENANCY

5.41 When the interest or estate which the parties to a financial remedy application have in a property is a tenancy and not ownership of the property, different considerations arise from those already considered. In principle, the court must deal with the application in the same way as any other, namely by application of the s 25 factors. However, there are additional matters to be borne in mind.

5.42 Perhaps, at the outset, it should be made clear that most of the tenancies which will be the subject of an application will be local authority or social housing tenancies. This is because most tenancies in the private sector are now shorthold tenancies which are likely to contain a covenant against assignment (see below) or to be of so short a period as not to be worth transferring.

5.43 It has been held[1] that a tenancy is 'property' for the purposes of s 24(1)(a) and is therefore capable of being transferred pursuant to an order. There are two ways in which such an order may be obtained, and the choice will depend on the terms of the tenancy.

[1]   *Thompson v Thompson* [1976] Fam 25, CA.

5.44 While the court has jurisdiction to make an order for transfer of a tenancy under s 24(1)(a), it should not exercise its discretion to do so when its order would be rendered ineffective by a covenant against assignment or where it would interfere with the statutory duties and discretion of a local housing authority[1]. If, therefore, there is a covenant against assignment, so that the tenant has contractually agreed not to assign, it has been said that it is doubtful that the court would transfer the tenancy[2].

[1]   See *Regan v Regan* [1977] 1 WLR 84; *Hale v Hale* [1975] 1 WLR 931. See also *Newlon Housing Trust v Alsulaimen* [1997] 1 FLR 914, CA.
[2]   Most recently in *Newlon Housing Trust v Alsulaimen* (above).

5.45 However, this statement may be subject to doubt, at least as far as council tenants are concerned, since in another decision of the Court of

Appeal[1] it was described as out of date on the ground that, since the Housing Act 1980, council tenants had security of tenure and even the right to buy.

[1] *Jones v Jones* [1997] 1 FLR 27, CA.

5.46 In any event, the position would be different where the local housing authority had expressly declined to become involved on behalf of either party but made it clear that it had no objection to transfer.

5.47 In a case where s 24 could not be invoked, an application for transfer of tenancy may be made under FLA 1996, Sch 7. This empowers the court to order the transfer of a protected or statutory tenancy, a statutory tenancy within the meaning of the Rent (Agriculture) Act 1976, a secure tenancy within the meaning of the Housing Act 1985, s 79, or an assured tenancy or assured agricultural tenancy within the meaning of Pt I of the Housing Act 1988. In the case of spouses, past or present, the court has jurisdiction to make an order whenever it has power to make a property adjustment order.

5.48 It will be noted that shorthold tenancies are not included in the list of tenancies which may be transferred. However, secure tenancies are included, and the Act provides a procedure for allowing landlords to be heard and provides a checklist for the guidance of the court. It is for this reason that it can be said that even where there is a covenant against assignment, the court has jurisdiction to consider an application under this statute.

5.49 The procedure for applying for a transfer of tenancy under FLA 1996, Sch 7 is set out in FPR, Pt 8, Chapter 7.

Chapter 6

SETTLEMENT OF PROPERTY ORDERS AND VARIATION OF SETTLEMENTS

INTRODUCTION

6.1 As was seen in CHAPTER 5, when dealing with transfer of property orders, settlement of property orders and transfer of property orders are both types of property adjustment order and, to a large extent, overlap. For example, a *Mesher* order[1], often regarded as a typical transfer of property order, is in reality a settlement of property order. The distinction is, for most purposes, immaterial, and in CHAPTER 5 the general principles governing the making of all such orders involving property were considered. In this chapter, therefore, it is proposed to consider only the special characteristics of settlement orders and also the subject of variation of settlement.

[1]   *Mesher v Mesher and Hall* [1980] 1 All ER 126, CA.

STATUTORY PROVISION

6.2 The power to order settlement of property or variation of settlement is contained in s 24 of MCA 1973 which provides that on granting a decree of divorce, a decree of nullity of marriage, or a decree of judicial separation or at any time thereafter (whether, in the case of a decree of divorce or of nullity of marriage, before or after the decree is made absolute) the court may make one or more of the following orders, that is to say[1]:

'(b)   an order that a settlement of such property as may be so specified, being property to which a party to the marriage is so entitled, be made to the satisfaction of the court for the benefit of the other party to the marriage and of the children of the family or either or any of them;

(c)   an order varying for the benefit of the parties to the marriage and of the children of the family or either or any of them any ante-nuptial or post-nuptial settlement (including such a settlement made by will or codicil) made on the parties to the marriage, other than one in the form of a pension arrangement (within the meaning of section 25D . . .);

(d)   an order extinguishing or reducing the interest of either of the parties to the marriage under any settlement, other than one in the form of a pension arrangement (within the meaning of section 25D . . .).'

[1]   MCA 1973, s 24(1).

6.3 These orders are, therefore, only capable of being made after decree. There is no provision for any interim relief of this nature.

WHAT IS A SETTLEMENT?

6.4 This is considered in more detail at **6.9**.

6.5 With the exception of *Mesher* and *Martin*[1] type orders, settlement orders are quite rare today. The reason for this is the comparatively sophisticated range of orders of other kinds available under the statute, and the fact that settlements of land are unusual in any circumstances in contemporary conditions. It is therefore not proposed to spend much time considering the requirements for settlement orders.

[1]   *Martin v Martin* [1976] Fam 335.

6.6 It should, however, be noted that the power to settle is not limited in any way. When, therefore, the court considers that a settlement order is appropriate, it may do so in a wide variety of ways[1]. Since, with the exception of *Mesher* or *Martin* orders, this will be quite unusual, it is not proposed to consider the matter further here.

[1]   For an example, see *Tavoulareas v Tavoulareas* [1998] 2 FLR 418, CA.

VARIATION OF SETTLEMENT

6.7 As has been seen, the statute confers on the court wide jurisdiction to vary or discharge settlements. This was once an important part of the court's jurisdiction on marriage breakdown, but has become comparatively rare. When marriage settlements were common and the court had restricted powers, the power to vary the settlement was clearly significant. Now that such settlements are less common and, in any event, the court enjoys wide discretionary powers, it is unusual for the court to have to exercise this branch of its jurisdiction. A modern example of a case in which the court would have had no means of providing for a party (in terms of pension provision) except by way of variation of settlement is *Brooks v Brooks*, considered at **6.11**.

6.8 Having said that, it must also be said that the approach of the court when dealing with such applications must be exactly the same as in any other financial remedy application. The s 25 factors must be observed, and the interest of either party under a settlement is one of the assets to be brought into the calculations under s 25(2)(a). It will be for the court to consider the settlement in the light of the overall picture, and to decide how, if at all, it should be varied.

6.9 The first matter to be proved is, of course, that there is an ante-nuptial or post-nuptial settlement. The court interprets the term 'settlement' in a liberal manner and is not constrained by conveyancing concepts. The form is not the most important element; settlements can range from the strict settlement which would be easily recognised by a chancery lawyer to a mere covenant to pay periodic amounts. The settlement may be contained in a separation agreement, a will or codicil, or any document.

6.10 What is important is that the settlement provide for the financial benefit of one of the spouses and with reference to their married state[1]. A mere gift between spouses, or by a third party to a spouse, does not of itself create a settlement. An agreement to pay sums of money to a spouse after the marriage came to an end has been held to lack the required nuptial element[2].

[1] *Prescott (formerly Fellowes) v Fellowes* [1958] P 260, CA.
[2] *Young v Young* [1962] P 27, CA.

6.11 In *Brooks v Brooks*[1], the parties had married in 1977 and in 1980 the husband's company set up a non-contributory pension scheme for him. It included the right for him to elect on retirement to give up a portion of his pension to provide on his death a deferred pension to his spouse or other person financially dependent on him. It was held that this was a post-nuptial settlement which the court could vary. The significance of *Brooks v Brooks* in terms of pensions has now diminished due to the effect of the Welfare Reform and Pensions Act 1999 (WRPA 1999) (see CHAPTER 10).

[1] [1996] 1 AC 375, [1995] 2 FLR 13, HL.

6.12 In his speech, Lord Nicholls conceded the wide interpretation given to 'settlement' and said that the disposition must be one which makes some form of continuing provision for both or either of the parties to the marriage, with or without provision for their children. A disposition which conferred an immediate, absolute interest in an item of property would not constitute a settlement; in such a case, the appropriate remedy (if remedy were needed) would be a property transfer order or property settlement order. The authorities had consistently given a wide meaning to settlement in this context and had spelled out no precise limitation. A disposition which created interests in succession in specified property would cause no difficulty, nor where such interests were concurrent but discretionary. Concurrent joint interests, such as where parties to a marriage hold the matrimonial home as joint tenants or tenants in common, were 'near the borderline' but there was (rightly) authority[1] for holding this to be within the scope of the section. Income provision from settled property would readily qualify, and it was 'only a short step' to include income provision which took the form of an obligation by one party to the marriage to make periodical payments to the other.

[1] In *Brown v Brown* [1959] P 86.

6.13 In *Charamalous v Charamalous*[1] it was held that, provided it existed at the date of the order, the court has jurisdiction under s 24(1)(c) to vary a settlement that, at the date it was made, was ante- or post-nuptial, notwithstanding that, prior to the date of the order, the features that made it nuptial had been removed. In this case the court accorded primacy to the ancillary relief regime over the trust regime and emphasised the incapacity of individuals to elect out of it. The nuptial character or otherwise of a settlement was held to be a question of fact.

[1] [2004] 2 FLR 1093, CA.

6.14 For a recent example of a case where the court found that there was not a post-nuptial settlement see *K v K*[1].

[1] [2007] EWHC 3485 (Fam).

6.15 In *AB V CB (Financial Remedy: Variation of Trust)*[1] the facts were that in 2005 the parties moved into a farmhouse owned by the husband's parents. In 2009 a trust was established in relation to the farmhouse. The principal beneficiary was the husband and the main discretionary beneficiaries were the parties' children. The wife obtained a financial remedy order but the trustees applied for permission to appeal. Mostyn J reserved the matter to himself and found that although the wife had not seen the trust deed prior to execution, she knew that it was intended that it would stay in the family and after it had been used by them, it would revert back to the family estate.

[1]   [2014] EWHC 2998 (Fam).

6.16 The trustees argued that the trust was not a nuptial settlement. Mostyn J concluded that it was a nuptial settlement as it satisfied the test proposed by Lord Nicholls in *Brooks v Brooks*; the trust was '[an] arrangement which makes some form of continuing provision for both or either of the parties to [the] marriage'. He also dismissed the trustees' submission that the only nuptial element which was capable of variation by the court under s 24(1)(c) of the MCA 1973 was the husband's right to occupy. However, the trust included a clause that gave the trustees specific powers to advance all of the property to the husband during his lifetime, thus all of the property contained within the trust was regarded as a variable nuptial settlement.

6.17 The judge held that the wife was to receive £23,000 from the trust outright (the value of her contributions), and an additional award of £134,000 on the terms of a life tenancy. The additional element was designed to reflect the sharing principle in relation to the matrimonial home while, at the same time, recognising the existence and purpose of the trust. The total award to the wife (£157,000) corresponded to half the net value of the farmhouse. This decision was appealed by the trustees sub nom *P v P (Variation of Post-Nuptial Settlement)*[1]. The appeal was dismissed and the approach of Mostyn J upheld.

[1]   [2015] EWCA Civ 447.

6.18 For the issue of when a trust was in contemplation of marriage and whether a non-nuptial settlement may become nuptialised later see *Joy v Joy-Morancho and Others (No 3)*[1] and *K v K (Ancillary Relief: Deed of Appointment)*[2].

[1]   [2015] EWHC 2507 (Fam).
[2]   [2007] EWHC 3485 (Fam).

6.19 For examples of the court finding that there were ante-nuptial settlements see *N v N and F Trust*[1] and *NR v AB*[2].

[1]   [2005] EWHC 2908 (Fam).
[2]   [2016] EWHC 277 (Fam).

6.20 The powers of the court to vary the settlement are wide:

- the capital or income can be given to either party or to the[1] children;
- the interest of a party under the settlement can be extinguished;
- the settlement may be terminated; the property contained in the settlement may be resettled[2].

[1]   See eg *E v E* [1990] 2 FLR 233; *Jump v Jump* [1883] 8 PD 159.
[2]   *Bacon v Bacon* [1947] P 151.

6.21 When the property contained in the settlement is the matrimonial home, the various options adopted in transfer of property orders may be employed. The court has the power to require separate representation of children where there may be a conflict of interest[1], and other third parties must be given the right to be heard[2]. It has been held that, on an application under this section the court has power to remove a trustee[3].

[1]   FPR 9.11.
[2]   FPR 9.13.
[3]   *E v E (Financial Provision)* [1990] 2 FLR 233, per Ewbank J; for a different, albeit older, view, see *Compton v Compton and Hussey* [1960] P 201.

6.22 In the older cases it was held that the court would not interfere with the terms of a settlement more than was necessary to do justice between the parties[1]. Clearly, today the court has wide powers of redistribution, and is more prepared to intervene in the parties' affairs than was once the case. Nevertheless, in a 1989 case[2] dealing with a post-nuptial settlement, Ewbank J said that his first consideration was the welfare of the children and the second consideration was that he should not interfere with the settlement more than was necessary for the purposes of the s 25 factors. In another more recent case[3] involving a lump sum (and not variation of settlement), Thorpe J said that the discretionary powers of the court to adjust capital shares between the parties should not be exercised unless there was a manifest need for intervention upon the application of the s 25 criteria; it might be said that this statement of principle echoes the older cases on this subject and is equally valid in this context. As always, these older cases must be re-read in the light of *White v White*[4] and *Miller/McFarlane*[5] and, indeed, now *Radmacher v Granatino*[6].

[1]   See eg *Smith v Smith and Graves* (1887) 12 PD 102; *Ulrich v Ulrich and Felton* [1968] 1 All ER 67; *Egerton v Egerton* [1949] 2 All ER 238, CA.
[2]   *E v E* [1990] 2 FLR 233.
[3]   *H v H (Financial Provision: Capital Allowance)* [1993] 2 FLR 335 at 348.
[4]   [2001] 1 AC 596.
[5]   [2006] 1 FLR 1186.
[6]   [2010] UKSC 42.

6.23 The law on variation of post-nuptial settlements is extensively reviewed in *Ben Hashem v Al Sharif*[1]. Here, it was held that, while the jurisdiction to vary such a settlement under s 24(1)(c) of MCA 1973 is unfettered and, in theory, unlimited, a settlement should not be interfered with more than is necessary to do justice between the parties.

[1]   [2008] EWHC 2380 (Fam).

Chapter 7

ORDERS FOR SALE

INTRODUCTION

7.1 The effect of a financial remedy order is frequently that property must be sold. This may happen as a direct result of the order, for example if the former matrimonial home is to be sold, or perhaps when some asset has to be sold to provide a lump sum for one of the parties. This chapter will consider briefly the types of order for sale which may be made and the law and practice involved.

ORDER FOR SALE UNDER SECTION 24A OF MCA 1973

7.2 Statutory power of sale is provided by s 24A which provides that[1]:

'(1)   Where the court makes under section 23 or 24 of this Act a secured periodical payments order, an order for the payment of a lump sum or a property adjustment order, then, on making that order or at any time thereafter, the court may make a further order for the sale of such property as may be specified in the order, being property in which or in the proceeds of sale of which either or both of the parties to the marriage has or have a beneficial interest, either in possession or reversion.'

[1]   MCA 1973, s 24A(1).

7.3 This power of sale is, therefore, ancillary to the principal capital order which has been made, and is only exercisable if such an order has been made[1]. (Although an order under s 24A cannot be made prior to the making of a financial provision or property adjustment order, in exceptional circumstances an order can be made under Pt IV FLA 1996 by the termination of one party's home rights under s 33(3)(e) FLA and order for sale under FPR 20.2(1)(c)(v). See *BR v VT (Financial Remedies: Interim Order for Sale)*[2] per Mostyn J.) However, in *WS v HS (Sale of Matrimonial Home)*[3] Cobb J disagreed and held that an order for sale can only be made on or after the making of a financial remedies order.

[1]   *Thompson v Thompson* [1986] Fam 38.
[2]   [2015] EWHC 2727 (Fam).
[3]   [2018] EWFC 11.

7.4 An order for a lump sum, property adjustment or secured provision takes effect only on decree absolute, so no order could be made under this section to take effect before that time[1]. Subject to that proviso, the order may be made either at the same time as making the principle order or at any time thereafter;

however, it must be the case that the court could not make such an order if the principal order had been complied with.

[1]   MCA 1973, s 24A(3).

7.5 The order may contain a provision that it shall not take effect until the occurrence of an event specified by the order or the expiration of a period so specified. The court has, therefore, considerable discretion as to the terms which it imposes.

7.6 In *TJB v RJB (Financial Order: Declaration)*[1] Holman J made it clear per curiam that a court in England and Wales may make an order for sale under s 24A MCA to give effect to a financial remedies order without this being spelled out in the order itself and regardless of the location of the property.

[1]   [2016] EWHC 1171 (Fam).

7.7 Section 24A also contains further provisions ancillary to the power to order sale. It is provided that any order for sale may contain such consequential or supplementary provisions as the court thinks fit and, without prejudice to the generality of those provisions, may include[1]:

'(a)   provision requiring the making of a payment out of the proceeds of sale of the property to which the order relates, and
(b)   provision requiring any such property to be offered for sale to a person or class of persons specified in the order.'

[1]   MCA 1973, s 24A(2).

7.8 The order could, therefore, for example, require the sale of a property owned by the respondent, and the payment of a lump sum from the proceeds of sale with the balance to be paid to the respondent; or the sale of a jointly owned former matrimonial home, with a requirement that one of the parties to the marriage and his or her cohabitant be entitled to bid. It is not uncommon for such orders to provide that the property be sold for the best offer received in excess of a certain figure.

7.9 What the order cannot do is require payments to third parties such as creditors who have no connection with the property or the sale[1] thereof; it would be proper to include an order for payment of estate agents' charges but not for payment of debts owed by the parties.

[1]   *Burton v Burton* [1986] 2 FLR 419.

7.10 When the property in respect of which a sale is sought is owned jointly by one of the parties and a third party, it is provided that[1]:

' . . . before deciding whether to make an order under this section in relation to that property, it shall be the duty of the court to give that other person an opportunity to make representations with respect to the order; and any representations made by that other person shall be included among the circumstances to which the court is required to have regard under section 25(1) . . . '

[1]   MCA 1973, s 24A(6).

7.11 It follows from this that the court must direct service of all relevant proceedings on the third party; procedure for this is considered in more detail in CHAPTER 16. In *Ram v Ram (No 2)*[1] it was held that the court's power under s 24A is limited to property in which either or both of the parties has or have a beneficial interest in possession or reversion. Thus, where a bankruptcy order has been made and the property therefore vested in the trustee, the bankrupt has no beneficial interest even after his discharge.

[1]   [2004] EWCA Civ 1684, [2005] 2 FLR 75.

How is jurisdiction exercised?

7.12 There is no separate set of guidelines applicable to orders under s 24A. An order under this section is an order to which s 25 applies, and the exercise of the court's discretion will be governed by the usual s 25 factors. An order under s 24A may be made if the court considers it necessary to do so to achieve its purpose pursuant to s 25.

Interim orders

7.13 There is no power to make an interim order for sale under s 24A or, indeed, under any other provision. This is considered in more detail at **4.8**.

FPR 2010, rule 9.24

7.14 FPR 9.24(1) provides that, where the court has made an order under MCA 1973, s 24A, the Matrimonial and Family Proceedings Act 1984, s 17(2), or the Civil Partnership Act 2004, Sch 5, Pt 3 or Sch 7, para 9(4), it may order any party to deliver up to the purchaser or any other person possession of the land, including any interest in, or right over, land, receipt of rents or profits relating to it, or both.

7.15 It has been held that RSC Ord 31, r 1 did not permit the court to order an interim sale of a property pending the final resolution of an application for ancillary relief[1].

[1]   *Wicks v Wicks* [1998] 1 FLR 470, CA.

THE TRUSTS OF LAND AND APPOINTMENT OF TRUSTEES ACT 1996

7.16 Under s 30 of the Law of Property Act 1925 (LPA 1925), when property was held on trust for sale (which was always the case when jointly owned) either trustee could apply to the court for an order for sale, which would be granted unless, for example, it could be found that the purposes for which the trust was established (such as the provision of a family home) had not been fulfilled. Section 30 has now been repealed by the Trusts of Land and Appointment of Trustees Act 1996 (TOLATA 1996) and, for the purposes of this chapter, the important part of this statute is s 14 which permits the court to order sale.

7.17 The difference between s 14 and LPA 1925, s 30 is that there is now no presumption as to an order for sale. Instead, the court is directed by s 15 to have regard to various matters such as the intentions of the persons who created the trust, the purposes for which the property is held, the welfare of any minor occupying the property, and the interests of any secured creditor.

7.18 It is unlikely that it will be necessary to make an application under s 14 in the course of an application for financial relief. Nevertheless, the statutory powers exist, and it may be necessary to have them in mind as a fallback position in some situations.

7.19 This was in fact the case in *Miller-Smith v Miller-Smith*[1]. Here it was held that where the court is confronted by an application under TOLATA 1996 between separated spouses it should ask itself whether the issues raised by the application can reasonably be left to be resolved within an application for financial relief following divorce. In the circumstances of this case, where the house was larger than required to meet the wife's needs and it was unlikely that the financial relief proceedings would be determined within another year, the Court of Appeal upheld a decision that the house should be sold.

[1]   [2009] EWCA Civ 1297, [2010] 1 FLR 1402.

7.20 For further discussion in the context of insolvency, see CHAPTER 12.

Chapter 8

AVOIDANCE OF DISPOSITION AND OTHER INJUNCTIONS

INTRODUCTION

8.1 The course of an application for a financial remedy does not always run smoothly. Sometimes, orders are not obeyed, parties are less than frank, and, in extreme cases, there may be a concerted effort to defeat the just entitlement of one of the parties by the other party. The court therefore has to have powers to overcome such stratagems.

8.2 These powers may be summarised as follows:

(a)   the power to prevent or set aside a disposition under s 37 of the MCA 1973;
(b)   a similar power under the inherent jurisdiction of the court;
(c)   the power to grant a freezing injunction;
(d)   the power to grant a search order.

8.3 These powers and remedies will be considered in turn. The first is by far the most common.

APPLICATIONS UNDER SECTION 37 OF MCA 1973 FOR AN AVOIDANCE OF DISPOSITION ORDER

8.4 It is provided that[1]:

'(2)   Where proceedings for financial relief are brought by one person against another, the court may, on the application of the first-mentioned person—
(a)   if it is satisfied that the other party to the proceedings is, with the intention of defeating the claim for financial relief, about to make any disposition or to transfer out of the jurisdiction or otherwise deal with any property, make such order as it thinks fit for restraining the other party from so doing or otherwise for protecting the claim;
(b)   if it is satisfied that the other party has, with that intention, made a reviewable disposition and that if the disposition were set aside financial relief or different financial relief would be granted to the applicant, make an order setting aside the disposition;
(c)   if it is satisfied, in a case where an order has been obtained under any of the provisions mentioned in subsection (1) above by the applicant

against the other party, that the other party has, with that intention, made a reviewable disposition, make an order setting aside the disposition;

and an application for the purposes of paragraph (b) above shall be made in the proceedings for the financial relief in question.'

[1]   MCA 1973, s 37(2).

8.5 Section 37(2) refers to s 37(1) which is a definition section. There, it is provided that, for the purposes of s 37[1]:

' . . . "financial relief" means relief under any of the provisions of sections 22, 23, 24, 24B, 27, 31 (except subsection (6)) and 35 above, and any reference in this section to defeating a person's claim for financial relief is a reference to preventing financial relief from being granted to that person, or to that person for the benefit of a child of the family, or reducing the amount of any financial relief which might be so granted, or frustrating or impeding the enforcement of any order which might be or has been made at his instance under any of those provisions.'

[1]   MCA 1973, s 37(1).

8.6 By FPR 2.3 an order for avoidance of disposition is a financial order. By r 9.3 an avoidance of disposition order means, in addition to orders under MCA 1973, s 37, orders under similar provisions in the statutes relating to financial relief after overseas divorce and dissolution of civil partnerships. Orders after overseas divorce are considered in CHAPTER 15, and this book is not concerned with civil partnerships. Issues arising out of the remedy under s 37 will now be considered in turn.

Two types of remedy

8.7 Section 37 gives the right to apply for two distinct remedies. The first, which is pre-emptive, is the power of the court to prevent a disposition before it has been made. Thus, for example, a spouse who threatened to transfer assets to another person, or to squander some asset, could be ordered not to do so; banks or other financial institutions can be served with copies of any order made which would normally have the result of freezing transactions.

8.8 The second is the power to undo or set aside any disposition which has been made. Where a spouse transfers assets to another with the intention of putting them out of reach of the court, the person to whom the assets were transferred can be ordered to transfer them back so that they may form part of the funds available for distribution between the parties. This provision itself falls into two categories, namely the power to set aside in anticipation of the hearing of an application for a financial remedy, and the power to set aside at or after the hearing. Separate factors obviously govern these two remedies, but there are a number of common factors which will be considered.

The requirement for an application for a financial remedy

8.9 Section 37 is a remedy ancillary to an application for a financial remedy; there cannot be a free-standing s 37 application. Subsection (2) begins by requiring that financial proceedings are brought by one person against another, and there can be no application under s 37 unless this has happened. Where the applicant is a petitioner, or a respondent who has filed an answer, the application for a financial remedy contained in the petition or answer will be deemed sufficient for this purpose, although it would normally be considered right to require a Form A to have been issued; s 37 is a discretionary remedy, and the court would not normally think it right to make an order unless satisfied that the application for financial relief was to proceed.

8.10 The application for financial relief may be filed at court at the same time as the s 37 application. In cases of urgency, the court will accept an undertaking to file the application by a fixed date.

8.11 'Financial relief' is defined by s 37(1) as, in effect, an application for either a financial provision order, a property adjustment order, an order for maintenance pending suit, an order on the ground of neglect to maintain, or a variation order.

Only the applicant can apply

8.12 After reciting the need for an application for financial relief by one person against another, s 37(2) sets out the remedies which may be granted 'on the application of the first mentioned person', ie the applicant for financial relief. A respondent to such an application who had made no prayer for financial relief in an answer would have no right to apply under s 37. This is perhaps a formal hurdle only because all the respondent would have to do would be to file a notice of application, but the point should be noted.

What is a 'disposition'?

8.13 The section provides that 'disposition' does not include provision made by will or codicil, but that it does include any conveyance, assurance or gift of property of any description, whether made by an instrument or otherwise[1]. Apart from this, no attempt is made to define the term, but clearly it includes any act, deed or transaction which has the effect of transferring ownership or possession from one person to another. It has been held to include a legal charge on real property[2]. It has also been held that failure to deal with property, as opposed to a positive dealing, is not a disposition[3]. A notice to quit a periodic tenancy is not a disposition and cannot be set aside under s 37[4].

[1] MCA 1973, s 37(6).
[2] *Whittingham v Whittingham* [1979] Fam 9, CA.
[3] *Crittenden v Crittenden* [1990] 2 FLR 361, CA.
[4] *Newlon Housing Trust v Alsulaimen* [1998] 2 FLR 690, HL.

'With the intention of defeating the claim for financial relief'

8.14 The court must be satisfied that, in the case of a pre-emptive application, the disposition or transfer is to be made, or, in the case of a post-disposition or transfer application, has been made, with the intention of defeating the applicant's claim for financial relief. The onus of proof is on the applicant, and if this burden is not discharged the order cannot be made. However, it has been held that the question which the judge must ask himself is whether he is 'satisfied', and that it is inappropriate to add tests such as 'beyond reasonable doubt' or 'on the balance of probabilities'[1].

[1]   *K v K (Avoidance of Reviewable Disposition)* (1983) 4 FLR 31, CA.

8.15 To some extent, the task of the applicant is made easier by s 37(1) which goes some way to defining 'defeating the claim'. Here, it is said that this means any of the following[1]:

(a)   preventing (any) financial relief from being granted to the applicant, either for herself or for a child;

(b)   reducing the amount of any financial relief which might otherwise be granted;

(c)   frustrating or impeding the enforcement of any order for financial relief which might be made or which has been made.

The court will therefore have to find that one of these results is more likely than not to happen if an order is not made.

[1]   MCA 1973, s 37(1).

8.16 This leaves the question of proving 'intention'. Where it is found that one of the outcomes set out above is likely to occur, the court would have no difficulty in deducing that the respondent to the application intended that to happen. A person is deemed to intend the normal consequences of his actions, and where, for example, the inevitable result of a transfer of a property to someone else would be that the funds available for distribution between the spouses would be diminished, it would almost inevitably have to be found that the transferor had intended that consequence.

8.17 Different factors might arise where there could be more than one reason for the disposition or transfer, particularly where it could also be said that the funds available for distribution would not be diminished. For example, a person whose livelihood depended on the sale and purchase of assets should not be prevented from trading for no other reason than a pending financial remedy application, and a person involved in any business should not be subjected to unusual and unreasonable restrictions. In the context of marriage breakdown, it is not unusual for the parties to be both deeply suspicious of each other and resentful of any interference with their normal activities. The court has to distinguish these cases from those where there is evidence that some deliberate attempt to defeat the claim is being or has been made[1].

[1]   See *Smith v Smith* (1973) Fam Law 80; the court must be satisfied that a disposition is in fact about to take place, and also that its intention is to defeat the applicant's claim. There is no general power to freeze a party's assets pending the hearing of an application for financial relief.

8.18 In *Mubarak v Mubarik*[1] it was held that s 37 requires an actual intention to defeat a claim to be in existence at the time of the disposition; here, the court could not be satisfied that the husband had made the disposition with the intention of defeating the claim for ancillary relief (as opposed to tax evasion).

[1]   [2007] 2 FLR 364, Holman J.

Special considerations in applications to set aside dispositions

8.19 As has already been mentioned, the power to set aside a disposition is distinct from the power to prevent a disposition. Clearly, once a disposition or transfer has been made, it may be that third parties have acquired rights in the property concerned, and in this situation different considerations arise from those which arise when it is sought to prevent a disposition from taking place. The various relevant factors will now be considered.

Reviewable dispositions

8.20 For a disposition or transfer to be set aside, it has to be 'reviewable'. This term is defined by the section. First, it is provided that[1]:

> '(4) Any disposition made by the other party to the proceedings for financial relief in question (whether before or after the commencement of those proceedings) is a reviewable disposition for the purposes of subsection (2)(b) and (c) above unless it was made for valuable consideration (other than marriage) to a person who, at the time of the disposition, acted in relation to it in good faith and without notice of any intention on the part of the other party to defeat the applicant's claim for financial relief.'

[1]   MCA 1973, s 37(4).

8.21 The significance of this is that it will be presumed that any disposition is reviewable unless the respondent to the application (and the transferee) can establish all the matters mentioned, namely:

(a)   valuable consideration (for this purpose, marriage does not count);
(b)   transferee acting in good[1] faith;
(c)   transferee without any notice of transferor's intention to defeat applicant's claim.

The onus will therefore be on the respondent or transferee to satisfy the court of these matters. This applies to any transfer or disposition which the respondent has made[2].

[1]   See *Whittingham v Whittingham* [1979] Fam 9, CA; at the very least lack of good faith involves lack of honesty, and may require something akin to fraud.
[2]   There is no general rule that anyone acquiring an interest in property from someone he knows to be divorced thereby has notice of an application for financial relief. However, the facts may indicate constructive notice. A bank may be under an obligation to make inquiries, and a lender who knows that an aspirant borrower has been involved in divorce proceedings is obliged to ask him whether his spouse has any potential interest in a property sought to be charged; however, it is under no obligation to verify information given by the borrower unless the spouse is in occupation of the property. See *Whittingham v Whittingham* (above); *B v B (P Ltd Intervening) (No 2)* [1995] 1 FLR 374, CA.

8.22 The limitations of s 37 were demonstrated by the decision in *Ansari v Ansari*[1]. Here, the husband and a third party had conspired to defeat the wife's claim; a house which was owned by the husband was transferred to the third party who then charged it to a bank for a large sum. The bank had notice of the wife's family home rights. The wife's application to set aside the charge failed, on the ground that the husband was not a party to the bank's charge which was therefore not a reviewable disposition made by 'the other party'. It was also held, per curiam, that even if the charge had been a reviewable disposition, the bank would have been able to rely on s 37(4). The fact that the bank had notice of the wife's rights did not mean that it had notice of the husband's intention to defeat the wife's claims.

1   [2008] EWCA Civ 1456.

Presumption of intention to defeat claim in some cases

8.23 The section goes further. It is provided that[1]:

'(5)   Where an application is made under this section with respect to a disposition which took place less than three years before the date of the application or with respect to a disposition or other dealing with property which is about to take place and the court is satisfied –
(a)   in a case falling within subsection (2)(a) or (b) above, that the disposition or other dealing would (apart from this section) have the consequence, or
(b)   in a case falling within subsection (2)(c) above, that the disposition has had the consequence,
of defeating the applicant's claim for financial relief, it shall be presumed, unless the contrary is shown, that the person who disposed of or is about to dispose of or deal with the property did so, or, as the case may be, is about to do so, with the intention of defeating the applicant's claim for financial relief.'

1   MCA 1973, s 37(5).

8.24 This subsection therefore erects a further hurdle which the respondent or transferee must cross. Where the disposition was either less than 3 years before the application, or, in the case of an application to prevent a disposition, has not yet been made, and it is established to the satisfaction of the court that its effect will be to defeat the applicant's claim for financial relief (as defined in s 37(1): see **8.11**) it will be presumed that the intention was or is to defeat the claim for financial relief unless the respondent is able to prove the contrary.

Consequential directions

8.25 When an order is made setting aside a disposition, the court must give consequential directions as it thinks fit for giving effect to the order, including directions requiring the making of any payments or the disposal of any property.

How will the court exercise its discretion?

8.26 Even if the court finds in favour of the applicant on the issues of intention to defeat the claim, etc the position remains that the court 'may' make an order under s 37; the final disposal is subject to the discretion of the court. Clearly, each case will turn on its own facts, and, as always, the factors set out in s 25 apply.

8.27 In deciding whether or not to grant an order under s 37(2)(a) (a pre-emptive order), and assuming that the intention on the part of the respondent had been proved, the court would normally feel obliged to make an order unless it could be demonstrated that the disposition or transfer need not affect the final result because there would be more than enough capital left to provide for any order which the court could conceivably make.

8.28 In deciding whether or not to set aside a disposition, the same consideration will apply, but the court will also have to weigh up the hardship which would be caused to the transferee if the disposition were set aside against the hardship which would be caused to the applicant if it were not set aside.

8.29 In *Joy v Joy*[1] Sir Peter Singer made an order setting aside a charge over a Bentley car given by a husband in favour of his solicitor to secure his costs.

[1]   [2014] EWCA Civ 520.

Foreign property

8.30 It has been held that an order under s 37 can be granted even though the property in question is outside England and Wales[1]. The court might, in the exercise of its discretion, decline to make any order which would be unenforceable, but that would not per se prevent an application being made and an order granted in appropriate cases.

[1]   *Hamlin v Hamlin* [1986] 1 FLR 61, CA.

Procedure

8.31 By FPR 9.6(1) the Part 18 procedure applies to applications for an avoidance of a disposition order. By r 9.6(2) the application may be made without notice to the respondent.

8.32 In *ND v KP (ex parte application)*[1] Mostyn J re-affirmed the principle that an ex parte order is an exceptional remedy and should only be sought where there is good cause and clear evidence. An application for an ex parte order should only be made where there is positive evidence that to give notice would lead to irretrievable prejudice to the applicant. This was in fact a case involving a freezing order, but it is submitted that his Lordship's comments apply to all forms of without notice application.

[1]   [2011] EWHC 457 (Fam).

8.33 Rule 18.2 confirms that an applicant may use the Part 18 procedure where the application is made within existing proceedings. The procedure is set out in rr 18.4–18.12. Briefly, an application must be filed which must set out what order the applicant is seeking and why the order is sought. A draft of the order sought must be attached to the application. Part 17 requires the application notice to be verified by a statement of truth if the applicant intends to rely on the notice as evidence. The applicant seems, therefore, to have the choice of either putting all the supporting evidence in the notice of application and verifying it by a statement of truth, or of filing a separate statement which would also need to be so verified.

8.34 When an order is made without notice, or where the applicant is proceeding on notice, at least 7 days' notice of the hearing or return date as the case may be, must be given.

8.35 Rule 2.62 of the now repealed FPR 1991 provided that where practicable an application for an avoidance of disposition order should be heard at the same time as any related application for ancillary relief. There seems to be no corresponding provision in the 2010 Rules, though the commonsense of the previous provision is clear.

Forms

8.36 For guidance as to forms and precedents please see Lexis Nexis' *Family Law Precedents Service*.

APPLICATIONS FOR AVOIDANCE OF DISPOSITION UNDER THE INHERENT JURISDICTION OF THE COURT

8.37 As has been seen, s 37 contains a series of requirements which the court must find to have been fulfilled before an order under that section may be made. However, there may be occasions when, although the evidence might not support a positive finding under s 37, the justice of the case demands that some injunctive relief be granted. In such circumstances, it has been held that the court is not powerless, since it may invoke its inherent jurisdiction. Whether or not the county court enjoys any inherent jurisdiction may be a matter for debate. Normal practice is that applications invoking the inherent jurisdiction are transferred to the High Court and heard by a judge.

8.38 In *Shipman v Shipman*[1] it was held that, although the requirements of s 37 (including in particular the intention to defeat the wife's claim) could not be met, the court had an inherent jurisdiction to freeze assets which might be put beyond the reach of the applicant; in deciding whether or not to exercise its discretion in favour of the applicant, the court was not bound by the many restrictions and safeguards which must be observed when granting a world-wide freezing injunction (as to which see **8.42** et seq).

[1] [1991] 1 FLR 250, Anthony Lincoln J; see also *Roche v Roche* (1981) Fam Law 243, CA, and *Walker v Walker* (1983) 4 FLR 455.

8.39 Another example of the court's ability to grant an injunction to preserve the status quo is provided by the decision of Thorpe J in *Poon v Poon*[1]. In that case, the parties were directors and shareholders of a family company. Proceedings for ancillary relief were pending, and the wife proposed to remove the husband from his position in the company and replace him with her current boyfriend; she was in a position to do this since other members of her family were also shareholders. Thorpe J said that, pending a final hearing, every effort was made to preserve the status quo. Although the company was a separate entity, it was not an entity in which any other individual or non-family member had any interest; it was unthinkable that the wife should be allowed to proceed to emasculate the husband's interest. Accordingly, an injunction was granted restraining the wife from placing her proposals before the general meeting.

1   [1994] 2 FLR 857.

8.40 However, a word of caution may be in order. The inherent jurisdiction of the court was considered by the Court of Appeal in *Wicks v Wicks*[1], a case which dealt with a different issue, namely the power of the court to order an interim sale of property, and it was held that, for that purpose at least, the court did not have inherent jurisdiction. Ward LJ pointed out that the inherent jurisdiction related to the procedural and not the substantive law:

> 'Under the cloak of ensuring fair play, the judge was in fact making orders affecting the parties' substantive rights, and that must be governed by the general law and rules, not by resort to a wide judicial discretion derived from the court's inherent jurisdiction . . . The reality [in *Wicks*] is that the wife is seeking the enforcement of rights which the Matrimonial Causes Act 1973 does not grant her. She wants an order for sale before s 24A allows the court to order it.'

1   [1998] 1 FLR 470, CA; discussed in more detail at **4.9**.

8.41 It remains to be seen whether these comments as to the inherent jurisdiction will ever be used to overturn the line of authorities referred to in this section, or, indeed, whether it would be held that these injunctions affected the substantive rather than the procedural rights of the parties. For the time being the decisions remain good law, and at least one of them is a decision of the Court of Appeal. However, the possibility of development should not be ignored.

FREEZING INJUNCTIONS

8.42 Freezing injunctions were originally called *Mareva* injunctions after the name of the vessel in the leading case on the subject[1]. Although this was a mercantile case, the principles laid down are applicable to family cases.

1   *Mareva Cia Naviera SA v International Bulkcarriers SA, The Mareva* [1980] 1 All ER 213n, CA.

8.43 The essence of such an injunction is that the respondent to the application is forbidden to remove from the jurisdiction of the court (ie from England and Wales) funds or property until the trial of the action or matter. The onus is on the applicant to show that it is likely that she will recover a capital sum or property at the final hearing and that there is a danger that the court's order may be emasculated by the respondent removing funds out of the court's reach.

8.44 The statutory basis is s 37 of the Senior Courts Act 1981 (SCA 1981). This is applied to the county court by the County Courts Act 1984 (CCA 1984), s 38. The county court, therefore, has jurisdiction in a family matter[1], but under normal circumstances a freezing injunction, particularly where the issues are contested, should be transferred to the High Court[2]. A freezing injunction may be worldwide (ie applying to assets outside the jurisdiction) or limited to assets within the jurisdiction.

See *VS v RE*[3] where Mostyn J criticized a party who had issued an application for a freezing order and an order for sale in the High Court under the mistaken belief that only that High Court had jurisdiction to make such an order. FPR 33.1 makes clear that the rules as to enforcement in Part 33 apply to an application to the High Court or the Family Court to enforce an order made in family proceedings. Cases should be heard in the High Court only in very limited and exceptional circumstances[4].

[1] See MFPA 1984, s 32.
[2] *Practice Direction (Family Business: Distribution of Business)* [1992] 3 All ER 151.
[3] [2018] EWFC 30.
[4] See President's Guidance of 28 February 2018, [2018] Fam Law 440.

8.45 In *UL v BK (Freezing orders: Safeguards: Standard Examples)*[1] Mostyn J summarised the principles and safeguards relevant to freezing injunctions. Standard examples for such orders are appended to the judgment.

(1)   The court has a general power to preserve specific tangible assets which are the subject matter of the claim. Such applications do not necessarily require the same safeguards as a freezing order.

(2)   Where a freezing order capable of covering all the respondent's assets it is essential that all principles and safeguards are applied.

(3)   In applications for freezing orders the applicant must show clear evidence of unjustified dealing with assets giving rise to the conclusion that there is a solid risk of dissipation of the assets to the applicant's prejudice.

(4)   The evidence must set out clear facts and their source/basis.

(5)   Ex parte application must be confined to cases of exceptional urgency. The respondent must be give short, informal notice unless it is essential he is not made aware of the application.

(6)   Ex parte or short notice application impose on the applicant a high duty of candour. Breach of that duty will likely lead to the discharge of the order.

(7)   All the safeguards must be applied on short/no notice applications. The applicant must draw the court's attention to any variation of the safeguards and justify them.

[1] [2013] EWHC 1735 (Fam).

8.46 The law and practice relating to freezing injunctions is clearly both complicated and of a specialist nature, and it is not proposed to say more in detail about it in this book. The rules relating to such applications are contained in Part 20 and essential material is contained in Practice Direction 20A in the FPR.

8.47 For a full and very detailed analysis of the jurisdiction to make freezing orders in connection with financial remedy proceedings see *C v C and another (Freezing Orders: Jurisdiction)*[1].

[1] [2015] EWHC 2795 (Fam).

SEARCH ORDERS

8.48 Similar comments to those contained in the previous paragraph apply to search orders. These orders were originally called *Anton Piller* orders after the eponymous case[1] in which they were first made, were of mercantile or commercial origin, and have been adapted for use in family proceedings[2]. Such orders now have a statutory basis in s 7 of the Civil Procedure Act 1997. The Practice Direction referred to above also governs practice and procedure in these cases.

[1] *Anton Piller KG v Manufacturing Processes Ltd* [1976] Ch 55, [1976] 1 All ER 779, CA.
[2] See *Emanuel v Emanuel* [1982] 2 All ER 342; *Kepa v Kepa* (1983) 4 FLR 515.

8.49 A search order may be granted where it appears that the respondent to the application has in his possession documents or other material relevant to the application for financial relief, that he has not disclosed them, and that there is a real possibility that he may destroy them before an application can be made inter partes. The order is therefore always made ex parte, and its effect is that the applicant or her agent is empowered to enter the respondent's premises and to seize and remove documents or material of the classes specified in the order. By s 7 of the 1997 Act, an order may be made against 'any person'.

8.50 The order is, therefore, extremely drastic and has been described as being 'at the extremity of the court's powers'[1]. Such orders are therefore rarely made, and where it eventually appears that the search was fruitless, severe penalties in costs will be inflicted on the applicant[2]. It remains to be seen whether the decision of Moylan J in *Imerman v Imerman*[3] results in an increase of search applications in respect of allegedly improperly retained documents.

[1] *Anton Piller KG v Manufacturing Processes Ltd* (above), per Ormrod LJ.
[2] As in *Burgess v Burgess* [1996] 2 FLR 34.
[3] [2009] EWHC 3486 (Fam), [2010] 2 FLR 752.

8.51 An application for a search order made in county court proceedings must be transferred to the High Court.

Chapter 9

CONSENT ORDERS

INTRODUCTION

9.1 Not all applications for a financial order result in a final contested hearing. Some applications are agreed from the outset; some become agreed in the course of the proceedings but before the final hearing; and yet more are settled at the doors of the court. The principles applicable to these different classes of case are the same, but there are differences in procedure.

9.2 A consent order is defined by MCA 1973 as 'an order in the terms applied for to which the respondent agrees'[1]; in effect, it is an order which both parties to the application for financial relief ask the court to make without hearing evidence or argument. Before considering the procedural steps necessary for a consent order and the requirements to be observed when drafting such an order, it will be necessary to consider the duty of the court on such occasions, and the general principles applicable to applications for consent orders.

[1]   MCA 1973, s 33A(3).

9.3 The circumstances in which a consent order may be set aside are considered in detail in CHAPTER **18**.

THE DUTY OF THE COURT

9.4 It is a fundamental principle of family law in England and Wales that the rights of the parties are not finally declared until the court has made an order endorsing their agreement; any attempt to oust the jurisdiction of the court is likely to fail, and the parties cannot know that their agreement is final until the court has made an order incorporating its terms[1].

[1]   *Pounds v Pounds* [1994] 1 FLR 775, CA. See also **1.199** as to agreements generally.

9.5 It is a further fundamental principle that the court has a duty to scrutinise and approve whatever agreement is put before it. The position was authoritatively established in *Livesey (formerly Jenkins) v Jenkins*[1], where the position as to consent orders was summarised as follows:

- the jurisdiction of the court to make orders for financial relief is derived entirely from statute, namely MCA 1973;
- the function of the court when making such orders is exactly the same when the application is by consent as when the hearing is contested;

- s 25 of MCA 1973 prescribes a list of matters to which the court is required to have regard;
- it follows that the court must consider the merits of any consent application in the light of the s 25 factors, and only make the order if it appears to be just and reasonable.

Livesey v Jenkins was specifically approved by Lord Wilson in *Vince v Wyatt*[2].

[1]   [1985] AC 424, HL.
[2]   [2015] UKSC 14.

9.6 The position was well set out in a later case[1], where it was said that in consent applications for financial relief:

> ' . . . the court does not act, it has been said, as a rubber stamp. The judge will be concerned, whether the order be made by consent or imposed after argument, to be satisfied that the criteria of ss 25 and 25A of the Matrimonial Causes Act 1973 have been duly applied.'

[1]   *Pounds v Pounds* [1994] 1 FLR 775, CA.

9.7 Having said that, it should also be said that the function of the court is not to scrutinise the agreed terms and evidence in the same way as it would on a defended hearing[1]. It is submitted that the court's role is limited to satisfying itself that the proposed order is within the band of reasonable discretion and that it does not, on the face of it, offend any obvious principle. For a case where there was a dispute as to whether an agreement had been made at all, see *Xydhias v Xydhias*[2] discussed at **1.236**.

[1]   *Pounds v Pounds* [1994] 1 FLR 775, CA.
[2]   [1999] 1 FLR 683, CA.

9.8 It follows from what has been said that the court cannot perform its statutory functions unless it has the information and material on which to base its assessment. When the question of setting aside consent orders is considered in CHAPTER **18**, the importance of full and frank disclosure will become apparent; this was one of the major issues in *Livesey v Jenkins*. Another important result of that case was that it became necessary to establish procedures to give the court the required information when it was considering a consent application, and this will now be considered.

INFORMATION REQUIRED BY THE COURT

9.9 After some uncertainty following *Livesey v Jenkins* as to what would be required by the court in order to carry out its investigations, statutory authority was provided by s 33A of MCA 1973. This provides that[1]:

> ' . . . on an application for a consent order for financial relief the court may, unless it has reason to think that there are other circumstances into which it ought to inquire, make an order in the terms agreed on the basis only of the prescribed information furnished with the application.'

'Prescribed' means prescribed by rules of court, and these are to be found in FPR 9.26.

[1]   MCA 1973, s 33A(1).

9.10 This provides that the applicant must file two copies of a draft of the order in the terms sought, one of which must be endorsed with a statement signed by the respondent to the application signifying agreement. Further, each party must file with the court and serve on the other party, a statement of information in the form referred to in Practice Direction 5A. Where each party's statement of information is contained in one form, it must be signed by both the applicant and respondent to certify that they have read the contents of the other party's statement. Where each party's statement of information is in a separate form, the form of each party must be signed by the other party to certify that they have read the contents of the statement contained in that form.

9.11 Practice Direction 5A requires the statements of information to contain the following:

'(a) the duration of the marriage, the age of each party and of any minor or dependent child of the family;

(b) an estimate in summary form of the approximate amount of value of the capital resources and net income of each party and of any minor child of the family;

(c) what arrangements are intended for the accommodation of each of the parties and any minor child of the family;

(d) whether either party has remarried or has any present intention to marry or to cohabit with another person;

(dd) where the order includes provision to be made under s 24B, 25B or 25C of the Act of 1973, a statement confirming that the person responsible for the pension arrangement in question has been served with the documents required by rule 2.70(11) and that no objection to such an order has been made by that person within 14 days from such service;

(e) where the terms of the order provide for a transfer of property, a statement confirming that any mortgagee of the property has been served with notice of the application and that no objection to such a transfer has been made by the mortgagee within 14 days from such service; and

(f) any other especially significant matters.'

9.12 Unless the court directs otherwise, the applicant and the respondent need not attend the hearing of an application for a consent order. Normally, the district judge would only require parties to attend where, on the face of it, the order seemed unfair or something needed to be explained.

EXCEPTIONS TO THE GENERAL RULE

9.13 Sometimes a consent order is requested at a hearing where the parties have come to an agreement. In such circumstances, by FPR 9.26(5) the court may dispense with the filing of the statements of information and give directions for the information which would otherwise be required to be given in such a statement in such a manner as it thinks fit. Normally, where the parties had filed Form E and counsel or solicitors had filed a case outline, no further documentation should be required.

9.14 It is important to make the point that there are no other circumstances in which the statements may be dispensed with. It cannot be emphasised too strongly that:

(i)   Form D81 must be completed as at the date of the form – i.e. before implementation of the proposed order.

(ii)   Form D81 cannot be waived because 'forms E have been filed' or 'we discussed something along these lines with the DJ at the hearing, who nodded'. D81 is mandatory under FPR 9.26(1)(b) and is essential to confirm the application has been served on any relevant third parties, the court has power to make the orders sought and there is a record of disclosure.

(iii)   It would save much time for all concerned if those submitting orders briefly explained the net effect of the order and any reasons behind it in either box 9 of the form or a covering letter.

9.15 A diversion from the established practice was approved by Coleridge J in *S v P*[1]. His Lordship directed that draft consent orders approved by the collaborative law process could be approved in the Urgent Ex Parte Applications List without it being necessary to go through the normal procedure. This procedure could only be used where every aspect of the documentation was agreed, the hearing was not more than 10 minutes, and the documentation was lodged with the judge the night before. It was emphasised that this procedure would be kept under review and the implication is that it must not be allowed to get out of hand.

[1]   [2008] 2 FLR 2040.

NOTES ON DRAFTING CONSENT ORDERS

9.16 It is clearly important that all orders should be correctly drafted. This is particularly important in the case of consent orders. In the first place, the drafting of the order is in the hands of the parties' advisers, who therefore assume responsibility for the order and any defects in it. In the second place, in most cases of a consent order, the application is considered by the court in the absence of the parties, and any matter which requires amendment or further inquiry by the court results in delay and, probably, additional cost for the lay client[1]. The following paragraphs include common causes of query by the court.

[1]   For an example of the problems which can be caused by lack of care in a drafting order, see *McGladdery v McGladdery* [1999] 2 FLR 1102.

The distinction between matters which may be ordered and those which may not

9.17 In *Livesey v Jenkins* it was pointed out that the powers of the court in respect of financial relief are entirely statutory; if the power to make a certain order cannot be identified in MCA 1973, that order cannot be made[1]:

> 'When a consent order is drafted it is essential that all its terms should come clearly within the court's powers conferred on it by sections 23 and 24 of the Act of 1973.'

However, it should not be thought that the powers of the court are exclusively limited to those orders contained in MCA 1973 Pt II. As was pointed out by Mostyn J in *CH v WH (Power to Order Indemnity)*[2], under s 31E(1)(a) of the

MFPA 1984 the Family Court may make any order which could have been made by the High Court if the proceedings were in the High Court; the High Court has power, as part of its equitable jurisdiction, to order an indemnity. If awarded, that represents a legal right in favour of the person so indemnified, and the court can award an injunction in support of a legal right. To order someone who has been ordered to indemnify the other party in respect of a mortgage to use his or her best endeavours to keep up the mortgage payments is in the nature of an injunction in support of a legal right and can therefore be ordered by the Family Court.

1   *Livesey v Jenkins* [1984] AC 424, HL, per Lord Brandon.
2   2 [2017] EWHC 2379 (Fam)..

9.18 Having said that, frequently there are matters of fact which the parties wish to have recorded, or agreements which are essential to the proper performance of the overall arrangement which the parties have made which cannot be brought within the terms of the statute but which, nevertheless, should appear in the order. One of the most common reasons for rejection of a consent order is a failure on the part of the draftsman to recognise the difference between the various parts of the order.

9.19 The distinction which must be made is between recitals of fact, recitals of agreement, undertakings, and orders. These will be considered in turn.

Recitals of fact

9.20 Most of the important factual matters, such as the declared means of the parties, will have been set out in the form filed with the court, so it should not normally be necessary to recite detailed facts in the preamble to the order itself. Nevertheless, there are certain matters which it may be thought helpful for the court to have on the face of the order (eg that the former matrimonial home has been sold and the proceeds divided in certain proportions). There may also be important matters which have been in dispute, and which the party agreeing to compromise wishes to have placed on record unambiguously, so that if it later appeared that any such recited matter was not true it would be easier for that party to establish that he or she was misled.

The court has jurisdiction to entertain applications to be released from an undertaking and, where appropriate, to substitute a new undertaking. The merits of any such application would normally be considered under the principles of s 31(7) MCA 1973. See further under Variation at **13.21** et seq, post.

Recitals of agreement

9.21 An agreement should be recited in the preamble to the order if it is an integral part of the overall settlement between the parties, but is not a matter which could properly be worded as an undertaking (as to which, see below). This might be the case, for example, where one party agreed that the other should be given the proceeds of a sale, or be allowed to occupy premises until sale. It would also be the case where one party agreed to indemnify the other in respect of liability under a contract. In the event of a breach of any such agreement, the remedy of the aggrieved party would be to institute separate proceedings for breach of contract rather than trying to enforce the order in the preamble to which the agreement was recited.

9.22 Another useful recital in an agreement (or of the existence of an agreement) would arise when the parties had made a written agreement for the support of a child pursuant to s 8(5) of CSA 1991[1].

[1] See also the Child Maintenance (Written Agreements) Order 1993, SI 1993/620; but note **11.11**.

9.23 In *T v R (Maintenance after Remarriage: Agreement)*[1] a recital in a consent order was construed by the court as constituting a maintenance agreement within s 34 MCA 1973.

[1] [2016] EWFC 26.

Undertakings

9.24 The difference between an agreement and an undertaking is that in the case of an undertaking the person giving the undertaking is making a promise to the court and not to the other party[1]. The expectation is therefore that the court would be able to punish any breach of undertaking, for example by committal to prison.

[1] Though, for the sake of completeness, it may be wise for the undertaking to be expressed as being to the court and to the other party.

9.25 In *Livesey v Jenkins*, Lord Brandon drew the distinction between obligations which could be the subject of an order of the court and those which could not, pointed out that the latter should be drawn as undertakings, and observed that 'such undertakings are, needless to say, enforceable as effectively as direct order'[1]. This statement clearly has the unanimous authority of the highest court and must be taken to be correct. Nevertheless, the position is not entirely free from doubt, and it may be that not all undertakings are as easily enforceable as has been suggested.

[1] [1984] AC 424, HL.

9.26 Until the decision of the Court of Appeal in *Mubarak v Mubarak*[1], there was no doubt that an undertaking by one party to pay money to the other party is capable of being enforced by judgment summons[2].

[1] [2001] 1 FLR 698.
[2] *Symmons v Symmons* [1993] 1 FLR 317.

9.27 In an effort to resolve the debates which have raged as to the enforcement of undertakings, Practice Direction 33A now contains detailed guidance. It is provided that any undertaking for the payment of money that has effect as if it was an order made under MCA 1973, Pt 2 may be enforced as if it was an order and Pt 33 applies accordingly.

9.28 The form of any such undertaking must be endorsed with a notice setting out the consequences of disobedience, as follows:

'If you fail to pay any sum of money which you have promised the court that you would pay, a person entitled to enforce the undertaking may apply to the court for an order. If it is proved that you have had the means to pay the sum but you have refused or neglected to pay that sum, you may be sent to prison.'

9.29 The person giving the undertaking must make a signed statement to the effect that he or she understands the terms of the undertaking being given and the consequences of failure to comply with it, as follows:

'I understand the undertaking that I have given, and that if I break my promise to the court to pay any sum of money, I may be sent to prison.'

9.30 The statement need not be given before the court in person (this would obviously be impracticable in the case of consent orders). It may be endorsed on the court copy of the undertaking or may be filed in a separate document such as a letter.

Dismissal of claims and clean break orders

9.31 This is mentioned only for the purpose of underlining what was said on the subject of the clean break in CHAPTER 2. The justification for a clean break is one of the most common reasons for inquiry and delay in the making of consent orders. The court must ask itself in every case whether, if the case were being considered on a contested basis, the claims of the parties would be dismissed. In CHAPTER 2 at **2.70** et seq, it is suggested that it may be that the Court of Appeal, by its dicta in recent decisions, has reminded courts that a clean break should certainly not be imposed as a matter of course, and only after careful consideration to ensure that the statutory criteria are met.

Some common faults

9.32 Most of the possible pitfalls have been suggested above. However, care should also be taken to ensure that all dates for the commencement of certain actions, and all matters of detail such as mortgage accounts or insurance policies are inserted; if there are blank spaces left in a form of order this will cause delay. It is important that the prescribed statement of information should be completed in full. While not, strictly speaking, a fault, one matter which is frequently not provided for is interest on any overdue sum ordered to be paid. It would avoid doubt if this were always included.

9.33 For the complications which may arise from poor drafting of an order involving foreign property see *BG v BA (Deceased)*[1]. For an example of a reminder of the need for care in drafting consent orders see *Besharova v Berezovsky*[2].

[1]   [2015] EWHC 3947 (Fam).
[2]   [2016] EWCA Civ 161.

FORMS

9.34 A full range of standard financial and enforcement orders, is available as a zip file on the judiciary website (www.judiciary.gov.uk/publications/practice

-guidance-standard-financial-and-enforcement-orders) and, for a modest sub-scription, as an online drafting tool from http://www.familyorders.co.uk, supported by a handbook (*Standard Family Orders Handbook: Volume One* by HHJ Edward Hess, Class Legal, 2018).

Chapter 10
PENSIONS

INTRODUCTION

10.1 After the matrimonial home, a pension fund is often the most substantial investment a family will hold. Pensions may confer the right to a lump sum on retirement, the right to an income stream for life, and the right to substantial benefits payable to dependents on death before or during retirement. Following the enactment of the new pension 'freedoms' in the Taxation of Pensions Act 2014, they may also open up access to a source of potentially significant liquid capital for those over 55.

10.2 There has long been concern that pensions are the Cinderella asset in divorce proceedings: overlooked and treated badly. Many divorcing couples have avoided proper scrutiny of pensions, perhaps keen to focus on more immediate worries as to income and housing, perhaps put off by the perceived complexity of the topic[1]. Where pensions have been considered, there has been concern that a too simplistic approach is sometimes adopted, focussing on uninterrogated cash equivalent valuations and the offsetting of pension claims against other assets. Poor advice about pensions on divorce has been a fruitful area for professional negligence claims against lawyers in recent years. There have also been criticisms that different courts were taking an inconsistent approach to pension issues, and that a lack of agreed standards was leading to varied approaches amongst experts instructed to advise.

[1] Of 369 court files studied by the Pension Action Group, 80% revealed at least one relevant pension, but only 14% contained a pension order.

10.3 These concerns led to the formation in June 2017 of the Pension Advisory Group (PAG), a multi-disciplinary group of lawyers, judges, actuaries and financial advisers, with the aim of improving understanding of pension issues on divorce and enabling more consistent and fairer outcomes. In July 2019 the PAG published its report 'A Guide to the Treatment of Pensions on Divorce'. This is required reading for all those seeking to understand and proffer advice in this area of the law. The report has the endorsement of the President of the Family Division. It has been quoted in reported appellate decisions[1]. In *W v H*[2] HHJ Hess, a co-chair of the PAG (with Francis J) commented that the report should "be treated as being prima facie persuasive in the areas it has analysed, although of course susceptible to judicial oversight and criticism". In January 2021 a further document has been published: 'A Survival Guide to Pensions on Divorce', written for the lay reader by Law for

Life with help from PAG. This accessible guide has been endorsed by the President of the Family Division and the Family Justice Council.

1   See the decisions of HHJ Robinson on appeal from the District Bench in *KM v CV* [2020] EWFC B22 and *RH v SV* [2020] EWFC B23.
2   *W v H* [2020] EWFC B10 at para 59.

10.4 Just as with any other assets on divorce, pensions are dealt with by applying the principles of sharing and needs and the factors in MCA 1973, s 25, to achieve a fair outcome. The combined effect of ss 25(2)(a) and 25(B)(1)(a) is that pensions must be considered as a financial resource, even if the pension benefits will not be received for many years to come. Under ss 25(2)(h) and 25(B)(1)(b), the value of benefits to be lost on divorce, namely widow/widower benefits on death, must also be considered.

What is a pension: income or capital?

10.5 A pension already in payment is to be treated as a current income stream, albeit derived not from future endeavour but from past efforts, whether during or before the marriage[1]. How should a divorcing couple treat a pension that is not already in payment, and may not be accessible to them for many years to come? Is it to be viewed as income, albeit deferred? Or should it be viewed as a capital asset, albeit illiquid? The answer to this question will depend on the facts of each case. If the parties are likely to draw lump sums from the pension (whether because a lump sum is payable as of right or because they are commuting part of the potential income stream to a tax-free lump sum or using the new pension freedoms) then this will be treated as capital. If the pension fund, or part of it, is to be used to fund income in retirement (whether by purchasing an annuity or by some form of income drawdown) it is usually treated as deferred income, even though a cash equivalent value will be ascribed to the fund and will look temptingly like a pot of cash at the bottom of the asset schedule. In many cases, pension assets will be intended to fund *both* a lump sum or sums in retirement *and* an income stream. The court will want to ensure that the overarching treatment of the pension assets is fair, whatever form it takes.

1   Per Thorpe LJ in *Martin-Dye v Martin-Dye* [2006] EWCA Civ 681, [2006] 2 FLR 901 para 48: 'a pension in payment is no more than a whole life income stream . . . it cannot be sold, commuted for cash or offered as security for borrowings. It has no capacity for capital appreciation' and para 65 'a pension sharing order should have been adopted'.

HOW DID WE GET TO WHERE WE ARE NOW? A SHORT HISTORY OF PENSIONS ON DIVORCE

10.6 Until 1996, the courts had no specific powers to deal with pension assets on family breakdown. If the divorcing spouses were still relatively young, accrued pensions were often ignored altogether, as being assets that would not be available to either party 'in the foreseeable future'. Where the pension would be available to one spouse within the next few years, the court might make a deferred lump sum order, to take effect provided the non-pensioned spouse survived until the pension award was made. Pensions in payment could be used to fund periodical payments, or maintenance awards could be varied when the time came, to take into account pension income upon retirement. The estimated value of pension assets could also be offset against other capital assets to be retained by the non-pensioned spouse.

10.7 For divorce petitions filed on or after 1 July 1996, the Pensions Act 1995 introduced pension attachment orders, formerly known as 'earmarking'. These powers are found in MCA 1973, ss 25B–25D. For the first time, orders to share pension benefits could be made directly against pension trustees in divorce, nullity and judicial separation proceedings. Attachment orders are not a separate form of financial provision order. They are orders for periodical payments and lump sums against benefits held by the pension scheme member. They provide for a proportion of spouse A's pension payments (lump sum and/or income) to be paid directly to (former) spouse B by the pension provider at the time of payment. Whilst the introduction of pension attachment marked a significant step forward in the fair treatment of pensions on family breakdown, the orders have some manifest disadvantages, most notably the extinguishing of benefits on spouse A's death, notwithstanding that spouse B may still have years to live and be reliant on the payments.

10.8 The Welfare Reform and Pensions Act 1999 introduced pension sharing on divorce or nullity for petitions filed on or after 1 December 2000. For the first time, spouses at the end of a marriage (but not on judicial separation) could seek the transfer of pension assets into pension funds held in their own names and under their own control, often as part of a clean break. The court's powers to order a pension share are found in MCA 1973, ss 21A and 24B–24D.

10.9 The Taxation of Pensions Act 2014, effective from 6 April 2015, provides for a much greater degree of flexibility in the way pension capital can be accessed by individuals reaching the minimum pension age, currently 55. Subject to paying the appropriate levels of tax (which can be high), many (but not all) pension funds can now be accessed by way of uncapped income drawdown or encashment of all or part of the fund as a lump sum.

10.10 The long and still evolving history of legislation affecting pensions on divorce can still set traps for the unwary. Bear in mind the following points:

(i)   On those rare occasions when an application for financial relief on divorce has been much delayed (for example *Wyatt v Vince*)[1], pension sharing or attachment orders may not be available, if the petition was filed before the law changed.

(ii)   The power to make a pension sharing order under MCA 1973, s 31(7B)(ba) on an application to vary a longstanding periodical payments order is not available for those cases where the petition was filed before 1 December 2000.

(iii)   When pension attachment and pension sharing were designed, the new pension freedoms were not contemplated. Since the introduction of the freedoms in 2015, they may be used by less scrupulous spouses to access and dissipate pension funds before appropriate pension sharing orders can be implemented. Existing attachment orders may also be vulnerable to fund dissipation. Applications under MCA 1973, s 37 to prevent transfers out of the pension fund, or appropriate undertakings in the alternative, may have to be considered.

[1] *Wyatt v Vince* [2015] UKSC 14.

THE ORDERS AVAILABLE TO THE COURT

10.11 The ways in which a pension may now be dealt with by the court on marriage breakdown can be summarised as follows:

(i)   As a general resource to be offset against other assets, under MCA 1973, ss 25 and 25B.
(ii) By way of an attachment of a lump sum and/or pension income, under MCA 1973, ss 25B–25D.
(iii) By way of a pension sharing order (PSO), under MCA 1973, ss 21A and 24B–24D.

A combination of these options can be used if appropriate. The options will be considered in detail in later sections of this chapter.

TYPES OF PENSION

10.12 For our purposes, the bewildering array of different non-state pension types can be divided into two broad categories: defined benefit schemes and defined contribution schemes.

(i)   In a *defined benefit* scheme, the beneficiary receives a pension on retirement calculated by reference to a formula based on their salary and the number of years' service they have accrued. These schemes are common in the public sector and in many substantial companies. The benefits are predictable and are not dependent on market fluctuations. A lump sum may be payable as of right, or by commuting a part of the pension income.
(ii) *Defined contribution* schemes, by contrast, invest the pension contributions, to create a fund to be accessed on retirement. The amount of benefits payable in retirement will depend on the level of contributions and the performance of the investments and therefore the size of the fund. Until the 2014 pension freedoms were introduced, in general no more than 25% of the value of the fund could be accessed as a (tax-free) lump sum. The balance of the fund was commonly used to buy an annuity (an insurance-based income received on a regular basis, usually for life). Compulsory purchase of an annuity was abolished in 2011 and since 2015 the ways of accessing the fund have been considerably relaxed, to allow the withdrawal of uncapped income and/or capital, subject to paying the appropriate rate of tax.

10.13 Public service pensions are defined benefit schemes. They are unfunded schemes, paid out of current taxation and are approved by Parliament. Self-contained schemes exist for civil servants, the judiciary, local government employees, armed forces personnel, teachers, NHS staff, policemen, firefighters and MPs. This list is by no means exhaustive. Long serving staff will often have accrued benefits in more than one scheme, as successive governments have responded to rising life expectancies by introducing new, and usually less generous, provisions. Armed Forces personnel, for example, may have joined the AFPS 05 (or even the AFPS 75 – closed to new members on 5 April 2005). Personnel aged 47 and under on 1 April 2015 were transferred to AFPS 15.

10.14 Many large employers in the private sector also run defined benefit schemes, approved by HMRC. Increasingly, where these still exist, benefits are calculated on a career-average salary, rather than a final salary. Some of these schemes are currently underfunded, in that the investments in the scheme are unlikely to be sufficient to pay the promised pensions in retirement to all the scheme members. This is considered further in the section below on instructing experts (at **10.34**(iv)).

10.15 'Occupational', or 'work-based' money purchase schemes are defined contribution schemes set up by employers, into which both employer and employee make regular contributions. They are a type of personal pension, in that the employee has an account with a financial institution providing the pension. The benefits depend on the performance of the investments. For employers, these schemes are cheaper and less risky than defined benefit schemes. The employer makes no guarantees as to the level of pension to be received, but simply makes payments into the scheme on a regular basis and channels the employee's contribution through payroll deductions. Some schemes offered by employers are 'stakeholder' pensions, meaning that they meet minimum standards set by the government, with low and flexible minimum contributions, capped charges and a default investment strategy for those who do not wish to choose a strategy themselves. Auto enrolment requires all employers to enrol their employees (currently aged between 22–66 and earning over £10,000) into a pension scheme, unless the employee specifically opts out. Small self-administered pension schemes (SSAS) are another type of occupational money purchase scheme typically set up for key employees or directors of private companies, usually with a maximum of 11 members.

10.16 Personal pensions can simply be set up by an individual as a defined contribution scheme. Contributions are then made by the individual to the pension company from net income and the tax already paid is reclaimed and also invested. Stakeholder pensions are available, for those who want to take a low-cost, straightforward approach. At the other end of the scale, for those who seek maximum control over their personal pension plan investments, SIPPS (self-invested personal pensions) allow the holder to make their own unique investment decisions using a full range of investments approved by HMRC.

State pensions

10.17 State pensions should not be overlooked. There are two discrete systems to consider: the New State Pension (for those reaching retirement age on or after 6 April 2016) and the Old State Pension (for those reaching retirement age before 6 April 2016).

10.18 The Old State Pension is a tiered pension scheme, comprising the Basic State Pension and, potentially, the Additional State Pension. The Basic State Pension is based upon an individual's National Insurance contributions. The Additional State Pension is an earnings-related component of the state pension, comprising the State Earnings Related Pension Scheme (SERPS) from 1978 to 2002 and the State Second Pension (S2P) from 2002 to 2016. Many people with occupational or private pension schemes 'contracted-out' of the Additional State Pension in favour of accruing benefits within their private pension instead. There is a third tier within the Old State Pension for those who accrued state pension benefits before 1975, namely the Graduated Retirement Benefit, but the extra pension payable is usually modest, in the sum of a few pounds per week.

10.19 The New State Pension is a single-tier system based on National Insurance contributions. Those with a 35-year qualifying NI record will receive the full amount, £175.20 per week in 2020/21. For those individuals with a higher state pension entitlement under the Old State Pension than the maximum New State Pension (calculated as at 6 April 2016), the difference is known as the Protected Payment, and will be paid in addition to the New State Pension sum.

10.20 The State Pension Credit (not to be confused with a pension credit on divorce under a PSO) is an income-related welfare benefit for those whose retirement income does not reach minimum levels (£173.75 for a single person and £265.20 for a couple in 2020/21).

VALUATION

10.21 The valuation methodology prescribed by the regulations for use in divorce proceedings is the cash equivalent (CE)[1]. The same methodology is used both for pensions in payment and pensions not yet in payment (a change effected in 2008, when the terms cash equivalent of benefits – for pensions in payment – and cash equivalent transfer value were abandoned in favour of the unified CE). The CE is simply the sum for which one pension arrangement will transfer a pension liability to an alternative pension arrangement to extinguish their liability to the pension holder. It takes the value of the pension rights in today's terms on the basis that the member left service at the time the valuation request was received. The CE does not therefore include any valuation of expectations based on future service and future salary increases. It also does not include any benefits payable on death in service.

[1] Pensions on Divorce etc (Provision of Information) Regulations 2000, SI 2000/1048, reg 3 and the Divorce etc (Pensions) Regulations 2000, SI 2000/1123, reg 3.

10.22 The CE can be thought of as having two roles in valuing pensions on divorce. It is a *starting point* for *valuing* the benefits in the pension. It is also the *end point* for *implementation* of a pension sharing order: all pension sharing orders must be expressed as a percentage of the CE[1].

[1] MCA 1973, s 21A(1)(b) and *H v H (Financial Relief: Pensions)* [2010] 2 FLR 173, affirmed in *Finch v Baker* [2021] EWCA Civ 72 at para 31.

10.23 The CE will usually be specified on the annual pension benefits statement supplied by the scheme trustees to the scheme member. If this is not to hand, or a more up-to-date figure is required, the member can request (or the court can order) a CE valuation. A charge will not be made for this, unless more than one request is made within 12 months, or the member has reached or is about to reach retirement age or the request is expedited (within 3 months)[1]. Form P, the Pension Inquiry Form, may be used to obtain more information about pension rights, and this may be directed by the court at the first appointment[2]. It is good practice in all cases to serve Form P on pension trustees at an early point, to ensure all the relevant information is to hand.

[1] Pensions on Divorce etc (Charging) Regulations 2000, SI 2000/1049, reg 3.
[2] FPR 9.15(7)(c).

10.24 It is vital to recognise that the CE is only a *starting point* in the valuation exercise. In cases where all the pensions are straightforward defined contribution schemes and there are no complicating factors such as a wide disparity in the spouses' ages, imminent retirement or guaranteed annuity rates, then the CE may be a sufficient measure of a pension's value for the purposes of a divorce settlement. However, it is usually foolhardy to rely solely on a CE for a defined benefit scheme or a small self-administered pension scheme (SSAS). Further information about the value of the pension will also be required in a number of other circumstances and all this will be explored below as we consider the role of experts in the proceedings.

10.25 State pension values will also be an important piece of the valuation jigsaw and information about state pension rights should be obtained at an early stage in all cases. Form BR19 should be completed to obtain an estimate of pension entitlement. Form BR20 will provide an estimate of shareable state pension rights on divorce.

WHAT ARE YOU TRYING TO ACHIEVE?

10.26 Before consideration is given to the detail of the negotiation, it is important to consider the bigger picture: what is it the parties are trying to achieve? Consider the following questions:

(i)   Is it a case governed primarily by the imperative of meeting the *needs* of the parties and any children, or are the assets sufficient that the *sharing* principle is more fully engaged?

(ii)   If the parties are trying to achieve equality of division, do they mean (a) equality of *income* in retirement, or (b) equality of the *capital* accrued in the pension funds, on a fair valuation basis?

Keeping in mind the answers to these questions will help to ensure that the process remains focussed and proportionate.

10.27 The vast majority of cases, even where the assets run into a few millions, will still be needs based. A careful analysis of the income-producing potential of the pension fund is likely to be important, and this may well require expert assistance. Where the assets are large, by contrast, the line between pension and non-pension assets has been blurred by the greater access to pensions bestowed by the Taxation of Pensions Act 2014. In *SJ v RA*[1] Nicholas Francis QC (as he then was) observed, in the context of a 'big money' case 'the recent . . . changes to pensions regulations will mean that pension investments are virtually to be treated as bank accounts to people over 55'.

[1]   *SJ v RA* [2014] EWHC 4054.

10.28 Where the focus of settlement is aimed at meeting the parties' needs, the timing and source of the payments into the pension funds may not be very relevant. Just as with other types of assets, it is not usually possible to 'ring-fence' pensions as being accrued prior to the marriage (or after separation), where the focus is on meeting needs. By contrast, in a case where the totality of the assets ensures that needs can be comfortably met, it may be necessary to consider whether pensions accrued before or after the cohabitation are to be treated as non-matrimonial assets, and so not ordinarily to be distributed according to the sharing principle (although the court will retain a level of discretion as to the level of any sharing).

10.29 In *W v H*[1] HHJ Hess commented 'in a needs case, the approach [as to ring-fencing/apportionment of pension accrued outside the relationship] needs to be treated with more caution. Where the pensions concerned represent the sole or main mechanism for meeting the post-retirement income needs of both parties, and where the income produced by the pension funds after division falls short of producing a surplus over needs, then it is difficult to see that excluding any portion of the pension has justification'. In *Finch v Baker*[2] the Court of Appeal curtly dismissed an argument that increases in a pension since separation should be taken into account in limiting the pension to be shared, commenting 'this was an irrelevant issue because the outcome was dictated by needs which completely subsumed any argument there might otherwise have been as to whether any part of the wealth represented marital property'. See also **10.82** and **10.83** below.

[1]   *W v H* [2020] EWFC B10 per HHJ Hess: a first instance decision of a circuit judge and so not binding authority, but persuasive given the judge's role as co-chair of PAG.
[2]   *Finch v Baker* [2021] EWCA Civ 72 at para 60.

10.30 The primary purpose of a pension is to provide an income in retirement. Where pension assets are fairly significant and/or the spouses are older, then the focus is likely to be on considering their income needs in retirement and ensuring that the pensions are divided to enable them to meet those needs, or to achieve equality of income if those needs are likely to be similar or cannot yet be predicted. However, there will also be cases where the focus will instead be on dividing the current *capital* value of the pensions, rather than the future income. Such cases could include short marriages, 'big money' cases or younger parties in their twenties, thirties or early forties with defined contribution schemes, where projections about future income streams are likely to be speculative. Dividing the capital value equally will not necessarily give the same income in retirement. The spouses may have different ages and life expectancies. Different types of pension may produce different amounts of income from superficially similar CE values. In cases where the focus is on capital division (whether through a pension share or offsetting) expert analysis of the 'true' or 'fair' value of the pension may be required.

EXPERT EVIDENCE

10.31 Pensions are complicated. Traps for the unwary abound. Yet the just conduct of litigation must include its expeditious and proportionate conduct, saving expense[1]. How should the case be prepared, bearing in mind these principles, but also that errors in analysing pension assets can have lifelong consequences for the standard of living of the divorcing spouses, and potentially involve hundreds of thousands of pounds even in 'middle money' cases?

[1]   Extracted from FPR 1.1 – the overriding objective.

When should an expert be instructed?

10.32 The test for instruction of an expert in family proceedings is one of 'necessity'. The court must be of the opinion that the expert evidence is *necessary* to assist the court to resolve the proceedings[1]. This test is significantly more stringent than the old test, pre–2010, of what was 'reasonably required'. The Court of Appeal has defined 'necessary' as having 'a meaning lying somewhere between 'indispensable' on the one hand and 'useful', 'reasonable' or 'desirable' on the other hand, having the connotation of the imperative, what is demanded rather than what is merely optional, reasonable or desirable'[2].

[1]   FPR 25.4(3).
[2]   Munby P in *Re H-L (A child)* [2013] 2 FLR 1434 quoting with approval from *Re P (Placement Orders: Parental Consent)* [2008] 2 FLR 625.

10.33 Some first instance decisions from the High Court over the last few years might suggest at first blush that the courts will apply the test of necessity to limit significantly the use of experts in the context of pensions on divorce. In *SJ v RA*[1] Nicholas Francis QC observed 'in cases where distribution is being made on a basis which is not guided by need it is, in my judgement, incorrect to distribute a pension fund on the basis of equality of income and there is no need for actuarial reports in the overwhelming majority of such cases. I should expect courts to be most reluctant in the future, in bigger money cases, to provide permission for actuarial reports on the issue of how to effect equality of income'. However, note that the judge very expressly limited his comments to bigger money cases where needs are not the magnetic factor. The parties in the case were also old enough to access their funds immediately under the new pension freedoms. In *WS v WS*[2] the court at a case management hearing had declined to allow a single joint expert on the issue of pensions, on the basis that submissions from counsel would suffice. However, a team of pensions experts have made the point that the lack of expert analysis of the taxation of the pension, specifically as to the testing of the pensions against the Lifetime Allowance, may have led the parties and thus the court into error in considering the net assets likely to be available and the financial consequences of the options[3]. In contrast to the High Court approach in these 'bigger money' case examples, the Family Justice Council's guidance for litigants 'Sorting out Finances on Divorce', published in 2016, warns the parties 'this is complicated!' and specifically suggests that the cost of legal and financial advice and an actuary's report may be an 'investment worth making'[4]. The PAG 'Guide to the Treatment of Pensions on Divorce' and the 'Survival Guide to Pensions on

Divorce' both emphasise the point that expert advice will very often be necessary in 'smaller' or 'middle' money cases, to investigate the income streams to be produced and/or whether the CEs represent fair and comparable valuations and/or the most practical way to implement a pension share.

1 See **10.27**, fn 1.
2 *WS v WS* (Financial Remedies: Pension Offsetting) [2015] EWHC 3941 (Fam).
3 [2016] Fam Law 504.
4 At pp 43–44.

10.34 So when might an expert report be necessary? Of course, each case is fact specific and must be considered on its own merits, but it is suggested that the following situations are likely to make the instruction of an expert necessary:

(i) The presence of a defined benefit scheme of anything more than a very modest size. According to the team of pensions experts[1] 'the capital values (. . . CEs) of defined benefit pensions rarely represent a fair reflection of the value of the pension benefits, in terms of the cost of generating equivalent guaranteed benefits. Where significant defined benefits are concerned it remains fundamental to obtain a pension sharing/actuarial report or there would be a significant risk of an unfair settlement and destroying the value of the matrimonial assets'. Bear in mind also that CEs for public sector pensions are calculated using tables from the Government Actuary's Department and a discount figure prescribed by the Treasury. This discount rate is higher than that used by most actuaries considering private sector schemes, with the result that CEs provided for public sector schemes tend to be lower than those in the private sector for the same benefits.

(ii) The presence of guarantees in defined contribution pensions. These are a feature of some older pension contracts. They may guarantee annuity rates or a 'GMP' guaranteed minimum pension (ie guaranteeing the income in retirement, irrespective of fund performance) and/or they may guarantee a minimum value for the fund at a specified retirement age. The presence of income guarantees can render the CE effectively meaningless. The presence of fund guarantees at a certain age can make the timing of the pension sharing exercise critical. If the parties wait until the guarantee becomes effective, the CE of the pension can increase markedly, literally overnight, as the pension holder reaches the defined age.

(iii) Uniformed service schemes provide particularly dramatic examples both as to how the CE can mislead as to the real value of a pension fund and of CE values increasing overnight. Members reaching a defined length of service can leave with a pension payable immediately. Leaving prior to that point in time will result in only a deferred pension payable from a much later age. Remember that the CE provides a figure assuming that the member left service at the time of the valuation request. Future service is not accounted for. Simply relying on the CE can mean that the valuation of the pension, and the predicted timescales for the receipt of benefits, can be wholly misleading.

(iv) The presence of an underfunded defined benefit scheme also raises issues that are highly likely to justify expert assistance. Many private sector final salary schemes fall into this category. Underfunded schemes are permitted to reduce CEs in some circumstances (to ensure that members do not simply take their cash and flee), although they are then obliged to offer an unreduced pension at the member's retirement age. The reduced CE in these circumstances would not give a reliable figure for comparison with other pension or non-pension assets. Additionally, in the event that a pension sharing order is made against a reduced CE the scheme will be obliged to implement an internal transfer on a full unreduced basis, but there is no obligation to implement an external transfer to another pension provider on an unreduced basis. An external transfer out of the fund could therefore lead to a significant reduction in the benefits taken by the receiving spouse, compared with the value in reality of the benefits the member retains. Regulated financial advice will be needed as to whether to opt for an internal transfer (knowing the scheme is underfunded) or an external transfer with a potentially reduced transfer value.

(v) Where the parties are older – perhaps in their late 40s to early 50s or above – and the case is one based primarily on needs, it becomes more important to focus on their income needs in retirement and how the pensions can be divided to meet these needs. Calculating these incomes, taking account of state pension entitlements and working out an efficient way to share the pensions may well require expert assistance. The expert will be able to advise on which particular pensions to share, to maximise the value of the matrimonial assets and minimise implementation costs.

(vi) Where the spouses are of significantly differing ages, particular issues can arise requiring careful consideration, especially where the aim is to equalise incomes in retirement. Where a pension already in payment is to be shared with a spouse too young to access the benefits for years to come, the pension holder will experience a drop in income without there being any immediate benefit for the pension claimant. This is explored further under the heading 'income gap syndrome' at **10.49** below. Even if the spouses are of similar ages, some schemes (particularly the uniformed services, such as the armed forces, police and firefighters) allow scheme members to take benefits much earlier than the spouse with a PSO.

(vii) Cases where the pensions are reasonably significant but the parties wish to consider offsetting as part of their approach may well require expert assistance, even where the pensions are straightforward defined contribution schemes without guarantees or underfunding issues. It will be important to ensure that the effect of taxation on the benefits within the pension scheme is understood and that the CE represents a fair comparative value of all the benefits within the pension fund.

(viii) The presence of a small self-administered scheme (SSAS) within the pension assets is likely to call for expert help. Such schemes are usually found within smaller owner-managed businesses, and may be described as a 'directors' retirement scheme'. The assets within the scheme may include commercial premises and loans to companies, making the valuation exercise complicated. Assets within the pension may be illiquid, leading to problems implementing any PSO.

(ix) Cases where the pensions are large enough to raise issues as to the lifetime allowance will merit expert advice, in particular as to the tax consequences of the available options and strategies to mitigate the tax liability. The lifetime allowance is the total amount that can be accrued in pensions savings before incurring a tax charge. The amount for the tax year 2020/21 is £1,073,100 (although some people have a higher allowance). The charge is payable when funds are taken form the scheme, whether as a lump sum or income. The lifetime allowance is complicated and specialist tax advice is highly likely to be useful and proportionate. Lifetime allowance limits will be relevant to many middle-income families – doctors, senior teachers, dentists, senior army officers and others on similar incomes – and do not just impact the wealthy.

(x) Where an individual is keen to rebuild their pension pot after divorce, care must be taken to understand the Money Purchase Annual Allowance (MPAA). This is a mechanism designed to prevent people drawing down their pension funds under the new freedoms and then re-investing in pensions to claim tax relief. Where the MPAA is triggered (by certain drawdowns and lump sums taken from a pension) subsequent investments into pension funds exceeding £4,000 per year will then be heavily taxed. Financial advice will be necessary if the MPAA may be in issue.

(xi) Where one party has a serious diagnosed medical condition likely to impact on their life expectancy, expert advice will assist in ensuring that pension value is not destroyed on transferring pension assets offering guaranteed lifetime incomes away from the spouse likely to survive for longer.

(xii) Even in the absence of the above factors, in any case where the pensions exceed around £100,000, expert advice is likely to be necessary and proportionate.

[1]   [2016] Fam Law 618.

10.35 In what circumstances might it *not* be necessary to obtain an expert's report? Again, all cases are fact specific, but it *may* be acceptable to proceed on the basis of the CE values without further analysis where:

(i) The pensions are defined contribution schemes and you are confident there are no issues as to annuity, fund or income guarantees and the parties are similar ages, or are content to proceed to equalise capital values rather than incomes in retirement.

(ii) The parties are young (in their twenties or thirties). Here, even if there are modest defined benefit schemes, the spouses may take the view, especially if both are working in pensioned employment, that there are so many years to go before retirement that any modest departure from 'equality' through the sharing of CEs can be tolerated, given the time left to them to build up further pension assets. However, expert advice will still probably be needed where there is a uniformed service scheme (potentially providing significant benefits from a fairly young age) or the defined benefit assets are significant.

(iii) The marriage is short, with no children, and the parties are not so near retirement that it is necessary to examine income needs in retirement.

(iv) The pension assets are modest, so that the cost of instructing an expert is not proportionate, even if the schemes have (non-uniformed service) defined benefits. Pension assets totalling less than around £100,000 may fall into this category.

(v) 'Big money' cases where the pensions form a relatively insignificant part of the totality of the assets and/or the aim is to distribute the capital value of the assets according to the sharing principle rather than to meet income needs. This was the situation in *SJ v RA*[1].

(vi) The sole pension is a defined benefit scheme offering an internal transfer only.

(vii) Both parties hold pension assets, which are all defined benefit schemes and relatively modest, but the CEs are comparable, on examination of the likely future benefits, and any minor disparity in values can be compensated for by limited adjustments elsewhere in the assets. Again, the cost of instructing an expert in such a case may not be proportionate.

[1] See **10.27**, fn 1.

What type of expert should be instructed?

10.36 There is currently no professional qualification or regulatory system for those offering expert advice as to the treatment of pensions on family breakdown. Experts may be actuaries, and many (but not all) actuaries are members of the Institute and Faculty of Actuaries (IFA). Others with expertise in this field may be Independent Financial Advisers, regulated by the Financial Conduct Authority (FCA). Financial planners, or others holding themselves out as having expertise in this area (possibly with justification) may not be regulated by the IFA or FCA. It is good practice, before an expert is selected, to check that the expert has appropriate qualifications and experience, and that they are adequately insured with appropriate peer review, ongoing training and complaint handling arrangements. The PAG has coined the term 'PODE' for pension on divorce experts, and recommends that any PODE producing a report should self-certify in the report as to their competence and regulation[1].

[1] PAG 'A Guide to the Treatment of Pensions on Divorce', Appendices C and D.

10.37 Independent Financial Advisers may be best placed to advise spouses on the taxation consequences of income drawdown, the MPAA and the Lifetime Allowance. IFAs may also be well placed to advise on the selection of an appropriate retirement age and the various notions of equalisation. An IFA can also advise on the destination fund for an external transfer, or the relative merits of internal and external transfers. Where actuarial calculations are required as to incomes in retirement, the 'true' comparative value of a fund or the value of a pension for offsetting, then an actuary is often better placed to prepare the report, and many IFAs will defer to the mathematical expertise of an actuary. One approach might be for the spouses to consult an IFA first, to discuss their retirement strategy and taxation issues, before an actuary is instructed as a single joint expert to prepare a report dealing with income and valuation issues. However, this approach will, obviously, increase costs and may not be necessary or proportionate in many cases.

155

How to instruct the expert

10.38 Where the parties are negotiating outside the court process, in the hope of submitting a consent order in due course, then the choice of expert and the timing and content of the instruction will simply be a matter for agreement between the spouses. Where Form A has been issued to trigger the court timetable leading to a first appointment, then the parties must comply with Pt 25 of the Family Procedure Rules 2010 (FPR). FPR 25.6 provides that a formal written Pt 18 application must be made, no later than the first appointment. It must include the information set out in FPR 25.7 and Practice Direction 25D, such as the type of expert, the CVs and availability of those proposed, the issues to be considered and the costs and timescales of the proposed instruction. An expert will usually be appointed to advise the court and the parties as a single joint expert witness.

10.39 All too often, the judge at a first appointment is faced with an oral application for a 'pensions report'. The court is then unable to make a proper evaluation of the application in accordance with the factors set out in FPR 25.5, which include the questions to be asked and the impact of the report on the timetable for the proceedings. Proper compliance with Pt 25, with a well-considered and properly researched application, will give the application the best chance of succeeding, and the litigation the best chance of progressing in a properly timetabled and proportionate way. Bear in mind that the instruction may well take 3–5 months from start to finish, as the expert is likely to seek further information from the various pension schemes before the report can be prepared.

10.40 The letter of instruction itself does not have to be attached to the application for permission, but it is good practice to prepare a draft to set out the proposed questions. The letter of instruction should be kept short and focussed. A 'scattergun' approach of asking for calculations based on multiple scenarios involving different retirement ages and acquest periods should be avoided. It will simply increase the costs and provide the spouses with a confusing array of different figures over which they can argue. Keep firmly in mind the question: 'what are the parties trying to achieve?'. Is it a case where the parties are seeking to equalise incomes in retirement? Or is it a case where they seek to equalise the capital in their pensions, based on 'true values'? Are you therefore instructing the expert to prepare calculations to share incomes in retirement, or to share the pensions as capital, or to advise on both options? Is an offsetting calculation required? The PAG has prepared an excellent specimen letter of instruction at Appendix E of their report. Signed letters of authority from both parties should be included with the instruction, to enable the expert to seek any further information required with a minimum of delay.

PENSION SHARING IN DETAIL

10.41 Pension sharing enables the court at the time of divorce or nullity to share a member's pension rights so that the receiving spouse can establish their own pension fund under their own control. It can only be achieved by a court order, whether by consent or after judicial determination. The power to order pension sharing is founded by MCA 1973, ss 21A and 24B–24D.

Pension sharing orders are not available for divorce petitions issued before 1 December 2000 or within judicial separation proceedings. All pension arrangements and unfunded public service schemes can be shared, save only for pensions payable to holders of the Great Offices of State (Prime Minister, Lord Chancellor and Speaker) and dependents' pensions where those are the only rights held by a person in a pension scheme. A pension sharing order (PSO) operates to transfer a specified portion of the scheme member's rights to the other party. A 'pension debit' is applied to the transferor's fund, reducing the value of his fund or benefits, and a 'pension credit' is established for the benefit of the transferee. The parties will then have separate pension rights in their own names, completely independent of each other. The transferee's rights will not be extinguished by the death of the other party or their own re-marriage: he (or she) has the security of pension rights under his own control, just as if he had accrued them himself. The pension share operates as a clean break order between the spouses.

10.42 The pension sharing order must specify a percentage figure. It cannot be expressed as 'such percentage as will give a particular sum'[1]. The value of the pension fund will vary over time and this gives rise to what has become known as 'moving target syndrome'. The negotiations between the parties or the court hearing will have proceeded using the CE valuation of the pension. The benefits are then revalued by the pension scheme for the purpose of implementing the order on the 'transfer day', which is the day the pension sharing order takes effect. Market fluctuations and further contributions or service will mean that this valuation differs from the CE valuation used in the negotiations or court hearing. The pension share will then be finally implemented on the 'valuation day', when the benefits are again revalued to take account of market fluctuations, but not contributions and salary accruals[2]. There is little that can be done to ameliorate 'moving target syndrome' save to be aware of it, to advise clients of it and to ensure that the implementation of the order proceeds without undue delay. The only practical option to mitigate the issue may be for the pension holder to stop making contributions after the CE is provided and before the order is implemented. In *Finch v Baker*[3] the Court of Appeal expressly declined to interfere with an order simply because the figures on the valuation day differed from the assumptions made by the judge at the final hearing, commenting that such changes are an inevitable feature of pension sharing.

[1]   MCA 1973, s 21A(1)(b) and *H v H (Financial Relief: Pensions)* [2010] 2 FLR 173, FD.
[2]   Welfare Reform and Pensions Act 1999, s 29.
[3]   *Finch v Baker* [2021] EWCA Civ 72.

10.43 The pension sharing order can proceed as either an 'internal transfer' or an 'external transfer'. An internal transfer establishes the receiving spouse as a member of the pension scheme in their own right. An external transfer creates a pension fund in the receiving spouse's name with a different pension provider. In an unfunded public service scheme, only an internal transfer is permitted. In all other cases, an external transfer must be offered as an option, and an internal transfer may or may not be offered. If a choice is offered between an internal or an external transfer, then independent financial advice should be sought. Similarly, if only an external transfer is available, independent advice will be needed to select the most appropriate receiving pension scheme. Lawyers should be careful not to stray into giving financial advice as to the destination of the pension assets.

Sharing state pension rights

10.44 The Basic State Pension, accrued under the Old State Pension for those reaching retirement age before 6 April 2016, cannot be shared through a PSO. However, those in the Old State Pension can substitute their ex-spouse's National Insurance contribution record for their own where this is financially beneficial, provided they make the application before re-marrying. This is done by sending a certified copy of the decree absolute and their spouse's NI number to the Department for Work and Pensions. Women who divorce when they are already over the state pension age and who reached pension age before 6 April 2016 should notify the DWP as soon as possible, as the uplift is not added automatically to their pensions already in payment.

10.45 Any Additional State Pension (SERPS or S2P) accrued under the Old State Pension can be shared, in just the same way as occupational and private pensions. The person whose Additional State Pension is to be shared must have reached state pension age prior to 6 April 2016 (though they may have chosen to defer taking their pension benefits). The valuation of the scheme rights is obtained by submitting form BR20.

10.46 The New State Pension, commencing on 6 April 2016, cannot be shared. Individuals in the New State Pension (those reaching retirement age on or after 6 April 2016) also cannot substitute their former spouse's NI contribution history for their own[1]. There are, however, two limited circumstances where a pension share can be ordered against Additional State Pension (ASP) rights even though the former spouse is in the New State Pension:

(i)   Where the petition for divorce was issued before 6 April 2016, Form BR20 is used to obtain a valuation, and the DWP Pensions Service is advised of the petition issue date, to ensure that the full ASP benefits are valued. The percentage pension share is then ordered through a PSO and the Pensions Service calculates at the point of implementation the additional amount of pension to be added to the claimant's state pension.

(ii)   Where an individual in the New State Pension has a Protected Payment (ie an enhanced New State Pension based on NI contributions under the old system) the Protected Payment element of the New State Pension can be shared. The value of the Protected Payment amount is obtained using form BR20. The PSO will be for the specified percentage of the weekly Protected Payment, to be added to the claimant's own state pension.

---

[1]   It is important, therefore, for everyone in the New State Pension to build up their own NI record. In families with children under 12 and one high earner and one non-working spouse, the non-working partner should register for child benefit, even if they then choose not to receive a payment (which would be clawed back if made) to ensure they receive the NI credits that come with the CB claim.

Restrictions on pension sharing

10.47 If there has already been a pension sharing order in relation to *this marriage*, then no pension sharing order (or attachment order) is possible in relation to the same pension arrangement or shareable state scheme rights[1]. This issue may arise in particular if pension sharing is being considered on a variation application under MCA 1973, s 31. However, if a prior pension sharing order has been made in relation to a *different spouse* following a previous marriage, then a further PSO can be made against the same pension scheme. By contrast, a prior pension *attachment* order in force against a pension, from any marriage, operates to prevent any PSO against that pension scheme.

[1]   MCA 1973, s 24B(3) and (4).

Potential disadvantages of pension sharing

10.48 Implementing a pension sharing order can be costly. A pension scheme is entitled to make a charge for PSO services, and this charge can range from nothing at all to several thousand pounds. It is important to enquire about the costs of implementation at an early stage, and factor these into the negotiations. Form P gathers this information, which is also often published by the scheme within notes to assist divorcing scheme members. Some schemes allow the fees to be deducted from the pension share itself, but this is by no means universally permitted. The pension annex attached to the order allows the arrangements for the payment of fees to be specified. If the annex is silent on this point, then the default provision is that the pension holder is liable for all the fees.

10.49 *Income gap syndrome:* Where one former spouse is entitled to access their pension significantly before the other spouse, problems may arise. One spouse may be much older than the other and either be in receipt of their pension already, or be contemplating taking it soon. Alternatively, the spouses may be of similar ages, but if the pension was accrued through uniformed service (military, police, firefighters) the pension holder will be entitled to draw their pension at a much younger age than the spouse in receipt of the PSO. The making of a pension sharing order in these circumstances can result in an immediate or imminent drop in income for the pension holder, but with no corresponding benefit to the other spouse for many years to come.

10.50 It is not possible to make a deferred pension sharing order to try and mitigate this problem. Nor is it possible to defer serving the PSO on the pension provider. The *application* for a PSO could be adjourned so that the income of the older pension holder is not reduced until such time as the pension claimant is old enough to claim pension benefits (at least 55) but this is a risky strategy, not least because it could leave the divorced pension claimant without either a pension share or death benefits in the event that the pension holder dies before the matter is finalised. Careful planning is usually the only option, recognising the income gap problem and working to distribute all the available income and capital assets to ensure the parties can best meet their needs both now and in the future, taking expert advice.

10.51 It may be important to exercise care in choosing against which particular scheme(s) to implement a PSO, if a spouse has more than one pension investment. Some schemes charge exit or transfer penalties. Some schemes may be underfunded, or may have valuable guarantees that would be lost or eroded on transfer. The costs of implementation may vary widely between schemes and it may be better to incur one fee than to implement a share against a number of different schemes, each incurring a fee. If an expert is instructed, the instruction should include a request for advice on the most efficient way of implementing a pension share.

Making and implementing the pension sharing order

10.52 The order itself will refer to the attached pension sharing annex, which will set out the details of the parties, the percentage to be transferred and the arrangements for paying the fees. A separate annex is used for each separate pension to be shared. The form allows the beneficiary of the PSO to specify whether they will take an internal or external transfer (where there is a choice) but it is not obligatory to complete this part.

10.53 The wording of the order usually includes the phrase 'it being agreed between the parties that in the event of [A] predeceasing [B] after this order has taken effect but before its implementation [B] shall have [A's] personal representative's consent to an application for leave to appeal out of time against the terms of this order', where A is the PSO beneficiary and B is the pension holder. This phrase is designed to protect the surviving party in the event of the PSO beneficiary dying in the period between the transfer day (when the order formally takes effect) and the valuation day (when the benefits actually move between pension pots). Should this happen, the pension benefits may be lost to everyone. The order would not have been implemented to transfer the benefits to A, but the benefits may still be lost to B as the order will be in effect. In such circumstances, rare though they will be, the parties will want to ensure that the PSO can be unravelled with the least practical difficulty.

10.54 A copy of the application in Form A must be served on the pension provider at the outset, just as soon as their identity is known. This is often honoured in the breach, but it is important: an adviser could be considered negligent if funds were accessed by the scheme member to thwart a pension sharing order before it can take effect, if the notice provisions have not been fully complied with. It is good practice to submit the draft PSO and annex to the pension scheme for approval before the order is submitted to the court, although this is not a formal requirement of the rules (unlike with pension attachment orders, where prior submission for approval is compulsory). This ensures that any issues with regard to implementing the order or accurately defining the scheme and any associated AVCs or related closed schemes are resolved before the order has been sealed.

10.55 A pension sharing order takes effect on the later of 7 days following the period for an appeal, or the date of the decree absolute. The period for appeal is currently 21 days, so the earliest date a PSO can take effect is 28 days after the date of approval by the court (or on the decree absolute date if later). The court is obliged to serve the order on the trustees, but it is sensible for the party benefitting from the order to send a copy to the trustees and to ask for confirmation that it has been safely received[1]. The decree absolute should also be sent as soon as it is available. The trustees of the pension have a maximum period of 4 months in which to implement the order, beginning on the later of the day on which the order takes effect and the day they have all the relevant documents (ie the sealed order and annex, and the decree absolute)[2].

---

[1] For a detailed analysis of the date when the order takes effect and the importance of informing trustees, see the article 'Protecting the Pension Sharing Order' at February [2021] Fam Law, p 266.

[2] Welfare Reform and Pensions Act 1999, ss 29(7) and 34.

10.56 Following the introduction of the pension freedoms by the Taxation of Pensions Act 2014, it is sensible to send the order to the trustees as soon as it is sealed and to send the decree absolute later, if it is not yet available. This ensures that the trustees are on notice of the order without delay, as part of a strategy to ensure that the pension is not accessed by a pension holder aged 55 or over, to strip it of benefits before the PSO can be implemented. It is also good practice to seek an undertaking from the pension holder, recorded in the court order, that the pension benefits will not be accessed until the pension sharing order has taken effect. If an undertaking is refused and there are real concerns that a spouse may use the pension freedoms to thwart the PSO, then an order restraining the disposition of pension assets may have to be sought, under MCA 1973, s 37.

10.57 The timing of the application for decree absolute requires careful thought. The earliest a PSO can take effect is 28 days after the order is made. If the decree absolute has been granted already, and the pension holding spouse unfortunately dies before the order takes effect but after decree absolute, the receiving spouse may find themselves in an invidious position: neither the holder of an effective PSO, nor a widow/er entitled to death benefits. It may therefore be wise to delay applying for the decree absolute until after the 28-day period (or the conclusion of any appeal), to ensure that the PSO becomes effective immediately on the making of the decree. Of course, this strategy does mean that other aspects of the court order (lump sums and property adjustment orders etc) are not enforceable until the decree absolute is granted, so there is no one best practice and clients may have to take a view on what seems most important: immediate enforceability of other aspects of the court order or insuring against a possible loss of pension rights. Should the scheme member die *after* the order has taken effect, but before the PSO has been implemented, the beneficiary's pension credit is secure.

10.58 Where the pension to be shared is already in payment, the pension claimant is entitled to the income from the date the PSO *took effect*, not from the later date of actual implementation. Most pension schemes continue to make the full payment to the pension holder until *implementation*, resulting in an overpayment that must then be clawed back. Holders of pensions in payment that are to be shared should be warned of this likelihood: they will have money deducted from their income to clawback sums overpaid to them between the order taking effect and implementation, in addition to the loss of income resulting from implementation of the PSO itself. Care must also be taken to limit the term of any interim maintenance payable pending the implementation of the PSO, to ensure that the pension holder is not penalised twice. Interim maintenance might be limited to 2 or 3 months after the order, to allow a reasonable period for implementation, but no more.

'Reverse' pension sharing

10.59 The pension freedoms introduced in 2015 mean that, for the over 55s, pension assets can now, in many instances, be unlocked to release immediate liquid capital, subject to paying the appropriate rate of tax. Unfunded public sector schemes cannot be accessed under the new freedoms, but other defined benefit or defined contribution occupation schemes can be accessed by transferring the benefits to a private pension scheme. Financial Conduct Authority rules require that authorised advice must be given before a transfer out of a scheme with safeguarded benefits.

10.60 In some cases, one spouse may have a pension fund that would be of more use to the parties if it could be cashed in, but the holding spouse is under the age of 55. It may be, for example, that the fund is fairly small and so will yield little income in retirement, but the capital locked up would make a significant difference to the housing fund available to meet the parties' needs now. If the other spouse is over 55, one option may be to transfer the pension to the older spouse, even if they are the party with the better overall pension provision, simply to enable the pension to be accessed as liquid capital, as part of an overall settlement.

PENSION ATTACHMENT IN DETAIL

10.61 Pension attachment (formerly known as 'earmarking') is available for petitions filed after 1 July 1996, including petitions for judicial separation. Attachment orders are not a separate form of financial provision order: they are orders for periodical payments and lump sums under MCA 1973, s 23, to be paid directly from the pension scheme to the receiving non-member spouse. They are therefore effectively a form of enforcement of a periodical payments or lump sum order. The statutory provisions are found in MCA 1973, ss 25B–25D.

10.62 An attachment order can attach a percentage of:

(i)   the member's pension in retirement and/or
(ii)   any lump sum payable to the member on retirement and/or
(iii)   any lump sum payable on death in service, or on death after leaving service but before retirement, or on death after retirement.

The order is directed to those responsible for the pension arrangement, who will make the payments directly to the receiving spouse. Pension attachment income is taxable in the hands of the pension member but not in the hands of the receiving spouse.

10.63 The court can require the pension member to commute pension benefits to create or enhance a lump sum (s 25B(7)). The court can also require the pension member to nominate the other party to receive death benefits (s 25C(2)(b)). The court can also order a member to take the pension benefits, by means of an injunction or the appointment of a receiver under the Senior Courts Act 1981, s 37[1]. Pension trustees can be ordered to exercise their discretion as to paying a lump sum in favour of the receiving spouse (s 25C(2)(a).

[1]   *Blight v Brewster* [2012] EWHC 165 (Ch).

Disadvantages of pension attachment

10.64 A periodical payments attachment order will cease upon the death of the pension holder. It can only therefore provide limited financial security in retirement. It will also cease on the remarriage of the receiving party. The payments will only become due on the scheme member choosing to draw the pension; there is no provision in the legislation for the court to set the date. Whilst s 37 of the Senior Courts Act 1981 provides a way around this problem, it is a cumbersome and expensive route. Pension attachment prevents a clean break between the spouses. The orders are also subject to variation and so lack certainty: an attached periodical payments order can be varied at any time and an attached lump sum order can also be varied, even as to amount, at any time before death. These disadvantages mean that pension *sharing*, with its clean break and certainties, is now the more common approach to pension provision on divorce.

10.65 The pension freedoms introduced by the Taxation of Pensions Act 2014 also introduce risks for the recipients of pension attachment orders. If the member spouse chooses to use the freedoms to draw on or transfer the pension funds, the receiving spouse could be left without access to the anticipated benefits. Undertakings, injunctions, s 37 MCA 1973 applications or variations of existing orders may be required to preserve the assets in the pension and prevent the intention of the order from being thwarted. A proposed transfer out of funds from an attached pension to another scheme must be notified to the receiving spouse by the pension trustees[1], but there is no requirement on trustees to notify a recipient spouse where the scheme holder proposes to access scheme benefits by drawing down or taking lump sums in a way that would reduce the periodical payments.

[1]   Divorce etc (Pensions) Regulations 2000, SI 2000/1123, regs 4 and 5.

When might pension attachment still be useful?

10.66 Attachment orders may still be useful in 'income gap' cases. If a pension is already in payment to the scheme member, and their spouse is younger but needs income now, then a pension sharing order would not be effective. The making of a PSO would reduce the income payable to the member, without yielding any immediate benefit to their spouse. An attached periodical payments order would preserve the current income and share it between the parties. The effect could also, of course, be achieved through making a periodical payments order, but the pension attachment has the added benefit of reliability. An attached lump sum order could ensure that liquid capital is made available to a younger spouse. The pension member could take lump sum benefits from the scheme, to be paid to their spouse as an attached lump sum, whether immediately or deferred.

10.67 Perhaps the most useful ongoing role for attachment orders is to secure the payment of death benefits on divorce. On death of a spouse before retirement, an order under s 25C(2) can provide for the lump sum (or part of it) to be paid to a former spouse. Bear in mind, however, that even these orders are liable to be varied prior to the death of either party, for example if the member should acquire new financial responsibilities to a second family. Attachment of death benefits can save the cost of buying separate life cover for a financially dependent former spouse. Remember that it is not possible to have a pension sharing and an attachment order against the same pension. However, in some defined benefit schemes, the death in service benefit is established under a trust separate to the main pension, and in these circumstances a pension attachment against the death benefits could still provide life cover at no additional cost, even where a PSO is also made.

Restrictions on pension attachment

10.68 A pension attachment order may not be made in relation to a pension arrangement which is the subject of a pension sharing order for the same parties. If, however, the pension sharing order relates to a different marriage, then an attachment order may be made for the same pension fund.

Making and implementing the pension attachment order

10.69 The pension provider must be served with the application in Form A, or with a draft of the order on a consent application, and may request a copy of the pension section of Form E[1]. The pension provider may choose to file a statement in answer and even attend the first appointment. The form of the order must be expressed as a percentage and attach a completed pension attachment annex – Form P2 – for each arrangement. The court or a party serves the order: it is good practice for the party benefitting from the order to serve it and request an acknowledgment form the pension trustees. The beneficiary should also ensure that the pension trustees have their up to date contact details. An order for attached periodical payments or an attached lump sum is exempt from the Legal Aid Agency's statutory charge.

[1]   FPR 9.33 and 9.34.

PENSION OFFSETTING

10.70 Pension offsetting is not a type of pension order at all. Rather, it is a trade-off, whereby one party's rights to receive pension income and/or lump sums in future is taken into account in dividing up other, non-pension assets. The spouse without the pension will take a greater share of the other available assets, in lieu of receiving an interest in the pension itself. Research in 2014 found that pension offsetting remained at that time the most common way of resolving pension disparities on divorce[1].

[1] Pensions on divorce: an empirical study by Hilary Woodward and Mark Sefton https://orca. cf.ac.uk/56702/1/14%2002%2024%20KF%20final.pdf.

10.71 How, though, are the benefits held within the pension to be valued and compared with other assets such as cash or houses? Concern as to a lack of understanding and consistency in this area was one of the main drivers in establishing the PAG. Within the discretionary framework of the section 25 exercise, it is important to avoid the use of arbitrary figures or unjustified assumptions in establishing the asset values used as the basis for the discretionary distributive decisions.

10.72 Offsetting may suit the parties' priorities, for example the desire of a primary carer to retain the family home. It may be the only feasible option, for example if the pensions are held abroad or the assets in a SSAP are illiquid. It may be a pragmatic and proportionate approach, for example if the funds are too small to justify the costs of a pension sharing exercise. The key issue is to identify an appropriate value for the pension(s) to be offset. A combination of offsetting and pension sharing can be used where appropriate. By definition, offsetting is only available where there are sufficient non-pension assets to compensate the receiving spouse.

10.73 In considering whether offsetting represents the right approach, spouses and their advisers should remember that the orthodox view, set out by Thorpe LJ in *Martin-Dye v Martin-Dye*[1] in 2006, repeated by the PAG[2] and endorsed in *W v H*[3] is that pensions are very different from other classes of assets and that to blur the distinction between categories through offsetting runs a risk of unfairness. An analogy of comparing 'apples with pears' is often quoted. Where practical, pensions should usually be dealt with by pension sharing orders and other assets should be dealt with separately by lump sum or property adjustment orders. Offsetting should be approached with caution.

[1] *Martin-Dye v Martin-Dye* [2006] 2 FLR 901.
[2] At p 35.
[3] *W v H* [2020] EWFC B10.

10.74 Different approaches are available to value the pension benefits for offsetting purposes:

(i)   In cases involving simple defined contribution schemes (with no guarantees), SIPPs containing straightforward assets, cases with only small pensions or some 'big money' cases, offsetting can be achieved without PODE valuation advice, by simply taking the up-to-date CE and applying a discount to take account of tax and the 'utility' of holding non-pension assets.

(ii)   In other cases, a PODE should be instructed, to arrive at a fair value (or a range of fair values) for the pension asset(s) to be offset, based on the *value of the benefits to the pension holder*, then discounting for tax, with the parties or court finally to consider whether any further utility discount is justified on the facts. There are a number of different valuation methodologies from which to choose.

(iii)   A third option is to consider offsetting from the perspective of the *cost to the non-pension holder of acquiring equivalent benefits*. Again, different methodologies are available, although PODE advice may not be needed to obtain the figures.

We will consider these approaches in turn.

10.75 The CE *may* be an adequate starting point, but the many cautions against over-reliance on the CE set out at **10.34** should all be borne in mind. Secondly, the effect of taxation must be considered, to arrive at a comparable figure for non-pension assets. Pension benefits will be partly tax-free and partly taxed at the pension holder's marginal rate. By contrast, the spouse retaining non-pension assets may be able to make tax-efficient choices. For example, they could choose to hold the offset cash in an ISA, and/or invest it in a pension fund and claim tax relief. Lastly, consideration must be given as to what, if any, discount should be applied for the perceived 'utility' of having liquid capital now rather than money locked in pension assets. The utility discount reflects both an element for accelerated receipt and a discretionary value judgment about holding cash over other forms of assets. The Family Justice Council's publication 'Sorting Out Finances on Divorce', designed to assist litigants in person, suggests that in practice 'the present value of £1 is often discounted between 20% and 40% when comparing current assets with the value of £1 of pension CE which can only be drawn in the future', to adjust for a combination of tax *and* utility[1]. The PAG have suggested a refinement to this general approach, recommending an adjustment of 15% where the pension is likely to be accessed by a basic-rate taxpayer and 30% where the pension holder is likely to pay higher rate tax, *before* any additional utility adjustment is applied[2]. The 'utility' discount is, uncomfortably, a 'finger in the wind' value judgment. Is it really right, for example, to factor in much of a utility discount for the 'liquidity' and 'advantage' of retaining the family home to house the children? If justified on the facts, a *utility* adjustment may be in the range of a further 0–25%, bearing in mind that the more accessible the pension cash (for example if the parties are over 55), the lower the utility adjustment, if any, is likely to be. An adjustment may be appropriate where the offsetting is likely to exclude the pension holder from buying owner-occupied accommodation for years or perhaps indefinitely. The question of what, if any, utility adjustment to apply is one for the parties to agree or the judge to determine.

[1]   2016, pp 46–47.
[2]   A Guide to the Treatment of Pensions on Divorce, para 7.31, p 41.

10.76 An alternative to relying on the CE and making a broad working assumption about applying a discount for tax and utility, is to instruct a PODE to calculate a figure to be used for offsetting, based on valuing the benefits retained by the pension holder. The actuary may use a 'Defined Contribution Fund Equivalent' (DCFE) valuation, being the gross replacement value of a defined benefit pension based on buying an annuity, or an 'actuarial value' with adjustments made to reflect that an annuity is unlikely to be purchased. Either calculation is then adjusted for tax. Alternatively, the valuation may calculate the capital value in a pension if the tax-free lump sum is paid out and then the balance is drawn down, subject to tax (a 'realisable value'). The question of any further utility discount is for the parties or the court to decide, and is not a matter for the PODE. This overall approach has the benefit of yielding a clearer picture of the real value of the pension, and it avoids the dangerous ground of over-reliance on the CE. There will obviously be a cost for the expert's report, and so it is not a proportionate approach in all cases. It may be appropriate for the expert to complete calculations based on a range of methods, to provide the parties and the court with options to consider.

10.77 A third offsetting approach is to calculate the cost of buying an annuity in the insurance market to replace the 'lost' share of pension benefits from the perspective of the non-pension holder and to provide a guaranteed income in retirement, usually for life. In the current economic climate, this is likely to give rise to the highest potential offset lump sum and has led to some influential judicial comment at first instance that it is an unrealistic approach[1]. A team of pension experts writing in May 2016[2], whilst acknowledging that there has been a significant fall in the number of annuity purchases following the removal of income withdrawal limits in April 2015, nonetheless offered the combined view that 'where the main objective is a guaranteed lifelong income and there is little appetite for investment risk the most appropriate option for many is likely to remain an annuity'. If one party has a defined benefit, copper-bottomed, index-linked, guaranteed income for life, then fairness may require at least some consideration of the cost of replicating that for the other spouse.

[1] For example Mr Nicholas Francis QC (as he then was) in *SJ v RA* [2014] EWHC 4054 (Fam) at para 83: 'I suspect that annuities will, in the overwhelming majority of cases, become a thing of the past' and Mostyn J in *BJ v MJ (Financial Order: Overseas Trusts)* [2011] EWHC 2708 (Fam) at para 75 'No one nowadays seriously would think of buying an annuity'.
[2] May [2016] Fam Law, pp 618–620.

10.78 An alternative basis for assessing the offset lump sum from the perspective of loss to the non-pension holder has been to use the *Duxbury* algorithm, to calculate the lump sum needed to fund the 'lost' share of retirement income. This was the approach adopted in the first instance decision of HHJ Lord Meston QC in *WS v WS* (a case where permission for a single joint expert witness had been refused at an earlier hearing)[1]. However, the PAG point out[2] that *Duxbury* may not be entirely suited to calculating a comparison with pension income and may lead to offsetting figures that are too low. The *Duxbury* calculation assumes a currently unrealistic rate of return on investments compared with inflation. Aiming for a market-beating rate of return will always carry enhanced risk. The *Duxbury* assumptions are based on replacing lost earned income, with all its inherent uncertainties about workforce insecurity, whereas pension capital 'unlike any attempted capitalisation of earning capacity . . . does not depend on the application of future effort but . . . is in the bag'[3]. 50% of *Duxbury* recipients can be assumed to outlive the lump sum calculated to provide the income, given that the calculations are based on average life expectancy, and so those settling for a *Duxbury* lump sum in lieu of a pension share will either need to live below the assumed standard of living in the hope of outliving their average assumed life expectancy, or accept that they will have run out of money in that happy eventuality. The *Duxbury* algorithm also assumes a full state pension is payable, which may not be the case. An alternative to the *Duxbury* algorithm may be to use the *Ogden* tables familiar to civil litigators, but not (yet) conventionally adopted in family cases. In Appendix U to the Guide to the

Treatment of Pensions on Divorce, the PAG consider the potential for the future development of Ogden-style tables to provide greater consistency and clarity in valuing pension assets for offsetting.

1   WS *v* WS (Financial Remedies: Pension Offsetting) [2015] EWHC 3941 (Fam).
2   A Guide to the Treatment of Pensions on Divorce, para 7.27, p 40.
3   Per Wilson LJ (as he then was) in *Vaughan v Vaughan* [2007] EWCA Civ 1085 at para 25.

10.79 In summary, there are various different methodologies available to calculate a 'fair' value for offsetting purposes and the role of any PODE instructed may extend to making alternative calculations and highlighting the strengths and weaknesses of each one. Competing approaches can produce widely differing figures: in *WS v WS* (where there was no expert advice) the annuity-based figure contended for by the husband was £1.2–1.3 million whereas the wife's *Duxbury* offer was £425,000. Even where the basic approach to be adopted is agreed to be a discounted lump sum based on PODE advice (the option outlined in **10.76** above) different methodologies available to be used by PODEs in making their calculations can produce very different outcomes. The 'utility' adjustment is an unpredictable value judgment. Even where there is expert evidence before the court, the judge may choose to depart from this in the exercise of his/her wide discretion. In *JS v RS*[1], Sir Peter Singer, when faced with an SJE's recommended offset figure, viewed it as 'very significantly excessive' and, whilst accepting that he was 'thus left in the unsatisfactory position where I must alight upon an amount which will necessarily be arbitrary' substituted a much lower figure. If annuity-based figures represent the iciest tip of one pole for offsetting figures and a *Duxbury* calculation represents the iciest tip of the other, then sensible negotiation or the application of judicial discretion may yield an answer somewhere in between.

1   *JS v RS* [2015] EWHC 2921 (Fam) at paras 74 and 75.

10.80 Where offsetting has been used as the approach for resolving pension issues on divorce, always consider including a recital on the face of the order to explain this and to give a thumbnail sketch of the figures used and how these were arrived at. This, together with some further explanation in the D81 forms on submission of a consent order, will assist the judge asked to make the order as well as anyone considering the rationale behind the order in the years to come.

THE SECTION 25 EXERCISE

10.81 The division of pension assets is, ultimately, only one strand of the overall discretionary exercise of distributing assets fairly between spouses on the ending of a relationship. The principles of sharing and of meeting needs, and the factors in MCA 1973, s 25, apply to this part of the exercise, just as they apply to the inter-linked decisions as to how to distribute all the other assets. A fair outcome may be to share pension assets equally (whether based on a sharing of pensions as capital or pensions as income), but the application of the s 25 factors may lead in some cases to a departure from equality. In particular, contribution arguments are often raised as to the period when pension assets were accrued, in an effort by one spouse to exclude from the matrimonial division pension assets acquired before the relationship, or after the separation. Arguments may also be raised as to the effect of one party's ill health on the pension distribution. The Court of Appeal has issued a reminder in *Finch v Baker*[1] that the court's powers under s 25 are exercised in a broad, discretionary manner and not necessarily with the expectation of achieving mathematical precision, even in the realm of pensions.

[1] *Finch v Baker* [2021] EWCA Civ 72 at para 54.

Discounting for pre-marital pension contributions?

10.82 It may be argued by one spouse that unmatched pension assets brought in to the relationship at the start should be left out of account, as non-matrimonial property. Just as with all other classes of assets, this argument is likely to carry little or no weight in cases where the principal consideration is meeting the needs of the parties and any dependent children (see **10.28** above). If reasonable needs cannot be met without recourse to non-matrimonial property, then that property will not be ringfenced in the matrimonial division. In *RH v SV*[1] the Circuit Judge commented 'the fact that a wife as a litigant in person accepted that her share was limited to the period of cohabitation should not in itself have affected the [first instance] judge's reasoning, as he would have been perfectly entitled to share the whole pension pot if justified by needs'. Where, however, the case is to be decided largely on principles of sharing and entitlement, because the parties' needs are capable of being met from the matrimonial resources, some recognition of pre-existing pension assets may be appropriate. If so, how should this be achieved? A straight-line discount of years of cohabitation divided by years of pension contribution is a simple calculation and is often put forward. Such an approach ignores complicating factors such as the presence of investment returns over the course of the marriage on the pre-existing capital ('passive growth') and the probability that pension accrual has not proceeded evenly over all the years but has accelerated with promotions during the later years when the parties were married. However, any more sophisticated approach may call for a disproportionate gathering of data and an over-complicated expert analysis. When faced with this issue in *M v M*[2], (a case based on entitlement not need) HHJ Wildblood QC concluded that 'the extent of the discount is not capable of being proved on actuarial figures or a strict mathematical basis and so there must be an element of discretion'. Where mathematical methods are to be attempted, the options are explored at Appendix S of the Guide to the Treatment of Pensions on Divorce. Just as with other asset classes, if the marriage has been long and the parties have tended to pool their resources, it is less likely to be appropriate to exclude assets as having been acquired pre-marriage[3].

[1] *RH v SV* [2020] EWFC B23 per HHJ Robinson.
[2] *M v M* [2015] EWFC B63 at para 89, the first instance decision of a Circuit Judge and DFJ, so not binding authority but persuasive.
[3] *N v F* [2011] EWHC Fam per Mostyn J at para 14.

Discounting for post-marital pension contributions?

10.83 The pension assets will be valued near to the time of trial or negotiation (and then revalued for the implementation of any pension sharing order at the transfer day and valuation day). Where there has been a lengthy period of separation, it *may* be appropriate for unmatched contributions made by the pension-holding spouse in the period since the separation to be acknowledged through an adjustment to the pension shares or offset. Passive growth of assets accumulated during the marriage would, however, usually be shared, and it may well be argued successfully that even active contributions founded on an earning capacity built up during the marriage should not be stripped out, especially where the other spouse does not have the income capacity to make similar pension contributions. The argument to exclude post-separation pension accrual may be strongest where the separation has been very long and the contributions come from 'a truly new venture which has no connection to the marital partnership or the assets of the partnership'[1]. But again, if the needs of the parties or their dependent children demand that such assets are shared, that will be the outcome. In *KM v CV* the wife, a police officer, succeeded at first instance in ringfencing her pension on the basis that she had made unmatched contributions to the fund in the years since separation. In allowing the husband's appeal, HHJ Robinson commented 'the [district] judge appears to have been led into error by an over-emphasis on the non-matrimonial accrual of part of the pension and of contributions over needs . . . the correct approach must be to conduct a comparative analysis of the parties' respective income and needs in retirement, taking into account all the section 25 criteria, including health, needs and contributions . . . only then can a fair decision be reached'[2].

[1] *JL v SL (No 2) (Appeal: Non-matrimonial Property)* [2015] EWHC 360 (Fam) per Mostyn J at para 42.
[2] *KM v CV* [2020] EWFC B22, per HHJ Robinson: an appellate decision of a circuit judge and so not binding authority, but persuasive.

Health issues

10.84 A significantly impaired life expectancy may mean that enhanced annuities are available to one spouse, or that the amounts to be drawn down from a pension fund each year can be increased. In such a case (and again assuming that meeting the needs of the parties does not predominate), should the ill or disabled spouse receive a smaller portion of the available pension capital? Such an outcome could tend to equalise *incomes* in retirement, but on the basis of the ill or disabled spouse receiving an unequal capital share. There is no definitive guidance on the issue from an appellate court, but when faced with this point at first instance in *M v M*[1], HHJ Wildblood QC based his approach on an equalisation of capital values (with a cross check in considering the income consequences of his order). The PAG however recommend in *A Guide to the Treatment of Pensions on Divorce*[2] that a clearly diagnosed medical condition with a substantial probability of impaired life expectancy should be reflected in the calculations.

[1] See 10.79, fn 1.
[2] A Guide to the Treatment of Pensions on Divorce, para 12.5, p 62.

10.85 Where the pension is a public-sector scheme, the pension income is calculated using standard actuarial tables prescribed by the Government Actuary's Department. These assume an average life expectancy and will not be adjusted for ill health or life-shortening disability. In these circumstances, it makes financial sense for the pension assets to be retained predominantly by the spouse with the longer life expectancy. That person is more likely to receive an income for longer and so receive a fuller value from the scheme. Transferring to (or retaining) the public-sector pension assets in the name of the partner with the reduced life expectancy would have the effect of destroying part of the probable value of the combined assets. Again, however, meeting the parties' needs during their respective lifetimes must be the primary aim.

THE PENSION PROTECTION FUND

10.86 The Pension Protection Fund (PPF) was set up by the Pensions Act 2004 and came into effect from 5 April 2005. It is a fund of last resort, set up to pay compensation to members of eligible *defined benefit* schemes where the employer is insolvent and there are insufficient funds in the scheme to provide at least PPF level of pension benefits. As at 2021 the PPF manage £36 billion of assets and hundreds of transferred pension schemes for 276,000 members. PPF compensation is funded in part by a levy paid by all eligible pension schemes and in part from the funds of schemes transferring in to the PPF. Where a scheme is accepted into the PPF, the members of the scheme receive the following compensation:

- 100% of pension benefits for those who have already reached normal scheme retirement age;
- 90% of accrued pension benefits from age 65 for all other members.

PPF compensation is capped at £41,461 (2020/21), rising in line with wage inflation. The 90% maximum for those in schemes entering the PPF who are below their scheme's normal pension age will therefore be £37,315. The cap is increased for those with 21 or more years' service in the original scheme and also varies by age. PPF compensation in payment rises in line with the CPI, capped at 2.5%.

10.87 Entering the PPF is a lengthy process. Following a 'qualifying insolvency event' (administration, appointment of a receiver or winding up) the appointed insolvency practitioner will notify the PPF, which then has 28 days to decide if the scheme is eligible. If it is, an Assessment Period begins, which will take at least a year, and often more. If, at the end of the Assessment Period, the actuarial valuation confirms that the scheme cannot pay at least PPF levels of benefits, the scheme will transfer formally into the PPF. Not all schemes that begin the process end up in the PPF: some companies may be rescued as a going concern or be bought by a purchaser who takes responsibility for the pension scheme liabilities. Search facilities on the PPF website can be used to establish whether a scheme is being assessed or has transferred into the PPF. FPR 9.37 and 9.39 place obligations on scheme members where the PPF is involved to notify their spouse and to obtain valuations of the compensation rights where an application has been made for a financial remedy on divorce.

10.88 PPF compensation is a matter to which the court must have regard[1] and it can be shared or attached on divorce[2]. The application is made in Form A for a pension compensation sharing order and/or a pension compensation attachment order. PPF compensation does not, however, include payment of death in service lump sums and so these cannot be attached. Once a scheme is in the PPF all its assets are transferred to the PPF and valuations are provided by the PPF Board. Pension sharing and attachment orders can no longer be made: only compensation orders. Those pension schemes that have notified the PPF of an insolvency event but have not yet transferred into the PPF (ie those within the first 28 days or in the Assessment Period) will still issue CEs (although these may be reduced) and pension sharing or attachment orders may still be made. If the PPF assumes responsibility for the scheme at the end of the Assessment Period, any outstanding pension sharing or attachment orders are implemented by the PPF. If a fund against which a pension sharing order has already been made subsequently transfers into the PPF, then the PPF is substituted for the trustees or managers of the previous scheme and PPF compensation replaces any pension benefits previously payable. The person entitled to the pension credit is treated as if he or she had been a member of the relevant scheme immediately before the Assessment period and the PPF compensation is calculated, including by reference to the cap. If a PPF compensation order is contemplated, don't forget to serve the PPF Board with the application, draft order and sealed order[3]. The detail of the order is drafted in a pension compensation sharing or attachment annex.

[1]   MCA 1973, s 25(2)(a) and (h) and s 25(E)(1).
[2]   MCA 1973, ss 21B and 24E–24G and 25–25G.
[3]   For the detail of what is required see FPR 9.40–9.45.

10.89 For those defined benefit pension schemes which are ineligible for the PPF because the insolvency event happened before 5 April 2005, the Financial Assistance Scheme (FAS) may assist members at risk of losing their pension benefits. The FAS closed to new schemes on 1 September 2016. Unlike the PPF, it is a top-up scheme, paying compensation in addition to that paid by the original pension scheme, to a maximum of 90% of the original pension accrued, subject to a cap. FAS compensation *cannot* be subject to pension sharing, attachment or compensation orders, but it can and should be taken into account as a resource available to the pension member.

10.90 PPF and FAS schemes only assist those in certain defined *benefit* schemes, where the insolvent employer has made but cannot keep its pension pledges. If a pension firm holding defined *contribution* assets fails, this will not be covered by the PPF or FAS. However, the FSCS may pay compensation to an individual if the failed pension firm was regulated by the Prudential Regulation Authority or the Financial Conduct Authority. Any such compensation would be an asset to take into account in divorce proceedings.

INTERNATIONAL ISSUES

10.91 Two distinct scenarios can arise:

•   the spouses are divorcing in England and Wales, but one or more pension funds are held abroad;
•   the parties have divorced overseas, but require a pension order in this jurisdiction as one or more of the pension funds is held in England or Wales.

Pension orders against pensions in other jurisdictions

10.92 In relation to pension orders against pensions in other jurisdictions:

(i)   Many British families hold pension assets with Scottish pension funds. Scottish pension providers will usually implement an English/Welsh pension sharing order. In the unlikely event of a problem, a certificate can be applied for under Sch 6 of the Civil Jurisdiction and Judgments Act 1982.

(ii)   It is not possible for the courts in England and Wales to make a pension sharing order or a pension attachment order directly against a foreign pension[1].

(iii)   It may still, however, be possible to access the foreign pension funds to bring them within the English divorce settlement. In some jurisdictions, anti-alienation restrictions (preventing the transfer of pension funds away from the pension holder) do not exist, and a simple lump sum order (immediate or deferred) can be made. An (unattached) periodical payments order might be made. Some jurisdictions have an equivalent to the provisions in the Matrimonial and Family Proceedings Act 1984, Pt III, allowing for a pension order to be made in that jurisdiction following an English divorce. If the pension holder will cooperate, it may be possible to transfer the pension funds into an English pension arrangement, thus making them amenable to an English pension order. Offsetting may be an appropriate remedy where there are sufficient other funds. It may be possible to vary an overseas pension as a nuptial settlement under MCA 1973, s 24(1)(c).

(iv)   Bespoke expert advice might be necessary and proportionate as to how the pension will be treated in the jurisdiction where it is based. For example, in Australia pensions may be split by agreement and without the necessity of a court order. In Germany pensions are divided administratively on divorce, irrespective of where the divorce has taken place, and it is important to be aware of this, to avoid double compensation.

[1]   *Goyal v Goyal* [2016] EWFC 50.

Pension orders following an overseas divorce

10.93 English pension providers will not implement orders made by a foreign court, and so a mirror order in this jurisdiction will be required. The application is made under the Matrimonial and Family Proceedings Act 1984, Pt III. Jurisdiction to make such an application is governed by s 15 of the Act. This is complicated and beyond the scope of this chapter to explain in detail, but is most often based on the domicile of either party or on one party's habitual residence in England or Wales for at least a year prior to the application. The existence of a former matrimonial home in this jurisdiction is not of itself enough to found jurisdiction. If the English court does not have jurisdiction, the foreign pension order may remain unenforceable, unless and until the English pension can be transferred abroad or the assets are withdrawn from within the pension fund. Some examples of successful Pt III applications for pension orders are *Schofield v Schofield*[1] where a pension sharing order was made against the husband's British Army pension following a

German divorce and *Barnett v Barnett*[2] where a pension sharing order was made against the husband's British miner's pension after Bulgarian divorce proceedings.

[1]   [2011] EWCA Civ 174.
[2]   [2014] EWHC 2678 (Fam).

VARIATION

10.94 Pension orders are variable as follows:

(i)   A pension sharing order (or compensation sharing order) may be varied under s 31 MCA 1973 *only* where the application to vary is made *both* before the order has taken effect and before decree absolute is granted. After either of these events, the PSO can no longer be varied.

(ii)   A pension attachment order for periodical payments remains variable under s 31(2)(b).

(iii)   An order for a pension attachment lump sum is variable under s 31(2)(e), as an exception to the general rule that capital orders cannot be varied.

(iv)   A pension attachment of death benefits can be varied, save that an order attaching a member's death in service benefits cannot be varied after the death of one of the parties.

10.95 On an application to vary or discharge any type of variable order under s 31, a pension sharing order (or compensation sharing order) may be made under s 31(7B), provided always the petition was filed after 1 December 2000 and a previous PSO has not been made against this pension between these parties. For example, on an application to vary or discharge a periodical payments order, the court may make a PSO to effect a clean break between the parties, as part of its ongoing duty to consider whether the party in whose favour the order was made may adjust to the termination of the payments without undue hardship[1].

[1]   MCA 1973, s 25A(2).

ENFORCEMENT AND PENSION ORDERS

10.96 Pension sharing orders are not presently available as a *direct* method of enforcement. However, enforcement of periodical payments arrears and/or unpaid lump sum orders (or any other judgment debt) may be made against pension assets, pursuant to the rule in *Blight v Brewster*, a first instance decision of Mr Gabriel Moss QC sitting as a deputy High Court judge[1]. The debtor, who held a pension, was ordered to delegate his power of election as to drawing a lump sum from his pension to the creditor's solicitor as a receiver. The solicitor was then authorised to make the election for drawdown of a lump sum from the pension. A third-party debt order then channelled the lump sum directly to the creditor. The method will only work to the extent that the pension assets can be accessed as a lump sum – ie for debtors aged 55 and over. Form D50K should be used to make the application[2].

[1]   *Blight v Brewster* [2012] EWHC 165 (Ch).

2   For more information as to the theory and practice see Joseph Rainer's article in Family Law
    Week 'Enforcement against Pensions in Financial Remedies Cases: the neglected option' [2018
    archive – familylawweek.co.uk]. An article by Beverley Morris and Philip Cayford QC – 'An
    effective method of enforcement? *Blight v Brewster*' at February [2017] Fam Law provides an
    example of the method operating in practice.

10.97 The case of *Amin v Amin*[1] provides an example of a wife's application
for a pension sharing order being adjourned, to see if the husband complied
with orders to transfer a property to the wife and pay a lump sum. Upon the
husband's non-compliance, the judge made a PSO on the wife's 'enforcement'
application, using a broad-brush approach to equate sums in the pension with
sums outstanding under the unpaid non-pension orders.

1   *Amin v Amin* [2017] EWCA Civ 1114.

SAME SEX RELATIONSHIPS

10.98 The courts' powers to deal with pensions on divorce extend, applying
identical principles, to parties dissolving same sex unions, by virtue of the Civil
Partnership Act 2004 and the Marriage (Same Sex Couples) Act 2013.
However, survivor's benefits in occupational pension schemes have operated
differently for same sex couples, compared with couples of opposite sexes. An
exception in the Equality Act 2010 provides that it is not discrimination to
limit the provision of survivor's benefits to same sex couples to service after
5 December 2005, when civil partnerships were first introduced. In July 2017
the Supreme Court ruled that the different treatment of death benefits for same
sex couples, limiting the benefits to post-December 2005 service, was incompatible with EU law and that pension schemes should not therefore exclude
benefits accrued before 5 December 2005 in calculating death benefits in
respect of members in civil partnerships or same sex marriages[1]. Public service
pension schemes are consulting on changes to remove gender discrimination in
survivor entitlements and the House of Commons Library has published a
detailed briefing paper[2] setting out the position as to pension rights for those
in civil partnerships and same sex marriages. Practitioners should therefore be
aware that survivor's benefits for same sex couples (and thus the benefits to be
lost on dissolution) may be mis-quoted by schemes still applying, unlawfully,
the 5 December 2005 cut-off date in making any payments or calculating
quotations.

1   *Walker v Innospec and others* [2017] UKSC 47.
2   Number CBP-03035 15 February 2019.

BANKRUPT SPOUSES AND PENSIONS

10.99 The Insolvency Act 1986 explicitly excludes pension rights from the
estate of a bankrupt. Pension assets will therefore remain available to the
divorcing spouses even after or within a bankruptcy. However, a trustee in
bankruptcy may apply to the court under the Insolvency Act 1986, s 342A to
recoup pension contributions where these were excessive or designed to keep
assets out of the hands of creditors. In *Horton v Henry*[1], the Court of Appeal
clarified that a bankrupt could not be compelled to draw down lump sums and
income from his pension to make them available to creditors, although the use

of receivership as an enforcement mechanism in *Blight v Brewster*[2] as described at **10.96** above provides an exception to this rule.

1   *Horton v Henry* [2016] EWCA Civ 989.
2   *Blight v Brewster* [2012] EWHC 165 (Ch).

Chapter 11
CHILDREN

INTRODUCTION

11.1 Any attempt to describe the significance of children in financial remedy cases is bound to result in a somewhat muddled account. The welfare of any minor children of the family is the first consideration of the court[1], but this does not mean that their interests take precedence over those of the adults in the case; the meaning of the 'first consideration' is considered in more detail at **1.52**. It certainly does not mean that the court must make orders for the support of children before it may deal with their parents; indeed, as will be seen, in most cases the court is precluded by statute from doing so.

[1] MCA 1973, s 25(1).

11.2 The complicating factor in cases involving children is the CSA 1991, which is intended to provide support for most children. It will, therefore, be necessary to consider the principles of this Act at the outset, after which the principles for dealing with those cases in which the court has jurisdiction will be examined.

THE CHILD SUPPORT ACT 1991

11.3 The present law, which has been considerably amended, may be summarised as follows:

(a) In cases involving 'natural' children (ie children of both parties, whether by birth or adoption) jurisdiction to make orders for financial support was removed from the courts and originally vested in the Child Support Agency (CSA)[1] and now in its successor the Child Maintenance Service (CMS). The CMS has responsibility for the enforcement and collection of any maintenance required to be paid.

(b) A person with the care of children is described as 'the person with care' (PWC) and the other parent is the 'non-resident parent' (NRP). A child is only subject to the Act if he or she was a 'qualifying child', ie a child of the PWC and the NRP who lives with the person with care, and where all three are habitually resident in the UK.

(c) Child maintenance is calculated under the Act according to a formula prescribed by the Act. In the original version of the formula there was no room for discretion or variation; indeed, one of the purposes of the Act was to depart from what was described as the 'discredited discretionary system' adopted by the courts. When it was found that

> this resulted in hardship, attempts were made to make the formula more flexible, but the principle that all jurisdiction must be derived from the Act remains.

1   CSA 1991, s 8(3).

11.4 This is not the place for a detailed examination of the principles of the 1991 Act[1]. Instead, the following matters will be considered:

(a)   the basic principles of the formula; and
(b)   exceptions to the Act.

1   For a helpful introduction, see the articles by James Pirrie and Michelle Counley at [2020] Fam Law 1530 and 1670 and [2021] Fam Law 124.

11.5 The significance of the Act in relation to cases to which it does not apply and where the court has jurisdiction will be considered at **11.20**.

Basic principles of the formula

11.6 The parents of a qualifying child are called the parent with care (PWC) and the non-resident parent (NRP). What used to be called a 'maintenance assessment' is now a 'maintenance calculation'. The income of the PWC is ignored and the calculation is based entirely on the income of the NRP, being a percentage of his gross income depending on the number of children.

11.7 From the beginning of the child support system the formula for determining how much a NRP should pay has been contained in para 2 of Sch 1 to the CSA 1991. This has now been amended by para 3 of Sch 4 to the Child Maintenance and Other Payments Act 2008 (CMOPA 2008), which was brought into effect by statutory instrument[1] on 10 December 2012. The general rule now is that the basic rate is a percentage of the gross weekly income of the NRP calculated as follows:

- 12% where the NRP has one qualifying child;
- 16% where the NRP has two qualifying children;
- 19% where the NRP has three or more qualifying children.

1   Child Maintenance and Other Payments Act 2008 (Commencement No 10 and Transitional Provisions) Order 2012, SI 2012/3042. See also the Child Support Maintenance Calculation Regulations 2012, SI 2012/2677 and the Child Support (Miscellaneous Amendments) Regulations 2018, SI 2018/1279.

11.8 This is therefore on the face of it a simple calculation. If, for example, the NRP earns £400 per week gross and has one qualifying child the child support maintenance will be £48 per week. Where there are two children it would be £64 per week and where there are three or more children it would be £76 per week.

11.9 However, the calculation is not as simple as might appear at first sight since, in effect, CSA 1991 reintroduces a two-tier system of earnings of the NRP, so that higher earners do not pay the full basic rate. Where the gross weekly income of the non-resident parent exceeds £800 (or £41,600 per annum) the percentages mentioned above apply only to the first £800, but the slice of the income above £800 per week is subject to deduction of the following percentages:

- one qualifying child 9%;
- two qualifying children 12%;
- three or more qualifying children 15%.

11.10 There is a cap, or limit, on the income of the NRP that is taken into account. After the changes of 2000 this figure was £2,000 per week net; it is now[1] £800 per week gross (equivalent to £153,846 per annum) plus a percentage of the balance over that figure depending on whether he has one qualifying child (9%), two qualifying children (12%) or three or more qualifying children (15%). (For the position as to top-up orders, where income exceeds £3,000 per week, see **11.15** below.)

[1] From 10 December 2012: see CSA 1991, s 3 above.

11.11 However, the calculation contains two other complications. The first of these relates to 'relevant other children' of the NRP. Relevant other children are defined as children other than qualifying children in respect of whom the NRP or his or her partner receives child benefit or such other children as may be[1] prescribed; as there has never been any other class of children it may be assumed that this is a complete definition.

[1] CSA 1991, Sch 1, para 10C(2).

11.12 In effect, therefore, other relevant children are children of the NRP or his or her partner who are living with the NRP. No account is taken of the income of the partner, whether as child maintenance or otherwise.

11.13 The allowance which is made is by way of a deduction from the gross income of the NRP before it falls to be considered for deduction of the basic rate. The percentages are:

- 11% for one relevant other child;
- 14% for two relevant children;
- 16% for three or more relevant children[1].

[1] CMOPA 2008, Sch 4, para 3(3), amending CSA 1991, Sch 1, para 2.

11.14 Gross weekly income is determined in such manner as prescribed by regulations[1]. These regulations may in particular provide for the CMS to estimate any income or make an assumption as to any fact where, in its view, the information at its disposal is unreliable, insufficient or relates to an untypical period in the life of the non-resident parent[2].

[1] CSA 1991, Sch 1, para 10(1).
[2] CSA 1991, Sch 1, para 10(2).

11.15 The system contains a large number of exceptions, special cases etc which are detailed and need not be considered here. The following are the principal matters of which the reader should be aware. As always with child support, the calculation is more complex than might appear to be the case, and the stages through which the calculation must go are outlined below.

(1)   No child maintenance is payable when the NRP has a net income of below £7 or his income is of a prescribed description (eg students and prisoners).

(2)   When the NRP's net income is £100 per week or less, or he receives any benefit, pension or allowance prescribed for this purpose, or he or his partner receive any benefit prescribed for this purpose, and the nil rate does not apply, the flat rate of £7 per week applies.

(3)   Where the NRP has a partner who is also an NRP, and the partner is a person with respect to whom a maintenance calculation is in force, and the NRP or his partner receive any benefit prescribed for this purpose, the nil rate applies.

(4)   When neither the nil rate nor a flat rate applies, and the NRP's net income is between £100 and £200 per week, the reduced rate applies[1].

(5)   When none of the previous categories is applicable, the basic rate applies. This is a percentage of the net weekly income of the NRP and is 15% where there is one qualifying child, 20% for two children and 25% for three or more.

(6)   Income of the NRP exceeding £3,000 per week is ignored. The maximum sum payable under a maintenance calculation is therefore £500 per week, but the provisions as to applications to the court for 'top-up' orders are maintained.

(7)   Where the NRP has more than one qualifying child, living with different PWCs, the rate of maintenance liability is divided by the number of qualifying children and shared among the PWCs according to the number of qualifying children living with that PWC.

(8)   The amount of the maintenance calculation may be reduced if the NRP has one or more qualifying children with him for more than a certain number of nights per annum. The amount of decrease in respect of each child is as follows:

Number of nights with NRP	*Fraction to subtract*
52 to 103	One-seventh
104 to 155	Two-sevenths
156 to 174	Three-sevenths
175 or more	One-half

[1]   Reduced rate is defined in CSA 1991, Sch 1, para 3.

11.16 If the PWC is providing for more than one qualifying child of the NRP, the applicable decrease is the sum of the appropriate fractions in the table divided by the number of qualifying children. If the applicable fraction is one-half in relation to any qualifying child in the care of the PWC, the total amount payable to the PWC is then to be further decreased by £7 for each such child. Finally, if the application of these provisions would reduce the weekly amount of child support payable by the NRP to the PWC to less than £5 per week, the NRP has to pay £5 per week.

WHEN MAY APPLICATIONS BE MADE TO THE COURT?

11.17 As was explained above, one of the principal features of the 1991 Act is that it is intended that the jurisdiction of the court shall be excluded and replaced by that of the Secretary of State. In *R (Kehoe) v Secretary of State for Work and Pensions*[1] it was held that the intention of the 1991 Act was to replace – except as expressly retained by the Act itself – any pre-existing rights of either a child or parent to periodical payments for the maintenance of that child. The applicant mother had no right that she could exercise against the father and accordingly she could not assert that she had an arguable civil right that entitled her under Art 6(1) of ECHR to a determination by the court. However, the Act itself contains various exceptions to this principle, and further exceptions have been provided for as a result of the CSA's inability to handle all the tasks originally intended for it. These may be summarised as follows.

[1] [2004] EWCA Civ 225, [2004] 1 FLR 1132. Upheld on appeal at [2005] UKHL 48, [2005] 2 FLR 1249, HL. The PWC had no right she could enforce against the NRP apart from judicial review. The maintenance obligation was enforceable only by the Secretary of State.

(a) Cases where the Secretary of State does not have jurisdiction

11.18 The Secretary of State has jurisdiction only where the child is under 18 years of age and is the natural or adopted child of a person with care and a non-resident parent, and all three are habitually resident in the UK. It follows that stepchildren, children aged over 18, and cases where any one of the parties or child are not habitually resident are excluded from the jurisdiction of the Secretary of State and fall within the jurisdiction of the court.

(b) Applications to the court permitted by the Act

11.19 The Act allows applications to the court to be made in addition to a calculation by the Secretary of State in certain cases:

(i)   'Topping up', ie when the maximum amount payable under the formula has been reached; in such cases the court may make an order for such additional amount as is appropriate[1].

(ii) Additional educational expenses. An order may be made 'solely for the purposes of requiring the person making or securing the making of periodical payments fixed by the order to meet some or all of the expenses incurred in connection with the provision of . . . instruction or training'[2]. The most obvious way in which this might be used is to obtain an order for the payment of school fees, but the provision is not limited to this.

(iii) Disabled or blind children. Where a disability living allowance is paid to or in respect of a child, or no such allowance is paid but the child is disabled, an order may be made solely for the purpose of requiring the person making the payments 'to meet some or all of any of the expenses attributable to the child's disability'[3].

In the case of (i) above, it is a prerequisite that a maintenance calculation has been made. This is not necessary in the two other cases.

[1]   CSA 1991, s 8(6).
[2]   CSA 1991, s 8(7).
[3]   CSA 1991, s 8(8). By s 8(9), a child is disabled if he is blind, deaf or dumb or is substantially and permanently handicapped by illness, injury, mental disorder or congenital deformity or such other disability as may be prescribed.

(c) Certain consent orders

11.20 A court may make an order where 'a written agreement (whether or not enforceable) provides for the making, or securing, by a non-resident parent of the child of periodical payments to or for the benefit of the child; and the maintenance order which the court makes is, in all material respects, in the same terms as that agreement'[1]. In order to be satisfied of its jurisdiction, therefore, the court may need to see a copy of the written agreement. It should also be noted that the CSA 1991 provides that 'nothing in this Act shall be taken to prevent any person from entering into a maintenance agreement'[2].

[1]   CSA 1991, s 8(5).
[2]   CSA 1991, s 9(2).

(d) Capital orders

11.21 There is nothing in the CSA 1991 to prevent a lump sum order or a property adjustment order in favour of a child (but see **11.40**).

(e) Applications under 'transitional provisions'

11.22 It was always envisaged that the Agency (now the Child Maintenance Service) would not be able to take on all cases immediately and that there would have to be a phased take up. What began as transitional provisions seem to have achieved a degree of permanence, but there seems little point in summarising the position further since, with the advent of the new formula, this will be a diminishing problem.

(f) Variation and duration of orders

11.23 As was noted above, the court has jurisdiction to make orders for child maintenance where there is no maintenance calculation in effect and the parties have agreed the terms of such order in writing. Such an order, once made, may be varied. Until the coming into force of the new provisions in 2003, this prevented any application for a maintenance calculation under s 4 of the 1991 Act. The position after implementation of the new provisions was different. By s 4(10) of the 1991 Act, as amended by CSPSSA 2000, the Secretary of State could make a maintenance calculation, provided that one year has elapsed from the date of the order. Advisers should therefore be aware that any agreement made and reflected in a consent order may last only for one year, and the message would seem to be that orders should, as far as possible, be in terms similar to those of a maintenance calculation.

APPLICATIONS TO THE COURT

11.24 For the purposes of this book, it will be assumed that any application to the court in respect of children will be made under the provisions of MCA 1973. For the sake of completeness, however, it should be noted that, where the court has jurisdiction, applications may be made under the provisions of Sch 1 to the Children Act 1989. The principles governing the exercise of the court's discretion under the 1989 Act are virtually identical to those under MCA 1973.

11.25 The rules governing the procedure for applications in respect of children are contained in Chapter 3 of Pt 9 of the FPR. It is provided that the following persons may apply for an order:

* any person in whose favour a residence order has been made with respect to a child of the family, and any applicant for such an order;
* any other person who is entitled to apply for a residence order with respect to a child;
* a local authority, where an order has been made under s 31(1)(a) of the 1989 Act placing a child in its care;
* the Official Solicitor, if appointed the children's guardian of a child of the family under r 16.24; and
* a child of the family who has been given permission to apply for a financial remedy.

Jurisdiction

11.26 The powers of the court to make financial provision orders and property adjustment orders have been set out in the chapters applicable to each of the various forms of relief (eg periodical payments, lump sum, etc). It will be noted that in each case the court has jurisdiction to make an order of the kind described for the benefit of a child of the family. 'Child of the family' is defined as, in relation to the parties to a marriage[1]:

'(a) a child of both those parties; and
(b) any other child, not being a child who is placed with those parties as foster parents by a local authority or voluntary organisation, who has been treated by both of those parties as a child of their family.'

[1]   MCA 1973, s 52(1).

Age limits

11.27 The basic principle is that 'no financial provision order and no order for a transfer of property under s 24(1)(a) . . . shall be made in favour of a child who has attained the age of eighteen'[1]. It is also provided that the term specified in any order for periodical payments or secured periodical payments in favour of a child[2]:

'(a)   shall not in the first instance extend beyond the date of the birthday of the child next following his attaining the upper limit of the compulsory school age . . . unless the court considers that in the circumstances of the case the welfare of the child requires that it should extend to a later date; and

(b)   shall not in any event, subject to subsection (3) below, extend beyond the date of the child's eighteenth birthday.'

[1]   MCA 1973, s 29(1).
[2]   MCA 1973, s 29(2).

11.28 Section 29(3) will be considered below. However, the principle is that no order may be made in respect of a child who is aged over 18, or which extends beyond the age of 18. The court has no power to make an order on the application of a parent for a child who is over the age of 18 when the application is made. At the time of the application the child must be 'a child' as defined in s 105 CA 1989[1]. Moreover, any periodic order for a child should not extend beyond the child's seventeenth birthday unless the court considers that the welfare of the child requires such an order.

[1]   *DN v UD (Sch 1 Children Act: Capital Provision)* [2020] EWHC 627 (Fam).

11.29 However, there is an exception to this principle. It is provided that the limitations on orders for children aged over 18 or extending beyond that age shall not apply[1]:

' . . . if it appears to the court that—

(a)   the child is, or will be, or if an order were made without complying with either or both of those provisions would be, receiving instruction at an educational establishment or undergoing training for a trade, profession or vocation, whether or not he is also, or will also be, in gainful employment; or

(b)   there are special circumstances which justify the making of an order without complying with either or both of those provisions.'

[1]   MCA 1973, s 29(3).

11.30 The effect of this is that when a child is, or will be, in education or training, whether full-time or part-time, an order may be made for or to him. 'Special circumstances' are not defined, but would probably include cases where the 'child' was unable to be self-sufficient because of some mental or physical disability.

11.31 The usual wording of an order for a child under the age of 17 is that the payments continue 'until the said child shall attain the age of 17 years or ceases full-time education if later or further order'.

Principles on which the court exercises its jurisdiction

11.32 When the court exercises its jurisdiction in respect of a child, it is directed to have regard in particular to the following matters[1]:

'(a)   the financial needs of the child;

(b)   the income, earning capacity (if any), property and other financial resources of the child;

(c)   any physical or mental disability of the child;

(d) the manner in which he was being and in which the parties to the marriage expected him to be educated or trained;

(e) the considerations mentioned in relation to the parties to the marriage in paragraphs (a), (b), (c) and (e) of subsection (2).'

The matters referred to in (e) are the income, capital, etc of each of the parties, their needs, obligations and responsibilities, the standard of living enjoyed by the family and any mental or physical disability of either party.

[1] MCA 1973, s 25(3).

11.33 In addition to the matters prescribed above, when the court is exercising its powers against a party to the marriage in favour of a child of the family who is not the child of that party, the court is directed to have regard[1]:

'(a) to whether that party assumed any responsibility for the child's maintenance, and, if so, to the extent to which, and the basis upon which, that party assumed such responsibility and to the length of time for which that party discharged such responsibility;

(b) to whether in assuming and discharging such responsibility that party did so knowing that the child was not his or her own;

(c) to the liability of any other person to maintain the child.'

[1] MCA 1973, s 25(4).

Periodic orders for children

11.34 The quantification of an order for periodical payments for a child must be approached on the same basis as any other periodical payments order, ie by assessing the reasonable needs and requirements of the child in the light of the statutory factors set out above and then determining the ability of the parents to provide for such needs and requirements. Both parents have an obligation to provide for a child, and the court would normally expect this obligation to be regarded as a prior responsibility by both of them. However, this principle must be tempered by the recognition of the fact that the 'non-resident parent' has to maintain himself and discharge any proper responsibilities which he may have assumed; the latter may include a new family[1]. In one case it was said that[2]:

'The respondent husband is entitled to order his life in such a way as will hold in reasonable balance the responsibilities to his existing family which he carries into his new life, as well as his proper aspirations for that new future. In all life, for those who are divorced as well as for those who are not divorced, indulging one's whims or even one's reasonable desires must be held in check by the constraints imposed by limited resources and compelling obligations.'

[1] See eg *R v R* [1988] 1 FLR 89, CA.
[2] *Delaney v Delaney* [1990] 2 FLR 457, CA, at 461, per Ward J.

11.35 Whatever view is eventually taken of the parents' ability to pay, it is normally necessary to make a provisional assessment of the child's needs. In many cases, the formula prescribed by the CSA 1991 will assist as a starting point, and a 'child support calculation' is always useful in such cases. Indeed, in *E v C (Child Maintenance)*[1], where a family proceedings court had declined to vary an order for £5 per week against a father who was unemployed and in receipt of benefit, Douglas Brown J allowed the appeal and observed that the justices would have done well to consider what a child support assessment would have been (in the instant case it would have been a nil assessment). While that assessment would not have been binding on the court, it would have been strongly persuasive. It was the practice of professional judges to ask about a child support assessment, and it would be helpful for justices to do likewise.

¹ [1996] 1 FLR 472.

11.36 Support for this view is now to be found in *GW v RW (Financial Provision: Departure from Equality)*¹, a case involving very substantial assets. It was held that, in fixing a child maintenance award in a case where the Agency lacked jurisdiction, the appropriate starting point was almost invariably the figure thrown up by the new child support rules.

¹ [2003] EWHC 611 (Fam), [2003] 2 FLR 108, Nicholas Mostyn QC.

11.37 In *TM v TM (Minors)(Child Maintenance: Jurisdiction and Departure from Formula)*¹ Mostyn J, applying *GW v RW (Financial Provision: Departure from Equality)*² held that where the court makes a child maintenance order the starting point should almost invariably be the amount arrived at by the application of the formula prescribed by the CSA 1991. In *CB v KB (Financial Remedies: Calculation of Income Streams and Child Support)*³ Mostyn J pursued this line of argument and said that, although it is not 'written in marble', in every case where the gross annual income of the non-resident parent does not exceed £650,000 the starting point for calculating child support should be the result of the formula, ignoring the cap of £156,000. For gross incomes exceeding £650,000 the result given using the formula should be the starting point with full discretionary freedom to depart from it having regard to the scale of the excess. It is fair to say that this statement is not universally accepted and, as Mostyn J suggests, it is certainly not a binding rule. Nevertheless it might be a useful starting point.

¹ [2016] Fam Law 15.
² [2003] 2 FLR 108.
³ [2019] EWFC 78.

11.38 These cases are, therefore, authority for always considering as a first step what a child support calculation would be in all cases involving a child. It could not be the last word, since the court is bound by s 25(3) and (4) and not by the CSA 1991 when dealing with children's cases, but it would at least be a useful starting point. It is suggested that these principles supersede the earlier practice of adopting income support figures (in lower income cases) or the National Foster Care Association recommendations (in cases of greater affluence) as a starting point.

11.39 Different considerations apply in very 'big money' cases. In *M v M (Financial Relief: Substantial Earning Capacity)*¹ the award was for £25,000 pa per child, increasing to £35,000 pa for a child with special needs. In the celebrated case of *McCartney v Mills McCartney*² the award was for £35,000 pa for one child aged 4, plus school fees and the cost of a nanny not to exceed £30,000 pa. All sums were index-linked.

¹ [2004] 2 FLR 236.
² [2008] 1 FLR 1508.

Capital provision for children

11.40 As was observed when the exceptions to the CSA 1991 were being considered, there is nothing in the Act to prevent a lump sum order or property adjustment order in favour of a child, even when a child support calculation is in force. However, it must be said that such orders are rare, since it is difficult to show that a child, as distinct from the parent with whom he lives, has a need or reasonable requirement for capital. There is, in principle, no justification for the children to expect to share in their parents' capital assets on or after the dissolution of marriage[1], although settlement orders may be made in exceptional cases[2].

[1] *Lilford (Lord) v Glyn* [1979] 1 All ER 441; *Kiely v Kiely* [1988] 1 FLR 248, CA.
[2] See eg *Tavoulareas v Tavoulareas* [1998] 2 FLR 418, CA.

11.41 An example of a capital order for children in somewhat unusual circumstances is *V v V (Child Maintenance)*[1], where the father, having invited the judge to determine the level of child maintenance, then refused to consent to the judge's proposed order. The judge awarded the children lump sums, saying that, in those circumstances, it was right to seek to reflect the balance of the provision in another form of order.

[1] [2001] 2 FLR 799, Wilson J.

11.42 The cases brought under the Children Act 1989, Sch 1, in which property has been ordered to be transferred for the benefit of children, support this general proposition. Such cases have been brought when the parents have not been married and so the parent with care (normally the mother) has been unable to apply for provision in her own right[1]. The orders for transfer of capital to provide a home have all provided for the property to be held on trust until the majority of the child and then to return to the transferor. In *Phillips v Peace*[2] it was held that in an application under Sch 1 only one settlement of property order could be made.

[1] See eg *A v A (Minor: Financial Provision)* [1994] 1 FLR 657; *T v S (Financial Provision for Children)* [1994] 2 FLR 883; *Phillips v Peace* [1996] 2 FLR 230; *J v C (Child: Financial Provision)* [1999] 1 FLR 152. For the position where the mother was a joint owner of the house see *Re B (Child: Property Transfer)* [1999] 2 FLR 418.
[2] [2004] EWHC 3180 (Fam), [2005] 2 FLR 1212.

11.43 An interesting insight into financial provision for a child is provided by *K v K (Ancillary Relief: Pre-nuptial Agreement)*[1]. The important point is that, after a short marriage where there had been a pre-nuptial agreement, the wife was held to her agreement as to capital. However, the judge also ordered the husband to provide a home and furnishings for the mother and child at a cost of £1.2m (to revert to him in due course) and £15,000 pa for the child.

[1] [2003] 1 FLR 120.

11.44 Given this decision, the decision of the Court of Appeal in *Re P (Child: Financial Provision)*[1] is also of interest, although it was clearly a most unusual case. Here, the parties were not married and the child was aged 2 years. The father was described as 'fabulously rich'. The court decided that a home in central London was appropriate and ordered the father to provide £1m for this purpose, £100,000 for decoration and furnishing, and £70,000 pa periodical payments, on the basis that the father undertook to pay school fees. The Court of Appeal gave further guidance as to the quantum of financial support for children in *F v G (Child: Financial Provision)*[2]. It was held that, although standard of living is not a factor which appears in the Children Act 1989, Sch 1, para 4(1), it is clearly among the totality of circumstances which the court must hold in view. The extent to which the unit of primary carer and child have become accustomed to a particular level of lifestyle can impact legitimately on an evaluation of a child's needs. The remainder of the case is an interesting example of the way the court may exercise its discretion but, as each case is fact-specific, no further comment need be made here.

[1]   [2003] EWCA Civ 837, [2003] 2 FLR 865.
[2]   [2004] EWHC 1848 (Fam), [2005] 1 FLR 261.

11.45 In *W v J (Child: Variation of Periodical Payments)*[1] it was held that there was no jurisdiction to make an order for increased periodical payments for a child to cover legal costs to be incurred in forthcoming litigation between the parties.

[1]   [2003] EWHC 2657 (Fam), [2004] 2 FLR 300.

School fees

11.46 As was seen above, provision for school fees or other educational expenses is an area where the court always retains jurisdiction, whether or not a child support calculation has been or might be made. Since the Finance Act 1988, there has been no tax advantage to be gained by any particular form of order.

11.47 In *T v T (Financial Provision: Private Education)*[1] the husband applied to be relieved of his obligation under a consent order to pay school fees. The application was dismissed and the husband ordered to pay £254,680.71 lump sum for fees. Bennett J held that he could afford to do so even if he had to sell some assets. This would still leave him securely housed. However, sub nom *Tracey v Tracey*[2], the Court of Appeal allowed in part the husband's appeal. This was allowed on the facts, important information not having been before Bennett J, and the lump sum was reduced. However, the principle was not affected.

[1]   [2005] EWHC 2119 (Fam), [2006] 1 FLR 903.
[2]   [2006] EWCA Civ 734, [2007] 1 FLR 196.

INTERIM APPLICATIONS

11.48 The situation may (indeed, frequently does) arise in which a parent with the care of a child, normally the mother, is left without any support for a child, and, whether or not she seeks to recover any periodical payments or maintenance payment suit for herself, wishes to obtain support for a child. In many such cases the provisions of the CSA 1991 prohibit her from applying to the court for an order for the child, but the Child Maintenance Service (previously the Child Support Agency) may well take many months to deal with any application under s 4.

11.49 In such cases, there is nothing to prevent the court from making an order for the mother which includes support for the child. Such an order has to be expressed as remaining in force 'until a child support calculation is made'. When the order is made up partly of the mother's maintenance and partly the child's, the court would add the words 'whereupon this order shall be reduced by the amount of any such calculation'. Such an order would not be possible where the mother had remarried. Indeed, any such order is only legitimate where there is a genuine and substantial amount of spousal support in the order; where the order in reality relates only to children, it is not legitimate[1].

[1]   *Dorney-Kingdom v Dorney-Kingdom* [2000] 2 FLR 855, CA.

11.50 Orders of the kind approved in *Dorney-Kingdom* are often known as 'Segal orders', in tribute to the district judge who first devised this formula. This approach was recently approved again in *AB v CD (Jurisdiction: Global Maintenance Orders)*[1].

[1]   [2017] EWHC 3164 (Fam).

Chapter 12

INSOLVENCY AND RIGHTS OF CREDITORS

INTRODUCTION

12.1 In this chapter it is intended to consider the effect on the parties of the bankruptcy of one of them. It also seems convenient at this point to consider the position of one or both of the parties when a creditor has a charge, whether by virtue of a mortgage deed or a charging order, over the matrimonial home. The two situations are different, but the effect on the party who is not insolvent or object of the judgment or charge may seem to be similar; a third party is perceived to wish to deprive that party of what she regards as hers.

THE INSOLVENCY ACT 1986 AND SALE OF THE MATRIMONIAL HOME

12.2 When a person becomes bankrupt, the whole of his estate vests in his trustee in bankruptcy[1], who is then under an obligation to realise the bankrupt's assets for the benefit of the creditors. One of the assets will be any property in which the bankrupt has a legal or beneficial interest, and this will frequently include the matrimonial home. If a property is held by the bankrupt and another as joint tenants, the bankruptcy severs the joint[2] tenancy; the result of this is that the trustee and the other co-owner hold the property as tenants in common in equal shares. Where the property was held as tenants in common, the trustee holds the share which the bankrupt previously held.

[1]   IA 1986, s 306.
[2]   *Re Gorman (A Bankrupt)* [1990] 2 FLR 284.

12.3 The trustee is then in the position of any joint owner in the sense that he may apply to the court for an order for sale, previously under s 30 of the Law of Property Act 1925 (LPA 1925) and now under s 14 of the Trusts of Land and Appointment of Trustees Act 1996 (TOLATA 1996)[1]. However, the trustee is in a different position from other joint owners because the Insolvency Act 1986 (IA 1986) prescribes the duties of the court in such circumstances. It is provided[2] that, on application for an order for sale, the court shall make such order:

' . . .   as it thinks just and reasonable having regard to—
  (a)   the interests of the bankrupt's creditors,

> (b)   the conduct of the spouse or former spouse, so far as contributing to the bankruptcy,
>
> (c)   the needs and financial resources of the spouse or former spouse,
>
> (d)   the needs of any children, and
>
> (e)   all the circumstances of the case other than the needs of the bankrupt.'

1   As to when time begins to run for the purposes of the Limitation Act 1980, s 20(1), see *Gotham v Doodes* [2006] EWCA Civ 1080, [2007] 1 FLR 373; the right to receive the money could not predate an order for sale. Until the order for sale, the charge is merely a deferred charge.

2   By IA 1986, s 336(4).

12.4 It will be seen that the court is afforded a certain degree of discretion when considering such applications. However, it is further provided[1] that when the application is made more than one year after the bankruptcy the court 'shall assume, unless the circumstances of the case are exceptional, that the interests of the bankrupt's creditors outweigh all other considerations'.

1   By IA 1986, s 336(5).

12.5 The result of these provisions is that applications for orders for sale are rarely made before one year has elapsed, and, when they are eventually made, there is little or no dispute that an order must be made. It is clearly difficult to prove that the circumstances of a particular case are exceptional, and the courts have accepted the clear intention of the insolvency legislation which puts the interests of the creditors to the forefront. In one case[1], the fact that the wife and children would be rendered homeless was described as 'not an exceptional circumstance. It is a normal circumstance and is the result, the all too obvious result, of a husband having conducted the financial affairs of the family in a way that has led to bankruptcy'. In another case, Hoffmann J decided that, since the half share which the bankrupt's wife would receive would not be sufficient to rehouse her and the children, the order for sale and possession should not be enforced until the youngest child was 16 years old. The Court of Appeal allowed the trustee's appeal and said that an order for immediate sale should have been made. The eviction of the wife, with all the consequent problems, was not exceptional but was 'one of the melancholy consequences of debt and improvidence with which every society has been familiar'[2]. A similar result was reached in *Barca v Mears*[3] but it should be noted that in that case the learned judge said that the *Re Citro* approach might be incompatible with Convention rights and might need re-examining in light of the European Convention.

1   *Re Lowrie (A Bankrupt)* [1981] 3 All ER 353.
2   *Re Citro (A Bankrupt)* [1991] Ch 142, CA.
3   [2004] EWHC 2170 (Ch).

12.6 However, it is not impossible to prove exceptional circumstances[1]. In *Re Holliday*[2], the husband had presented his own petition in bankruptcy as a tactical move to defeat his wife's claims. No creditors were pressing and he was in a position to discharge his debts out of income. The judge postponed sale for 5 years. In *Re Bailey*[3], although an order for sale was made, it seems to have been accepted that if a house had been specially converted to meet the needs of a disabled child, the circumstances could properly be described as exceptional.

¹   For another example of the application of the relevant principles leading to an order for sale, see the judgment of Lawrence Collins J in *Dean v Stout* [2005] EWHC 3315 (Ch), [2006] 1 FLR 725.
²   [1981] 3 All ER 353.
³   [1977] 1 WLR 278.

12.7 In *Judd v Brown*¹, the fact that the wife was suffering from cancer and had to undergo a course of chemotherapy was held to be an exceptional circumstance and the trustee's application for an order for sale was refused. A slightly different result was reached in *Re Raval (A Bankrupt)*², where the bankrupt's wife suffered from schizophrenia and it was thought that 'adverse life events' might cause a relapse. The former matrimonial home was the only asset but there was a substantial equity. Possession was suspended for one year.

¹   [1998] 2 FLR 360.
²   [1998] 2 FLR 718.

12.8 In *Re Bremner*¹, the bankrupt husband was aged 79, suffering from cancer, and unlikely to survive more than 6 months. It was held that the wife's need to care for him was distinct from the husband's needs and was exceptional; sale was deferred with marketing not to begin until 3 months after the husband's death.

¹   [1999] 1 FLR 912. See also *Claughton v Charalamabous* [1999] 1 FLR 740, CA (the court must make a value judgment and look at all the circumstances); the process leaves little scope for interference by an appellate court.

12.9 An example to the contrary is *Donohoe v Ingram*¹ where the bankrupt's partner applied for sale to be postponed on the ground that the home was needed for the children and the creditors would be paid in full by 2017. It was held that the case was not sufficiently similar to *Holliday* to permit a deviation from the usual *Re Citro* approach.

¹   [2006] 2 FLR 1084.

12.10 In *Mekarska v Ruiz and Bowden (Trustee in Bankruptcy)*¹ a wife's application to annul the husband's bankruptcy was refused, partly because at the date of the bankruptcy order he was plainly unable to pay his debts and his motivation in petitioning had not been to defeat the wife's claims. *Per curiam*, the judge said that where a person affected by a bankruptcy order considers that the order should not have been made, they must act immediately to have it annulled or suspended.

¹   [2011] EWHC 913 (Fam).

12.11 The position of a spouse who has no legal or beneficial interest in the home is different from that of the spouse with such an interest, in that when the house is sold she will recover nothing. However, in terms of her right of occupation, her position is very similar. A spouse with no legal or beneficial interest has matrimonial home rights¹, which include the right not to be evicted save by order of the court. A former spouse has similar rights provided an order to that effect has been made before decree absolute². A trustee in bankruptcy who wishes to obtain a possession order must apply to the court having jurisdiction in the bankruptcy³. The factors which the court must take into account are those already set out above where the spouse is a joint owner. In *Byford v Butler*[4] it was held that a wife who had continued to live in the former matrimonial home after the bankruptcy was entitled to credit for mortgage interest paid, subject to the trustee's right to set off occupation rent.

[1]   FLA 1996, s 30.
[2]   FLA 1996, s 33(5).
[3]   IA 1986, s 336(3).
[4]   [2004] 1 FLR 56.

12.12 Finally, in this section, the position of a bankrupt spouse who has the care of children must be considered. A person who has a beneficial interest in a property, has been made bankrupt, and who has living with him in the property any person under the age of 18 has the right not to be evicted without order of the court[1]. On an application for sale made by a trustee, the court must have regard to 'the interests of the creditors, to the bankrupt's financial resources, to the needs of the children, and to all the circumstances of the case other than the needs of the bankrupt'[2]. There is a similar provision in respect of applications made one year after the bankruptcy to that set out above[3].

[1]   IA 1986, s 337(2).
[2]   IA 1986, s 337(5).
[3]   IA 1986, s 337(6).

Effect of bankruptcy on order for financial relief

12.13 All that has been said so far in this chapter assumes that the bankruptcy has pre-dated any order for financial relief; once the bankruptcy occurs, there is normally little point in considering such applications, and the provisions of the IA 1986 apply. Where a party has presented his or her own petition for bankruptcy in order to defeat the claim of the other in principle the other party may apply to annul the bankruptcy on the ground that it should not have been made under s 282(1)(a). However, the onus of proof lies on the applicant and if, in fact, the bankrupt was unable to pay his debts on the date of the bankruptcy, his motives are irrelevant[1].

[1]   *Whig v Whig* [2008] 1 FLR 453.

12.14 What must now be considered is the position when a bankruptcy order is made after an order for financial relief has been made, and what effect, if any, the bankruptcy will have on that order and its implementation.

12.15 The answer to this will depend on the type of order which has been made, and each must be considered in turn. It should, however, be noted that the same regime and rationales apply when there has not been an order but a transfer pursuant to an agreement which has not led to an order[1].

[1]   *Segal v Pasram* [2008] 1 FLR 271.

Property adjustment orders

12.16 The court has no jurisdiction to make a property adjustment order against a bankrupt spouse[1]. A common danger which may be encountered by a party in whose favour a property adjustment order has been made is that the transaction, ie the transfer of property pursuant to the order, may be set aside on an application by the trustee in bankruptcy. The trustee has the right to apply to the court[2] for an order to set aside any transaction 'at an undervalue' made within a specified period before the day of the presentation of the bankruptcy petition. The fact that the transfer has been made pursuant to an order of the court does not prevent it from being the object of such an application[3].

1   *McGladdery v McGladdery* [1999] 2 FLR 1102.
2   Under IA 1986, s 339.
3   MCA 1973, s 39.

12.17 However, in *Mountney v Treharne*[1], where the court had ordered the transfer of a house to the wife but a bankruptcy order was made in respect of the husband before the transfer was signed, it was held that the order had the effect of conferring on the wife an equitable interest in the property at the moment it took effect, ie on decree absolute. The trustee in bankruptcy therefore took the property subject to the wife's equitable interest[2]. For the position in a similar case involving pension policies see **12.28**.

1   [2002] EWCA Civ 1174, [2002] 2 FLR 930, CA.
2   This would not have been the case had decree absolute not been pronounced.

12.18 The specified period is 5 years unless it can be shown that the other party was not insolvent at the date of the transaction and that he did not become insolvent because of it, in which case it is 2 years[1].

1   See IA 1986, s 341.

12.19 Whether or not a transaction was at an undervalue will depend on the facts of the case. For example, if it could be shown that a former husband and wife had agreed to transfer the property of one of them to the other in an attempt to defeat creditors, and had obtained an order of the court to that effect, it is virtually certain that the transaction would be set aside. On the other hand, it was thought that, if an order for transfer of property were made for the housing of a spouse and children in the normal way and after consideration of the s 25 factors, it might be difficult to establish that the transaction was at an undervalue and that this might also be the case where the property transferred was on a clean break basis, and in settlement of all a wife's claims including her right to periodical payments.

12.20 This may have been clarified by the decision of the Court of Appeal in *Hill v Haines*[1]. Here, in the proceedings for financial relief, the district judge had ordered, inter alia, that the husband transfer to the wife all his interest in the former matrimonial home. The husband was subsequently made bankrupt. Following the bankruptcy, trustees of the bankrupt were appointed and they applied for an order to set aside the transfer of property pursuant to s 339 of the IA 1986. The application was refused and the trustees appealed against the refusal of their application. They submitted that the transfer was a transaction at an undervalue either under s 339(3)(a) or (c) of the Act in view of the fact that the property adjustment order had not involved the respondent giving consideration and certainly not such that could be measured in money or money's worth within the meaning of s 339(3)(c). The wife submitted that a transferee under a transfer made pursuant to a property transfer order was to be regarded as having given consideration equivalent to the value of the property being transferred, unless the case was an exceptional one where it could be demonstrated that the property transferred was obtained by fraud or some broadly similar exceptional circumstance. The appeal was allowed. The judge held that the district judge had been wrong to conclude that the transfer of the property pursuant to the order made in favour of the respondent by the matrimonial court was not a transaction at an undervalue. The transaction had been at an undervalue by application of s 339(3)(a) of the Act and in any event on an application of s 339(3)(c).

[1]   [2007] EWHC 1012 (Ch), [2007] All ER (D) 72 (May).

12.21 However, to the relief of most financial remedy practitioners, this was not the last word. The wife's appeal was allowed by the Court of Appeal[1] which held that the judge had been wrong to find that that parties to an ancillary relief order do not give consideration. The ability of a spouse to apply for financial relief is a right conferred by law, and the court may make an order entitling one party to property at the expense of the other. That property is prima facie the value of the right. Release or compromise of a claim can therefore constitute valuable consideration.

[1]   See [2008] 1 FLR 1192, CA.

12.22 A different result was obtained in *Avis v Turner and Avis*[1] where it was held that where there is a financial relief order postponing sale until certain events (eg a *Martin* or *Mesher* order) the bankrupt's share is not protected from an application by the trustee under s 339 until the occurrence of the events. Section 335A(3) gives priority to the interests of the creditors save in specified circumstances.

[1]   [2008] 1 FLR 482, CA. See also the same case reported at [2008] Fam Law 1185 where, on the facts, it was held that the circumstances of the case were not exceptional.

12.23 Any disposition of property made by a bankrupt between the date of the presentation of the petition and the date of the bankrupt's property vesting in the trustee is void unless made with the consent of the court or subsequently ratified by the court[1].

[1]   IA 1986, s 284(1).

Lump sum orders

12.24 The point made at **12.11** should be noted; for these purposes, a lump sum payment would be a disposition of property. Subject to that point, the issues arising as to lump sums are:

(a)   whether or not a lump sum could be set aside by the court on the trustee's application;
(b)   whether it can be enforced against a bankrupt's estate;
(c)   irrespective of (b), whether an order will be made against a bank-rupt's estate.

12.25 As to the first point, it would seem that, for the lump sum to be successfully attacked by the trustee, it would have to constitute a preference[1]. When a bankrupt has given a preference within the time specified by the IA 1986, the court may make such order as is necessary to restore the position to what it would have been had the preference not been made[2]. The specified times are the same as those applicable to transfers at an undervalue (see above). The fact that the lump sum had been paid pursuant to an order of the court would not prevent it from being classed as a preference[3].

1   For example, see *Trowbridge v Trowbridge* [2003] 2 FLR 231 where the court granted relief under both s 37 MCA and s 423 IA 1986. See also *B v IB (Order to set aside disposition under Insolvency Act)* [2013] EWHC 3755 (Fam) where a widow was allowed to proceed with an application under s 423 IA 1986 to set aside a gift of shares made before the husband's death, even though he had not actually been insolvent.
2   IA 1986, s 340(1) and (2).
3   IA 1986, s 340(6).

12.26 There is no mention in the IA 1986 of a lump sum constituting a transfer at an undervalue, and no authority as to whether this might be possible.

12.27 The second point may arise when a lump sum order has been made and the paying party then becomes bankrupt (or, as may be the case, is already bankrupt). Any obligation arising under an order made in family or domestic proceedings is not provable in bankruptcy[1]. The effect of this is that, so long as the bankrupt remains bankrupt, the order cannot be enforced against his estate. However, it also follows that the order survives the bankruptcy and may be enforced after the bankrupt's discharge, or during the bankruptcy by other methods, for example a judgment summons.

1   Insolvency (England and Wales) Rules 2016, r 14.2(2)(c). See also *Woodley v Woodley (No 2)* [1993] 2 FLR 477, CA.

12.28 In *Re Nunn (Bankruptcy: Divorce: Pension Rights)*[1] the husband was ordered to pay one-half of the lump sums which he would receive under his pension policies. He was then made bankrupt. It was held that the wife had no rights as against the trustee in bankruptcy; the court lacked jurisdiction to make an order for payment in any form which created an equitable interest or security.

1   [2004] 1 FLR 1123.

12.29 Finally, the jurisdiction of the court to make an order against an undischarged bankrupt must be considered. In view of what has been said above, there will be little point in such an application in most cases. However, there is no reason in principle why such an order should not be made; the only restriction is that the court must consider the bankrupt's ability to pay[1]. In one case[2], it was shown that there would be a substantial surplus in the bankruptcy, and an order for a lump sum of £450,000 was upheld. The only caveat was that the judge must have a clear picture of the assets and liabilities of the bankrupt so that he can determine what assets the bankrupt will have in the foreseeable future.

1   *Woodley v Woodley (No 2)* (above).
2   *Hellyer v Hellyer* [1996] 2 FLR 579, CA.

12.30 In *Young v Young*[1] Moor J held that he was not precluded from making a substantial lump sum order against the husband even though he was an undischarged bankrupt as long as account was taken of the level of debts, statutory interest and costs of the insolvency and this was put in the balance when determining the amount of the lump sum.

¹ [2013] EWHC 3637 (Fam).

12.31 The fact that a spouse seeks a bankruptcy order in order to defeat a claim for financial relief is not a matter which the court may take into account under s 37 of the MCA 1973. In such a case, the appropriate remedy is to apply to the bankruptcy court for an annulment of the bankruptcy[1]. In *Paulin v Paulin*[2] it was said that an individual who was made bankrupt on his own petition who was shown to have made a dishonest statement of his affairs and on the date of presentation of the petition to have had assets substantially exceeding liabilities would find it difficult to resist annulment of the bankruptcy.

¹ *F v F (Divorce: Insolvency: Annulment of Bankruptcy Order)* [1994] 1 FLR 359. See also *Couvaras v Wolf* [2002] 2 FLR 107.
² [2009] EWCA Civ 221, [2009] 2 FLR 354.

Periodical payments orders

12.32 Orders for periodic maintenance for a spouse or child are probably the class of order for financial relief which is most vulnerable to attack after bankruptcy. After bankruptcy, the income of the bankrupt may be claimed by the trustee as part of the bankrupt's estate[1]. The court may make an income payments order, which requires the bankrupt to make payments from his income to the trustee for the benefit of the[2] creditors; this order may continue to have effect after discharge from bankruptcy[3].

¹ IA 1986, s 307(1).
² IA 1986, ss 310(1) and 385(1).
³ IA 1986, ss 310(5) and 280(2)(c).

12.33 When assessing the amount of an income payments order, the court must leave the bankrupt with sufficient to meet the reasonable domestic needs of the bankrupt and his family, defined in this context as the persons who are living with the bankrupt and are dependent on him[1]. It is therefore not difficult to see that any order for periodical payments made before bankruptcy is at great risk of not being paid in full or even at all once the paying party is made bankrupt.

¹ IA 1986, ss 310(2) and 385(1).

12.34 An order for periodical payments or maintenance pending suit is not provable in the bankruptcy[1]. Similarly, although an order for costs made in ancillary relief proceedings is a 'bankruptcy debt' within the meaning of s 382(1) of the IA 1986, it has been held that it would be difficult to envisage any circumstances in which the court could properly make a bankruptcy order based on such an unprovable debt[2]. On the other hand, an order in favour of a bankrupt may be claimed by the trustee by way of an application for an income payments order[3].

¹ Insolvency (England and Wales) Rules 2016, r 14.2(2)(c).
² *Levy v Legal Services Commission* [2001] 1 FLR 435, CA. See also *Wehmeyer v Wehmeyer* [2001] 2 FLR 84.
³ IA 1986, ss 310(1) and 283(1)(b).

THE RIGHTS OF THIRD-PARTY CREDITORS

12.35 In general, while the court must take account of the proper liabilities of either party when performing the s 25 exercise[1], it does not have to put the interests of creditors before those of the parties to the marriage and the children. There is no jurisdiction to make an order for payment to any person other than the parties or a child.

1   MCA 1973, s 25(2)(b).

12.36 The only exception to this general rule is the position of a creditor which has a secured interest over any property which is the object of an application by either party. When procedure is considered in Chapter 16, it will be seen that a mortgagee or chargee is one of the persons who must be served with notice of any application for a property adjustment order, and who have the right to be heard on the application. This is not normally a situation which causes difficulty, since the court would not order transfer of any property if the transferee was unable to maintain the mortgage payments from some source of funds, whether private or public.

12.37 However, some difficulties have arisen and may arise when either a mortgagee has a charge which is repayable on demand, or is a creditor which has obtained a charging order to secure a judgment debt. The position is most difficult when only one of the parties is liable in respect of the judgment debt and the charging order is over that party's interest in a jointly owned property and a dispute arises as to whether the interests of the non-liable party and the family or those of the creditor are to have precedence. Such a dispute will not normally arise on the application for the charging order itself, but more commonly arises on an application for an order for sale or on an application to vary the charging order.

12.38 In *Harman v Glencross*[1], it was held that, in such a case, the application for the charging order to be varied should be transferred to the Family Division or to the divorce county court (this would now be the family court), so that the court might be fully apprised of all the circumstances of the case. The court should strike a balance between the creditor's normal expectation that an order enforcing a money judgment lawfully obtained would be made, and the hardship to the wife and children that such an order could entail. Where, as in this case, the wife's right of occupation would not be adequately protected under the LPA 1925, s 30, an order with *Mesher*-type terms would normally be appropriate.

1   [1984] FLR 652, FD.

12.39 It was also said in this case that where the application for the charging order to be made absolute is heard before the commencement of divorce proceedings, the court should normally make the order sought. Where the interim charging order has been made after the filing of the petition, the court considering the application for the final charging order should bear in mind that the court is holding the balance not only between the wife and the husband but also between the wife and the judgment creditor, and should make only such order as is necessary to protect the wife's right to occupy the home.

12.40 In another case[1], it was held that there was no automatic predominance for either claim. Every case depended on striking a fair balance between the normal expectations of the creditor and the hardship to the wife and children if an order were made. The use of the term 'hardship' necessarily implied that there would be instances in which a wife and/or children would be compelled, in the interests of justice to the judgment creditor, to accept a provision for their accommodation which fell below the level of adequacy. The court, having weighed all the circumstances, was required to make only such orders as might be necessary to protect the wife's right to occupy the home, albeit not on a permanent basis.

[1] *Austin-Fell v Austin-Fell and Midland Bank* [1989] 2 FLR 497.

12.41 By virtue of the TOLATA 1996, trusts are no longer trusts for sale and the court should therefore be able to take a more balanced view of competing interests[1].

[1] See *Mortgage Corporation v Shaire* [2000] 1 FLR 973. For an example of the disadvantaged position of a spouse as against the creditors of a bankrupt, see *Ram v Ram, Ram and Russell* [2004] EWCA Civ 1452, [2005] 2 FLR 63.

12.42 This issue was argued on behalf of a wife in *Bank of Ireland Mortgages v Bell and Bell*[1] where a judge at first instance had refused to order the sale of a property on the application of the creditor on the grounds that it had been purchased as a family home, was occupied by the wife and son, and the wife was in poor health. On appeal, it was held that while s 15 of the TOLATA 1996 had given scope for some change to the court's previous practice, a powerful consideration was whether a creditor was receiving proper recompense for being kept out of his money of which repayment was overdue. Here, the house had ceased to be the family home when the husband left, the son was nearly 18 and the wife's ill health might at best have justified only postponement of the sale. Sale was ordered.

[1] [2001] 2 FLR 809, CA.

Chapter 13

VARIATION

INTRODUCTION

13.1 The orders which may be made under the MCA 1973 may be divided into those which can be reconsidered and, if appropriate, changed or varied, and those which are 'final orders' and which cannot normally be changed. With certain limited exceptions, only periodic orders can be varied. The general principle of the MCA 1973 is that a capital order cannot be varied, save as to detail.

13.2 The statutory powers to vary are contained in s 31 of the MCA 1973, which must be considered in detail. There is some case law in relation to the way the courts should approach such cases, and this must also be considered.

STATUTORY PROVISIONS

What orders can be varied?

13.3 Section 31 begins by defining the types of order to which it applies. Since s 31 is intended to be a comprehensive code, it may be taken that unless an order appears in the list of orders in s 31(2), it cannot be varied.

13.4 It is provided that[1]:

'(2)   This section [ie s 31] applies to the following orders, that is to say—
    (a)   any order for maintenance pending suit and any interim order for maintenance;
    (b)   any periodical payments order;
    (c)   any secured periodical payments order;
    (d)   any order made by virtue of section 23(3)(c) or 27(7)(b) above (provision for payment of a lump sum by instalments);
    (dd)   any deferred order made by virtue of section 23(1)(c) (lump sums) which includes provision made by virtue of—
        (i)   section 25B(4), or
        (ii)   section 25C,
        (provision in respect of pension rights);
    (e)   any order for a settlement of property under section 24(1)(b) or for a variation of settlement under section 24(1)(c) or (d) above, being an order made on or after the grant of a decree of judicial separation;
    (f)   any order made under section 24A(1) above for the sale of property;

       (g)   a pension sharing order under section 24B above which is made at a time before the decree has been made absolute.'

[1]   MCA 1973, s 31(2).

13.5 The powers of the court in respect of each of these types of order are set out in s 31(1). It is provided that:

'(1) Where the court has made an order to which this section applies, then, subject to the provisions of this section and of section 28(1A) above, the court shall have power to vary or discharge the order or to suspend any provision thereof temporarily and to revive the operation of any provision so suspended.'

Section 28(1A) is the section of the Act which empowers the court to direct that no further applications may be made. The reference to s 28(1A) therefore reminds the court that, when such a direction has been given, the order may not be varied.

13.6 The principles observed by the court when considering an application will be set out at **13.20** et seq. First, however, some particular considerations applicable to certain types of orders must be considered.

Capital orders

13.7 As was seen above, lump sum orders and property adjustment orders cannot be varied and they are not included in the list of variable orders in s 31(2). Little more need be said, save that when any dispute arises as to the precise meaning of an order, the question which must be asked is whether the order was intended to be, and can reasonably be construed as being, a final resolution of all issues between the parties. Where that is the case, and the order is in effect a lump sum order, property adjustment order or settlement of property order, it must be a final order and cannot be varied[1].

In *SR v HR*[2] the husband had failed to comply with three property adjustment orders and then was declared bankrupt. A judge had discharged the three orders and replaced them with a new order. On appeal, Mostyn J set aside that order, making clear that the only capital orders which can be varied under s 31 MCA 1973 are orders for a lump sum payable by instalments. However, while a lump sum order cannot be varied, there is nothing to prevent a judge at first instance providing a potential alternative to the lump sum where it is thought that the paying party may default in payment of the lump sum, provided, of course, that this provision is made in the original order[3].

[1]   See *Dinch v Dinch* [1987] 2 FLR 162, HL; *Peacock v Peacock* [1991] 1 FLR 324; *Hill v Hill* [1998] 1 FLR 198, CA.
[2]   [2018] EWHC 606 (Fam).
[3]   *Amin v Amin* [2017] EWCA Civ 1114.

13.8 A lump sum order payable by instalments can by varied (see **4.5**). This power to vary extends to quantum as well as to timing, but this is not the case where the order is merely for a series of lump sums payable at different times[1]. In *Myerson v Myerson* the availability of the power to vary was given as one reason for declining to allow an appeal against a consent order[2].

[1]   *Hamilton v Hamilton* [2013] EWCA Civ 13.

[2]   [2009] EWCA Civ 282, [2009] 2 FLR 147.

Maintenance pending suit and periodical payments

13.9 When an order of this type is varied the court has power to remit any arrears which have accrued[1]. It may also, of course, either increase or decrease the rate of payment or discharge the order.

[1]   MCA 1973, s 31(2A).

13.10 Since November 1998, the court has also enjoyed the valuable power[1] to substitute a lump sum order or property adjustment order when it discharges a periodical payments order and also, where the petition was filed on or after 1 December 2000, to make a pension sharing order. This in effect allows the court to capitalise maintenance. When substituting a lump sum order on discharging a periodical payments order, the court is not limited to a mathematical calculation of the capital equivalent of the ongoing periodical payments but may consider what lump sum would be fair in all the circumstances[2]. The court may also order that no further applications may be made for periodical payments, secured periodical payments, or an extension of any term granted by the court.

[1]   MCA 1973, s 31(7A) and (7B), introduced by FLA 1996, Sch 8, para 7; the remedy established by *S v S* [1987] 1 FLR 71 is now therefore obsolete.
[2]   *Cornick v Cornick (No 3)* [2001] 2 FLR 1240, Charles J.

13.11 In *Pearce v Pearce*[1] Thorpe LJ summarised his general conclusions on this issue as follows:

(1)   On dismissing an entitlement to future periodical payments, the court's function is not to reopen capital claims but to substitute for the periodical payments order such other order or orders as will both fairly compensate the payee and at the same time complete the clean break.
(2)   In surveying what substitute order or orders should be made, first consideration should be given to the option of carving out of the payor's pension funds a pension for the payee equivalent to the discharged periodical payments order.

[1]   [2003] EWCA Civ 1054, [2003] 2 FLR 1144.

13.12 In *Mills v Mills*[1] Lord Wilson said that the first step in a capitalisation on variation exercise is a calculation of the amount of periodical payments to which, in the absence of capitalisation, the payee would have been entitled. Those payments cannot include a sum in respect of capital sums compromised in the original settlement.

[1]   [2018] UKSC 38.

13.13 When the court decides to vary or discharge a periodical payments order or secured periodical payments order it may direct that the variation or discharge shall not take effect until the expiration of such period as may be specified in the order[1].

[1]   MCA 1973, s 31(10).

13.14 *Variation*

Secured periodical payments

13.14 The comments made above apply equally to secured periodical payments. There is also a provision[1] to deal with the position where a person liable to make secured payments has died. In principle, an order for secured periodical payments survives the death of the paying party; his obligation was to provide the security for the payments, and these will continue after his death. It is therefore provided that the person entitled to payments or the personal representatives of the deceased may apply for an order for the proceeds of sale of a property to be used for securing the payments, but, save with permission of the court, no such application may be made later than 6 months after the date on which representation in regard to the deceased's estate is taken out.

[1] MCA 1973, s 31(6).

Lump sum payable by instalments

13.15 As has already been said, in principle, a lump sum order cannot be varied. The provision in s 31(2) is limited to the question of payment by instalments. It only applies when the court's original order provided for payment by instalments rather than by one single payment. The power of the court is, therefore, to reduce or increase the size of the instalments or to change the frequency of the payments. In practice, of course, the court could render a lump sum order ineffective by so reducing the instalments that it would never be paid, but this would be unusual.

Provision in respect of pension rights

13.16 Pensions are dealt with in detail in CHAPTER 10. The types of orders which are covered by s 31(2)(dd) are, first, orders under s 25B(4) which enable the court to 'attach' a pension lump sum, and secondly, orders under s 25C which contain a similar power including the power to compel the trustees or a party with pension rights to nominate the other party as the payee. The essential nature of these provisions is that a deferred order is made requiring the trustees of a pension scheme to make a payment or payments out of the scheme to the party who is not the scheme member at some future date.

13.17 The effect of this provision is that the court may vary any such order, whether it is of a periodic or capital nature at any time after the order is made. This might be before the order had come into effect.

13.18 It is provided that, in respect of these types of orders, s 31 shall cease to apply on the death of either of the parties to the marriage[1].

[1] MCA 1973, s 31(2B).

Settlement of property or variation of settlement

13.19 The powers of the court under s 31 in relation to these types of orders are limited[1] to orders made in judicial separation proceedings and also to applications:

' . . . made in proceedings—
(a)   for the rescission of the decree of judicial separation by reference to which the order was made, or
(b)   for the dissolution of the marriage in question.'

[1]   MCA 1973, s 31(4).

13.20 This provision therefore recognises that a decree of judicial separation leaves the parties still married to each other. If the decree itself is rescinded, any justification for the order must fall away, and if the marriage is dissolved, the court has wider powers as to a clean break, and the position may need to be reconsidered.

'Variation' of undertakings

13.21 In *Birch v Birch*[1] the Supreme Court held that an application to be released from an undertaking combined with an offer to substitute a new undertaking was not to be confused with an application to vary. There was settled authority that the court had jurisdiction to entertain such an application. The merits of any such application should be decided in accordance with s 31(7) MCA 1973. See also *A v A (Financial Remedies: Variation of Undertaking)*[2] where it was held that a finding that there has been a significant change of circumstances since an undertaking was given does not lead inevitably to release from the undertaking. All it does is open the door to consideration of the change of circumstances in the light of all other relevant factors.

[1]   [2017] UKSC 53.
[2]   [2018] EWHC 340 (Fam).

THE PRINCIPLES ON WHICH THE COURT EXERCISES ITS DISCRETION

13.22 The principles which govern the exercise of the court's discretion are contained in s 31(7) and fall into three parts. First, it is provided that[1]:

' . . . the court shall have regard to all the circumstances of the case, first consideration being given to the welfare while a minor of any child of the family who has not attained the age of eighteen . . . '

This provision requires little comment. The meaning of 'the first consideration' has already been considered at **1.52**.

[1]   MCA 1973, s 31(7).

13.23 Secondly, it is provided that[1]:

13.23 *Variation*

'. . . the circumstances of the case shall include any change in any of the matters to which the court was required to have regard when making the order to which the application relates.'

1   MCA 1973, s 31(7).

13.24 Thirdly, it is provided that[1]:

'(a)   in the case of a periodical or secured periodical payments order made on or after the grant of a decree of divorce or nullity of marriage, the court shall consider whether in all the circumstances and after having regard to any such change it would be appropriate to vary the order so that payments under the order are required to be made or secured only for such further period as will in the opinion of the court be sufficient . . . to enable the party in whose favour the order was made to adjust without undue hardship to the termination of those payments.'

1   MCA 1973, s 31(7)(a).

13.25 Then, in a provision which applies only to secured periodical payments, it is also provided that[1]:

'(b)   in a case where the party against whom the order was made has died, the circumstances of the case shall also include the changed circumstances resulting from his or her death.'

1   MCA 1973, s 31(7)(b).

The clean break on variation applications

13.26 The significance of the reference to termination of payments is clear. On a variation application, the court must perform the same task of inquiry into whether or not there should be a clean break as would be performed on an original application. The principles of the clean break are considered in detail at **2.70** et seq and need not be considered further here, save to say that the courts have adopted a variety of approaches to the termination of payments on a variation application, depending on the circumstances of the case[1].

1   See eg *Morris v Morris* [1985] FLR 1176; *Sandford v Sandford* [1986] 1 FLR 412; *Richardson v Richardson (No 2)* [1994] 2 FLR 1051; *Ashley v Blackman* [1988] Fam 85; *Jones v Jones* [2000] 2 FLR 307.

13.27 In *Fleming v Fleming*[1] it was held that on an application for variation the court was under a duty to consider terminating financial dependence provided such outcome could be achieved without undue hardship and that this principle was much enhanced where there was a previous term order.

1   [2004] 1 FLR 667.

Changes in circumstances

13.28 The court must consider all the circumstances including any change there may have been in any of the matters to which it was originally directed to have regard under s 25. The requirement to have regard to all the circumstances therefore dictates a complete review of all relevant matters; the changes since the order was made are merely one of the aspects to be considered. It is not correct merely to look at what has changed since the order was made[1].

[1]   *Lewis v Lewis* [1977] 3 All ER 992, CA.

13.29 Having said that, it is inevitable that the court will require some change in the circumstances before it varies an order; otherwise, a dissatisfied litigant could apply repeatedly for variation as a method of appeal or challenge. The starting point must be that the order was correctly made. In a case[1] involving variation of a consent order, it was said that 'the court should not adopt an approach which differs radically from the approach taken by the parties themselves in assessing quantum of maintenance when the original order was made'; the same could be said of the approach adopted by the court in a contested case.

[1]   *Boylan v Boylan* [1988] 1 FLR 282 per Booth J.

13.30 Some comparatively recent cases demonstrate, in different ways, the tendency of the courts to try not to depart radically from the spirit of the original order. In *VB v JP*[1] the original order had allocated 34% of the husband's net income to the wife and children when he was earning £340,000 pa net. At the time of the variation application, his earnings had increased to £450,000 pa net. At the request of the husband, the wife had given up her career to fulfil a domestic role. The order was increased from £34,000 pa to £65,000 pa which continued to give the wife about 33% of the husband's income, the President holding that *Miller/McFarlane* principles did not apply to variation applications. A similar result was obtained in *Lauder v Lauder*[2].

[1]   [2008] 1 FLR 742, Sir Mark Potter P.
[2]   [2007] 2 FLR 802, Baron J.

13.31 In *Hvorostovsky v Horostovsky*[1] it was said that there was much to be said for trial judges directing themselves by reference to Charles J's rule of fairness in *Cornick v Cornick (No 3)*[2] (see **13.10**) namely that, as an income fall justifies an application for downwards variation so an income rise justifies an upward variation[3].

[1]   [2009] EWCA Civ 791.
[2]   [2001] 2 FLR 1240.
[3]   One might think that practitioners did not need Charles J or even the Court of Appeal to explain this simple truth.

13.32 In *North v North*[1] it was held that a paying party is not an insurer against all financial hazards, nor is he responsible for needs created by the other's financial mismanagement. A similar result occurred in *Mills v Mills*[2] where it was held that the court was entitled to decline to increase a periodical payments order to enable the payee to fund her housing costs where she had been awarded a capital sum to enable her to buy a home in the original order.

[1]   [2008] 1 FLR 158.
[2]   [2018] UKSC 38.

13.33 In *Primavera v Primavera*[1], the husband was ordered to pay the wife periodical payments of £10,000 pa less tax, and a lump sum of £72,000. The wife was a beneficiary of her mother's estate, part of which was a house. The wife agreed to sell her share of the house to one of her daughters for the district valuer's valuation, which was considerably less than the true value, with the result that she received much less than she would otherwise have done. She applied to vary her periodical payments, and Booth J increased the order to £28,000 pa. The husband was a wealthy man. On appeal, Booth J's conclusion that there was no reason why the wife should not have regarded the inheritance as hers to do with as she wished was upheld. However, it was emphasised that an important factor was that the husband was wealthy and well able to pay the increased order; the position might be very different where the parties were of more modest means and the inheritance would have made a material difference to the total means of both parties. It was also held that, although financial mismanagement by a party was not a relevant factor in this case, it could well be a relevant circumstance in an appropriate case.

[1]   [1992] 1 FLR 16, CA.

13.34 Useful guidance was given by Charles J in *McFarlane v McFarlane*[1]. Readers will be familiar with this case (see **1.21** et seq) from when it was before the House of Lords; this was the wife's application for a variation of the periodical payments order made then. Since the previous hearings the husband's income had increased. The approach adopted by the court and agreed by the parties was to use the concept of the husband's surplus income after deducting payments for children and essential living expenses and then to give consideration to what an application of the surplus (plus the wife's own capital and other income) would be likely to produce for the wife for the rest of her life. The husband planned to retire in 2014. The wife was awarded 40% of the husband's income up to £750,000, 20% of the balance up to £1m, and 10% of any income above that figure. Charles J emphasised that it would be wrong to isolate the principle of compensation and treat it as if it were a damages claim.

[1]   [2009] EWHC 891 (Fam), [2009] 2 FLR 1322.

PROCEDURE

13.35 An application to vary is contained within the definition of 'financial remedy'[1]. There are therefore no separate rules applicable to such an application, and it should be conducted according to the normal rules applicable to financial remedies[2].

[1]   FPR 2.3.
[2]   See CHAPTER 16.

FORMS OF ORDER

13.36 For guidance as to forms and precedents please see Lexis Nexis' *Family Law Precedents Service*.

VARIATION SUBJECT TO CONDITIONS

13.37 In *Mubarak v Mubarik*[1] the husband applied to vary. He was in default of earlier orders and had been found to be dishonest. It was held that

Hadkinson v Hadkinson[2] was still good law and was an important discretionary power of last resort – see also *Corbett v Corbett*[3]. The court could impose conditions on the husband proceeding with his application. It must consider:

(a)   whether the husband was in contempt;

(b)   whether he caused an impediment to the course of justice;

(c)   whether there was any other effective way of securing justice;

(d)   whether the contempt was wilful;

(e)   whether it was appropriate to impose conditions and if so what would be appropriate.

[1]   [2004] EWCA 1158 (Fam), [2004] 2 FLR 932.
[2]   [1952] P 285.
[3]   [2003] EWCA Civ 559, [2003] 2 FLR 385.

13.38 A similar result may be found in *Laing v Laing*[1]. Here, the district judge had made it a condition of the continuation of the husband's variation application that he pay arrears of periodical payments and also reduced periodical payments to the wife. The husband appealed. The President held that the jurisdiction to make such an order was not dependent on the amount of the arrears but on the situation of the parties, the circumstances of the non-payment, and the effect of the non-payment on the course of justice in the particular case. Key questions were whether justice was being impeded and whether there was no other effective method of securing compliance with the order. It was not limited to breaches of a capital sum order.

[1]   [2007] EWHC 3152 (Fam), Sir Mark Potter P.

13.39 In *Assoun v Assoun (No 1)*[1] it was held that a Hadkinson order is draconian and should not be commonplace, and a rigorous application of the procedural requirements is necessary[2]. Nevertheless, in the instant case the husband had been the author of his own misfortune, having disregarded orders and procedure, and he was held to be bound by the order.

[1]   [2017] EWCA Civ 21.
[2]   Application should be made under FPR Pt 18 on an application notice stating the order being applied for and the reasons therefor.

Chapter 14
MISCELLANEOUS APPLICATIONS

INTRODUCTION

14.1 In this chapter, it is intended to deal with certain types of application which, although they must be mentioned, do not merit a chapter to themselves. They are:

(a) applications under MCA 1973, s 27;
(b) applications under MCA 1973, s 10(2);
(c) alteration of agreements.

APPLICATIONS UNDER MCA 1973, SECTION 27

14.2 The marginal note to s 27 of the MCA 1973 reads 'Financial provision in cases of neglect to maintain', and the section is intended to provide a remedy for financial relief exercisable by courts exercising family jurisdiction. The essential difference from the other types of relief described in this book is that the exercise of the jurisdiction conferred by s 27 does not depend on the grant of a decree of divorce, nullity or judicial separation nor even the filing of a petition. It is a 'free-standing' remedy, and the application is by way of an originating application.

14.3 Before 1970, applications for neglect to maintain were quite common, but for some time, s 27 has been little used. It was thought that it might assume a more prominent role when FLA 1996 came into force but that is now, at most, an academic possibility.

14.4 It is provided that either party to a marriage may apply to the court for an order on the ground that the other party[1]:

'(a) has failed to provide reasonable maintenance for the applicant, or
(b) has failed to provide, or to make a proper contribution towards, reasonable maintenance for any child of the family.'

Jurisdiction to make the order is the same as in other matrimonial causes[2].

[1] MCA 1973, s 27(1).
[2] MCA 1973, s 27(2).

14.5 The orders which the court may make in favour of the applicant are orders for periodical payments, secured periodical payments, and a lump sum[1]. There is jurisdiction to make similar orders for a child, but the effect of CSA

1991, s 8 reduces the value of those provisions. The court may also make a lump sum order for the purpose of enabling any liabilities or expenses to be met[2]; this is a similar provision to that contained in s 23(3)[3]. The court also has jurisdiction to make interim orders[4].

[1] MCA 1973, s 27(6).
[2] MCA 1973, s 27(7).
[3] See **4.11**.
[4] MCA 1973, s 27(5).

14.6 In deciding whether or not the respondent has failed to provide reasonable maintenance for the applicant, and, if so, what order to make, the court is directed to[1]:

' . . . have regard to all the circumstances of the case including the matters mentioned in section 25(2) above and where an application is also made under this section in respect of a child of the family who has not attained the age of eighteen, first consideration shall be given to the welfare of the child while a minor.'

The court has therefore to take account of the usual s 25 factors[2]. Since the marriage has not yet been dissolved, the termination of the parties' financial dependence on each other does not arise.

[1] MCA 1973, s 27(3).
[2] See Chapter 1.

14.7 There are few authorities under the modern law to indicate how the courts exercise their discretion; this may be because s 27 has been little used, and also, perhaps, because when used the orders are often only of temporary duration. The duty of both parties to a marriage to maintain each other is an established part of English law[1]; what is reasonable will depend on the circumstances of the case.

[1] *Northrop v Northrop* [1968] P 74, CA.

14.8 The wording of the statute was changed in 1978[1], the old formula of 'wilful neglect to maintain' being replaced by the present 'failure to maintain'. It had been held that the common law rule that a husband has no duty to maintain a wife who has committed adultery which he has not connived at, nor by his conduct conduced to, applied to the duty to provide reasonable maintenance under s 27[2]. However, it is thought that the change in the wording of the statute, which omits the word 'wilful' and introduces some general guidelines, means that the law is no longer simply a procedure for enforcing the common law duty to maintain, and therefore that the rule that adultery is a bar no longer applies[3].

[1] By Domestic Proceedings and Magistrates' Courts Act 1978, s 63(1); see also MFPA 1984, s 4.
[2] *Gray v Gray* [1976] Fam 324; *Newmarch v Newmarch* [1978] Fam 79.
[3] This certainly was the intention of the Law Commission; see Law Com No 77, paras 2.15, 9.11, and 9.24(c).

14.9 There is no separate procedure for making applications under s 27 (this is a change from the previous position). An application under s 27 is defined by FPR 2.3 as a financial remedy; FPR 9.1 states that Part 9 applies to applications for a financial remedy, and FPR 9.5(2) specifically refers to s 27 applications and requires them to be issued in a divorce county court. The procedure is therefore the same as for any other financial relief application.

APPLICATIONS UNDER MCA 1973, SECTION 10(2)

14.10 In 1969, for the first time, the law of divorce was changed to allow 'no fault' divorce[1]. For the first time, a divorce could be granted on the ground that the parties had lived apart for 2 years and the respondent consented to the grant of a decree, or that they had lived apart for 5 years even though the respondent did not consent to the grant of a decree; in the latter case, an 'innocent party' could be divorced against her will. These provisions are now s 1(2)(d) and (e) of the 1973 Act.

[1]   Divorce Reform Act 1969, s 2.

14.11 Because of these then novel provisions, it was thought right to include in the legislation special protection for respondents in such cases, and this protection survives unchanged in the modern law as s 10(2). The only significant advantage which can be obtained by an application under s 10(2) as opposed to a conventional application for a financial remedy is that the filing of the notice of application prevents the grant of decree absolute[1], which can, in appropriate cases, be postponed until proper provision has been made. When an application under s 10(2) is made, it is common to apply for other financial remedies in the usual way at the same time.

[1]   MCA 1973, s 10(3).

14.12 The section therefore applies where the court has granted a decree nisi under s 1(2)(d) or (e) and the respondent applies for her financial position to be considered; when the decree was also on the basis of one of the other facts in s 1 the section does not apply[1]. The application must clearly be made before decree absolute or it will lose its purpose.

[1]   MCA 1973, s 10(2).

14.13 It is provided that the court hearing the application[1]:

' . . .   shall consider all the circumstances, including the age, health, conduct, earning capacity, financial resources and financial obligations of each of the parties, and the financial position of the respondent as, having regard to the divorce, it is likely to be after the death of the petitioner should the petitioner die first . . . '

[1]   MCA 1973, s 10(3).

14.14 The statute imposes two duties on the court: first, to consider the age, health and general financial position of the parties and any issue of conduct which may be relevant, and, secondly, to consider what the position of the respondent would be if the petitioner died first. Section 10(3) then continues:

' . . .   and, subject to subsection (4) below, the court shall not make the decree absolute unless it is satisfied—
(a)   that the petitioner should not be required to make any financial provision for the respondent, or
(b)   that the financial provision made by the petitioner for the respondent is reasonable and fair or the best that can be made in the circumstances.'

14.15 The court must, therefore, satisfy itself either that no financial provision need be made, or that the provision made is fair and reasonable, or the best in the circumstances. The latter case (best in the circumstances) would apply where the provision made was inadequate but there were insufficient funds to do better.

14.16 As indicated, there is provision for exception made in s 10(4) which provides that the court may, if it thinks fit, make the decree absolute notwithstanding the requirements of s 10(3), if[1]:

> '(a) it appears that there are circumstances making it desirable that the decree should be obtained without delay, and
> (b) the court has obtained a satisfactory undertaking from the petitioner that he will make such financial provision for the respondent as the court may approve.'

Both parts of this requirement must be met before the court could act under s 10(4).

[1] MCA 1973, s 10(4).

14.17 As was said in the introduction to this part, the only separate usefulness of s 10(2) is to hold up decree absolute until all financial matters have been concluded. When the person in need of protection is the petitioner, an application under s 10(2) is unnecessary as well as impossible. In *Wickler v Wickler*[1], where the respondent applied for decree absolute under s 9(2) of MCA 1973, the petitioner having failed to apply, it was held that the court had power to refuse the application unless and until he complied with orders as to ancillary relief. There always will be a residue of cases where a respondent feels that the only way to ensure proper relief is to make an application under s 10(2); these will nearly always be cases where she will lose all rights under the husband's pension scheme on the grant of decree absolute[2].

[1] [1998] 2 FLR 326, Bracewell J.
[2] For examples, see *Cumbers v Cumbers* [1975] 1 All ER 1, CA; *Grigson v Grigson* [1974] 1 All ER 748, CA; *Garcia v Garcia* [1991] 3 All ER 451, CA.

14.18 By FPR 2.3 an application under s 10(2) is defined as a financial remedy. The Part 9 procedure therefore applies. Further details are given in CHAPTER 16.

ORDERS FOR ALTERATION OF AGREEMENTS DURING LIFETIMES OF PARTIES

14.19 Section 35 of the MCA 1973 applies where there is a maintenance agreement subsisting, and each of the parties is, for the time being, either domiciled in or resident in England and Wales[1]. In those circumstances, either party may apply to the court for an order making such alterations in the agreement[2]:

> '(i) by varying or revoking any financial arrangements contained in it, or
> (ii) by inserting in it financial arrangements for the benefit of one of the parties to the agreement or a child of the family,
>
> as may appear to that court to be just having regard to all the circumstances, including, if relevant, the matters mentioned in section 25(4) above; and the agreement shall have effect thereafter as if any alteration made by the order had been made by agreement between the parties and for valuable consideration.'

Section 25(4) refers to the liability of a step-parent. This is the only specific s 25 factor to be mentioned. Otherwise, the court must consider all the circumstances.

1   MCA 1973, s 35(1).
2   MCA 1973, s 35(2).

14.20 In *T v R (Maintenance after Remarriage: Agreement)*[1] a recital in a consent order was construed by the court as constituting a maintenance agreement within s 34 MCA 1973.

1   [2016] EWFC 26.

14.21 Before it can make such an order, the court must be satisfied either[1]:

'(a)   that by reason of a change in the circumstances in the light of which any financial arrangements contained in the agreement were made or, as the case may be, financial arrangements were omitted from it (including a change foreseen by the parties when making the agreement), the agreement should be altered so as to make different, or, as the case may be, so as to contain, financial arrangements, or

(b)   that the agreement does not contain proper financial arrangements with respect to any child of the family.'

The second provision may now be of little effect due to CSA 1991.

1   MCA 1973, s 35(2).

14.22 There are other matters of detail in the section. It should be noted that application may be made to a magistrates' court under s 35, provided the parties are resident in England and Wales and at least one of the parties resides in the area of that court[1]. The powers of the magistrates are limited to issues of periodical payments[2].

1   MCA 1973, s 35(3).
2   MCA 1973, s 35(3).

14.23 By FPR 2.3 an application under s 35 is defined as a financial remedy. The procedure under Part 9 therefore applies.

Chapter 15

FINANCIAL RELIEF AFTER OVERSEAS DIVORCE

INTRODUCTION

15.1 The various forms of financial relief described in this book, with the exception of applications under s 27 of the MCA 1973, all depend on the grant of a decree of divorce, nullity or judicial separation (or at least the filing of a petition for such relief). Without a petition and, in the case of a final order, a decree, the court can do nothing. The type of relief about to be described in this chapter is different, in that the basis for jurisdiction is an overseas divorce or other order. There are two stages in such applications. First, the court must grant permission to apply. Secondly, the court will adjudicate on the application; in this case, the relief it may grant is practically identical to that which would be granted after a decree of the English and Welsh courts.

JURISDICTION

15.2 It is provided that an application for financial relief may be made where[1]:

'(a)   a marriage has been dissolved or annulled, or the parties to a marriage have been legally separated, by means of judicial or other proceedings in an overseas country[2], and
(b)   the divorce, annulment or legal separation is entitled to be recognised as valid in England and Wales.'

Remarriage of the applicant is a bar to an application in relation to that marriage[3].

---

[1]   MFPA 1984, s 12(1).
[2]   In *MET v HAT (Interim Maintenance)* [2013] EWHC 4247 (Fam) the husband had pronounced divorce by bare talaq which, it seemed, would have been recognised in his native country. The wife's application under Pt III of the MFPA 1984 was dismissed on the ground that relief could only be granted where there had been a recognised overseas divorce 'by means of judicial or other proceedings'.
      However, the wife obtained further expert evidence to the effect that the triple talaq was void as such but took effect as a single talaq which was a proceedings divorce entitled to recognition in England and Wales. When the matter returned to court – see *MET v HAT (Interim Maintenance) (No 2)* [2014] EWHC 717 (Fam) the judge Mostyn J 'completely revised' his previous view and awarded substantial maintenance pending suit.
[3]   MFPA 1984, s 12(2).

15.3 The classes of divorce etc which would be recognised as valid are those set out in the Recognition of Divorces and Legal Separations Act 1971, ss 2–6.

15.4 Jurisdiction therefore depends on the existence of a divorce etc which would be recognised and on the requirements of MFPA 1984, s 15, which provides that the court shall have jurisdiction if any of the following three jurisdictional requirements are satisfied:

(1)   domicile of either party at the date of application for leave or as at the divorce etc;

(2)   the habitual residence of either party for one year ending with either the application for leave or the divorce etc;

(3)   either party having, at the date of the application for leave, a beneficial interest in possession in a dwelling-house in England and Wales which was at some time in the marriage a matrimonial home of the parties to the marriage.

15.5 If the proposed respondent is domiciled in a contracting State within the meaning of the Civil Jurisdiction and Judgments Act 1982[1], a further complication may arise. The general theme of the 1982 Act is that a respondent who is in a contracting State must be sued there. However, the Act does not apply to rights in property arising out of a matrimonial relationship, nor to maintenance.

[1]   Most countries in western Europe are contracting States.

APPLICATIONS FOR PERMISSION

15.6 The first step the applicant must take is to apply for permission, and it is provided that the court shall not grant permission unless it considers that there is substantial ground for the making of an application for such an order[1]. Clearly, the court would first have to be satisfied that it had jurisdiction, as explained above. However, that would not be an end of the matter, since s 16 provides that[2]:

' . . . the court shall consider whether in all the circumstances of the case it would be appropriate for such an order to be made by a court in England and Wales, and if the court is not satisfied that it would be appropriate the court shall dismiss the application.'

[1]   MFPA 1984, s 13.
[2]   MFPA 1984, s 16(1).

15.7 There follows a list of the matters to which the court must have particular regard. These include[1]:

•   the connection which the parties have with England and Wales, the country where the divorce etc was granted, or any other country;

•   the financial benefit which the applicant or a child has or is likely to have received in the foreign proceedings;

•   the financial relief awarded by any foreign court and the likelihood of any such order being complied with;

•   the right to apply in any other jurisdiction;

•   availability of property in this country;

- length of time since divorce etc.

[1]   MFPA 1984, s 16(2)(a)–(i).

15.8 The procedure for an application is contained in FPR, Pt 6. The application must be made in the Principal Registry except where FPR 9.26 applies (this relates to consent orders and provides that the application may be made to the court where the consent application is proceeding). The application must be heard by a judge but not a district judge. However, when permission is granted, the court may direct that the substantive application may be heard by a district judge of the Principal Registry.

15.9 The applicant may apply for an order that the application be made without notice, but some reason for this must be given; where the application is without notice, the respondent has the right to apply to set the order aside. The procedure to be followed is that set out in Pt 18.

15.10 The application for permission is a crucial step. The court has to be satisfied as to the 'substantial ground for the making of an application', and if, on the application for permission, it is clear that if permission were granted the substantive application would fail, permission should not be granted[1]. The burden is on the person bringing the application, and it was held, in a case where there had been a connection with England before the marriage but the connection with the foreign jurisdiction was now stronger, that permission should not be granted[2].

[1]   *Holmes v Holmes* [1989] Fam 47, CA.
[2]   *Z v Z (Financial Provision: Overseas Divorce)* [1992] 2 FLR 291.

15.11 It has been held that the mischief which the Act was designed to redress is a narrow one, and does not include the case of a foreign court of competent jurisdiction making an order which has neither been appealed nor impugned[1]. While there is no absolute rule of law that permission will not be granted where the sole motive is to enforce a foreign order, in practice permission will only rarely be granted in such circumstances[2]. Permission was refused in one case where the wife, wisely or unwisely, had allowed the breakdown of her marriage to be referred to the courts in France; she was not to be allowed to relitigate here an issue which had been taken to its conclusion there[3]. In another case, it was held that it was essential to demonstrate that the applicant was suffering some injustice before the court could find that there was a substantial ground[4] but in a later decision of the Court of Appeal it was said that the judge had gone too far and his decision should not be followed[5].

[1]   *Hewitson v Hewitson* [1995] Fam 100, CA.
[2]   *Jordan v Jordan* [1999] 2 FLR 1069, CA.
[3]   *M v M (Financial Provision after Foreign Divorce)* [1994] 1 FLR 399.
[4]   *N v N (Foreign Divorce: Financial Relief)* [1997] 1 FLR 900, per Cazalet J.
[5]   *Jordan v Jordan* (above).

15.12 The relationship between the grant of permission and the substantive application was considered in detail in *Agbaje v Agbaje* which is examined at **15.18**.

15.13 Since permission is granted without a hearing the respondent to the application clearly has the right to apply on notice to set aside the grant of permission. In *Potanina v Potanin*[1] it was held that In respect of any subsequent application to set aside the grant of permission, unless it is clear that the respondent can deliver a 'knock-out blow' the court 'should' adjourn an application to set aside to be heard with the substantive application. This followed the judgement of Munby LJ in *Traversa v Freddi*[2].

[1] [2021] EWCA Civ 702.
[2] [2009] EWHC 2101 (Fam).

ORDERS WHICH MAY BE MADE

15.14 Once the vital step of obtaining permission has been taken (and assuming that the order is not set aside), the applicant may proceed with the application for financial relief. The powers of the court are contained in ss 14, and 17–26 of MFPA 1984. Broadly speaking, the court has power to make all the types of order it could make if the divorce etc had been granted in England and Wales, including avoidance of disposition. The matters to which the court must have regard are contained in s 18, and are similar to those in s 25.

15.15 Examples of cases where substantive orders have been made after the grant of permission are found in two recent cases. In *A v S (Financial Relief After Overseas US Divorce and Financial Proceedings)*[1] the parties had been divorced in Texas, and the Texan court had made an order in financial proceedings awarding the wife almost nothing, based on the Texan doctrine of community of property. Before the marriage, the wife lived in a house in England which the husband had purchased for her occupation; after the marriage she had moved to live with him in Texas. The Texan court ordered her to leave the house in England to which she had returned, and she applied for relief in the English court. Bodey J held that extreme caution had to be exercised when a mature foreign jurisdiction had already adjudicated and there was also a problem because the wife had repeatedly lied in the Texan proceedings. Nevertheless, there was an injustice which could be remedied by the application of the discretionary approach, and the wife had a real need for financial help. It was only appropriate to intervene to the minimum extent necessary so as to remedy the injustice perceived. The wife was awarded £60,000.

[1] [2003] 1 FLR 431.

15.16 In *Vilanova v Vilanov and another*[1] Holman J said that he would have entertained an application for 50% of the assets but made an order for under 30% in recognition of the difficulties in such cases, including those of enforcement.

[1] [2019] EWHC 1107 (Fam).

15.17 In *M v L (Financial Relief After Overseas Divorce)*[1] there had been a 30-year delay between divorce and the application. The fact that the divorce had been in South Africa was anomalous, since the case should always have been an English one. The wife had remained dependent on the husband through voluntary payments. Coleridge J declined to divide the husband's capital on modern principles, but made an award of periodical payments based on what it would be reasonable for her to have in all the circumstances.

[1]   [2003] 2 FLR 425.

15.18 The decision of the Supreme Court in *Agbaje v Agbaje*[1] is the first important guidance to be issued on a review of a substantive order under Pt III and also contains guidance as to the relationship between the grant of permission and the approach of the court on making a substantive order. The facts of the case need not be set out in detail. Essentially, Coleridge J made an order granting a Nigerian wife £275,000; this was set aside by the Court of Appeal. It was said that the judge had failed to address the issue of comity and had not identified why this was an exceptional case; the parties' connection with Nigeria was more significant than with England and the Nigerian court, which had made an award to the wife, had not done her a serious injustice.

[1]   [2010] UKSC 13, [2010] 1 FLR 1813.

15.19 The decision of the Court of Appeal was set aside by the Supreme Court and the decision of Coleridge J restored. The following guidance was given in the speech of Lord Collins:

(1)   The principal object of the filter mechanism is to prevent wholly unmeritorious claims being pursued to oppress or blackmail a former spouse. The threshold is not high; 'substantial' means 'solid'.

(2)   Once a judge has given reasons for deciding that the threshold has been crossed, the approach to setting aside should be (as under the CPR) exercised only where there is a compelling reason to do so.

(3)   Section 16 does not require the court to consider whether it is appropriate for an order to be made but only whether it is appropriate for an order to be made by the court of England and Wales. It does not determine the criteria by which the question of whether financial provision should be made is determined.

(4)   Part III contains no reference to hardship, injustice or exceptionality. Hardship and injustice are not pre-conditions.

(5)   Mere disparity between the award made by the foreign court and what would be awarded on an English divorce is insufficient to trigger the application of Pt III. Nor is hardship or injustice a condition, but if either factor is present it may make it appropriate for an order to be made.

(6)   The following general principles should be applied. First, primary consideration should be given to the welfare of any children of the marriage. Secondly, it will never be appropriate to make an order which gives the claimant more than he or she would have been awarded had all the proceedings taken place within this jurisdiction. Thirdly, where possible, the order should have the result that provision is made for the reasonable needs of both spouses. Subject to this, the court has a broad discretion.

15.20 The decision in *Agbaje* was followed in *Traversa v Freddi*[1] where it was said that it is inevitable in practice that the court will look comparatively at the parties' respective degrees of closeness with the two jurisdictions involved. In this case, it was held that the foreign jurisdiction had not produced an overall unjust result.

¹   [2009] EWHC 2101 (Fam), [2010] 1 FLR 324, Charles J.

15.21 In *Z v A (Financial Remedy after Overseas Divorce)*¹ Coleridge J after observing that the proper interpretation of ss 16–18 was set out in *Agjabe v Agjabe* (supra), particularly at paras [70] and [73] per Lord Collins, added that there was a scale of award dependent on the parties' connections (or lack of connections) with this jurisdiction. He said that where the English connections were very strong there was no reason why the application should not proceed as if it were made in purely English proceedings under MCA 1973. This emphasis appears to be a new element in the guidance and it will be interesting to see if it is repeated by higher courts.

¹   [2012] EWHC 1434 (Fam).

15.22 In *MA v SK: S Investments v MA (Financial Relief after Overseas Divorce)*¹ Moor J made it clear that the law on this topic is contained in the speech of Lord Collins in *Agjabe* (supra); he did not propose to repeat those important paragraphs but distilled the following principles:

(a)   The intention of the Act was the alleviation of the adverse consequences of no, or no adequate, financial provision being made by a foreign court in a situation where there were substantial connections with England and Wales.

(b)   The situation is different from an application that is made pursuant to the Matrimonial Causes Act 1973 as Lord Collins makes plain that some of the matters to be considered under s 16 may be relevant to s 18, and vice versa.

(c)   It is not the purpose of Pt III to allow a spouse with some English connections to make an application in England and to take advantage of what may well be the more generous approach in England to financial provision, particularly in so-called big-money cases, although there is no condition of exceptionality.

(d)   Hardship or injustice is not a condition of the exercise of the jurisdiction but, if either factor is present, it may make it appropriate in the light of all the circumstances, for an order to be made and may affect the nature of the provision ordered.

(e)   The amount of the financial provision will depend on all the circumstances of the case and there is no rule that it should be the minimum amount required to overcome injustice. It will never be appropriate to give the claimant more than she or he would have been awarded had all the proceedings taken place within this jurisdiction. Where possible, the order should have the result that provision is made for the reasonable needs of each spouse. Subject to these principles, the court has a broad discretion.

(f)   The grant of leave does not inevitably trigger a full blown claim for all forms of financial relief.

¹   [2015] EWHC 887 (Fam).

15.23 In *Zimina v Zimin*¹ King LJ helpfully summarised the law and procedural steps as follows (at para 47):

'Whilst the proper application of the *Agbaje* principles is not always straight forward, it is clear for the purposes of the present case that:

i) The legislative purpose is to alleviate the adverse consequence of no, or no adequate financial provision having been made by a foreign court in a situation where there are substantial connections with England.

ii) The duties under section 16 and section 17 together impose two interrelated duties ie to consider whether "in all the circumstances of the case" England and Wales is an appropriate venue and, secondly, whether an order should be made "having regard to all the circumstances" including the matters in section 25(2)(a)-(h) of the Matrimonial Causes Act 1973.

iii) Part III cannot be used to "top up" foreign provision in order to make it equate to an English award; it follows that mere disparity will be insufficient to "trigger" the application of Part III.

iv) No element of exceptionality is required and neither injustice nor hardships are preconditions. The order need not be the minimum amount required to avoid injustice.

v) In considering quantum the court has a broad discretion subject to three principles:

a) Primary consideration is to be given to the needs of any children

b) It is never appropriate to make an order which gives a claimant more than she would have been awarded had all the proceedings taken place within this jurisdiction

c) Where possible the order should have the result that provision is made for the reasonable needs of each spouse.'

Similar guidance was given in *NN v AS and Others*[2].

1   [2017] EWCA Civ 1429.
2   [2018] EWHC 2973 (Fam).

15.24 In *Vasilyeva v Shemyakin*[1] Williams J observed that whether the grant of leave ultimately translates into a decision following consideration of the s 16 factors that it is appropriate for the English court to grant relief or whether it is appropriate to make an order after consideration of the s 18 factors is to prejudge the ultimate questions.

1   [2019] EWHC 932 (Fam).

Chapter 16
PROCEDURE

INTRODUCTION

16.1 The Family Procedure Rules 2010 (FPR) Pt 9 and the accompanying practice directions, which came into force on 6 April 2011, set out the rules for dealing with applications for a financial remedy. FPR 2.3 defines this term to include a wide range of family proceedings within which courts can make financial orders including applications under Sch 1 of the Children Act 1989 and the Civil Partnership Act 2004 and applications after foreign divorce under part III of the Matrimonial and Family Proceedings Act 1984[1]. The court's powers to make orders which were formerly known as ancillary relief orders are now collectively defined as 'financial orders' and that terminology is used in this chapter.

[1] Applications under the Married Women's Property Act 1882, the Trusts of Land and Appointment of Trustees Act 1996, the Inheritance (Provision for Family and Dependents) Act 1975 or for a tenancy transfer under the Family Law Act 1996 are not 'applications for financial remedies' governed by FPR Pt 9.

16.2 Although the FPR made substantial amendments to the rules and practice dealing with many aspects of family proceedings, the provisions relating to applications for financial orders have not changed significantly from the ancillary relief procedural rules which had been in operation since 2000. FPR follow a style similar to the Civil Procedure Rules 1998 (CPR) and at their heart have the overriding objective which is set out in Pt 1 of the FPR. In addition to considering the specific provisions for financial orders set out in Pt 9 of the Rules, the practitioner will also need to be familiar with other aspects of the rules which apply to all family proceedings (including those for financial orders) such as the provisions relating to experts (Pt 25), costs (Pt 28), evidence (Pts 22–24 and the rules about statements of truth at Pt 17), hearings and bundles (Pt 27) and the court's general case management powers (Pt 4).

16.3 There have been relatively few significant procedural amendments to FPR Pt 9 since it was introduced in April 2011 (with the exception of the amendments relating to the fast track procedure for maintenance applications referred to later in this chapter). It has, however, been a time which has encompassed what has been described by the immediate past President of the Family Division, Sir James Munby, as 'the largest reform of the family justice system in our professional lives . . . amounting to a cultural revolution'. These reforms, which included the introduction of the Family Court in April 2014, have seen a range of organisational changes, including the introduction nationwide of the Financial Remedies Courts (FRCs) as a subset of the

Family Court. The FRCs cover all parts of England and Wales in 18 zones with a lead judge for each. Judges ticketed to hear financial remedy cases are listed in an organogram[1], the intention being to ensure that all financial remedy cases are case managed and heard by a suitably trained and experienced judge. Since the onset of the COVID-19 pandemic almost all financial remedies work has been conducted by video hearing, and the use of electronic bundles is now universal. Consent orders are dealt with by the Digital Consent Orders scheme and the Digital Contested Cases scheme is, at the time of writing, in the process of being rolled out, to allow the uploading of and access to documents via a portal. The family orders project has provided a set of standard templates for orders, available online and used by all family courts. It is hoped eventually that all family money claims may be dealt with in the FRCs in accordance with a single set of rules and procedures, to remove current anomalies such as the inability of the Family Court to deal with claims under the Trusts of Land and Appointment of Trustees Act 1996[2].

[1]   https://www.judiciary.uk/announcements/financial-remedy-court-organogram.
[2]   See the 17th View from the President's Chambers, per Sir James Munby, June [2017] Fam Law p 609 and comments of McFarlane P in his message dated 24 February 2021.

ISSUE OF PROCEEDINGS

16.4 The application for a financial order may be made in the petition for divorce (or civil partnership dissolution) or at any time thereafter[1], subject to the prohibition on applications after remarriage in MCA 1973, s 28(3). The divorce petition form D8 (in use from September 2017) contains a single question at section 10.1 as to whether the applicant wishes to apply for a financial order, to be answered 'yes' or 'no'. A follow-up question at section 11.3 asks whether the order sought is for the applicant or the children. Answering 'yes' at section 10.1 does not lead to any action by the court at that stage. To start the financial remedy timetable leading to a hearing requires the filing of a completed Form A or Form A1. Conversely, answering 'no' at section 10.1 in the petition does not prevent a subsequent Form A/A1 application for a financial order. A respondent to the petition may also file a Form A or Form A1 at any time after the petition is issued, whether or not they have filed an answer to the decree proceedings.

[1]   FPR 9.4.

16.5 MCA 1973, s 28(3) imposes an absolute bar on the court's jurisdiction to consider an application for a financial remedy after the applicant's remarriage, if the application has not been made prior to the remarriage. The only exception to this rule is that an application for a pension sharing order may be made after remarriage. Provided the *application* has been made before the remarriage, the proceedings may continue and orders may be made after the remarriage. What then constitutes making the application? Filing a Form A is certainly sufficient. It is presumed that ticking the box at section 10.1 will be sufficient, even in the absence of Form A, although this has not yet been established in a reported case. A respondent to the decree proceedings who seeks a financial remedy must be careful to file a Form A (or an answer to the petition, formally seeking financial relief) before any remarriage. An acknowledgment of service does not amount to an application for financial relief[1], (although it has been proposed that a question similar to that posed in section 10.1 of the petition may be incorporated into the acknowledgment, in which case an affirmative answer may be sufficient to qualify as an 'application' and avoid the 'remarriage trap'). The fact that the other party has made an application does not found a jurisdiction for the court to make orders in favour of the party who has not applied[2].

1   *Hargood (formerly Jenkins) v Jenkins* [1978] Fam 148, [1978] 2 WLR 969, FD.
2   Obiter comments of Dunn LJ in *Robin v Robin* (1983) 4 FLR 632, CA, considered in *Whitehouse-Piper v Stokes* [2009] 1 FLR 983, CA, at para 5. In *Whitehouse-Piper v Stokes* the court transferred a property to a husband who had not himself applied, on the basis that the wife had made an application for a property transfer, and it is perfectly possible to apply for an order against oneself: *Dart v Dart* [1996] 2 FLR 286, [1997] 1 FCR 21, [1996] Fam Law 607, CA.

16.6 Applications may also be made for financial remedies for a child. The list of potential applicants is set out in FPR 9.10, and includes parents, guardians, any person named in a child arrangements order as a person with whom the child is to live, a local authority with a care order and the child him/herself. A child applicant may require separate representation, as set out in FPR 9.11.

THE OVERRIDING OBJECTIVE

16.7 FPR Pt 1 sets out the 'overriding objective' of the rules. The overriding objective applies when the court exercises any powers set out under the FPR, or interprets any rule. The overriding objective is to enable the court to deal with cases justly, having regard to any welfare issues involved. This includes ensuring that a case is dealt with expeditiously and fairly; in ways which are proportionate to the nature, importance and complexity of the issues; ensuring that the parties are on an equal footing; saving expense; and allotting to the case an appropriate share of the court's resources, while taking into account the need to allot resources to other cases. These provisions follow closely the overriding objective which is a central feature of the CPR.

ISSUING THE APPLICATION

Mediation Information and Assessment Meetings

16.8 Section 10(1) of the Children and Families Act 2014 and FPR Pt 3 provides that, before making a relevant family application, a person must attend a mediation information and assessment meeting (MIAM). A financial remedy application falls within the definition of relevant family applications set out in PD3A, paragraph 13(1). This statutory requirement reflects the policy of successive governments to encourage the use of mediation and other non-court dispute resolution options instead of court proceedings, where possible, to resolve family disputes. Mediation itself is entirely voluntary, though encouraged, but attendance at a MIAM, to be given information about mediation, is compulsory before an application is issued, unless a valid exemption can be claimed. The exemptions to the MIAM attendance requirement are set out in r 3.8, and include where the applicant is bankrupt, where the parties are in agreement and there is no dispute to mediate, where the application is urgent or made without notice or where the location of the other party is unknown or overseas. There is also a MIAM exemption where there is evidence of domestic violence. The forms of evidence required in cases of domestic abuse are set out in PD3A at para 20. When issuing an application for a financial order, Form A includes a section which must be completed by the applicant or his solicitor giving details of any exemptions claimed from attending at a MIAM. Where the applicant has attended a MIAM, the form must also be completed by the mediator. At the first hearing, the court will consider whether a MIAM has been attended and whether any exemption has been validly claimed and evidenced, and may direct the applicant or parties to attend a MIAM and adjourn the proceedings pending attendance (PD3A, para 37).

Where to issue Form A

16.9 With effect from 15 February 2021 applications for financial remedies should be issued in the hub court of one of the FRC zones[1] (as opposed to a Regional Divorce centre). FPR 5.4 does not stipulate at which zone hub the application must be issued. The applicant can therefore issue the application in the zone hub that he or she prefers. However, were the application to be issued in a non-local zone then the court may, either of its own motion or on the application of the other party, use its powers under FPR 29.17 and 29.18 to transfer the case to be heard elsewhere, most likely in a local zone. The application is made in Form A (or Form A1 where the application concerns periodical payments only: see the explanation of the fast track procedure at 16.56 below). Practitioners should also complete an allocation questionnaire[2], to ensure that cases with complex features can be allocated to be heard by an experienced district judge or circuit judge. Allocation decisions are made on paper on receipt of the application[3]. A party may request the court to reconsider this decision at a hearing[4]. In the FRCs the allocation will frequently be made to a level of judge different from that specified by the Family Court (Composition and Distribution of Business) Rules 2014[5] in order to reflect complexity or the efficient use of local resources. It is unlikely that a court will wish to change such an allocation without very good reason and is unlikely that a separate hearing will be permitted for such a request to be considered.

[1]   The hub courts are for these purposes: Central Family Court, Birmingham, Nottingham, Newport, Swansea, Liverpool, Sheffield, Newcastle, Leeds, Medway, Manchester, Peterborough, Oxford, Bristol, Bournemouth, Plymouth, Wrexham and Preston.
[2]   To be found at the Third Schedule of the Financial Remedies Guide to Good Practice Protocol November 2019.
[3]   In accordance with the Second Schedule of the Financial Remedies Guide to Good Practice Protocol November 2019.
[4]   FPR 29.19.
[5]   SI 2014/840.

Delay in making the application

16.10 In *Vince v Wyatt*[1] the Supreme Court confirmed that there is no limitation period for seeking orders for financial provision or property adjustment following a divorce, as an order may be made on granting a decree of divorce, 'or at any time thereafter'[2]. Even after an inordinate delay, where the application was made 30 years after the divorce, the applicant was entitled to bring her application, although the consequences of delay may well reduce or even eliminate provision for the applicant. Whilst the court has power to strike out an application pursuant to FPR 4.4, this is of limited reach and has to be construed without reference to whether the application has a real prospect of success. There is no equivalent of the CPR's application for summary judgment in an application for a financial remedy. An application will be struck out for disclosing 'no reasonable grounds' on which it could be brought only if it is legally incoherent or untenable, for example because the applicant has remarried before the application is made. *Roocroft v Ball*[3] provides a further example of the court declining to use the provisions of FPR 4.4 to strike out an application (here in the context of setting aside a consent order), although the court may where appropriate use its case management powers to conduct an abbreviated hearing. In *A v B*[4] Baker J (as he then was) declined to strike out the husband's long-delayed application for financial orders, but arranged an abbreviated hearing at which the husband's claim was considered and dismissed on its merits[5]

[1]   *Vince v Wyatt* [2015] UKSC 14.
[2]   MCA 1973, s 23(1).
[3]   *Roocroft v Ball* [2016] EWCA Civ 1009.
[4]   *A v B (Financial Remedies: Application to Strike Out)* [2018] EWFC 4.
[5]   *A v B (Financial Remedies) (No 2)* [2018] EWFC 45.

16.11 An application under MCA 1973, s 10(2) for the court to consider the financial position of a respondent to a separation-based divorce, whilst rare in practice, is made in Form B. Other than in s 10(2) applications, the parties to a financial remedies application are referred to as 'the applicant' and 'the respondent'. A respondent to the main suit may therefore be the applicant in the financial remedy application.

16.12 At the stage of filing Form A, Form A1 or Form B, no statement or other evidence is filed. The parties receive a notice from the court in Form C, informing them of the date of the first appointment (FA) and the requirements as to the filing of evidence. Form C sets out the timetable in the form of an order, and compliance is therefore required. The court allocates a date for hearing of the first appointment not less than 12 weeks and not more than 16 weeks after the date of issue[1].

[1]   FPR 9.12.

SERVICE AND PARTIES

16.13 Form C and the application must then be served on the respondent to the application. This is usually done by the court within 4 days of the filing of the application. If the applicant wishes to serve the respondent they must notify the court and then do so within 4 days of receiving the notice of hearing from the court, and must file a certificate of service at or before the first appointment. Methods of service are set out in FPR Pt 6. The documents are usually sent by post either to the solicitors who are on the record as acting for a party or to the party in person where no solicitor is on the record. Service by email must comply with PD6A, which requires, broadly, that consent for email service must have been given. Service out of the jurisdiction is governed by PD6B.

Service on third parties

16.14 FPR 9.13 and 9.31 set out the rules for notifying other interested parties that an application has been made. The rules are often honoured in the breach, but compliance is important: negligence claims may follow if things go wrong and, for example, mortgagees and pension trustees have not been served. Given the new freedoms for the over 55s to draw uncapped funds from some pensions, it is obviously important to alert those responsible for administering a pension that an application has been made. If the application seeks pension sharing or pension attachment orders it must be served on the person responsible for the pension arrangement (or on the Pension Protection Fund Board if the PPF has taken responsibility for the scheme and pension compensation orders are sought). When the application is for a property adjustment order, a copy of the application must be served by the applicant on any mortgagee. When the application is for a variation of settlement, a copy of the application must be served by the applicant on the trustees of the settlement and on the settlor if living. In the case of an application for avoidance of disposition, the application must be sent by the applicant to the person in whose favour the disposition is alleged to have been made. A certificate of service on these third parties should be filed by the applicant no later than 14 days before the first hearing. Any third party served may request a copy of forms E (or any relevant part) and may also file an answer to the application within 14 days of service.

Joinder of parties

16.15 Sometimes it is necessary to join other parties into the litigation, if there is a dispute between a spouse and a third party as to the beneficial ownership of property. A spouse may assert that the other spouse is beneficially entitled to a property held in the name of a third party. Alternatively, a third party may assert they have a beneficial interest in property held by one or both spouses. It is important to establish the size of the matrimonial 'pot' before the court proceeds to conduct the discretionary exercise of deciding how that pot should be apportioned between the spouses. A financial remedy order will only bind the parties to the proceedings and it will therefore be necessary to join third parties to ensure an order governing ownership of property will bind them and become enforceable, as well as to ensure the third party has a voice in the proceedings. Joinder of third parties to family proceedings is governed by the court's wide case management powers in FPR 4.1, the application of the overriding objective in FPR 1.1 and the court's duty under FPR 1.4 to manage cases, which specifies that the court's duties of active case management include identifying at an early stage the issues and who should be a party to the proceedings. FPR 9.26B enables the court to add a party if it is 'desirable' so that the court can resolve all matters in dispute in the proceedings, or to remove a party if it is not desirable for him or her to continue to be a party to the proceedings. Such orders can be made on the court's own initiative or following an application made in accordance with the Pt 18 procedure using form D11. Any such application must be supported by evidence setting out the proposed new party's interest in, or connection with, the proceedings (unless the court directs otherwise).

16.16 The approach to be taken in cases involving a dispute as to ownership involving a third party was summarised by Nicholas Mostyn QC, then sitting as a deputy High Court judge, in *TL v ML and others (Ancillary Relief: Claim against Assets of Extended Family)*[1] in which he stated that where a dispute arises about the ownership of property in financial relief proceedings between a spouse and a third party the following steps should ordinarily happen:

(1) the third party should be joined to the proceedings at the earliest opportunity;

(2) directions should be given for the issue to be fully pleaded by points of claim and points of defence;

(3) separate witness statements should be directed in relation to the dispute; and

(4) the dispute should be directed to be heard separately as a preliminary issue before the financial dispute resolution appointment.

[1] *TL v ML and others (Ancillary Relief: Claim against Assets of Extended Family* [2005] EWHC 2860 (Fam), [2006] 1 FLR 1263 at para 36.

16.17 However, proportionality must always be considered, and not every case will require the expensive process of a preliminary issue hearing. In *Shield v Shield*[1] Nicholas Francis QC (as he then was) suggested that in some cases it may be more cost effective to deal with the issue of beneficial ownership only if the matter has not settled at FDR. In *Fisher Meredith v JH and PH*[2] Mostyn J identified a distinction between cases where one spouse asserts a property held by a third party is in fact the property of the other spouse (where the full *TL v ML* procedure should ordinarily be followed to establish the size of the asset pot, with the party making the assertion obligated to organise the joinder) and cases where a spouse argues that a property in which they hold the legal title in fact belongs beneficially to another. In the latter case, it may be more appropriate to proceed to FDR, where the judge can express a preliminary view on the ownership of the asset, based on the evidence so far. In *Behbehani v Behbehani and Others*[3], the Court of Appeal went one step further in stating that where a spouse is seeking a *transfer [or sale] of property* asserted to belong to a third party, that party must ordinarily be joined to the proceedings, but where a spouse is seeking another form of financial provision, such as a lump sum, based on an overall assertion as to the respondent's wealth which is disputed on the basis that an asset is alleged to be owned by a third party, joinder of the third party may not be necessary or proportionate. The extent of the wealth can simply be established as a matter of evidence.

[1] *Shield v Shield* [2014] EWHC 23 at para 108, upheld on appeal at [2014] EWCA Civ 1136.
[2] *Fisher Meredith v JH and PH* [2012] EWHC 408 (Fam) at paras 42–44 and 51.
[3] *Behbehani v Behbehani and Others* [2019] EWCA Civ 2301 at para 69.

SPECIAL RULES RELATING TO PENSIONS

16.18 Specific rules relating to the action required by a person with pension rights are set out in FPR 9.30. Broadly, the pension holder must request a cash equivalent valuation of the pension within 7 days of being notified of the date of the first appointment and must then promptly supply the information to the other party (with contact details for the pension trustees or administrators, to enable service on them). However, if the pension holder is already in possession of a CE valuation not more than 12 months old (at the date of the first hearing), then this will suffice and a further request need not be made. Similar provisions apply where the application is for compensation for a pension in the Pension Protection Fund (PPF) or in an assessment period for transfer to the PPF[1]. Information relating to each party's pension rights must be set out in the Form E Financial Statement. At the first appointment the court may direct any party with pension rights to file and serve a Pension Inquiry Form (Form P) completed in full or in part as the court may direct[2]. It is good practice to use form P to gather information about pensions at an early stage, without waiting for a court direction. It is also good practice to obtain information about state pension entitlements at the outset of a case, using forms BR19 and BR20.

[1]   FPR 9.37–9.45.
[2]   FPR 9.15(7)(c).

FILING OF EVIDENCE

16.19 Evidence in applications for a financial order under the MCA 1973 or the Civil Partnership Act 2004, or for an order after a foreign divorce, is given by each party completing Form E. Form E1 is used for applications under Sch 1 of the Children Act 1989 and applications for maintenance other than periodical payments under the MCA. Form E2 is used in an application for variation of financial remedy orders and fast-track periodical payments applications (see **16.56** below). The appropriate form must be filed at court and simultaneously exchanged not less than 35 days before the date of the first appointment (FA)[1]. The Form C hearing notice will set out the filing date, in the form of a court order. Form E is a comprehensive document which requires the parties to set out full details of the marriage, their children, their property and income and financial needs and obligations, and enables them to provide information about any specific MCA 1973, s 25 matter (such as contributions) on which they rely. Form E is a statement verified by a statement of truth. The form should be completed with true, comprehensive and realistic information, and solicitors should advise clients of their duty to give full and frank disclosure and of the consequences of giving incomplete or misleading answers. These consequences can include prosecution for fraud, proceedings for contempt of court, adverse costs orders or simply presenting an open goal for cross examination and/or losing the sympathy and trust of the court. It is intended that the information contained in Form E will be all the information which the court will need in the majority of cases. There is, however a duty of ongoing full and frank disclosure, so any significant developments in a party's financial circumstances must be notified promptly, and updating disclosure is usually ordered prior to any final hearing.

[1]   FPR 9.14(1).

16.20 Form E must have attached to it all the documents required by the form itself and any other documents necessary to clarify or explain any of the information contained in the form. It may not annex or exhibit any other documents[1]. The form helpfully sets out in highlighted boxes all the documents required. These include any property valuation obtained within the last 6 months, a recent mortgage statement, bank or building society statements for the past 12 months, surrender value quotations in respect of any life insurance policies, the last 2 years' accounts and any other document used as a basis for the valuation of business assets, a cash equivalent valuation of pension rights and the last three pay slips and most recent P60. At this stage, no further disclosure may be requested or given. In *J v J*[2] Mostyn J said that, while the obligation to give documentation supporting the valuation of a business may require a party to append a short accountant's letter justifying the figure set out in the form, it was quite wrong to append 'a very full expert's report'. Where a party is unavoidably prevented from annexing any document required by Form E, he must at the earliest opportunity serve copies of that document on the other party and file a copy with the court together with a written explanation of the failure to send it with Form E[3].

[1]   FPR 9.14(2).
[2]   *J v J* [2014] EWHC 3654 (Fam).
[3]   FPR 9.14(3).

16.21 The intention is that in relatively simple cases it should be possible to use the first appointment (FA) as a financial dispute resolution (FDR) appointment but this cannot happen where one side is waiting for information and documents from the other. Proper preparation for the FDA is impossible where one party fails to comply with the Form C timetable. Exchange of the Forms E must be simultaneous. The date of the FA may be vacated only with permission of the court. If the FA is drawing near without one party complying with the timetable the applicant should file (but not exchange) their own form E and may apply without notice to the district judge for an order that the respondent file and exchange his Form E within, say, 7 days of the service of the order upon him, with a penal notice attached. If this does not produce the desired result, it may well be that the court will make an adverse costs order to be paid within 14 days, if the FA is ineffective and has to be adjourned.

OTHER DOCUMENTS TO BE SERVED

16.22 At least 14 days before the hearing of the FA (the date will be set out in the Form C order and notice of hearing), each party must file at court and serve on the other an important series of documents, designed to clarify the case and narrow the issues[1]. These are as follows:

- a concise statement of the issues between the parties;
- a chronology;
- a questionnaire setting out by reference to the concise statement of issues any further information or documents requested from the other party, or a statement that no further information and documents are requested; and
- a notice stating whether or not that party will be in a position at the FA to proceed on that occasion to an FDR appointment (Form G).

[1]   FPR 9.14(5).

THE STATEMENT OF APPARENT ISSUES

16.23 One of the documents which both parties must file at court and serve on each other before the FA is the statement of apparent issues. In a well-prepared case this should be a central document for the judge at the FA, since the principal purpose of that hearing is to define succinctly the issues in the case. It is essential, therefore, that the parties and their advisers should have contemplated the issues and committed their thoughts to writing before the FA. The Forms E of both parties will have stated the terms of the orders which each party seeks, and it should therefore be possible to identify the issues in the case. It is not necessary to set out a laborious list of each and every factual issue on which the parties do not agree. For example, it would be unnecessary to record evidential disputes as to elements of the quantum of income needs.

16.24 Proper issues might read, for example:

• 'The wife asserts that the matrimonial home should be transferred to her, to provide a home for herself and the children, subject to a charge in favour of the husband to be realised when the children all leave full-time education; the husband says that the wife's housing needs can be met by a lump sum payment of £x which should be paid to her from the proceeds of sale of the home'.

• 'The husband states that there should be a clean break on payment to the wife of £x and says that the wife could acquire an earning capacity of £y per annum and make herself self-sufficient within 12 months. The wife says that her earning capacity is uncertain and unpredictable, and that, in any event, as long as the children are of school age, there should be no dismissal of her claims. She seeks periodical payments of £z until the children are all in secondary education, on an extendable term'.

• 'The wife asserts that her separate capital amounts to £x, acquired in the following manner [brief details] and that this sum should be ring-fenced from the sharing of the matrimonial resources. The husband asserts that the case should be decided primarily on the basis of the parties' needs and in any event asserts that the assets have been mingled and have acquired a matrimonial nature'.

It is unnecessary to continue at great length. In most cases the document can be limited to one or two sides of text.

QUESTIONNAIRES AND REQUESTS FOR DOCUMENTS

16.25 It is fundamental to current procedure that no further disclosure of documents may be sought or given after the filing of Forms E and before the FA (although this sometimes happens on a voluntary basis, where both parties are keen to use the first hearing as a dispute resolution hearing). The intention of the rule[1] is that the 35 days between the exchange of the Forms E and the FA shall be taken up with deciding what further information and documentation is needed, and formulating the questionnaire and request for documents. The importance of these provisions and, in particular, the court's control over the disclosure and inspection process, was emphasised by the Court of Appeal in its decision in *Imerman v Imerman*[2], when considering an appeal brought by a husband (following a first instance decision by Moylan J) concerning the wife's ability to use documents obtained by her brothers from the hard drive of a computer system that they had shared with the husband. At first instance these documents had been admitted as evidence in accordance with the long standing approach taken by the family courts following the decision in *Hildebrand v Hildebrand*[3] which had allowed the use in evidence of confidential private documents obtained by one spouse concerning the financial affairs of the other, provided that no force or interception was used to obtain the documents and that copies of the documents found were produced and the original documents returned to the other party. As part of its reasoning for overturning Moylan J's decision and disapproving the way in which the '*Hildebrand*' approach had been used in family cases, the Court of Appeal in *Imerman* emphasised that it was only at the point at which a party is required to file and serve Form E that the duty arises to provide disclosure. The court and the rules then closely regulate the process of discovery and decisions as to what is relevant, proportionate and admissible, balancing the parties' rights to privacy and a fair trial. In the *Imerman* case, when the documents from the husband's computer had been downloaded prior to exchange of Forms E, the husband had been under no current duty of financial disclosure.

[1]   FPR 9.14(4).
[2]   *Imerman v Imerman* [2010] EWCA Civ 908, [2010] 2 FLR 814.
[3]   *Hildebrand v Hildebrand* [1992] 1 FLR 244.

16.26 The questionnaire and request for documents must be filed at court and served on the other party not later than 14 days before the hearing of the FA, by the date set out in the Form C order[1]. It is important to observe this date, not only because it is a requirement of both the rules and the Form C order, but also because consideration of the detailed questionnaire, and deletion of disproportionate or unnecessary questions, is an important judicial function at the FA. Few judges are happy to order the answering of a questionnaire that has not yet even been prepared and which they have not scrutinised. Considerable care should be taken in drafting the questionnaire, for two main reasons. First, the questionnaire is likely to represent the only opportunity to seek missing information and clarification. Following the FA, no party may seek the production of any further documents before the FDR, unless the court gives permission[2]. It is therefore intended that the district judge at the FA shall deal comprehensively and finally with all issues of disclosure and questionnaires, and those orders will be based on the requests before him/her. Secondly, the questionnaire must be a proportionate focus on those significant issues in dispute between the parties which need to be resolved in order to achieve a fair outcome. Questions about issues that are of little or no significance to the outcome of the case (such as enquiries as to past holiday destinations) will simply increase costs and are likely to be deleted by the judge. Questions should therefore be tightly focused on the practical information and documents that are really needed before the case can be resolved. Likewise, questions which are really cross-examination points, simply challenging the other party's version of events or casting aspersions, should be avoided.

[1]   FPR 9.14(5).
[2]   FPR 9.16(1).

THE FIRST APPOINTMENT

16.27 The FA is conducted by a district judge, unless the case has been allocated to the High Court in accordance with Mr Justice Mostyn's 'Statement on the Efficient Conduct of Financial Remedy Hearings Allocated to a

High Court Judge' issued with the approval of the President of the Family Division in February 2016, in which case it may be heard by a High Court judge. Mostyn J's statement, which gives detailed guidance as to the thresholds justifying a High Court process and the procedures to be followed, must be read carefully in all such cases. The parties to the case must attend every hearing in addition to their lawyers, unless the court otherwise directs[1]. Provision for an accelerated FA procedure on the papers, or for a paper hearing in some circumstances, is explored at **16.31** below. By the time of the FA, the Forms E, questionnaires, chronologies and statements of issues should be on the court file, and the judge should have read them in advance. The other vital document which each party must produce no later than one day before the FA is a written estimate of the costs incurred by that party up to the date of the hearing and expected to be incurred up to the FDR, in Form H[2]. This document should have been notified to the client in advance, and is an open statement, the contents of which the judge is likely to comment on in the presence of the parties.

[1]   FPR 9.15(8).
[2]   FPR 9.27.

16.28 In order to improve the prospects of settlement at the FA, it is helpful for the court to have a case summary and a schedule of assets showing concisely the resources and assets available to the parties, agreed where possible. This enables the court and the parties to focus upon those issues which are relevant to resolving the dispute between them. Many practitioners routinely produce documents of this kind at the FA, and this is encouraged by PD 9A, para 4.1 which provides that the parties should, if possible, exchange and file an agreed summary of the case, a schedule of assets agreed between them and details of any directions that they seek. Where full agreement has not been possible in preparing these documents, the differences should be marked up on a single document, rather than the judge being presented with competing versions. In practical terms, although not mandated by the rules, many judges find it helpful for the parties to bring evidence of their mortgage capacity and housing needs (ie realistic sample property particulars) to the FA, as this increases the chance of the hearing being used to resolve the whole dispute.

16.29 The objective of the judge at the FA is stated in FPR 9.15(1) as 'defining the issues and saving costs'. The judge's specific duties are set out in FPR 9.15(2) and (3). The judge must decide to what extent questionnaires should be answered and further documents be produced. S/he must direct and control any necessary valuations and expert evidence, and decide whether any further evidence is required from the parties (for example, on issues as to contributions, mortgage capacity, housing need or – rarely – conduct). In all this, s/he will be guided by an understanding of the real issues in the case and by the overriding objective. The judge will be able to exercise the wide-ranging case management powers set out in FPR Pt 4 to define and limit the issues and direct the just and proportionate conduct of the case.

16.30 The judge must then consider the future progress of the case. This will involve a decision as to whether the FA is to be treated as the FDR appointment[1]. Both parties should have filed and served Form G indicating whether they will be in a position to proceed to FDR there and then, but, even where they have not so indicated, the judge may treat the appointment as an FDR[2]. If the FDR is not conducted there and then, the judge <u>must</u> direct the listing of an FDR, unless there are 'exceptional reasons' that make such a course inappropriate[3]. Such reasons may include a decision to adjourn the case to allow for mediation or another form of alternative dispute resolution such as a private FDR, or the need to list a preliminary issues hearing, for example where a third party has been joined in a dispute as to property ownership. In some cases, the court may decide to list a case for an abbreviated hearing on one discrete issue which is likely to determine the case. An example of the latter is the decision of Coleridge J in *Crossley v Crossley*[4]. Here, the parties, both of mature age and independently wealthy, had married late in life after making a pre-nuptial agreement to the effect that, in the event of divorce, neither would make any claim on the other. When, after divorce, the wife applied for financial relief, the husband issued a notice to show cause why her application should not be resolved in accordance with the agreement. Coleridge J agreed with this approach, ordered Forms E with no documentation, and adjourned the FA to resolve the issue. The wife's appeal against this approach was dismissed; it was held that, while the agreement was only one aspect of the case and did not relieve the court of its duty to consider all the s 25 factors, in this case it was of magnetic importance. The rules should not be a straitjacket and the overriding objective governed all. The judge had a duty to identify issues at an early stage and deal with the case in a manner proportionate to the issues. A party wishing to avail himself of the procedure for an abbreviated hearing should issue a notice to show cause returnable at the FA, supported by a witness statement. The case of *A v B* noted at **16.10** provides a more recent example of the abbreviated hearing approach.

[1] FPR 9.15(7).
[2] FPR 9.15(7)(b).
[3] FPR 9.15(4).
[4] *Crossley v Crossley* [2007] EWCA Civ 1491, [2008] 1 FLR 1467.

16.31 An accelerated FA procedure, approved by Mostyn and Moor JJ on behalf of the High Court Judiciary, is set out in the fourth schedule of the Financial Remedies Guide to Good Practice Protocol, released in November 2019. This applies to cases in which the parties have been able to agree all directions well in advance, where on the particular facts of the case personal attendance is likely to have little purpose and where the costs of attending would probably outweigh the benefits. An application must be submitted to the court with a consent order setting out the directions sought (using the template provided for the purpose) together with the first appointment documents *at least 14 days* before the FA hearing. The draft order will be considered on the papers and either approved, or not approved with short reasons (in which latter case attendance at the FA will still be required). It is intended that the accelerated approach will only apply to a limited number of cases, where the benefits of attending at an early stage in front of a judge to discuss the case and hear the judge's views is outweighed by the need for further proportionate and agreed steps in the litigation prior to an attended hearing. In the majority of cases, attendance at the FA continues to be crucial: to control the evidence, questionnaires and the use of experts and for the judge to speak directly to the parties about the issues and the costs at an early stage in the proceedings, in order to encourage settlement and a proportionate and rational approach to the litigation. Outside the strict parameters of the accelerated procedure, an approach which is sometimes encountered, of solicitors simply submitting 'agreed directions' at the very last minute and then failing to turn up for the FA without prior judicial agreement ('meaning no disrespect to the court'), is likely to be deprecated[1]!

1   It should however be noted that the Central Family Court issued a Notice on 24 April 2020 (as the courts accommodated the new pandemic reality of remote hearings) approving FA 'paper hearings' where directions have not been agreed but a summary of the directions sought, a response to the other party's proposed directions and any objections to questions are filed and served at least 7 days before the FA, with a bundle filed no later than the day before the hearing. The judge may then decide to adjudicate on the directions at the hearing, but on the papers. This notice applies only to the CFC, but other courts have been prepared to countenance similar approaches during the pandemic. It remains the case that the FA should be attended (usually remotely) unless and until the judge authorises an unattended hearing.

EXPERT EVIDENCE

16.32 Expert evidence may be necessary to assist the court and the parties to resolve the proceedings. For example:

* valuation evidence may be necessary if the parties cannot agree the valuation to be used for a property;
* in the case of a family business, expert evidence may be needed to value the business and to advise on liquidity and the tax consequences of sharing the value in the business or drawing funds from it;
* evidence may be needed from a pensions expert to understand the percentages for a pension sharing order or the value of pensions for offsetting;
* evidence may be required from an accountant as to liability for CGT if the parties own more than one property.

In financial remedy proceedings (in contrast to proceedings relating to children) a party can *obtain* an expert's report without seeking permission from the court. However, an expert's report cannot be *put before the court* (in any form) without the court's permission[1]. FPR Pt 25 and the accompanying practice directions (particularly PD25B and PD25C) govern the use and instruction of experts in financial proceedings. The court must be of the opinion that the expert evidence is *necessary* to assist the court to resolve the proceedings[2]. This test is significantly more stringent than the old test, pre-2010, of what was 'reasonably required'. The Court of Appeal has defined 'necessary' as having 'a meaning lying somewhere between 'indispensable' on the one hand and 'useful', 'reasonable' or 'desirable' on the other hand, having the connotation of the imperative, what is demanded rather than what is merely optional, reasonable or desirable'[3]. In deciding whether to grant permission the court will consider the factors set out in r 25.5(2), namely the issues to which the evidence would relate, the questions that the court would require the expert to answer, the impact on the timetable, duration and conduct of the case, any failure to comply with the rules dealing with the way in which the application is to be made and the cost of the expert evidence. It is the duty of experts to help the court on matters within their expertise. Their overriding duty is to the court rather than to the person by whom they were instructed or paid.

1   FPR 25.4(2).

2   FPR 25.4(3).
3   Munby P in *Re H-L (A child)* [2013] 2 FLR 1434 quoting with approval from *Re P (Placement Orders: Parental Consent)* [2008] 2 FLR 625.

16.33 The court has power to direct that the expert evidence is given by one expert, instructed by both parties as a single joint expert witness (SJE)[1]. It will be rare that the court will consider it necessary and proportionate for each party to instruct their own separate expert. In *J v J*[2] Mostyn J criticised a judge for allowing the parties each to obtain reports from a separate expert leading to a substantial increase in costs, emphasising that PD25D, para 2.1 mandates the use of an SJE 'wherever possible'. If the identity of the SJE cannot be agreed, the judge will select the expert from a list prepared by the parties (or otherwise direct how the expert will be chosen). The judge can also settle the terms of the letter of instruction where this cannot be agreed, or refer this issue to arbitration[3]. Where the parties are obtaining expert assistance without seeking the court's permission (for example if the court's timetable has not yet started), PD25D, para 2.1 encourages them to agree to instruct an SJE.

1   FPR 25.11.
2   *J v J* [2014] EWHC 3654 (Fam), [2015] Fam Law 372.
3   As per Moor J in *CM v CM* [2019] EWFC 16.

16.34 The application for permission to put expert evidence before the court should be made as soon as possible and in any event no later than the first appointment. It should be made as a formal, written, on notice application under FPR Pt 18 in Form D11, with details of the type of expertise considered necessary, the name of the expert where practicable and the issues that the expert is to address, together with a draft order. Care should be taken before making the application to contact the expert(s) proposed, to confirm their willingness and availability to do the work, the timescales involved and the likely cost[1]. Only then can the judge considering the application properly apply the test in r 25.5(2). Simply arriving at the FA and making a vague and unresearched oral application for expert assistance is not acceptable and may be refused, or lead to an adverse costs order if it causes the hearing to have to be adjourned.

1   FPR PD25D, para 3.3.

16.35 If permission is given, the expert evidence should be given in a written report and must comply with the detailed requirements as to form and content set out in PD25B, para 9.1. FPR 25.10 sets out a mechanism for proportionate questions, intended to seek clarification of the report, to be put to the expert within 10 days of receipt and to be answered within the timescale specified by the court. Failure by the expert to answer the questions may lead to the party who instructed the expert being unable to rely on the expert report and/or being unable to recover the expert's fees from the other party even if a costs order is made. Any communications with the SJE must be copied to the other party. The court will only direct an expert to attend to give oral evidence if it is necessary in the interests of justice to do so[1]. The costs of an SJE are the joint and several responsibility of the parties, unless the court orders otherwise. After the final hearing the expert should be informed in writing by the instructing party about the court's determination and the use made of the expert's evidence.

1   FPR 25.9(2).

THE FINANCIAL DISPUTE RESOLUTION HEARING

16.36 The purpose of the FDR appointment is to give the parties an opportunity to put their fundamental positions to the judge and to each other, and for the judge to make such comments as he or she may consider to be helpful to assist the parties to reach a settlement without the need for a fully contested final hearing. It is useful for solicitors and/or counsel and their clients to be available at least an hour before the appointed time (earlier if a conference with counsel is necessary) to enable negotiations before going into court. The FDR process, involving time in court and time negotiating outside court, will frequently take place over the course of a whole day. The Family Justice Council has published a Best Practice Guidance note as to the conduct of FDRs (December 2012) and this is required reading for practitioners and judges.

16.37 The FDR appointment is a privileged occasion; it must be treated as a meeting held for the purposes of discussion and negotiation at which the parties use their best endeavours to reach agreement on the matters in issue between them[1]. Anything said at the FDR is not admissible in any subsequent proceedings (save where an offence is committed at the hearing). The media are not permitted to attend and the hearing takes place in chambers to which the public are not admitted. The hearing is intended to enable the parties to discuss the case and their negotiating positions openly and without reservation. All offers and responses, including without prejudice offers, must be filed at court at least 7 days before the hearing, and will be returned at the conclusion of the hearing so that they are not kept on the court file. Costs schedules, including estimates of the costs to final hearing if settlement is not reached, must be filed in Form H. A judge who has conducted an FDR may only do one of three things at its conclusion: make a consent order; give directions for trial; or adjourn for a further FDR. A judge who has conducted an FDR process that has not resulted in a settlement will have no further involvement with the financial application. A judge making a consent order at the conclusion of a successful FDR cannot then decide subsidiary issues that the parties fail to agree[2]. The FDR judge also cannot deal with any matters of enforcement or variation of an order made at or subsequent to an FDR. This strict provision against further involvement with the case cannot be waived by the court or by the agreement of the parties, given the mandatory wording of FPR 9.17(2)[3].

[1] FPR 9.17.
[2] *Myerson v Myerson* [2008] EWCA Civ 1376.
[3] *Shokrollah-Babaee v Shokrollah-Babaee* [2019] EWHC 2135 (Fam) per Holman J.

16.38 The role of the judge at an FDR is to provide an early neutral evaluation of the case and then to help the parties to bridge the gap between them. The court cannot, of course, resolve any matters of factual dispute, but the judge will provide an overview of the principles to be applied and will comment on matters in dispute and the necessity and proportionality of pursuing these to trial. For example, the judge may explore with a party whether the likely cost of pursuing an 'add-back' argument to trial is wise in the context of a case where the magnetic factor is likely to be meeting the housing needs of the parties and their children. The judge will consider the amounts really in dispute between the parties, by examining the net effect of their most recent offers, and will express a view on the likely costs of continuing with the litigation and the proportionality of a contested hearing. Where possible, the judge is likely to express an opinion on the range of probable outcomes. Where parties have unrealistic expectations the judge will help them to understand the likely realities of the process. A preliminary view on issues of disputed fact may be expressed, based on the evidence available so far. Having expressed a view, the judge will encourage the parties to continue their negotiations outside the court room.

16.39 At the conclusion of the FDR appointment, if an agreement is reached, the court will make a final order by consent where possible, and advocates should come prepared to draft an order to be perfected that same day. An order can, however, only be perfected where Decree Nisi (DN) has already been pronounced. The necessity of having the DN before an order can be made was highlighted in *K v K (Financial Remedy Final Order Prior to Decree Nisi)*[1] where an order purportedly made prior to DN was set aside as a nullity. In cases where there is no DN, or where an agreement in principle has been reached but the parties are awaiting a point of clarification before matters can be finalised, the agreement should be recorded in formal signed Heads of Agreement and labelled as a *Xydhias* agreement[2]. Such an agreement is binding on the parties, but lacks the status of a court order. Should either party seek to resile from the agreement, the other party may issue a notice to show cause as to why the agreement should not be upheld and approved as a court order. Formal agreements properly arrived at with competent legal advice will generally be upheld by the court unless an injustice would be done.

[1]   *K v K (Financial Remedy Final Order Prior to Decree Nisi)* [2016] EWFC 23, [2017] 1 FLR 541, [2016] Fam Law 804.
[2]   *Xydhias v Xydhias* [1999] 1 FLR 683, CA.

16.40 Where the DN has been pronounced and full agreement has been reached, but it is not possible to draft a formal consent order on the day of the hearing, the Heads of Agreement should be labelled as a *Rose v Rose*[1] unperfected order of the court. A *Rose* order has been approved by the court and has all the status of an order, but simply requires the formal drafting process. A *Rose* order can only be undone by the usual formal processes common to all orders, of set aside or appeal. Where Heads of Agreement are drafted at the end of a successful FDR, it is important to record on the face of the document whether it is a *Xydhias* agreement or a *Rose* unperfected order, and the judge should explain the consequences of the label to the parties.

[1]   *Rose v Rose* [2002] 1 FLR 978, CA.

16.41 If the FDR does not result in an agreement, the appointment may be adjourned for a further FDR if that seems likely to assist the parties, or the judge may give directions to prepare for and list a final hearing. This will include the filing of evidence, with updating disclosure documentation and narrative statements from the parties setting out their evidence on each of the relevant factors listed in MCA 1973, s 25. Where a witness statement is to be made by a person unable to read it (for example because the maker is not fluent in English and a translator has been used) the requirements of PD22A as to certifying the witness statement must be complied with. This is no mere formality: the witness statement may not be used in evidence unless it has been properly translated and this is certified, and a party could therefore end up at the final hearing with no s 25 evidence if PD22A is ignored. Many cases will now be listed for final hearings by video platform, and the court is likely to confirm the format of the final hearing on the face of the order. If an attended hearing is directed, but some evidence is to be given by video link (for example because a witness is abroad, or because allegations of domestic abuse make it inappropriate for both parties to sit in the same room) this must be notified to the court at the earliest opportunity and it will be the responsibility of the party calling the witness to make the practical arrangements with the court office in good time. The time estimate for the final hearing will be canvassed, to include a realistic period for the judge to consider and deliver a reasoned *ex tempore* judgment. If an FDR does not result in either an adjourned FDR listing or a consent order, each party must file and serve an open proposal for settlement within 21 days of the FDR (or such other date as the court directs)[1].

[1]   FPR 9.27A.

16.42 For those who can afford them, 'private FDRs' offer an alternative to the court FDR process. These are examined in more detail in CHAPTER 22 at **22.19-22.20.** If a private FDR is agreed, the court will record this in a recital to the order made at the FA, usually listing a short directions appointment to take place after the private FDR, or alternatively adjourning the proceedings generally.

16.43 One of the principal reasons why cases involving substantial assets reach a final hearing and cannot be resolved before then is that there is a genuine dispute as to the amount of the assets, coupled with allegations of lack of good faith and failure to disclose. In *OS v DS (Oral Disclosure: Preliminary Hearing)*[1] Coleridge J devised a novel procedure for resolving such issues at an early stage. At a directions appointment he ordered a 3-day preliminary/oral discovery hearing, to take oral evidence from the husband and resolve questions of joinder. This enabled the judge to make findings and for the parties then to resolve the issues with great savings of costs and court time. It is unlikely that this procedure will be used in more than a small proportion of cases but it remains a useful tool to bear in mind in appropriate cases. The wide case management powers in FPR Pt 4 and the central importance of the overriding objective facilitate creative approaches of this kind.

[1]   [2004] EWHC 2376 (Fam), [2005] 1 FLR 675.

THE FINAL HEARING

16.44 The final hearing will not be heard by the judge who conducted the FDR. No later than 14 days before the hearing the applicant must file with the court and serve on the respondent an open statement of the orders he or she invites the court to make and the respondent must do likewise no later than 7 days after receipt of the applicant's proposals[1]. A failure to comply with this rule will be taken into account when the court considers whether to make costs orders. Each party must file with the court and serve on the other at least 14 days before the hearing a statement of costs in Form H1 setting out costs up to and including the final hearing and including the costs to be incurred implementing an order. The judge will expect advocates to produce a single chronology and schedule of assets, marked up with any disputed figures or dates, as per guidance given to FRC judiciary by Mostyn J in March 2021 further to the comments of Cohen J in *AG v VD*[2].

[1]   FPR 9.28, in addition to the new requirement for offers no later than 21 days after FDR, in FPR 9.27A.
[2]   *AG v VD* [2021] EWFC 9 at paras 8 and 144.

16.45 The detail of the conduct of the final hearing is likely to depend on whether or not the parties are represented by advocates. Where both are, the hearing will usually observe the traditional route of opening submissions and applications, evidence in chief, cross examination and re-examination of the applicant and any witnesses, followed by the same process for the respondent, closing submissions from the advocates and then an oral (or reserved written) judgment. Where one or both parties is a litigant in person, the judge may swear in the parties at the outset of the hearing, so that everything they say has the quality of evidence, and may then adopt a more inquisitorial approach.

PROCEDURE ON DRAFTING AND SUBMITTING THE ORDER

16.46 Whether the order results from a contested final hearing, or from agreement within or without the court process, a formal written order must be drafted, sealed by the court and served. A full range of standard financial and enforcement orders, is available as a zip file on the judiciary website (www.judiciary.gov.uk/publications/practice-guidance-standard-financial-and-enforcement-orders) and, for a modest subscription, as an online drafting tool from http://www.familyorders.co.uk, supported by a handbook (*Standard Family Orders Handbook: Volume One* by HHJ Edward Hess, Class Legal, 2018). Detailed information on the drafting of consent orders is given in CHAPTER 9.

16.47 The order and any annexes must be sealed by the court, which cannot be done until after the pronouncement of the Decree Nisi. The order becomes enforceable only on the making of the Decree Absolute. Where a pension sharing order is made, the timing of the Decree Absolute may be crucial; see **10.57**. If pension orders of any kind have been made (sharing, attachment or compensation) the sealed order and annex(es) should be served on the pension trustees or administrators (or the PPF Board), having already been served on them in draft form for comment before sending to the court. Any expert who has provided a report should be notified of the outcome in writing by the instructing party[1].

[1]   FPR 25.19.

16.48 A consent order, other than one approved by the judge already at a hearing as a *Rose v Rose* order, must be submitted to the court with a completed and signed Statement of Information in Form D81. The use of this form is made mandatory by FPR 9.26, unless specifically dispensed with by the court. The form fulfils three purposes. First, it gives the judge, in considering whether or not to approve the order, the information necessary for the court to consider the s 25 factors and the overall fairness of the order. Secondly, it confirms that the requirements of service on mortgagees and pension providers have been satisfied and that the court has the power to make any pension order sought. Thirdly, it confirms that each party is aware of the disclosed financial position of the other party. This record will be critical if subsequent non-disclosure is alleged. The financial information given should be stated for each party *before* implementation of the proposed order. In anything other than the most simple and obvious case, it will greatly assist the judge considering the order to submit a short covering letter (or alternatively to complete box 9 in the form) to state briefly the net effect of the order and why the parties consider this to be fair. Such a brief explanation may pre-empt the judge's queries and prevent the order from being returned with a list of questions. It is not always easy to gauge the net effect of an order from the information on the form and in the draft order. Where one or both parties is not represented, it is important to confirm in a covering letter or on the face of the documents that they are aware of the significance of the order and their entitlement to seek legal advice on its contents and effect. If the judge is not satisfied that the order represents a fair outcome and is properly and comprehensively drafted, he or she may return it with queries, or may list a short hearing at which the parties will be required to attend.

TRANSPARENCY IN FINAL HEARINGS

16.49 Should the final hearing take place in public, with members of the general public allowed to attend and the media permitted to report details of the identity of the parties, or should it take place in private? If the hearing is held in private, members of the public are not admitted without the express permission of the judge. Accredited members of the press and legal bloggers (lawyers permitted to attend under a pilot scheme running from 1 October 2018 to 31 December 2021 pursuant to FPR PD 36J) may attend a private hearing, but must not report what they hear and see in a way that identifies the parties (unless the reporting restrictions are lifted by the judge). FPR 27.10 starts from the proposition that family court hearings will take place in private. In *Fields v Fields* Holman J set out his views as follows[1]:

'For reasons which I have explained in my judgment in *Luckwell v Limata* [2014] EWHC 502 (Fam) at paragraphs 2 to 5, there is, in my view, a pressing need for more openness in divorce financial remedy proceedings . . . The family courts must be more transparent and there is no good basis for making an exception of financial cases. Such cases are heard in public on appeal to the Court of Appeal and the Supreme Court, and the law reports and press reporting are riddled with considerable intimate and financial detail of many financial cases on appeal. Accredited journalists are, in any event, entitled to be present even when the court is sitting in private, subject to strict and limited exceptions. To permit the presence of accredited journalists, but then tightly to restrict what they can report, creates a mere illusion of transparency. For these reasons I decided at the outset of the hearing to exercise the discretion under the FPR 2010, r 27.10, to direct that the bulk of the hearing (including now the delivery of this judgment) should be in public.'

In *DL v SL*[2], however, Mostyn J came to a diametrically opposed conclusion, on the basis that matrimonial financial proceedings are a category of court business so personal and private that in almost every case heard at first instance the right to privacy should trump the right to freedom of expression. On balance, the majority of family judges currently favour the latter analysis and approach, and the vast majority of first instance hearings continue to be heard in private. The admission into the court room of accredited media representatives and legal bloggers, whilst required in their reporting to anonymise the parties, strikes a balance between opening up the family courts to proper scrutiny whilst respecting the parties' rights to privacy.

1   *Fields v Fields* [2015] EWHC 1670 (Fam).
2   *DL v SL* [2015] EWHC 2621 (Fam).

DISCLOSURE ORDERS AGAINST THIRD PARTIES

16.50 A problem which sometimes arises is that a person who is not a party to the case, and who cannot therefore ordinarily expect to be bound by orders made in the case, fails to produce for inspection a document which is potentially important for the preparation of the case. To solve this problem, FPR 21.2 sets out the procedure for an application 'under any Act' for an order that a non-party shall disclose specific documents necessary to dispose fairly of the proceedings or save costs. The most common classes of persons against whom orders are sought are the cohabitant of one of the parties, and some person or body (such as a bank, or business partner) with whom the other party has a financial relationship. The statutes referenced by FPR 21.2 are the Bankers Books Evidence Act 1879, s 7 (direct evidence from a bank account) and the Senior Courts Act 1981, s 34(2)[1] (production from a non-party).

1   Applied to the Family Court by virtue of the Matrimonial and Family Proceedings Act 1984, s 31J .

16.51 An application for an order for disclosure against a third party is made to a district judge, using the FPR, Pt 18 procedure and Form D11. It must be supported by evidence setting out all factual matters relied upon and endorsed with a signed statement of truth. The application can be made without notice in appropriate circumstances. The application should specify the order sought, with details of the documents to be disclosed. It will normally be the case that the other party has refused or failed on request to produce the evidence which is sought, and the statement should give particulars of this refusal or failure. In general, the third party should be compensated in costs, unless the court disapplies this principle in view of the third party's conduct[1].

1   CPR 46.1(2) and (3).

16.52 FPR 21.2(6) provides that no person shall be compelled by an order to produce any document which he could not be compelled to produce at the final hearing. The court will bear in mind that, when the documents sought are the personal documents of the third party, he or she is entitled to privacy and should not normally be required to disclose them to others. The court must, therefore, be satisfied that there is *prima facie* evidence that the documents relate to a relevant issue in the proceedings, that disclosure is a proportionate response, and that the evidence which they will provide cannot be obtained in any other reasonable way, or by the drawing of adverse inferences. For example, if disclosure is sought from a cohabitant, it must be established that the financial position of the cohabitant is relevant to an issue to be decided in the case such as to make it necessary to see the cohabitant's documents. Two examples from the case law archive (on the previous similar provisions under the 1991 rules) illustrate the jurisdiction in practice. In *Frary v Frary*[1] the husband cohabited with a wealthy woman with whom he said he had no financial relationship and who did not support him. On appeal, a disclosure order was set aside. It was observed that the rule merely brought forward the time at which a witness might be compelled to attend court. In this case, the applicant wife had no intention of calling the third party at the final hearing, neither she nor the respondent had made any secret of their relationship and there was no particular relevance in the precise limits of the third party's means. There was nothing to make it a proper exercise of the court's powers to order the third party, a stranger to the proceedings, to attend and be examined at the trial or to produce documents in advance. By contrast, in *D v D (Production Appointment)*[2], the husband's attempts to obtain proper disclosure of the wife's considerable means had been obstructed and frustrated. Thorpe J made a production order requiring the wife's accountant to attend and produce his files, such disclosure being on a broad basis in view of the earlier obstructions and having the effect of overriding any professional privilege. In *M v M (Ancillary Relief: Conduct: Disclosure)*[3] it was held that the existing case law on disclosure against a third party had been strengthened rather than weakened by Art 8 of the ECHR.

[1] *Frary v Frary* [1993] 2 FLR 696.
[2] *D v D (Production Appointment)* [1995] 2 FLR 497.
[3] *M v M (Ancillary Relief: Conduct: Disclosure* [2006] Fam Law 923.

INTERIM ORDERS

Interim income orders

16.53 A problem which may arise is that an applicant for a financial order is in urgent need of interim support and cannot wait for up to 16 weeks until the first hearing, at which there may or may not be time to resolve interim maintenance issues. A party may therefore apply at any stage of the proceedings for an order for maintenance pending suit, interim periodical payments or an interim variation order[1]. It is implicit that such an application can be made only where a full application for a financial order is pending, so one or other party must have issued Form A/A1. The application for an interim order is made as a FPR Pt 18 application. Where the application is made before Forms E have been filed, the parties must file statements giving information about their means. An urgent hearing will then be listed by the court.

[1] FPR 9.7(1).

Interim capital orders

16.54 An interim order for sale of a property is probably not available under the MCA 1973. The court has jurisdiction to make substantive orders under MCA 1973, ss 23 and 24 only after Decree Nisi, and orders for sale under MCA 1973, s 24A can only be made following a substantive order for secured periodical payments, a lump sum or a property adjustment[1]. The Court of Appeal in *Wicks v Wicks*[2] confirmed in 1998 that the court has no power to grant an interim order for sale under procedural rather than substantive rules. This was further considered in 2018 by Cobb J in *WS v HS (Sale of*

Matrimonial Home)[3], who concluded that the wording of FPR 20.2(1)(c)(v) ('the court may grant the following interim remedies . . . an order . . . for the sale of relevant property . . . which for any other good reason it is desirable to sell quickly') does not of itself found a jurisdiction to make an interim order for sale of a house where this is not founded on any statutory provision. Cobb J's decision is at variance with the earlier decision in 2015 of Mostyn J in *BR v VT (Financial Remedies: Interim)*[4], where an interim order for sale *was* made on the basis of FPR 20.2(1)(c)(v), the judge also stating that before vacant possession could be ordered the court would have to apply the test in the Family Law Act 1996, s 33 to terminate a party's occupation rights. Mostyn J has described the difference in opinion with Cobb J as 'regrettable' and the issue awaits either clarification by the Court of Appeal, or statutory reform. Both judges are agreed that the Married Women's Property Act 1882 and the Trusts of Land and Appointment of Trustees Act 1996 provide statutory routes to an order for interim sale and vacant possession, and so it would be wise to issue such applications if an order for interim sale must be sought.

[1]   Or following an order under MCA 1973, s 22ZA for payments in respect of legal services, so could this route be a statutory basis under the MCA 1973 for an interim order for sale?
[2]   *Wicks v Wicks* [1998] 1 FLR 470.
[3]   *WS v HS (Sale of Matrimonial Home)* [2018] EWFC 11.
[4]   *BR v VT (Financial Remedies: Interim)* [2015] EWHC 2727 (Fam).

Other interim orders

16.55 FPR 20.2(1) sets out a menu of interim orders available to the court. These include the power to order the inspection of relevant property and the entry onto land for that purpose (which could be used if one party is obstructing a property valuation or to inspect computer files for crypto currency assets); the power to direct the preparation of accounts (which could be helpful if up-to-date information is needed for a business valuation) and the power to direct the payment of income from property until an application is decided (useful if the parties cannot agree on receipt of rental income). Such orders will only be granted if proportionate and necessary to resolve the issues in the case, and with due regard to the privacy of individuals not involved in the litigation.

THE 'FAST-TRACK' PROCEDURE

16.56 FPR 9.9B and FPR 9.18 apply a fast-track procedure for applications in which only a periodical payments order is sought (for ex-spouses, civil partners or unmarried parents under Sch 1 to the Children Act 1989) or for variation of a periodical payments order where the remedies sought do not include replacement of the order with a capital order (for a lump sum, property adjustment or pension order). An application is made in Form A1, after attendance at a MIAM unless exemptions apply, but the court will fix a first hearing date not less than 6 weeks and no more than 10 weeks after the date of the filing of the application. The financial statement form will be in the abbreviated Form E2 and must be exchanged by the parties and filed with the court not more than 21 days after issue of the application. The court is required to determine the application at the first hearing unless there are good reasons not to do so, may use the first hearing as an FDR if appropriate and will give directions for the filing of further evidence and the listing of any further hearing if the case cannot be resolved[1].

[1]   FPR 9.20.

16.57 An application may be made for the court to apply the ordinary financial order procedure to a fast-track application (FPR 9.18A). The reasons for seeking this direction must be set out in the application, or by the respondent within 7 days of service of the application, and the court will then determine without notice to the parties and before the first hearing which form of procedure will apply to the application and make directions accordingly. The court may also order of its own motion the transfer of the proceedings to the standard track at any stage in the proceedings[1].

[1]   FPR 9.9B(4).

THE PD9A PROTOCOL

16.58 One of the innovations of the CPR, which apply to civil proceedings other than family proceedings, was the introduction of protocols which govern how practitioners deal with the preparation of cases up to the issue of proceedings. These protocols have the force of law in the sense that the court may refer to them once proceedings have been issued when deciding whether or not various orders should be made, and when deciding issues of costs. The FPR contain a protocol attached to PD 9A. It is required reading for all practitioners and, in particular, the following points should be noted:

(a)   making an application to the court is not to be seen as a hostile step or a last resort, but is a way of controlling the timetable and disclosure;

(b)   while there is sometimes an advantage in preparing disclosure and negotiating before proceedings are commenced, solicitors must bear in mind the advantages of a court timetable and a court managed process;

(c)   solicitors should consider at an early stage and keep under review whether mediation and/or collaborative law would be appropriate;

(d)   proportionality and the overriding objective must be borne in mind at all times;

(e)   parties should seek to clarify their claims and identify the issues as soon as possible; and

(f)   correspondence should be focused and constructive and avoid exacerbating hostility.

COURT BUNDLES

16.59 Practitioners are reminded of the importance of complying with the court bundles Practice Direction FPR, PD 27A, which applies to all hearings in the family court and in the Family Division of the High Court. A bundle is required in all cases (except for in urgent applications to the extent that it is impossible to comply with it). The bundle must contain copies of only those documents which are relevant to the hearing and which it is necessary for the court to read or will actually be referred to during the hearing. Correspondence and bank and credit card statements should not therefore be included in the court bundle (unless it is necessary for the court to read them or they will actually be referred to during the hearing). The bundle must contain within its preliminary documents an up to date case summary limited to six A4 pages and a statement of the issues to be determined at the hearing and at the final hearing, as well as a chronology (limited to 10 pages) and position statements by each party including a summary of the order that they seek (limited to three pages). Skeleton arguments are expressly limited to no more than 20 pages. Unless the court has specifically directed otherwise (which it will only do if such a direction is necessary to enable the proceedings to be disposed of justly) the bundle is to consist of no more than 350 pages. E-bundles are permitted within the FRCs and senior judiciary including the President have issued general guidance on the preparation and filing of PDF bundles[1]. Responsibility for preparing the bundle lies with the applicant unless he is a litigant in person. In that event, the respondent's solicitor will be required to prepare the bundle, the contents of which should be agreed between the parties as far as reasonably practicable. The bundle must be lodged no later than 2 working days before the hearing. On a number of occasions senior judges have criticised practitioners for failing to comply with PD27A[2]. All practitioners should be familiar with the detail of the requirements to avoid sanctions which may include the adjournment of the case, condemnation in open court and costs sanctions.

[1] www.judiciary.uk/wp-content/uploads/2020/05/GENERAL-GUIDANCE-ON-PDF-BUNDLE S-f-1.pdf.
[2] See for example Holman J in *Seagrove v Sullivan* [2014] EWHC 4110 (Fam) and Cohen J in *AG v VD* [2021] EWFC 9 at para 144(iii).

LITIGANTS IN PERSON

16.60 Many litigants represent themselves in financial remedy proceedings, a few through choice but most through economic necessity. The judge responsible for case managing proceedings involving litigants in person (LIPs) has a duty to explain the court procedures and the requirements of orders clearly, and ensure that orders are drafted in a way that the parties can understand. For example, the meaning of phrases such as 'filing and serving' documents and 'section 25 statements' may not be readily apparent. Managing expectations as to the eventual outcome of the case, at the FA and FDR stages, may also require substantial judicial input. Anecdotally, more cases now proceed to a final hearing, as litigants in person do not always fully appreciate the parameters of a reasonable settlement and sometimes lack the trust, confidence and knowledge necessary to negotiate successfully with their opponent. Guidelines for lawyers dealing with LIPs has been published jointly by the Law Society, Bar Council and CILEX, dated June 2015. The Family Justice Council's 'Guidance on Financial Needs on Divorce' (2nd edition, April 2018) is a useful resource for LIPs, as is Law for Life's 'A Survival Guide to Pensions on Divorce' published in January 2021.

COMMUNICATING WITH THE COURT

16.61 Any communications between a party and the court (unless purely routine) must be disclosed to, and if in writing copied to, the other party, under FPR 5.7 introduced in April 2020. The rule provides an exception if there is a compelling reason not to comply, stated in the communication. The communication must state on its face that it is being copied to the other party. A communication that does not comply with the rule will be returned without being considered by the court.

RELIEF FROM SANCTIONS

16.62 The court's wide case management powers include the ability to grant relief from a sanction imposed by a rule or court order, following default. For example, an order may exclude an issue from consideration at the final hearing unless evidence is filed by a certain time. If the date is missed a successful application for relief from sanction will be necessary before the issue can be resurrected. If a witness statement is not filed in time, FPR 22.10 prohibits the calling of the witness to give oral evidence at the final hearing, and again an application for relief would be required. Any application under FPR 4.5 must be supported by evidence and the court will consider all the circumstances including the checklist of factors at FPR 4.6.

Chapter 17
COSTS AND FUNDING

INTRODUCTION

17.1 The term 'costs' is used in this chapter to refer to the sums a court can order to be paid by one party[1] to another party towards their legal expenses. 'Funding' is used to describe the arrangements a client makes to remunerate his own advisers.

[1] Or even a non-party – see **17.37-17.38** below.

17.2 Costs and funding are rightly a cause of significant concern, both for the parties to litigation and for the courts. Case reports abound in which a judge of the High Court comments on the haemorrhaging of money to fund legal costs running into the hundreds of thousands of pounds[1]. On the District Bench, two scenarios present themselves all too often at final hearings: the represented parties where there will be so little left after the costs of the litigation are paid that it becomes almost (or actually) impossible for the family and their children to be adequately rehoused; and the litigant in person, represented throughout all the interim stages, who has run out of funding for the final and crucial hearing.

[1] For recent examples, see *AW v AH and Others* [2020] EWFC 22, where the husband's conduct of the litigation had contributed to the wife running up costs of £545,000; *MB v EB (No 2)* [2019] EWHC 3676 (Fam) where the total costs incurred ran to £1.25 million, 'grossly disproportionate to what was in issue' per Cohen J; *RM v TM* [2020] EWFC 41 per Deputy High Court Judge Robert Peel QC: 'the difference between the parties' offers is £191,000. The legal costs are three times that figure. It is hard to express what a calamitous waste of resources this has been' and *AG v VD* [2021] EWFC 9 per Cohen J: 'the parties have lost all perspective of what this case is really about . . . they have sought to argue every point . . . and have thus between them expended some £2.1m on costs'.

17.3 Family litigation presents several unique challenges on the issue of costs. All the costs come ultimately out of the one pot of money that must be stretched to provide for the needs of two separate households. The subjects of the litigation – one's home and family – do not allow for a detached and coolly rational approach. Unlike a claimant in a civil case, who usually has a choice whether to proceed with the litigation or not, a litigant in family proceedings is caught up in a situation that intimately affects his or her daily life and which must be resolved.

17.4 The rules and case law on costs continue to develop to try to ensure that litigants are kept fully informed of their liability for costs (both incurred and anticipated) and that litigation is conducted in a proportionate and cost-effective way. It is the duty of the legal profession not to make the difficult situation of family breakdown worse through an insupportable burden of costs. However, ultimately, how to litigate and how to spend his or her money (or at any rate the money which he or she can access) remains a decision for the client, duly informed and advised on the consequences and risks of their approach and within the boundaries of proportionate case conduct set by the court.

COSTS: THE STARTING POINT

17.5 Costs in the Family Court are in the discretion of the court: Senior Courts Act 1981 s 51. The court has a wide discretion to determine by whom and to what extent costs are paid, subject to rules of court. 'The court may at any time make such order as to costs as it thinks just': FPR 28.1. Aspects of the Civil Procedure Rules on costs at CPR Pts 44–47 are specifically applied to costs in family proceedings, subject to defined exceptions, the most important exception being that the general rule in civil proceedings – that an unsuccessful party will be ordered to pay the costs of the successful party ('costs follow the event') – is not applicable in proceedings concerning family money.

COSTS: THE 'GENERAL RULE' AND THE 'CLEAN SHEET'

17.6 Costs in proceedings concerning family finances will fall into one of two distinct camps:

(i)   those governed by the 'general rule' set out in FPR 28.3(5) that the court will not make an order requiring one party to pay the costs of another party; or

(ii)   those governed by the starting point of a 'clean sheet'.

The general rule

17.7 The general rule that no order for costs will be made applies to 'financial remedy proceedings' as defined in FPR 28.3(5). This uses the definition of 'financial order' from FPR 2.3(1) but specifically excludes orders for interim maintenance payments, orders for legal services payments and other interim orders. The definition of proceedings <u>included</u> under the general rule covers applications on divorce or dissolution for:

- an order for periodical payments (other than interim orders);
- a lump sum order;
- a property adjustment order;
- a variation order, including an interim variation order[1];
- a pension sharing order;
- a pension compensation order;
- financial relief after an overseas divorce/dissolution.

[1]   FPR PD 28A, para 4.2(a).

17.8 Although the general rule in these application is that a costs order will not be made, and each party will therefore be left to meet their own costs, the court is empowered, in the exercise of its discretion, to make a costs order. FPR 28.3(6) states 'the court may make an order requiring one party to pay the costs of another party at any stage of the proceedings where it is appropriate to do so because of the conduct of a party in relation to the proceedings (whether before or during them)'.

17.9 FPR 28.3(7) provides a checklist of factors for the judge to consider in deciding what, if any, costs orders to make:

(a)   any failure by a party to comply with these rules, any order of the court or any practice direction which the court considers relevant;

(b)   any open offer to settle made by a party;

(c)   whether it was reasonable for a party to raise, pursue or contest a particular allegation or issue;

(d)   the manner in which a party has pursued or responded to the application or a particular allegation or issue;

(e)   any other aspect of a party's conduct in relation to proceedings which the court considers relevant; and

(f)   the financial effect on the parties of any costs order.

17.10 The approach is based on litigation conduct, although paragraph (f) also requires the court to pay regard to the financial consequences of making a costs order (which presumably therefore includes affordability, although the lack of an obvious means to pay is not necessarily a bar to making an order[1]). Costs orders can be made at either (or both) interim and final hearings. Only open offers can be considered by the court as it exercises its discretion. Offers made on a 'without prejudice' basis, even if marked 'without prejudice save as to costs' cannot be referred to[2].

[1]   *Joy v Joy-Morancho* [2015] EWHC 2507 (Fam), where Sir Peter Singer made a costs order against the husband following 'aberrant conduct' despite the wife having identified no source of funds from which he could meet the award. The judge considered the financial effect on the parties of a costs order, but decided that the 'manifest unfairness' to the wife if no order was made should justify an order.

[2]   FPR 28.3(8): without prejudice offers are not admissible at any stage of proceedings governed by FPR 28.3, except at FDR.

17.11 Concern about proportionality of costs expenditure expressed repeatedly over the years in published judgments has led to the inclusion since May 2019 of the following paragraph in Practice Direction 28A[1]:

'In considering the conduct of the parties for the purposes of rule 28.3(6) and (7) (including any open offers to settle), the court will have regard to the obligation of the parties to help the court to further the overriding objective (see rules 1.1 and 1.3) and will take into account the nature, importance and complexity of the issues in the case. This may be of particular significance in applications for variation orders and interim variation orders or other cases where there is a risk of the costs becoming disproportionate to the amounts in dispute. The court will take a broad view of conduct for the purposes of this rule and will generally conclude that to refuse openly to negotiate reasonably and responsibly will amount to conduct in respect of which the court will consider making an order for costs. This includes in a 'needs' case where the applicant litigates unreasonably resulting in the costs incurred by each party becoming disproportionate to the award made by the court. Where an order for costs is made at an interim stage the court will not usually allow any resulting liability to be reckoned as a debt in the computation of the assets.'

The paragraph was cited by Cohen J in *MB v EB (No 2)*[1] in limiting the husband's costs from the £650,000 claimed to £150,000. In *OG v AG*[2], having referred to PD28A, Mostyn J commented 'if, once the financial landscape is clear, you do not openly negotiate reasonably, then you will likely suffer a penalty in costs. This applies whether the case is big or small, or whether it is being decided by reference to needs or sharing'.

[1] FPR PD28A, para 4.4.
[1] *MB v EB (No 2)* [2019] EWHC 3676 (Fam).
[2] *OG v AG* [2020] EWFC 52 at para 31.

17.12 Practical examples of costs orders made disapplying the general rule at an interim stage may include an order against a party who has failed to prepare for a hearing by complying with court directions, necessitating an adjournment, or against a party who has taken a wholly unreasonable stance in instructing an expert, incurring additional costs. At a final hearing, costs orders may be made to reflect the court's assessment of the litigation conduct over the case as a whole (whilst taking care not to penalise a party twice where an interim costs order has already been made). Conduct justifying the sanction of the court can include (but is not limited to) failures to disclose or to negotiate, intransigence, oppressive enquiry, a lack of honesty or pursuit of unwinnable or irrelevant issues. In AW v AH and Others[1] Roberts J ordered the husband to pay 60% of the wife's costs, in the exercise of the court's 'generous discretion'. The husband had failed to provide the wife with a coherent narrative for his substantial disclosure, depriving her of a reasonable opportunity to settle and necessitating that the case be examined forensically at a trial. The award reflected that the husband should be given some incentive to restore his financial position and that in the later stages of the case he had been more forthcoming.

[1] *AW v AH and Others* [2020] EWFC 22.

17.13 Litigation misconduct is generally punished by way of a costs order, rather than increasing the substantive award made to the 'wronged' party. In *Ezair v Ezair*[1] the Court of Appeal overturned the judge's order of an enhanced lump sum intended to penalise the husband in costs and remitted the case for a distinct costs order to be quantified to mark the litigation misconduct. The substantive order should reflect the factors in s 25 and only rarely will conduct be relevant in that exercise. However, the Court of Appeal's decision not to overturn the first instance judge in the 'unusual and unfortunate' case of *Rothschild v De Sousa*[2] stands as an example of litigation misconduct falling within MCA 1973, s 25(2)(g) so as to affect the substantive award, on the basis that money spent on legal costs is no longer available to meet the parties' needs or to be shared. Whilst acknowledging that litigation misconduct will generally be reflected only in a costs order, the court commented that there are nevertheless cases where conduct, including conduct in separate but related proceedings, should be taken into account in determining the overall award.

[1] *Ezair v Ezair* [2012] EWCA Civ 893.
[2] *Rothschild v De Sousa* [2020] EWCA Civ 1215.

17.14 The court should generally avoid making a costs order 'by the back door' in awarding a party a lump sum with which to pay off debts incurred in litigating, where a costs order is otherwise not justified. In *Daga v Bangur*[1] the husband pursued a needs case, which did not find favour with the court. Holman J commented 'his only pressing need is to clear his debts, but they are entirely referable to the costs which he has incurred in these proceedings. If I were to order him to pay a lump sum with which to pay off these debts, that would be tantamount to making an order for costs in his favour, which could not be justifiable'. Similarly, where a wife invested her capital in the unsuccessful pursuit of financial relief after an overseas divorce, in *NN v AS and others*[2], Roberts J stated 'it is not a legitimate use of the court's powers to order a lump sum in a Pt III application to make good any deficiency in the calculation of future needs in order to address a shortfall which has arisen as a result of litigation costs'.

[1]   *Daga v Bangur* [2018] EWFC 91 at para 66.
[2]   *NN v AS and others* [2018] EWHC 2973 (Fam) at para 294.

17.15 CPR 44.2(6) and (7) apply to costs orders made under FPR 28.3[1]. This rule provides the court with a menu of potential approaches to costs orders. The non-definitive list sets out that a court may order a party to pay:

(a)   a proportion of another party's costs;
(b)   a stated amount in respect of another party's costs;
(c)   costs from or until a certain date only;
(d)   costs incurred before proceedings have begun;
(e)   costs relating to particular steps taken in the proceedings;
(f)   costs relating only to a distinct part of the proceedings; and
(g)   interest on costs from or until a certain date, including a date before judgment.

Where the court would otherwise consider making an order under paragraph (f), it must instead, if practicable, make an order under paragraphs (a) or (c).

[1]   By application of FPR 28.3(3); the rest of CPR 44.2 (except (8) – see **17.29** below) does not apply to costs in financial remedy proceedings through a combination of FPR 28.2(1) and 28.3(2).

17.16 Where costs orders are made against both parties, the court may set them off against each other[1]. Alternatively, where both parties have been guilty of litigation conduct that might ordinarily sound in costs, the court in the exercise of its broad discretion may simply make no order for costs.

[1]   As happened in *RM v TM* [2020] EWFC 41, Deputy High Court Judge Robert Peel QC.

The clean sheet

17.17 For cases falling outside the general rule, what approach does the court take to the award of costs? The court here starts with a 'clean sheet' and the ability to exercise a broad discretion. However, the judge must start somewhere as s/he mentally stares at a blank canvas, and a line of authority, stretching back to *Gojkovic (No 2)*[1] in 1991 and approved by the Court of Appeal in *Solomon v Solomon and others*[2] in 2013 confirms that the starting point should be that costs 'follow the event' (ie the 'loser' faces a costs order against him), although that approach may be displaced more easily than in civil proceedings.

1   *Gojkovic v Gojkovic (No 2)* [1991] 2 FLR 233 per Butler-Sloss LJ.
2   *Solomon v Solomon and others* [2013] EWCA Civ 1095.

17.18 In deciding what, if any, order to make in 'clean sheet' cases, the court will have regard to CPR 44.2(4) and (5) (specifically disapplied for 'general rule' cases, but applicable to 'clean sheet' situations). The court will have regard to 'all the circumstances' including:

(a)   the conduct of all the parties;
(b)   whether a party has succeeded on part of his case, even if he has not been wholly successful; and
(c)   any . . . admissible offer to settle made by a party which is drawn to the court's attention.

The conduct of the parties includes:

(a)   conduct before, as well as during, the proceedings;
(b)   whether it was reasonable for a party to raise, pursue or contest a particular allegation or issue;
(c)   the manner in which a party has pursued or defended his case or a particular allegation or issue; and
(d)   whether a claimant who has succeeded in his claim, in whole or in part, exaggerated his claim.

17.19 The 'clean sheet' approach applies to applications for financial remedies excluded from the specific definition of 'financial remedy proceedings' in FPR 28.3(4)(b). The list of 'clean sheet' situations <u>includes</u>:

- maintenance pending suit/interim periodical payments;
- other forms of interim order[1];
- applications to set aside a financial remedy order[2];
- Schedule 1 Children Act applications;
- preliminary issue applications;
- intervenor proceedings;
- strike out applications under FPR 4.4;
- applications for relief from sanction under FPR 4.6;
- applications to set aside or implement awards made in arbitration;
- enforcement of family orders;
- applications for payment in respect of legal services under MCA 1973, s 22ZA.

1   As per FPR 9.7(1)(e). In the writer's view this does not include interim applications regarding interlocutory case management decisions, such as an application to instruct an expert, which will usually fall within the general (r 28.3) rule, although if the application seeks the indulgence of the court, for example to extend a time limit, ordinarily the applicant should expect an order that they pay the other party's costs of that application.
2   FPR 28.3(9) and FPR 9.9A.

17.20 The case of *Crowther v Crowther & Others*[1] provides an example of an indemnity costs order made applying the 'clean sheet' approach in preliminary issue proceedings. Lieven J criticised the wife's "fairly extraordinary" litigation conduct in making allegations of significant fraud and conspiracy but then withdrawing the allegations shortly before the trial of a preliminary issue. The judge declined to defer the decision as to the preliminary issue costs to the end of the proceedings as a whole, an approach the wife had argued would enable the husband's alleged poor litigation conduct to be taken into account, commenting that this was largely irrelevant to the issue of whether the wife should pay the preliminary issue costs. Costs were ordered against the wife on an indemnity basis[2], with a payment on account[3].

1   *Crowther v Crowther & Others* [2020] EWHC 3555 (Fam).
2   See **17.28** below.
3   See **17.30** below.

COSTS: PRACTICAL ISSUES

Informing the client about costs

17.21 For many years parties have been required to file and exchange estimates of their costs in Form H, to be considered by the judge at each hearing. The form was until 2020 retrospective in documenting the costs incurred, contributing to the situation in many cases where the incurring of disproportionate costs only became visible after the event, when the damage had already been done. This situation contrasted with the much more interventionist approach to costs adopted in recent years in civil litigation, where costs in smaller matters are often fixed and an active judicial role is taken to budget for and cap costs in higher value matters. After many years of judicial lamentation that 'something must be done'[1] in family proceedings to control disproportionate costs, a significant amendment to FPR 9.27 came into force in July 2020.

1   See for example Munby J in *KSO v MJO and others* [2008] EWHC 3031 (Fam) where 71.7% of the matrimonial pot had been lost in costs: 'something must be done . . . we simply cannot go on as we are' and Mostyn J in *J v J* [2014] EWHC 3654 (Fam): 'the time has come when lawmakers in this country, whether they are legislators or judges, must stop saying "something must be done" and actually do something'.

17.22 Form H (the estimate of costs) and its sister form H1 (the statement of costs) now require estimates of costs to be lodged and exchanged, predicting the costs up to the next hearing and the final hearing. No later than one day before the first appointment, parties must file and exchange Form H recording their estimates of costs not only up to that hearing but also up to and including the FDR if a settlement is not reached. No later than one day before the FDR the exercise is repeated, with a Form H to record an estimate of costs to the final hearing. No later than 14 days before a final hearing, Form H1 is required, to state all costs incurred or expected to be incurred up to the end of the final hearing and in implementing an order.

17.23 The amounts set out in the forms must be noted by the court and recorded as a recital to the order made at the hearing. Any failure to comply will also be recorded and the default must then be rectified. Judges are likely to take a more interventionist role, questioning the reasons for any large disparity in costs expenditure between the parties, challenging costs figures that appear disproportionate, and referring to the forms when quantifying costs orders, particularly where estimates have been exceeded.

How to make a claim for costs

17.24 At interim hearings, in addition to filing Form H, any party seeking a costs order must make it plain to the other party in open correspondence or a skeleton argument served before the hearing that a costs order will be sought and file a statement of costs in Form N260 (if they seek a summary assessment of the amount of the costs)[1].

[1]   FPR PD28A, para 4.5.

17.25 At the final hearing, the court will have the costs information from both parties in Form H1. The costs incurred (or to be incurred) and not yet paid will appear on the assets schedule as a liability (except for unpaid interim costs orders – excluded by virtue of FPR PD28A, para 4.4). Costs already paid will, of course, have disappeared from the assets schedule, and will only be visible on Form H. What if one party's costs already paid exceed those already spent by the other party? If this issue is simply ignored, and the remaining assets are shared, the party who has been more economical with their legal spend will end up subsidising part of the costs spend of the other party. Judges are able to rectify such potential unfairness by using their case and costs discretion. If the costs expenditure is egregious a sum can be added back into the assumed assets of the unreasonable party, as happened in *RH v RH*[1], although this is likely to be rare. Alternatively, the spending could be recognised as litigation misconduct sufficient to influence the substantive result, as in *Rothschild v De Souza* (see **17.13** above). This could be the result even in a needs case: in *R v B and others*[2] Moor J commented that, in order to achieve a fair outcome, the court must be entitled to prioritise the needs of the party who has not been guilty of misconduct.

[1]   *RH v RH* [2008] EWHC 347 (Fam) per Singer J.
[2]   *R v B* [2017] EWFC 33 at para 85.

Quantifying costs

17.26 On relatively straightforward applications lasting less than one day, where a Form N260 has been filed, the court may summarily assess the costs, on a fairly rough-and-ready basis having heard brief submissions. The Form N260 should be served on the other side at least 24 hours before the hearing. Any failure to do so will not be fatal to the costs claim but will be taken into account by the court in deciding what order to make about costs[1]. A summary assessment will not give approval to disproportionate or unreasonable costs[2].

[1]   CPR PD 44, paras 9.5 and 9.6.
[2]   CPR PD 44, para 9.10.

17.27 If a summary assessment of costs is not appropriate, the court may adjourn the assessment of costs to a detailed assessment hearing. CPR Pt 47 sets out the rules for the detailed assessment process.

17.28 The judge will need to decide the basis of a costs assessment. There are two choices: assessment on a standard basis (the norm, as the name implies) or assessment on an indemnity basis. Indemnity costs are intended to mark the court's disapproval of aspects of the paying party's conduct and are relatively rare in practice. The paying party's conduct must have been unreasonable to a high degree. When assessing on the standard basis, the court will only allow costs that are proportionate to the matters in issue. Disproportionate costs will be disallowed, even if reasonably or even necessarily incurred. Costs unreasonably incurred or unreasonable in amount will also be disallowed. Any doubts as to reasonableness and proportionality will be resolved in favour of the *paying* party[1]. Indemnity costs will be assessed without a focus on proportionality. Costs unreasonably incurred or unreasonable in amount will be disallowed but doubts as to reasonableness will be resolved in favour of the *receiving* party[2].

1   CPR 44.3 (1) and (2).
2   CPR 44.3 (1) and (3).

Paying costs

17.29 Unless the court orders otherwise, costs must be paid within 14 days of the date of the order, otherwise enforcement action can be taken[1]. When a costs order is made but the client will struggle to pay within 14 days, the court should be asked either, within its discretion, to allow a longer period for payment or to state explicitly that the order will not be enforced until the conclusion of the financial remedy proceedings. This latter allows the costs liability to be discharged as part of the overall division of assets at the end of the case

1   CPR 44.7.

17.30 Where a costs order is made that costs should be paid subject to detailed assessment, the court will order the paying party to make payment of a reasonable sum on account of costs, unless there is a good reason not to do so[1]. What constitutes a reasonable sum is a matter for the judge, but something like 60-70% of the costs estimated by the receiving party might be appropriate. An order for a payment on account remains in force (as with every other aspect of the order) if the order is subject to an appeal (unless specifically stayed pending appeal by the lower or appellate court).

1   CPR 44.2(8).

COSTS: PROTECTING THE CLIENT'S POSITION

17.31 As we have seen, clients must be kept informed of their own costs and those of the other party, through the exchange of Forms H/H1. Where the other party is conducting the case unreasonably, they should be placed on notice of a potential application for costs, and Form N260 should be filed and served if a summary assessment of costs may be appropriate. Beyond these practical steps, the most important costs protection (other than conducting the litigation reasonably and proportionately) will be to make sensible and reasonable open offers to settle.

17.32 FPR 9.27A was bolstered in July 2020 to mandate the exchange of open proposals to settle by no later than 21 days after an unsuccessful FDR or no later than 42 days before a final hearing if there has been no FDR. This new provision is in addition to the existing requirement under rule 9.28 to file and serve a detailed open statement of the orders the court is asked to make either 14 (applicant) or 7 (respondent) days before a final hearing. As set out in paragraph 11 above, the court 'will generally conclude that to refuse openly to negotiate reasonably and responsibly will amount to conduct in respect of which the court will consider making an order for costs'[1].

[1]   FPR PD28A, para 4.4.

17.33 Tactically, there has been something of a reluctance to commit one's best offer to open correspondence. It can skew the negotiations if the other party views the offer simply as an opening gambit. There is a perceived danger that the judge will be tempted to decide the case 'somewhere in the middle' of the open positions and that one's offer should be tempered to reflect that risk. The changes introduced by FPR 9.27A and PD 28A in 2019 and 2020 should combine to mitigate these concerns. A well-pitched open offer will not only protect the offeror in costs, but to spurn such an offer will leave the other party vulnerable to a costs order. Litigants can also take heart from Moor J's words in *MAP v MFP*[1]: 'litigants must be encouraged to make open proposals as early as possible that are designed to encourage settlement. If the other party spurns such an offer, the court is entitled to ignore it completely and decide the case entirely on the merits. I will have no hesitation in a suitable case in awarding an applicant more than an open offer he or she has made if that is justified'.

[1]   *MAP v MFP (Financial Remedies: Add Back)* [2015] EWHC 627 (Fam) at para 87.

COSTS: FUTURE DEVELOPMENTS

17.34 There is a groundswell of support[1] for amending the current costs rule in FPR 28.3 to introduce something akin to the *Calderbank* offer, named after the 1976 case in which Cairns LJ proposed the approach[2]. Until the possibility was swept away in financial remedy proceedings in April 2006, settlement offers could be made on the basis that they were without prejudice (and thus would not be seen by the judge) except on the issue of costs. After judgment had been delivered, an offer marked as 'without prejudice save as to costs' could be shown to the judge and relied upon when the question of costs fell to be considered. It remains possible to negotiate on a 'without prejudice' basis, but the offers cannot be shown to the judge (except at FDR) and can never be relied on in seeking costs. *Calderbank* offers are no longer possible in financial remedy proceedings by virtue of FPR 28.3(8) but they remain permissible in 'clean sheet' situations to which FPR 28.3 does not apply.

[1]   See for example comments of Francis J in *ABX v SBX (DX Intervening)* [2018] EWFC 81 at para 2 and the article by K Gerrard and W Longrigg in *Family Law*, April 2019, p 369.
[2]   *Calderbank v Calderbank* [1976] Fam 93.

17.35 The *Calderbank* principle was abolished in 2006 in favour of the current position that the starting point in financial remedy cases is usually that each party will bear their own costs. The old *Calderbank* approach did have disadvantages. It operated on a 'cliff edge' basis. Equalling or beating a *Calderbank* offer, even by a small margin, opened the door to an order that the 'losing' party would have a significant liability for costs. Carefully crafted judicial orders, stretching the resources to provide for essential needs, could be wholly undermined by the costs consequences of a failure to guess the outcome of a discretionary process with sufficient accuracy. Defining who had 'beaten' an offer in the mosaic of a final order dealing with different types of assets and financial provision could became a hotly contested topic, with large costs sums at stake. However, *Calderbank* proposals undoubtedly encouraged sensible negotiations and settlements at an early stage. The risks of failing to guess the outcome correctly and being liable not just for one's own costs but for a substantial proportion of the other party's costs as well, focussed minds. Under the current system of each party usually being liable only for their own costs, the risks inherent in litigating to the bitter end are reduced and the incentive to settle is correspondingly reduced as well.

17.36 In response to the concerns that the post-*Calderbank* costs regime was not incentivising early settlement, the Family Procedure Rule Committee set up a judicially led working group (the Costs Working Group) to investigate and make proposals for reform. A consultation has been held on amending the rules to allow *Calderbank* offers to be taken into account as part of the consideration of 'conduct' when the court is weighing up whether to make a costs order, but perhaps avoiding the 'cliff edge' approach inherent in the original *Calderbank* scheme. The Rules Committee considered the responses to the consultation during 2020 and further developments are awaited at the time of writing.

17.37 Costs capping has been mooted in recent years, for example by Mostyn J in *J v J*[1]. The suggestion, based on an argument that autonomy in costs expenditure cannot be justified when the funds are coming from a finite pot over which the other party has a claim, is that the court could impose a cap for each phase of the proceedings. It remains no more than a suggestion at present and the Family Court does not possess such powers. The only current instances of judicial ability to cap costs in family proceedings remain the potential capping of expenditure on expert fees and the example of capping recoverable costs on appeal (analogous to the possibility of a cap on appeal costs under CPR 52.19) set by Peter Jackson J in granting permission to appeal in *TF v FF*[2].

[1] *J v J* [2014] EWHC 3654 (Fam) at para 13.
[2] *TF v FF* [2013] EWHC 390 (Fam).

COSTS: ORDERS AGAINST NON-PARTIES AND LAWYERS

17.38 Costs order against non-parties are exceptional but may sometimes be made. The case law setting the framework for the making of such orders comes largely from civil cases[1]. 'Exceptional' is not a high bar and means no more than 'outside the ordinary run of cases where parties pursue or defend claims for their own benefit and at their own expense'[2]. A fair procedure must be adopted, giving the potential payer the opportunity to be heard and the procedure will usually be summary, especially where the non-party has had a close connection with the proceedings.

[1] Notably *Symphony Group plc v Hodgson* [1994] QB 179 and *Dymocks v Franchise Systems (NSW) v Todd* [2004] UKPC 39.
[2] *Dymocks* at para 25 per Lord Brown.

17.39 Such orders may be made against non-party funders of the litigation. This will not include those such as friends or family, or commercial funders, who have simply assisted access to justice, even if some financial reward results. However, if the third party has a personal or commercial interest in the outcome of the litigation and has been a driving or facilitating force behind it, they may be exposed to a risk of a costs order. Where an order is made requiring a commercial funder to pay costs, there is no rule that the costs liability should be capped at the level of the funding provided. That might be a just outcome, but it is not a rule and does not limit the discretion of the court[1]. Occasionally, a costs order may be made against an expert who has conspicuously failed in their duty to the court and thereby caused wasted costs[2].

[1] *Chapelgate Credit Opportunity Master Fund Ltd v Money and another* [2020] EWCA Civ 246.
[2] *Re ABCDEF (Fact Finding: Honour Based Violence)* [2019] EWHC 406 (Fam).

17.40 On rare occasions a lawyer in a case may be made personally responsible for paying costs incurred by another party or may be required to forfeit their own costs, under the wasted costs jurisdiction established by the Senior Courts Act 1981, s 51(6). The bar for such applications is set high. Fearlessly defending or advancing one's client's position on instructions, or adopting a course that hindsight shows to have been unwise, will not be sufficient. The conduct must be improper, unreasonable or 'negligent', the latter having a non-technical meaning and including a failure to act with the competence reasonably to be expected of the legal profession[1]. The jurisdiction has been described as draconian[2] and even a finding that costs have been wasted through improper, unreasonable or negligent conduct will not obligate the court to make an order, but will only open the door to a discretion. The procedure to be adopted should be summary but fair, allowing the legal representative a reasonable opportunity to formulate and present a response[3]. The court may act on its own initiative to raise the issue, or on the application of a party to the proceedings[4].

[1] *Ridehalgh v Horsefield* [1994] 2 FLR 194, CA and *Fisher Meredith v JH and PH* [2012] 2 FLR 536, FD.
[2] *Re A Barrister (Wasted Costs Order)* [1993] QB 293, CA.
[3] CPR 46.8.
[4] CPR PD 46, para 5.

COSTS ON APPEAL

17.41 Appeals in family proceedings are not covered by either of the two different 'general rules' in civil or financial remedy proceedings. Appeals do not come within the definition of 'financial remedy proceedings' in FPR 28.3(4) and so are excluded from the principle that ordinarily no order for costs will be made. Appeals are also specifically excluded by CPR 1998 r 44.2 (3) from the general rule in civil proceedings that costs should 'follow the event'. Costs on appeal are therefore subject to the 'clean sheet' approach with its starting point of costs to follow the event, which may however be displaced in the exercise of the wide judicial discretion.

17.42 Appeals do not come within FPR 28.3 and therefore are not subject to the prohibition on the admissibility of *Calderbank* offers at FPR 28.3(8). *Calderbank* offers may be referred to when appeal costs fall to be decided.

FUNDING

17.43 The Legal Aid, Sentencing and Punishment of Offenders Act 2012 (LASPO 2012) effectively removed legal aid funding from the vast majority of financial remedies litigation. Most clients must now either pay their way from their own resources, source an alternative stream of funding or conduct the case as best they can as a litigant in person, possibly accessing Direct Access counsel or unbundled legal services from time to time. This section offers a brief introduction to funding legal costs in a post-LASPO world.

17.44 Lawyers are not often prepared nowadays to wait until the end of the case to be paid, as this amounts to agreeing to fund the litigation through an interest-free advance of their time. In any event the disbursements of court and expert fees must still be paid before the outcome of the litigation is known. If a firm is prepared to wait for payment, an assignment is permitted of such of the capital to be recovered in the proceedings as is needed to meet the costs, secured by a formal deed, following the ruling in *Sears Tooth v Payne Hicks Beach* in 1997[1].

[1]   *Sears Tooth v Payne Hicks Beach* [1997] 2 FLR 116.

17.45 Solicitors are entitled in any event, even where the client has not signed a deed of assignment, to recoup unpaid costs from money or property recovered or preserved where the lawyer has been instrumental in the recovery or preservation, whether by way of judgment or settlement. The lawyer will have an equitable lien over the sums recovered or preserved[1]. The Solicitors Act 1974, s 73 provides for the solicitor to be able to register a charge against real property recovered or preserved in the litigation. A court declaration of entitlement to the remedy (using the Pt 18 procedure following assessment of the bill), can be enforced by a charge registered at the Land Registry[2].

[1]   *Gavin Edmondson Solicitors v Haven Insurance Company Ltd* [2018] UKSC 21.
[2]   The writer is indebted to David Burrows' article in *Family Law*, December 2020, p,1703, which gives further details.

17.46 Litigation loans are available from some commercial funders, subject to credit checks and an assessment that funds are likely to be available at the end of the proceedings to discharge the loan. There will be fees for setting up the loan and the borrower will have to take independent advice. The funder will require reports on progress in the litigation and the interest rate is likely to be significant. Such loans should never be treated as a licence to litigate without restraint (and the funders will want to know if the borrower is refusing to follow legal advice). However, such loans, used moderately and in suitable cases, can increase access to justice. Family members may sometimes be prepared to assist with loans to meet legal costs, but such informal lending may be treated as a 'soft' loan and a low priority for repayment in any final hearing.

17.47 The court has the power under MCA 1973, s 22ZA, to order one party to pay the other an amount to enable that party to obtain legal services for the purposes of the proceedings. The court must be satisfied that the applicant for the order would not reasonably be able to obtain appropriate legal services without the order, in particular by way of a Sears Tooth agreement or litigation loan. Where one party litigates unreasonably, funds transferred under a legal services payment order may be recouped by way of a costs cap, as happened in *MB v EB*[1]. The wife had funded the husband's costs to the tune of £236,000 under a s 22ZA order. He claimed a sum of £650,000 to cover his costs. Cohen J capped the husband's costs at £150,000, commenting that it was not for the wife to bankroll litigation unreasonably conducted against her. The topic of orders under s 22ZA is covered in more detail in Chapter 2.

1   *MB v EB (No 2)* [2020] EWHC 3676 (Fam).

17.48 Increasingly, solicitors are offering 'unbundled' services to clients, to meet the needs of those who seek advice and representation but cannot afford or do not wish to have a full legal service. Unbundled services offer help with clearly defined tasks for a fixed fee, without the solicitor being placed on the court record as formally acting for the client. Tasks may include drafting a Form E or first appointment documents, attending at a hearing or preparing a consent order. The Court of Appeal held in *Minkin v Lesley Landsberg (Practising as Barnet Family Law)*[1] that solicitors may offer unbundled services without being held liable for matters beyond those in their client retainer. The Law Society has published guidance on offering unbundled services, available on its website[2].

1   *Minkin v Lesley Landsberg (Practising as Barnet Family Law]* [2015] EWCA Civ 1152.
2   For a discussion of unbundling in practice, see 'To unbundle or bundle – that is the question' by Nick Astley, March [2017] Fam Law 314.

17.49 Where parties are agreed on their settlement and seek only practical help with drafting a consent order and obtaining the court's approval, that work may be carried out jointly on behalf of them both, provided the work does not favour one party to the detriment of the other and there are no 'red flags' identified such as risk of abuse or lack of full disclosure[1].

1   *JK v MK ("amicable" intervening)* [2020] EWFC 2.

Chapter 18

APPEALS AND SETTING ASIDE

INTRODUCTION

18.1 The appeals to be considered in this chapter are appeals in financial remedy cases. These are therefore appeals, in the family court, from district judge to circuit judge, and in the High Court from district judge to High Court judge, and thereafter, in both courts, to the Court of Appeal. Not all challenges to district judge's orders are appeals, however, and in this chapter we also consider applications to set aside district judges' consent orders.

18.2 The rules governing the procedure for appeals in the family court and the High Court are now identical[1] and are contained in Pt 30 of the FPR and in Practice Direction PD 30A. The various elements of these will now be considered in turn. It should be noted that the same rules, eg as to time limits, apply whether the appeal is from the district judge or the circuit or High Court judge.

[1] FPR 30.1.

PERMISSION REQUIRED

18.3 Rule 30.3 deals with permission to appeal. An appellant or respondent requires permission to appeal against a decision in proceedings where the decision appealed against was made by a district judge or a costs judge, unless para (2) applies (which is not the case here), or as provided by the Practice Direction. An application for permission to appeal may be made to the lower court at the hearing at which the decision to be appealed was made; or to the appeal court in an appeal notice. Permission to appeal an order of a district judge is a new provision and dissatisfied practitioners should therefore be sure to make the application at the conclusion of the hearing.

18.4 Where the lower court refuses an application for permission to appeal, a further application for permission to appeal may be made to the appeal court. An application refused by the district judge may therefore be made to the circuit or High Court judge.

18.5 Such applications are normally considered without a hearing, but where, in such a case, the application is refused, the person seeking permission may request the decision to be reconsidered at a hearing[1]. A request for a hearing in such a case must be made within 7 days of service of the notice of refusal[2].

[1] FPR 30.4 and 30.5.
[2] FPR 30.3(6).

18.6 Rule 30.7 provides that permission to appeal may be given only where the court considers that the appeal would have a real prospect of success, or there is some other compelling reason why the appeal should be heard.

18.7 An order giving permission may limit the issues to be heard, and be made subject to conditions[1]. As an example of conditions, in *C v C (Appeal: Hadkinson Order)*[2] it was held that there is power to require a sum of money to be deposited as a condition of appealing an order of a district judge. See also *Radmacher v Granatino*[3] at **18.18**.

[1] FPR 30.8.
[2] [2010] EWHC 1656 (Fam), [2011] 1 FLR 434, Eleanor King J.
[3] [2008] EWCA Civ 1304.

18.8 Under certain circumstances an appeal in a case which has been heard by a district judge in the county court may be transferred to the High Court for hearing by a High Court judge where it appears to the district judge, whether on the application of a party or otherwise, that the appeal raises a difficult or important question, whether of law or otherwise.

18.9 It should, however, be noted that para 4.1B of FPR PD 30A provides that the court should not ordinarily grant permission to appeal where the matters complained of would be better dealt with on an application to set aside a financial remedy order under FPR 9.9A, an inherent jurisdiction order under FPR 12.42B or a return order or non-return order under FPR 12.52A. FPR PD 30A adds that such an application would be appropriate if the proposed appeal does not in fact allege an error of the court on the materials that were before the court at the time the order was made. However, it clarifies this by adding that by way of exception, permission to appeal may still be given where (i) a litigant alleges both that the court erred on the materials before it and that a ground for setting aside exists; or (ii) as the case may be, the order which it is sought to set aside includes a pension sharing order or pension compensation sharing order and the court may be asked to consider making orders under s 40A(5) or s 40B(2) MCA 1973.

TIME LIMITS

18.10 An appellant must file the appellant's notice at the appeal court within such period as may be directed by the lower court (which may be longer or shorter than 21 days). However, where the court makes no such direction, the time limit is 21 days after the date of the decision of the lower court against which the appellant wishes to appeal[1]. The appellant's notice must be served on the respondent to the appeal as soon as practicable and in any event within 7 days[2].

[1] FPR 30.4(2).
[2] FPR 30.4(4).

18.11 A respondent to an appeal who either is seeking permission to appeal from the appeal court, or wishes to ask the appeal court to uphold the order of the lower court for reasons different from or additional to those given by the lower court, must file a respondent's notice. The time for filing such notice depends on a number of factors; it must be filed within:

(a)   such period as may be directed by the lower court; or
(b)   where the court makes no such direction, 14 days beginning with whichever of the following dates is appropriate:
- the date on which the respondent is served with the appellant's notice where permission to appeal was given by the lower court; or permission to appeal is not required;
- the date on which the respondent is served with notification that the appeal court has given the appellant permission to appeal; or
- the date on which the respondent is served with notification that the application for permission to appeal and the appeal itself are to be heard together[1].

1   FPR 30.5(4) and (5).

18.12 Any application to vary the time required for appeal must be made to the appeal court. The parties to an appeal may not agree to vary the times[1].

1   FPR 30.7(1) and (2).

ROUTES OF APPEAL

18.13 The question of to whom or to what level of judge an appeal lies is dealt with in PD30A, para 2.1. Appeal from a district judge of the county court lies to a circuit judge (normally one who is 'ticketed' to deal with such appeals). Appeals from a district judge in a district registry of the High Court or from a district judge of the Principal Registry or a costs judge go to a High Court judge. Appeals from circuit judges, recorders and High Court judges go to the Court of Appeal.

CONTENTS OF NOTICE

18.14 Unsurprisingly, it is provided that the appeal notice must state the grounds of appeal[1]. Once served, the appeal notice may not be amended except with permission of the appeal court[2]. The appeal court may strike out the whole or part of an appeal notice, set aside permission to appeal in whole or in part, or impose or vary conditions upon which an appeal may be brought[3]. However, it is provided that the court will only exercise these powers where there is a compelling reason for doing so[4].

1   FPR 30.6.
2   FPR 30.9.
3   FPR 30.10(1).
4   FPR 30.10(2).

POWERS OF APPELLATE COURT

18.15 Rule 30.11 provides that the appellate court has all the powers of the lower court. It may:

(a)   affirm, set aside or vary any order or judgment made or given by the lower court;
(b)   refer any application or issue for determination by the lower court;
(c)   order a new hearing;
(d)   make orders for the payment of interest;
(e)   make a costs order[1].

The appeal court may exercise its powers in relation to the whole or part of an order of the lower court[2].

[1]   FPR 30.11(2).
[2]   FPR 30.11(3).

18.16 As to the principles applicable to the exercise of the appellate court's discretion, it is worth noting that these are the same whether the appellate court consists of a circuit or High Court judge on appeal from a district judge or the Court of Appeal on appeal from the circuit or High Court judge. The new rules in fact more or less repeat the amended FPR 1991, r 8.1(3) which was inserted in 2003. Rule 30.12 in its entirety reads as follows:

'(1) Every appeal will be limited to a review of the decision of the lower court unless—
  (a)   an enactment or practice direction makes different provision for a particular category of appeal; or
  (b)   the court considers that in the circumstances of an individual appeal it would be in the interests of justice to hold a re-hearing.

(2) Unless it orders otherwise, the appeal court will not receive—
  (a)   oral evidence; or
  (b)   evidence which was not before the lower court.

(3) The appeal court will allow an appeal where the decision of the lower court was—
  (a)   wrong; or
  (b)   unjust because of a serious procedural or other irregularity in the proceedings in the lower court.

(4) The appeal court may draw any inference of fact which it considers justified on the evidence.

(5) At the hearing of the appeal a party may not rely on a matter not contained in that party's appeal notice unless the appeal court gives permission.'

18.17 In *IC v RC (Slip Rule)*[1] it was held that an appellate court will allow an appeal only where the decision of the lower court was wrong or unjust because of a serious procedural or other irregularity. The slip rule (FPR 29.16) can be used to correct an order to give effect to the court's intention.

[1]   [2020] EWHC 2997 (Fam).

18.18 Permission to appeal may be made subject to conditions[1]. In *Radmacher v Granatino*[2] the Court of Appeal held that the appellant wife's gross and subsisting breaches of an order made this an extreme case and that the husband should be protected in the event that the appeal failed. Permission was granted subject to the wife paying a sum of money into the joint names of the solicitors and giving security for costs.

1   CPR 52.3(7).
2   [2008] EWCA Civ 1304.

18.19 The following are some examples of how the Court of Appeal has exercised its discretion as to whether or not to allow appeals. These were cases using almost identical rules and guidelines to the new rules.

- In *Brisset v Brisset*[1] it was found that the circuit judge had been procedurally improper on an appeal from the district judge. His order was set aside and the court conducted its own appeal from the district judge.
- In *Fallon v Fallon*[2] a High Court judge declined to allow an appeal even though the district judge had clearly made a mistake of fact in his calculations and deliberations. The appeal was allowed.
- In *Lyons v Lyons*[3] an appeal was allowed where the trial judge had made an obvious error. It was said that it was unfortunate that the errors had not been taken up when the judgment was delivered.
- In *Kaur v Matharu*[4] a circuit judge on hearing an appeal allowed fresh (oral) evidence. On appeal it was held that the judge was clearly wrong. Although the court was not strictly bound by *Ladd v Marshall*[5] its discretion to admit fresh evidence should only be exercised in exceptional circumstances and when it was in the interests of justice so to do.
- In *N v N (Financial Order: Appellate Role)*[6] a circuit judge had failed to direct himself correctly on the appellate function, based his decision to allow an appeal on a view of the evidence fundamentally at variance with the district judge's findings and erroneously exercised an independent discretion. The Court of Appeal held that these were compelling circumstances which justified giving permission for a second appeal and for allowing the appeal.

1   [2009] EWCA Civ 679, [2009] 2 FLR 1451.
2   [2008] EWCA Civ 1653.
3   [2010] EWCA Civ 177.
4   [2010] EWCA Civ 930.
5   [1954] 1 WLR 1489.
6   [2011] EWCA Civ 940.

18.20 For a case where an appeal was allowed on grounds of error of law (which can include a failure to give proper reasons, a failure to apply the statutory test under s 25 MCA, and a failure to take account of relevant factors) see *V v V (Prenuptial Agreement)*[1].

1   [2011] EWHC 3230 (Fam).

MATERIAL OMISSIONS

18.21 PD30A, paras 4.6–4.9 deal with the procedure where a party's advocate considers that there is a material omission from the judgment of the lower court. Before the drawing of the order the advocate should notify the lower court of the omission so that the court can consider this, rather than using the omission as an immediate ground of appeal. Where an application for permission to appeal on the ground of an omission is made to the lower court that court must consider the issue and, if it agrees that there was an omission, correct the omission. It may adjourn if necessary to consider the issue.

18.22 Where such an application is made to the appeal court, that court may, if it considers that there was an omission, adjourn the application and ask the lower court to correct the omission.

PROCEDURE

18.23 The procedure for appeals, including detail as to bundles of documents, skeleton arguments etc will be found in PD30A, para 5 et seq.

APPLICATIONS TO SET ASIDE CONSENT ORDERS

18.24 Since an order made by consent is made with the express agreement of the parties, there are clearly only limited grounds on which it might be set aside; an appeal cannot lie on the merits of the order, in the usual way. Any challenge to a consent order has, therefore, to attack the fundamental basis of the order, and there are four recognised ways of doing this. They are by alleging:

(a)   non-disclosure of some essential matter;
(b)   fraud or misrepresentation;
(c)   supervening events which invalidate the whole basis of the order; and
(d)   undue influence[1].

These possibilities will be considered in turn, with (a) and (b) being considered together since, as will be seen, they are essentially variations on the same basic allegation, namely that the respondent to the application has in some way misled the applicant[2].

[1]   *Tomney v Tomney* [1983] Fam 15. See also *L v L* below; pressure falling short of undue influence will not suffice.
[2]   For a lengthy and comprehensive analysis of the various grounds on which an ancillary relief order may be challenged, see the judgment of Munby J in *L v L* [2006] EWHC 956 (Fam). Inter alia, his Lordship said that an order can never be set aside on the ground of bad legal advice.

18.25 The power of the court to set aside an order is contained in MFPA 1984, s 31F(6) which provides as follows:

'(6) The family court has power to vary, suspend, rescind or revive any order made by it, including—
(a)   power to rescind an order and re-list the application on which it was made,
(b)   power to replace an order which for any reason appears to be invalid by another which the court has power to make, and
(c)   power to vary an order with effect from when it was originally made.'

The relevant rule provision is FPR 9.9A which provides that:

'(1) In this rule—
(a)   "financial remedy order" means an order or judgment that is a financial remedy, and includes—

        (i)   part of such an order or judgment; or
        (ii)   a consent order; and
  (b)   "set aside" means—
        (i)   in the High Court, to set aside a financial remedy order pursuant to section 17(2) of the Senior Courts Act 1981 and this rule;
        (ii)   in the family court, to rescind or vary a financial remedy order pursuant to section 31F(6) of the 1984 Act.

(2) A party may apply under this rule to set aside a financial remedy order where no error of the court is alleged.

(3) An application under this rule must be made within the proceedings in which the financial remedy order was made.

(4) An application under this rule must be made in accordance with the Part 18 procedure, subject to the modifications contained in this rule.

(5) Where the court decides to set aside a financial remedy order, it shall give directions for the rehearing of the financial remedy proceedings or make such other orders as may be appropriate to dispose of the application.'

18.26 Finally, guidance is given by FPR PD 9A, para 13.5 which provides that:

'An application to set aside a financial remedy order should only be made where no error of the court is alleged. If an error of the court is alleged, an application for permission to appeal under Part 30 should be considered. The grounds on which a financial remedy order may be set aside are and will remain a matter for decisions by judges. The grounds include (i) fraud; (ii) material non-disclosure; (iii) certain limited types of mistake; (iv) a subsequent event, unforeseen and unforeseeable at the time the order was made, which invalidates the basis on which the order was made.'

18.27 In *CB v EB*[1] Mostyn J reviewed the various authorities and said that the set aside power contained in s 31F(6) was not a break with the past but was no more than a power vested in divorce courts since 1986. He added that, insofar as the language of PD 9A para 13.5 suggests otherwise, it is misleading.

[1]   [2020] EWFC 72.

18.28 The two means of attacking a consent order are applications for leave to appeal out of time and applications to set aside the order; the first is made by the normal appellate route from the court which made the order, while the second is made to the court which made the order[1]. It would seem that the former is more appropriate in the case of events occurring after the date of the order while the latter would be appropriate in the case of non-disclosure or fraud.

[1]   See *B-T v B-T (Divorce Procedure)* [1990] 2 FLR 1 per Ward J.

Non-disclosure, fraud and misrepresentation

18.29 The duty of full and frank disclosure has already been mentioned above, and was one of the principal issues in *Livesey (formerly Jenkins) v Jenkins*[1]. In that case the parties had settled their litigation by means of a consent order, but the wife had omitted to tell her former husband, or even her own solicitors, that she was intending to remarry; that remarriage was a significant matter and something which she should have disclosed. In his speech, Lord Brandon emphasised that the parties were under the same obligation as to complete disclosure in cases of consent orders as in contested proceedings, and said that in order to do justice to the husband it was necessary to set the order aside.

¹   See **9.5**.

18.30 This decision confirmed a number of earlier decisions, notably *Robinson v Robinson (Disclosure)*¹, where it was held that there was a duty on litigants in matrimonial proceedings to make full and frank disclosure of their property and financial resources; the power to set aside orders was not limited to cases of fraud and mistake but extended to material non-disclosure.

¹   (1983) 4 FLR 102, CA.

18.31 It was emphasised in *Livesey v Jenkins* that not every example of non-disclosure would result in the order being set aside. Orders will not be set aside if the disclosure would not have made any substantial difference to the order which the court would have made¹:

> 'It will only be in cases where the absence of full and frank disclosure has led to the court making, either in contested proceedings or by consent, an order that is substantially different from the order which would have been made if such disclosure had taken place that a case for setting aside can possibly be made good.'

¹   *Livesey v Jenkins* [1984] AC 424, HL, per Lord Brandon.

18.32 In *Vicary v Vicary*¹, a consent order was made on the basis that the husband's assets, including his shares in a private company, were £430,000. He did not disclose the fact that negotiations were taking place for the sale of the company, and, shortly thereafter, he sold his shares for £2.8m. The order was set aside².

¹   [1992] 2 FLR 271, CA.
²   See also *Thompson v Thompson* [1991] 2 FLR 530, CA.

18.33 In *Rose v Rose*¹ a consent order was made in August 2001. At an FDR hearing the wife had claimed that her relationship with a boyfriend had cooled. However, the husband subsequently adduced evidence to show that they had planned to buy a house in Italy and spend part of each year there. He applied to set aside the consent order, but the wife successfully applied for a summary order striking out his application. It was held that the operative date for non-disclosure was the date of the order. On that date the husband had been aware of the relationship and had chosen not to cross-examine her on it. Even if the husband were able to prove non-disclosure, it was utterly unlikely that the wife's interest would be confined to a life interest in property as he now suggested. It was emphasised that a delay of one year in making an application of this kind is 'wholly unreasonable'².

¹   [2003] EWHC 505 (Fam), [2003] 2 FLR 197.
²   A point repeated in *Shaw v Shaw* [2002] EWCA Civ 1298, [2002] 2 FLR 1204, CA.

18.34 Parties who applied on trivial grounds will be penalised in costs. In another case, the fact that there is no jurisdiction to vary a lump sum order nor to award a second lump sum was advanced to support the point that consent orders should not lightly be set aside¹.

¹   *Redmond v Redmond* [1986] 2 FLR 173.

18.35 In *Kingdon v Kingdon*[1] the husband failed to disclose that he had purchased shares in a new company which led to his being required to sell other shares resulting in a net gain for him of £1.2m. He continued to present a misleading picture and the wife applied to set aside the consent order. The trial judge found that there had been a material non-disclosure, but declined to set aside the whole order, instead ordering the husband to pay an additional lump sum. The Court of Appeal dismissed the wife's appeal against this decision; there was no need to dismantle the consent order but merely to add to it. The court relied on the judgment of Thorpe LJ in *Williams v Lindley* (see **18.54**). In this case, however, re-consideration of all the s 25 factors was not necessary.

[1]   [2010] EWCA Civ 1251.

18.36 For a very clear case of material non-disclosure vitiating a consent order see *C v C (Financial Orders: Non-Disclosure: Set-Aside)*[1]. The husband had failed completely to disclose his interest in one company and his attribution of a nil value to his shares in another company was shown to be 'a disingenuous half-truth'. As to the test to be applied, Coleridge J said 'the test in relation to materiality is that there has to be a strong possibility that the court would have made a substantially different order'. By way of contrast, in *Sharland v Sharland*[2] the Court of Appeal upheld a lower court's finding that although the husband's evidence had been dishonest and, had the court known what it now knew, it was inconceivable that it would not have regarded the facts as relevant, nevertheless, any order made would not have been substantially different to that arrived at in the heads of agreement and so the non-disclosure was not material.

[1]   [2013] Fam Law 953.
[2]   [2014] EWCA Civ 95.

18.37 Some of the issues arising in these cases have been resolved by the decisions of the Supreme Court in *Sharland v Sharland*[1] and *Gohill v Gohill (No 2)*[2].

[1]   [2015] UKSC 60.
[2]   [2015] UKSC 61.

18.38 *Sharland v Sharland* was a case of fraud involving a consent order. There were various procedural complications and arguments which need not concern us here; the central point was that the husband had failed to disclose the fact that there were plans for an initial public offering (IPO) in respect of his company and the husband had given evidence to the effect that there no such plans. The wife applied to set aside the order. The Court of Appeal (Briggs LJ dissenting) had declined to set it aside. That court and the Supreme Court proceeded on the basis that this was a plain case of fraudulent misrepresentation.

18.39 Giving the sole judgment of the Supreme Court (starting at para 32), Lady Hale ruled as follows:

'There was no need to decide whether the greater flexibility which the court now has in cases of innocent or negligent misrepresentation in contract should also apply to innocent or negligent misrepresentation or non- disclosure in consent orders whether in civil or in family cases. It was clear from *Dietz* and *Livesey* that the misrepresentation or non-disclosure must be material to the decision that the court made at the time. But this case was a case of fraud, and it would be extraordinary if the victim of a fraudulent misrepresentation, which had led her to compromise her claim to financial remedies in a matrimonial case, were in a worse position than the victim of a fraudulent misrepresentation in an ordinary contract case, including a contract to settle a civil claim. As was held in *Smith v Kay* (1859) VII HLC 749, a party who has practised deception with a view to a particular end, which has been attained by it, could not be allowed to deny its materiality. Furthermore, the court was in no position to protect the victim from the deception, or to conduct its statutory duties properly, because the court too has been deceived. The only exception was where the court was satisfied that, at the time when it made the consent order, the fraud would not have influenced a reasonable person to agree to it, nor, had it known then what it knows now, would the court have made a significantly different order, whether or not the parties had agreed to it. However, the burden of satisfying the court of that must lie with the perpetrator of the fraud. It would be wrong in this case to place upon the victim the burden of showing that it would have made a difference.'

18.40 In other words, the general principle is that 'fraud unravels all' but this is not absolute; if the fraudster (the burden being on him) can satisfy the court that the fraud did not vitiate consent or that the facts fraudulently concealed or averred would not, if known, have led the court to make a significantly different order, the order might not be set aside. However, the starting point remains that the fraud undermines the order.

18.41 The facts and procedural history of *Gohill v Gohill* were highly complicated and need not be recited in detail here; suffice it to say that it concerned the wife's application to set aside a consent order on the ground of fraudulent non-disclosure and, subsequent to the making of the consent order, the husband, a solicitor, was imprisoned for money-laundering. One of the principal points made by Lord Wilson was that the principles propounded in *Ladd v Marshall* (see **18.19** above) have no relevance to the determination of an application to set aside a financial order on the ground of fraudulent non-disclosure. On the issue of accidental, innocent or negligent misrepresentation or non-disclosure, Lord Neuberger said that it will still be necessary to show that the omission or distortion was material to the final order.

18.42 *AB v CD (Financial Remedy: Consent Order: Non-Disclosure)*[1] was a post-*Sharland* application to set aside a consent order on the basis of non-disclosure by the wife. The judge found that the evidence did not prove that there had been deliberate fraud or deception perpetrated by the wife. It was therefore for the husband to prove that that the non-disclosure was material; the onus of proof lay on him. The judge had no hesitation in this case in finding that it was material. Had the husband known of the potential investment in the wife's company by a third party he would not have agreed the terms of the consent order.

[1]   [2016] EWHC 10 (Fam).

18.43 In *N v N (Periodical Payments: Non-Disclosure)*[1] where an application to set aside based on alleged non-disclosure failed. McFarlane LJ summarised the law as follows:

'As a matter of law, however, the need for finality at the conclusion of financial provision proceedings following divorce is supported by restricting the court's ability to reopen such decisions following contested proceedings to cases where there has either been material non-disclosure or there has been a significant supervening event in the period following the making of the order (*Barder v Caluori* [1988] AC 20). A finding of material non-disclosure must be established on the evidence and after an appropriate and fair trial process during which that evidence is evaluated.'

1   [2014] EWCA Civ 314.

New or supervening circumstances

18.44 As has already been said, there is no jurisdiction to vary a lump sum order or property adjustment order on the ground of new circumstances or otherwise. Nevertheless, some procedure has to exist to deal with the kind of case where the whole factual basis on which the order was made has disappeared.

18.45 In *Barder v Caluori*[1], a consent order was made by which the husband was ordered to transfer his interest in the former matrimonial home to the wife. One of the principal reasons for this order was that the wife had the care of the children. Shortly thereafter, the wife killed the children and herself. On appeal to the House of Lords, the principal issue was whether leave to appeal out of time should have been granted, but the reasons given in the speech of Lord Brandon may be applied to an application to the judge at first instance. Lord Brandon said that the court might properly exercise its discretion to grant leave to appeal out of time from an order for financial provision or property transfer on the ground of new events provided four conditions were met. These conditions were:

(1)   that new events have occurred since the making of the order which invalidate the basis or fundamental assumption upon which the order was made, so that, if leave to appeal out of time were given, the appeal would be certain, or very likely, to succeed;
(2)   that the new events should have occurred within a relatively short time of the order having been made. While that time could not be precisely defined, Lord Brandon thought it extremely unlikely that it could be as long as a year, and that in most cases it would be no more than a few months;
(3)   that the application should be made reasonably promptly in the circumstances of the case; and
(4)   that the grant of leave should not prejudice third parties who have acquired in good faith and for valuable consideration interests in property which is the subject matter of the order.

1   [1988] AC 20, sub nom *Barder v Barder (Caluori Intervening)* [1987] 2 FLR 480, HL.

18.46 Inevitably, circumstances change after orders are made, and it must be emphasised that the courts will not set aside an order merely on the ground that things are now different from how they appeared at the time of the order[1]. In *Walkden v Walkden*[2] the husband had stated the value of his shares as £216,000 in his Form E. After a consent order was made he sold them for £1.8m. The Court of Appeal held that a court should first consider whether the consent order was vitiated by misrepresentation, fraud, undue influence or non-disclosure. If not, it should then consider whether there was a '*Barder* event'. Here there was no vitiating factor and no *Barder* event because the sale was not unforeseen or unforeseeable and there had been no dramatic change in the company's performance. In *Judge v Judge*[3] it was held that an application to set aside an order is not an application for ancillary relief and so the general rule that costs do not follow the event did not apply. In *Richardson v Richardson*[4] Thorpe LJ emphasised that '*Barder* jurisprudence' is to be kept within very strict limits; clearly such applications are not encouraged. It seems that there are several common grounds for such applications which may conveniently be summarised as follows.

[1]   See eg *McGladdery v McGladdery* [1999] 2 FLR 1102.
[2]   [2009] EWCA Civ 627, [2010] 1 FLR 174.
[3]   [2009] EWCA Civ 1458, [2009] 1 FLR 1287.
[4]   [2011] EWCA Civ 79.

(1)   Disputes as to the value of an asset

18.47   The position was summarised in *Cornick v Cornick*[1]. Where an asset which was correctly valued at the time of the order changes value within a relatively short period because of the natural processes of price fluctuation, leave to appeal should not be granted (and the order should not be set aside).

[1]   [1994] 2 FLR 530.

18.48   Where a wrong value was placed on an asset at the time of the order and, had this been known, a different order would have been made, provided that this was not the fault of the person alleging the mistake, leave to appeal may be granted (and the order set aside).

18.49   Where something unforeseen and unforeseeable has occurred since the date of the order which has altered the value of the assets so dramatically as to bring about a substantial change in the balance of the assets brought about by the order, then, provided the other three *Barder* conditions are met, the *Barder* principles may apply. The circumstances in which these conditions might apply are rare[1].

[1]   See eg *Middleton v Middleton* [1998] 2 FLR 821, CA.

18.50   At a time of rapid fluctuation of property prices, it is natural that there should be second thoughts about the wisdom of some consent orders. However, it will always be necessary to show that the facts fall within the principles set out above. For example, in one case[1] the Court of Appeal granted leave to appeal out of time on the ground that the actual value of a house was so much lower than the agreed valuation that the applicant could not be rehoused on the division of the proceeds of sale originally agreed. In another[2], the division of the proceeds of sale would have been enough to rehouse the parties had the husband not 'disgracefully' delayed the sale by more than 3 years, and leave to appeal was granted on the basis that the fundamental assumption underlying the order, namely that the wife would be able to rehouse herself, had been falsified. However, in another case[3], where the value of a house at the time of the order was £340,000 and at the time of the hearing of the application for leave to appeal 3 years later £250,000, leave to appeal was refused.

1   *Heard v Heard* [1995] 1 FLR 970, CA.
2   *Hope-Smith v Hope-Smith* [1989] 2 FLR 56, CA.
3   *B v B (Financial Provision: Leave to Appeal)* [1994] 1 FLR 219. See also, for a contrary decision, *Heard v Heard* [1995] 1 FLR 970, CA.

18.51 In *Kean v Kean*[1] a consent order was made in 2000 on the basis that the property was worth £500,000 to £550,000. No formal valuation was obtained. In the summer of 2001 the property was sold for £765,000 and the wife sought leave to appeal out of time. This application was refused on the ground that the estimate of the value was not a basis of, nor a fundamental assumption underlying the agreement. It was not certain that the court would have made a different order if the true value had been known. Moreover, the wife had to take some responsibility since she had been advised to take separate advice and had refused.

1   [2002] 2 FLR 28.

18.52 In *B v B (Ancillary Relief: Consent Order: Appeal out of Time)*[1] a wife sought leave to appeal on the ground, inter alia, of an error in valuation at trial. It was held that there was no evidence of an incorrect valuation at the date of the hearing and that none of the *Barder* conditions applied.

1   [2007] EWHC 2472 (Fam), [2008] 1 FLR 1279.

(2) Remarriage or cohabitation

18.53 It has been seen above that in *Livesey v Jenkins* the fact that the wife failed to disclose to the husband her intention to remarry undermined the basis on which the order was made and was sufficient to enable the court to set it aside. This will, of course, not always be the case[1]. In another case[2], where the wife had remarried since the order, it was held that the fact of her remarriage did not affect her entitlement to capital and this would have been the case even if she had been remarried at the time of the order. It is therefore necessary to demonstrate that the basis on which the order was made has been falsified before the application will stand any chance of success.

1   See eg *Cook v Cook* [1988] 1 FLR 521, CA.
2   *B v B (Financial Provision: Leave to Appeal)* (above).

18.54 In *Williams v Lindley*[1] a consent order of 70/30 in favour of a wife had been made after the wife had denied any relationship with a certain man. Soon thereafter she married the man in question. A circuit judge refused the husband's application for a re-hearing but this was allowed by the Court of Appeal. It was held that the main foundation of the wife's case had been undermined, and Thorpe LJ added that, when approaching the 'supervening event', greater flexibility was needed; the court should move away from rigid prescription and reconsideration of all the s 25 factors was necessary.

1   [2005] EWCA Civ 103, [2005] 2 FLR 710.

18.55 In *Dixon v Marchant*[1] a husband claimed that he had been led to make a consent order capitalising the wife's periodical payments by her assertion that she was not cohabiting and did not intend to do so. Seven months later she remarried. His appeal was dismissed. The court held that he had to show on an objective test that there was a common assumption made by the parties and shared by the court that for an indefinite period to be measured in years rather than weeks or months the wife would not remarry.

[1]   [2008] 1 FLR 655, CA.

(3)   Death

18.56 The same principles apply in the case of the death of a party. It might be thought that where the basis of an order was the provision of a home for one party, the death of that party would invalidate the whole order, but that would be an over-simplistic view of the law. Death was, clearly, the background to *Barder v Caluori*, considered at **18.45**, and the principles set out there need not be repeated.

18.57 In *Amey v Amey*[1], there had been an agreement between the parties which they intended to have approved by means of a consent order. However, before they could do so, the wife died. The husband sought to set aside the agreement. It was held that the mere fact of the wife's death was not sufficient; the agreement had been a fair distribution of assets on the basis of the wife's entitlement, and the only ground for setting it aside would be if the death had undermined the fundamental assumptions on which the order was made.

[1]   [1992] 2 FLR 89.

18.58 In *Barber v Barber*[1], an order was made for the wife to have more than half the proceeds of sale of the former matrimonial home on the assumption that, though she was ill, she had at least 5 years to live. She died 3 months after the order was made. The order was set aside in part, on the ground that its fundamental basis had been invalidated. It was held that the proper approach was to start again and make an order on the basis of what the court would have done had it known at the date of the order what it now knew. This followed the decision of the court in *Smith v Smith (Smith and Others Intervening)*[2], which established similar principles.

[1]   [1993] 1 FLR 476, CA.
[2]   [1991] 2 FLR 432, CA.

18.59 In *Reid v Reid*[1] the facts were that a consent order had awarded the wife £99,000 on a clean break basis. She had disclosed the fact that she suffered from ill health. Fifteen days after decree absolute she died. The husband sought leave to appeal out of time. The court held that her death 2 months after the order was a new event and attracted *Barder* principles. It was not reasonably foreseeable; the husband's needs had not been fully met by the order and the wife's death had invalidated the parties' perceptions of her needs. The husband would receive a lump sum of £37,000; the executor's arguments based on entitlement and contributions were not appropriate where assets were very limited.

[1]   [2004] 1 FLR 736, Wilson J.

18.60 In *WA v The Estate of HA deceased and others*[1] the wife was 'fabulously wealthy'. A consent order was made that the husband receive £17.3m payable by two instalments. Twenty-two days later he committed suicide. The wife appealed the consent order. Moor J held that the husband's death was not foreseeable. The issue therefore was whether or not the award was needs based or a 'sharing' award. He held that it was needs based and so had been invalidated by the death of the husband. This was an exceptional example of a case meeting the *Barder* guidelines. The award was reduced to £5m.

[1] [2015] EWHC 2233 (Fam).

(4)   Other matters

18.61 For the sake of completeness, reference should be made to *Crozier v Crozier*[1], where an application was made to set aside a clean break order with nominal maintenance for a child on the ground that the Child Support Agency, which had come into being since the making of the order, seemed likely to require the husband to pay a substantial amount by way of child maintenance. The application was refused, partly on the ground that parties could never agree to contract out of liability for a child.

[1] [1994] 1 FLR 126.

18.62 In *S v S (Ancillary Relief: Consent Order)*[1] a consent order was made for a payment of £800,000 to the wife on a clean break basis one month before the House of Lords decision in *White v White*. The wife applied to set aside the order on the ground of a supervening event. The application was dismissed. It was held that, while a change in the law could be a supervening event, it must be unforeseeable. At the time of the order, the House was considering its judgment, and a change in the law was foreseeable.

[1] [2002] 1 FLR 992.

18.63 During the 'credit crunch' many orders were made at a time when values, whether of shares or properties, were considerably greater than they were later, and it was widely anticipated that this would give rise to applications to set aside consent (and, indeed, other) orders. The decision of the Court of Appeal in *Myerson v Myerson*[1] was therefore awaited with keen interest.

[1] [2009] EWCA Civ 282.

18.64 In this case, the consent order had divided the assets, valued at the time at £25m, at 57% to the husband and 43% to the wife. The husband's retained assets were largely made up of his shareholding in his company. At the time of the order the shares were worth £15m (each share was valued at £2.99). By the time of the appeal the shares were trading at 27.5p. The husband had paid the first instalment (£7m) of a lump sum totalling £9.5m in April 2008. He had submitted that the original judge's jurisdiction should be extended to fundamentally rewrite the order at a future hearing as the order was no longer fair and the husband could not perform his remaining obligations (ie the lump sum instalments).

18.65 Thorpe LJ rejected the appeal even though it had 'dramatic features'. He relied on *Cornick*, and agreed with Hale J's reasoning in that case that the 'natural processes of price fluctuation' should not constitute a *Barder* event. He also added four other factors in this case that prevent the appeal succeeding:

(i)   the husband, with all his knowledge and experience, had agreed the compromise;

(ii)   the husband, in attempting to vary and offer the wife shares instead, was seeking to relieve himself of the consequences of his speculation;

(iii)   he still has the opportunities as 'unusual opportunities are created for the most astute in a bear market'; and

(iv)   the husband has already invoked the statutory power of variation concerning the instalments.

18.66 He went on as follows:

'There may be many who are contemplating an attempt to reopen an existing ancillary relief order on the grounds of subsequently encountered financial eclipse. All in that situation should ponder Hale J's analytical characterisation and ask themselves whether the events upon which they intend to rely can be bought within either the second or the third category. Even then they would be well advised to heed the warning that very few successful applications have been reported. I echo the words of Hale J that the natural processes of price fluctuation, whether in houses, shares, or any other property, and however dramatic, do not satisfy the *Barder* test.'

APPEAL OR SETTING ASIDE?

18.67 Where non-disclosure is alleged it would seem that the applicant to set aside has the choice of proceeding by way of appeal or by way of application to the first instance judge. In *Harris v Manahan*[1] it was clear that Thorpe and Ward LJJ held different opinions as to which was the most appropriate course. In the recent case of *Musa v Karim*[2] Thorpe LJ repeated that it was open to the applicant to choose the most suitable route and added that this difference of opinion needed to be resolved.

[1]   [1997] 1 FLR 205, CA.
[2]   [2012] EWCA Civ 1332, [2013] Fam Law 16.

18.68 In *MAP v RAP (Consent Order: Appeal: Incapacity)*[1] Mostyn J had to consider the proper route for an application to set aside a consent order on the ground of incapacity. His Lordship was clear:

'18. I am of the view that the appeal route is mandatory in respect of a consent order made by a district judge where there is no real challenge to the validity of the consent order per se. So, for example, if a challenge is being made under the famous case of *Barder v Barder*, then it seems to me that the Practice Direction fully applies and the appeal route is the only available route. Indeed, this is a view that has been adopted by Lady Justice Gloster recently in a decision of hers – admittedly only refusing permission in the Court of Appeal called *Cart v Cart*.

19. I believe that it is right also to characterise an appeal which is based on non-disclosure as being one that falls on the side of the line where an appeal is the appropriate route, although I accept that two views could be taken as to whether the fact of non-disclosure if proved in fact destroys any consensual element to the order under attack. But as this case, as I am satisfied, for reasons I have already given, that this case is not a non-disclosure case, I need say no more about that.

20. However, where the ground of attack against the order is that there was no true consent, either because it had been withdrawn (which is said to be the case here), or because one of the parties purportedly giving consent was incapacitated, then I do not believe that the final sentence in para.14 of the Practice Direction applies, and that it is appropriate for the application for revocation of the order to proceed under Rule 4.1(6).'

¹ [2013] EWHC 4784 (Fam).

18.69 These issues were reviewed by Sir James Munby P in *CS v ACS and Anor*¹. His Lordship held to be ultra vires a statement in Practice Direction 30A at para 14.1 to the effect that an appeal was the only way to apply to set aside an order and that it remained open to apply either to the original court or by way of appeal. This conclusion was endorsed by Lady Hale at para 41 of her judgment in *Sharland v Sharland* at **18.36**.

¹ [2015] EWHC 1005 (Fam).

PROCEDURE ON REHEARING

18.70 In *Goddard-Watts v Goddard-Watts*¹ Moylan J was conducting a rehearing following the set aside of an earlier order on the grounds of non-disclosure. Moylan J stated that it was not necessary to start again from scratch; much of the evidence in the earlier case which was non-contentious might be accepted, and the important issues might be isolated. His Lordship continued (at para 88) as follows:

'I agree with Mr Pointer that I am conducting a rehearing. But I do not agree that, merely because this is a rehearing, the only way of achieving a fair outcome is to give the wife an award based on the current values of the assets. I must determine what is fair *now* and I must do so by reference to all the circumstances of the case. These include the current resources available to the parties but also the division which was effected in 2010 *and* the fact that this was procured by non-disclosure.'

¹ [2016] EWHC 3000 (Fam).

18.71 Unusually, the same case came before the court again in November 2019¹ on a second application to set aside the order for non-disclosure. Holman J followed the guidance in *Sharland v Sharland*² and found that there was further non-disclosure and that it was not possible to say that there was not a real prospect of the wife doing better at a final hearing and that she was entitled to reopen the case.

¹ [2019] EWHC 3367 (Fam).
² [2014] EWCA Civ 95.

Chapter 19

ENFORCEMENT

INTRODUCTION

19.1 The aim of this chapter is to give an overview of the types of enforcement action most likely to be of practical use to clients and their advisers facing non-compliance with a court order. FPR Pt 33 sets out the main principles of enforcement for the family lawyer, with significant cross-reference to the CPR 1998.

19.2 A creditor may use more than one method of enforcement at the same time[1]. A judgment can be enforced after 6 years, but not any claim for interest on that judgment[2]. However, under MCA 1973, s 32(1) the permission of the court is required to enforce arrears of maintenance more than 12 months old at the date of the application to enforce[3].

[1] FPR 33.2 incorporating CPR 70.2(2)(b).
[2] Execution of a judgment is not a 'fresh action' and so is not caught by the statutory 6-year time limit in s 24 Limitation Act 1980: *Lowsley v Forbes* [1998] UKHL 34.
[3] See further **19.13**.

APPLICATIONS FOR ENFORCEMENT BY 'SUCH MEANS AS THE COURT MAY CONSIDER APPROPRIATE'

19.3 Under FPR 33.3(2)(b) a creditor under an order of the Family Court can apply for 'an order for such method of enforcement as the court may consider appropriate'. This provides a straightforward and low-cost route to a variety of practical enforcement options.

19.4 The applicant completes form D50K, a simple three-page form submitted with a modest court fee (£50 at the time of writing). The form complies with FPR 33.3 (1) in that it states the amount due under the order, shows how this figure is arrived at, and is verified by a statement of truth.

19.5 The application will lead to an order that the respondent (debtor) must attend court with documentation, to be questioned on oath by a judge or magistrates as to his or her assets and means[1]. If the questioning takes place before a judge, the court may, if it considers it appropriate, proceed immediately (and without a further application, hearing or fee) to make an attachment of earnings order, a charging order, a third-party debt order, or to direct the issue of a warrant of control. If the questioning takes place before magistrates, their powers are limited to making an attachment of earnings order and any other enforcement order will require a transfer to the District Bench and an adjournment of the hearing. If the applicant seeks consideration of options not limited to attachment of earnings, it is worth highlighting this in a covering letter with the application, to secure an appropriate initial listing before a district judge. *Kaur v Randhawa*[2] stands as an example of a FPR 33.3(2)(b) application. Having heard evidence, Mostyn J proceeded immediately to make a final third party debt order. An interim order, used on an ex parte basis to secure funds pending a final hearing, was not required. *Quan v Bray*[3] provides a further case example, this time of a wife failing to establish that the husband had any assets or income within the jurisdiction against which any enforcement order could be made. The wife's application in form D50K was stayed generally, and Holman J declined to give directions on a judgment summons application not yet actually issued by the wife. He also emphasised that the costs of enforcement processes must be kept proportionate to the sums at stake.

[1]   CPR 71(6) and (7).
[2]   *Kaur v Randhawa* [2015] EWHC 1592 (Fam).
[3]   *Quan v Bray* [2019] EWFC 46.

19.6 What if the respondent does not attend the hearing? The court should be asked to give directions for a further hearing, clearly mandating the respondent's attendance and attaching a penal notice to that requirement. Standard order template 4.8[1] can be adapted for the purpose. The order, specifying the hearing date, should then be personally served on the respondent. Service by the court bailiff can be requested (form D89, current fee £100). If there is still no attendance, the court should be asked to issue a bench warrant for the respondent's arrest (template order 5.7).

[1]   Promulgated with the Practice Guidance of 30 November 2017.

APPLICATIONS FOR PARTICULAR ENFORCEMENT REMEDIES FOR THE PAYMENT OF MONEY

19.7 The procedure under FPR 33.3(2)(b) for the court to decide on the method of enforcement is intended to be convenient and cost-effective, but there is nothing to prevent a creditor with some knowledge of the debtor's finances from choosing a particular method (or methods) of enforcement and pursuing those specifically.

Attachment of earnings

19.8 Applications to enforce maintenance orders in the Family Court are governed by FPR 33.19 and Pt 39. The definition of 'maintenance order' is wide and can include a lump sum as well as orders for periodical payments, together with any costs ordered in the proceedings when the original order was made[1]. Unusually, an attachment of earnings order can be made even at the time the maintenance order itself is made, before any arrears have accrued[2]. It stands as the only type of enforcement action that can be invoked prospectively. More often, an application is made once arrears have started to accrue. The application can be made against wages or salary, including bonus, commission or overtime and against pension payments (other than social security or disability pensions). Statutory sick pay is included in pay that may be attached, but tax credits are excluded[3]. Orders cannot be made against the income of the self-employed.

[1] The definition is found in Sch 1 to the Attachment of Earnings Act 1971 (AtEA 1971) (per FPR 39.2) and includes periodical or other payments made under Pt II of the MCA 1973 (emphasis added). Costs are included by virtue of s 25(2) of the AtEA 1971 Act. In the event that a judgment debt does not come within the definition of a 'maintenance order' – for example a costs order in the main divorce suit – then FPR Pt 39 will not apply but an attachment of earnings order may still be sought under CPR Pt 89.

[2] FPR 39.1(1) and (2).

[3] Attachment of Earnings Act 1971, s 24.

19.9 The application must comply with FPR 33.3(1), namely that it must be accompanied by a statement verified by a statement of truth and setting out the amount due and how that calculation is arrived at. Court form FE15 has been prescribed for the purpose in the Family Court[1]. The application fee at the time of writing is £34. A copy of the sealed maintenance order must be filed with the application. The application may seek an order in respect of ongoing maintenance, arrears accrued, or both. If the creditor seeks to enforce arrears due for more than 12 months, permission must be sought in the notice of application[2]. If the creditor knows the identity of the debtor's employer, the court can be asked at any stage to issue a form N338 for completion by the employer with information about the debtor's earnings[3], and it makes sense to request this at the time the application is made if the employer is known. The court will fix a date for a hearing on receipt of the application. The debtor is sent a reply form FE17 and the application is served on him by the court, usually by post[4].

[1] FPR 39.21 applies to the uncommon situation of enforcing a maintenance order made in the High Court (as distinct from an order made in the Family Court by a judge of High Court level).

[2] FPR 39.20, although see **19.13** below.

[3] FPR 39.7.

[4] FPR 39.6(1) and 6.23.

19.10 If the debtor cooperates, or his employer provides information in form N338, the court can make an attachment of earnings order, authorising the employer to deduct sums regularly from the debtor's earnings, to satisfy the liability under the original order. The judge must set a normal deduction rate (NDR) and a protected earnings rate (PER) below which the debtor's net earnings will not be reduced. If the debtor is cooperative and keen to avoid his employer being involved in the enforcement process the attachment of earnings order may be suspended, in that the debtor is permitted to make the payments voluntarily, but if he does not the order will automatically be served on the employer for the deductions to begin.

19.11 If the debtor fails to cooperate by either returning the reply form or making payment to the creditor, the court will issue a form endorsed with a penal notice for the creditor to arrange to be served personally on the debtor, requiring the debtor to specify his earnings[1]. If there is still no compliance, a hearing will be listed to consider whether the debtor has committed an offence under s 23(2)(c) of the Attachment of Earnings Act 1971 (failing to comply with the order to provide information) and the debtor must be served personally with not less than 5 days' notice of the hearing date. If the debtor fails to attend an adjourned hearing after personal service, a committal order may be made for a maximum of 14 days (of which the debtor would serve 7), and such an order may be suspended, giving the debtor a further opportunity for compliance[2]. The committal is for the offence under s 23 of the 1971 Act, rather than for contempt of court. In practice, rather than committing the debtor to prison, the judge will usually make an order under s 23(1A) of the Attachment of Earnings Act 1971, requiring the debtor to be brought before the court following arrest, to give a final opportunity for compliance.

[1]   FPR 39.9(1) and s 14(1) Attachment of Earnings Act 1971.
[2]   FPR 39.11.

19.12 If the debtor is a member of the armed forces, an application should be made instead to the relevant service authority for a deduction from service pay under the Armed Forces Act 2006 and the Armed Forces (Forfeitures and Deductions) Regulations 2009[1], as service pay is not subject to the Attachment of Earnings Act 1971.

[1]   SI 2009/1109.

19.13 The decision as to whether to give permission to enforce arrears accrued more than 12 months before the application is within the court's discretion. There is no presumption that leave should only be granted in special circumstances[1], but given the starting point that leave is required, some cogent explanation for the delay is generally expected if the applicant is to persuade the court to grant permission to enforce. In *Tattersall v Tattersall*[2] the Court of Appeal commented that the application for permission may be made informally, especially where the relevant arrears are only a little out of date, but this approach is in contrast with the apparent requirement for more formality in FPR 39.20.

[1]   *Lumsden v Lumsden* (unreported), 11 November 1998, CA.
[2]   *Tattersall v Tattersall* [2018] EWCA Civ 1978 at para 31.

Third party debt orders

19.14 A third party debt order requires a third party (often a bank[1]) to pay money standing to the credit of a judgment debtor directly to the judgment creditor. FPR 33.24 imports CPR Pt 72, subject to some minor amendments. The process is useful if the creditor is aware, at least in broad terms, of the debtor's banking arrangements or some other funds held to the debtor's order.

[1]   But it may be any third party holding monies to the credit of the debtor, for example a solicitor in a client account (subject to the solicitor's lien for costs).

19.15 The application must be made to the court which made the original order to be enforced (unless the case has since been transferred)[1]. The order can be made by the District Bench or above, but not by lay justices. The application is made in form N349. The fee at the time of writing is £77. The application is initially considered by a judge on the papers. If appropriate, an interim order is made, directing the third party not to make any payment reducing the balance in the account(s) to below the sum of the judgment until further order. The interim order is served (usually by the court) firstly on the third party, to enable the funds in the account to be protected before the debtor becomes aware of the process[2]. On receipt of the order the third party must search their records for any funds held for the debtor.

1   FPR 33.24(1A).
2   CPR 72.5.

19.16 A hearing on notice to the debtor (and third party) is fixed for not less than 28 days after the interim order is made. If the debtor or third party object to the making of a final order they must file and serve written evidence setting out the grounds for the objection[1]. A debtor in hardship may apply for a 'hardship payment order'[2]. At the final hearing the court may either make a final order authorising the release of the funds to the creditor, or dismiss the application and discharge the order, or summarily decide any disputed issues or give directions for such issues to be tried[3].

1   CPR 72.8(1).
2   CPR 72.7.
3   CPR 72.8(6).

Charging orders

19.17 A charging order secures a debt against an asset, usually land, but also securities (tradeable financial assets such as shares). The application is made under the Charging Orders Act 1979, FPR 33.25 and FPR Pt 40 and PD 40A. The application form is FE6 (for land) and FE7 (for securities). At the time of writing the court fee is £38. A creditor may apply in a single application notice for charging orders over more than one asset, but the court will draw separate orders relating to each asset charged[1].

1   FPR PD 40A, para 1.4.

19.18 The application is initially dealt with on paper and an interim order may be made, imposing a charge over the debtor's interest in the asset to which the application relates[1]. It is the applicant creditor's responsibility to serve the debtor, any co-owner, the debtor's spouse or civil partner and any other known creditor[2]. A certificate of service must be produced at the hearing. Form RX1 should be used to register a Form K restriction at the Land Registry for registered land.

1   FPR 40.5(2)(a).
2   FPR 40.6 – and see FPR 40.6(3)(e) and (f) for further detail about service if the interest is held under a trust or is in securities.

19.19 A hearing on notice is fixed. Any objections to the making of a final order (which may be from a spouse or co-owner and not just from the debtor) must be notified at least 7 days before the hearing. At the final hearing the court may either make a final order confirming the continuation of the charge, or dismiss the application and discharge the interim order, or summarily decide any disputed issues, or give directions for such issues to be tried or make any other order the court considers appropriate[1]. After the hearing the final order must be served on all those given notice of the interim order[2].

1   FPR 40.8(2).
2   FPR 40.8(4).

19.20 A charging order acts only to secure the debt. The property cannot be sold without payment of the secured sum, but of itself the charge does not lead to any money changing hands. The Family Court (as well as the High Court and the County Court) can enforce a charging order by an order for sale[1]. Further information on orders for possession and sale is given in **19.32-19.36** below.

[1]   *VS v RE* [2018] EWFC 30 and FPR PD 40A, para 4.1.

Warrants of control

19.21 Parts 83 and 84 of the CPR 1998 are applied in family enforcement proceedings, by virtue of FPR 33.1(2). Form N323 is used to apply for a warrant of control, for the Family Court enforcement agent (in practice the court bailiff) to seize the debtor's goods to be sold to satisfy the debt. The court fee at the time of writing is £100. There is no upper limit for the sums involved in the Family Court, so amounts enforceable by High Court Enforcement Officers in civil proceedings remain enforceable by the bailiff in the Family Court. The detail of the process is governed by the Taking Control of Goods Regulations 2013[1].

[1]   SI 2013/1894.

19.22 If an application is pending for variation of a financial order no warrant of control may be issued without the permission of the court[1].

[1]   FPR 33.20.

19.23 For an example of an application to the Family Court for a 'writ of control' that went spectacularly wrong due to numerous errors in the application and court process, see *Gladwell v Gladwell*[1]. Enforcement officers attended the husband's home to enforce the purported writ and the matter was eventually transferred to Mostyn J in the High Court on the husband's challenge to the process. Ordering the sums taken from the husband to be returned to him, Mostyn J confirmed that the process should never have purported to involve the High Court or have been transferred there. Only a full High Court judge or above can sanction the transfer of a case from the Family Court to the High Court[2] (and any suggestion to the contrary in FPR 33.4(3) must be considered incorrect). Mostyn J transferred the matter back to the District Bench in the Family Court, deeming the wife's original application to have been an application for general enforcement in form D50K.

[1]   *Gladwell v Gladwell* [2019] EWFC 32.
[2]   FPR 29.17 (3) and (4), noting that many cases in the Family Court are heard at High Court judge *level*, but this is not the same as them being heard in the High Court.

Orders to obtain information from judgment debtors

19.24 Part 71 of the CPR 1998 is applied in family enforcement proceedings, by virtue of FPR 33.23. The application is made in the Family Court in form N316 and the fee is £50. Given that the questioning is conducted by a court officer (not a judge or magistrate) and there is no option for the court to proceed straight to making an appropriate enforcement order, this process is inferior to the D50K procedure (see **19.3-19.6** above) which is likely to be used in preference.

JUDGMENT SUMMONS

19.25 The judgment summons procedure is based on s 5 of the Debtors Act 1869. A debtor proved to be in default, having had the means to pay but refusing or neglecting to pay, may be committed to prison for a period of up to 6 weeks (of which he would serve half). The process can be used in respect of 'maintenance orders', defined broadly by the Administration of Justice Act 1970, Sch 8 and FPR 33.9 to include lump sum and school fees orders as well as orders for periodical payments.

19.26 The liberty of the citizen is at stake and therefore the process must be viewed as quasi-criminal, attracting a range of safeguards to comply with Art 6 of the European Convention on Human Rights. There can be no shortcuts[1].

[1] *Quan v Bray* [2019] EWFC 46, although the court does have power to waive procedural defects if satisfied no injustice has been caused.

19.27 FPR 33.9-33.17 governs the process. The application is made in form D62 and at the time of writing the court fee is £73. The application must be accompanied by all the written evidence on which the applicant proposes to rely, together with a copy of the court order to be enforced[1]. The application is made in the Family Court to whichever designated family judge area is most convenient in the view of the creditor, having regard to the place where the debtor lives or works[2]. It will be allocated to the level of judge who last dealt with the proceedings and only a judge of the same level (or above) who made the original order may commit for a breach of that order[3].

[1] FPR 33.10(2).
[2] FPR 33.10(1).
[3] Family Court (Composition and Distribution of Business) Rules 2014, SI 2014/840, r 17(5).

19.28 A hearing will be listed on receipt of the application and the debtor must be served not less than 14 days before the hearing. At this stage, service may be either personal or by first class post (unless the court directs personal service only)[1]. However, if the debtor does not attend the first hearing having been served only by post, the court may not commit him at that hearing. If the debtor attends court, or fails to attend having been served personally (when he should also be offered travelling expenses[2]), he may be committed to prison, provided the creditor proves the necessary default to the criminal standard[3].

[1] FPR 33.11(3)–(6).
[2] Although expenses are not an essential prerequisite for committal under the Debtors Act 1869 - only for imprisonment for non-attendance under s 110(2) County Courts Act 1984 - the tendering of reasonable expenses is good practice.
[3] FPR 33.14(1) and (3).

19.29 The burden of proof remains on the applicant creditor at all times to prove that the debtor:

(a)   has, or has had, since the date of the [original] order the means to pay the sum in respect of which he is in default, and

(b)   has refused or neglected, or refuses or neglects, to pay that sum[1].

[1]   Debtors Act 1869, s 5(2) and FPR 33.14.

19.30 The creditor must prove both limbs of the test to the criminal standard, so that the court is sure of them. The debtor cannot be compelled to give evidence. The debtor should be reminded by the judge of their right to remain silent (but that adverse inferences may be drawn from silence) and the privilege against self-incrimination, and should be offered reasonable opportunity to obtain legal advice and representation, for which criminal legal aid may be available. The hearing takes place in open court. The creditor cannot simply rely on findings in the original proceedings to prove the means to pay, since those findings would have been based on the lower civil standard of proof[1]. Statements made under compulsion (for example in questioning during a general enforcement process) also cannot be relied on (although documents produced as a result of such processes may be used)[2]. A variation application or general enforcement hearing should not be listed alongside a judgment summons, as that effectively deprives the debtor of his right to silence.

[1]   *Prest v Prest* [2015] EWCA Civ 714 per McFarlane LJ at para 55.
[2]   *Mohan v Mohan* [2013] EWCA Civ 586.

19.31 The orders available to the court on hearing a judgment summons and finding the default proved comprise:

- an order for immediate imprisonment of up to 6 weeks. Serving a term of imprisonment does not extinguish the debt, which may still subsequently be enforced. Only one term of imprisonment can be imposed for an unpaid amount, although fresh arrears could then trigger a second judgment summons application. Payment of the sums due whilst incarcerated will lead to the debtor's immediate release; or
- a suspended order for committal, suspended on terms that the amount due plus costs and any further sums accruing, are paid either by a specified time or by instalments[1]; or
- an order re-timetabling the payments due under the original order plus costs, either by a specified time or by instalments[2]; or
- an order adjourning the committal application, in the expectation that the imminent prospect of a custodial sentence will induce compliance[3]; or
- an attachment of earnings order under s 3(4) Attachment of Earnings Act 1971 (requiring proof of means only to the civil standard); and/or
- an order to remit arrears, or part of them.

[1]   FPR 33.16(2).
[2]   FPR 33.16(1).
[3]   See for example *Rogan v Rogan* [2018] EWHC 2512 (Fam) and [2019] EWHC 814 (Fam).

ORDERS FOR SALE OF PROPERTY AND OBTAINING VACANT POSSESSION OF LAND

19.32 Enforcement against a property owned by an uncooperative debtor requires (i) an order for sale, then (ii) an order for possession followed by (iii) a warrant of possession, to achieve vacant possession.

19.33 If the court makes an order for payment of a lump sum or a for property adjustment order, a secured periodical payments order or a legal services payment order (MCA 1973, s 22ZA) then, upon making that order or at any time thereafter the court can make an order for a sale of property under MCA 1973, s 24A. Such orders are most frequently made at the same time as other orders on divorce, but an order for sale can prove a useful avenue for enforcement, as the right to apply is not lost on the making of a clean break and there need be no link between the original order and the property to be sold. The case could be restored to court for consideration on notice of the making of an order for sale under the 'liberty to apply' provision, using Form FP2 under FPR Pt 18. Either one or both spouses must have a beneficial interest in the property and the order will only take effect on or after decree absolute.

19.34 In the alternative, an order for payment of money could be secured against property owned by the debtor by way of a charging order (see **19.17-19.20** above) and then an application could be made under CPR 73.10C for the charging order to be enforced through a sale of the property, using the CPR Pt 8 procedure. The Family Court has jurisdiction to make an order for sale to enforce a charging order made in family proceedings against a sole owner[1]. An order for sale to enforce a charging order is not inevitable and requires the court to balance the rights of the creditor against those of the debtor, particularly where the property is the debtor's home, which engages Art 8 rights under the European Convention on Human Rights.

[1]   *VS v RE* [2018] EWFC 30. Also note: where the charging order has been imposed on the beneficial interest of a joint owner, TOLATA 1996 proceedings in the civil court may be necessary to establish the extent of that interest before the charging order can be enforced.

19.35 Once an order for sale of a property has been made, how can it be enforced if the owners and/or occupiers refuse to cooperate? If the order for sale has been made under either MCA 1973, s 24A or in 'any proceedings relating to land' then the court has power to order any party to deliver up possession of the land to a purchaser or any other person under both FPR 9.24 and CPR 40.17. Once an order for possession has been made, an application can be brought in the Family Court for a warrant of possession to be issued to a bailiff, requiring him to take physical possession of the land and give it to the person in whose favour the order was made, evicting the occupiers. A warrant for possession is governed by CPR 83.26. Form N325 is used to make the application for a warrant for possession of land and the fee at the time of writing is £110.

19.36 Where an order provides for the sale of a matrimonial home, the order should make clear who is entitled to occupy the home pending sale and on what terms, to include whether any rent is payable to the non-occupying spouse. Where an occupying spouse refuses to vacate pending sale, it is probably preferable for any further court application to be made to the Family Court (for variation or enforcement) rather than as possession proceedings in the County Court[1].

[1]   *Derhalli v Derhalli* [2021] EWCA Civ 112.

OTHER USEFUL ENFORCEMENT OPTIONS

Execution of documents by a third party such as a judge

19.37 Where compliance with an order requires a document to be signed, such as a contract for sale, a transfer deed or a stock transfer form, but the respondent refuses or neglects to sign or cannot be found, the High Court and the Family Court can nominate a third party to sign the document(s) in place of the original signor, under s 39 of the Senior Courts Act 1981.

19.38 There must first be an order directing the person to sign the document, usually within a reasonable period (this could be made at the same time as the substantive orders if non-compliance is a potential concern). A Pt 18 application is then used (Form FP2) to restore the matter before the court, with supporting evidence in the form of a witness statement and attachments evidencing that the respondent is aware of the order but has refused/neglected to sign or the efforts made to trace the respondent. The application can be made without notice, for example if the respondent cannot be found, and is usually dealt with on the papers, although the judge may direct a hearing. Commonly, the district judge is nominated to sign in place of the respondent, although the judge could also direct another person to sign, such as a partner in the conveyancing firm handling the sale.

Committal for contempt of court

19.39 The only route to commit a *debtor* to prison is via a judgment summons (see **19.25-19.31** above). The FPR Pt 37 committal route is not available for breach of orders or undertakings for non-payment of money[1].

[1]   *Olu-Williams v Olu-Williams* [2018] EWHC 2464 (Fam) per Williams J at para 43.

19.40 Breach of other types of order (or undertaking) can however lead to committal proceedings for contempt of court. A new Pt 37 was introduced to the FPR from 1 October 2010, intended to simplify and clarify the process. The procedure is quasi-criminal and attracts safeguards to ensure the protection of the defendant's Art 6 rights, including clarity in the requirements of the original order, clear warning of the consequences of breach by way of a penal notice and personal service, clarity in the allegations faced, a hearing (usually) in public, a right to silence, access to legal advice and representation and a requirement that the claimant proves the allegations to the criminal standard, namely that that the court is sure of them. The new Pt 37 is short and clear in setting out the application process and procedural requirements and is therefore not repeated here.

Surrender of passport

19.41 In *Young v Young*[1] Mostyn J summarised the powers of the court to grant a temporary injunction restricting the movement of a party to litigation, including the power to impound the party's passport pending disposal of a financial remedy claim. The power is only available up to judgment and not thereafter and should be used with caution and as a short-term measure only.

The court must be satisfied that there is a good cause of action for a substantive award. The applicant must establish there is probable cause to believe the respondent is likely to quit the jurisdiction and that their presence in the jurisdiction is needed for a proper trial process. The Family Court may make any order which could be made by the High Court if the proceedings were in the High Court, under s 31E of the Matrimonial and Family Proceedings Act 1984.

1   *Young v Young* [2012] EWHC 138 (Fam) at para 26.

'Hadkinson' orders

19.42 A *Hadkinson*[1] order is a discretionary power of the court to require an existing obligation imposed by court order to be complied with before a further application by the contemnor will be considered.

1   *Hadkinson v Hadkinson* [1952] 2 All ER 567.

19.43 In *De Gafforj v De Gafforj*[1] a husband was permitted to pursue his appeal only on condition that he paid sums outstanding under a legal services payment order and costs. Failing this, his appeal would be dismissed. Peter Jackson LJ emphasised that a *Hadkinson* order is draconian in its effect as it affects rights of access to a court. It should be used as an exceptional case management order of last resort and should not be used as 'enforcement by the back door'. It requires the court to be satisfied that the respondent is in deliberate and continuing contempt resulting in an impediment to justice where there is no other realistic and effective remedy. The order must be proportionate to the problem and go no further than is necessary.

1   *De Gafforj v De Gafforj (Appeal – Hadkinson Order)* [2018] EWCA Civ 2070.

19.44 In *HR v DS*[1] a husband was prevented from proceeding with an appeal (as to a costs order in Family Law Act 1996 proceedings) until he had paid arrears of child maintenance accrued in different (but related) family proceedings. In *Laing v Laing*[2] the husband was required to make good arrears of maintenance before his application to vary could proceed. In *C v C*[3] the court required funds to pay a lump sum to be brought onshore as a condition for an appeal continuing. Eleanor King J made the point that the failure to pay a lump sum can constitute an impediment to justice by leading to numerous applications to the court and costs out of proportion to the issues.

1   *HR v DS* [2019] 2425 (Fam).
2   *Laing v Laing* [2005] EWHC 3152 (Fam).
3   *C v C (Appeal: Hadkinson Order)* [2011] FLR 434.

Adjourning an aspect of financial provision and adjusting subsequent provision in the event of non-compliance with another part of the order

19.45 In *Amin v Amin*[1] Moylan J had awarded a lump sum to the wife and adjourned her application for a pension sharing order, recording that in principle she was entitled to receive 50% of the value of the pension. The case was adjourned to give the husband the opportunity to raise the lump sum by selling assets located abroad. The husband paid nothing. At the restored hearing to consider enforcement of the lump sum and the adjourned issue of the pension sharing order the judge increased the PSO to 76% of the husband's pension, on the wife undertaking not to enforce a financially equivalent part of the lump sum order. This approach was upheld on appeal.

[1]   *Amin v Amin* [2017] EWCA Civ 1114.

Means of payment order

19.46 The court has power[1], usually exercised on its own initiative or on oral application, to order that a periodical payments order or lump sum order by instalments is paid by standing order or direct debit and to require a bank account to be opened for that purpose.

[1]   Under the Maintenance Enforcement Act 1991, s 1 for a debtor ordinarily resident in England and Wales.

Undertakings

19.47 An undertaking to pay money may be enforced as if it was an order, and so applying FPR Pt 33, provided the form of the undertaking as signed accords with the warning notice set out in FPR PD 33A, para 2.2[1].

[1]   FPR PD 33A para 2.1.

Bankruptcy

19.48 After a bankruptcy order is made the bankrupt will no longer have the 'means to pay' and so a committal order under a judgment summons will not be made (or will be set aside if made in absence) unless the debtor's conduct prior to the bankruptcy is sufficient to satisfy the stringent test under s 5 of the Debtors Act 1869[1].

[1]   *Woodley v Woodley (No 2)* [1993] 2 FLR 477, CA.

19.49 Unpaid lump sums and orders for costs are provable in bankruptcy. Any unpaid balance will also survive the bankruptcy and may be enforced after the bankrupt is discharged.

Receivership and freezing injunctions

19.50 The court has the power under s 37(1) of the Senior Courts Act 1981 to appoint a receiver, such as a chartered accountant, to collect in money due to a debtor. The power is used sparingly, in situations of financial complexity, in part due to the expense. The application is governed by FPR 33.22 and CPR Prt 69. An example of an appointment, used to collect outstanding sums under orders for child maintenance, is found in *Maughan v Wilmot*[1] where Mostyn J summarised the applicable law at paras 17–20 of the judgment. Enforcement of periodical payments arrears and/or unpaid lump sum orders may be made against pension assets via receivership, pursuant to the rule in *Blight v Brewster*[2], a first instance decision of Mr Gabriel Moss QC sitting as a deputy High Court judge. The debtor, who held a pension, was ordered to delegate his power of election as to drawing a lump sum from his pension to the creditor's solicitor as a receiver. The solicitor was then authorised to make the election for drawdown of a lump sum from the pension. A third-party debt order then channelled the lump sum directly to the creditor. The method will only work to the extent that the pension assets can be accessed as a lump sum – ie for debtors aged 55 and over. Form D50K should be used to make the application.

1   *Maughan v Wilmot* [2014] EWHC 1288 (Fam).
2   *Blight v Brewster* [2012] EWHC 165 (Ch).

19.51 The court also has power, under s 37(3) of the Senior Courts Act 1981 to grant an injunction freezing certain assets where there are grounds for believing they may be transferred or dissipated to defeat an award. Further details are provided in CHAPTER 8.

Registering a maintenance order in the magistrates' court

19.52 Following the establishment of the unified Family Court in April 2014 the previous procedure under the Maintenance Orders Act 1958 to register a maintenance order in the magistrates' court, whereby responsibility for collection of sums due became that of the justices' administration, has been rendered obsolete.

INTER-RELATIONSHIP OF ENFORCEMENT AND VARIATION

19.53 A periodical payments order may be varied by the court under MCA 1973, s 31, as may the instalments due under a lump sum payable by instalments. A creditor seeking to enforce an order may often be faced with a reactive cross-application to vary the maintenance or instalments.

19.54 An order remains due and enforceable unless and until the court makes a different order. The application for variation will not therefore, unless and until successfully resolved in the payer's favour, absolve him or her from compliance with the original order. The court dealing with enforcement does, however, have power to remit arrears, and must give permission for arrears older than 12 months to be enforced.

19.55 In *Tattershall v Tattershall*[1] the Court of Appeal determined that there is no principle requiring a judge to adjourn an enforcement application pending determination of a variation application, commenting "'the objections to such a principle are obvious. It would enable the process to be too easily manipulated, if not subverted'[2]. The decision as to how to proceed is a case management decision for the judge and whilst there may be some merit in first determining a variation application, the party seeking the variation is expected to progress that application without undue delay.

1   *Tattershall v Tattershall* [2018] EWCA Civ 1978.
2   [2018] EWCA Civ 1978 at para 32.

RECIPROCAL ENFORCEMENT OF CROSS-BORDER ORDERS

19.56 This complicated topic is beyond the scope of this book. The tables in Part 1 of *Family Court Practice* (the Red Book) (C1(1)–C1(15)) provide an excellent starting point.

ENFORCEMENT AGAINST CRYPTO-ASSETS

19.57 The existence of crypto-assets can present practical problems in tracing financial resources and enforcing orders. Tracing companies may be able to track crypto-assets, but enforcement directly against the assets is likely to prove very challenging if the holder is uncooperative. Cost-effective enforcement is likely to focus on other conventional assets held by the debtor, with the D50K process used to obtain information. Committal by way of the judgment summons process or an application for the appointment of a receiver may offer alternative routes.

FUTURE REFORM?

19.58 The Law Commission reported on enforcement of family orders in December 2016, making a series of recommendations in Chapter 21 to simplify and bolster court processes. The government committed in 2018 to taking forward recommendations not requiring primary legislation (ie reforms that can be achieved through changes in court rules and practice directions, court administration and the provision of guidance) but there is no current commitment to introduce reforms requiring primary legislation.

Chapter 20

THE IMPACT OF THE HUMAN RIGHTS ACT 1998

INTRODUCTION

20.1 The Human Rights Act 1998 (HRA 1998) incorporates into English law rights set out in the European Convention on Human Rights (ECHR). Human rights are 'basic rights and freedoms that belong to every person in the world, from birth until death . . . regardless of where you are from, what you believe or how you choose to live your life . . . based on shared values like dignity, fairness, equality, respect and independence'[1]. The ECHR was drafted in 1950 in the aftermath of the atrocities and genocide of the Second World War

[1] The UK Equality and Human Rights Commission definition.

20.2 In the two decades since the HRA 1998 came into force in October 2000 it has permeated every aspect of our legal system, and the law on financial remedies following family breakdown is no exception. In particular, the rights to a fair trial (Art 6), respect for a person's private and family life, home and correspondence (Art 8); the right to freedom of expression (Art 10) and the right to marry and start a family (Art 12) have impacted on practice and procedure in the Family Court.

A VERY BRIEF OVERVIEW OF THE HRA 1998

20.3 Section 1 of the HRA 1998 incorporates 16 articles of the Convention and its protocols into English law. Only the articles and protocols listed at section 1 are incorporated; articles and protocols not listed are specifically excluded. (As an example, Article 5 of Protocol 7, providing for equality of rights and responsibilities of spouses, is therefore not incorporated into English law).

20.4 Section 2 of the HRA 1998 requires English courts to take into account any judgments of the European Court of Human Rights or opinions or decisions of the European Commission of Human Rights. Legislation must, so far as possible, be read and given effect in a way which is compatible with the Convention rights (s 3 HRA 1998). In cases where primary legislation cannot be interpreted in a way compatible with a Convention right, the higher courts (High Court and above) can make a declaration that the legislation is incompatible (s 4 HRA 1998). Such a declaration does not affect the continuing validity of the statute or the outcome of the particular case before the court, but the government may then choose to act to remedy the incompatibility.

20.5 Public authorities, and this includes courts and tribunals, must act in a way which is compatible with the incorporated Convention rights, unless they are prohibited from doing so by primary legislation (s 6 HRA 1998). If a person is a victim of an unlawful act by a public authority, they may rely on the Convention rights in any legal proceedings (HRA 1998, s 7(1)(b)) or bring a separate legal claim against the authority in an appropriate court or tribunal under HRA 1998, s 7(1)(a). Damages may be awarded by a court with a power to award damages in civil proceedings (HRA 1998, s 8).

20.6 At the risk of stating the obvious, the European Commission on Human Rights and its European Court of Human Rights are part of a completely different legal system from the European Union (EU) and its European Court of Justice (ECJ). For the time being at least, UK membership of the Convention and its court are unaffected by Brexit. The Convention and its court are part of the Council of Europe, which has 47 member states, including Russia, Turkey and the UK. The Political Declaration agreed in October 2019 as part of the UK's withdrawal from the European Union records that the UK will continue to respect the framework of the Convention as part of a wider ongoing commitment on both sides to human rights, democratic principles and the rule of law[1].

[1]   Paragraphs 6 and 7 of the Political Declaration Setting out the Framework for the Future Relationship between the EU and the UK, 19 October 2019.

THE EFFECT OF THE HRA 1998 IN PRACTICE: SOME HIGHLIGHTS

20.7 In the determination of civil rights and obligations (as well as criminal charges) 'everyone is entitled to a fair and public hearing within a reasonable time by an independent and impartial tribunal established by law. Judgment shall be pronounced publicly but the press and public may be excluded from all or part of the trial . . . where the interests of juveniles or the private life of the parties so require, or to the extent strictly necessary in the opinion of the court in special circumstances where publicity would prejudice the interests of justice' (Art 6).

20.8 The right to a fair trial is absolute, in that it cannot be balanced against the rights of other individuals or the public interest[1]. The only balancing permitted concerns what constitutes a fair trial and any limitations must satisfy the test of proportionality. The constituent elements of the right include assistance with interpretation if required, time to prepare a case, access to legal advice of a person's own choosing (with public funding 'when the interests of justice so require') and the right to call witnesses and cross examine.

[1]   Although strictly speaking Art 6 is a limited right – the government is entitled to derogate from the right in a time of war or national emergency.

20.9 Whilst the right to a fair trial is an absolute right, other rights are 'qualified' including those under Arts 8 (respect for private and family life) and

10 (freedom of expression). Qualified rights may need to be balanced against other people's rights, to achieve a fair and proportionate outcome. A public authority may interfere with a qualified right if it is a necessary and proportionate way of achieving a legitimate aim.

20.10 The judgment summons enforcement procedure under the Debtors Act 1969 provided an early example of the changes to existing domestic law wrought by the HRA 1998. *Mubarak v Mubarak (No 1)*[1] established that a debtor facing enforcement proceedings in which he is at risk of imprisonment is entitled to the protections of a quasi-criminal procedure. The burden of proving deliberate disobedience to a court order is on the applicant for committal, the debtor is not a compellable witness and must be warned by the judge of his right to silence and arrangements must be made for the debtor to obtain legal advice if he wishes to do so. *Iqbal v Iqbal*[2] provides a more recent example of wholesale failures by the court to accord a husband a fair quasi-criminal process and a reasoned judgment in enforcement hearings.

[1]   *Mubarak v Mubarak (No 1)* [2001] 1 FLR 698, CA.
[2]   *Iqbal v Iqbal* [2017] EWCA Civ 19.

20.11 The right to a 'public hearing' does not necessarily require the court to sit in public[1]. Indeed FPR 27.10 creates a starting point that family proceedings (other than before the Court of Appeal) will usually be heard in private. However, 'duly accredited representatives' of the press and legal bloggers are entitled to attend even private hearings[2], although the court may impose restrictions on what they can report after balancing the right to respect for private life and family life (Art 8) against the right to freedom of expression (Art 10). Judges are encouraged to publish anonymised judgments in cases where they have sat in private. Lykiardopulo v Lykiardopulo[3] provides an example of the court deciding to publish a judgment without anonymisation in proceedings where the husband had conspired to present a perjured case and hide assets, although the court recognised that un-anonymised publication was the exception in financial relief proceedings, where private information is required to be disclosed under compulsion.

[1]   *B v UK; P v UK* [2001] 2 FCR 221, ECtHR.
[2]   FPR 27.11(2)(f) and PD36J.
[3]   *Lykiardopulo v Lykiardopulo* [2010] EWCA Civ 1315.

20.12 The right to a fair trial under Art 6 does not extend to the state providing free legal advice or free interpretation services for the impecunious in financial remedy claims, but an application for an adjournment to permit a party to obtain such assistance must be considered by the court in the light of Art 6. If there really is no alternative for a party struggling to communicate with the court, then a judge may be persuaded that the duties imposed on the court by the HRA 1998 necessitate HMCTS arranging an interpreter. Allowances for a financially weaker party's costs to be funded by the stronger party (under MCA 1973, s 22ZA) also raise issues of Art 6 rights, as expressed in the overriding objective where justice includes 'ensuring that the parties are on an equal footing'[1].

[1]   FPR 1.1(2)(c).

20.13 The Art 8 right to respect for private and family life, home and correspondence has also fed into significant changes in English legal practice since 2000. The old *'Hildebrand'*[1] approach whereby spouses sometimes pre-empted disclosure by helping themselves to documents they 'stumbled across' in briefcases and filing cabinets has been firmly laid to rest by the Court of Appeal in *Imerman v Tchenguiz and Others*[2]. Confidentiality can exist between spouses and the way parties live their lives is relevant in determining the fact-specific question of whether a document carries a reasonable expectation of privacy. Confidentiality is not dependent upon documents having been locked away. Communications concerned with an individual's private life, personal finances and business dealings are often confidential and it is a breach of confidence (actionable as a tort) for one spouse, without the other's consent, to examine or to take copies of documents whose contents are (or ought to have been) appreciated by that spouse to be confidential to the other party[3]. Any information obtained in contravention of these principles must immediately be returned to the owner and no copies may be retained by the client or their legal advisers (whether hard copies or soft). The spouse who has read the documents may, however, rely on their memory of what they have read (other than privileged material) for a number of potential purposes: to seek specific disclosure; to challenge the other party's stated case; to apply for freezing or search orders; to apply for an order that the documents are retained (unread) by solicitors or released to independent counsel to advise the parties and the court on their relevance and admissibility[4].

[1] *Hildebrand v Hildebrand* [1992] 1 FLR 244.
[2] *Imerman v Tchenguiz and Others* [2010] EWCA Civ 908.
[3] [2010] EWCA Civ 908 at para 69.
[4] *UL v BK (Freezing Orders: Safeguards: Standard Examples)* [2013] EWHC 1735 (Fam).

20.14 The court has a broad discretion (as stated in FPR 22.1) to exclude or allow into evidence confidential information and documents obtained improperly. This will require a balancing exercise between competing rights under the EHCR: the constituent rights of what constitutes a fair trial against the rights of privacy and confidentiality. In *Arbili v Arbili*[1] the husband showed a lack of candour in explaining how he had obtained information, which was anyway of limited relevance. The wife had been cooperative in providing corroborated updating disclosure. The balance in that case, including considerations of delay and cost, fell against allowing reliance on the information obtained in breach of confidentiality. In *Lifely v Lifely*[2] (a farming inheritance appeal from the Chancery Division) the balance fell the other way: the court permitted reliance on highly private but also highly relevant material (a diary) obtained in questionable circumstances.

[1] *Arbili v Arbili* [2015] EWCA Civ 542.
[2] *Lifely v Lifely* [2008] EWCA Civ 904.

20.15 Disclosure of evidence from third parties also raises issues of respect for private and family life, home and correspondence. In *M v M (Third Party: Subpoena: Financial Conduct)*[1] the court approved a limited set of enquiries of the husband's girlfriend, including partially redacted bank statements but excluding the estate accounts of her late father, on the grounds that Art 8 required disclosure to be limited to that which was necessary and proportionate. FPR 21.2 now sets out the test: an order for non-party disclosure may only be made where it is necessary to dispose fairly of the proceedings or to save costs.

[1]   *M v M (Third Party: Subpoena: Financial Conduct)* [2006] EWHC 2250 (Fam).

20.16 A very practical example of human rights law enhancing legal remedies in practice in a family case comes from *McCann v UK*[1]. It had long been recognised as problematic that a joint tenant unilaterally serving a notice to quit on a council or social landlord would terminate the other spouse's occupancy and potentially lose the valuable resource of a secure tenancy, without redress. In *McCann* the European Court of Human Rights ruled that the absence of any right for the husband to have the proportionality of the tenancy surrender reviewed by an independent court or tribunal amounted to a violation of his Art 8 rights.

[1]   *McCann v UK* [2008] 2 FLR 899, ECtHR.

Chapter 21

THE PROCEEDS OF CRIME ACT 2002, MONEY LAUNDERING AND CRIMINAL PROPERTY

INTRODUCTION

21.1 The Proceeds of Crime Act 2002 (POCA 2002) sets out a statutory scheme for the recovery of criminal assets. The intention behind the legislation is to deny criminals the use of their assets, to recover the proceeds of crime and to disrupt and deter criminal behaviour. While a trial is pending, the Crown Court may freeze property suspected to be the proceeds of crime, by making a restraint order. On sentencing in the Crown Court, the judge may make a confiscation order if the defendant is found (on a balance of probabilities) to have a 'criminal lifestyle' and to have benefitted from his 'general criminal conduct' or alternatively has benefitted from his 'particular criminal conduct'. Where a conviction has not been possible (perhaps because the potential defendant is abroad) a civil recovery application may be made to the High Court by, for example, the Director of Public Prosecutions or the Director of the National Crime Agency (NCA). The NCA also has the power to undertake tax investigations and raise a tax demand where there is a reasonable suspicion that a person has accrued income or gains thorough criminal activity..

21.2 What does this have to do with the family lawyer and applications for financial relief in the Family Court? There are three main reasons why a financial remedies lawyer should have some knowledge of POCA:

(i)   POCA 2002 imposed anti-money laundering obligations on the legal profession, and the 'customer due diligence' obligations are now applied to family lawyers by the amended Money Laundering, Terrorist Financing and Transfer of Funds (Information on the Payer) Regulations 2017[1] (Money Laundering Regulations 2017).

(ii)   There was concern, when POCA 2002 was first introduced, that family lawyers were at significant risk of committing criminal offences under the Act by facilitating the retention or transfer of criminal property, for example if some of a family's money may have stemmed from tax evasion or other criminal activities. Reports to the NCA by family lawyers were made frequently from the coming into force of POCA 2002 until the concerns were largely laid to rest by the Court of Appeal in *Bowman v Fels*[2]. However, in cases of tax evasion, the court itself may authorise information being passed to the tax authorities

(iii) What of the situation whereby confiscation orders, civil recovery orders or tax demands may deplete (or have already depleted) the resources in the matrimonial pot? Should the Family Court proceedings or the POCA 2002 proceedings have priority? How can the 'innocent' spouse best protect an appropriate share of the matrimonial assets or any assets in their own name that may have the status of a 'tainted gift'[3].

[1] SI 2017/692.
[2] [2005] EWCA Civ 226.
[3] POCA 2002, s 77.

ANTI-MONEY LAUNDERING REGULATIONS

21.3 The Money Laundering Regulations introduced and subsequently amended since 2003 define the professionals subject to the full regulatory regime by work type rather than professional status. Conveyancers were fully regulated from the beginning, but family lawyers, as litigators, initially were not. Many mixed solicitors' firms applied the same regime to all departments for checking client identities and monitoring the movement of funds, but specialist family law firms or departments previously had the option of exempting themselves from full compliance.

21.4 Since January 2020, this has changed, with the introduction of the Money Laundering and Terrorist Financing (Amendment) Regulations 2019[1], amending the Money Laundering Regulations 2017[2]. Whilst litigators remain outside the definition of 'independent legal professional' in reg 12, family solicitors are now almost certainly caught by the expanded definition of 'tax adviser' within reg 11. Formerly limited to those who provided direct advice on taxation issues, the category is now expanded to add those who provide aid or assistance in connection with tax affairs including through a third party. Merely referring a client to an HMRC website with an explanation of why it might be of specific interest, referring a client to an accountant for tax advice to assist the resolution of proceedings, or providing tailored information and assistance about the tax consequences of separation are now sufficient to fall within the definition of 'tax adviser' (notwithstanding anything excluding responsibility for tax advice in the terms of business document) and thus to bring the family lawyer fully within the class of professionals subject to the regulations.

[1] SI 2019/1511.
[2] SI 2017/692.

21.5 Regulated solicitors must apply to the Solicitors Regulation Authority to be recorded as a firm subject to the Money Laundering Regulations 2017. A Money Laundering Reporting Officer must be appointed. Full 'customer due diligence' checks are required to establish the identity of the client and the purpose and intended nature of the instructions. Obligations on barristers, who do not hold client money and often receive instructions via another supervised professional, have traditionally been lighter, but at the time of writing the Bar Council are working to update their guidance. An explanation of the steps required to comply with the money laundering regulations is beyond the scope of this book, but the Legal Sector Affinity Group publish and update detailed guidance, approved by HM Treasury[1].

[1]   Legal Sector Affinity Group Anti-Money Laundering Guidance for the Legal Sector 2021.

CRIMINAL OFFENCES UNDER POCA 2002 AND REPORTING TO THE NATIONAL CRIME AGENCY AND HMRC

21.6 The investigation of a family's finances at the end of a marriage can reveal assets tainted by unlawful acquisition. At the top end of this scale, the whole of a family's wealth may be built on drug crime or large-scale fraud. At the bottom end, some money may have reached the family as undeclared cash received outside the accounts of a small business or sole trader, or the company credit card may have been used for some personal spending.

Tax fraud and disclosure to HMRC

21.7 It is a fundamental tenet of financial remedy litigation that full and frank disclosure, to the court and to the other party, is required on an on-going basis. The proceedings are usually heard in private and FPR 29.12 protects the confidentiality of documents produced under the compulsion of the duty of disclosure. The permission of the court is required to disclose documents to third parties, including HMRC. In *S v S*[1] the wife's brother had sent a copy of the court's judgment, inferring tax evasion by the husband, to the Revenue. In *A v A; B v B*[2] Charles J considered whether to send papers himself from the case to HMRC. In *The Commissioners for HM Revenue and Customs v Charman*[3], HMRC applied for documents to be disclosed. In *Bloom v Bloom*[4] the wife applied for judgments including findings against the husband of serious fraud to be disclosed to the tax authorities. In all these cases, the court had to balance two competing public interests: the interest of encouraging full and frank disclosure in family litigation and the interest of encouraging financial propriety and the proper payment of tax. In *S v S*, *A v A; B v B* and *Charman* the balance fell in favour of not ordering disclosure of the case papers outside the proceedings. Absent a clear finding of tax evasion or serious criminal conduct, the court is unlikely to make or sanction disclosure, bearing in mind the starting point of confidentiality and the public interest in avoiding a system where full disclosure is disincentivised by the real risk of onward transmission to the tax authorities. *Bloom* however stands as an example of the court authorising disclosure to the tax authorities following findings against the husband of calculated, grave and repeated financial crimes.

[1]   *S v S (Inland Revenue: Tax Evasion)* [1997] 2 FLR 774 per Wilson J.
[2]   *A v A; B v B* [2000] 1 FLR 701.
[3]   *The Commissioners for HM Revenue and Customs v Charman* [2012] EWHC 1448 (Fam) per Coleridge J.
[4]   *Bloom v Bloom* [2018] EWFC B10, Mr Recorder Cusworth QC.

21.8 In cases where tax fraud is identified, lawyers should inform the client of the option to make an approach to HMRC to admit the irregularity and come to an arrangement to pay what is due and avoid prosecution, under the Hansard procedure[1].

[1] The revised statement of policy made in response to a Parliamentary Question on 7 November 2002.

Criminal offences under POCA 2002

21.9 POCA 2002 created a number of criminal offences. In the early years after the Act came into force there was real concern among family lawyers that they may be held criminally liable in cases where they advised a family whose assets were in part derived from tax evasion or other crimes. POCA 2002, s 328 makes it a criminal offence to assist someone to acquire, retain, use or control criminal property. Section 330 creates the offence of failing to disclose a known or suspected money laundering offence. 'Tipping off' a client by informing them of disclosure of suspected offences to the authorities is also an offence (s 333A). Following the coming into force of the sections creating these (and other) offences in February 2003 there were numerous reports from the profession to the NCA and delays as litigators awaited consent to proceed from the NCA, unable to tell their client what the problem was. How could legal professional protect themselves from committing a crime under the Act whilst also complying with their duties to their clients, including the duty to respect legal professional privilege?

21.10 The 2005 decision of the Court of Appeal in *Bowman v Fels*[1] confirmed that s 328 of POCA 2002 was not intended to cover or affect the ordinary course of litigation by legal professionals. Any step taken in litigation, from the issuing of proceedings through interlocutory decisions to final judgment, would not fall within the concept of involvement in an arrangement to 'facilitate the acquisition, retention, use or control of criminal property'. The court also took the view that the obligations imposed by s 328 should not be interpreted as meaning legal professional privilege is to be overridden or that a lawyer is to breach his duties to his client and the court not to disclose documents received in confidential litigation. Additionally, POCA 2002, s 328 does not extend to the negotiating of a settlement 'in a litigious context'. Arbitration and mediation of disputes, as well as the ordinary negotiation of consent orders, are covered by the protection afforded by *Bowman v Fels*, provided the settlement is conducted within a context of existing or contemplated legal proceedings and the negotiation, arbitration or litigation is not a mere pretext for the acquisition or retention of criminal property.

[1] [2005] EWCA Civ 226.

21.11 Section 330 POCA 2002 creates an offence for a person within the MLR regulated sector (now including most solicitors engaged in family law – see **21.4** above) of failing to disclose that another person is engaged in money laundering. The duty to disclose arises not merely when the regulated lawyer actually knows or suspects the offence, but also where they have reasonable grounds for knowing or suspecting. However, s 330(6) provides a statutory defence to the offence of failing to report. Where the information comes to a legal adviser in 'privileged circumstances', no offence is committed by the failure to disclose. 'Privileged circumstances' means information communicated by a client in connection with the giving or seeking of legal advice or in connection with actual or contemplated legal proceedings.

CRIMINAL PROPERTY

21.12 Where assets result from criminal activity, the Crown Court may make restraint or confiscation orders against money or property in the defendant's possession or against tainted gifts made to third parties. Civil recovery orders and NCA tax demands may also deplete the assets available within matrimonial financial proceedings. Where such orders under POCA are made or contemplated, what is the inter-relationship with financial remedy proceedings? Criminals and drug dealers and their spouses are subject to the Matrimonial Causes Act 1973, just as other families, yet there are public policy arguments in favour of criminal proceeds being restored to the victims of crime rather than distributed to the families of offenders. Where there are competing claims to assets between a spouse and the state, who should prevail?

21.13 The jurisdiction to make restraint and confiscation orders under POCA 2002 is reserved to the Crown Court, whereas financial remedy proceedings will take place in the Family Court. Two sets of court proceedings may run alongside each other, and the question also arises: which should go first?

21.14 There are no hard and fast rules to either of the questions posed above. As so often in family law, the answer is: it depends on the circumstances. Important factors in the determination will be the extent to which the spouse was complicit in the criminal activities or had knowledge of the criminal enterprise, and the extent to which the asset was funded with criminal proceeds.

21.15 Where it is clear that a spouse was not involved in criminality and there are assets for distribution untainted by crime, it may be that the MCA 1973 proceedings will take place first, and only once the spouse's needs and entitlement to a fair settlement have been met will the remaining assets be considered for confiscation. In *Webber v Webber*[1] the Crown had conceded that the wife was entitled to 50% of a joint property. Sir Mark Potter P concluded that the pre-POCA approach, where a single High Court judge would consider both sets of proceedings together, could no longer apply given the exclusive jurisdiction of the Crown Court over confiscation and restraint orders. Potter P made arrangements for the financial relief application to be considered first, with the Crown Court judge then able to assess whether the amount available for confiscation was the half share conceded by the Crown or a different figure further to the decision in the family proceedings.

[1]   *Webber v Webber* [2006] EWHC 2893 (Fam).

21.16 In cases where the matrimonial assets substantially comprise tainted assets, the confiscation order proceedings are likely to take place first in time. The 'innocent' spouse is then left to apply to the Crown Court for a determination under s 10A POCA 2002 as to the spouse's interest in the assets considered for confiscation. For example, if a couple own a property as joint owners and it was not purchased using criminal funds, the Crown Court judge may declare that the spouse has a 50% interest in the asset, enabling that share to be ring-fenced from the confiscation order. The determination will be limited to a relatively straightforward assessment of the property ownership, and will not be used to investigate more complicated assertions of beneficial interests under trust principles or the type of needs and contribution arguments often used in the Family Court to adjust property shares.

21.17 Where a confiscation order has been made but not complied with, enforcement proceedings may be taken under POCA 2002, including an application to the Crown Court for an enforcement receiver to be appointed under s 50. A reasonable opportunity must be provided for any person holding an interest in property subject to seizure, to make representations to the court[1]. This provides an opportunity for a co-owning spouse to argue that the receiver should not sell property transferred to the spouse in consequence of a financial relief order.

[1] POCA 2002, s 51(8).

21.18 In *Gibson v Revenue & Customs*[1], a confiscation order was made against the husband, attributing the entire equity of the family home to him. Mrs Gibson contested this in the enforcement proceedings. On appeal, the wife was permitted to retain her half share of the property which had been bought in joint names and where the prosecution had conceded that the joint purchase had taken place before the proceeds of crime were used to pay the mortgage. The wife was not seeking any transfer in her favour, but only to retain an asset to which she was already entitled. She had not been convicted of any offence and no confiscation order had been made against her.

[1] *Gibson v Revenue & Customs* [2008] EWCA Civ 645.

21.19 In *Stodgell v Stodgell*[1] it was common ground that the wife was not implicated in the husband's substantial tax fraud. He was convicted of offences and a confiscation order made, which was not paid. The Court of Appeal held that 'while non-complicity in the crime is a necessary condition for the wife to succeed in a [financial] relief claim as a matter of discretion where she is in competition with a confiscation order, such non-complicity is not a sufficient condition'. In financial relief proceedings the court refused to exercise the matrimonial discretion in the wife's favour, to award her a lump sum. Her application was adjourned to be considered only once the confiscation order had been discharged in full. The confiscation order prevailed, on the basis that, if the husband had paid his taxes, the amount available for distribution to the spouses would have been nil.

[1] *Stodgell v Stodgell* [2009] EWCA Civ 243.

21.20 Just as a spouse may seek to intervene in confiscation or enforcement proceedings under ss 10A or 51(8), so the CPS may seek to intervene in financial relief proceedings to ensure that assets are not distributed in the family proceedings if they ought to be available for confiscation. Where a restraint order is in place in Crown Court proceedings, the Family Court is obliged to hear representations from the CPS before any orders are made concerning the subject matter of the restraint order[1].

[1] POCA 2002, s 58.

21.21 Transfers to third parties, including a spouse, that act to defeat a confiscation order can be set aside. In *Re B (Confiscation Order)*[1] the husband's transfer of his half share in the matrimonial home, made shortly before his guilty plea to tax fraud and the making of a confiscation order, was set aside on the application of HMRC. Although the transfer was made on advice in an attempt to put the family finances on an even keel and not with the intention of evading a confiscation order, it had the status of a tainted gift (no consideration had been paid) and was set aside in the Administrative Court.

[1] *Re B (Confiscation Order)* [2008] EWHC 690 (Admin) per Cranston J.

21.22 If the CPS seeks to use documents created or disclosed in family proceedings within criminal proceedings, an application to the Family Court will be required, presumably to be determined by balancing the competing policy considerations, just as in the examples relating to disclosure to the tax authorities in **21.7** above. If a party seeks disclosure of a witness statement from confiscation proceedings into the family proceedings, the consent of the Crown Court judge or of the author of the statement needs to be obtained under Criminal Procedure Rule 33.8, unless the statement has been put in evidence at a hearing held in public.

Chapter 22

NON-COURT DISPUTE RESOLUTION, ARBITRATION AND 'PRIVATE FDRS'

INTRODUCTION

22.1 At every stage in the proceedings, there is a positive duty on the court to consider whether non-court dispute resolution is appropriate[1].There are many practical incentives for the parties to consider alternatives to the full court process. The courts are very busy and the existing backlog of cases has been exacerbated by the effects of the pandemic. Most practitioners will have some experience of waiting many months for a listing, only to find it vacated at short notice, even the day before, due to judicial unavailability. Non-court dispute resolution allows the parties themselves to choose the process, its timetable, and the identity of their mediator, arbitrator or neutral evaluator (not 'private judge': the use of this term is discouraged[2]). Although the parties themselves must pay for this individual's time and the venue or platform for the process, this may save costs in the long-run, as the quicker process will avoid both the need for updating documentation and the tendency for correspondence and ancillary disputes to fill the weeks spent waiting for a hearing. Privacy can be assured: there is no risk of a hearing in public or (for the more well-known) being spotted in a court waiting room or entering the building.

[1]　FPR 3.3.
[2]　A judge in the context of the legal system is appointed publicly by HM The Queen and takes oaths of office. There can be no such individual as a 'private judge'.

MEDIATION

22.2 All those intending to apply to the court for a financial remedy[1] must file a form FM1 with their application, either confirming attendance at a Mediation Information and Assessment Meeting (MIAM) or claiming an exemption from the requirement to attend. The list of exemptions can be found at FPR 3.8.

[1]　Defined in FPR PD 3A, para 13.

22.3 A MIAM is conducted by an authorised family mediator. The mediator must provide information about the principles, process and different models of mediation and other forms of non-court dispute-resolution and assess the suitability of mediation as a means of resolving the dispute. Risks of domestic abuse and harm must also be assessed. If there has been no MIAM attendance

311

and the court is not satisfied that a MIAM exemption has been validly claimed, the judge may direct the parties to attend a MIAM, adjourning the proceedings for this to take place[1].

1   FPR 3.9 and 3.10.

22.4 Whilst MIAM attendance is compulsory (subject to exemption), mediation itself is a voluntary process. The mediator does not decide the dispute: they act as an impartial enabler, facilitating the parties to reach their own decisions. The mediator cannot advise, but will use their experience to keep the discussion focussed and realistic and ensure access to the necessary information. Mediation usually happens as a series of meetings with the parties and mediator(s) in the same room, but the mediator(s) can shuttle between participants in different rooms if required. Decisions reached in mediation are recorded in a memorandum of understanding (MoU). The MoU is a confidential and non-binding record of the mediation process. Once advice has been taken, the MoU (or any varied or subsequent version of the agreement, following advice) can be converted into a consent order for approval by the court. Mediation is a confidential process (subject to any overriding legal obligations to report concerns as to illegal acts or safeguarding issues) and the discussions or MoU will not be referred to in evidence in any court proceedings, unless both parties agree to waive this privilege

22.5 Legal aid is available for mediation, subject to means. By empowering the parties to make and 'buy into' their own decisions it can provide a comparatively swift, cost-effective and durable method of achieving a workable settlement. 'All Issues' mediation can enable decision-making in the round as to arrangements for children and marital assets. However, in higher-conflict cases, those involving abuse, cases where the issues are more complicated or where full and frank disclosure cannot be assured, mediation may not be suitable.

22.6 The Family Mediation Council maintains a register of family mediators and a Code of Practice, with an accreditation and complaints process maintained by the Family Mediation Standards Board.

COLLABORATIVE LAW

22.7 Collaborative law involves specially trained lawyers throughout the process. Each party attends a series of four-way meetings with their lawyer and the collaborative lawyer acting for the other spouse, designed to resolve issues out of court. Other professionals can be called in to assist, such as financial or pensions experts, or consultants with a therapeutic background. The provision of bespoke advice to each party is therefore an integral part of the procedure. Crucially, the parties and their lawyers agree to an exclusively out-of-court process, without an underlying threat of litigation: if the collaboration does not resolve all issues, other lawyers will step in to take the case to court or arbitration. In the four-way settlement meetings information is shared, proposals are offered and alternatives are evaluated, all with the benefit of advice. As with mediation, collaborative law provides the parties with a high degree of control over the process and the outcome, but it is not suitable for everyone. An agreement is likely to be recorded in a consent order for submission to the court.

ARBITRATION

22.8 Arbitration is a quasi-adversarial process, built upon a fundamental agreement to arbitrate as an alternative to court proceedings. The parties to the dispute select an arbitrator for the specific expertise and experience he or she will bring. The spouses and arbitrator will choose the process and timescale to resolve the dispute. The arbitrator can make case management decisions, appoint experts and determine interim awards. Some arbitrations involve oral evidence from witnesses, some are considered on a combination of written evidence and written and oral submissions and others are determined solely on paper. All will result in a detailed written decision with reasons, which is binding on the parties (unless successfully overturned: see **22.13–22.16** below).

22.9 Arbitration has a long pedigree in resolving commercial disputes and is governed by the Arbitration Act 1996. Since 2012, the Institute of Family Law Arbitrators (IFLA) has proffered its financial arbitration scheme (followed in 2016 by a further scheme for resolving disputes about children). The parties enter into a formal contract to arbitrate in Form ARB1FS. It is a mandatory requirement of the IFLA rules that the arbitrator will decide the substance of the dispute only in accordance with the laws of England and Wales. Dual qualified arbitrators can determine disputes as to both children and finances, either sequentially or at one composite hearing. Once considered the preserve of the wealthy, seeking privacy and able to afford a private process, it is now 'widely anticipated that parties in modest asset cases (including litigants in person) will increasingly use the arbitration process . . . as the courts cope with a backlog of cases'[1].

[1]   Per King LJ in *Haley v Haley* [2020] EWCA Civ 1369 at para 5. Mr and Mrs Haley were a case in point: a modest-asset family who turned to arbitration when their two-day listing in September 2019 for a final hearing before the District Bench was vacated with one week's notice due to 'judicial unavailability'.

22.10 The use of arbitration as an alternative to a court adjudication has received the enthusiastic backing of the senior judiciary. In *S v S (Financial Remedies: Arbitral Award)*[1] Sir James Munby P approved a consent order submitted to the court following an arbitration conducted under the IFLA scheme, commenting: 'where the consent order . . . is founded on an arbitral award under the IFLA Scheme or something similar (and the judge will, of course, need to check that the order does indeed give effect to the arbitral award and is workable) the judge's role will be simple. The judge will not need to play the detective unless something leaps off the page to indicate that something has gone so seriously wrong in the arbitral process as fundamentally to vitiate the arbitral award. Although recognising that the judge is not a rubber stamp, the combination of (a) the fact that the parties have agreed to be bound by the arbitral award, (b) the fact of the arbitral award (which the judge will of course be able to study) and (c) the fact that the parties are putting the matter before the court by consent, means that it can only be in the rarest of cases that it will be appropriate for the judge to do other than approve the order. With a process as sophisticated as that embodied in the IFLA Scheme it is difficult to contemplate such a case'[2]. On 23 November 2015 the President's *Practice Guidance: Arbitration in the Family Court* was published[3].

[1]   [2014] 1 FLR 1257.
[2]   [2014] 1 FLR 1257 at para 21.
[3]   Although some parts of this guidance now need revisiting further to the CA decision in *Haley v Haley* [2020] EWCA Civ 1369, and redrafted guidance is expected shortly.

22.11 Where court proceedings have already commenced and the parties then agree to arbitrate, the court should be invited to stay the financial remedy proceedings pending delivery of the arbitral award. An application notice with a copy of the signed ARB1FS and a draft consent order to stay the proceedings should be lodged and is likely to be dealt with on the papers[1].

[1]   *Practice Guidance: Arbitration in the Family Court*, 23 November 2015, paras 7-10.

Applying for an order to reflect the award, by consent

22.12 Not every award needs to be brought before the Family Court for an order to be made. The parties may simply decide to operate in accordance with the award with no need for an order to reflect it. However, if the parties desire the certainty of a clean break order, or the availability of enforcement mechanisms or a remedy that can only be granted by the court such as a pension sharing order, then the arbitral award should be drafted into a consent order for submission to the court in the usual way. Forms D81 will be required, and a copy of the signed form ARB1FS and the arbitrator's award should also be lodged. The application will be scrutinised by a judge on the papers in the usual way (checking for fairness and clear and correct drafting) and the court will retain the ability to seek clarification through correspondence or to list a hearing, but the parties can usually expect the settlement to be approved.

Challenge to the arbitrator's award

22.13 What if one (or both) of the parties do not like the arbitrator's decision and seek to challenge the award? What role should the court have in such a challenge? How can a party seeking adherence to the award secure compliance?

22.14 Until the Court of Appeal handed down its decision in *Haley v Haley*[1] in October 2020 it was thought that the court's role in a challenge to an arbitral award was very constrained, being limited to challenges as to jurisdiction or on a point of law, or those based on serious irregularity, mistake or a supervening (*Barder*-type) event. Challenges based on an assertion that the award was 'wrong' or 'unfair' or 'unjust' would therefore almost never get off the ground, prior to October 2020. A challenge to the facts found by the arbitrator was also bound to fail prior to the Court of Appeal's decision in *Haley*, absent a mistake or supervening event.

[1]   [2020] EWCA Civ 1369.

22.15 This line of case law has been overturned by the Court of Appeal in *Haley*. In family proceedings, unlike in civil proceedings, the court has a fundamental role in assessing whether an outcome reached outside the courtroom is 'fair'. The authority for the orders for financial provision comes from the court, not from the agreement of the parties themselves. The parties have agreed to arbitrate, but have not agreed to be bound by any particular outcome in the arbitration. Whilst the fact that the parties have agreed to arbitration is an important factor for the court to weigh, of itself it cannot oust the duty of the court to consider fairness in the round, bearing in mind all the s 25 criteria.

22.16 A party who believes that an arbitral award is wrong, and should not be binding upon them and approved as a consent order, can put their objections to the court through the 'notice to show cause' process. Likewise, a party seeking for the court to make an order reflecting the terms of the arbitral award can also use the same procedure. The court will initially 'triage' the case on paper, similar to the permission to appeal filter in the appellate jurisdiction, before a financial remedy circuit judge or a High Court judge. The test to be applied by the court is the appeals test under the MCA 1973, namely whether the decision is 'wrong' or 'unjust because of a serious procedural or other irregularity'[1]. There should be no gloss applied to the word 'wrong'. It is not necessary for the decision to be 'plainly wrong' or so wrong it 'leaps off the page'. If the court at the paper triage stage 'takes the view that the objection made to the award by one of the parties would not pass the permission to appeal test, it can make an order in the terms of the arbitral award without more ado and penalise the reluctant party in costs'[2]. If the court considers there is a real prospect of the objecting party succeeding in demonstrating that the arbitral award is wrong or unjust, then the matter can be set down for a hearing, confined to a review and without oral evidence or fresh information unless the judge considers that it would be in the interests of justice to hold a re-hearing and/or require evidence[3].

[1] FPR 30.12.
[2] Per King LJ in *Haley* at para 96.
[3] Analogous to FPR 30.12(1)(b) and (2).

22.17 Arbitration can also be used to deal with subsidiary decisions on disputed issues in cases otherwise proceeding through the court system. In *CM v CM*[1] Moor J expressed his dismay at facing cross-applications from the parties to decide the exact wording of a letter of instruction to an expert, where the precise issues on which the expert was to report had already been delineated at the First Appointment. Commenting that High Court judges did not have time to draft letters of instruction, Moor J considered it 'exactly the sort of matter that should be referred to an arbitrator who is accredited by the Institute of Family Law Arbitrators'.

[1] *CM v CM* [2019] EWFC 16.

22.18 Practitioners should also bear in mind the potential role of single issue or even limited multiple issue arbitrations in support of mediation and the collaborative process. If the negotiations have become stuck on one or two issues, a decision from a third-party arbitrator may break the 'log-jam,' allowing the remainder of the case to be resolved on a mediated or collaborative basis.

PRIVATE FDRS

22.19 Early neutral evaluation of the parties' respective cases and an expert indication of the likely range of outcomes is a cornerstone of the court process for financial remedies and takes place at the Financial Dispute Resolution hearing (FDR). Parties who wish to choose their evaluator and have control over the timing of the process, ensuring that sufficient time can be devoted to a thorough consideration in adequate surroundings, now have the option (if they can afford it) to choose a 'private FDR'. In a message dated 24 February 2021 the President of the Family Division, Sir Andrew McFarlane, welcomed the increasing use of private FDRs, noting they appear to have a high rate of success and also free up court time for those cases that require a judicial hearing.

22.20 Retired judges or eminent legal professionals offer their services for a day or half day, plus reading time. In the event that agreement is reached at or soon after the private FDR, a consent order can be submitted to the court for approval in the usual way. If agreement is not reached, the court can be asked to give directions for a final hearing, either by approving agreed directions or by convening a short case-management hearing after the FDR. If a case is already proceeding down the court route when the parties select a private FDR, the court can be applied to, again usually by consent, to vacate any court-listed FDR and list a short directions appointment after the private FDR, to be vacated if it is not in fact required.

Chapter 23
FUTURE DEVELOPMENTS

INTRODUCTION

23.1 Family law is always subject to legislative change, and the purpose of this chapter is to alert the reader to the possible shape of things to come. As has been seen in this book, many of the most important developments over recent years have been judge-made and some might think that the law as it now stands needs a period of consolidation rather than reform. However, the will of Parliament is unpredictable and it is inevitable that there will be some changes, though probably not in ways one could predict.

REFORM OF MCA 1973, SECTION 25

23.2 During the parliamentary passage of the FLA 1996, the then Lord Chancellor announced his intention of considering whether anything could be learned from the Scottish system of ancillary relief with a view to improving the system in England and Wales. This statement aroused little attention, but it became clear that these ideas were being pursued when the then parliamentary secretary in the Lord Chancellor's Department, Mr Geoffrey Hoon, announced, at the annual conference of the Solicitors Family Law Association in 1998 that the government was giving favourable consideration to adopting the Scottish concept of a presumption of equal sharing of matrimonial property (as defined in the Family Law (Scotland) Act 1985), and making pre-nuptial contracts enforceable, subject to various safeguards. This gave rise to some debate, although the only formal consultation which the government carried out was to invite the Lord Chancellor's Advisory Group on Ancillary Relief to comment. In the event, the Advisory Group advised against amendment of s 25 in this way, and no more came of the proposal. As will be seen later, the desire to change has not gone away and it calls for more clarity in the law which has recently been renewed.

23.3 The decisions of the House of Lords in *White v White* and *Miller/McFarlane* (as to which see Chapter 1) do not seem to have stopped the calls for a more predictable and formulaic approach. No doubt conscious of this continuing debate, in *Charman v Charman*[1] the Court of Appeal added a postscript entitled 'Changing the Law'. At the end of a lengthy review of the history, the court identified the new problems which have arisen as follows:

'[116] However a social change that was not perhaps recognised in that decision was the extent to which the origins and the volume of big money cases were shifting.

317

Most of the big money cases pre-*White* involved fortunes created by previous generations. The removal of exchange control restrictions in 1979, a policy that offered a favourable tax regime to very rich foreigners domiciled elsewhere, and a new financial era dominated by hedge-funds, private equity funds, derivative traders and sophisticated off-shore structures meant that very large fortunes were being made very quickly. These socio-economic developments coincided with a retreat from the preference of English judges for moderation. The present case well illustrates that shift. At trial Mr Pointer achieved for his client an award of £48 million. Before us he freely conceded that he could not have justified an award of more than £20 million on the application of the reasonable requirements principle. Thus, in very big money cases, the effect of the decision in *White* was to raise the aspirations of the claimant hugely. In big money cases the *White* factor has more than doubled the levels of award and it has been said by many that London has become the divorce capital of the world for aspiring wives. Whether this is a desirable result needs to be considered not only in the context of our society but also in the context of the European Union of which we are a singular Member State, in the sense that we are a common law jurisdiction amongst largely Civilian fellows and that in the determination of issues ancillary to divorce we apply the lex fori and decline to apply the law more applicable to the parties.

[117] In the case of *Cowan* the need for legislative review in the aftermath of the case of *White* was articulated: see paragraphs 32, 41 and 58. Undoubtedly the decision in *White* did not resolve the problems faced by practitioners in advising clients or by clients in deciding upon what terms to compromise.

[118] However this court adopted a cautious approach both in *Cowan* and in the later case of *Lambert*. In his submission Mr Singleton drew attention to an article by Joanna Miles in International Journal of Law, Policy and the Family 19 (2005) 242. He told us that he had incorporated the article in his argument for Mrs McFarlane in the House of Lords. The article criticises the earlier decision of this court in the conjoined appeals of *McFarlane* and *Parlour* [2005] Fam 171 for having declined the opportunity to identify principles underpinning the exercise of judicial discretion under the Act of 1973. The article is particularly interesting in that it demonstrates that the principles discussed in the article (needs, entitlement and compensation), were subsequently the principles identified by the House of Lords in deciding the conjoined appeals of *Miller* and *McFarlane*.'

¹   [2007] EWCA Civ 503 at para [106] et seq.

23.4 Later, in relation to the European aspects, the court had this to say:

'[124] Any harmonisation within the European region is particularly difficult, given that the Regulation Brussels I is restricted to claims for maintenance and the Regulation Brussels II Revised expressly excludes from its application the property consequence of divorce. In the European context this makes sense because in Civilian systems the property consequences of divorce are dealt with by marital property regimes. Almost uniquely our jurisdiction does not have a marital property regime and it is scarcely appropriate to classify our jurisdiction as having a marital regime of separation of property. More correctly we have no regime, simply accepting that each spouse owns his or her own separate property during the marriage but subject to the court's wide distributive powers in prospect upon a decree of judicial separation, nullity or divorce. The difficulty of harmonising our law concerning the property consequences of marriage and divorce and the law of the Civilian Member States is exacerbated by the fact that our law has so far given little status to pre-nuptial contracts. If, unlike the rest of Europe, the property consequences of divorce are to be regulated by the principles of needs, compensation and sharing, should not the parties to the marriage, or the projected marriage, have at the least the opportunity to order their own affairs otherwise by a nuptial contract? The White Paper, "Supporting Families", not only proposed specific reforms of section 25 but also to give statutory force to nuptial contracts. The government's subsequent abdication has not been accepted by specialist practitioners. In 2005 Resolution published a well argued report urging the government to give statutory force to nuptial contracts. The report was subsequently fully supported by the Money and Property Sub-Committee of the Family Justice Council.'

The significance of the European aspects has of course been reduced now that this country has left the European Union.

23.5 The Court of Appeal recommended research by the Law Commission, and particularly stressed the need to reform the law to include the enforceability of pre-nuptial contracts[1]. The calls to reform the law to make pre-nuptial contracts enforceable as such have become ever more strident and it seems highly likely that this will be a prime candidate for reform, particularly in a period when a higher than ever proportion of marriages are second and subsequent marriages.

[1] Though it has to be said that this would not have achieved very much in *Charman*. When the parties married they had no money and would, no doubt, have agreed equal sharing at that stage.

23.6 So far, no Government has shown signs of wishing to embark on the time-consuming and unpredictable task of family law reform and there are many other issues demanding the attention of any government. The absence of any government intervention was commented on in the judgement of Moylan LJ recently in *XW v XH*[1]. It has fallen to individual members of both houses of Parliament to take the initiative and, in January 2017 Baroness Deech, not for the first time, introduced a private members Bill, the Divorce (Financial Provision) Bill in the House of Lords. This measure has passed its second reading and was in Committee stage before the dissolution of parliament in anticipation of the 2017 general election. It has therefore now died and would have to be renewed in the next parliament. The purpose of the Bill was to bring the law of England and Wales more into line with that of Scotland and to end the 'dependency for life' idea. Baroness Deech is firmly committed to this reform, but her Bill has not been without its critics, notably Lord Wilson, whose experience in these matters is of course unrivalled.

[1] [2019] EWCA Civ 2262.

23.7 Following the close of the consultation on agreements in 2011 (as to which, see **23.9** below) the Law Commission decided to consider two other significant aspects of the financial consequences of divorce and dissolution. (The Government announced that decision in February 2012 as part of its response to the Family Justice Review.)

23.8 These two aspects, which are the subject of a supplementary consultation, are:

(1)   the law relating to financial needs on divorce and dissolution; and
(2)   the legal status of 'non-matrimonial property'.

23.9 The Law Commission reported[1] in due course and its conclusions are well summarised at paras 1.6–1.8 of its report as follows:

'1.6 We think that the objective of independence is the right one. We are therefore not advocating an overall change in the courts' approach. That is in line with the view of most of our consultees, many of whom were very keen not to detract from the courts' discretion.

1.7 However, we do think that action is needed. Although the law is largely well-understood by family lawyers, it is inaccessible to the general public and there is evidence that the courts in different areas of the country do not always apply the law consistently.

1.8 **We recommend** that the meaning of "financial needs" be clarified in guidance published by the Family Justice Council. Clarification will ensure that the term is applied consistently by the courts, reinforcing judicial best practice. It will also give people without legal representation access to a clear statement of their responsibilities and the objective of eventual independence that a financial settlement should strive to achieve.'

[1] LC 343 April 2014.

23.10 At para 1.11 the Law Commission continued as follows:

'1.11 **We recommend** that legislation be enacted to introduce "qualifying nuptial agreements". These would be enforceable contracts, not subject to the scrutiny of the courts, which would enable couples to make contractual arrangements about the financial consequences of divorce or dissolution. In order for an agreement to be a "qualifying" nuptial agreement, certain procedural safeguards would have to be met. Qualifying agreements could not, however, be used to contract out of "financial needs.'

23.11 In April 2014 it was announced that the government had asked the Family Justice Council to publish clarification of the meaning of 'needs'. No mention was made of the Law Commission's recommendations as to legislating regarding pre-nuptial contracts.

ENFORCEMENT

23.12 Changes in the law and practice regarding enforcement of financial remedy orders have been recommended by a Law Commission report[1] on this topic. The report is clear that there is a need for reform; at para 1.4 it records the following:

'Non-compliance with family financial orders is a significant problem. We estimate that on average there are 4,200 enforcement cases in relation to family financial orders each year. Although data on the total amount of money that goes unpaid each year through non-compliance with family financial orders is not routinely collected, we estimate that it is approximately £15 – 20 million. Further, these figures are likely to be an underestimate as they do not account for those individuals who are not receiving what they are owed under a family financial order but who do not take enforcement action. They may not take action due to a lack of understanding of the system, a feeling that they need legal representation that they cannot afford, concerns about their relationship with the debtor, or simply a lack of faith that action will achieve compliance.'

[1] Enforcement of Family Financial Orders (2016) Law Com No 370.

23.13 The report recommends a number of changes, most of which can be achieved by Practice Directions. These reforms may briefly be summarised as follows:

(1)   Judges should be directed to consider whether any terms as to enforcement should be included whenever a family financial order is made.

(2)   Judges should be directed to consider noting for the court file a summary of their main findings in relation to the debtor's assets that may be relevant to future enforcement proceedings.

(3)   An enforcement liaison judge should be appointed in each designated family judge area. The enforcement liaison judge will help to build expertise in enforcement in his or her area and oversee and improve the management of enforcement proceedings, as well as providing training and information to other judges and being a point of contact for judges with enforcement questions. The enforcement liaison judge may also hear any particularly complex enforcement cases.

(4)   Rules should require the debtor to provide financial disclosure before the first hearing. This disclosure would enable the creditor and court to consider appropriate enforcement action at that hearing, make an enforcement order or make any necessary direction. We recommend that disclosure should be provided in a standard form designed for the purposes of enforcement (an 'Enforcement Financial Statement').

(5)   The law should be clarified to ensure that the enforcement methods available on a general enforcement application can be made without the need for the debtor to make a further, specific application for that order.

(6)   In addition to the powers the court already has, the court should be able to make orders disqualifying debtors from driving, prohibiting them from travelling out of the UK and orders against a debtor's pension, on a general enforcement application.

23.14 Some of these recommendations were canvassed and made over 12 years ago in a report of the Lord Chancellor's Advisory Group on Ancillary Relief (as it was then called). Not all those recommendations found their way into the FPR and it is encouraging to see that, however belatedly, they may now have some chance of implementation.

THE FAMILY JUSTICE REVIEW

23.15 The Family Justice Review, which was commenced in 2010, produced its interim report in 2011. Although most of the report is concerned with children's cases the possibility of reform and simplification of the law relating to financial remedies is mentioned, almost in passing. It remains to be seen what changes may be proposed in the final report. Any such changes would of course require primary legislation.

THE EUROPEAN ELEMENT

23.16 Readers will not need reminding that the Government has taken this country out of the European Union. It remains to be seen what will happen to the many regulations, eg as to jurisdiction, which are made by the EU and which currently affect law and practice in England and Wales.

PROCEDURE

23.17 The Financial Remedies Working Party of the Family Justice Council has considered procedural issues and has now reported, as summarised below:

- There should be one unified procedure for all financial remedy applications.
- Standard forms should be rationalised so that there should be only one Form E (Form E1 and E2 should be discontinued).
- Once Form A is issued by one party to a marriage or a civil partnership, all possible applications by both parties are deemed to have been made and may be granted or dismissed by the court without further application.
- The FDR hearing should feature in all cases as a compulsory requirement and that generally no listing for a final hearing should be given until an FDR hearing has taken place.
- The parties should attend the first appointment prepared to treat it as an FDR.
- The pilot accelerated first appointment procedure currently in use at the Central Family Court should be adopted nationwide.
- The costs working party of the FPRC should be invited to give consideration to costs issues, including the issues of fixed price costing and judicial costs capping.
- Litigants in person supported by McKenzie friends have to be weighed up, especially in relation to what they charge and, if they are allowed to speak, the length and the tone of the hearings.
- There should be standard form orders in financial remedy proceedings.
- Recommendations are made in relation to arbitration in family proceedings.

It remains to be seen which, if any, of these proposed reforms will be implemented.

Chapter 24

A SUMMING UP

INTRODUCTION

24.1 Throughout this book, a number of recurring themes have appeared. One of the problems of writing any book of this kind is that the separate chapters on individual topics may appear to the reader to be self-contained, whereas the lessons to be learned from many of them apply across the board and should be borne in mind generally. Nevertheless, it would be irksome for the reader if the same messages were driven home in every chapter.

24.2 For these reasons, it has been thought appropriate to include in this final chapter the principal matters which anyone involved in a financial remedy application should have in mind. First, the generally accepted principles on which the courts decide these matters will be outlined, with accompanying references as to where a longer exposition may be found. Then, some of the practical lessons for the conduct of an application will be considered.

THE PRIMACY OF THE STATUTE

24.3 Applications for a financial remedy are governed by s 25 of MCA 1973, which is a self-contained code which directs the court's attention to certain specified factors. Decided cases are of some assistance, but they can never replace the words of the statute.

24.4 Subject to the 'first consideration' of the welfare of the minor children, no single factor within s 25 is intrinsically more important than the others. All of them must be considered. In most cases, the facts of the case will mean that there is a 'gravitational pull' towards one or more factors which assume particular significance, but this does not mean that all the factors should not be considered. This paragraph should be borne in mind when reading all that now follows. Whatever the importance of cases such as *White v White* and *Miller/McFarlane*, and whatever stress is placed on 'sharing' and 'equality', time and again one is reminded that the speeches in the House were not some form of statutory amendment and that one must begin always with the statute.

THE IMPORTANCE OF FINDING THE FACTS

24.5 Notwithstanding what was said above, no case can proceed without accurate findings under s 25(2)(a). Until the income and capital of each of the parties is ascertained, the court cannot begin to consider whether the assets should be redistributed in accordance with any of the other factors. When determining the facts, the usual rules of evidence apply. The fact that a hearing is in chambers and may seem relatively informal should not deceive a practitioner or litigant into thinking that rules of evidence do not apply nor that the court will make findings of fact on less than the normal civil standard of proof.

24.6 The court will be concerned, where this is relevant, to decide what is and is not 'matrimonial property', ie property acquired during the marriage (or any relevant period of pre-marital cohabitation) which is neither property inherited by either of the parties nor property which they owned well before the marriage or relevant period of cohabitation. However, it must be emphasised that this does not mean that such property is then excluded from the calculations. Generally speaking, the longer the marriage the less inclined a court will be to hive off any particular asset. Moreover, in cases where assets are not sufficient to meet the needs of both parties and one party has a greater need than the other, it is unlikely that this aspect of the matter will be decisive.

NO MATHEMATICAL STARTING POINT

24.7 There is no 'one-third rule' nor any other fractional starting point. When a judge has decided how the assets of the parties should be divided (if at all) in accordance with the s 25 factors, he may cross-check his proposals by considering the proportions of the joint assets which each party would have, but there is no absolute proportion with which either party must be left. The yardstick of equality (see below) is a useful cross-check at the end of the calculation to ensure fairness. However, having said that, it is a reasonable inference from the judgment of the Court of Appeal in *Charman v Charman*[1] and several other recent cases that the concept of 'sharing' derived from *Miller v Miller* implies equal sharing and that this is now considerably more of a starting point than once it was.

[1] [2007] EWCA Civ 503, [2007] All ER (D) 425 (May) at [65]. See also the discussion in CHAPTER 1.

REASONABLE NEEDS AND ABILITY TO PROVIDE

24.8 The reasonable needs as to capital and income of both parties must be considered. These will vary in every case, but will depend on the age and health of the parties in the light of the history of the marriage, and the responsibilities which they both have, particularly to children of the family. How far these needs can be met will depend on the means available.

THE IMPORTANCE OF HOUSING

24.9 The most important requirement for most people is to be housed, and the primary task of the court in average income and capital cases should be to ensure that both are housed. Where there are dependent children, the housing of the parent with the care of the children must come first, even if this means that the other party is not rehoused as he would wish. However, rehousing of a parent with children does not mean that that parent must live in the former matrimonial home. The housing of the other parent is an important priority also, and where a parent and children can be adequately rehoused in cheaper accommodation with a proportion of the proceeds of sale, to enable the other parent to be rehoused, this should be done.

NO REDISTRIBUTION FOR ITS OWN SAKE

24.10 When either or both parties have capital, there is no presumption that it must be redistributed. Redistribution is only appropriate if required to do justice between the parties in the light of the s 25 factors. However, this must be balanced against what is said in the next paragraph.

THE YARDSTICK OF EQUALITY

24.11 When the court has performed its statutory functions of investigating all the s 25 factors, it must first arrive at a provisional and tentative view as to what is required before comparing that provisional view with what the result would be on the basis of equal division. If the provisional view does not approximate to equal division, the court must be able to articulate and express reasons, based on the s 25 criteria, as to why it should not do so. Where there are no such reasons, it must be presumed that fairness means sharing and hence equality should prevail.

SELF-SUFFICIENCY

24.12 The court must have regard to the possibility of self-sufficiency and a clean break in every case. Nevertheless, a clean break should not be imposed where the evidence does not suggest that self-sufficiency will be achieved.

PENSIONS NOT A SEPARATE REGIME

24.13 The only reason for making the following point is the recent date of the legislative changes. Pensions are not a separate form of assets which must be re-allocated according to some discrete code. The extent to which the court will consider pensions relevant, and make orders in respect of them, will depend entirely on the application of the s 25 factors.

SOME PRACTICAL HINTS ON PREPARING A CASE

24.14 Practitioners acting for a party to financial remedy proceedings should bear in mind all that has been said above. Certain practical questions emerge and should be asked in every case and these are set out below. However, one useful first step, once the basic information has been absorbed, is to ask what kind of case it is that is now before you. What seems to be the overriding factor? Is it a case where assets exceed needs or one where needs will exhaust any assets and one party or perhaps both will have to suffer a financial loss? Imagine you are the judge; how will you approach the case?

(a)   What are the assets and incomes of both parties?

(b)   Have the parties made any agreement, whether pre or post- nuptial before the litigation began? If so, what is its significance? Will the court uphold it or is there some vitiating factor?

(c)   What are the needs of the parties? In particular:
   (i)   Where will the parent with care of a child (if any) live?
   (ii)   Where will the other party live?

(d)   What are the income needs of the parties, in particular your client? Be realistic; do not merely compile a wish list. What will it cost him or her to live?

(e)   How can these needs be met? Can your client support himself or herself? Are there other sources of funds?

(f)   What is the position as to pensions?

(g)   Can there be a clean break? Why should there not be a clean break?

(h)   Having considered all the s 25 factors, is there some particular factor which is relevant to this case?

(i)   Finally, what would be the position if there were equal division? Is there some s 25 factor which makes equal division unjust?

APPENDIX
LEGISLATION

MATRIMONIAL CAUSES ACT 1973

A1.1

. . .

PART II

FINANCIAL RELIEF FOR PARTIES TO MARRIAGE AND CHILDREN
OF FAMILY

Financial provision and property adjustment orders

21 Financial provision and property adjustment orders

(1) The financial provision orders for the purposes of this Act are the orders for periodical or lump sum provision available (subject to the provisions of this Act) under section 23 below for the purpose of adjusting the financial position of the parties to a marriage and any children of the family in connection with proceedings for divorce, nullity of marriage or judicial separation and under section 27(6) below on proof of neglect by one party to a marriage to provide, or to make a proper contribution towards, reasonable maintenance for the other or a child of the family, that is to say—

<ul style="list-style:none">
<li>(a) any order for periodical payments in favour of a party to a marriage under section 23(1)(a) or 27(6)(a) or in favour of a child of the family under section 23(1)(d), (2) or (4) or 27(6)(d);</li>
<li>(b) any order for secured periodical payments in favour of a party to a marriage under section 23(1)(b) or 27(6)(b) or in favour of a child of the family under section 23(1)(e), (2) or (4) or 27(6)(e); and</li>
<li>(c) any order for lump sum provision in favour of a party to a marriage under section 23(1)(c) or 27(6)(c) or in favour of a child of the family under section 23(1)(f), (2) or (4) or 27(6)(f);</li>
</ul>

and references in this Act (except in paragraphs 17(1) and 23 of Schedule 1 below) to periodical payments orders, secured periodical payments orders, and orders for the payment of a lump sum are references to all or some of the financial provision orders requiring the sort of financial provision in question according as the context of each reference may require.

(2) The property adjustment orders for the purposes of this Act are the orders dealing with property rights available (subject to the provisions of this Act) under section 24 below for the purpose of adjusting the financial position of the parties to a marriage and any children of the family on or after the grant of a decree of divorce, nullity of marriage or judicial separation, that is to say—

<ul style="list-style:none">
<li>(a) any order under subsection (1)(a) of that section for a transfer of property;</li>
<li>(b) any order under subsection (1)(b) of that section for a settlement of property; and</li>
</ul>

    (c)   any order under subsection (1)(c) or (d) of that section for a variation of settlement.

[21A Pension sharing orders]

[(1) For the purposes of this Act, a pension sharing order is an order which—

    (a)   provides that one party's—

        (i)   shareable rights under a specified pension arrangement, or

        (ii)   shareable state scheme rights,

be subject to pension sharing for the benefit of the other party, and

    (b)   specifies the percentage value to be transferred.

(2) In subsection (1) above—

    (a)   the reference to shareable rights under a pension arrangement is to rights in relation to which pension sharing is available under Chapter I of Part IV of the Welfare Reform and Pensions Act 1999, or under corresponding Northern Ireland legislation,

    (b)   the reference to shareable state scheme rights is to rights in relation to which pension sharing is available under Chapter II of Part IV of the Welfare Reform and Pensions Act 1999, or under corresponding Northern Ireland legislation, and

    (c)   "party" means a party to a marriage.]

NOTES

Amendment
    Inserted by the Welfare Reform and Pensions Act 1999, s 19, Sch 3, paras 1, 2.
        Date in force: 1 December 2000: see SI 2000/1116, art 2(e).

[21B Pension compensation sharing orders]

[(1) For the purposes of this Act, a pension compensation sharing order is an order which—

    (a)   provides that one party's shareable rights to PPF compensation that derive from rights under a specified pension scheme are to be subject to pension compensation sharing for the benefit of the other party, and

    (b)   specifies the percentage value to be transferred.

(2) In subsection (1)—

    (a)   the reference to shareable rights to PPF compensation is to rights in relation to which pension compensation sharing is available under Chapter 1 of Part 3 of the Pensions Act 2008 or under corresponding Northern Ireland legislation;

    (b)   "party" means a party to a marriage;

    (c)   "specified" means specified in the order.]

NOTES

Amendment
    Inserted by the Pensions Act 2008, s 120, Sch 6, Pt 1, paras 1, 2.
        Date in force: 6 April 2011: see SI 2011/664, art 2(3), Schedule, Pt 2.

[21C Pension compensation: interpretation]

[In this Part—

    "PPF compensation" means compensation payable under the pension compensation provisions;

    "the pension compensation provisions" means—

        (a)   Chapter 3 of Part 2 of the Pensions Act 2004 (pension protection) and any regulations or order made under it,

        (b)   Chapter 1 of Part 3 of the Pensions Act 2008 (pension compensation on divorce etc) and any regulations or order made under it, and

(c) any provision corresponding to the provisions mentioned in paragraph (a) or (b) in force in Northern Ireland.]

NOTES

Amendment
    Inserted by the Pensions Act 2008, s 120, Sch 6, Pt 1, paras 1, 2.
        Date in force: 6 April 2011: see SI 2011/664, art 2(3), Schedule, Pt 2.

Ancillary relief in connection with divorce proceedings, etc

22 Maintenance pending suit
[(1)] On a petition for divorce, nullity of marriage or judicial separation, the court may make an order for maintenance pending suit, that is to say, an order requiring either party to the marriage to make to the other such periodical payments for his or her maintenance and for such term, being a term beginning not earlier than the date of the presentation of the petition and ending with the date of the determination of the suit, as the court thinks reasonable.
[(2) An order under this section may not require a party to a marriage to pay to the other party any amount in respect of legal services for the purposes of the proceedings.
(3) In subsection (2) "legal services" has the same meaning as in section 22ZA.]

NOTES

Amendment
    Sub-s (1): numbered as such by the Legal Aid, Sentencing and Punishment of Offenders Act 2012, s 49(1)(a).
        Date in force: 1 April 2013: see SI 2013/773, art 2.
    Sub-ss (2), (3): inserted by the Legal Aid, Sentencing and Punishment of Offenders Act 2012, s 49(1)(b).
        Date in force: 1 April 2013: see SI 2013/773, art 2.

[22ZA Orders for payment in respect of legal services]
[(1) In proceedings for divorce, nullity of marriage or judicial separation, the court may make an order or orders requiring one party to the marriage to pay to the other ("the applicant") an amount for the purpose of enabling the applicant to obtain legal services for the purposes of the proceedings.
(2) The court may also make such an order or orders in proceedings under this Part for financial relief in connection with proceedings for divorce, nullity of marriage or judicial separation.
(3) The court must not make an order under this section unless it is satisfied that, without the amount, the applicant would not reasonably be able to obtain appropriate legal services for the purposes of the proceedings or any part of the proceedings.
(4) For the purposes of subsection (3), the court must be satisfied, in particular, that—

    (a) the applicant is not reasonably able to secure a loan to pay for the services, and
    (b) the applicant is unlikely to be able to obtain the services by granting a charge over any assets recovered in the proceedings.

(5) An order under this section may be made for the purpose of enabling the applicant to obtain legal services of a specified description, including legal services provided in a specified period or for the purposes of a specified part of the proceedings.
(6) An order under this section may—

    (a) provide for the payment of all or part of the amount by instalments of specified amounts, and
    (b) require the instalments to be secured to the satisfaction of the court.

(7) An order under this section may direct that payment of all or part of the amount is to be deferred.

(8)   The court may at any time in the proceedings vary an order made under this section if it considers that there has been a material change of circumstances since the order was made.

(9)   For the purposes of the assessment of costs in the proceedings, the applicant's costs are to be treated as reduced by any amount paid to the applicant pursuant to an order under this section for the purposes of those proceedings.

(10)   In this section "legal services", in relation to proceedings, means the following types of services—

    (a)   providing advice as to how the law applies in the particular circumstances,

    (b)   providing advice and assistance in relation to the proceedings,

    (c)   providing other advice and assistance in relation to the settlement or other resolution of the dispute that is the subject of the proceedings, and

    (d)   providing advice and assistance in relation to the enforcement of decisions in the proceedings or as part of the settlement or resolution of the dispute,

and they include, in particular, advice and assistance in the form of representation and any form of dispute resolution, including mediation.

(11)   In subsections (5) and (6) "specified" means specified in the order concerned.]

NOTES

Amendment
    Inserted by the Legal Aid, Sentencing and Punishment of Offenders Act 2012, s 49(2).
        Date in force: 1 April 2013: see SI 2013/773, art 2.

[22ZB Matters to which court is to have regard in deciding how to exercise power under section 22ZA]

[(1)   When considering whether to make or vary an order under section 22ZA, the court must have regard to—

    (a)   the income, earning capacity, property and other financial resources which each of the applicant and the paying party has or is likely to have in the foreseeable future,

    (b)   the financial needs, obligations and responsibilities which each of the applicant and the paying party has or is likely to have in the foreseeable future,

    (c)   the subject matter of the proceedings, including the matters in issue in them,

    (d)   whether the paying party is legally represented in the proceedings,

    (e)   any steps taken by the applicant to avoid all or part of the proceedings, whether by proposing or considering mediation or otherwise,

    (f)   the applicant's conduct in relation to the proceedings,

    (g)   any amount owed by the applicant to the paying party in respect of costs in the proceedings or other proceedings to which both the applicant and the paying party are or were party, and

    (h)   the effect of the order or variation on the paying party.

(2)   In subsection (1)(a) "earning capacity", in relation to the applicant or the paying party, includes any increase in earning capacity which, in the opinion of the court, it would be reasonable to expect the applicant or the paying party to take steps to acquire.

(3)   For the purposes of subsection (1)(h), the court must have regard, in particular, to whether the making or variation of the order is likely to—

    (a)   cause undue hardship to the paying party, or

    (b)   prevent the paying party from obtaining legal services for the purposes of the proceedings.

(4)   The Lord Chancellor may by order amend this section by adding to, omitting or varying the matters mentioned in subsections (1) to (3).

(5)   An order under subsection (4) must be made by statutory instrument.

(6)   A statutory instrument containing an order under subsection (4) may not be made unless a draft of the instrument has been laid before, and approved by a resolution of, each House of Parliament.

(7)   In this section "legal services" has the same meaning as in section 22ZA.]

NOTES

Amendment
>   Inserted by the Legal Aid, Sentencing and Punishment of Offenders Act 2012, s 50.
>   Date in force: 1 April 2013: see SI 2013/773, art 2.

23 Financial provision orders in connection with divorce proceedings, etc

(1) On granting a decree of divorce, a decree of nullity of marriage or a decree of judicial separation or at any time thereafter (whether, in the case of a decree of divorce or of nullity of marriage, before or after the decree is made absolute), the court may make any one or more of the following orders, that is to say—

(a)   an order that either party to the marriage shall make to the other such periodical payments, for such term, as may be specified in the order;

(b)   an order that either party to the marriage shall secure to the other to the satisfaction of the court such periodical payments, for such term, as may be so specified;

(c)   an order that either party to the marriage shall pay to the other such lump sum or sums as may be so specified;

(d)   an order that a party to the marriage shall make to such person as may be specified in the order for the benefit of a child of the family, or to such a child, such periodical payments, for such term, as may be so specified;

(e)   an order that a party to the marriage shall secure to such person as may be so specified for the benefit of such a child, or to such a child, to the satisfaction of the court, such periodical payments, for such term, as may be so specified;

(f)   an order that a party to the marriage shall pay to such person as may be so specified for the benefit of such a child, or to such a child, such lump sum as may be so specified;

subject, however, in the case of an order under paragraph (d), (e) or (f) above, to the restrictions imposed by section 29(1) and (3) below on the making of financial provision orders in favour of children who have attained the age of eighteen.

(2)   The court may also, subject to those restrictions, make any one or more of the orders mentioned in subsection (1)(d), (e) and (f) above—

(a)   in any proceedings for divorce, nullity of marriage or judicial separation, before granting a decree; and

(b)   where any such proceedings are dismissed after the beginning of the trial, either forthwith or within a reasonable period after the dismissal.

(3)   Without prejudice to the generality of subsection (1)(c) or (f) above—

(a)   an order under this section that a party to a marriage shall pay a lump sum to the other party may be made for the purpose of enabling that other party to meet any liabilities or expenses reasonably incurred by him or her in maintaining himself or herself or any child of the family before making an application for an order under this section in his or her favour;

(b)   an order under this section for the payment of a lump sum to or for the benefit of a child of the family may be made for the purpose of enabling any liabilities or expenses reasonably incurred by or for the benefit of that child before the making of an application for an order under this section in his favour to be met; and

(c)   an order under this section for the payment of a lump sum may provide for the payment of that sum by instalments of such amount as may be specified in the order and may require the payment of the instalments to be secured to the satisfaction of the court.

(4)   The power of the court under subsection (1) or (2)(a) above to make an order in favour of a child of the family shall be exercisable from time to time; and where the court makes an order in favour of a child under subsection (2)(b) above, it may from time to time, subject to the restrictions mentioned in subsection (1) above, make a further order in his favour of any of the kinds mentioned in subsection (1)(d), (e) or (f) above.

(5)   Without prejudice to the power to give a direction under section 30 below for the settlement of an instrument by conveyancing counsel, where an order is made under subsection (1)(a), (b) or (c) above on or after granting a decree of divorce or nullity of marriage, neither the order nor any settlement made in pursuance of the order shall take effect unless the decree has been made absolute.

[(6)   Where the court—

(a)   makes an order under this section for the payment of a lump of sum; and
(b)   directs—

(i)   that payment of that sum or any part of it shall be deferred; or
(ii)   that that sum or any part of it shall be paid by instalments,

the court may order that the amount deferred or the instalments shall carry interest at such rate as may be specified by the order from such date, not earlier than the date of the order, as may be so specified, until the date when payment of it is due.]

NOTES

Amendment
    Sub-s (6): inserted by the Administration of Justice Act 1982, s 16.

24 Property adjustment orders in connection with divorce proceedings, etc
(1)   On granting a decree of divorce, a decree of nullity of marriage or a decree of judicial separation or at any time thereafter (whether, in the case of a decree of divorce or of nullity of marriage, before or after the decree is made absolute), the court may make any one or more of the following orders, that is to say—

(a)   an order that a party to the marriage shall transfer to the other party, to any child of the family or to such person as may be specified in the order for the benefit of such a child such property as may be so specified, being property to which the first-mentioned party is entitled, either in possession or reversion;

(b)   an order that a settlement of such property as may be so specified, being property to which a party to the marriage is so entitled, be made to the satisfaction of the court for the benefit of the other party to the marriage and of the children of the family or either or any of them;

(c)   an order varying for the benefit of the parties to the marriage and of the children of the family or either or any of them any ante-nuptial or post-nuptial settlement (including such a settlement made by will or codicil) made on the parties to the marriage[, other than one in the form of a pension arrangement (within the meaning of section 25D below)];

(d)   an order extinguishing or reducing the interest of either of the parties to the marriage under any such settlement[, other than one in the form of a pension arrangement (within the meaning of section 25D below)];

subject, however, in the case of an order under paragraph (a) above, to the restrictions imposed by section 29(1) and (3) below on the making of orders for a transfer of property in favour of children who have attained the age of eighteen.

(2)   The court may make an order under subsection (1)(c) above notwithstanding that there are no children of the family.

(3)   Without prejudice to the power to give a direction under section 30 below for the settlement of an instrument by conveyancing counsel, where an order is made under this section on or after granting a decree of divorce or nullity of marriage, neither the order nor any settlement made in pursuance of the order shall take effect unless the decree has been made absolute.

NOTES

Amendment
> Sub-s (1): in paras (c), (d) words ", other than one in the form of a pension arrangement (within the meaning of section 25D below)" in square brackets inserted by the Welfare Reform and Pensions Act 1999, s 19, Sch 3, paras 1, 3.
>> Date in force: 1 December 2000 (except in relation to proceedings in which the decree is granted were begun before that date): see SI 2000/1116, art 2(e) and the Welfare Reform and Pensions Act 1999, s 85(4).

[24A Orders for sale of property]

[(1)   Where the court makes [an order under section 22ZA or makes] under section 23 or 24 of this Act a secured periodical payments order, an order for the payment of a lump sum or a property adjustment order, then, on making that order or at any time thereafter, the court may make a further order for the sale of such property as may be specified in the order, being property in which or in the proceeds of sale of which either or both of the parties to the marriage has or have a beneficial interest, either in possession or reversion.

(2)   Any order made under subsection (1) above may contain such consequential or supplementary provisions as the court thinks fit and, without prejudice to the generality of the foregoing provision, may include—

> (a)   provision requiring the making of a payment out of the proceeds of sale of the property to which the order relates, and
> (b)   provision requiring any such property to be offered for sale to a person, or class of persons, specified in the order.

(3)   Where an order is made under subsection (1) above on or after the grant of a decree of *divorce or* nullity of marriage, the order shall not take effect unless the decree has been made absolute.

(4)   Where an order is made under subsection (1) above, the court may direct that the order, or such provision thereof as the court may specify, shall not take effect until the occurrence of an event specified by the court or the expiration of a period so specified.

(5)   Where an order under subsection (1) above contains a provision requiring the proceeds of sale of the property to which the order relates to be used to secure periodical payments to a party to the marriage, the order shall cease to have effect on the death or re-marriage of[, or formation of a civil partnership by,] that person.

[(6)   Where a party to a marriage has a beneficial interest in any property, or in the proceeds of sale thereof, and some other person who is not a party to the marriage also has a beneficial interest in that property or in the proceeds of sale thereof, then, before deciding whether to make an order under this section in relation to that property, it shall be the duty of the court to give that other person an opportunity to make representations with respect to the order; and any representations made by that other person shall be included among the circumstances to which the court is required to have regard under section 25(1) below.]]

NOTES

Amendment
> Inserted by the Matrimonial Homes and Property Act 1981, s 7.
> Sub-s (1): words "an order under section 22ZA or makes" in square brackets inserted by the Legal Aid, Sentencing and Punishment of Offenders Act 2012, s 51.
>> Date in force: 1 April 2013: see SI 2013/773, art 2.

Sub-s (5): words ", or formation of a civil partnership by," in square brackets inserted by the Civil Partnership Act 2004, s 261(1), Sch 27, para 42.

Date in force: 5 December 2005: see SI 2005/3175, art 2(2).

Sub-s (6): inserted by the Matrimonial and Family Proceedings Act 1984, s 46(1), Sch 1.

[24B Pension sharing orders in connection with divorce proceedings etc]

[(1)   On granting a decree of divorce or a decree of nullity of marriage or at any time thereafter (whether before or after the decree is made absolute), the court may, on an application made under this section, make one or more pension sharing orders in relation to the marriage.

(2)   A pension sharing order under this section is not to take effect unless the decree on or after which it is made has been made absolute.

(3)   A pension sharing order under this section may not be made in relation to a pension arrangement which—

(a)   is the subject of a pension sharing order in relation to the marriage, or

(b)   has been the subject of pension sharing between the parties to the marriage.

(4)   A pension sharing order under this section may not be made in relation to shareable state scheme rights if—

(a)   such rights are the subject of a pension sharing order in relation to the marriage, or

(b)   such rights have been the subject of pension sharing between the parties to the marriage.

(5)   A pension sharing order under this section may not be made in relation to the rights of a person under a pension arrangement if there is in force a requirement imposed by virtue of section 25B or 25C below which relates to benefits or future benefits to which he is entitled under the pension arrangement.]

NOTES

Amendment

Inserted by the Welfare Reform and Pensions Act 1999, s 19, Sch 3, paras 1, 4.

Date in force: 1 December 2000 (except that a pension sharing order may not be made if the proceedings in which the decree is granted were begun before that date): see SI 2000/1116, art 2(e) and the Welfare Reform and Pensions Act 1999, s 85(3)(a).

[24C Pension sharing orders: duty to stay]

[(1)   No pension sharing order may be made so as to take effect before the end of such period after the making of the order as may be prescribed by regulations made by the Lord Chancellor.

(2)   The power to make regulations under this section shall be exercisable by statutory instrument which shall be subject to annulment in pursuance of a resolution of either House of Parliament.]

NOTES

Amendment

Inserted by the Welfare Reform and Pensions Act 1999, s 19, Sch 3, paras 1, 4.

Date in force (for the purpose only of the exercise of any power to make regulations): 11 November 1999: see the Welfare Reform and Pensions Act 1999, s 89(5)(a).

Date in force (for remaining purposes): 1 December 2000: see SI 2000/1116, art 2(e).

[24D Pension sharing orders: apportionment of charges]

[If a pension sharing order relates to rights under a pension arrangement, the court may include in the order provision about the apportionment between the parties of any charge under section 41 of the Welfare Reform and Pensions Act 1999 (charges in respect of pension sharing costs), or under corresponding Northern Ireland legislation.]

NOTES

Amendment

> Inserted by the Welfare Reform and Pensions Act 1999, s 19, Sch 3, paras 1, 4.
> Date in force: 1 December 2000: see SI 2000/1116, art 2(e).

[24E Pension compensation sharing orders in connection with divorce proceedings]

[(1)   On granting a decree of divorce or a decree of nullity of marriage or at any time thereafter (whether before or after the decree is made absolute), the court may, on an application made under this section, make a pension compensation sharing order in relation to the marriage.

(2)   A pension compensation sharing order under this section is not to take effect unless the decree on or after which it is made has been made absolute.

(3)   A pension compensation sharing order under this section may not be made in relation to rights to PPF compensation that—

(a)   are the subject of pension attachment,

(b)   derive from rights under a pension scheme that were the subject of pension sharing between the parties to the marriage,

(c)   are the subject of pension compensation attachment, or

(d)   are or have been the subject of pension compensation sharing between the parties to the marriage.

(4)   For the purposes of subsection (3)(a), rights to PPF compensation "are the subject of pension attachment" if any of the following three conditions is met.

(5)   The first condition is that—

(a)   the rights derive from rights under a pension scheme in relation to which an order was made under section 23 imposing a requirement by virtue of section 25B(4), and

(b)   that order, as modified under section 25E(3), remains in force.

(6)   The second condition is that—

(a)   the rights derive from rights under a pension scheme in relation to which an order was made under section 23 imposing a requirement by virtue of section 25B(7), and

(b)   that order—

(i)   has been complied with, or

(ii)   has not been complied with and, as modified under section 25E(5), remains in force.

(7)   The third condition is that—

(a)   the rights derive from rights under a pension scheme in relation to which an order was made under section 23 imposing a requirement by virtue of section 25C, and

(b)   that order remains in force.

(8)   For the purposes of subsection (3)(b), rights under a pension scheme "were the subject of pension sharing between the parties to the marriage" if the rights were at any time the subject of a pension sharing order in relation to the marriage or a previous marriage between the same parties.

(9)   For the purposes of subsection (3)(c), rights to PPF compensation "are the subject of pension compensation attachment" if there is in force a requirement imposed by virtue of section 25F relating to them.

(10)   For the purposes of subsection (3)(d), rights to PPF compensation "are or have been the subject of pension compensation sharing between the parties to the marriage" if they are or have ever been the subject of a pension compensation sharing order in relation to the marriage or a previous marriage between the same parties.]

NOTES

Amendment

> Inserted by the Pensions Act 2008, s 120, Sch 6, Pt 1, paras 1, 3.

Date in force: 6 April 2011: see SI 2011/664, art 2(3), Schedule, Pt 2.

[24F Pension compensation sharing orders: duty to stay]

[(1) No pension compensation sharing order may be made so as to take effect before the end of such period after the making of the order as may be prescribed by regulations made by the Lord Chancellor.

(2) The power to make regulations under this section shall be exercisable by statutory instrument which shall be subject to annulment in pursuance of a resolution of either House of Parliament.]

NOTES

Amendment
>   Inserted by the Pensions Act 2008, s 120, Sch 6, Pt 1, paras 1, 3.
>>   Date in force (for certain purposes): 6 March 2011: see SI 2011/664, art 2(2), Schedule, Pt 1.
>>   Date in force (for remaining purposes): 6 April 2011: see SI 2011/664, art 2(3), Schedule, Pt 2.

[24G Pension compensation sharing orders: apportionment of charges]

[The court may include in a pension compensation sharing order provision about the apportionment between the parties of any charge under section 117 of the Pensions Act 2008 (charges in respect of pension compensation sharing costs), or under corresponding Northern Ireland legislation.]

NOTES

Amendment
>   Inserted by the Pensions Act 2008, s 120, Sch 6, Pt 1, paras 1, 3.
>   Date in force: 6 April 2011: see SI 2011/664, art 2(3), Schedule, Pt 2.

[25 Matters to which court is to have regard in deciding how to exercise its powers under ss 23, 24[, 24A, 24B and 24E]]

(1) It shall be the duty of the court in deciding whether to exercise its powers under section 23, 24[, 24A[, 24B or 24E]] above and, if so, in what manner, to have regard to all the circumstances of the case, first consideration being given to the welfare while a minor of any child of the family who has not attained the age of eighteen.

(2) As regards the exercise of the powers of the court under section 23(1)(a), (b) or (c), [section 22A or 23 above to make a financial provision order in favour of a party to a marriage or the exercise of its powers under section 23A,] 24 [, 24A[, 24B or 24E]] above in relation to a party to the marriage, the court shall in particular have regard to the following matters—

>   (a)   the income, earning capacity, property and other financial resources which each of the parties to the marriage has or is likely to have in the foreseeable future, including in the case of earning capacity any increase in that capacity which it would in the opinion of the court be reasonable to expect a party to the marriage to take steps to acquire;
>   (b)   the financial needs, obligations and responsibilities which each of the parties to the marriage has or is likely to have in the foreseeable future;
>   (c)   the standard of living enjoyed by the family before the breakdown of the marriage;
>   (d)   the age of each party to the marriage and the duration of the marriage;
>   (e)   any physical or mental disability of either of the parties to the marriage;
>   (f)   the contributions which each of the parties has made or is likely in the foreseeable future to make to the welfare of the family, including any contribution by looking after the home or caring for the family;
>   (g)   the conduct of each of the parties, if that conduct is such that it would in the opinion of the court be inequitable to disregard it;

(h)   in the case of proceedings for divorce or nullity of marriage, the value to each of the parties to the marriage of any benefit . . . which, by reason of the dissolution or annulment of the marriage, that party will lose the chance of acquiring.

(3)   As regards the exercise of the powers of the court under section 23(1)(d), (e) or (f), (2) or (4), 24 or 24A above in relation to a child of the family, the court shall in particular have regard to the following matters—

(a)   the financial needs of the child;

(b)   the income, earning capacity (if any), property and other financial resources of the child;

(c)   any physical or mental disability of the child;

(d)   the manner in which he was being and in which the parties to the marriage expected him to be educated or trained;

(e)   the considerations mentioned in relation to the parties to the marriage in paragraphs (a), (b), (c) and (e) of subsection (2) above.

(4)   As regards the exercise of the powers of the court under section 23(1)(d), (e) or (f), (2) or (4), 24 or 24A above against a party to a marriage in favour of a child of the family who is not the child of that party, the court shall also have regard—

(a)   to whether that party assumed any responsibility for the child's maintenance, and, if so, to the extent to which, and the basis upon which, that party assumed such responsibility and to the length of time for which that party discharged such responsibility;

(b)   to whether in assuming and discharging such responsibility that party did so knowing that the child was not his or her own;

(c)   to the liability of any other person to maintain the child.

NOTES

Amendment

Substituted by the Matrimonial and Family Proceedings Act 1984, s 3.

Section heading: words ", 24A, 24B and 24E" in square brackets substituted by the Pensions Act 2008, s 120, Sch 6, Pt 1, paras 1, 4(1), (2).

Date in force: 6 April 2011: see SI 2011/664, art 2(3), Schedule, Pt 2.

Sub-s (1): words in square brackets beginning with the reference to ", 24A" substituted by the Welfare Reform and Pensions Act 1999, s 19, Sch 3, paras 1, 5(a).

Date in force: 1 December 2000: see SI 2000/1116, art 2(e).

Sub-s (1): words ", 24B or 24E" in square brackets substituted by the Pensions Act 2008, s 120, Sch 6, Pt 1, paras 1, 4(1), (3).

Date in force: 6 April 2011: see SI 2011/664, art 2(3), Schedule, Pt 2.

Sub-s (2): words in square brackets beginning with the reference to ", 24A" substituted by the Welfare Reform and Pensions Act 1999, s 19, Sch 3, paras 1, 5(b).

Date in force: 1 December 2000: see SI 2000/1116, art 2(e).

Sub-s (2): words ", 24B or 24E" in square brackets substituted by the Pensions Act 2008, s 120, Sch 6, Pt 1, paras 1, 4(1), (3).

Date in force: 6 April 2011: see SI 2011/664, art 2(3), Schedule, Pt 2.

Sub-s (2): in para (h) words omitted repealed by the Pensions Act 1995, s 166(2); for savings see SI 1996/1675, arts 4, 5.

Date in force: 1 August 1996: see SI 1996/1675, art 3(b).

[25A Exercise of court's powers in favour of party to marriage on decree of divorce or nullity of marriage]

[(1)   Where on or after the grant of a decree of divorce or nullity of marriage the court decides to exercise its powers under section 23(1)(a), (b) or (c), 24[, 24A[, 24B or 24E]] above in favour of a party to the marriage, it shall be the duty of the court to consider whether it would be appropriate so to exercise those powers that the financial obligations of each party towards the other will be terminated as soon after the grant of the decree as the court considers just and reasonable.

(2)   Where the court decides in such a case to make a periodical payments or secured periodical payments order in favour of a party to the marriage, the court shall in particular consider whether it would be appropriate to require those payments to be

made or secured only for such term as would in the opinion of the court be sufficient to enable the party in whose favour the order is made to adjust without undue hardship to the termination of his or her financial dependence on the other party.

(3) Where on or after the grant of a decree of divorce or nullity of marriage an application is made by a party to the marriage for a periodical payments or secured periodical payments order in his or her favour, then, if the court considers that no continuing obligation should be imposed on either party to make or secure periodical payments in favour of the other, the court may dismiss the application with a direction that the applicant shall not be entitled to make any future application in relation to that marriage for an order under section 23(1)(a) or (b) above.]

NOTES

Amendment
   Inserted by the Matrimonial and Family Proceedings Act 1984, s 3.
   Sub-s (1): words in square brackets beginning with the reference to ", 24A" substituted by the Welfare Reform and Pensions Act 1999, s 19, Sch 3, para 1, 6.
      Date in force: 1 December 2000: see SI 2000/1116, art 2(e).
   Sub-s (1): words ", 24B or 24E" in square brackets substituted by the Pensions Act 2008, s 120, Sch 6, Pt 1, paras 1, 5.
      Date in force: 6 April 2011: see SI 2011/664, art 2(3), Schedule, Pt 2.

[25B Pensions]

[(1) The matters to which the court is to have regard under section 25(2) above include—

   (a)   in the case of paragraph (a), any benefits under a pension [arrangement] which a party to the marriage has or is likely to have, and

   (b)   in the case of paragraph (h), any benefits under a pension [arrangement] which, by reason of the dissolution or annulment of the marriage, a party to the marriage will lose the chance of acquiring,

and, accordingly, in relation to benefits under a pension [arrangement], section 25(2)(a) above shall have effect as if "in the foreseeable future" were omitted.

(2) . . .

(3) The following provisions apply where, having regard to any benefits under a pension [arrangement], the court determines to make an order under section 23 above.

(4) To the extent to which the order is made having regard to any benefits under a pension [arrangement], the order may require the [person responsible for] the pension [arrangement] in question, if at any time any payment in respect of any benefits under the [arrangement] becomes due to the party with pension rights, to make a payment for the benefit of the other party.

[(5) The order must express the amount of any payment required to be made by virtue of subsection (4) above as a percentage of the payment which becomes due to the party with pension rights.]

(6) Any such payment by the [person responsible for the arrangement]—

   (a)   shall discharge so much of [his] liability to the party with pension rights as corresponds to the amount of the payment, and

   (b)   shall be treated for all purposes as a payment made by the party with pension rights in or towards the discharge of his liability under the order.

(7) Where the party with pension rights [has a right of commutation under the arrangement, the order may require him to exercise it to any extent]; and this section applies to [any payment due in consequence of commutation] in pursuance of the order as it applies to other payments in respect of benefits under the [arrangement].

[(7A) The power conferred by subsection (7) above may not be exercised for the purpose of commuting a benefit payable to the party with pension rights to a benefit payable to the other party.

(7B) The power conferred by subsection (4) or (7) above may not be exercised in relation to a pension arrangement which—

(a)   is the subject of a pension sharing order in relation to the marriage, or

(b)   has been the subject of pension sharing between the parties to the marriage.

(7C) In subsection (1) above, references to benefits under a pension arrangement include any benefits by way of pension, whether under a pension arrangement or not.]]

NOTES

Amendment

Inserted with savings by the Pensions Act 1995, s 166(1); for savings see SI 1996/1675, regs 4, 5.

Sub-s (1): word "arrangement" in square brackets in each place it occurs substituted by the Welfare Reform and Pensions Act 1999, s 21, Sch 4, para 1(1), (2).

Date in force: 1 December 2000: see SI 2000/1116, art 2(e).

Sub-s (2): repealed by the Welfare Reform and Pensions Act 1999, ss 21, 88, Sch 4, para 1(1), (2), Sch 13, Pt II.

Date in force: 1 December 2000: see SI 2000/1116, art 2(e), (g).

Sub-s (3): word "arrangement" in square brackets substituted by the Welfare Reform and Pensions Act 1999, s 21, Sch 4, para 1(1), (4).

Date in force: 1 December 2000: see SI 2000/1116, art 2(e).

Sub-s (4): word "arrangement" in square brackets in each place it occurs substituted by the Welfare Reform and Pensions Act 1999, s 21, Sch 4, para 1(1), (5)(a).

Date in force: 1 December 2000: see SI 2000/1116, art 2(e).

Sub-s (4): words "person responsible for" in square brackets substituted by the Welfare Reform and Pensions Act 1999, s 21, Sch 4, para 1(1), (5)(b).

Date in force: 1 December 2000: see SI 2000/1116, art 2(e).

Sub-s (5): substituted by the Welfare Reform and Pensions Act 1999, s 21, Sch 4, para 1(1), (6).

Date in force: 1 December 2000: see SI 2000/1116, art 2(e).

Sub-s (6): words "person responsible for the arrangement" in square brackets substituted by the Welfare Reform and Pensions Act 1999, s 21, Sch 4, para 1(1), (7)(a).

Date in force: 1 December 2000: see SI 2000/1116, art 2(e).

Sub-s (6): in para (a) word "his" in square brackets substituted by the Welfare Reform and Pensions Act 1999, s 21, Sch 4, para 1(1), (7)(b).

Date in force: 1 December 2000: see SI 2000/1116, art 2(e).

Sub-s (7): words from "has a right" to "to any extent" in square brackets substituted by the Welfare Reform and Pensions Act 1999, s 21, Sch 4, para 1(1), (8)(a).

Date in force: 1 December 2000: see SI 2000/1116, art 2(e).

Sub-s (7): words "any payment due in consequence of commutation" in square brackets substituted by the Welfare Reform and Pensions Act 1999, s 21, Sch 4, para 1(1), (8)(b).

Date in force: 1 December 2000: see SI 2000/1116, art 2(e).

Sub-s (7): word "arrangement" in square brackets substituted by the Welfare Reform and Pensions Act 1999, s 21, Sch 4, para 1(1), (8)(c).

Date in force: 1 December 2000: see SI 2000/1116, art 2(e).

Sub-ss (7A)–(7C): inserted by the Welfare Reform and Pensions Act 1999, s 21, Sch 4, para 1(1), (9).

Date in force: 1 December 2000: see SI 2000/1116, art 2(e).

[25C Pensions: lump sums]

[(1) The power of the court under section 23 above to order a party to a marriage to pay a lump sum to the other party includes, where the benefits which the party with pension rights has or is likely to have under a pension [arrangement] include any lump sum payable in respect of his death, power to make any of the following provision by the order.

(2) The court may—

(a)   if the [person responsible for the pension arrangement in question has] power to determine the person to whom the sum, or any part of it, is to be paid, require [him] to pay the whole or part of that sum, when it becomes due, to the other party,

(b)   if the party with pension rights has power to nominate the person to whom the sum, or any part of it, is to be paid, require the party with pension rights to nominate the other party in respect of the whole or part of that sum,

(c)   in any other case, require the [person responsible for the pension arrangement] in question to pay the whole or part of that sum, when it becomes due, for the benefit of the other party instead of to the person to whom, apart from the order, it would be paid.

(3) Any payment by the [person responsible for the arrangement] under an order made under section 23 above by virtue of this section shall discharge so much of [his] liability in respect of the party with pension rights as corresponds to the amount of the payment.

[(4) The powers conferred by this section may not be exercised in relation to a pension arrangement which—

(a)   is the subject of a pension sharing order in relation to the marriage, or

(b)   has been the subject of pension sharing between the parties to the marriage.]]

NOTES

Amendment

Inserted with savings by the Pensions Act 1995, s 166(1); for savings see SI 1996/1675, arts 4, 5.

Sub-s (1): word "arrangement" in square brackets substituted by the Welfare Reform and Pensions Act 1999, s 21, Sch 4, para 2(1), (2).

Date in force: 1 December 2000: see SI 2000/1116, art 2(e).

Sub-s (2): in para (a) words "person responsible for the pension arrangement in question has" in square brackets substituted by the Welfare Reform and Pensions Act 1999, s 21, Sch 4, para 2(1), (3)(a)(i).

Date in force: 1 December 2000: see SI 2000/1116, art 2(e).

Sub-s (2): in para (a) word "him" in square brackets substituted by the Welfare Reform and Pensions Act 1999, s 21, Sch 4, para 2(1), (3)(a)(ii).

Date in force: 1 December 2000: see SI 2000/1116, art 2(e).

Sub-s (2): in para (c) words "person responsible for the pension arrangement" in square brackets substituted by the Welfare Reform and Pensions Act 1999, s 21, Sch 4, para 2(1), (3)(b).

Date in force: 1 December 2000: see SI 2000/1116, art 2(e).

Sub-s (3): words "person responsible for the arrangement" in square brackets substituted by the Welfare Reform and Pensions Act 1999, s 21, Sch 4, para 2(1), (4)(a).

Date in force: 1 December 2000: see SI 2000/1116, art 2(e).

Sub-s (3): word "his" in square brackets substituted by the Welfare Reform and Pensions Act 1999, s 21, Sch 4, para 2(1), (4)(b).

Date in force: 1 December 2000: see SI 2000/1116, art 2(e).

Sub-s (4): inserted by the Welfare Reform and Pensions Act 1999, s 21, Sch 4, para 2(1), (5).

Date in force: 1 December 2000: see SI 2000/1116, art 2(e).

[25D Pensions: supplementary]

[(1) Where—

(a)   an order made under section 23 above by virtue of section 25B or 25C above imposes any requirement on the person responsible for a pension arrangement ("the first arrangement") and the party with pension rights acquires rights under another pension arrangement ("the new arrangement") which are derived (directly or indirectly) from the whole of his rights under the first arrangement, and

(b)   the person responsible for the new arrangement has been given notice in accordance with regulations made by the Lord Chancellor,

the order shall have effect as if it had been made instead in respect of the person responsible for the new arrangement.]

(2) [The Lord Chancellor may by regulations]—

(a)   in relation to any provision of sections 25B or 25C above which authorises the court making an order under section 23 above to require the [person responsible for a pension arrangement] to make a payment for the benefit of the other party, make provision as to the person to whom, and the terms on which, the payment is to be made [(ab) make, in relation to payment under a mistaken belief as to the continuation in force of a provision included by virtue of section 25B or 25C above in an order under section 23 above, provision about the rights or liabilities of the payer, the payee or the person to whom the payment was due,]

(b) require notices to be given in respect of changes of circumstances relevant to such orders which include provision made by virtue of sections 25B and 25C above,

[(ba) make provision for the person responsible for a pension arrangement to be discharged in prescribed circumstances from a requirement imposed by virtue of section 25B or 25C above,]

(c) ...

(d) ...

[(e) make provision about calculation and verification in relation to the valuation of—

    (i) benefits under a pension arrangement, or

    (ii) shareable state scheme rights,

for the purposes of the court's functions in connection with the exercise of any of its powers under this Part of this Act,]

...

[(2A) Regulations under subsection (2)(e) above may include—

(a) provision for calculation or verification in accordance with guidance from time to time prepared by a prescribed person, and

(b) provision by reference to regulations under section 30 or 49(4) of the Welfare Reform and Pensions Act 1999.

(2B) Regulations under subsection (2) above may make different provision for different cases.

(2C) Power to make regulations under this section shall be exercisable by statutory instrument which shall be subject to annulment in pursuance of a resolution of either House of Parliament.]

[(3) In this section and sections 25B and 25C above—

"occupational pension scheme" has the same meaning as in the Pension Schemes Act 1993;

"the party with pension rights" means the party to the marriage who has or is likely to have benefits under a pension arrangement and "the other party" means the other party to the marriage;

"pension arrangement" means—

    (a) an occupational pension scheme,

    (b) a personal pension scheme,

    (c) a retirement annuity contract,

    (d) an annuity or insurance policy purchased, or transferred, for the purpose of giving effect to rights under an occupational pension scheme or a personal pension scheme, and

    (e) an annuity purchased, or entered into, for the purpose of discharging liability in respect of a pension credit under section 29(1)(b) of the Welfare Reform and Pensions Act 1999 or under corresponding Northern Ireland legislation;

"personal pension scheme" has the same meaning as in the Pension Schemes Act 1993;

"prescribed" means prescribed by regulations;

"retirement annuity contract" means a contract or scheme approved under Chapter III of Part XIV of the Income and Corporation Taxes Act 1988;

"shareable state scheme rights" has the same meaning as in section 21A(1) above; and "trustees or managers", in relation to an occupational pension scheme or a personal pension scheme, means—

> (a)   in the case of a scheme established under a trust, the trustees of the scheme, and
>
> (b)   in any other case, the managers of the scheme.

(4) In this section and sections 25B and 25C above, references to the person responsible for a pension arrangement are—

> (a)   in the case of an occupational pension scheme or a personal pension scheme, to the trustees or managers of the scheme,
>
> (b)   in the case of a retirement annuity contract or an annuity falling within paragraph (d) or (e) of the definition of "pension arrangement" above, the provider of the annuity, and
>
> (c)   in the case of an insurance policy falling within paragraph (d) of the definition of that expression, the insurer.]]

NOTES

Amendment

Inserted with savings by the Pensions Act 1995, s 166(1); for savings see SI 1996/1675, art 5.
Sub-s (1): substituted by the Welfare Reform and Pensions Act 1999, s 21, Sch 4, para 3(1), (2).

> Date in force: 1 December 2000: see SI 2000/1116, art 2(e).

Sub-s (2): words "The Lord Chancellor may by regulations" in square brackets substituted by the Welfare Reform and Pensions Act 1999, s 21, Sch 4, para 3(1), (3)(a).

> Date in force: 11 November 1999: see the Welfare Reform and Pensions Act 1999, s 89(5)(a).

Sub-s (2): in para (a) words "person responsible for a pension arrangement" in square brackets substituted by the Welfare Reform and Pensions Act 1999, s 21, Sch 4, para 3(1), (3)(b).

> Date in force: 11 November 1999: see the Welfare Reform and Pensions Act 1999, s 89(5)(a).

Sub-s (2): para (ab) inserted by the Welfare Reform and Pensions Act 1999, s 21, Sch 4, para 3(1), (3)(c).

> Date in force: 11 November 1999: see the Welfare Reform and Pensions Act 1999, s 89(5)(a).

Sub-s (2): para (ba) inserted by the Welfare Reform and Pensions Act 1999, s 21, Sch 4, para 3(1), (3)(d).

> Date in force: 11 November 1999: see the Welfare Reform and Pensions Act 1999, s 89(5)(a).

Sub-s (2): paras (c), (d) repealed by the Welfare Reform and Pensions Act 1999, ss 21, 88, Sch 4, para 3(1), (3)(e), Sch 13, Pt II.

> Date in force: 11 November 1999: see the Welfare Reform and Pensions Act 1999, s 89(5)(a).

Sub-s (2): para (e) substituted by the Welfare Reform and Pensions Act 1999, s 21, Sch 4, para 3(1), (3)(f).

> Date in force: 11 November 1999: see the Welfare Reform and Pensions Act 1999, s 89(5)(a).

Sub-s (2): final words omitted repealed by the Welfare Reform and Pensions Act 1999, ss 21, 88, Sch 4, para 3(1), (3)(g), Sch 13, Pt II.

> Date in force: 11 November 1999: see the Welfare Reform and Pensions Act 1999, s 89(5)(a).

Sub-ss (2A)–(2C): inserted by the Welfare Reform and Pensions Act 1999, s 21, Sch 4, paras 3(1), (4).

> Date in force: 11 November 1999: see the Welfare Reform and Pensions Act 1999, s 89(5)(a).

Sub-ss (3), (4): substituted by the Welfare Reform and Pensions Act 1999, s 21, Sch 4, para 3(1), (5).

> Date in force: 1 December 2000: see SI 2000/1116, art 2(e).

[25E The Pension Protection Fund]

[(1) The matters to which the court is to have regard under section 25(2) include—

> (a)   in the case of paragraph (a), any PPF compensation to which a party to the marriage is or is likely to be entitled, and

(b)   in the case of paragraph (h), any PPF compensation which, by reason of the dissolution or annulment of the marriage, a party to the marriage will lose the chance of acquiring entitlement to,

and, accordingly, in relation to PPF compensation, section 25(2)(a) shall have effect as if "in the foreseeable future" were omitted.

(2)   Subsection (3) applies in relation to an order under section 23 so far as it includes provision made by virtue of section 25B(4) which—

(a)   imposed requirements on the trustees or managers of an occupational pension scheme for which the Board has assumed responsibility in accordance with Chapter 3 of Part 2 of the Pensions Act 2004 (pension protection) or any provision in force in Northern Ireland corresponding to that Chapter, and

(b)   was made before the trustees or managers of the scheme received the transfer notice in relation to the scheme.

(3)   The order is to have effect from the time when the trustees or managers of the scheme receive the transfer notice—

(a)   as if, except in prescribed descriptions of case—

(i)   references in the order to the trustees or managers of the scheme were references to the Board, and

(ii)   references in the order to any pension or lump sum to which the party with pension rights is or may become entitled under the scheme were references to any PPF compensation to which that person is or may become entitled in respect of the pension or lump sum, and

(b)   subject to such other modifications as may be prescribed.

(4)   Subsection (5) applies to an order under section 23 if—

(a)   it includes provision made by virtue of section 25B(7) which requires the party with pension rights to exercise his right of commutation under an occupational pension scheme to any extent, and

(b)   before the requirement is complied with the Board has assumed responsibility for the scheme as mentioned in subsection (2)(a).

(5)   From the time the trustees or managers of the scheme receive the transfer notice, the order is to have effect with such modifications as may be prescribed.

(6)   Regulations may modify section 25C as it applies in relation to an occupational pension scheme at any time when there is an assessment period in relation to the scheme.

(7)   Where the court makes a pension sharing order in respect of a person's shareable rights under an occupational pension scheme, or an order which includes provision made by virtue of section 25B(4) or (7) in relation to such a scheme, the Board subsequently assuming responsibility for the scheme as mentioned in subsection (2)(a) does not affect—

(a)   the powers of the court under section 31 to vary or discharge the order or to suspend or revive any provision of it, or

(b)   on an appeal, the powers of the appeal court to affirm, reinstate, set aside or vary the order.

(8)   Regulations may make such consequential modifications of any provision of, or made by virtue of, this Part as appear to the Lord Chancellor necessary or expedient to give effect to the provisions of this section.

(9)   In this section—

"assessment period" means an assessment period within the meaning of Part 2 of the Pensions Act 2004 (pension protection) (see sections 132 and 159 of that Act) or an equivalent period under any provision in force in Northern Ireland corresponding to that Part;

"the Board" means the Board of the Pension Protection Fund;

"occupational pension scheme" has the same meaning as in the Pension Schemes Act 1993;

"prescribed" means prescribed by regulations;

. . .

"regulations" means regulations made by the Lord Chancellor;

"shareable rights" are rights in relation to which pension sharing is available under Chapter 1 of Part 4 of the Welfare Reform and Pensions Act 1999 or any provision in force in Northern Ireland corresponding to that Chapter;

"transfer notice" has the same meaning as in section 160 of the Pensions Act 2004 or any corresponding provision in force in Northern Ireland.

(10)   Any power to make regulations under this section is exercisable by statutory instrument, which shall be subject to annulment in pursuance of a resolution of either House of Parliament.]

NOTES

Amendment

Inserted by the Pensions Act 2004, s 319(1), Sch 12, para 3.
Date in force: 1 January 2006: see SI 2005/3331, art 2(3), Schedule, Pt 3.
Sub-s (9): definition "PFF compensation" (omitted) repealed by the Pensions Act 2008, ss 120, 148, Sch 6, Pt 1, paras 1, 6, Sch 11, Pt 4.
Date in force: 6 April 2011: see SI 2011/664, art 2(3), Schedule, Pt 2.

[25F Attachment of pension compensation]

[(1)   This section applies where, having regard to any PPF compensation to which a party to the marriage is or is likely to be entitled, the court determines to make an order under section 23.

(2)   To the extent to which the order is made having regard to such compensation, the order may require the Board of the Pension Protection Fund, if at any time any payment in respect of PPF compensation becomes due to the party with compensation rights, to make a payment for the benefit of the other party.

(3)   The order must express the amount of any payment required to be made by virtue of subsection (2) as a percentage of the payment which becomes due to the party with compensation rights.

(4)   Any such payment by the Board of the Pension Protection Fund—

(a)   shall discharge so much of its liability to the party with compensation rights as corresponds to the amount of the payment, and

(b)   shall be treated for all purposes as a payment made by the party with compensation rights in or towards the discharge of that party's liability under the order.

(5)   Where the party with compensation rights has a right to commute any PPF compensation, the order may require that party to exercise it to any extent; and this section applies to any payment due in consequence of commutation in pursuance of the order as it applies to other payments in respect of PPF compensation.

(6)   The power conferred by subsection (5) may not be exercised for the purpose of commuting compensation payable to the party with compensation rights to compensation payable to the other party.

(7)   The power conferred by subsection (2) or (5) may not be exercised in relation to rights to PPF compensation that—

(a)   derive from rights under a pension scheme that were at any time the subject of a pension sharing order in relation to the marriage, or a previous marriage between the same parties, or

(b)   are or have ever been the subject of a pension compensation sharing order in relation to the marriage or a previous marriage between the same parties.]

NOTES

Amendment
> Inserted by the Pensions Act 2008, s 120, Sch 6, Pt 1, paras 1, 7.
>> Date in force: 6 April 2011: see SI 2011/664, art 2(3), Schedule, Pt 2.

[25G Pension compensation: supplementary]

[(1) The Lord Chancellor may by regulations—

    (a)   make provision, in relation to any provision of section 25F which authorises the court making an order under section 23 to require the Board of the Pension Protection Fund to make a payment for the benefit of the other party, as to the person to whom, and the terms on which, the payment is to be made;

    (b)   make provision, in relation to payment under a mistaken belief as to the continuation in force of a provision included by virtue of section 25F in an order under section 23, about the rights or liabilities of the payer, the payee or the person to whom the payment was due;

    (c)   require notices to be given in respect of changes of circumstances relevant to orders under section 23 which include provision made by virtue of section 25F;

    (d)   make provision for the Board of the Pension Protection Fund to be discharged in prescribed circumstances from a requirement imposed by virtue of section 25F;

    (e)   make provision about calculation and verification in relation to the valuation of PPF compensation for the purposes of the court's functions in connection with the exercise of any of its powers under this Part.

(2) Regulations under subsection (1)(e) may include—

    (a)   provision for calculation or verification in accordance with guidance from time to time prepared by a prescribed person;

    (b)   provision by reference to regulations under section 112 of the Pensions Act 2008.

(3) Regulations under subsection (1) may make different provision for different cases.

(4) The power to make regulations under subsection (1) is exercisable by statutory instrument which shall be subject to annulment in pursuance of a resolution of either House of Parliament.

(5) In this section and section 25F—

"the party with compensation rights" means the party to the marriage who is or is likely to be entitled to PPF compensation, and "the other party" means the other party to the marriage;

"prescribed" means prescribed by regulations.]

NOTES

Amendment
> Inserted by the Pensions Act 2008, s 120, Sch 6, Pt 1, paras 1, 7.
>> Date in force (for certain purposes): 6 March 2011: see SI 2011/664, art 2(2), Schedule, Pt 1.
>> Date in force (for remaining purposes): 6 April 2011: see SI 2011/664, art 2(3), Schedule, Pt 2.

26 Commencement of proceedings for ancillary relief, etc

(1) Where a petition for divorce, nullity of marriage or judicial separation has been presented, then, subject to subsection (2) below, proceedings for maintenance pending suit under section 22 above, for a financial provision order under section 23 above, or for a property adjustment order may be begun, subject to and in accordance with rules of court, at any time after the presentation of the petition.

(2) Rules of court may provide, in such cases as may be prescribed by the rules—

  (a) that applications for any such relief as is mentioned in subsection (1) above shall be made in the petition or answer; and

  (b) that applications for any such relief which are not so made, or are not made until after the expiration of such period following the presentation of the petition or filing of the answer as may be so prescribed, shall be made only with the leave of the court.

Financial provision in case of neglect to maintain

27 Financial provision orders, etc, in case of neglect by party to marriage to maintain other party or child of the family

[(1) Either party to a marriage may apply to the court for an order under this section on the ground that the other party to the marriage (in this section referred to as the respondent)—

  (a) has failed to provide reasonable maintenance for the applicant, or

  (b) has failed to provide, or to make a proper contribution towards, reasonable maintenance for any child of the family.]

[(2) The court may not entertain an application under this section unless it has jurisdiction to do so by virtue of the Maintenance Regulation and Schedule 6 to the Civil Jurisdiction and Judgments (Maintenance) Regulations 2011.]

[(3) Where an application under this section is made on the ground mentioned in subsection (1)(a) above, then, in deciding—

  (a) whether the respondent has failed to provide reasonable maintenance for the applicant, and

  (b) what order, if any, to make under this section in favour of the applicant,

the court shall have regard to all the circumstances of the case including the matters mentioned in section 25(2) above, and where an application is also made under this section in respect of a child of the family who has not attained the age of eighteen, first consideration shall be given to the welfare of the child while a minor.]

[(3A) Where an application under this section is made on the ground mentioned in subsection (1)(b) above then, in deciding—

  (a) whether the respondent has failed to provide, or to make a proper contribution towards, reasonable maintenance for the child of the family to whom the application relates, and

  (b) what order, if any, to make under this section in favour of the child,

the court shall have regard to all the circumstances of the case including the matters mentioned in [section 25(3)(a) to (e)] above, and where the child of the family to whom the application relates is not the child of the respondent, including also the matters mentioned in [section 25(4)] above.

(3B) In relation to an application under this section on the ground mentioned in subsection (1)(a) above, [section 25(2)(c) above] shall have effect as if for the reference therein to the breakdown of the marriage there were substituted a reference to the failure to provide reasonable maintenance for the applicant, and in relation to an application under this section on the ground mentioned in subsection (1)(b) above, [section 25(2)(c) above (as it applies by virtue of section 25(3)(e) above)] shall have effect as if for the reference therein to the breakdown of the marriage there were substituted a reference to the failure to provide, or to make a proper contribution towards, reasonable maintenance for the child of the family to whom the application relates.]

(5) Where on an application under this section it appears to the court that the applicant or any child of the family to whom the application relates is in immediate need of financial assistance, but it is not yet possible to determine what order, if any, should be made on the application, the court may make an interim order for

maintenance, that is to say, an order requiring the respondent to make to the applicant until the determination of the application such periodical payments as the court thinks reasonable.

(6)   Where on an application under this section the applicant satisfies the court of any ground mentioned in subsection (1) above, the court may make [any one or more of the following orders], that is to say—

(a)   an order that the respondent shall make to the applicant such periodical payments, for such term, as may be specified in the order;

(b)   an order that the respondent shall secure to the applicant, to the satisfaction of the court, such periodical payments, for such term, as may be so specified;

(c)   an order that the respondent shall pay to the applicant such lump sum as may be so specified;

(d)   an order that the respondent shall make to such person as may be specified in the order for the benefit of the child to whom the application relates, or to that child, such periodical payments, for such term, as may be so specified;

(e)   an order that the respondent shall secure to such person as may be so specified for the benefit of that child, or to that child, to the satisfaction of the court, such periodical payments, for such term, as may be so specified;

(f)   an order that the respondent shall pay to such person as may be so specified for the benefit of that child, or to that child, such lump sum as may be so specified;

subject, however, in the case of an order under paragraph (d), (e) or (f) above, to the restrictions imposed by section 29(1) and (3) below on the making of financial provision orders in favour of children who have attained the age of eighteen.

[(6A)   An application for the variation under section 31 of this Act of a periodical payments order or secured periodical payments order made under this section in favour of a child may, if the child has attained the age of sixteen, be made by the child himself.

[(6B)   Where a periodical payments order made in favour of a child under this section ceases to have effect on the date on which the child attains the age of sixteen or at any time after that date but before or on the date on which he attains the age of eighteen, then if, on an application made to the court for an order under this subsection, it appears to the court that—

(a)   the child is, will be or (if an order were made under this subsection) would be receiving instruction at an educational establishment or undergoing training for a trade, profession or vocation, whether or not he also is, will be or would be in gainful employment; or

(b)   there are special circumstances which justify the making of an order under this subsection,

the court shall have power by order to revive the first mentioned order from such date as the court may specify, not being earlier than the date of the making of the application, and to exercise its power under section 31 of this Act in relation to any order so revived.]

(7)   Without prejudice to the generality of subsection (6) above, an order under this section for the payment of a lump sum—

(a)   may be made for the purpose of enabling any liabilities or expenses reasonably incurred in maintaining the applicant or any child of the family to whom the application relates before the making of the application to be met;

(b)   may provide for the payment of that sum by instalments of such amount as may be specified in the order and may require the payment of the instalments to be secured to the satisfaction of the court.

(8) . . .

NOTES

Amendment

> Sub-s (1): substituted by the Domestic Proceedings and Magistrates' Courts Act 1978, s 63(1).
> Sub-s (2): substituted by SI 2011/1484, reg 9, Sch 7, para 6(1), (2).
> > Date in force: 18 June 2011: see SI 2011/1484, reg 1(1).
> Sub-s (3): substituted by the Matrimonial and Family Proceedings Act 1984, s 4.
> Sub-ss (3A), (3B): substituted by the Domestic Proceedings and Magistrates' Courts Act 1978, s 63(2); words in square brackets substituted by the Matrimonial and Family Proceedings Act 1984, s 46(1), Sch 1, para 13.
> Sub-s (6): words in square brackets substituted by the Domestic Proceedings and Magistrates' Courts Act 1978, s 63(3).
> Sub-s (6A): inserted by the Domestic Proceedings and Magistrates' Courts Act 1978, s 63(4).
> Sub-s (6B): inserted by the Domestic Proceedings and Magistrates' Courts Act 1978, s 63(4); substituted by the Family Law Reform Act 1987, s 33(1), Sch 2, para 52.
> Sub-s (8): repealed by the Domestic Proceedings and Magistrates' Courts Act 1978, s 63(5), 89(2)(b), Sch 3.

Additional provisions with respect to financial provision and property adjustment orders

28 Duration of continuing financial provision orders in favour of party to marriage, and effect of remarriage [or formation of civil partnership]

(1) [Subject in the case of an order made on or after the grant of a decree of divorce or nullity of marriage to the provisions of sections 25A(2) above and 31(7) below, the term to be specified in a periodical payments or secured periodical payments order in favour of a party to a marriage shall be such term as the court thinks fit, except that the term shall not begin before or extend beyond the following limits], that is to say—

  (a) in the case of a periodical payments order, the term shall begin not earlier than the date of the making of an application for the order, and shall be so defined as not to extend beyond the death of either of the parties to the marriage or, where the order is made on or after the grant of a decree of divorce or nullity of marriage, the remarriage of[, or formation of a civil partnership by,] the party in whose favour the order is made; and

  (b) in the case of a secured periodical payments order, the term shall begin not earlier than the date of the making of an application for the order, and shall be so defined as not to extend beyond the death or, where the order is made on or after the grant of such a decree, the remarriage of[, or formation of a civil partnership by,] the party in whose favour the order is made.

[(1A) Where a periodical payments or secured periodical payments order in favour of a party to a marriage is made on or after the grant of a decree of divorce or nullity of marriage, the court may direct that that party shall not be entitled to apply under section 31 below for the extension of the term specified in the order].

(2) Where a periodical payments or secured periodical payments order in favour of a party to a marriage is made otherwise than on or after the grant of a decree of divorce or nullity of marriage, and the marriage in question is subsequently dissolved or annulled but the order continues in force, the order shall, notwithstanding anything in it, cease to have effect on the remarriage of[, or formation of a civil partnership by,] that party, except in relation to any arrears due under it on the date of the remarriage [or formation of the civil partnership].

(3) If after the grant of a decree dissolving or annulling a marriage either party to that marriage remarries [whether at any time before or after the commencement of this Act] [or forms a civil partnership], that party shall not be entitled to apply, by reference to the grant of that decree, for a financial provision order in his or her favour, or for a property adjustment order, against the other party to that marriage.

NOTES

Amendment

> Section heading: words "or formation of civil partnership" in square brackets inserted by the
> Civil Partnership Act 2004, s 261(1), Sch 27, para 43(1), (5).
>> Date in force: 5 December 2005: see SI 2005/3175, art 2(2).
> Sub-s (1): words from "Subject in the case" to "the following limits" in square brackets
> substituted by the Matrimonial and Family Proceedings Act 1984, s 5.
> Sub-s (1): in paras (a), (b) words ", or formation of a civil partnership by," in square brackets
> inserted by the Civil Partnership Act 2004, s 261(1), Sch 27, para 43(1), (2).
>> Date in force: 5 December 2005: see SI 2005/3175, art 2(2).
> Sub-s (1A): inserted by the Matrimonial and Family Proceedings Act 1984, s 5(2).
>> Date in force: 12 October 1984: see the Matrimonial and Family Proceedings Act
>> 1984, s 47(1)(a).
> Sub-s (2): words ", or formation of a civil partnership by," and "or formation of the civil
> partnership" in square brackets inserted by the Civil Partnership Act 2004, s 261(1), Sch 27,
> para 43(1), (3).
>> Date in force: 5 December 2005: see SI 2005/3175, art 2(2).
> Sub-s (3): words "whether at any time before or after the commencement of this Act" in
> square brackets inserted by the Matrimonial and Family Proceedings Act 1984, s 5.
> Sub-s (3): words "or forms a civil partnership" in square brackets inserted by the Civil
> Partnership Act 2004, s 261(1), Sch 27, para 43(1), (4).
>> Date in force: 5 December 2005: see SI 2005/3175, art 2(2).

29 Duration of continuing financial provision orders in favour of children, and age limit on making certain orders in their favour

(1)   Subject to subsection (3) below, no financial provision order and no order for a transfer of property under section 24(1)(a) above shall be made in favour of a child who has attained the age of eighteen.

(2)   The term to be specified in a periodical payments or secured periodical payments order in favour of a child may begin with the date of the making of an application for the order in question or any later date [or a date ascertained in accordance with subsection (5) or (6) below] but—

> (a)   shall not in the first instance extend beyond the date of the birthday of the child next following his attaining the upper limit of the compulsory school age [(construed in accordance with section 8 of the Education Act 1996)] [unless the court considers that in the circumstances of the case the welfare of the child requires that it should extend to a later date]; and

> (b)   shall not in any event, subject to subsection (3) below, extend beyond the date of the child's eighteenth birthday.

(3)   Subsection (1) above, and paragraph (b) of subsection (2), shall not apply in the case of a child, if it appears to the court that—

> (a)   the child is, or will be, or if an order were made without complying with either or both of those provisions would be, receiving instruction at an educational establishment or undergoing training for a trade, profession or vocation, whether or not he is also, or will also be, in gainful employment; or

> (b)   there are special circumstances which justify the making of an order without complying with either or both of those provisions.

(4)   Any periodical payments order in favour of a child shall, notwithstanding anything in the order, cease to have effect on the death of the person liable to make payments under the order, except in relation to any arrears due under the order on the date of the death.

[(5)   Where—

> (a)   a *maintenance assessment* [maintenance calculation] ("the *current assessment* [current calculation]") is in force with respect to a child; and

> (b)   an application is made under Part II of this Act for a periodical payments or secured periodical payments order in favour of that child—

>> (i)   in accordance with section 8 of the Child Support Act 1991, and

        (ii)   before the end of the period of 6 months beginning with the making of the *current assessment* [current calculation]

the term to be specified in any such order made on that application may be expressed to begin on, or at any time after, the earliest permitted date.

(6) For the purposes of subsection (5) above, "the earliest permitted date" is whichever is the later of—

      (a)   the date 6 months before the application is made; or

      (b)   the date on which the *current assessment* [current calculation] took effect or, where successive *maintenance assessments* [maintenance calculations] have been continuously in force with respect to a child, on which the first of *those assessments* [those calculations] took effect.

(7) Where—

      (a)   a *maintenance assessment* [maintenance calculation] ceases to have effect *or is cancelled* by or under any provision of the Child Support Act 1991; and

      (b)   an application is made, before the end of the period of 6 months beginning with the relevant date, for a periodical payments or secured periodical payments order in favour of a child with respect to whom that *maintenance assessment* [maintenance calculation] was in force immediately before it ceased to have effect *or was cancelled,*

the term to be specified in any such order made on that application may begin with the date on which that *maintenance assessment* [maintenance calculation] ceased to have effect *or, as the case may be, the date with effect from which it was cancelled,* or any later date.

(8) In subsection (7)(b) above—

      (a)   where the *maintenance assessment* [maintenance calculation] ceased to have effect, the relevant date is the date on which it so ceased; *and*

      (b)   *where the maintenance assessment was cancelled, the relevant date is the later of—*

           (i)   *the date on which the person who cancelled it did so, and*

           (ii)   *the date from which the cancellation first had effect.*]

NOTES

Amendment

Sub-s (2): words "or a date ascertained in accordance with subsection (5) or (6) below" in square brackets inserted by SI 1993/623, art 2, Sch 1, para 2.

Sub-s (2): in para (a) words "(construed in accordance with section 8 of the Education Act 1996)" in square brackets substituted by the Education Act 1996, s 582(1), Sch 37, para 136.
     Date in force: 1 September 1997: see SI 1997/1623, art 2(2).

Sub-ss (5)–(8): inserted by SI 1993/623, art 2, Sch 1, para 2.

Sub-s (5): in para (a) words "maintenance assessment" in italics repealed and subsequent words in square brackets substituted by the Child Support, Pensions and Social Security Act 2000, s 26, Sch 3, para 3(1), (2)(a).
     Date in force (in relation to certain cases): 3 March 2003: see SI 2003/192, arts 3, 8, Schedule.
     Date in force (for remaining purposes): to be appointed: see the Child Support, Pensions and Social Security Act 2000, s 86(2).

Sub-s (5): in para (a) words "current assessment" in italics repealed and subsequent words in square brackets substituted by the Child Support, Pensions and Social Security Act 2000, s 26, Sch 3, para 3(1), (2)(b).
     Date in force (in relation to certain cases): 3 March 2003: see SI 2003/192, arts 3, 8, Schedule.
     Date in force (for remaining purposes): to be appointed: see the Child Support, Pensions and Social Security Act 2000, s 86(2).

Sub-s (5): in para (b)(ii) words "current assessment" in italics repealed and subsequent words in square brackets substituted by the Child Support, Pensions and Social Security Act 2000, s 26, Sch 3, para 3(1), (2)(b).
     Date in force (in relation to certain cases): 3 March 2003: see SI 2003/192, arts 3, 8, Schedule.

Date in force (for remaining purposes): to be appointed: see the Child Support, Pensions and Social Security Act 2000, s 86(2).

Sub-s (6): in para (b) words "current assessment" in italics repealed and subsequent words in square brackets substituted by the Child Support, Pensions and Social Security Act 2000, s 26, Sch 3, para 3(1), (2)(b).

Date in force (in relation to certain cases): 3 March 2003: see SI 2003/192, arts 3, 8, Schedule.

Date in force (for remaining purposes): to be appointed: see the Child Support, Pensions and Social Security Act 2000, s 86(2).

Sub-s (6): in para (b) words "maintenance assessments" in italics repealed and subsequent words in square brackets substituted by the Child Support, Pensions and Social Security Act 2000, s 26, Sch 3, para 3(1), (2)(c).

Date in force (in relation to certain cases): 3 March 2003: see SI 2003/192, arts 3, 8, Schedule.

Date in force (for remaining purposes): to be appointed: see the Child Support, Pensions and Social Security Act 2000, s 86(2).

Sub-s (6): in para (b) words "those assessments" in italics repealed and subsequent words in square brackets substituted by the Child Support, Pensions and Social Security Act 2000, s 26, Sch 3, para 3(1), (2)(d).

Date in force (in relation to certain cases): 3 March 2003: see SI 2003/192, arts 3, 8, Schedule.

Date in force (for remaining purposes): to be appointed: see the Child Support, Pensions and Social Security Act 2000, s 86(2).

Sub-s (7): in para (a) words "maintenance assessment" in italics repealed and subsequent words in square brackets substituted by the Child Support, Pensions and Social Security Act 2000, s 26, Sch 3, para 3(1), (2)(a).

Date in force (in relation to certain cases): 3 March 2003: see SI 2003/192, arts 3, 8, Schedule.

Date in force (for remaining purposes): to be appointed: see the Child Support, Pensions and Social Security Act 2000, s 86(2).

Sub-s (7): in para (a) words "or is cancelled" in italics repealed by the Child Support, Pensions and Social Security Act 2000, s 85, Sch 9, Pt I.

Date in force (in relation to certain cases): 3 March 2003: see SI 2003/192, arts 3, 8, Schedule.

Date in force (for remaining purposes): to be appointed: see the Child Support, Pensions and Social Security Act 2000, s 86(2).

Sub-s (7): in para (b) words "maintenance assessment" in italics repealed and subsequent words in square brackets substituted by the Child Support, Pensions and Social Security Act 2000, s 26, Sch 3, para 3(1), (2)(a).

Date in force (in relation to certain cases): 3 March 2003: see SI 2003/192, arts 3, 8, Schedule.

Date in force (for remaining purposes): to be appointed: see the Child Support, Pensions and Social Security Act 2000, s 86(2).

Sub-s (7): in para (b) words "or was cancelled" in italics repealed by the Child Support, Pensions and Social Security Act 2000, s 85, Sch 9, Pt I.

Date in force (in relation to certain cases): 3 March 2003: see SI 2003/192, arts 3, 8, Schedule.

Date in force (for remaining purposes): to be appointed: see the Child Support, Pensions and Social Security Act 2000, s 86(2).

Sub-s (7): words "maintenance assessment" in italics repealed and subsequent words in square brackets substituted by the Child Support, Pensions and Social Security Act 2000, s 26, Sch 3, para 3(1), (2)(a).

Date in force (in relation to certain cases): 3 March 2003: see SI 2003/192, arts 3, 8, Schedule.

Date in force (for remaining purposes): to be appointed: see the Child Support, Pensions and Social Security Act 2000, s 86(2).

Sub-s (7): words "or, as the case may be, the date with effect from which it was cancelled" in italics repealed by the Child Support, Pensions and Social Security Act 2000, s 85, Sch 9, Pt I.

Date in force (in relation to certain cases): 3 March 2003: see SI 2003/192, arts 3, 8, Schedule.

Date in force (for remaining purposes): to be appointed: see the Child Support, Pensions and Social Security Act 2000, s 86(2).

Sub-s (8): in para (a) words "maintenance assessment" in italics repealed and subsequent words in square brackets substituted by the Child Support, Pensions and Social Security Act 2000, s 26, Sch 3, para 3(1), (2)(a).

Date in force (in relation to certain cases): 3 March 2003: see SI 2003/192, arts 3, 8, Schedule.

Date in force (for remaining purposes): to be appointed: see the Child Support, Pensions and Social Security Act 2000, s 86(2).

Sub-s (8): para (b) and word "and" immediately preceding it repealed by the Child Support, Pensions and Social Security Act 2000, s 85, Sch 9, Pt I.
> Date in force (in relation to certain cases): 3 March 2003: see SI 2003/192, arts 3, 8, Schedule.
> Date in force (for remaining purposes): to be appointed: see the Child Support, Pensions and Social Security Act 2000, s 86(2).

30 Direction for settlement of instrument for securing payments or effecting property adjustment

Where the court decides to make a financial provision order requiring any payments to be secured or a property adjustment order—

(a) it may direct that the matter be referred to one of the conveyancing counsel of the court for him to settle a proper instrument to be executed by all necessary parties; and

(b) where the order is to be made in proceedings for *divorce*, nullity of marriage *or judicial separation* it may, if it thinks fit, defer the grant of the decree in question until the instrument has been duly executed.

Variation, discharge and enforcement of certain orders, etc

31 Variation, discharge, etc, of certain orders for financial relief

(1) Where the court has made an order to which this section applies, then, subject to the provisions of this section [and of section 28(1A) above], the court shall have power to vary or discharge the order or to suspend any provision thereof temporarily and to revive the operation of any provision so suspended.

(2) This section applies to the following orders, that is to say—

(a) any order for maintennce pending suit and any interim order for maintenance;

(b) any periodical payments order;

(c) any secured periodical payments order;

(d) any order made by virtue of section 23(3)(c) or 27(7)(b) above (provisions for payment of a lump sum by instalments);

[(dd) any deferred order made by virtue of section 23(1)(c) (lump sums) which includes provision made by virtue of—

(i) section 25B(4), . . .

(ii) section 25C, [or]

[(iii) section 25F(2),]

(provision in respect of pension rights [or pension compensation rights]);]

(e) any order for a settlement of property under section 24(1)(b) or for a variation of settlement under section 24(1)(c) or (d) above, being an order made on or after the grant of a decree of judicial separation;

[(f) any order made under section 24A(1) above for the sale of property;]

[(g) a pension sharing order under section 24B above[, or a pension compensation sharing order under section 24E above,] which is made at a time before the decree has been made absolute].

[(2A) Where the court has made an order referred to in subsection (2)(a), (b) or (c) above, then, subject to the provisions of this section, the court shall have power to remit the payment of any arrears due under the order or of any part thereof.]

[(2B) Where the court has made an order referred to in subsection (2)(dd)(ii) above, this section shall cease to apply to the order on the death of either of the parties to the marriage.]

(3) The powers exercisable by the court under this section in relation to an order shall be exercisable also in relation to any instrument executed in pursuance of the order.

(4)   The court shall not exercise the powers conferred by this section in relation to an order for a settlement under section 24(1)(b) or for a variation of settlement under section 24(1)(c) or (d) above except on an application made in proceedings—

(a)   for the rescission of the decree of judicial separation by reference to which the order was made, or

(b)   for the dissolution of the marriage in question.

[(4A)   In relation to an order which falls within paragraph (g) of subsection (2) above ("the subsection (2) order")—

(a)   the powers conferred by this section may be exercised—

(i)   only on an application made before the subsection (2) order has or, but for paragraph (b) below, would have taken effect; and

(ii)   only if, at the time when the application is made, the decree has not been made absolute; and

(b)   an application made in accordance with paragraph (a) above prevents the subsection (2) order from taking effect before the application has been dealt with.

(4B)   No variation of a pension sharing order[, or a pension compensation sharing order,] shall be made so as to take effect before the decree is made absolute.

(4C)   The variation of a pension sharing order[, or a pension compensation sharing order,] prevents the order taking effect before the end of such period after the making of the variation as may be prescribed by regulations made by the Lord Chancellor.]

(5)   [Subject to subsections (7A) to [(7G)] below and without prejudice to any power exercisable by virtue of subsection (2)(d), (dd)[, (e) or (g)] above or otherwise than by virtue of this section,] no property adjustment order [or pension sharing order] [or pension compensation sharing order] shall be made on an application for the variation of a periodical payments or secured periodical payments order made (whether in favour of a party to a marriage or in favour of a child of the family) under section 23 above, and no order for the payment of a lump sum shall be made on an application for the variation of a periodical payments or secured periodical payments order in favour of a party to a marriage (whether made under section 23 or under section 27 above).

(6)   Where the person liable to make payments under a secured periodical payments order has died, an application under this section relating to that order [(and to any order made under section 24A(1) above which requires the proceeds of sale of property to be used for securing those payments) may be made by the person entitled to payments under the periodical payments order] or by the personal representatives of the deceased person, but no such application shall, except with the permission of the court, be made after the end of the period of six months from the date on which representation in regard to the estate of that person is first taken out.

[(7)   In exercising the powers conferred by this section the court shall have regard to all the circumstances of the case, first consideration being given to the welfare while a minor of any child of the family who has not attained the age of eighteen, and the circumstances of the case shall include any change in any of the matters to which the court was required to have regard when making the order to which the application relates, and—

(a)   in the case of a periodical payments or secured periodical payments order made on or after the grant of a decree of divorce or nullity of marriage, the court shall consider whether in all the circumstances and after having regard to any such change it would be appropriate to vary the order so that payments under the order are required to be made or secured only for such further period as will in the opinion of the court be sufficient [(in the light of any proposed exercise by the court, where the marriage has been dissolved, of its powers under subsection (7B) below)] to enable the party in whose favour the order was made to adjust without undue hardship to the termination of those payments;

(b)   in a case where the party against whom the order was made has died, the circumstances of the case shall also include the changed circumstances resulting from his or her death.]

[(7A) Subsection (7B) below applies where, after the dissolution of a marriage, the court—

(a)   discharges a periodical payments order or secured periodical payments order made in favour of a party to the marriage; or

(b)   varies such an order so that payments under the order are required to be made or secured only for such further period as is determined by the court.

(7B) The court has power, in addition to any power it has apart from this subsection, to make supplemental provision consisting of any of—

(a)   an order for the payment of a lump sum in favour of a party to the marriage;

(b)   one or more property adjustment orders in favour of a party to the marriage;

[(ba) one or more pension sharing orders;]

[(bb) a pension compensation sharing order;]

(c)   a direction that the party in whose favour the original order discharged or varied was made is not entitled to make any further application for—

(i)   a periodical payments or secured periodical payments order, or

(ii)   an extension of the period to which the original order is limited by any variation made by the court.

(7C) An order for the payment of a lump sum made under subsection (7B) above may—

(a)   provide for the payment of that sum by instalments of such amount as may be specified in the order; and

(b)   require the payment of the instalments to be secured to the satisfaction of the court.

(7D) [Section 23(6)] above [applies] where the court makes an order for the payment of a lump sum under subsection (7B) above as [it applies where the court] makes such an order under [section 23] above.

(7E) If under subsection (7B) above the court makes more than one property adjustment order in favour of the same party to the marriage, each of those orders must fall within a different paragraph of section 21(2) above.

(7F) Sections 24A and 30 above apply where the court makes a property adjustment order under subsection (7B) above as they apply where it makes such an order under section 23A above.]

[(7G) Subsections (3) to (5) of section 24B above apply in relation to a pension sharing order under subsection (7B) above as they apply in relation to a pension sharing order under that section.]

[(7H) Subsections (3) to (10) of section 24E above apply in relation to a pension compensation sharing order under subsection (7B) above as they apply in relation to a pension compensation sharing order under that section.]

(8) The personal representatives of a deceased person against whom a secured periodical payments order was made shall not be liable for having distributed any part of the estate of the deceased after the expiration of the period of six months referred to in subsection (6) above on the ground that they ought to have taken into account the possibility that the court might permit an application under this section to be made after that period by the person entitled to payments under the order; but this subsection shall not prejudice any power to recover any part of the estate so distributed arising by virtue of the making of an order in pursuance of this section.

[(9) The following are to be left out of account when considering for the purposes of subsection (6) above when representation was first taken out—

(a)   a grant limited to settled land or to trust property,

(b)   any other grant that does not permit any of the estate to be distributed,

(c)   a grant limited to real estate or to personal estate, unless a grant limited to the remainder of the estate has previously been made or is made at the same time,

(d)   a grant, or its equivalent, made outside the United Kingdom (but see subsection (9A) below).

(9A)   A grant sealed under section 2 of the Colonial Probates Act 1892 counts as a grant made in the United Kingdom for the purposes of subsection (9) above, but is to be taken as dated on the date of sealing.]

[(10)   Where the court, in exercise of its powers under this section, decides to vary or discharge a periodical payments or secured periodical payments order, then, subject to section 28(1) and (2) above, the court shall have power to direct that the variation or discharge shall not take effect until the expiration of such period as may be specified in the order.]

[(11)   Where—

(a)   a periodical payments or secured periodical payments order in favour of more than one child ("the order") is in force;

(b)   the order requires payments specified in it to be made to or for the benefit of more than one child without apportioning those payments between them;

(c)   a *maintenance assessment* [maintenance calculation] ("*the assessment* [the calculation]") is made with respect to one or more, but not all, of the children with respect to whom those payments are to be made; and

(d)   an application is made, before the end of the period of 6 months beginning with the date on which *the assessment* [the calculation] was made, for the variation or discharge of the order,

the court may, in exercise of its powers under this section to vary or discharge the order, direct that the variation or discharge shall take effect from the date on which *the assessment* [the calculation] took effect or any later date.

(12)   Where—

(a)   an order ("the child order") of a kind prescribed for the purposes of section 10(1) of the Child Support Act 1991 is affected by a *maintenance assessment* [maintenance calculation];

(b)   on the date on which the child order became so affected there was in force a periodical payments or secured periodical payments order ("the spousal order") in favour of a party to a marriage having the care of the child in whose favour the child order was made; and

(c)   an application is made, before the end of the period of 6 months beginning with the date on which the *maintenance assessment* [maintenance calculation] was made, for the spousal order to be varied or discharged,

the court may, in exercise of its powers under this section to vary or discharge the spousal order, direct that the variation or discharge shall take effect from the date on which the child order became so affected or any later date.

(13)   For the purposes of subsection (12) above, an order is affected if it ceases to have effect or is modified by or under section 10 of the Child Support Act 1991.

(14)   Subsections (11) and (12) above are without prejudice to any other power of the court to direct that the variation of discharge of an order under this section shall take effect from a date earlier than that on which the order for variation or discharge was made.]

[(15)   The power to make regulations under subsection (4C) above shall be exercisable by statutory instrument which shall be subject to annulment in pursuance of a resolution of either House of Parliament.]

NOTES

Amendment

Sub-s (1): words "and of section 28(1A) above" in square brackets inserted by the Matrimonial and Family Proceedings Act 1984, s 6.

Sub-s (2): para (dd) inserted with savings by the Pensions Act 1995, s 166(3)(a); for savings see SI 1996/1675, arts 4, 5.

Sub-s (2): in para (dd)(i) word omitted repealed by the Pensions Act 2008, ss 120, 148, Sch 6, Pt 1, paras 1, 8(1), (2)(a), Sch 11, Pt 4.

Date in force: 6 April 2011: see SI 2011/664, art 2(3), Schedule, Pt 2.

Sub-s (2): in para (dd)(ii) word "or" in square brackets inserted by the Pensions Act 2008, s 120, Sch 6, Pt 1, paras 1, 8(1), (2)(b) .

Date in force: 6 April 2011: see SI 2011/664, art 2(3), Schedule, Pt 2.

Sub-s (2): para (dd)(iii) inserted by the Pensions Act 2008, s 120, Sch 6, Pt 1, paras 1, 8(1), (2)(c).

Date in force: 6 April 2011: see SI 2011/664, art 2(3), Schedule, Pt 2.

Sub-s (2): in para (dd) words "or pension compensation rights" in square brackets inserted by the Pensions Act 2008, s 120, Sch 6, Pt 1, paras 1, 8(1), (2)(d).

Date in force: 6 April 2011: see SI 2011/664, art 2(3), Schedule, Pt 2.

Sub-s (2): para (f) inserted by the Matrimonial Homes and Property Act 1981, s 8(2)(a).

Sub-s (2): para (g) inserted by the Welfare Reform and Pensions Act 1999, s 19, Sch 3, paras 1, 7(1), (2).

Date in force: 1 December 2000: see SI 2000/1116, art 2(e).

Sub-s (2): in para (g) words ", or a pension compensation sharing order under section 24E above," in square brackets inserted by the Pensions Act 2008, s 120, Sch 6, Pt 1, paras 1, 8(1), (3).

Date in force: 6 April 2011: see SI 2011/664, art 2(3), Schedule, Pt 2.

Sub-s (2A): inserted by the Administration of Justice Act 1982, s 5.

Sub-s (2B): inserted with savings by the Pensions Act 1995, s 166(3)(b); for savings see SI 1996/1675, arts 4, 5.

Sub-ss (4A)–(4C): inserted by the Welfare Reform and Pensions Act 1999, s 19, Sch 3, para 7(3).

Date in force: 1 December 2000: see SI 2000/1116, art 2(e).

Sub-s (4B): words ", or a pension compensation sharing order," in square brackets inserted by the Pensions Act 2008, s 120, Sch 6, Pt 1, paras 1, 8(1), (4).

Date in force: 6 April 2011: see SI 2011/664, art 2(3), Schedule, Pt 2.

Sub-s (4C): words ", or a pension compensation sharing order," in square brackets inserted by the Pensions Act 2008, s 120, Sch 6, Pt 1, paras 1, 8(1), (5).

Date in force (for certain purposes): 6 March 2011: see SI 2011/664, art 2(2), Schedule, Pt 1.

Date in force (for remaining purposes): 6 April 2011: see SI 2011/664, art 2(3), Schedule, Pt 2.

Sub-s (5): words from "Subject to subsections" to "of this section," in square brackets inserted with savings by the Family Law Act 1996, s 66(1), Sch 8, para 16(5)(a); for savings see s 66(2), Sch 9, para 5 thereto.

Date in force: 1 November 1998: see SI 1998/2572, art 3.

Sub-s (5): reference to "(7G)" in square brackets substituted by the Welfare Reform and Pensions Act 1999, s 19, Sch 3, paras 1, 7(1), (4)(a).

Date in force: 1 December 2000: see SI 2000/1116, art 2(e).

Sub-s (5): words ", (e) or (g)" in square brackets substituted by the Welfare Reform and Pensions Act 1999, s 19, Sch 3, paras 1, 7(1), (4)(b).

Date in force: 1 December 2000: see SI 2000/1116, art 2(e).

Sub-s (5): words "or pension sharing order" in square brackets inserted by the Welfare Reform and Pensions Act 1999, s 19, Sch 3, paras 1, 7(1), (4)(c).

Date in force: 1 December 2000: see SI 2000/1116, art 2(e).

Sub-s (5): words "or pension compensation sharing order" in square brackets inserted by the Pensions Act 2008, s 120, Sch 6, Pt 1, paras 1, 8(1), (6).

Date in force: 6 April 2011: see SI 2011/664, art 2(3), Schedule, Pt 2.

Sub-s (6): words from "(and to any" to "payments order" in square brackets substituted by the Matrimonial Homes and Property Act 1981, s 8(2)(b).

Sub-s (7): substituted by the Matrimonial and Family Proceedings Act 1984, s 6.

Sub-s (7): in para (a) words from "(in the light" to "subsection (7B) below)" in square brackets inserted with savings by the Family Law Act 1996, s 66(1), Sch 8, para 16(6)(b); for savings see s 66(2), Sch 9, para 5 thereto.

Date in force: 1 November 1998: see SI 1998/2572, art 3.

Sub-ss (7A)–(7F): inserted by the Family Law Act 1996, s 66(1), Sch 8, para 16(7); for effect see s 66(2), Sch 9, para 6(2) thereto.

Date in force: 1 November 1998: see SI 1998/2572, art 3.

Sub-s (7B): para (ba) inserted by the Welfare Reform and Pensions Act 1999, s 19, Sch 3, paras 1, 7(1), (5).

Date in force: 1 December 2000 (except that a pension sharing order may not be made if the marriage was dissolved by a decree granted in proceedings begun before that date): see SI 2000/1116, art 2(e) and the Welfare Reform and Pensions Act 1999, s 85(3)(b).

Sub-s (7B): para (bb) inserted by the Pensions Act 2008, s 120, Sch 6, Pt 1, paras 1, 8(1), (7).
Date in force: 6 April 2011: see SI 2011/664, art 2(3), Schedule, Pt 2.

Sub-s (7D): words "Section 23(6)" in square brackets substituted by the Children and Families Act 2014, s 18(6), (7)(b)(i).
Date in force: 13 May 2014: see the Children and Families Act 2014, s 139(4).

Sub-s (7D): word "applies" in square brackets substituted by the Children and Families Act 2014, s 18(8)(a).
Date in force: 13 May 2014: see the Children and Families Act 2014, s 139(4).

Sub-s (7D): words "it applies where the court" in square brackets substituted by the Children and Families Act 2014, s 18(8)(b).
Date in force: 13 May 2014: see the Children and Families Act 2014, s 139(4).

Sub-s (7D): words "section 23" in square brackets substituted by the Children and Families Act 2014, s 18(6), (7)(b)(ii).
Date in force: 13 May 2014: see the Children and Families Act 2014, s 139(4).

Sub-s (7G): inserted by the Welfare Reform and Pensions Act 1999, s 19, Sch 3, paras 1, 7(1), (6).
Date in force: 1 December 2000: see SI 2000/1116, art 2(e).

Sub-s (7H): inserted by the Pensions Act 2008, s 120, Sch 6, Pt 1, paras 1, 8(1), (8).
Date in force: 6 April 2011: see SI 2011/664, art 2(3), Schedule, Pt 2.

Sub-ss (9), (9A): substituted, for sub-s (9) as originally enacted, by the Inheritance and Trustees' Powers Act 2014, s 7, Sch 3, para 1; for transitional provision see s 12(4).
Date in force: 1 October 2014: see SI 2014/2039, art 2.

Sub-s (10): inserted by the Matrimonial and Family Proceedings Act 1984, s 6.

Sub-ss (11)–(14): inserted by SI 1993/623, art 2, Sch 1, para 3.

Sub-s (11): in para (c) words "maintenance assessment" in italics repealed and subsequent words in square brackets substituted by the Child Support, Pensions and Social Security Act 2000, s 26, Sch 3, para 3(1), (3)(a).
Date in force (in relation to certain cases): 3 March 2003: see SI 2003/192, arts 3, 8, Schedule.
Date in force (for remaining purposes): to be appointed: see the Child Support, Pensions and Social Security Act 2000, s 86(2).

Sub-s (11): in para (c) words "the assessment" in italics repealed and subsequent words in square brackets substituted by the Child Support, Pensions and Social Security Act 2000, s 26, Sch 3, para 3(1), (3)(b).
Date in force (in relation to certain cases): 3 March 2003: see SI 2003/192, arts 3, 8, Schedule.
Date in force (for remaining purposes): to be appointed: see the Child Support, Pensions and Social Security Act 2000, s 86(2).

Sub-s (11): in para (d) words "the assessment" in italics repealed and subsequent words in square brackets substituted by the Child Support, Pensions and Social Security Act 2000, s 26, Sch 3, para 3(1), (3)(b).
Date in force (in relation to certain cases): 3 March 2003: see SI 2003/192, arts 3, 8, Schedule.
Date in force (for remaining purposes): to be appointed: see the Child Support, Pensions and Social Security Act 2000, s 86(2).

Sub-s (11): words "the assessment" in italics repealed and subsequent words in square brackets substituted by the Child Support, Pensions and Social Security Act 2000, s 26, Sch 3, para 3(1), (3)(b).
Date in force (in relation to certain cases): 3 March 2003: see SI 2003/192, arts 3, 8, Schedule.
Date in force (for remaining purposes): to be appointed: see the Child Support, Pensions and Social Security Act 2000, s 86(2).

Sub-s (12): in para (a) words "maintenance assessment" in italics repealed and subsequent words in square brackets substituted by the Child Support, Pensions and Social Security Act 2000, s 26, Sch 3, para 3(1), (3)(a).
Date in force (in relation to certain cases): 3 March 2003: see SI 2003/192, arts 3, 8, Schedule.
Date in force (for remaining purposes): to be appointed: see the Child Support, Pensions and Social Security Act 2000, s 86(2).

Sub-s (12): in para (c) words "maintenance assessment" in italics repealed and subsequent words in square brackets substituted by the Child Support, Pensions and Social Security Act 2000, s 26, Sch 3, para 3(1), (3)(a).
Date in force (in relation to certain cases): 3 March 2003: see SI 2003/192, arts 3, 8, Schedule.
Date in force (for remaining purposes): to be appointed: see the Child Support, Pensions and Social Security Act 2000, s 86(2).

Sub-s (15): inserted by the Welfare Reform and Pensions Act 1999, s 19, Sch 3, paras 1, 7(1), (7).

Date in force: 11 November 1999: see the Welfare Reform and Pensions Act 1999, s 89(5)(a).

32 Payment of certain arrears unenforceable without the leave of the court

(1)   A person shall not be entitled to enforce through the High Court or [the family court] the payment of any arrears due under an order for maintenance pending suit, an interm order for maintenance or any financial provision order without the leave of that court if those arrears became due more than twelve months before proceedings to enforce the payment of them are begun.

(2)   The court hearing an application for the grant of leave under this section may refuse leave, or may grant leave subject to such restrictions and conditions (including conditions as to the allowing of time for payment or the making of payment by instalments) as that court thinks proper, or may remit the payment of the arrears or of any part thereof.

(3)   An application for the grant of leave under this section shall be made in such manner as may be prescribed by rules of court.

NOTES

Amendment

Sub-s (1): words "the family court" in square brackets substituted by the Crime and Courts Act 2013, s 17(6), Sch 11, Pt 1, paras 58, 60.

Date in force: 22 April 2014: see SI 2014/954, art 2(a), (e); for transitional provision see art 3.

33 Orders for repayment in certain cases of sums paid under certain orders

(1)   Where on an application made under this section in relation to an order to which this section applies it appears to the court that by reason of—

(a)   a change in the circumstances of the person entitled to, or liable to make, payments under the order since the order was made, or

(b)   the changed circumstances resulting from the death of the person so liable,

the amount received by the person entitled to payments under the order in respect of a period after those circumstances changed or after the death of the person liable to make payments under the order, as the case may be, exceeds the amount which the person so liable or his or her personal representatives should have been required to pay, the court may order the respondent to the application to pay to the applicant such sum, not exceeding the amount of the excess, as the court thinks just.

(2)   This section applies to the following orders, that is to say—

(a)   any order for maintenance pending suit and any interim order for maintenance;

(b)   any periodicial payments order; and

(c)   any secured periodical payments order.

(3)   An application under this section may be made by the person liable to make payments under an order to which this section applies or his or her personal representatives and may be made against the person entitled to payments under the order or her or his personal representatives.

(4)   An application under this section may be made in proceedings in the High Court or [the family court] for—

(a)   the variation or discharge of the order to which this section applies, or

(b)   leave to enforce, or the enforcement of, the payment of arrears under that order;

but when not made in such proceedings shall be made to [the family court], and accordingly references in this section to the court are references to the High Court or [the family court], as the circumstances require.

(5)   . . .

(6) An order under this section for the payment of any sum may provide for the payment of that sum by instalments of such amount as may be specified in the order.

NOTES

Amendment

Sub-s (4): words "the family court" in square brackets in each place they occur substituted by the Crime and Courts Act 2013, s 17(6), Sch 11, Pt 1, paras 58, 61(1), (2).

Date in force: 22 April 2014: see SI 2014/954, art 2(a), (e); for transitional provision see art 3.

Sub-s (5): repealed by the Crime and Courts Act 2013, s 17(6), Sch 11, Pt 1, paras 58, 61(1), (3).

Date in force: 22 April 2014: see SI 2014/954, art 2(a), (e); for transitional provision see art 3.

[Consent orders]

[33A Consent orders for financial provision on property adjustment]

[(1) Notwithstanding anything in the preceding provisions of this Part of this Act, on an application for a consent order for financial relief the court may, unless it has reason to think that there are other circumstances into which it ought to inquire, make an order in the terms agreed on the basis only of the prescribed information furnished with the application.

(2) Subsection (1) above applies to an application for a consent order varying or discharging an order for financial relief as it applies to an application for an order for financial relief.

(3) In this section—

"consent order", in relation to an application for an order, means an order in the terms applied for to which the respondent agrees;

"order for financial relief" means an order under any of sections 23, 24, 24A[, 24B] or 27 above; and

"prescribed" means prescribed by rules of court.]

NOTES

Amendment

Inserted by the Matrimonial and Family Proceedings Act 1984, s 7.

Sub-s (3): in definition "order for financial relief" reference to ", 24B" in square brackets inserted by the Welfare Reform and Pensions Act 1999, s 19, Sch 3, paras 1, 8.

Date in force: 1 December 2000: see SI 2000/1116, art 2(e).

Maintenance agreements

34 Validity of maintenance agreements

(1) If a maintenance agreement includes a provision purporting to restrict any right to apply to a court for an order containing financial arrangements, then—

    (a)   that provision shall be void; but

    (b)   any other financial arrangements contained in the agreement shall not thereby be rendered void or unenforceable and shall, unless they are void or unenforceable for any other reason (and subject to sections 35 and 36 below), be binding on the parties to the agreement.

(2) In this section and in section 35 below—

"maintenance agreement" means any agreement in writing made, whether before or after the commencement of this Act, between the parties to a marriage, being—

    (a)   an agreement containing financial arrangements, whether made during the continuance or after the dissolution or annulment of the marriage; or

      (b)   a separation agreement which contains no financial arrangements in a case where no other agreement in writing between the same parties contains such arrangements;

"financial arrangements" means provisions governing the rights and liabilities towards one another when living separately of the parties to a marriage (including a marriage which has been dissolved or annulled) in respect of the making or securing of payments or the disposition or use of any property, including such rights and liabilities with respect to the maintenance or education of any child, whether or not a child of the family.

35 Alteration of agreements by court during lives of parties

(1)   Where a maintenance agreement is for the time being subsisting and each of the parties to the agreement is for the time being either domiciled or resident in England and Wales, then, subject to [subsections (1A) and (3)] below, either party may apply to the court . . . for an order under this section.

[(1A)   If an application or part of an application relates to a matter where jurisdiction falls to be determined by reference to the jurisdictional requirements of the Maintenance Regulation and Schedule 6 to the Civil Jurisdiction and Judgments (Maintenance) Regulations 2011—

      (a)   the requirement as to domicile or residence in subsection (1) does not apply to the application or that part of it, but

      (b)   the court may not entertain the application or that part of it unless it has jurisdiction to do so by virtue of that Regulation and that Schedule.]

(2)   If the court . . . is satisfied either—

      (a)   that by reason of a change in the circumstances in the light of which any financial arrangements contained in the agreement were made or, as the case may be, financial arrangements were omitted from it (including a change foreseen by the parties when making the agreement), the agreement should be altered so as to make different, or, as the case may be, so as to contain, financial arrangements, or

      (b)   that the agreement does not contain proper financial arrangements with respect to any child of the family,

then subject to [subsections] (4) and (5) below, [the court] may by order make such alterations in the agreement—

      (i)   by varying or revoking any financial arrangements contained in it, or

      (ii)   by inserting in it financial arrangements for the benefit of one of the parties to the agreement or of a child of the family,

as may appear to [the court] to be just having regard to all the circumstances, including, if relevant, the matters mentioned in [section 25(4)] above; and the agreement shall have effect thereafter as if any alteration made by the order had been made by agreement between the parties and for valuable consideration.

(3) . . .

(4)   Where [the court] decides to alter, by order under this section, an agreement by inserting provision for the making or securing by one of the parties to the agreement of periodical payments for the maintenance of the other party or by increasing the rate of the periodical payments which the agreement provides shall be made by one of the parties for the maintenance of the other, the term for which the payments or, as the case may be, the additional payments attributable to the increase are to be made under the agreement as altered by the order shall be such term as the court may specify, subject to the following limits, that is to say—

      (a)   where the payments will not be secured, the term shall be so defined as not to extend beyond the death of either of the parties to the agreement or the remarriage of[, or formation of a civil partnership by,] the party to whom the payments are to be made;

(b)   where the payments will be secured, the term shall be so defined as not to extend beyond the death or remarriage of[, or formation of a civil partnership by,] that party.

(5)   Where [the court] decides to alter, by order under this section, an agreement by inserting provision for the making or securing by one of the parties to the agreement of periodical payments for the maintenance of a child of the family or by increasing the rate of the periodical payments which the agreement provides shall be made or secured by one of the parties for the maintenance of such a child, then, in deciding the term for which under the agreement as altered by the order the payments, or as the case may be, the additional payments attributable to the increase are to be made or secured for the benefit of the child, the court shall apply the provisions of section 29(2) and (3) above as to age limits as if the order in question were a periodical payments or secured periodical payments order in favour of the child.

(6)   For the avoidance of doubt it is hereby declared that nothing in this section or in section 34 above affects any power of a court before which any proceedings between the parties to a maintenance agreement are brought under any other enactment (including a provision of this Act) to make an order containing financial arrangements or any right of either party to apply for such an order in such proceedings.

NOTES

Amendment

Sub-s (1): words "subsections (1A) and (3)" in square brackets substituted by SI 2011/1484, reg 9, Sch 7, para 6(1), (3)(a).
> Date in force: 18 June 2011: see SI 2011/1484, reg 1(1).

Sub-s (1): words omitted repealed by the Crime and Courts Act 2013, s 17(6), Sch 11, Pt 1, paras 58, 62(1), (2).
> Date in force: 22 April 2014: see SI 2014/954, art 2(a), (e); for transitional provision see art 3.

Sub-s (1A): inserted by SI 2011/1484, reg 9, Sch 7, para 6(1), (3)(b).
> Date in force: 18 June 2011: see SI 2011/1484, reg 1(1).

Sub-s (2): words omitted repealed by the Crime and Courts Act 2013, s 17(6), Sch 11, Pt 1, paras 58, 62(1), (3)(a).
> Date in force: 22 April 2014: see SI 2014/954, art 2(a), (e); for transitional provision see art 3.

Sub-s (2): word "subsections" in square brackets substituted by the Crime and Courts Act 2013, s 17(6), Sch 11, Pt 1, paras 58, 62(1), (3)(b).
> Date in force: 22 April 2014: see SI 2014/954, art 2(a), (e); for transitional provision see art 3.

Sub-s (2): words "the court" in square brackets in each place they occur substituted by the Crime and Courts Act 2013, s 17(6), Sch 11, Pt 1, paras 58, 62(1), (3)(c).
> Date in force: 22 April 2014: see SI 2014/954, art 2(a), (e); for transitional provision see art 3.

Sub-s (2): words "section 25(4)" in square brackets substituted by the Matrimonial and Family Proceedings Act 1984, s 46(1), Sch 1, para 13.

Sub-s (3): repealed by the Crime and Courts Act 2013, s 17(6), Sch 11, Pt 1, paras 58, 62(1), (4).
> Date in force: 22 April 2014: see SI 2014/954, art 2(a), (e); for transitional provision see art 3.

Sub-s (4): words "the court" in square brackets substituted by the Crime and Courts Act 2013, s 17(6), Sch 11, Pt 1, paras 58, 62(1), (5).
> Date in force: 22 April 2014: see SI 2014/954, art 2(a), (e); for transitional provision see art 3.

Sub-s (4): in paras (a), (b) words ", or formation of a civil partnership by," in square brackets inserted by the Civil Partnership Act 2004, s 261(1), Sch 27, para 44.
> Date in force: 5 December 2005: see SI 2005/3175, art 2(2).

Sub-s (5): words "the court" in square brackets substituted by the Crime and Courts Act 2013, s 17(6), Sch 11, Pt 1, paras 58, 62(1), (5).
> Date in force: 22 April 2014: see SI 2014/954, art 2(a), (e); for transitional provision see art 3.

36 Alteration of agreements by court after death of one party

(1)   Where a maintenance agreement within the meaning of section 34 above provides for the continuation of payments under the agreement after the death of one of the parties and that party dies domiciled in England and Wales, the surviving party or the

personal representatives of the deceased party may, subject to subsections (2) and (3) below, apply to the . . . court for an order under section 35 above.

(2)   An application under this section shall not, except with the permission of the . . . court, be made after the end of the period of six months from the date on which representation in regard to the estate of the deceased is first taken out.

(3)   . . .

(4)   If a maintenance agreement is altered by [the court] on an application made in pursuance of subsection (1) above, the like consequences shall ensue as if the alteration had been made immediately before the death by agreement between the parties and for valuable consideration.

(5)   The provisions of this section shall not render the personal representatives of the deceased liable for having distributed any part of the estate of the deceased after the expiration of the period of six months referred to in subsection (2) above on the ground that they ought to have taken into account the possibility that [the court] might permit an application by virtue of this section to be made by the surviving party after that period; but this subsection shall not prejudice any power to recover any part of the estate so distributed arising by virtue of the making of an order in pursuance of this section.

(6)   Section 31(9) above shall apply for the purposes of subsection (2) above as it applies for the purposes of subsection (6) of section 31.

(7)   . . .

NOTES

Amendment

> Sub-s (1): words omitted repealed by the Crime and Courts Act 2013, s 17(6), Sch 11, Pt 1, paras 58, 63(1), (2).
>> Date in force: 22 April 2014: see SI 2014/954, art 2(a), (e); for transitional provision see art 3.
> Sub-s (2): words omitted repealed by the Crime and Courts Act 2013, s 17(6), Sch 11, Pt 1, paras 58, 63(1), (3).
>> Date in force: 22 April 2014: see SI 2014/954, art 2(a), (e); for transitional provision see art 3.
> Sub-s (3): repealed by the Crime and Courts Act 2013, s 17(6), Sch 11, Pt 1, paras 58, 63(1), (4).
>> Date in force: 22 April 2014: see SI 2014/954, art 2(a), (e); for transitional provision see art 3.
> Sub-s (4): words "the court" in square brackets substituted by the Crime and Courts Act 2013, s 17(6), Sch 11, Pt 1, paras 58, 63(1), (5).
>> Date in force: 22 April 2014: see SI 2014/954, art 2(a), (e); for transitional provision see art 3.
> Sub-s (5): words "the court" in square brackets substituted by the Crime and Courts Act 2013, s 17(6), Sch 11, Pt 1, paras 58, 63(1), (5).
>> Date in force: 22 April 2014: see SI 2014/954, art 2(a), (e); for transitional provision see art 3.
> Sub-s (7): repealed by the Crime and Courts Act 2013, s 17(6), Sch 11, Pt 1, paras 58, 63(1), (4).
>> Date in force: 22 April 2014: see SI 2014/954, art 2(a), (e); for transitional provision see art 3.

Miscellaneous and supplemental

37 Avoidance of transactions intended to prevent or reduce financial relief

(1)   For the purposes of this section "financial relief" means relief under any of the provisions of sections 22, 23, 24, [24B,] 27, 31 (except subsection (6)) and 35 above, and any reference in this section to defeating a person's claim for financial relief is a reference to preventing financial relief from being granted to that person, or to that person for the benefit of a child of the family, or reducing the amount of any financial relief which might be so granted, or frustrating or impeding the enforcement of any order which might be or has been made at his instance under any of those provisions.

(2)　Where proceedings for financial relief are brought by one person against another, the court may, on the application of the first-mentioned person—

    (a)　if it is satisfied that the other party to the proceedings is, with the intention of defeating the claim for financial relief, about to make any disposition or to transfer out of the jurisdiction or otherwise deal with any property, make such order as it thinks fit for restraining the other party from so doing or otherwise for protecting the claim;

    (b)　if it is satisfied that the other party has, with that intention, made a reviewable disposition and that if the disposition were set aside financial relief or different financial relief would be granted to the applicant, make an order setting aside the disposition;

    (c)　if it is satisfied, in a case where an order has been obtained under any of the provisions mentioned in subsection (1) above by the applicant against the other party, that the other party has, with that intention, made a reviewable disposition, make an order setting aside the disposition;

and an application for the purposes of paragraph (b) above shall be made in the proceedings for the financial relief in question.

(3)　Where the court makes an order under subsection (2)(b) or (c) above setting aside a disposition it shall give such consequential directions as it thinks fit for giving effect to the order (including directions requiring the making of any payments or the disposal of any property).

(4)　Any disposition made by the other party to the proceedings for financial relief in question (whether before or after the commencement of those proceedings) is a reviewable disposition for the purposes of subsection (2)(b) and (c) above unless it was made for valuable consideration (other than marriage) to a person who, at the time of the disposition, acted in relation to it in good faith and without notice of any intention on the part of the other party to defeat the applicant's claim for financial relief.

(5)　Where an application is made under this section with respect to a disposition which took place less than three years before the date of the application or with respect to a disposition or other dealing with property which is about to take place and the court is satisfied—

    (a)　in a case falling within subsection (2)(a) or (b) above, that the disposition or other dealing would (apart from this section) have the consequence, or

    (b)　in a case falling within subsection (2)(c) above, that the disposition has had the consequence,

of defeating the applicant's claim for financial relief, it shall be presumed, unless the contrary is shown, that the person who disposed of or is about to dispose of or deal with the property did so or, as the case may be, is about to do so, with the intention of defeating the applicant's claim for financial relief.

(6)　In this section "disposition" does not include any provision contained in a will or codicil but, with that exception, includes any conveyance, assurance or gift of property of any description, whether made by an instrument or otherwise.

(7)　This section does not apply to a disposition made before 1st January 1968.

NOTES

Amendment

    Sub-s (1): reference to "24B," in square brackets inserted by the Welfare Reform and Pensions Act 1999, s 19, Sch 3, paras 1, 9.

        Date in force: 1 December 2000: see SI 2000/1116, art 2(e).

38 Orders for repayment in certain cases of sums paid after cessation of order by reason of remarriage [or formation of civil partnership]

(1)　Where—

    (a)　a periodical payments or secured periodical payments order in favour of a party to a marriage (hereafter in this section referred to as "a payments order") has ceased to have effect by reason of the remarriage of[, or formation of a civil partnership by,] that party, and

(b)   the person liable to make payments under the order or his or her personal representatives made payments in accordance with it in respect of a period after the date of the remarriage [or formation of the civil partnership] in the mistaken belief that the order was still subsisting,

the person so liable or his or her personal representatives shall not be entitled to bring proceedings in respect of a cause of action arising out of the circumstances mentioned in paragraphs (a) and (b) above against the person entitled to payments under the order or her or his personal representatives, but may instead make an application against that person or her or his personal representatives under this section.

(2)   On an application under this section the court [to which the application is made] may order the respondent to pay to the applicant a sum equal to the amount of the payments made in respect of the period mentioned in subsection (1)(b) above or, if it appears to the court that it would be unjust to make that order, it may either order the respondent to pay to the applicant such lesser sum as it thinks fit or dismiss the application.

(3)   An application under this section may be made in proceedings in the High Court or [the family court] for leave to enforce, or the enforcement of, payment of arrears under the order in question, but when not made in such proceedings shall be made to [the family court]; and accordingly references in this section to the court are references to the High Court or [the family court], as the circumstances require.

(4)   . . .

(5)   An order under this section for the payment of any sum may provide for the payment of that sum by instalments of such amount as may be specified in the order.

(6)   [An officer of the family court,] and the collecting officer under an attachment of earnings order made to secure payments under a payments order, shall not be liable—

(a)   in the case of [an officer of the family court,] for any act done by him[, in pursuance of a payments order requiring payments to be made to the court or an officer of the court,] after the date on which that order ceased to have effect by reason of the remarriage of[, or formation of a civil partnership by,] the person entitled to payments under it, and

(b)   in the case of the collecting officer, for any act done by him after that date in accordance with any enactment or rule of court specifying how payments made to him in compliance with the attachment of earnings order are to be dealt with,

if, but only if, the act was one which he would have been under a duty to do had the payments order not so ceased to have effect and the act was done before notice in writing of the fact that the person so entitled had remarried [or formed a civil partnership] was given to him by or on behalf of that person, the person liable to make payments under the payments order or the personal representatives of either of those persons.

(7)   In this section "collecting officer", in relation to an attachment of earnings order, means the officer of the High Court, [or the officer of the family court,] to whom a person makes payments in compliance with the order.

NOTES

Amendment
Section heading: words "or formation of civil partnership" in square brackets inserted by the Civil Partnership Act 2004, s 261(1), Sch 27, para 45(1), (4).
    Date in force: 5 December 2005: see SI 2005/3175, art 2(2).
    Sub-s (1): in para (a) words ", or formation of a civil partnership by," in square brackets inserted by the Civil Partnership Act 2004, s 261(1), Sch 27, para 45(1), (2)(a).
    Date in force: 5 December 2005: see SI 2005/3175, art 2(2).
    Sub-s (1): in para (b) words "or formation of the civil partnership" in square brackets inserted by the Civil Partnership Act 2004, s 261(1), Sch 27, para 45(1), (2)(b).
    Date in force: 5 December 2005: see SI 2005/3175, art 2(2).

Sub-s (2): words "to which the application is made" in square brackets inserted by the Crime and Courts Act 2013, s 17(6), Sch 11, Pt 1, paras 58, 64(1), (2).
> Date in force: 22 April 2014: see SI 2014/954, art 2(a), (e); for transitional provision see art 3.

Sub-s (3): words "the family court" in square brackets in each place they occur substituted by the Crime and Courts Act 2013, s 17(6), Sch 11, Pt 1, paras 58, 64(1), (3).
> Date in force: 22 April 2014: see SI 2014/954, art 2(a), (e); for transitional provision see art 3.

Sub-s (4): repealed by the Crime and Courts Act 2013, s 17(6), Sch 11, Pt 1, paras 58, 64(1), (4).
> Date in force: 22 April 2014: see SI 2014/954, art 2(a), (e); for transitional provision see art 3.

Sub-s (6): words "An officer of the family court," in square brackets substituted by the Crime and Courts Act 2013, s 17(6), Sch 11, Pt 1, paras 58, 64(1), (5)(a).
> Date in force: 22 April 2014: see SI 2014/954, art 2(a), (e); for transitional provision see art 3.

Sub-s (6): in para (a) words "an officer of the family court," in square brackets substituted by the Crime and Courts Act 2013, s 17(6), Sch 11, Pt 1, paras 58, 64(1), (5)(b)(i).
> Date in force: 22 April 2014: see SI 2014/954, art 2(a), (e); for transitional provision see art 3.

Sub-s (6): in para (a) words from ", in pursuance of" to "of the court," in square brackets substituted by the Crime and Courts Act 2013, s 17(6), Sch 11, Pt 1, paras 58, 64(1), (5)(b)(ii).
> Date in force: 22 April 2014: see SI 2014/954, art 2(a), (e); for transitional provision see art 3.

Sub-s (6): in para (a) words ", or formation of a civil partnership by," in square brackets inserted by the Civil Partnership Act 2004, s 261(1), Sch 27, para 45(1), (3)(a).
> Date in force: 5 December 2005: see SI 2005/3175, art 2(2).

Sub-s (6): words "or formed a civil partnership" in square brackets inserted by the Civil Partnership Act 2004, s 261(1), Sch 27, para 45(1), (3)(b).
> Date in force: 5 December 2005: see SI 2005/3175, art 2(2).

Sub-s (7): words "or the officer of the family court," in square brackets substituted by the Crime and Courts Act 2013, s 17(6), Sch 11, Pt 1, paras 58, 64(1), (6).
> Date in force: 22 April 2014: see SI 2014/954, art 2(a), (e); for transitional provision see art 3.

39 Settlement, etc, made in compliance with a property adjustment order may be avoided on bankruptcy of settlor

The fact that a settlement or transfer of property had to be made in order to comply with a property adjustment order shall not prevent that settlement or transfer from being [a transaction in respect of which an order may be made under [section 339 or 340 of the Insolvency Act 1986] (transfers at an undervalue and preferences)].

NOTES

Amendment
> First words in square brackets substituted by the Insolvency Act 1985, s 235, Sch 8, para 23; words in square brackets therein substituted by the Insolvency Act 1986, s 439(2), Sch 14.

40 Payments, etc, under order made in favour of person suffering from mental disorder

[(1)] Where the court makes an order under this Part of this Act requiring payments (including a lump sum payment) to be made, or property to be transferred, to a party to a marriage and the court is satisfied that the person in whose favour the order is made [("P") lacks capacity (within the meaning of the Mental Capacity Act 2005) in relation to the provisions of the order] then, subject to any order, direction or authority made or given in relation to [P under that Act], the court may order the payments to be made, or as the case may be, the property to be transferred, to [such person ("D") as it may direct].

[(2) In carrying out any functions of his in relation to an order made under subsection (1), D must act in P's best interests (within the meaning of that Act).]

NOTES

Amendment
> Sub-s (1): numbered as such by the Mental Capacity Act 2005, s 67(1), Sch 6, para 19.

Date in force: 1 October 2007: see SI 2007/1897, art 2(1)(d).
Sub-s (1): words from ""(P)" lacks capacity (within" to "of the order" in square brackets substituted by the Mental Capacity Act 2005, s 67(1), Sch 6, para 19(a).
Date in force: 1 October 2007: see SI 2007/1897, art 2(1)(d).
Sub-s (1): words "P under that Act" in square brackets substituted by the Mental Capacity Act 2005, s 67(1), Sch 6, para 19(b).
Date in force: 1 October 2007: see SI 2007/1897, art 2(1)(d).
Sub-s (1): words "such person ("D") as it may direct" in square brackets substituted by the Mental Capacity Act 2005, s 67(1), Sch 6, para 19(c).
Date in force: 1 October 2007: see SI 2007/1897, art 2(1)(d).
Sub-s (2): inserted by the Mental Capacity Act 2005, s 67(1), Sch 6, para 19(d).
Date in force: 1 October 2007: see SI 2007/1897, art 2(1)(d).

[40A Appeals relating to pension sharing orders which have taken effect]

[(1)   Subsections (2) and (3) below apply where an appeal against a pension sharing order is begun on or after the day on which the order takes effect.

(2)   If the pension sharing order relates to a person's rights under a pension arrangement, the appeal court may not set aside or vary the order if the person responsible for the pension arrangement has acted to his detriment in reliance on the taking effect of the order.

(3)   If the pension sharing order relates to a person's shareable state scheme rights, the appeal court may not set aside or vary the order if the Secretary of State has acted to his detriment in reliance on the taking effect of the order.

(4)   In determining for the purposes of subsection (2) or (3) above whether a person has acted to his detriment in reliance on the taking effect of the order, the appeal court may disregard any detriment which in its opinion is insignificant.

(5)   Where subsection (2) or (3) above applies, the appeal court may make such further orders (including one or more pension sharing orders) as it thinks fit for the purpose of putting the parties in the position it considers appropriate.

(6)   Section 24C above only applies to a pension sharing order under this section if the decision of the appeal court can itself be the subject of an appeal.

(7)   In subsection (2) above, the reference to the person responsible for the pension arrangement is to be read in accordance with section 25D(4) above.]

NOTES

Amendment

Inserted by the Welfare Reform and Pensions Act 1999, s 19, Sch 3, paras 1, 10.
Date in force: 1 December 2000: see SI 2000/1116, art 2(e).

[40B Appeals relating to pension compensation sharing orders which have taken effect]

[(1)   This section applies where an appeal against a pension compensation sharing order is begun on or after the day on which the order takes effect.

(2)   If the Board of the Pension Protection Fund has acted to its detriment in reliance on the taking effect of the order the appeal court—

  (a)   may not set aside or vary the order;

  (b)   may make such further orders (including a pension compensation sharing order) as it thinks fit for the purpose of putting the parties in the position it considers appropriate.

(3)   In determining for the purposes of subsection (2) whether the Board has acted to its detriment the appeal court may disregard any detriment which in the court's opinion is insignificant.

(4)   Section 24F (duty to stay) only applies to a pension compensation sharing order under this section if the decision of the appeal court can itself be the subject of an appeal.]

NOTES

Amendment
Inserted by the Pensions Act 2008, s 120, Sch 6, Pt 1, paras 1, 9.
    Date in force: 6 April 2011: see SI 2011/664, art 2(3), Schedule, Pt 2.

. . .

FAMILY PROCEDURE RULES 2010

SI 2010/2955

PART 1
OVERRIDING OBJECTIVE

1.1 The overriding objective

(1)   These rules are a new procedural code with the overriding objective of enabling the court to deal with cases justly, having regard to any welfare issues involved.

(2)   Dealing with a case justly includes, so far as is practicable—

  (a)   ensuring that it is dealt with expeditiously and fairly;

  (b)   dealing with the case in ways which are proportionate to the nature, importance and complexity of the issues;

  (c)   ensuring that the parties are on an equal footing;

  (d)   saving expense; and

  (e)   allotting to it an appropriate share of the court's resources, while taking into account the need to allot resources to other cases.

1.2 Application by the court of the overriding objective

The court must seek to give effect to the overriding objective when it—

  (a)   exercises any power given to it by these rules; or

  (b)   interprets any rule.

1.3 Duty of the parties

The parties are required to help the court to further the overriding objective.

1.4 Court's duty to manage cases

(1)   The court must further the overriding objective by actively managing cases.

[(2)   Active case management includes—

  (a)   setting timetables or otherwise controlling the progress of the case;

  (b)   identifying at an early stage—

    (i)   the issues; and

    (ii)   who should be a party to the proceedings;

  (c)   deciding promptly—

    (i)   which issues need full investigation and hearing and which do not; and

    (ii)   the procedure to be followed in the case;

  (d)   deciding the order in which issues are to be resolved;

  (e)   controlling the use of expert evidence;

  (f)   encouraging the parties to use [a non-court dispute resolution] procedure if the court considers that appropriate and facilitating the use of such procedure;

  (g)   helping the parties to settle the whole or part of the case;

  (h)   encouraging the parties to co-operate with each other in the conduct of proceedings;

  (i)   considering whether the likely benefits of taking a particular step justify the cost of taking it;

  (j)   dealing with as many aspects of the case as it can on the same occasion;

  (k)   dealing with the case without the parties needing to attend at court;

  (l)   making use of technology; and

  (m)   giving directions to ensure that the case proceeds quickly and efficiently.]

NOTES

Amendment
> Para (2): substituted by SI 2012/3061, rr 2, 3.
>> Date in force: 31 January 2013: see SI 2012/3061, r 1.
> Para (2): in sub-para (f) words "a non-court dispute resolution" in square brackets substituted by SI 2014/843, rr 2, 3.
>> Date in force: 22 April 2014: see SI 2014/843, r 1.

[1.5 The Welsh language]
[(1) Nothing in the overriding objective undermines the principles provided by section 1 of the Welsh Language (Wales) Measure 2011 that the Welsh language has official status in Wales or by section 22 of the Welsh Language Act 1993 that in any legal proceedings in Wales the Welsh language may be used by any person who desires to use it.
(2) The parties are required to assist the court to put into effect the principles set out in paragraph (1).]

NOTES

Amendment
> Inserted by SI 2018/1172, rr 2, 3.
>> Date in force: 10 December 2018: see SI 2018/1172, r 1.

PART 2
APPLICATION AND INTERPRETATION OF THE RULES

[2.1 Application of these Rules]
[Unless the context otherwise requires, these rules apply to family proceedings in—
> (a)   the High Court; and
> (b)   the family court.]

NOTES

Amendment
> Substituted by SI 2013/3204, rr 2, 3.
>> Date in force: 22 April 2014 (being the date on which the Crime and Courts Act 2013, s 17(3) is brought fully into force): see SI 2013/3204, r 1 and SI 2014/954, art 2(a); for transitional provisions and savings see SI 2013/3204, r 137 and SI 2014/954, art 3.

2.2 The glossary
(1) The glossary at the end of these rules is a guide to the meaning of certain legal expressions used in the rules, but is not to be taken as giving those expressions any meaning in the rules which they do not have in the law generally.
(2) Subject to paragraph (3), words in these rules which are included in the glossary are followed by "GL".
(3) The word "service", which appears frequently in the rules, is included in the glossary but is not followed by "GL".

2.3 Interpretation
(1)   In these rules—
["the 1958 Act" means the Maintenance Orders Act 1958;]
"the 1973 Act" means the Matrimonial Causes Act 1973;
"the 1978 Act" means the Domestic Proceedings and Magistrates' Courts Act 1978;
"the 1980 Hague Convention" means the Convention on the Civil Aspects of International Child Abduction which was signed at The Hague on 25 October 1980;
"the 1984 Act" means the Matrimonial and Family Proceedings Act 1984;
"the 1986 Act" means the Family Law Act 1986;
"the 1989 Act" means the Children Act 1989;

"the 1990 Act" means the Human Fertilisation and Embryology Act 1990;

"the 1991 Act" means the Child Support Act 1991;

"the 1996 Act" means the Family Law Act 1996;

"the 1996 Hague Convention" means the Convention on Jurisdiction, Applicable Law, Recognition, Enforcement and Co-Operation in Respect of Parental Responsibility and Measures for the Protection of Children;

"the 2002 Act" means the Adoption and Children Act 2002;

"the 2004 Act" means the Civil Partnership Act 2004;

"the 2005 Act" means the Mental Capacity Act 2005;

["the 2007 Hague Convention" means the Convention on the International Recovery of Child Support and other forms of Family Maintenance done at The Hague on 23 November 2007;]

"the 2008 Act" means the Human Fertilisation and Embryology Act 2008;

["the 2014 Act" means the Children and Families Act 2014;]

"adoption proceedings" means proceedings for an adoption order under the 2002 Act;

. . .

. . .

"application form" means a document in which the applicant states his intention to seek a court order other than in accordance with the Part 18 procedure;

"application notice" means a document in which the applicant states his intention to seek a court order in accordance with the Part 18 procedure;

["Article 11 form" means a form published by the Permanent Bureau of the Hague Conference under Article 11(4) of the 2007 Hague Convention for use in relation to an application under Article 10 of that Convention, and includes a Financial Circumstances Form as defined in rule 9.3(1) which accompanies such an application;]

"Assembly" means the National Assembly for Wales;

"bank holiday" means a bank holiday under the Banking and Financial Dealings Act 1971—

    (a)   for the purpose of service of a document within the United Kingdom, in the part of the United Kingdom where service is to take place; and

    (b)   for all other purposes, in England and Wales.

"business day" means any day other than—

    (a)   a Saturday, Sunday, Christmas Day or Good Friday; or

    (b)   a bank holiday;

"care order" has the meaning assigned to it by section 31(11) of the 1989 Act;

"CCR" means the County Court Rules 1981, as they appear in Schedule 2 to the CPR [. . .];

"child" means a person under the age of 18 years who is the subject of the proceedings; except that—

    (a)   in adoption proceedings, it also includes a person who has attained the age of 18 years before the proceedings are concluded; and

    (b)   in proceedings brought under the Council Regulation, the 1980 Hague Convention or the European Convention, it means a person under the age of 16 years who is the subject of the proceedings;

["child arrangements order" has the meaning given to it by section 8(1) of the 1989 Act;]

"child of the family" has the meaning given to it by section 105(1) of the 1989 Act;

"children and family reporter" means an officer of the Service or a Welsh family proceedings officer who has been asked to prepare a welfare report under section 7(1)(a) of the 1989 Act or section 102(3)(b) of the 2002 Act;

"children's guardian" means—

    (a)   in relation to a child who is the subject of and a party to specified proceedings or proceedings to which Part 14 applies, the person appointed in accordance with rule 16.3(1); and

    (b)   in any other case, the person appointed in accordance with rule 16.4;

"civil partnership order" means one of the orders mentioned in section 37 of the 2004 Act;

"civil partnership proceedings" means proceedings for a civil partnership order;

. . .

"civil restraint order" means an order restraining a party—

    (a)   from making any further applications in current proceedings (a limited civil restraint order);

    (b)   from making certain applications in specified courts (an extended civil restraint order); or

    (c)   from making any application in specified courts (a general civil restraint order);

. . .

"consent order" means an order in the terms applied for to which the respondent agrees;

. . .

"the Council Regulation" means Council Regulation (EC) No 2201/2003 of 27 November 2003 on jurisdiction and the recognition and enforcement of judgments in matrimonial matters and in matters of parental responsibility;

"court" means, subject to any rule or other enactment which provides otherwise, the High Court, [or the family court];

    (rule 2.5 relates to the power to perform functions of the court.)

. . .

"court officer" means [a member of court staff;]

"CPR" means the Civil Procedure Rules 1998;

"deputy" has the meaning given in section 16(2)(b) of the 2005 Act;

. . .

"detailed assessment proceedings" means the procedure by which the amount of costs is decided in accordance with Part 47 of the CPR;

"directions appointment" means a hearing for directions;

. . .

. . .

. . .

"the European Convention" means the European Convention on Recognition and Enforcement of Decisions concerning Custody of Children and on the Restoration of Custody of Children which was signed in Luxembourg on 20 May 1980;

"filing", in relation to a document, means delivering it, by post or otherwise, to the court office;

"financial order" means—

    (a)   an avoidance of disposition order;

    (b)   an order for maintenance pending suit;

    (c)   an order for maintenance pending outcome of proceedings;

    (d)   an order for periodical payments or lump sum provision as mentioned in section 21(1) of the 1973 Act, except an order under section 27(6) of that Act;

(e)   an order for periodical payments or lump sum provision as mentioned in paragraph 2(1) of Schedule 5 to the 2004 Act, made under Part 1 of Schedule 5 to that Act;

(f)   a property adjustment order;

(g)   a variation order;

(h)   a pension sharing order; . . .

(i)   a pension compensation sharing order; [or

(j)   an order for payment in respect of legal services;]

("variation order", "pension compensation sharing order" and "pension sharing order" are defined in rule 9.3.)

"financial remedy" means—

(a)   a financial order;

(b)   an order under Schedule 1 to the 1989 Act;

(c)   an order under Part 3 of the 1984 Act [except an application under section 13 of the 1984 Act for permission to apply for a financial remedy];

(d)   an order under Schedule 7 to the 2004 Act [except an application under paragraph 4 of Schedule 7 to the 2004 Act for permission to apply for an order under paragraph 9 or 13 of that Schedule];

(e)   an order under section 27 of the 1973 Act;

(f)   an order under Part 9 of Schedule 5 to the 2004 Act;

(g)   an order under section 35 of the 1973 Act;

(h)   an order under paragraph 69 of Schedule 5 to the 2004 Act;

(i)   an order under Part 1 of the 1978 Act;

(j)   an order under Schedule 6 to the 2004 Act;

(k)   an order under section 10(2) of the 1973 Act; or

(l)   an order under section 48(2) of the 2004 Act;

"hearing" includes a directions appointment;

"hearsay" means a statement made, otherwise than by a person while giving oral evidence in proceedings, which is tendered as evidence of the matters stated, and references to hearsay include hearsay of whatever degree;

["incoming protection measure" means a protection measure that has been ordered in a Member State of the European Union other than the United Kingdom or Denmark;]

"inherent jurisdiction" means the High Court's power to make any order or determine any issue in respect of a child, including in wardship proceedings, where it would be just and equitable to do so unless restricted by legislation or case law;

(Practice Direction 12D (Inherent Jurisdiction (including Wardship Proceedings)) provides examples of inherent jurisdiction proceedings.)

["judge" means—

(a)   in the High Court, a judge or a district judge of that court (including a district judge of the principal registry) or a person authorised to act as such; and

(b)   in the family court, a person who is—

(i)   the Lord Chief Justice;

(ii)   the Master of the Rolls;

(iii)   the President of the Queens Bench Division;

(iv)   the President of the Family Division;

(v)   the Chancellor of the High Court;

(vi)   an ordinary judge of the Court of Appeal (including the vice-president, if any, of either division of that court);

(vii)   the Senior President of Tribunals;

(viii) a puisne judge of the High Court;

(ix) a deputy judge of the High Court;

(x) a person who has been a judge of the Court of Appeal or a puisne judge of the High Court who may act as a judge of the family court by virtue of section 9 of the Senior Courts Act 1981;

(xi) the Chief Taxing Master;

(xii) a taxing master of the Senior Courts;

(xiii) a person appointed to act as a deputy for the person holding office referred to in sub-paragraph (xiii) or to act as a temporary additional officer for any such office;

(xiv) a circuit judge;

(xv) a Recorder;

(xvi) the Senior District Judge of the Family Division;

(xvii) a district judge of the principal registry;

(xviii) a person appointed to act as a deputy for the person holding office referred to in sub-paragraph (xvii) or to act as a temporary additional office holder for any such office;

(xix) a district judge;

(xx) a deputy district judge appointed under section 102 of the Senior Courts Act 1981 or section 8 of the County Courts Act 1984;

(xxi) a District Judge (Magistrates' Courts);

(xxii) a lay justice;

(xxiii) any other judge referred to in section 31C(1) of the 1984 Act who is authorised by the President of the Family Division to conduct particular business in the family court;]

"jurisdiction" means, unless the context requires otherwise, England and Wales and any part of the territorial waters of the United Kingdom adjoining England and Wales;

["justices' legal adviser" means a person authorised to exercise functions under section 67B of the Courts Act 2003 who has such qualifications as are prescribed by the Authorised Court Staff (Legal Advice Functions) Qualifications Regulations 2020;]

["lay justice" means a justice of the peace who is not a District Judge (Magistrates' Courts);]

"legal representative" means a—

(a) barrister;

(b) solicitor;

(c) solicitor's employee;

(d) manager of a body recognised under section 9 of the Administration of Justice Act 1985; or

(e) person who, for the purposes of the Legal Services Act 2007, is an authorised person in relation to an activity which constitutes the conduct of litigation (within the meaning of the Act),

who has been instructed to act for a party in relation to proceedings;

"litigation friend" has the meaning given—

(a) in relation to a protected party, by Part 15; and

(b) in relation to a child, by Part 16;

["the Maintenance Regulation" means Council Regulation (EC) No 4/2009 of 18th December 2008 on jurisdiction, applicable law, recognition and enforcement of decisions and co-operation in matters relating to maintenance obligations, including as applied in relation to Denmark by virtue of the Agreement made on 19th October 2005 between the European Community and the Kingdom of Denmark;]

"matrimonial cause" means proceedings for a matrimonial order;

"matrimonial order" means—

> (a)   a decree of divorce made under section 1 of the 1973 Act;
>
> (b)   a decree of nullity made on one of the grounds set out in [section 11, 12 or 12A] of the 1973 Act;
>
> (c)   a decree of judicial separation made under section 17 of the 1973 Act;

["non-court dispute resolution" means methods of resolving a dispute, including mediation, other than through the normal court process;]

"note" includes a record made by mechanical means;

"officer of the Service" has the meaning given by section 11(3) of the Criminal Justice and Court Services Act 2000;

"order" includes directions of the court;

"order for maintenance pending outcome of proceedings" means an order under paragraph 38 of Schedule 5 to the 2004 Act;

"order for maintenance pending suit" means an order under section 22 of the 1973 Act;

["order for payment for legal services" means an order under section 22ZA of the 1973 Act or an order under paragraph 38A of Part 8 of Schedule 5 to the 2004 Act;]

"parental order proceedings" has the meaning assigned to it by rule 13.1;

"parental responsibility" has the meaning assigned to it by section 3 of the 1989 Act;

"placement proceedings" means proceedings for the making, varying or revoking of a placement order under the 2002 Act;

"principal registry" means the principal registry of the Family Division of the High Court;

"proceedings" means, unless the context requires otherwise, family proceedings as defined in section 75(3) of the Courts Act 2003;

"professional acting in furtherance of the protection of children" includes—

> (a)   an officer of a local authority exercising child protection functions;
>
> (b)   a police officer who is—
>> (i)   exercising powers under section 46 of the Act of 1989; or
>>
>> (ii)   serving in a child protection unit or a paedophile unit of a police force;
>
> (c)   any professional person attending a child protection conference or review in relation to a child who is the subject of the proceedings to which the information regarding the proceedings held in private relates[;]
>
> (d)   an officer of the National Society for the Prevention of Cruelty to Children; [or]
>
> [(e)   a member or employee of the [Disclosure and Barring Service], being the body established under [section 87(1) of the Protection of Freedoms Act 2012];]

"professional legal adviser" means a—

> (a)   barrister;
>
> (b)   solicitor;
>
> (c)   solicitor's employee;

(d)   manager of a body recognised under section 9 of the Administration of Justice Act 1985; or

(e)   person who, for the purposes of the Legal Services Act 2007, is an authorised person in relation to an activity which constitutes the conduct of litigation (within the meaning of that Act),

who is providing advice to a party but is not instructed to represent that party in the proceedings;

"property adjustment order" means—

(a)   in proceedings under the 1973 Act, any of the orders mentioned in section 21(2) of that Act;

(b)   in proceedings under the 1984 Act, an order under section 17(1)(a)(ii) of that Act;

(c)   in proceedings under Schedule 5 to the 2004 Act, any of the orders mentioned in paragraph 7(1); or

(d)   in proceedings under Schedule 7 to the 2004 Act, an order for property adjustment under paragraph 9(2) or (3);

"protected party" means a party, or an intended party, who lacks capacity (within the meaning of the 2005 Act) to conduct proceedings;

["protection measure" has the meaning given to it in the Protection Measures Regulation;]

["Protection Measures Regulation" means the Regulation (EU) No 606/2013 of the European Parliament and of the Council of 12th June 2013 on mutual recognition of protection measures in civil matters;]

"reporting officer" means an officer of the Service or a Welsh family proceedings officer appointed to witness the documents which signify a parent's or guardian's consent to the placing of the child for adoption or to the making of an adoption order or a section 84 order;

"risk assessment" has the meaning assigned to it by section 16A(3) of the 1989 Act;

. . .

"RSC" means the Rules of the Supreme Court 1965 as they appear in Schedule 1 to the CPR [. . .];

"section 8 order" has the meaning assigned to it by section 8(2) of the 1989 Act;

"section 84 order" means an order made by the High Court under section 84 of the 2002 Act giving parental responsibility prior to adoption abroad;

"section 89 order" means an order made by the High Court under section 89 of the 2002 Act—

(a)   annulling a Convention adoption or Convention adoption order;

(b)   providing for an overseas adoption or determination under section 91 of the 2002 Act to cease to be valid; or

(c)   deciding the extent, if any, to which a determination under section 91 of the 2002 Act has been affected by a subsequent determination under that section;

"Service" has the meaning given by section 11 of the Criminal Justice and Court Services Act 2000;

"the Service Regulation" means Regulation (EC) No 1393/2007 of the European Parliament and of the Council of 13 November 2007 on the service in the Member States of judicial and extrajudicial documents in civil or commercial matters (service of documents), and repealing Council Regulation (EC) No 1348/2000, as amended from time to time and as applied by the Agreement made on 19 October 2005 between the European Community and the Kingdom of Denmark on the service of judicial and extrajudicial documents in civil and commercial matters;

"specified proceedings" has the meaning assigned to it by section 41(6) of the 1989 Act and rule 12.27;

"welfare officer" means a person who has been asked to prepare a report under section 7(1)(b) of the 1989 Act;

"Welsh family proceedings officer" has the meaning given by section 35(4) of the Children Act 2004.

(2)   In these rules a reference to—

    (a)   an application for a matrimonial order or a civil partnership order is to be read as a reference to a petition for—

        (i)   a matrimonial order [or];

        (ii)   . . .

        (iii)   a civil partnership order,

and includes a petition by a respondent asking for such an order;

    (b)   "financial order" in matrimonial proceedings is to be read as a reference to "ancillary relief";

    (c)   "matrimonial proceedings" is to be read as a reference to a matrimonial cause. . ..

(3)   [Where] these rules apply the CPR, they apply the CPR as amended from time to time.

[(4)   . . .]

NOTES

Amendment

    Para (1): definition "the 1958 Act" inserted by SI 2011/1328, rr 2, 4(a).
        Date in force: 18 June 2011: see SI 2011/1328, r 1.
    Para (1): definition "the 2007 Hague Convention" inserted by SI 2012/2806, rr 2, 4(a).
        Date in force: 20 December 2012: see SI 2012/2806, r 1.
    Para (1): definition "the 2014 Act" inserted by SI 2014/843, rr 2, 4(a).
        Date in force: 22 April 2014: see SI 2014/843, r 1.
    Para (1): definition "Allocation Order" (omitted) revoked by SI 2013/3204, rr 2, 4(a)(i).
        Date in force: 22 April 2014 (being the date on which the Crime and Courts Act 2013, s 17(3) is brought fully into force): see SI 2013/3204, r 1 and SI 2014/954, art 2(a); for transitional provisions and savings see SI 2013/3204, r 137 and SI 2014/954, art 3.
    Para (1): definition "alternative dispute resolution" (omitted) revoked by SI 2014/843, rr 2, 4(b).
        Date in force: 22 April 2014: see SI 2014/843, r 1.
    Para (1): definition "Article 11 form" inserted by SI 2012/2806, rr 2, 4(b).
        Date in force: 20 December 2012: see SI 2012/2806, r 1.
    Para (1): in definition "CCR" words omitted in square brackets inserted by SI 2012/2046, rr 2, 3(a)(i).
        Date in force: 30 September 2012: see SI 2012/2046, r 1.
    Para (1): in definition "CCR" words omitted revoked by SI 2014/667, rr 2, 3(a)(i).
        Date in force: 22 April 2014: see SI 2014/667, r 1; for transitional and saving provision see r 45.
    Para (1): definition "child arrangements order" inserted by SI 2014/843, rr 2, 4(d).
        Date in force: 22 April 2014: see SI 2014/843, r 1.
    Para (1): definition "civil partnership proceedings county court" (omitted) revoked by SI 2013/3204, rr 2, 4(a)(ii).
        Date in force: 22 April 2014 (being the date on which the Crime and Courts Act 2013, s 17(3) is brought fully into force): see SI 2013/3204, r 1 and SI 2014/954, art 2(a); for transitional provisions and savings see SI 2013/3204, r 137 and SI 2014/954, art 3.
    Para (1): definition "Commission" (omitted) revoked by SI 2012/2007, art 3(2), Schedule, Pt 2, para 125(a).
        Date in force: 1 August 2012: see SI 2012/2007, art 1(2).
    Para (1): definition "contact order" (omitted) revoked by SI 2014/843, rr 2, 4(e).
        Date in force: 22 April 2014: see SI 2014/843, r 1.
    Para (1): in definition "court" words "or the family court" in square brackets substituted by SI 2013/3204, rr 2, 4(b).
        Date in force: 22 April 2014 (being the date on which the Crime and Courts Act 2013, s 17(3) is brought fully into force): see SI 2013/3204, r 1 and SI 2014/954, art 2(a); for transitional provisions and savings see SI 2013/3204, r 137 and SI 2014/954, art 3.
    Para (1): definition "court of trial" (omitted) revoked by SI 2013/3204, rr 2, 4(a)(iii).

Date in force: 22 April 2014 (being the date on which the Crime and Courts Act 2013, s 17(3) is brought fully into force): see SI 2013/3204, r 1 and SI 2014/954, art 2(a); for transitional provisions and savings see SI 2013/3204, r 137 and SI 2014/954, art 3.

Para (1): in definition "court officer" words "a member of court staff" in square brackets substituted by SI 2013/3204, rr 2, 4(c).

Date in force: 22 April 2014 (being the date on which the Crime and Courts Act 2013, s 17(3) is brought fully into force): see SI 2013/3204, r 1 and SI 2014/954, art 2(a); for transitional provisions and savings see SI 2013/3204, r 137 and SI 2014/954, art 3.

Para (1): definition "designated county court" (omitted) revoked by SI 2013/3204, rr 2, 4(a)(iv).

Date in force: 22 April 2014 (being the date on which the Crime and Courts Act 2013, s 17(3) is brought fully into force): see SI 2013/3204, r 1 and SI 2014/954, art 2(a); for transitional provisions and savings see SI 2013/3204, r 137 and SI 2014/954, art 3.

Para (1): definition "district judge" (omitted) revoked by SI 2013/3204, rr 2, 4(a)(v).

Date in force: 22 April 2014 (being the date on which the Crime and Courts Act 2013, s 17(3) is brought fully into force): see SI 2013/3204, r 1 and SI 2014/954, art 2(a); for transitional provisions and savings see SI 2013/3204, r 137 and SI 2014/954, art 3.

Para (1): definition "district registry" (omitted) revoked by SI 2013/3204, rr 2, 4(a)(vi).

Date in force: 22 April 2014 (being the date on which the Crime and Courts Act 2013, s 17(3) is brought fully into force): see SI 2013/3204, r 1 and SI 2014/954, art 2(a); for transitional provisions and savings see SI 2013/3204, r 137 and SI 2014/954, art 3.

Para (1): definition "divorce county court" (omitted) revoked by SI 2013/3204, rr 2, 4(a)(vii).

Date in force: 22 April 2014 (being the date on which the Crime and Courts Act 2013, s 17(3) is brought fully into force): see SI 2013/3204, r 1 and SI 2014/954, art 2(a); for transitional provisions and savings see SI 2013/3204, r 137 and SI 2014/954, art 3.

Para (1): in definition "financial order" in sub-para (h) word omitted revoked by SI 2013/1472, rr 2, 3(a)(i).

Date in force: 8 July 2013: see SI 2013/1472, r 1.

Para (1): in definition "financial order" sub-para (j) and word "or" immediately preceding it inserted by SI 2013/1472, rr 2, 3(a)(ii).

Date in force: 8 July 2013: see SI 2013/1472, r 1.

Para (1): in definition "financial remedy" in sub-para (c) words from "except an application" to "a financial remedy" in square brackets inserted by SI 2012/679, rr 2, 3(a)(i).

Date in force: 6 April 2012: see SI 2012/679, r 1.

Para (1): in definition "financial remedy" in sub-para (d) words from "except an application" to "of that Schedule" in square brackets inserted by SI 2012/679, rr 2, 3(a)(ii).

Date in force: 6 April 2012: see SI 2012/679, r 1.

Para (1): definition "incoming protection measure" inserted by SI 2014/3296, rr 2, 3(a)(i).

Date in force: 11 January 2015: see SI 2014/3296, r 1(2); for transitional and saving provision see r 15.

Para (1): definition "judge" substituted by SI 2014/667, rr 2, 3(a)(iii).

Date in force: 22 April 2014: see SI 2014/667, r 1; for transitional and saving provision see r 45.

Para (1): definition "justices' legal adviser" substituted, for definition "justices' clerk" as originally enacted, by SI 2020/135, rr 2, 3.

Date in force: 6 April 2020: see SI 2020/135, r 1.

Para (1): definition "lay justice" inserted by SI 2014/667, rr 2, 3(a)(ii).

Date in force: 22 April 2014: see SI 2014/667, r 1; for transitional and saving provision see r 45.

Para (1): definition "the Maintenance Regulation" inserted by SI 2011/1328, rr 2, 4(b).

Date in force: 18 June 2011: see SI 2011/1328, r 1.

Para (1): in definition "matrimonial order" in para (b) words "section 11, 12 or 12A" in square brackets substituted by SI 2015/913, rr 2, 3.

Date in force: 1 July 2015: see SI 2015/913, r 1; for transitional provision see r 14.

Para (1): definition "non-court dispute resolution" inserted by SI 2014/843, rr 2, 4(c).

Date in force: 22 April 2014: see SI 2014/843, r 1.

Para (1): definition "order for payment for legal services" inserted by SI 2013/1472, rr 2, 3(b).

Date in force: 8 July 2013: see SI 2013/1472, r 1.

Para (1): in definition "professional acting in furtherance of the protection of children" in sub-para (c) semi-colon in square brackets substituted by SI 2012/679, rr 2, 3(b)(i).

Date in force: 6 April 2012: see SI 2012/679, r 1; for transitional provisions and savings see r 30 thereof.

Para (1): in definition "professional acting in furtherance of the protection of children" in sub-para (d) word "or" in square brackets inserted by SI 2012/679, rr 2, 3(b)(ii).

Date in force: 6 April 2012: see SI 2012/679, r 1; for transitional provisions and savings see r 30 thereof.

Para (1): in definition "professional acting in furtherance of the protection of children" sub-para (e) inserted by SI 2012/679, rr 2, 3(b)(iii).

Date in force: 6 April 2012: see SI 2012/679, r 1; for transitional provisions and savings see r 30 thereof.
Para (1): in definition "professional acting in furtherance of the protection of children" in sub-para (e) words "Disclosure and Barring Service" in square brackets substituted by SI 2012/3006, art 30(1), (2)(a).
Date in force: 1 December 2012: see SI 2012/3006, art 1(1).
Para (1): in definition "professional acting in furtherance of the protection of children" in sub-para (e) words "section 87(1) of the Protection of Freedoms Act 2012" in square brackets substituted by SI 2012/3006, art 30(1), (2)(b).
Date in force: 1 December 2012: see SI 2012/3006, art 1(1).
Para (1): definition "protection measure" inserted by SI 2014/3296, rr 2, 3(a)(ii).
Date in force: 11 January 2015: see SI 2014/3296, r 1(2); for transitional and saving provision see r 15.
Para (1): definition "Protection Measures Regulation" inserted by SI 2014/3296, rr 2, 3(a)(ii).
Date in force: 11 January 2015: see SI 2014/3296, r 1(2); for transitional and saving provision see r 15.
Para (1): definition "Royal Courts of Justice" (omitted) revoked by SI 2013/3204, rr 2, 4(a)(viii).
Date in force: 22 April 2014 (being the date on which the Crime and Courts Act 2013, s 17(3) is brought fully into force): see SI 2013/3204, r 1 and SI 2014/954, art 2(a); for transitional provisions and savings see SI 2013/3204, r 137 and SI 2014/954, art 3.
Para (1): in definition "RSC" words omitted in square brackets inserted by SI 2012/2046, rr 2, 3(a)(ii).
Date in force: 30 September 2012: see SI 2012/2046, r 1.
Para (1): in definition "RSC" words omitted revoked by SI 2014/667, rr 2, 3(a)(i).
Date in force: 22 April 2014: see SI 2014/667, r 1; for transitional and saving provision see r 45.
Para (2): in sub-para (a)(i) word "or" in square brackets inserted by SI 2014/3296, rr 2, 3(b)(i)(aa).
Date in force: 6 April 2015: see SI 2014/3296, r 1(3); for transitional and saving provision see r 15.
Para (2): sub-para (a)(ii) revoked by SI 2014/3296, rr 2, 3(b)(i)(bb).
Date in force: 6 April 2015: see SI 2014/3296, r 1(3); for transitional and saving provision see r 15.
Para (2): in sub-para (c) words omitted revoked by SI 2014/3296, rr 2, 3(b)(ii).
Date in force: 6 April 2015: see SI 2014/3296, r 1(3); for transitional and saving provision see r 15.
Para (3): word "Where" in square brackets substituted by SI 2014/667, rr 2, 3(b).
Date in force: 22 April 2014: see SI 2014/667, r 1; for transitional and saving provision see r 45.
Para (4): inserted by SI 2012/2046, rr 2, 3(c).
Date in force: 30 September 2012: see SI 2012/2046, r 1.
Para (4): revoked by SI 2014/667, rr 2, 3(c).
Date in force: 22 April 2014: see SI 2014/667, r 1; for transitional and saving provision see r 45.

. . .

2.8 Court's discretion as to where it deals with cases
The court may deal with a case at any place that it considers appropriate.

2.9 Computation of time
(1) This rule shows how to calculate any period of time for doing any act which is specified—
    (a)   by these rules;
    (b)   by a practice direction; or
    (c)   by a direction or order of the court.
(2) A period of time expressed as a number of days must be computed as clear days.
(3) In this rule "clear days" means that in computing the numbers of days—
    (a)   the day on which the period begins; and
    (b)   if the end of the period is defined by reference to an event, the day on which that event occurs,
are not included.
(4) Where the specified period is 7 days or less and includes a day which is not a business day, that day does not count.

(5) When the period specified—

    (a)   by these rules or a practice direction; or

    (b)   by any direction or order of the court,

for doing any act at the court office ends on a day on which the office is closed, that act will be in time if done on the next day on which the court office is open.

2.10 Dates for compliance to be calendar dates and to include time of day

(1) Where the court makes an order or gives a direction which imposes a time limit for doing any act, the last date for compliance must, wherever practicable—

    (a)   be expressed as a calendar date; and

    (b)   include the time of day by which the act must be done.

(2) Where the date by which an act must be done is inserted in any document, the date must, wherever practicable, be expressed as a calendar date.

(3) Where "month" occurs in any order, direction or other document, it means a calendar month.

[PART 3
NON-COURT DISPUTE RESOLUTION]

NOTES

Amendment
    Part 3: substituted by SI 2014/843, rr 2, 5.
        Date in force: 22 April 2014: see SI 2014/843, r 1.

[CHAPTER 1

INTERPRETATION]

NOTES

Amendment
    Part 3: substituted by SI 2014/843, rr 2, 5.
        Date in force: 22 April 2014: see SI 2014/843, r 1.

[In this Part—

    "allocation" means allocation of proceedings other than appeal proceedings to a level of judge;

    ["authorised family mediator" means a person identified by the Family Mediation Council as qualified to conduct a MIAM;]

    "domestic violence" means any incident, or pattern of incidents, of controlling, coercive or threatening behaviour, violence or abuse (whether psychological, physical, sexual, financial or emotional) between the prospective applicant and another prospective party;

    "family mediation information and assessment meeting" has the meaning given to it in section 10(3) of the 2014 Act.

    "harm" has the meaning given to it in section 31 of the Children Act 1989;

    "mediator's exemption" has the meaning given to it in Rule 3.8(2);

    "MIAM" means a family mediation information and assessment meeting;

    "MIAM exemption" has the meaning given to it in Rule 3.8(1);

    "MIAM requirement" is the requirement in section 10(1) of the 2014 Act for a person to attend a MIAM before making a relevant family application;

    "private law proceedings" has the meaning given to it in Rule 12.2;

    "prospective applicant" is the person who is considering making a relevant family application;

    "prospective party" is a person who would be likely to be a party to the proceedings in the relevant family application;

"prospective respondent" is a person who would be a likely respondent to the proceedings in the relevant family application; and
"relevant family application" has the meaning given to it in section 10(3) of the 2014 Act.]

NOTES

Amendment
    Part 3: substituted by SI 2014/843, rr 2, 5.
        Date in force: 22 April 2014: see SI 2014/843, r 1.
    Definition "authorised family mediator" substituted by SI 2015/1868, rr 2, 3.
        Date in force: 1 January 2016: see SI 2015/1868, r 1(3).

[CHAPTER 2

THE COURT'S DUTY AND POWERS GENERALLY]

NOTES

Amendment
    Part 3: substituted by SI 2014/843, rr 2, 5.
        Date in force: 22 April 2014: see SI 2014/843, r 1.

[3.2 Scope of this Chapter]
[This Chapter contains the court's duty and powers to encourage and facilitate the use of non-court dispute resolution.]

NOTES

Amendment
    Part 3: substituted by SI 2014/843, rr 2, 5.
        Date in force: 22 April 2014: see SI 2014/843, r 1.

[3.3 The court's duty to consider non-court dispute resolution]
[(1) The court must consider, at every stage in proceedings, whether non-court dispute resolution is appropriate.
(2) In considering whether non-court dispute resolution is appropriate in proceedings which were commenced by a relevant family application, the court must take into account—
    (a)   whether a MIAM took place;
    (b)   whether a valid MIAM exemption was claimed or mediator's exemption was confirmed; and
    (c)   whether the parties attempted mediation or another form of non-court dispute resolution and the outcome of that process.]

NOTES

Amendment
    Part 3: substituted by SI 2014/843, rr 2, 5.
        Date in force: 22 April 2014: see SI 2014/843, r 1.

[3.4 When the court will adjourn proceedings or a hearing in proceedings]
[(1) If the court considers that non-court dispute resolution is appropriate, it may direct that the proceedings, or a hearing in the proceedings, be adjourned for such specified period as it considers appropriate—
    (a)   to enable the parties to obtain information and advice about[, and consider using,] non-court dispute resolution; and
    (b)   where the parties agree, to enable non-court dispute resolution to take place.
(2) The court may give directions under this rule on an application or of its own initiative.

(3) Where the court directs an adjournment under this rule, it will give directions about the timing and method by which the parties must tell the court if any of the issues in the proceedings have been resolved.

(4) If the parties do not tell the court if any of the issues have been resolved as directed under paragraph (3), the court will give such directions as to the management of the case as it considers appropriate.

(5) The court or court officer will—

(a) record the making of an order under this rule; and

(b) arrange for a copy of the order to be served as soon as practicable on the parties.

(6) Where the court proposes to exercise its powers of its own initiative, the procedure set out in rule 4.3(2) to (6) applies.]

NOTES

Amendment

Part 3: substituted by SI 2014/843, rr 2, 5.
Date in force: 22 April 2014: see SI 2014/843, r 1.
Para (1): in sub-para (a) words ", and consider using," in square brackets inserted by SI 2014/3296, rr 2, 4.
Date in force: 6 April 2015: see SI 2014/3296, r 1(3); for transitional and saving provision see r 15.

. . .

PART 9
APPLICATIONS FOR A FINANCIAL REMEDY

CHAPTER 1

APPLICATION AND INTERPRETATION

[9.1 Application

[(1) The rules in this Part apply to an application for a financial remedy.

(2) This Part is subject to any provision made by or pursuant to Part 41 (proceeding by electronic means).

("Financial remedy" and "financial order" are defined in rule 2.3)]

NOTES

Amendment

Substituted by by SI 2020/135, rr 2, 9.
Date in force: 6 April 2020: see SI 2020/135, r 1.

9.2 . . .

. . .

NOTES

Amendment

Revoked by SI 2014/667, rr 2, 7.
Date in force: 22 April 2014: see SI 2014/667, r 1; for transitional and saving provision see r 45.

9.3 Interpretation

(1) In this Part—

"avoidance of disposition order" means—

(a) in proceedings under the 1973 Act, an order under section 37(2)(b) or (c) of that Act;

(b) in proceedings under the 1984 Act, an order under section 23(2)(b) or 23(3) of that Act;

(c)   in proceedings under Schedule 5 to the 2004 Act, an order under paragraph 74(3) or (4); or

(d)   in proceedings under Schedule 7 to the 2004 Act, an order under paragraph 15(3) or (4);

"the Board" means the Board of the Pension Protection Fund;

["fast-track procedure" means the procedure set out in Chapter 5;]

"FDR appointment" means a Financial Dispute Resolution appointment in accordance with rule 9.17;

["Financial Circumstances Form" means the Financial Circumstances Form published by the Permanent Bureau of the Hague Conference under Article 11(4) of the 2007 Hague Convention for use in relation to applications under Article 10 of that Convention;]

"order preventing a disposition" means—

(a)   in proceedings under the 1973 Act, an order under section 37(2)(a) of that Act;

(b)   in proceedings under the 1984 Act, an order under section 23(2)(a) of that Act;

(c)   in proceedings under Schedule 5 to the 2004 Act, an order under paragraph 74(2); or

(d)   in proceedings under Schedule 7 to the 2004 Act, an order under paragraph 15(2);

"pension arrangement" means—

(a)   an occupational pension scheme;

(b)   a personal pension scheme;

(c)   shareable state scheme rights;

(d)   a retirement annuity contract;

(e)   an annuity or insurance policy purchased, or transferred, for the purpose of giving effect to rights under an occupational pension scheme or a personal pension scheme; and

(f)   an annuity purchased, or entered into, for the purpose of discharging liability in respect of a pension credit under section 29(1)(b) of the Welfare Reform and Pensions Act 1999 or under corresponding Northern Ireland legislation;

"pension attachment order" means—

(a)   in proceedings under the 1973 Act, an order making provision under section 25B or 25C of that Act;

(b)   in proceedings under the 1984 Act, an order under section 17(1)(a)(i) of that Act making provision equivalent to an order referred to in paragraph (a);

(c)   in proceedings under Schedule 5 to the 2004 Act, an order making provision under paragraph 25 or paragraph 26; or

(d)   in proceedings under Schedule 7 to the 2004 Act, an order under paragraph 9(2) or (3) making provision equivalent to an order referred to in paragraph (c);

"pension compensation attachment order" means—

(a)   in proceedings under the 1973 Act, an order making provision under section 25F of that Act;

(b)   in proceedings under the 1984 Act, an order under section 17(1)(a)(i) of that Act making provision equivalent to an order referred in to paragraph (a);

(c)   in proceedings under Schedule 5 to the 2004 Act, an order under paragraph 34A; and

(d) in proceedings under Schedule 7 to the 2004 Act, an order under paragraph 9(2) or (3) making provision equivalent to an order referred to in paragraph (c);

"pension compensation sharing order" means—

(a) in proceedings under the 1973 Act, an order under section 24E of that Act;

(b) in proceedings under the 1984 Act, an order under section 17(1)(c) of that Act;

(c) in proceedings under Schedule 5 to the 2004 Act, an order under paragraph 19A ; and

(d) in proceedings under Schedule 7 to the 2004 Act, an order under paragraph 9(2) or (3) making provision equivalent to an order referred to in paragraph (c);

"pension sharing order" means—

(a) in proceedings under the 1973 Act, an order making provision under section 24B of that Act;

(b) in proceedings under the 1984 Act, an order under section 17(1)(b) of that Act;

(c) in proceedings under Schedule 5 to the 2004 Act, an order under paragraph 15; or

(d) in proceedings under Schedule 7 to the 2004 Act, an order under paragraph 9(2) or (3) making provision equivalent to an order referred to in paragraph (c);

"pension scheme" means, unless the context otherwise requires, a scheme for which the Board has assumed responsibility in accordance with Chapter 3 of Part 2 of the Pensions Act 2004 (pension protection) or any provision in force in Northern Ireland corresponding to that Chapter;

"PPF compensation" has the meaning given to it—

(a) in proceedings under the 1973 Act, by section 21C of the 1973 Act;

(b) in proceedings under the 1984 Act, by section 18(7) of the 1984 Act; and

(c) in proceedings under the 2004 Act, by paragraph 19F of Schedule 5 to the 2004 Act;

"relevant valuation" means a valuation of pension rights or benefits as at a date not more than 12 months earlier than the date fixed for the first appointment which has been furnished or requested for the purposes of any of the following provisions—

(a) the Pensions on Divorce etc (Provision of Information) Regulations 2000;

(b) regulation 5 of and Schedule 2 to the Occupational Pension Schemes (Disclosure of Information) Regulations 1996 and regulation 11 of and Schedule 1 to the Occupational Pension Schemes (Transfer Value) Regulations 1996;

(c) section 93A or 94(1)(a) or (aa) of the Pension Schemes Act 1993;

(d) section 94(1)(b) of the Pension Schemes Act 1993 or paragraph 2(a) (or, where applicable, 2(b)) of Schedule 2 to the Personal Pension Schemes (Disclosure of Information) Regulations 1987;

(e) the Dissolution etc (Pensions) Regulations 2005;

["standard procedure" means the procedure set out in Chapter 4;]

"variation order" means—

(a) in proceedings under the 1973 Act, an order under section 31 of that Act; or

        (b)   in proceedings under the 2004 Act, an order under Part 11 of Schedule 5 to that Act.

(2) . . .

[(3)

        (a)   Where an application is made under Article 56 of, and using the form in Annex VII to, the Maintenance Regulation, references in this Part to "financial statement" apply to the applicant as if for the words "financial statement" were substituted "the form in Annex VII to the Maintenance Regulation";

        [(aa)   where an application for establishment or modification of maintenance is made under Article 10 of the 2007 Hague Convention, references in this Part to "financial statement" apply to the applicant as if for "financial statement" there were substituted "Financial Circumstances Form;]

        (b)   [Sub-paragraphs (a) and (aa) do] not apply where the relief sought includes relief which is of a type to which the Maintenance Regulation [or the 2007 Hague Convention, as the case may be,] does not apply.]

NOTES

Amendment

    Para (1): definition "fast-track procedure" inserted by SI 2018/440, rr 2, 4(a).
        Date in force: 4 June 2018: see SI 2018/440, r 1; for transitional provision see r 12.
    Para (1): definition "Financial Circumstances Form" inserted by SI 2012/2806, rr 2, 7(a).
        Date in force: 20 December 2012: see SI 2012/2806, r 1.
    Para (1): definition "standard procedure" inserted by SI 2018/440, rr 2, 4(b).
        Date in force: 4 June 2018: see SI 2018/440, r 1; for transitional provision see r 12.
    Para (2): revoked by SI 2013/3204, rr 2, 22.
        Date in force: 22 April 2014 (being the date on which the Crime and Courts Act 2013, s 17(3) is brought fully into force): see SI 2013/3204, r 1 and SI 2014/954, art 2(a); for transitional provisions and savings see SI 2013/3204, r 137 and SI 2014/954, art 3.
    Para (3): inserted by SI 2011/1328, rr 2, 7.
        Date in force: 18 June 2011: see SI 2011/1328, r 1.
    Para (3): sub-para (aa) inserted by SI 2012/2806, rr 2, 7(b)(i).
        Date in force: 20 December 2012: see SI 2012/2806, r 1.
    Para (3): in sub-para (b) words "Sub-paragraphs (a) and (aa) do" in square brackets substituted by SI 2012/2806, rr 2, 7(b)(ii)(aa).
        Date in force: 20 December 2012: see SI 2012/2806, r 1.
    Para (3): in sub-para (b) words "or the 2007 Hague Convention, as the case may be," in square brackets inserted by SI 2012/2806, rr 2, 7(b)(ii)(bb).
        Date in force: 20 December 2012: see SI 2012/2806, r 1.

CHAPTER 2

PROCEDURE FOR APPLICATIONS

9.4 When an Application for a financial order may be made

An application for a financial order may be made—

        (a)   in an application for a matrimonial or civil partnership order; or

        (b)   at any time after an application for a matrimonial or civil partnership order has been made.

9.5 Where to start proceedings

(1) An application for a financial remedy must be filed—

        (a)   if there are proceedings for a matrimonial order or a civil partnership order which are proceeding in [the family court], in that court; or

        (b)   if there are proceedings for a matrimonial order or a civil partnership order which are proceeding in the High Court, in the registry in which those proceedings are taking place.

(2) . . .

(3) . . .

NOTES

Amendment

Para (1): in sub-para (a) words "the family court" in square brackets substituted by SI 2013/3204, rr 2, 23(a).

> Date in force: 22 April 2014 (being the date on which the Crime and Courts Act 2013, s 17(3) is brought fully into force): see SI 2013/3204, r 1 and SI 2014/954, art 2(a); for transitional provisions and savings see SI 2013/3204, r 137 and SI 2014/954, art 3.

Para (2): revoked by SI 2013/3204, rr 2, 23(b).

> Date in force: 22 April 2014 (being the date on which the Crime and Courts Act 2013, s 17(3) is brought fully into force): see SI 2013/3204, r 1 and SI 2014/954, art 2(a); for transitional provisions and savings see SI 2013/3204, r 137 and SI 2014/954, art 3.

Para (3): words omitted revoked by SI 2017/741, rr 2, 6.

> Date in force: 7 August 2017: see SI 2017/741, r 1(1); for transitional provision see r 9.

9.6 Application for an order preventing a disposition

(1) The Part 18 procedure applies to an application for an order preventing a disposition.

(2) An application for an order preventing a disposition may be made without notice to the respondent.

("Order preventing a disposition" is defined in rule 9.3.)

9.7 Application for interim orders

(1) A party may apply at any stage of the proceedings for—

    (a)   an order for maintenance pending suit;

    (b)   an order for maintenance pending outcome of proceedings;

    (c)   an order for interim periodical payments;

    (d)   an interim variation order;

    [(da)   an order for payment in respect of legal services; or]

    (e)   any other form of interim order.

[(2) An application for an order mentioned in paragraph (1) shall be made using the Part 18 procedure.]

(3) Where a party makes an application before filing a financial statement, the written evidence in support must—

    (a)   explain why the order is necessary; and

    (b)   give up to date information about that party's financial circumstances.

(4) Unless the respondent has filed a financial statement, the respondent must, at least 7 days before the court is to deal with the application, file a statement of his means and serve a copy on the applicant.

(5) An application for an order mentioned in paragraph (1)(e) may be made without notice.

NOTES

Amendment

Para (1): sub-para (da) substituted, for word "or" at end of sub-para (d), by SI 2013/1472, rr 2, 4(a).

> Date in force: 8 July 2013: see SI 2013/1472, r 1.

Para (2): substituted by SI 2013/1472, rr 2, 4(b).

> Date in force: 8 July 2013: see SI 2013/1472, r 1.

9.8 Application for periodical payments order at same rate as an order for maintenance pending suit

(1) This rule applies where there are matrimonial proceedings and—

    (a)   a decree nisi of divorce or nullity of marriage has been made;

    (b)   at or after the date of the decree nisi an order for maintenance pending suit is in force; and

    (c)   the spouse in whose favour the decree nisi was made has made an application for an order for periodical payments.

(2) The spouse in whose favour the decree nisi was made may apply, using the Part 18 procedure, for an order providing for payments at the same rate as those provided for by the order for maintenance pending suit.

9.9 Application for periodical payments order at same rate as an order for maintenance pending outcome of proceedings
(1) This rule applies where there are civil partnership proceedings and—
  (a) a conditional order of dissolution or nullity of civil partnership has been made;
  (b) at or after the date of the conditional order an order for maintenance pending outcome of proceedings is in force;
  (c) the civil partner in whose favour the conditional order was made has made an application for an order for periodical payments.
(2) The civil partner in whose favour the conditional order was made may apply, using the Part 18 procedure, for an order providing for payments at the same rate as those provided for by, the order for maintenance pending the outcome of proceedings.

[9.9A Application to set aside a financial remedy order]
[(1) In this rule—
  (a) "financial remedy order" means an order or judgment that is a financial remedy, and includes—
    (i) part of such an order or judgment; or
    (ii) a consent order; and
  (b) "set aside" means—
    (i) in the High Court, to set aside a financial remedy order pursuant to section 17(2) of the Senior Courts Act 1981 and this rule;
    (ii) in the family court, to rescind or vary a financial remedy order pursuant to section 31F(6) of the 1984 Act.
(2) A party may apply under this rule to set aside a financial remedy order where no error of the court is alleged.
(3) An application under this rule must be made within the proceedings in which the financial remedy order was made.
(4) An application under this rule must be made in accordance with the Part 18 procedure, subject to the modifications contained in this rule.
(5) Where the court decides to set aside a financial remedy order, it shall give directions for the rehearing of the financial remedy proceedings or make such other orders as may be appropriate to dispose of the application.]

NOTES

Amendment
  Inserted by SI 2016/901, rr 2, 4.
  Date in force: 3 October 2016: see SI 2016/901, r 1.

[9.9B Standard and fast-track procedures for financial remedy proceedings]
[(1) In this rule "order for periodical payments" means an order under—
  (a) section 23(1)(a), (b), (d) or (c) of the 1973 Act;
  (b) section 27(5) or (6)(a), (b), (d) or (e) of the 1973 Act;
  (c) paragraph 1(2)(a) or (b), 2(2)(a) or 9 of Schedule 1 to the 1989 Act;
  (d) paragraph 2(1)(a), (b), (d) or (e) of Schedule 5 to the 2004 Act;
  (e) paragraph 40 or 41(1)(a), (b), (d) or (e) of Schedule 5 to the 2004 Act.
(2) Subject to paragraph (3), an application for a financial remedy must be dealt with under the standard procedure.
(3) The fast-track procedure applies to—
  (a) any application where the financial remedy sought is only for an order for periodical payments;

(b) any application made under—
  (i) the 1978 Act;
  (ii) Schedule 6 to the 2004 Act;
  (iii) Article 56 of the Maintenance Regulation; or
  (iv) Article 10 of the 2007 Hague Convention;
(c) any application for the variation of an order for periodical payments, except where the applicant seeks the dismissal (immediate or otherwise) of the periodical payments order and its substitution with one or more of a lump sum order, a property adjustment order, a pension sharing order or a pension compensation sharing order.

(4) At any stage in the proceedings the court may order that an application proceeding under the fast-track procedure must proceed under the standard procedure. (Rule 9.18A provides for specific occasions when the court may direct that a case should proceed under the standard procedure.)]

NOTES

Amendment

Inserted by SI 2018/440, rr 2, 5.
  Date in force: 4 June 2018: see SI 2018/440, r 1; for transitional provision see r 12.

CHAPTER 3

APPLICATIONS FOR FINANCIAL REMEDIES FOR CHILDREN

9.10 Application by parent, guardian etc for financial remedy in respect of children
(1) The following people may apply for a financial remedy in respect of a child—
  (a) a parent, guardian or special guardian of any child of the family;
  (b) any person [who is named in a child arrangements order as a person with whom a child of the family is to live], and any applicant for such an order;
  (c) any other person who is entitled to apply for [a child arrangements order which names that person as a person with whom a child is to live];
  (d) a local authority, where an order has been made under section 31(1)(a) of the 1989 Act placing a child in its care;
  (e) the Official Solicitor, if appointed the children's guardian of a child of the family under rule 16.24; and
  (f) [subject to paragraph (1A),] a child of the family who has been given permission to apply for a financial remedy.
[(1A) Where the application is—
  (a) for the variation of an order under section 2(1)(c), 6 or 7 of the 1978 Act or paragraph 2(1)(c) of, or Part 2 or 3 of, Schedule 6 to the 2004 Act for periodical payments in respect of a child;
  (b) the application is made by the child in question; and
  (c) the child in question is aged 16 or over,
the child does not require permission to make the application.]
(2) ....

NOTES

Amendment

Para (1): in sub-para (b) words from "who is named" to "is to live" in square brackets substituted by SI 2014/843, rr 2, 13(a)(i).
  Date in force: 22 April 2014: see SI 2014/843, r 1.
Para (1): in sub-para (c) words from "a child arrangements" to "is to live" in square brackets substituted by SI 2014/843, rr 2, 13(a)(ii).
  Date in force: 22 April 2014: see SI 2014/843, r 1.
Para (1): in sub-para (f) words "subject to paragraph (1A)," in square brackets inserted by SI 2013/3204, rr 2, 24(a).

Date in force: 22 April 2014 (being the date on which the Crime and Courts Act 2013, s 17(3) is brought fully into force): see SI 2013/3204, r 1 and SI 2014/954, art 2(a); for transitional provisions and savings see SI 2013/3204, r 137 and SI 2014/954, art 3.
Para (1A): inserted by SI 2013/3204, rr 2, 24(b).
Date in force: 22 April 2014 (being the date on which the Crime and Courts Act 2013, s 17(3) is brought fully into force): see SI 2013/3204, r 1 and SI 2014/954, art 2(a); for transitional provisions and savings see SI 2013/3204, r 137 and SI 2014/954, art 3.
Para (2): revoked by SI 2014/843, rr 2, 13(b).
Date in force: 22 April 2014: see SI 2014/843, r 1.

9.11 Children to be separately represented on certain applications

(1) Where an application for a financial remedy includes an application for an order for a variation of settlement, the court must, unless it is satisfied that the proposed variation does not adversely affect the rights or interests of any child concerned, direct that the child be separately represented on the application.

(2) On any other application for a financial remedy the court may direct that the child be separately represented on the application.

(3) Where a direction is made under paragraph (1) or (2), the court may if the person to be appointed so consents, appoint—

(a)   a person other than the Official Solicitor; or

(b)   the Official Solicitor,

to be a children's guardian and rule 16.24(5) and (6) and rules 16.25 to 16.28 apply as appropriate to such an appointment.

[CHAPTER 4

STANDARD PROCEDURE]

NOTES

Amendment
Chapter heading: substituted by SI 2018/440, rr 2, 6.
Date in force: 4 June 2018: see SI 2018/440, r 1; for transitional provision see r 12.

9.12 Duties of the court and the applicant upon issuing an application

(1) When an application under this Part is issued[, except where Chapter 5 of this Part applies]—

(a)   the court will fix a first appointment not less than 12 weeks and not more than 16 weeks after the date of the filing of the application; and

(b)   subject to paragraph (2), within 4 days beginning with the date on which the application was filed, a court officer will—

(i)   serve a copy of the application on the respondent; and

(ii)   give notice of the date of the first appointment to the applicant and the respondent.

(2) Where the applicant wishes to serve a copy of the application on the respondent and on filing the application so notifies the court—

(a)   paragraph (1)(b) does not apply;

(b)   a court officer will return to the applicant the copy of the application and the notice of the date of the first appointment; and

(c)   the applicant must,—

(i)   within 4 days beginning with the date on which the copy of the application is received from the court, serve the copy of the application and notice of the date of the first appointment on the respondent; and

(ii)   file a certificate of service at or before the first appointment.

(Rule 6.37 sets out what must be included in a certificate of service.)

(3)   The date fixed under paragraph (1), or for any subsequent appointment, must not be cancelled except with the court's permission and, if cancelled, the court must immediately fix a new date.

[(4)   In relation to an application to which the Maintenance Regulation [or the 2007 Hague Convention] applies, where the applicant does not already know the address of the respondent at the time the application is issued, paragraph (2) does not apply and the court will serve the application in accordance with paragraph (1).]

NOTES

Amendment
>   Para (1): words ", except where Chapter 5 of this Part applies" in square brackets substituted by SI 2013/3204, rr 2, 26.
>   Date in force: 22 April 2014 (being the date on which the Crime and Courts Act 2013, s 17(3) is brought fully into force): see SI 2013/3204, r 1 and SI 2014/954, art 2(a); for transitional provisions and savings see SI 2013/3204, r 137 and SI 2014/954, art 3.
>   Para (4): inserted by SI 2011/1328, rr 2, 8.
>   Date in force: 18 June 2011: see SI 2011/1328, r 1.
>   Para (4): words "or the 2007 Hague Convention" in square brackets inserted by SI 2012/2806, rr 2, 8.
>   Date in force: 20 December 2012: see SI 2012/2806, r 1.

9.13 Service of application on mortgagees, trustees etc
(1)   Where an application for a financial remedy includes an application for an order for a variation of settlement, the applicant must serve copies of the application on—

>   (a)   the trustees of the settlement;
>   (b)   the settlor if living; and
>   (c)   such other persons as the court directs.

(2)   In the case of an application for an avoidance of disposition order, the applicant must serve copies of the application on the person in whose favour the disposition is alleged to have been made.

(3)   Where an application for a financial remedy includes an application relating to land, the applicant must serve a copy of the application on any mortgagee of whom particulars are given in the application.

(4)   Any person served under paragraphs (1), (2) or (3) may make a request to the court in writing, within 14 days beginning with the date of service of the application, for a copy of the applicant's financial statement or any relevant part of that statement.

(5)   Any person who—

>   (a)   is served with copies of the application in accordance with paragraphs (1), (2) or (3); or
>   (b)   receives a copy of a financial statement, or a relevant part of that statement, following an application made under paragraph (4),

may within 14 days beginning with the date of service or receipt file a statement in answer.

(6)   Where a copy of an application is served under paragraphs (1), (2) or (3), the applicant must file a certificate of service at or before the first appointment.

(7)   A statement in answer filed under paragraph (5) must be verified by a statement of truth.

9.14 Procedure before the first appointment
(1)   Not less than 35 days before the first appointment both parties must simultaneously exchange with each other and file with the court a financial statement in the form referred to in Practice Direction 5A.

(2)   The financial statement must—

>   (a)   be verified by [a statement of truth]; and
>   (b)   accompanied by the following documents only—
>   (i)   any documents required by the financial statement;

(ii) any other documents necessary to explain or clarify any of the information contained in the financial statement; and

(iii) any documents provided to the party producing the financial statement by a person responsible for a pension arrangement, either following a request under rule 9.30 or as part of a relevant valuation; and

(iv) any notification or other document referred to in rule 9.37(2), (4) or (5) which has been received by the party producing the financial statement.

[(2ZA) Paragraph (2A) applies where the court has determined that the procedure in this Chapter should apply to an application under Article 56 of the Maintenance Regulation or Article 10 of the 2007 Hague Convention.]

[(2A) The requirement of paragraph (2)(a) relating to verification by a statement of truth does not apply to the financial statement of either party where the application has been made under—

(a) Article 56 of the Maintenance Regulation, using the form in Annex VII to that Regulation; or

(b) Article 10 of the 2007 Hague Convention, using the Financial Circumstances Form,

and the relief sought is limited to a type to which that Regulation or that Convention, as appropriate, applies, but the court may at any time direct that the financial statement of either party shall be verified by a statement of truth.]

(3) Where a party was unavoidably prevented from sending any document required by the financial statement, that party must at the earliest opportunity—

(a) serve a copy of that document on the other party; and

(b) file a copy of that document with the court, together with a written explanation of the failure to send it with the financial statement.

(4) No disclosure or inspection of documents may be requested or given between the filing of the application for a financial remedy and the first appointment, except—

(a) copies sent with the financial statement, or in accordance with paragraph (3); or

(b) in accordance with paragraphs (5) and (6).

(Rule 21,1 explains what is meant by disclosure and inspection.)

(5) Not less than 14 days before the hearing of the first appointment, each party must file with the court and serve on the other party—

(a) a concise statement of the issues between the parties;

(b) a chronology;

(c) a questionnaire setting out by reference to the concise statement of issues any further information and documents requested from the other party or a statement that no information and documents are required; and

(d) a notice stating whether that party will be in a position at the first appointment to proceed on that occasion to a FDR appointment.

(6) Not less than 14 days before the hearing of the first appointment, the applicant must file with the court and serve on the respondent confirmation—

(a) of the names of all persons served in accordance with rule 9.13(1) to (3); and

(b) that there are no other persons who must be served in accordance with those paragraphs.

NOTES

Amendment

Para (2): in sub-para (a) words "a statement of truth" in square brackets substituted by SI 2012/679, rr 2, 16(a).

Date in force: 6 April 2012: see SI 2012/679, r 1; for transitional provisions and savings see r 30 thereof.

Para (2ZA): inserted by SI 2014/667, rr 2, 8.
    Date in force: 22 April 2014: see SI 2014/667, r 1; for transitional and saving
    provision see r 45.
Para (2A) (as inserted by SI 2011/1328, rr 2, 9): substituted by SI 2012/2806, rr 2, 9.
    Date in force: 20 December 2012: see SI 2012/2806, r 1.

9.15 Duties of the court at the first appointment

(1)   The first appointment must be conducted with the objective of defining the issues and saving costs.

(2)   At the first appointment the court must determine—

    (a)   the extent to which any questions seeking information under rule 9.14(5)(c) must be answered; and

    (b)   what documents requested under rule 9.14(5)(c) must be produced,

and give directions for the production of such further documents as may be necessary.

(3)   The court must give directions where appropriate about—

    (a)   the valuation of assets (including the joint instruction of joint experts);

    (b)   obtaining and exchanging expert evidence, if required;

    (c)   the evidence to be adduced by each party; and

    (d)   further chronologies or schedules to be filed by each party.

[(4)   The court must direct that the case be referred to a FDR appointment unless—

    (a)   the first appointment or part of it has been treated as a FDR appointment and the FDR appointment has been effective; or

    (b)   there are exceptional reasons which make a referral to a FDR appointment inappropriate.]

(5)   If the court decides that a referral to a FDR appointment is not appropriate it must direct one or more of the following—

    (a)   that a further directions appointment be fixed;

    (b)   that an appointment be fixed for the making of an interim order;

    (c)   that the case be fixed for a final hearing and, where that direction is given, the court must determine the judicial level at which the case should be heard.

([Under Part 3] the court may also direct that the case be adjourned if it considers that [non-court dispute resolution] is appropriate.)

(6)   In considering whether to make a costs order under rule 28.3(5), the court must have particular regard to the extent to which each party has complied with the requirement to send documents with the financial statement and the explanation given for any failure to comply.

(7)   The court may—

    (a)   where an application for an interim order has been listed for consideration at the first appointment, make an interim order;

    (b)   having regard to the contents of the notice filed by the parties under rule 9.14(5)(d), treat the appointment (or part of it) as a FDR appointment to which rule 9.17 applies;

    (c)   in a case where a pension sharing order or a pension attachment order is requested, direct any party with pension rights to file and serve a Pension Inquiry Form, completed in full or in part as the court may direct; and

    (d)   in a case where a pension compensation sharing order or a pension compensation attachment order is requested, direct any party with PPF compensation rights to file and serve a Pension Protection Fund Inquiry Form, completed in full or in part as the court may direct.

(8)   Both parties must personally attend the first appointment unless the court directs otherwise.

NOTES

Amendment
> Para (4): substituted by SI 2017/741, rr 2, 7.
>> Date in force: 7 August 2017: see SI 2017/741, r 1(1); for transitional provision see r 9.
> Words in parentheses below para (5): words "Under Part 3" in square brackets substituted by SI 2014/843, rr 2, 14(a).
>> Date in force: 22 April 2014: see SI 2014/843, r 1.
> Words in parentheses below para (5): words "non-court dispute resolution" in square brackets substituted by SI 2014/843, rr 2, 14(b).
>> Date in force: 22 April 2014: see SI 2014/843, r 1.

9.16 After the first appointment

(1) Between the first appointment and the FDR appointment, a party is not entitled to the production of any further documents except—

    (a) in accordance with directions given under rule 9.15(2); or

    (b) with the permission of the court.

(2) At any stage—

    (a) a party may apply for further directions or a FDR appointment;

    (b) the court may give further directions or direct that parties attend a FDR appointment.

9.17 The FDR appointment

(1) The FDR appointment must be treated as a meeting held for the purposes of discussion and negotiation.

(2) The judge hearing the FDR appointment must have no further involvement with the application, other than to conduct any further FDR appointment or to make a consent order or a further directions order.

(3) Not less than 7 days before the FDR appointment, the applicant must file with the court details of all offers and proposals, and responses to them.

(4) Paragraph (3) includes any offers, proposals or responses made wholly or partly without prejudice(GL), but paragraph (3) does not make any material admissible as evidence if, but for that paragraph, it would not be admissible.

(5) At the conclusion of the FDR appointment, any documents filed under paragraph (3), and any filed documents referring to them, must, at the request of the party who filed them, be returned to that party and not retained on the court file.

(6) Parties attending the FDR appointment must use their best endeavours to reach agreement on matters in issue between them.

(7) The FDR appointment may be adjourned from time to time.

(8) At the conclusion of the FDR appointment, the court may make an appropriate consent order.

(9) If the court does not make an appropriate consent order as mentioned in paragraph (8), the court must give directions for the future course of the proceedings including, where appropriate—

    (a) the filing of evidence, including up to date information; . . .

    (b) fixing a final hearing date [; and]

    [(c) any necessary directions for the filing of open proposals for settlement under rule 9.27A or rule 9.28.].

(10) Both parties must personally attend the FDR appointment unless the court directs otherwise.

NOTES

Amendment
> Para (9): in sub-para (a) word omitted revoked by SI 2020/135, rr 2, 10(a).
>> Date in force: 6 July 2020: see SI 2020/135, r 1.
> Para (9): in sub-para (b) word "; and" in square brackets substituted by SI 2020/135, rr 2, 10(b).

Date in force: 6 July 2020: see SI 2020/135, r 1.
Para (9): sub-para (c) inserted by SI 2020/135, rr 2, 10(c).
Date in force: 6 July 2020: see SI 2020/135, r 1.

. . .

CHAPTER 6

GENERAL PROCEDURE

9.24 Power to order delivery up of possession etc
(1) This rule applies where the court has made an order under—
    (a)   section 24A of the 1973 Act;
    (b)   section 17(2) of the 1984 Act;
    (c)   Part 3 of Schedule 5 to the 2004 Act; or
    (d)   paragraph 9(4) of Schedule 7 to the 2004 Act.
(2) When the court makes an order mentioned in paragraph (1), it may order any party to deliver up to the purchaser or any other person—
    (a)   possession of the land, including any interest in, or right over, land;
    (b)   receipt of rents or profits relating to it; or
    (c)   both.

9.25 Where proceedings may be heard
(1) Paragraph (2) applies to an application—
    (a)   for a financial order;
    (b)   under Part 3 of the 1984 Act; or
    (c)   under Schedule 7 to the 2004 Act.
(2) An application mentioned in paragraph (1) must be heard—
    (a)   . . .
    (b)   where the case is proceeding in the High Court—
        (i)   at the Royal Courts of Justice; or
        (ii)   in matrimonial or civil partnership proceedings, any court at which sittings of the High Court are authorised.
(3) . . .
(4) . . .
(5) . . .

NOTES

Amendment
    Para (2): sub-para (a) revoked by SI 2013/3204, rr 2, 33.
        Date in force: 22 April 2014 (being the date on which the Crime and Courts Act 2013, s 17(3) is brought fully into force): see SI 2013/3204, r 1 and SI 2014/954, art 2(a); for transitional provisions and savings see SI 2013/3204, r 137 and SI 2014/954, art 3.
    Paras (3)–(5): revoked by SI 2013/3204, rr 2, 33.
        Date in force: 22 April 2014 (being the date on which the Crime and Courts Act 2013, s 17(3) is brought fully into force): see SI 2013/3204, r 1 and SI 2014/954, art 2(a); for transitional provisions and savings see SI 2013/3204, r 137 and SI 2014/954, art 3.

9.26 Applications for consent orders for financial remedy
(1) Subject to paragraph (5) and to rule 35.2, in relation to an application for a consent order—
    (a)   the applicant must file two copies of a draft of the order in the terms sought, one of which must be endorsed with a statement signed by the respondent to the application signifying agreement; and
    (b)   each party must file with the court and serve on the other party, a statement of information in the form referred to in Practice Direction 5A.

(2)   Where each party's statement of information is contained in one form, it must be signed by both the applicant and respondent to certify that they have read the contents of the other party's statement.

(3)   Where each party's statement of information is in a separate form, the form of each party must be signed by the other party to certify that they have read the contents of the statement contained in that form.

(4)   Unless the court directs otherwise, the applicant and the respondent need not attend the hearing of an application for a consent order.

(5)   Where all or any of the parties attend the hearing of an application for a financial remedy the court may—

> (a)   dispense with the filing of a statement of information; and
>
> (b)   give directions for the information which would otherwise be required to be given in such a statement in such a manner as it thinks fit.

(6)   In relation to an application for a consent order under Part 3 of the 1984 Act or Schedule 7 to the 2004 Act, the application for permission to make the application may be heard at the same time as the application for a financial remedy if evidence of the respondent's consent to the order is filed with the application.

(The following rules contain provision in relation to applications for consent orders - rule 9.32 (pension sharing order), rule 9.34 (pension attachment order), rule 9.41 (pension compensation sharing orders) and rule 9.43 (pension compensation attachment orders.)

[9.26A Questions as to the court's jurisdiction or whether the proceedings should be stayed]

[(1)   This rule applies to applications for maintenance where a question as to jurisdiction arises under—

> (a)   the 1968 Convention;
>
> (b)   the 1988 Convention;
>
> (c)   the Lugano Convention; . . .
>
> (d)   the Maintenance Regulation[; or
>
> (e)   Article 18 of the 2007 Hague Convention].

(2)   If at any time after the issue of the application it appears to the court that it does not or may not have jurisdiction to hear an application, or that under the instruments referred to in paragraph (1) it is or may be required to stay the proceedings or to decline jurisdiction, the court must—

> (a)   stay the proceedings, and
>
> (b)   fix a date for a hearing to determine jurisdiction or whether there should be a stay or other order.

(3)   The court officer will serve notice of the hearing referred to at paragraph (2)(b) on the parties to the proceedings.

(4)   The court must, in writing—

> (a)   give reasons for its decision under paragraph (2), and
>
> (b)   where it makes a finding of fact, state such finding.

(5)   The court may with the consent of all the parties deal with any question as to the jurisdiction of the court, or as to whether the proceedings should be stayed, without a hearing.

(6)   In this rule—

> (a)   "the 1968 Convention" has the meaning given to it in the Civil Jurisdiction and Judgments Act 1982;
>
> (b)   "the 1988 Convention" and "the Lugano Convention" have the meanings given to them in rule 34.1(2).]

NOTES

Amendment
> Inserted by SI 2011/1328, rr 2, 13.
>> Date in force: 18 June 2011: see SI 2011/1328, r 1.
> Para (1): in sub-para (c) word omitted revoked by SI 2012/2806, rr 2, 12(a).
>> Date in force: 20 December 2012: see SI 2012/2806, r 1.
> Para (1): sub-para (e) and word "; or" immediately preceding it inserted by SI 2012/2806, rr 2, 12(b).
>> Date in force: 20 December 2012: see SI 2012/2806, r 1.

[9.26AA International Maintenance Obligations: Communication with the Central Authority for England and Wales]

[(1) Where the Lord Chancellor requests information or a document from the court officer for the relevant court for the purposes of Article 58 of the Maintenance Regulation or Articles 12 or 25(2) of the 2007 Hague Convention, the court officer shall provide the requested information or document to the Lord Chancellor forthwith.

(2) In this rule, "relevant court" means the court at which an application under Article 56 of the Maintenance Regulation or Article 10 of the 2007 Hague Convention has been filed.

[The Lord Chancellor is the Central Authority for England and Wales in relation to the 2007 Hague Convention and the Maintenance Regulation]]

NOTES

Amendment
> Inserted by SI 2012/2806, rr 2, 13.
>> Date in force: 20 December 2012: see SI 2012/2806, r 1.

[9.26B Adding or removing parties]

[(1) The court may direct that a person or body be added as a party to proceedings for a financial remedy if—

    (a)   it is desirable to add the new party so that the court can resolve all the matters in dispute in the proceedings; or

    (b)   there is an issue involving the new party and an existing party which is connected to the matters in dispute in the proceedings, and it is desirable to add the new party so that the court can resolve that issue.

(2) The court may direct that any person or body be removed as a party if it is not desirable for that person or body to be a party to the proceedings.

(3) If the court makes a direction for the addition or removal of a party under this rule, it may give consequential directions about—

    (a)   the service of a copy of the application form or other relevant documents on the new party; and

    (b)   the management of the proceedings.

(4) The power of the court under this rule to direct that a party be added or removed may be exercised either on the court's own initiative or on the application of an existing party or a person or body who wishes to become a party.

(5) An application for an order under this rule must be made in accordance with the Part 18 procedure and, unless the court directs otherwise, must be supported by evidence setting out the proposed new party's interest in or connection with the proceedings or, in the case of removal of a party, the reasons for removal.]

NOTES

Amendment
> Inserted by SI 2012/679, rr 2, 18.
>> Date in force: 6 April 2012: see SI 2012/679, r 1; for transitional provisions and savings see r 30 thereof.

[9.26C Method of making periodical payments]

[(1) This rule applies where under section 1(4) or (4A) of the Maintenance Enforcement Act 1991 the court orders that payments under a qualifying periodical maintenance order are to be made by a particular means.

(2) The court officer will record on a copy of the order the means of payment that the court has ordered.

(3) The court officer will notify in writing the person liable to make payments under the order how the payments are to be made.

(4) Where under section 1(4A) of the Maintenance Enforcement Act 1991 the court orders payment to the court by a method of payment under section 1(5) of that Act, the court officer will notify the person liable to make payments under the order of sufficient details of the account into which payments should be made to enable payments to be made into that account.

(5) Where payments are made to the court, the court officer will give or send a receipt to any person who makes such a payment and who asks for a receipt.

(6) Where payments are made to the court, the court officer will make arrangements to make the payments to—

    (a)   the person entitled to them; or

    (b)   if the person entitled to them is a child, to the child or to the person with whom the child has his or her home.

(7) The Part 18 procedure applies to an application under section 1(7) of the Maintenance Enforcement Act 1991 (application from an interested party to revoke, suspend, revive or vary the method of payment).

(8) Where the court makes an order under section 1(7) of the Maintenance Enforcement Act 1991 or dismisses an application for such an order, the court officer will, as far as practicable, notify in writing all interested parties of the effect of the order and will take the steps set out in paragraphs (2), (3) and (4), as appropriate.

(9) In this rule, "interested party" and "qualifying periodical maintenance order" have the meanings given in section 1(10) of the Maintenance Enforcement Act 1991.]

NOTES

Amendment
    Inserted by SI 2014/667, rr 2, 13.
        Date in force: 22 April 2014: see SI 2014/667, r 1; for transitional and saving provision see r 45.

[9.26D Court officer to notify subsequent marriage or formation of civil partnership of a person entitled to payments under a maintenance order]

[(1) This rule applies where—

    (a)   there is an order of a type referred to in paragraph (4) which requires payments to be made to the court or to an officer of the court; and

    (b)   the court is notified in writing by—

        (i)   the person entitled to receive payments under the order;

        (ii)   the person required to make payments under the order; or

        (iii)   the personal representative of such a person,

    that the person entitled to receive payments under the order has subsequently married or formed a civil partnership.

(2) The court officer will, where practicable, notify in writing the courts referred to in paragraph (3) of the notification of the subsequent marriage or formation of a civil partnership.

(3) The courts to be notified are—

    (a)   any other court which has made an order of a type referred to in paragraph (4);

    (b)   in the case of a provisional order made under section 3 of the 1920 Act or section 3 of the 1972 Act, the court which confirmed the order;

(c)   if an order of a type referred to in paragraph (4) has been transmitted abroad for registration under section 2 of the 1920 Act or section 2 of the 1972 Act, the court in which the order is registered; and

(d)   any other court in which an application to enforce the order has been made.

(4)   The orders are—

  (a)   those to which the following provisions apply—

     (i)   section 38 of the 1973 Act;

     (ii)   section 4(2) of the 1978 Act;

     (iii) paragraph 65 of Schedule 5 to the 2004 Act; and

     (iv) paragraph 26(2) of Schedule 6 to the 2004 Act; and

  (b)   an attachment of earnings order made to secure payments under an order referred to in sub-paragraph (a).

(5)   In this rule—

"the 1920 Act" means the Maintenance Orders (Facilities for Enforcement) Act 1920; and

"the 1972 Act" means the Maintenance Orders (Reciprocal Enforcement) Act 1972.]

NOTES

Amendment
Inserted by SI 2014/667, rr 2, 13.
    Date in force: 22 April 2014: see SI 2014/667, r 1; for transitional and saving provision see r 45.

[9.26E Enforcement and apportionment where periodical payments are made under more than one order]

[(1) This rule applies where periodical payments are required to be made by a payer to a payee under more than one periodical payments order.

(2) Proceedings for the recovery of payments under more than one order may be made in one application by the payee, which must indicate the payments due under each order.

(3) Paragraphs (4) and (5) apply where any sum paid to the court on any date by a payer who is liable to make payments to the court under two or more periodical payments orders is less than the total sum that the payer is required to pay to the court on that date in respect of those orders.

(4) The payment made will be apportioned between the orders in proportion to the amounts due under each order over a period of one year.

(5) If, as a result of the apportionment referred to in paragraph (4), the payments under any periodical payments order are no longer in arrears, the residue shall be applied to the amount due under the other order or, if there is more than one other order, shall be apportioned between the other orders in accordance with paragraph (4).

(6) In this rule—

"payee" means a person entitled to receive payments under a periodical payments order; and

"payer" means a person required to make payments under a periodical payments order.]

NOTES

Amendment
Inserted by SI 2014/667, rr 2, 13.
    Date in force: 22 April 2014: see SI 2014/667, r 1; for transitional and saving provision see r 45.

CHAPTER 7

ESTIMATES OF COSTS

[9.27 Estimates of Costs]

[(1) Except where paragraph (4) applies, not less than one day before every hearing or appointment, each party must file with the court and serve on each other party an estimate of the costs incurred by that party up to the date of that hearing or appointment.

(2) Not less than one day before the first appointment, each party must file with the court and serve on each other party an estimate of the costs that party expects to incur up to the FDR appointment if a settlement is not reached.

(3) Not less than one day before the FDR appointment, each party must file with the court and serve on each other party an estimate of the costs that party expects to incur up to the final hearing if a settlement is not reached.

(4) Not less than 14 days before the date fixed for the final hearing of an application for a financial remedy, each party ("the filing party") must (unless the court directs otherwise) file with the court and serve on each other party a statement giving full particulars of all costs in respect of the proceedings which the filing party has incurred or expects to incur, to enable the court to take account of the parties' liabilities for costs when deciding what order (if any) to make for a financial remedy.

(5) A costs estimate filed and served in accordance with paragraph (1), (2) or (3) and particulars of costs filed and served in accordance with paragraph (4) must include confirmation—

> (a)   that they have been served on each other party; and
>
> (b)   in the case of a party who is legally represented, that they have been discussed with the party on whose behalf they are provided.

(6) Each party must bring to a hearing or appointment a copy of any estimate of costs filed and served in accordance with paragraph (1), (2) or (3) and any particulars of costs filed and served in accordance with paragraph (4).

(7) The amount of—

> (a)   a costs estimate filed and served in accordance with paragraph (1), (2) or (3); and
>
> (b)   particulars of costs filed and served in accordance with paragraph (4),

(8) If a party fails to comply with paragraph (1), (2), (3) or (4)—

> (a)   this fact must be recorded in a recital to the order made at the hearing or appointment before which the costs estimate or particulars of costs should have been filed and served; and
>
> (b)   the court must direct that the relevant costs estimate or particulars of costs must be filed with the court and served on each other party within three days of the hearing or appointment or within such other time period as the court directs.

(Rule 28.3 makes provision for orders for costs in financial remedy proceedings.)

(Practice Direction 9A makes provision for statements of truth to be included in estimates of costs and particulars of costs filed and served in accordance with this rule.)]

NOTES

Amendment

> Substituted by SI 2020/135, rr 2, 12.
> Date in force: 6 July 2020: see SI 2020/135, r 1.

[9.27A Duty to make open proposals after a FDR appointment or where there has been no FDR appointment]

[(1) Where at a FDR appointment the court does not make an appropriate consent order or direct a further FDR appointment, each party must file with the court and serve on each other party an open proposal for settlement—

    (a)   by such date as the court directs; or

    (b)   where no direction is given under sub-paragraph (a), within 21 days after the date of the FDR appointment.

(2) Where no FDR appointment takes place, each party must file with the court and serve on each other party an open proposal for settlement—

    (a)   by such date as the court directs; or

    (b)   where no direction is given under sub-paragraph (a), not less than 42 days before the date fixed for the final hearing.]

NOTES

Amendment
    Substituted by SI 2020/135, rr 2, 13.
        Date in force: 6 July 2020: see SI 2020/135, r 1.

9.28 [Duty to make open proposals before a final hearing]

(1) Not less than 14 days before the date fixed for the final hearing of an application for a financial remedy, the applicant must (unless the court directs otherwise) file with the court and serve on the respondent an open statement which sets out concise details, including the amounts involved, of the orders which the applicant proposes to ask the court to make.

(2) Not more than 7 days after service of a statement under paragraph (1), the respondent must file with the court and serve on the applicant an open statement which sets out concise details, including the amounts involved, of the orders which the respondent proposes to ask the court to make.

NOTES

Amendment
    Provision heading: substituted by SI 2020/135, rr 2, 14
        Date in force: 6 July 2020: see SI 2020/135, r 1.

CHAPTER 8

PENSIONS

9.29 Application and interpretation of this Chapter

(1) This Chapter applies

    (a)   where an application for a financial remedy has been made; and

    (b)   the applicant or respondent is the party with pension rights.

(2) In this Chapter—

    (a)   in proceedings under the 1973 Act and the 1984 Act, all words and phrases defined in sections 25D(3) and (4) of the 1973 Act have the meaning assigned by those subsections;

    (b)   in proceedings under the 2004 Act—

        (i)   all words and phrases defined in paragraphs 16(4) to (5) and 29 of Schedule 5 to that Act have the meanings assigned by those paragraphs; and

        (ii)   "the party with pension rights" has the meaning given to "civil partner with pension rights" by paragraph 29 of Schedule 5 to the 2004 Act;

    (c)   all words and phrases defined in section 46 of the Welfare Reform and Pensions Act 1999 have the meanings assigned by that section.

9.30 What the party with pension rights must do when the court fixes a first appointment

(1) Where the court fixes a first appointment as required by rule 9.12(1)(a) the party with pension rights must request the person responsible for each pension arrangement under which the party has or is likely to have benefits to provide the information referred to in regulation 2(2) of the Pensions on Divorce etc (Provision of Information) Regulations 2000.

(The information referred to in regulation 2 of the Pensions on Divorce etc (Provision of Information) Regulations 2000 relates to the valuation of pension rights or benefits.)

(2) The party with pension rights must comply with paragraph (1) within 7 days beginning with the date on which that party receives notification of the date of the first appointment.

(3) Within 7 days beginning with the date on which the party with pension rights receives the information under paragraph (1) that party must send a copy of it to the other party, together with the name and address of the person responsible for each pension arrangement.

(4) A request under paragraph (1) need not be made where the party with pension rights is in possession of, or has requested, a relevant valuation of the pension rights or benefits accrued under the pension arrangement in question.

9.31 Applications for pension sharing orders

Where an application for a financial remedy includes an application for a pension sharing order, or where a request for such an order is added to an existing application for a financial remedy, the applicant must serve a copy of the application on the person responsible for the pension arrangement concerned.

9.32 Applications for consent orders for pension sharing

(1) This rule applies where—

    (a) the parties have agreed on the terms of an order and the agreement includes a pension sharing order;

    (b) service has not been effected under rule9.31; and

    (c) the information referred to in paragraph (2) has not otherwise been provided.

(2) The party with pension rights must—

    (a) request the person responsible for the pension arrangement concerned to provide the information set out in Section C of the Pension Inquiry Form; and

    (b) on receipt, send a copy of the information referred to in sub-paragraph (a) to the other party.

9.33 Applications for pension attachment orders

(1) Where an application for a financial remedy includes an application for a pension attachment order, or where a request for such an order is added to an existing application for a financial remedy, the applicant must serve a copy of the application on the person responsible for the pension arrangement concerned and must at the same time send—

    (a) an address to which any notice which the person responsible is required to serve on the applicant is to be sent;

    (b) an address to which any payment which the person responsible is required to make to the applicant is to be sent; and

    (c) where the address in sub-paragraph (b) is that of a bank, a building society or the Department of National Savings, sufficient details to enable the payment to be made into the account of the applicant.

(2) A person responsible for a pension arrangement who receives a copy of the application under paragraph (1) may, within 21 days beginning with the date of service of the application, request the party with the pension rights to provide that person with the information disclosed in the financial statement relating to the party's pension rights or benefits under that arrangement.

(3) If the person responsible for a pension arrangement makes a request under paragraph (2), the party with the pension rights must provide that person with a copy of the section of that party's financial statement that relates to that party's pension rights or benefits under that arrangement.

(4) The party with the pension rights must comply with paragraph (3)—

(a)   within the time limited for filing the financial statement by rule 9.14(1); or

(b)   within 21 days beginning with the date on which the person responsible for the pension arrangement makes the request,

whichever is the later.

(5) A person responsible for a pension arrangement who receives a copy of the section of a financial statement as required pursuant to paragraph (4) may, within 21 days beginning with the date on which that person receives it, send to the court, the applicant and the respondent a statement in answer.

(6) A person responsible for a pension arrangement who files a statement in answer pursuant to paragraph (5) will be entitled to be represented at the first appointment, or such other hearing as the court may direct, and the court must within 4 days, beginning with the date on which that person files the statement in answer, give the person notice of the date of the first appointment or other hearing as the case may be.

9.34 Applications for consent orders for pension attachment

(1) This rule applies where service has not been effected under rule9.33(1).

(2) Where the parties have agreed on the terms of an order and the agreement includes a pension attachment order, then they must serve on the person responsible for the pension arrangement concerned—

(a)   a copy of the application for a consent order;

(b)   a draft of the proposed order, complying with rule 9.35; and

(c)   the particulars set out in rule 9.33(1).

(3) No consent order that includes a pension attachment order must be made unless either—

(a)   the person responsible for the pension arrangement has not made any objection within 21 days beginning with the date on which the application for a consent order was served on that person; or

(b)   the court has considered any such objection, and for the purpose of considering any objection the court may make such direction as it sees fit for the person responsible to attend before it or to furnish written details of the objection.

9.35 Pension sharing orders or pension attachment orders

An order for a financial remedy, whether by consent or not, which includes a pension sharing order or a pension attachment order, must—

(a)   in the body of the order, state that there is to be provision by way of pension sharing or pension attachment in accordance with the annex or annexes to the order; and

(b)   be accompanied by a pension sharing annex or a pension attachment annex as the case may require, and if provision is made in relation to more than one pension arrangement there must be one annex for each pension arrangement.

9.36 Duty of the court upon making a pension sharing order or a pension attachment order

(1)   A court which varies or discharges a pension sharing order or a pension attachment order, must send, or direct one of the parties to send—

(a)   to the person responsible for the pension arrangement concerned; or

(b)   where the Board has assumed responsibility for the pension scheme or part of it, the Board;

the documents referred to in paragraph (4).

(2)   A court which makes a pension sharing order or pension attachment order, must send, or direct one of the parties to send to the person responsible for the pension arrangement concerned, the documents referred to in paragraph (4).

(3)   Where the Board has assumed responsibility for the pension scheme or part of it after the making of a pension sharing order or attachment order but before the documents have been sent to the person responsible for the pension arrangement in accordance with paragraph (2), the court which makes the pension sharing order or the pension attachment order, must send, or direct one of the parties to send to the Board the documents referred to in paragraph (4).

(4)   The documents to be sent in accordance with paragraph (1) to (3) are—

(a)   in the case of—

(i)   proceedings under the 1973 Act, a copy of the decree of judicial separation;

(ii)   proceedings under Schedule 5 to the 2004 Act, a copy of the separation order;

(iii)   proceedings under Part 3 of the 1984 Act, a copy of the document of divorce, annulment or legal separation;

(iv)   proceedings under Schedule 7 to the 2004 Act, a copy of the document of dissolution, annulment or legal separation;

(b)   in the case of divorce or nullity of marriage, a copy of the decree absolute under rule 7.31or 7.32; or

(c)   in the case of dissolution or nullity of civil partnership, a copy of the order making the conditional order final under rule 7.31 or 7.32; and

(d)   a copy of the pension sharing order or the pension attachment order, or as the case may be of the order varying or discharging that order, including any annex to that order relating to that pension arrangement but no other annex to that order.

(5)   The documents referred to in [paragraph (4)] must be sent—

(a)   in proceedings under the 1973 Act and the 1984 Act, within 7 days beginning with the date on which—

(i)   the relevant pension sharing or pension attachment order[, or any order varying or discharging such an order,] is made; or

(ii)   the decree absolute of divorce or nullity or decree of judicial separation is made,

whichever is the later; and

(b)   in proceedings under the 2004 Act, within 7 days beginning with the date on which—

(i)   the relevant pension sharing or pension attachment order[, or any order varying or discharging such an order,] is made; or

(ii)   the final order of dissolution or nullity or separation order is made,

whichever is the later.

NOTES

Amendment
    Para (5): words "paragraph (4)" in square brackets substituted by SI 2012/679, rr 2, 19(a).

Date in force: 6 April 2012: see SI 2012/679, r 1.
Para (5): in sub-para (a)(i) words ", or any order varying or discharging such an order," in square brackets inserted by SI 2012/679, rr 2, 19(b).
Date in force: 6 April 2012: see SI 2012/679, r 1; for transitional provisions and savings see r 30 thereof.
Para (5): in sub-para (b)(i) words ", or any order varying or discharging such an order," in square brackets inserted by SI 2012/679, rr 2, 19(b).
Date in force: 6 April 2012: see SI 2012/679, r 1; for transitional provisions and savings see r 30 thereof.

9.37 Procedure where Pension Protection Fund becomes involved with the pension scheme

(1) This rule applies where—

(a) rules 9.30 to 9.34 or 9.36 apply; and

(b) the party with the pension rights ("the member") receives or has received notification in compliance with the Pension Protection Fund (Provision of Information) Regulations 2005 ("the 2005 Regulations")—

(i) from the trustees or managers of a pension scheme, that there is an assessment period in relation to that scheme; or

(ii) from the Board that it has assumed responsibility for the pension scheme or part of it.

(2) If the trustees or managers of the pension scheme notify or have notified the member that there is an assessment period in relation to that scheme, the member must send to the other party, all the information which the Board is required from time to time to provide to the member under the 2005 Regulations including—

(a) a copy of the notification; and

(b) a copy of the valuation summary,

in accordance with paragraph (3).

(3) The member must send the information or any part of it referred to in paragraph (2)—

(a) if available, when the member sends the information received under rule 9.30(1); or

(b) otherwise, within 7 days of receipt.

(4) If the Board notifies the member that it has assumed responsibility for the pension scheme, or part of it, the member must—

(a) send a copy of the notification to the other party within 7 days of receipt; and

(b) comply with paragraph (5).

(5) Where paragraph (4) applies, the member must—

(a) within 7 days of receipt of the notification, request the Board in writing to provide a forecast of the member's compensation entitlement as described in the 2005 Regulations; and

(b) send a copy of the forecast of the member's compensation entitlement to the other party within 7 days of receipt.

(6) In this rule—

(a) "assessment period" means an assessment period within the meaning of Part 2 of the Pensions Act 2004; and

(b) "valuation summary" has the meaning assigned to it by the 2005 Regulations.

CHAPTER 9

PENSION PROTECTION FUND COMPENSATION

9.38 Application and interpretation of this Chapter

(1) This Chapter applies—

      (a)   where an application for a financial remedy has been made; and

      (b)   the applicant or respondent is, the party with compensation rights.

(2)   In this Chapter "party with compensation rights"—

      (a)   in proceedings under the 1973 Act and the 1984 Act, has the meaning given to it by section 25G(5) of the 1973 Act;

      (b)   in proceedings under the 2004 Act, has the meaning given to "civil partner with compensation rights" by paragraph 37(1) of Schedule 5 to the 2004 Act.

9.39 What the party with compensation rights must do when the court fixes a first appointment

(1)   Where the court fixes a first appointment as required by rule 9.12(1)(a) the party with compensation rights must request the Board to provide the information about the valuation of entitlement to PPF compensation referred to in regulations made by the Secretary of State under section 118 of the Pensions Act 2008.

(2)   The party with compensation rights must comply with paragraph (1) within 7 days beginning with the date on which that party receives notification of the date of the first appointment.

(3)   Within 7 days beginning with the date on which the party with compensation rights receives the information under paragraph (1) that party must send a copy of it to the other party, together with the name and address of the trustees or managers responsible for each pension scheme.

(4)   Where the rights to PPF Compensation are derived from rights under more than one pension scheme, the party with compensation rights must comply with this rule in relation to each entitlement.

9.40 Applications for pension compensation sharing orders

Where an application for a financial remedy includes an application for a pension compensation sharing order or where a request for such an order is added to an existing application for a financial remedy, the applicant must serve a copy of the application on the Board.

9.41 Applications for consent orders for pension compensation sharing

(1)   This rule applies where—

      (a)   the parties have agreed on the terms of an order and the agreement includes a pension compensation sharing order;

      (b)   service has not been effected under rule 9.40; and

      (c)   the information referred to in paragraph (2) has not otherwise been provided.

(2)   The party with compensation rights must—

      (a)   request the Board to provide the information set out in Section C of the Pension Protection Fund Inquiry Form; and

      (b)   on receipt, send a copy of the information referred to in sub-paragraph (a) to the other party.

9.42 Applications for pension compensation attachment orders

Where an application for a financial remedy includes an application for a pension compensation attachment order or where a request for such an order is added to an existing application for a financial remedy, the applicant must serve a copy of the application on the Board and must at the same time send—

      (a)   an address to which any notice which the Board is required to serve on the applicant is to be sent;

      (b)   an address to which any payment which the Board is required to make to the applicant is to be sent; and

(c)   where the address in sub-paragraph (b) is that of a bank, a building society or the Department of National Savings, sufficient details to enable the payment to be made into the account of the applicant.

9.43 Applications for consent orders for pension compensation attachment

(1)   This rule applies where service has not been effected under rule9.42.

(2)   Where the parties have agreed on the terms of an order and the agreement includes a pension compensation attachment order, then they must serve on the Board—

    (a)   a copy of the application for a consent order;

    (b)   a draft of the proposed order, complying with rule 9.44; and

    (c)   the particulars set out in rule 9.42.

9.44 Pension compensation sharing orders or pension compensation attachment orders

An order for a financial remedy, whether by consent or not, which includes a pension compensation sharing order or a pension compensation attachment order, must—

    (a)   in the body of the order, state that there is to be provision by way of pension compensation sharing or pension compensation attachment in accordance with the annex or annexes to the order; and

    (b)   be accompanied by a pension compensation sharing annex or a pension compensation attachment annex as the case may require, and if provision is made in relation to entitlement to PPF compensation that derives from rights under more than one pension scheme there must be one annex for each such entitlement.

9.45 Duty of the court upon making a pension compensation sharing order or a pension compensation attachment order

(1)   A court which makes, varies or discharges a pension compensation sharing order or a pension compensation attachment order, must send, or direct one of the parties to send, to the Board—

    (a)   in the case of—

        (i)   proceedings under Part 3 of the 1984 Act, a copy of the document of divorce, annulment or legal separation;

        (ii)   proceedings under Schedule 7 to the 2004 Act, a copy of the document of dissolution, annulment or legal separation;

    (b)   in the case of—

        (i)   divorce or nullity of marriage, a copy of the decree absolute under rule 7.32 or 7.33;

        (ii)   dissolution or nullity of civil partnership, a copy of the order making the conditional order final under rule 7.32 or 7.33;

    (c)   in the case of separation—

        (i)   in the matrimonial proceedings, a copy of the decree of judicial separation;

        (ii)   in civil partnership proceedings, a copy of the separation order; and

    (d)   a copy of the pension compensation sharing order or the pension compensation attachment order, or as the case may be of the order varying or discharging that order, including any annex to that order relating to that PPF compensation but no other annex to that order.

(2)   The documents referred to in paragraph (1) must be sent—

    (a)   in proceedings under the 1973 Act and the 1984 Act, within 7 days beginning with the date on which—

        (i)   the relevant pension compensation sharing or pension compensation attachment order is made; or

(ii)   the decree absolute of divorce or nullity or the decree of judicial separation is made,

whichever is the later; and

(b)   in proceedings under the 2004 Act, within 7 days beginning with the date on which—

(i)   the relevant pension compensation sharing or pension compensation attachment order is made; or

(ii)   the final order of dissolution or nullity or separation order is made,

whichever is the later.

. . .

PART 19

ALTERNATIVE PROCEDURE FOR APPLICATIONS

19.1 Types of application for which Part 19 procedure may be followed

(1)   The Part 19 procedure is the procedure set out in this Part.

(2)   An applicant may use the Part 19 procedure where the Part 18 procedure does not apply and—

(a)   there is no form prescribed by a rule or referred to in Practice Direction 5A in which to make the application;

(b)   the applicant seeks the court's decision on a question which is unlikely to involve a substantial dispute of fact; or

(c)   paragraph (5) applies.

[(2A) This Part is subject to any provision made by or pursuant to Part 41 (proceeding by electronic means).]

(3)   The court may at any stage direct that the application is to continue as if the applicant had not used the Part 19 procedure and, if it does so, the court may give any directions it considers appropriate.

(4)   Paragraph (2) does not apply if a practice direction provides that the Part 19 procedure may not be used in relation to the type of application in question.

(5)   A rule or practice direction may, in relation to a specified type of proceedings—

(a)   require or permit the use of the Part 19 procedure; and

(b)   disapply or modify any of the rules set out in this Part as they apply to those proceedings.

NOTES

Amendment
> Para (2A): inserted by SI 2020/135, rr 2, 23.
>> Date in force: 6 April 2020: see SI 2020/135, r 1.

19.2 Applications for which the Part 19 procedure must be followed

(1)   The Part 19 procedure must be used in an application made in accordance with—

(a)   section 60(3) of the 2002 Act (order to prevent disclosure of information to an adopted person);

(b)   section 79(4) of the 2002 Act (order for Registrar General to give any information referred to in section 79(3) of the 2002 Act); and

(c)   rule 14.21 (directions . . . regarding fathers without parental responsibility).

(2)   The respondent to an application made in accordance with paragraph (1)(b) is the Registrar General.

NOTES

Amendment
> Para (1): in sub-para (c) words omitted revoked by SI 2020/135, rr 2, 24.
>> Date in force: 6 April 2020: see SI 2020/135, r 1.

19.3 Contents of the application
Where the applicant uses the Part 19 procedure, the application must state—
  (a) that this Part applies;
  (b) either—
      (i) the question which the applicant wants the court to decide; or
      (ii) the order which the applicant is seeking and the legal basis of the application for that order;
  (c) if the application is being made under an enactment, what that enactment is;
  (d) if the applicant is applying in a representative capacity, what that capacity is; and
  (e) if the respondent appears or is to appear in a representative capacity, what that capacity is.
(Part 17 requires a statement of case to be verified by a statement of truth.)

19.4 Issue of application without naming respondents
(1) A practice direction may set out circumstances in which an application may be issued under this Part without naming a respondent.
(2) The practice direction may set out those cases in which an application for permission must be made by application notice before the application is issued.
(3) The application for permission—
  (a) need not be served on any other person; and
  (b) must be accompanied by a copy of the application which the applicant proposes to issue.
(4) Where the court gives permission, it will give directions about the future management of the application.

19.5 Acknowledgment of service
(1) Subject to paragraph(2), each respondent must—
  (a) file an acknowledgment of service within 14 days beginning with the date on which the application is served; and
  (b) serve the acknowledgment of service on the applicant and any other party.
(2) If the application is to be served out of the jurisdiction, the respondent must file and serve an acknowledgment of service within the period set out in Practice Direction 6B.
(3) The acknowledgment of service must—
  (a) state whether the respondent contests the application;
  (b) state, if the respondent seeks a different order from that set out in the application, what that order is; and
  (c) be signed by the respondent or the respondent's legal representative.

19.6 Consequence of not filing an acknowledgment of service
(1) This rule applies where—
  (a) the respondent has failed to file an acknowledgment of service; and
  (b) the time period for doing so has expired.
(2) The respondent may attend the hearing of the application but may not take part in the hearing unless the court gives permission.

19.7 Filing and serving written evidence
(1) The applicant must, when filing the application, file the written evidence on which the applicant intends to rely.
(2) The applicant's evidence must be served on the respondent with the application.

(3)   A respondent who wishes to rely on written evidence must file it when filing the acknowledgment of service.

(4)   A respondent who files written evidence must also, at the same time, serve a copy of that evidence on the other parties.

(5)   Within 14 days beginning with the date on which a respondent's evidence was served on the applicant, the applicant may file further written evidence in reply.

(6)   An applicant who files further written evidence must also, within the same time limit, serve a copy of that evidence on the other parties.

19.8 Evidence—general

(1)   No written evidence may be relied on at the hearing of the application unless—

    (a)   it has been served in accordance with rule19.7; or

    (b)   the court gives permission.

(2)   The court may require or permit a party to give oral evidence at the hearing.

(3)   The court may give directions requiring the attendance for cross-examination(GL) of a witness who has given written evidence.

(Rule 22.1 contains a general power for the court to control evidence.)

19.9 Procedure where respondent objects to use of the Part 19 procedure

(1)   A respondent who contends that the Part 19 procedure should not be used because—

    (a)   there is a substantial dispute of fact; and

    (b)   the use of the Part 19 procedure is not required or permitted by a rule or practice direction,

must state the reasons for that contention when filing the acknowledgment of service.

(2)   When the court receives the acknowledgment of service and any written evidence, it will give directions as to the future management of the case.

(Rule 19.7 requires a respondent who wishes to rely on written evidence to file it when filing the acknowledgment of service.)

(Rule 19.1(3) allows the court to make an order that the application continue as if the applicant had not used the Part 19 procedure.)

PART 20

INTERIM REMEDIES AND SECURITY FOR COSTS

CHAPTER 1

Interim Remedies

20.1 . . .

. . .

NOTES

Amendment
> Revoked by SI 2013/3204, rr 2, 67.
>> Date in force: 22 April 2014 (being the date on which the Crime and Courts Act 2013, s 17(3) is brought fully into force): see SI 2013/3204, r 1 and SI 2014/954, art 2(a); for transitional provisions and savings see SI 2013/3204, r 137 and SI 2014/954, art 3.

20.2 Orders for interim remedies

(1)   The court may grant the following interim remedies—

    (a)   an interim injunction(GL);

    (b)   an interim declaration;

    (c)   an order—

        (i)   for the detention, custody or preservation of relevant property;

        (ii)   for the inspection of relevant property;

   (iii) for the taking of a sample of relevant property;
   (iv) for the carrying out of an experiment on or with relevant property;
   (v) for the sale of relevant property which is of a perishable nature or which for any other good reason it is desirable to sell quickly; and
   (vi) for the payment of income from relevant property until an application is decided;
 (d) an order authorising a person to enter any land or building in the possession of a party to the proceedings for the purposes of carrying out an order under sub-paragraph (c);
 (e) an order under section 4 of the Torts (Interference with Goods) Act 1977 to deliver up goods;
 (f) an order (referred to as a 'freezing injunction(GL)')—
   (i) restraining a party from removing from the jurisdiction assets located there; or
   (ii) restraining a party from dealing with any assets whether located within the jurisdiction or not;
 (g) an order directing a party to provide information about the location of relevant property or assets or to provide information about relevant property or assets which are or may be the subject of an application for a freezing injunction(GL);
 (h) an order (referred to as a "search order") under section 7 of the Civil Procedure Act 1997 (order requiring a party to admit another party to premises for the purpose of preserving evidence etc);
 (i) an order under section 34 of the Senior Courts Act 1981 or section 53 of the County Courts Act 1984 (order in certain proceedings for disclosure of documents or inspection of property against a non-party);
 (j) an order for a specified fund to be paid into court or otherwise secured, where there is a dispute over a party's right to the fund;
 (k) an order permitting a party seeking to recover personal property to pay money into court pending the outcome of the proceedings and directing that, if money is paid into court, the property must be given up to that party;
 (l) an order directing a party to prepare and file accounts relating to the dispute;
 (m) an order directing any account to be taken or inquiry to be made by the court.

(2) In paragraph (1)(c) and(g), 'relevant property' means property (including land) which is the subject of an application or as to which any question may arise on an application.

(3) The fact that a particular kind of interim remedy is not listed in paragraph (1) does not affect any power that the court may have to grant that remedy.

20.3 Time when an order for an interim remedy may be made

(1) An order for an interim remedy may be made at any time, including—
 (a) before proceedings are started; and
 (b) after judgment has been given.

(Rule 5.3 provides that proceedings are started when the court issues an application form.)

(2) However—
 (a) paragraph (1) is subject to any rule, practice direction or other enactment which provides otherwise; and
 (b) the court may grant an interim remedy before an application has been started only if—

      (i)   the matter is urgent; or

      (ii)   it is otherwise desirable to do so in the interests of justice.

(3)   Where the court grants an interim remedy before an application has been started, it will give directions requiring an application to be started.

(4)   The court need not direct that an application be started where the application is made under section 33 of the Senior Courts Act 1981 or section 52 of the County Courts Act 1984 (order for disclosure, inspection etc before starting an application).

20.4 How to apply for an interim remedy

(1)   The court may grant an interim remedy on an application made without notice if it appears to the court that there are good reasons for not giving notice.

(2)   An application for an interim remedy must be supported by evidence, unless the court orders otherwise.

(3)   If the applicant makes an application without giving notice, the evidence in support of the application must state the reasons why notice has not been given.

(Part 4 lists general case-management powers of the court.)

(Part 18 contains general rules about making an application.)

20.5 Interim injunction to cease if application is stayed

If—

    (a)   the court has granted an interim injunction(GL) other than a freezing injunction(GL); and

    (b)   the application is stayed(GL) other than by agreement between the parties,

the interim injunction(GL) will be set aside(GL) unless the court orders that it should continue to have effect even though the application is stayed(GL).

CHAPTER 2

SECURITY FOR COSTS

20.6 Security for costs

(1)   A respondent to any application may apply under this Chapter of this Part for security for costs of the proceedings.

(Part 4 provides for the court to order payment of sums into court in other circumstances.)

(2)   An application for security for costs must be supported by written evidence.

(3)   Where the court makes an order for security for costs, it will—

    (a)   determine the amount of security; and

    (b)   direct—

        (i)   the manner in which; and

        (ii)   the time within which,

    the security must be given.

20.7 Conditions to be satisfied

(1)   The court may make an order for security for costs under rule 20.6 if—

    (a)   it is satisfied, having regard to all the circumstances of the case, that it is just to make such an order; and

    (b)   either—

        (i)   one or more of the conditions in paragraph (2) applies; or

        (ii)   an enactment permits the court to require security for costs.

(2)   The conditions are—

    (a)   the applicant is—

        (i)   resident out of the jurisdiction; but

(ii)   not resident in a Brussels Contracting State, [a State bound by the Lugano Convention,] [a State bound by the 2007 Hague Convention which is an EEA State,] a Regulation State [or a Maintenance Regulation State], as defined in section 1(3) of the Civil Jurisdiction and Judgments Act 1982[, . . .] or a Member State bound by the Council Regulation;

(b)   the applicant has changed address since the application was started with a view to evading the consequences of the litigation;

(c)   the applicant failed to give an address in the application form, or gave an incorrect address in that form;

(d)   the applicant has taken steps in relation to the applicant's assets that would make it difficult to enforce an order for costs against the applicant.

(3)   The court may not make an order for security for costs under rule 20.6 in relation to the costs of proceedings under the 1980 Hague Convention.

(Rule 4.4 allows the court to strike out(GL) a statement of case.)

[("EEA State" is defined in Schedule 1 to the Interpretation Act 1978).]

NOTES

Amendment

Para (2): in sub-para (a)(ii) words "a State bound by the Lugano Convention," in square brackets substituted by SI 2012/679, rr 2, 24(a).
Date in force: 6 April 2012: see SI 2012/679, r 1; for transitional provisions and savings see r 30 thereof.
Para (2): in sub-para (a)(ii) words from "a State bound" to "an EEA State," in square brackets inserted by SI 2012/2806, rr 2, 16(a).
Date in force: 20 December 2012: see SI 2012/2806, r 1.
Para (2): in sub-para (a)(ii) words "or a Maintenance Regulation State" in square brackets inserted by SI 2012/679, rr 2, 24(b).
Date in force: 6 April 2012: see SI 2012/679, r 1; for transitional provisions and savings see r 30 thereof.
Para (2): in sub-para (a)(ii) words omitted in square brackets inserted by SI 2011/1328, rr 2, 15.
Date in force: 18 June 2011: see SI 2011/1328, r 1.
Para (2): in sub-para (a)(ii) words omitted revoked by SI 2012/679, rr 2, 24(c).
Date in force: 6 April 2012: see SI 2012/679, r 1; for transitional provisions and savings see r 30 thereof.
Words "("EEA State" is defined in Schedule 1 to the Interpretation Act 1978)." in square brackets inserted by SI 2012/2806, rr 2, 16(b).
Date in force: 20 December 2012: see SI 2012/2806, r 1.

20.8 Security for costs of an appeal

The court may order security for costs of an appeal against—

(a)   an appellant;

(b)   a respondent who also appeals,

on the same grounds as it may order security for costs against an applicant under this Part.

. . .

PART 30

APPEALS

30.1 Scope and interpretation

(1)   The rules in this Part apply to appeals to—

(a)   the High Court; and

(b)   [the family court].

(2)   This Part does not apply to an appeal in detailed assessment proceedings against a decision of an authorised court officer.

(Rules [47.21 to 47.24] of the CPR deal with appeals against a decision of an authorised court officer in detailed assessment proceedings.)

(3)   In this Part—
"appeal court" means the court to which an appeal is made;
"appeal notice" means an appellant's or respondent's notice;
"appellant" means a person who brings or seeks to bring an appeal;
["costs judge" means—

    (a)   the Chief Taxing Master;

    (b)   a taxing master of the Senior Courts; or

    (c)   a person appointed to act as deputy for the person holding office referred to in paragraph (b) or to act as temporary additional officer for any such office;]

["district judge" means—

    (a)   the Senior District Judge of the Family Division

    (b)   a district judge of the Principal Registry of the Family Division;

    (c)   a person appointed to act as deputy for the person holding office referred to in paragraph (b) or to act as temporary additional officer for any such office;

    (d)   a district judge;

    (e)   a deputy district judge appointed under section 102 of the Senior Courts Act 1981 or section 8 of the County Courts Act 1984; or

    (f)   a District Judge (Magistrates' Courts);]

"lower court" means the court from which, or the person from whom, the appeal lies; and
"respondent" means—

    (a)   a person other than the appellant who was a party to the proceedings in the lower court and who is affected by the appeal; and

    (b)   a person who is permitted by the appeal court to be a party to the appeal.

(4)   This Part is subject to any rule, enactment or practice direction which sets out special provisions with regard to any particular category of appeal.

NOTES

Amendment

Para (1): in sub-para (b) words "the family court" in square brackets substituted by SI 2014/667, rr 2, 21(a).
    Date in force: 22 April 2014: see SI 2014/667, r 1; for transitional and saving provision see r 45.
Words in parentheses below para (2): words "47.21 to 47.24" in square brackets substituted by SI 2014/667, rr 2, 21(b).
    Date in force: 22 April 2014: see SI 2014/667, r 1; for transitional and saving provision see r 45.
Para (3): definition "costs judge" inserted by SI 2014/667, rr 2, 21(c).
    Date in force: 22 April 2014: see SI 2014/667, r 1; for transitional and saving provision see r 45.
Para (3): definition "district judge" inserted by SI 2014/667, rr 2, 21(c).
    Date in force: 22 April 2014: see SI 2014/667, r 1; for transitional and saving provision see r 45.

30.2 Parties to comply with the practice direction

All parties to an appeal must comply with Practice Direction 30A.

30.3 Permission

[(1)   Paragraphs (1B) and (2) of this rule set out when permission to appeal is, or is not, required under these rules to appeal against a decision or order of the family court.

(1A)   This rule does not apply where the route of appeal from a decision or order of the family court is to the Court of Appeal, namely where the appeal is against a decision or order made by a circuit judge or Recorder—

    (a)   in proceedings under—

        (i)   Part 4 of the 1989 Act (care and supervision);

        (ii)   Part 5 of the 1989 Act (protection of children);

        (iii)   paragraph 19(1) of Schedule 2 to the 1989 Act (approval by the court of local authority arrangements to assist children to live abroad); or

        (iv)   the 2002 Act (adoption, placement etc);

    (b)   in exercise of the family court's jurisdiction in relation to contempt of court where that decision or order was made in, or in connection with, proceedings referred to in sub-paragraph (a); or

    (c)   where that decision or order was itself made on an appeal to the family court.

(Appeals in the cases referred to in this paragraph are outside the scope of these rules. The CPR make provision requiring permission to appeal in those cases.)

(1B)   Permission to appeal is required under these rules—

    (a)   unless paragraph (2) applies, where the appeal is against a decision made by a circuit judge, Recorder, district judge or costs judge; or

    (b)   as provided by Practice Direction 30A.]

(2)   Permission to appeal is not required where the appeal is against—

    (a)   a committal order; . . .

    (b)   a secure accommodation order under section 25 of the 1989 Act[; or

    (c)   a refusal to grant habeas corpus for release in relation to a minor].

(3)   An application for permission to appeal may be made—

    (a)   to the lower court at the hearing at which the decision to be appealed was made; or

    (b)   to the appeal court in an appeal notice.

(Rule 30.4 sets out the time limits for filing an appellant's notice at the appeal court. Rule 30.5 sets out the time limits for filing a respondent's notice at the appeal court. Any application for permission to appeal to the appeal court must be made in the appeal notice (see rules 30.4(1) and 30.5(3).)

(4)   Where the lower court refuses an application for permission to appeal, a further application for permission to appeal may be made to the appeal court.

(5)   [Subject to paragraph (5A), where] the appeal court, without a hearing, refuses permission to appeal, the person seeking permission may request the decision to be reconsidered at a hearing.

[(5A)   Where a judge of the High Court or [in the family court, a judge of the High Court or] a Designated Family Judge refuses permission to appeal without a hearing and considers that the application is totally without merit, the judge may make an order that the person seeking permission may not request the decision to be reconsidered at a hearing.

(5B)   Rule 4.3(5) will not apply to an order that the person seeking permission may not request the decision to be reconsidered at a hearing made under paragraph (5A).]

(6)   A request under paragraph (5) must be filed within 7 days beginning with the date on which the notice that permission has been refused was served.

(7)   Permission to appeal may be given only where—

    (a)   the court considers that the appeal would have a real prospect of success; or

    (b)   there is some other compelling reason why the appeal should be heard.

(8)   An order giving permission may—

    (a)   limit the issues to be heard; and

(b)   be made subject to conditions.

(9) . . .

NOTES

Amendment

Paras (1), (1A), (1B): substituted, for para (1) as originally enacted, by SI 2016/891, art 3.
Date in force: 3 October 2016: see SI 2016/891, art 1.
Para (2): in sub-para (a) word omitted revoked by SI 2014/3296, rr 2, 11(a).
Date in force: 6 April 2015: see SI 2014/3296, r 1(3); for transitional and saving provision see r 15.
Para (2): sub-para (c) and the word "; or" immediately preceding it inserted by SI 2014/3296, rr 2, 11(b), (c).
Date in force: 6 April 2015: see SI 2014/3296, r 1(3); for transitional and saving provision see r 15.
Para (5): words "Subject to paragraph (5A), where" in square brackets substituted by SI 2013/530, rr 2, 5(a).
Date in force: 1 April 2013: see SI 2013/530, r 1.
Paras (5A), (5B): inserted by SI 2013/530, rr 2, 5(b).
Date in force: 1 April 2013: see SI 2013/530, r 1.
Para (5A): words "in the family court, a judge of the High Court or " in square brackets inserted by SI 2014/667, rr 2, 22(a).
Date in force: 22 April 2014: see SI 2014/667, r 1; for transitional and saving provision see r 45.
Para (9): revoked by SI 2014/667, rr 2, 22(b).
Date in force: 22 April 2014: see SI 2014/667, r 1; for transitional and saving provision see r 45.

30.4 Appellant's notice

(1)   Where the appellant seeks permission from the appeal court it must be requested in the appellant's notice.

(2)   Subject to paragraph (3), the appellant must file the appellant's notice at the appeal court within—

(a)   such period as may be directed by the lower court (which may be longer or shorter than the period referred to in sub-paragraph (b)); or

(b)   where the court makes no such direction, 21 days after the date of the decision of the lower court against which the appellant wishes to appeal.

[(3)   Where the appeal is against—

(a)   a case management decision; or

(b)   an order under section 38(1) of the 1989 Act,

the appellant must file the appellant's notice within 7 days beginning with the date of the decision of the lower court.]

(4)   Unless the appeal court orders otherwise, an appellant's notice must be served on each respondent and the persons referred to in paragraph (5)—

(a)   as soon as practicable; and

(b)   in any event not later than 7 days,

after it is filed.

(5)   The persons referred to in paragraph (4) are—

(a)   any children's guardian, welfare officer, or children and family reporter;

(b)   a local authority who has prepared a report under section 14A(8) or (9) of the 1989 Act;

(c)   an adoption agency or local authority which has prepared a report on the suitability of the applicant to adopt a child;

(d)   a local authority which has prepared a report on the placement of the child for adoption; and

(e)   . . ..

NOTES

Amendment

Para (3): substituted by SI 2014/667, rr 2, 23(a).

Date in force: 22 April 2014: see SI 2014/667, r 1; for transitional and saving provision see r 45.
Para (5): sub-para (e) revoked by SI 2014/667, rr 2, 23(b).
Date in force: 22 April 2014: see SI 2014/667, r 1; for transitional and saving provision see r 45.

30.5 Respondent's notice
(1) A respondent may file and serve a respondent's notice.
(2) A respondent who—
   (a) is seeking permission to appeal from the appeal court; or
   (b) wishes to ask the appeal court to uphold the order of the lower court for reasons different from or additional to those given by the lower court,
must file a respondent's notice.
(3) Where the respondent seeks permission from the appeal court it must be requested in the respondent's notice.
(4) [Subject to paragraph (4A), a respondent's notice] must be filed within—
   (a) such period as may be directed by the lower court; or
   (b) where the court makes no such direction, 14 days beginning with the date referred to in paragraph (5).
[(4A) Where the appeal is against a case management decision, a respondent's notice must be filed within—
   (a) such period as may be directed by the lower court; or
   (b) where the court makes no such direction, 7 days beginning with the date referred to in paragraph (5).]
(5) The date referred to in paragraph (4) is—
   (a) the date on which the respondent is served with the appellant's notice where—
      (i) permission to appeal was given by the lower court; or
      (ii) permission to appeal is not required;
   (b) the date on which the respondent is served with notification that the appeal court has given the appellant permission to appeal; or
   (c) the date on which the respondent is served with notification that the application for permission to appeal and the appeal itself are to be heard together.
(6) Unless the appeal court orders otherwise, a respondent's notice must be served on the appellant, any other respondent and the persons referred to in rule 30.4(5)—
   (a) as soon as practicable; and
   (b) in any event not later than 7 days,
after it is filed.
(7) Where there is an appeal against an order under section 38(1) of the 1989 Act—
   (a) a respondent may not, in that appeal, bring an appeal from the order or ask the appeal court to uphold the order of the lower court for reasons different from or additional to those given by the lower court; and
   (b) paragraphs (2) and (3) do not apply.

NOTES

Amendment
Para (4): words "Subject to paragraph (4A), a respondent's notice" in square brackets substituted by SI 2014/667, rr 2, 24(a).
Date in force: 22 April 2014: see SI 2014/667, r 1; for transitional and saving provision see r 45.
Para (4A): inserted by SI 2014/667, rr 2, 24(b).
Date in force: 22 April 2014: see SI 2014/667, r 1; for transitional and saving provision see r 45.

30.6 Grounds of appeal
The appeal notice must state the grounds of appeal.

30.7 Variation of time

(1)   An application to vary the time limit for filing an appeal notice must be made to the appeal court.

(2)   The parties may not agree to extend any date or time limit set by—

    (a)   these rules;

    (b)   Practice Direction 30A; or

    (c)   an order of the appeal court or the lower court.

(Rule 4.1(3)(a) provides that the court may extend or shorten the time for compliance with a rule, practice direction or court order (even if an application for extension is made after the time for compliance has expired).)

(Rule 4.1(3)(c) provides that the court may adjourn or bring forward a hearing.)

30.8 Stay

Unless the appeal court or the lower court orders otherwise, an appeal does not operate as a stay(GL) of any order or decision of the lower court.

NOTES

30.9 Amendment of appeal notice

An appeal notice may not be amended without the permission of the appeal court.

30.10 Striking out appeal notices and setting aside or imposing conditions on permission to appeal

(1)   The appeal court may—

    (a)   strike out(GL) the whole or part of an appeal notice;

    (b)   set aside(GL) permission to appeal in whole or in part;

    (c)   impose or vary conditions upon which an appeal may be brought.

(2)   The court will only exercise its powers under paragraph (1) where there is a compelling reason for doing so.

(3)   Where a party was present at the hearing at which permission was given that party may not subsequently apply for an order that the court exercise its powers under paragraphs (1)(b) or (1)(c).

30.11 Appeal court's powers

(1)   In relation to an appeal the appeal court has all the powers of the lower court.

(Rule 30.1(4) provides that this Part is subject to any enactment that sets out special provisions with regard to any particular category of appeal.)

(2)   The appeal court has power to—

    (a)   affirm, set aside(GL) or vary any order or judgment made or given by the lower court;

    (b)   refer any application or issue for determination by the lower court;

    (c)   order a new hearing;

    (d)   make orders for the payment of interest;

    (e)   make a costs order.

(3)   The appeal court may exercise its powers in relation to the whole or part of an order of the lower court.

(Rule 4.1 contains general rules about the court's case management powers.)

(4)   If the appeal court—

    (a)   refuses an application for permission to appeal;

    (b)   strikes out an appellant's notice; or

    (c)   dismisses an appeal,

and it considers that the application, the appellant's notice or the appeal is totally without merit, the provisions of paragraph (5) must be complied with.

(5)   Where paragraph (4) applies—

(a) the court's order must record the fact that it considers the application, the appellant's notice or the appeal to be totally without merit; and

(b) the court must at the same time consider whether it is appropriate to make a civil restraint order.

30.12 Hearing of appeals

(1) Every appeal will be limited to a review of the decision of the lower court unless—

(a) an enactment or practice direction makes different provision for a particular category of appeal; or

(b) the court considers that in the circumstances of an individual appeal it would be in the interests of justice to hold a re-hearing.

(2) Unless it orders otherwise, the appeal court will not receive—

(a) oral evidence; or

(b) evidence which was not before the lower court.

(3) The appeal court will allow an appeal where the decision of the lower court was—

(a) wrong; or

(b) unjust because of a serious procedural or other irregularity in the proceedings in the lower court.

(4) The appeal court may draw any inference of fact which it considers justified on the evidence.

(5) At the hearing of the appeal a party may not rely on a matter not contained in that party's appeal notice unless the appeal court gives permission.

[30.12A Appeal court's power to order that hearing of appeal be held in public]

[(1) This rule applies where by virtue of rule 27.10 the hearing of an appeal is to be held in private.

(2) The appeal court may make an order—

(a) for the hearing of the appeal to be in public;

(b) for a part of the hearing of the appeal to be in public; or

(c) excluding any person or class of persons from attending a public hearing of an appeal or any part of it.

(3) Where the appeal court makes an order under paragraph (1), it may in the same order or in a subsequent order—

(a) impose restrictions on the publication of the identity of—

(i) any party;

(ii) any child (whether or not a party);

(iii) any witness; or

(iv) any other person;

(b) prohibit the publication of any information which may lead to any such person being identified;

(c) prohibit the publication of any information relating to the proceedings from such date as the court may specify; or

(d) impose such other restrictions on the publication of information relating to the proceedings as the court may specify.

(4) A practice direction may provide for—

(a) circumstances (which may be of general application or applicable only to specified appeal courts or proceedings) in which the appeal court will ordinarily make an order under paragraph (1); and

(b) the terms of the order under paragraph (2) which the court will ordinarily make in such circumstances.]

NOTES

Amendment
>Inserted by SI 2018/1172, rr 2, 6.
>>Date in force: 10 December 2018: see SI 2018/1172, r 1.

30.13 Assignment of appeals to the Court of Appeal

(1)   Where the court from or to which an appeal is made or from which permission to appeal is sought ("the relevant court") considers that—

>(a)   an appeal which is to be heard by a county court or the High Court would raise an important point of principle or practice; or

>(b)   there is some other compelling reason for the Court of Appeal to hear it,

the relevant court may order the appeal to be transferred to the Court of Appeal.

[(2)   Paragraph (1) does not allow an application for permission to appeal to be transferred to the Court of Appeal.]

NOTES

Amendment
>Para (2): substituted by SI 2014/667, rr 2, 25.
>>Date in force: 22 April 2014: see SI 2014/667, r 1; for transitional and saving provision see r 45.

30.14 Reopening of final appeals

(1)   The High Court will not reopen a final determination of any appeal unless—

>(a)   it is necessary to do so in order to avoid real injustice;

>(b)   the circumstances are exceptional and make it appropriate to reopen the appeal; and

>(c)   there is no alternative effective remedy.

(2)   In paragraphs (1), (3), (4) and (6), "appeal" includes an application for permission to appeal.

(3)   This rule does not apply to appeals to [the family court].

(4)   Permission is needed to make an application under this rule to reopen a final determination of an appeal.

(5)   There is no right to an oral hearing of an application for permission unless, exceptionally, the judge so directs.

(6)   The judge will not grant permission without directing the application to be served on the other party to the original appeal and giving that party an opportunity to make representations.

(7)   There is no right of appeal or review from the decision of the judge on the application for permission, which is final.

(8)   The procedure for making an application for permission is set out in Practice Direction 30A.

NOTES

Amendment
>Para (3): words "the family court" in square brackets substituted by SI 2014/667, rr 2, 26.
>>Date in force: 22 April 2014: see SI 2014/667, r 1; for transitional and saving provision see r 45.

. . .

PART 32
REGISTRATION AND ENFORCEMENT OF ORDERS

CHAPTER 1

SCOPE AND INTERPRETATION OF THIS PART

32.1 Scope and interpretation
(1) This Part contains rules about the registration and enforcement of maintenance orders and custody orders.
[(2) In this Part, "the 1950 Act" means the Maintenance Orders Act 1950.]
(3) Chapter 2 of this Part relates to—
    (a) the registration of a maintenance order, made in the High Court or [the family court], in a court in Scotland or Northern Ireland in accordance with the 1950 Act; and
    (b) the registration of a maintenance order, made in Scotland or Northern Ireland, in the High Court in accordance with the 1950 Act.
. . .
[(4) Chapter 3 of this Part contains rules to be applied in the family court in relation to the registration in the family court of a maintenance order made in the High Court, in accordance with the 1958 Act.]
(5) Chapter 4 of this Part relates to the registration and enforcement of custody orders in accordance with the 1986 Act.
[(6) Chapter 5 of this Part relates to the ability of a court officer to take enforcement proceedings in relation to certain orders for periodical payments.]

NOTES

Amendment
    Para (2): substituted by SI 2011/1328, rr 2, 16.
        Date in force: 18 June 2011: see SI 2011/1328, r 1.
    Para (3): in sub-para (a) words "the family court" in square brackets substituted by SI 2013/3204, rr 2, 76(a)(i).
        Date in force: 22 April 2014 (being the date on which the Crime and Courts Act 2013, s 17(3) is brought fully into force): see SI 2013/3204, r 1 and SI 2014/954, art 2(a); for transitional provisions and savings see SI 2013/3204, r 137 and SI 2014/954, art 3.
    Para (3): words omitted revoked by SI 2013/3204, rr 2, 76(a)(ii).
        Date in force: 22 April 2014 (being the date on which the Crime and Courts Act 2013, s 17(3) is brought fully into force): see SI 2013/3204, r 1 and SI 2014/954, art 2(a); for transitional provisions and savings see SI 2013/3204, r 137 and SI 2014/954, art 3.
    Para (4): substituted by SI 2013/3204, rr 2, 76(b).
        Date in force: 22 April 2014 (being the date on which the Crime and Courts Act 2013, s 17(3) is brought fully into force): see SI 2013/3204, r 1 and SI 2014/954, art 2(a); for transitional provisions and savings see SI 2013/3204, r 137 and SI 2014/954, art 3.
    Para (6): inserted by SI 2013/3204, rr 2, 76(c).
        Date in force: 22 April 2014 (being the date on which the Crime and Courts Act 2013, s 17(3) is brought fully into force): see SI 2013/3204, r 1 and SI 2014/954, art 2(a); for transitional provisions and savings see SI 2013/3204, r 137 and SI 2014/954, art 3.

CHAPTER 2

REGISTRATION ETC OF ORDERS UNDER THE 1950 ACT

SECTION 1
Interpretation of this Chapter

32.2 Interpretation
In this Chapter—
    "the clerk of the Court of Session" means the deputy principal clerk in charge of the petition department of the Court of Session;

["the clerk of the court which made the order" means, in the case of a county court in Northern Ireland, the Chief Clerk for the appropriate court in Northern Ireland;]

. . .

["family court order" means a maintenance order made in the family court;]

"High Court order" means a maintenance order made in the High Court;

"maintenance order" means a maintenance order to which section 16 of the 1950 Act applies;

["Northern Irish order" means a maintenance order made by a court in Northern Ireland;]

"the register" means the register kept for the purposes of the 1950 Act;

"the registrar in Northern Ireland" means the chief registrar of the Queen's Bench Division (Matrimonial) of the High Court of Justice in Northern Ireland;

"registration" means registration under Part 2 of the 1950 Act and "registered" is to be construed accordingly; and

["Scottish order" means a maintenance order made by a court in Scotland].

NOTES

Amendment

Definition "the clerk of the court which made the order" inserted by SI 2013/3204, rr 2, 77(a).

　Date in force: 22 April 2014 (being the date on which the Crime and Courts Act 2013, s 17(3) is brought fully into force): see SI 2013/3204, r 1 and SI 2014/954, art 2(a); for transitional provisions and savings see SI 2013/3204, r 137 and SI 2014/954, art 3.

Definition "county court order" (omitted) revoked by SI 2013/3204, rr 2, 77(b).

　Date in force: 22 April 2014 (being the date on which the Crime and Courts Act 2013, s 17(3) is brought fully into force): see SI 2013/3204, r 1 and SI 2014/954, art 2(a); for transitional provisions and savings see SI 2013/3204, r 137 and SI 2014/954, art 3.

Definition "family court order" inserted by SI 2013/3204, rr 2, 77(c).

　Date in force: 22 April 2014 (being the date on which the Crime and Courts Act 2013, s 17(3) is brought fully into force): see SI 2013/3204, r 1 and SI 2014/954, art 2(a); for transitional provisions and savings see SI 2013/3204, r 137 and SI 2014/954, art 3.

Definition "Northern Irish order" substituted by SI 2013/3204, rr 2, 77(d).

　Date in force: 22 April 2014 (being the date on which the Crime and Courts Act 2013, s 17(3) is brought fully into force): see SI 2013/3204, r 1 and SI 2014/954, art 2(a); for transitional provisions and savings see SI 2013/3204, r 137 and SI 2014/954, art 3.

Definition "Scottish order" substituted by SI 2013/3204, rr 2, 77(e).

　Date in force: 22 April 2014 (being the date on which the Crime and Courts Act 2013, s 17(3) is brought fully into force): see SI 2013/3204, r 1 and SI 2014/954, art 2(a); for transitional provisions and savings see SI 2013/3204, r 137 and SI 2014/954, art 3.

SECTION 2
Registration etc of High Court and [family court] orders

NOTES

Amendment

Section heading: words "family court" in italics revoked and subsequent words in square brackets substituted by SI 2013/3204, rr 2, 78.

　Date in force: 22 April 2014 (being the date on which the Crime and Courts Act 2013, s 17(3) is brought fully into force): see SI 2013/3204, r 1 and SI 2014/954, art 2(a); for transitional provisions and savings see SI 2013/3204, r 137 and SI 2014/954, art 3.

32.3 Registration of a High Court order

(1) An application for the registration of a High Court order may be made by sending to a court officer at the court which made the order—

　(a)　a certified copy of the order; and

　(b)　a statement which—

　　　(i)　contains the address in the United Kingdom, and the occupation, of the person liable to make payments under the order;

(ii)   contains the date on which the order was served on the person liable to make payments, or, if the order has not been served, the reason why service has not been effected;

(iii)   contains the reason why it is convenient for the order to be enforced in Scotland or Northern Ireland, as the case may be;

(iv)   contains the amount of any arrears due to the applicant under the order;

(v)   confirms that the order is not already registered; and

(vi)   is verified by a statement of truth.

(2)   If it appears to the court that—

(a)   the person liable to make payments under the order resides in Scotland or Northern Ireland; and

(b)   it is convenient for the order to be enforced there,

the court officer will send the documents filed under paragraph (1) to the clerk of the Court of Session or to the registrar in Northern Ireland, as the case may be.

(3)   On receipt of a notice of the registration of a High Court order in the Court of Session or the Court of Judicature of Northern Ireland, the court officer (who is the prescribed officer for the purposes of section 17(4) of the 1950 Act) will—

(a)   enter particulars of the notice of registration in the register;

(b)   note the fact of registration in the court records; and

(c)   send particulars of the notice to the principal registry.

32.4 Notice of Variation etc of a High Court order

(1)   This rule applies where a High Court order, which is registered in the Court of Session or the Court of Judicature of Northern Ireland, is discharged or varied.

(2)   A court officer in the court where the order was discharged or varied will send a certified copy of that order to the clerk of the Court of Session or the registrar in Northern Ireland, as the case may be.

32.5 Cancellation of registration of a High Court order [by the court of registration]

(1)   This rule applies where—

(a)   the registration of a High Court order registered in the Court of Session or the Court of Judicature of Northern Ireland is cancelled under section 24(1) of the 1950 Act; and

(b)   notice of the cancellation is given to a court officer in the court in which the order was made (who is the prescribed officer for the purposes of section 24(3)(a) of the 1950 Act).

(2)   On receipt of a notice of cancellation of registration, the court officer will enter particulars of the notice in . . . the register.

NOTES

Amendment

Provision heading: words "by the court of registration" in square brackets inserted by SI 2013/3204, rr 2, 79(a).

Date in force: 22 April 2014 (being the date on which the Crime and Courts Act 2013, s 17(3) is brought fully into force): see SI 2013/3204, r 1 and SI 2014/954, art 2(a); for transitional provisions and savings see SI 2013/3204, r 137 and SI 2014/954, art 3.

Para (2): words omitted revoked by SI 2013/3204, rr 2, 79(b).

Date in force: 22 April 2014 (being the date on which the Crime and Courts Act 2013, s 17(3) is brought fully into force): see SI 2013/3204, r 1 and SI 2014/954, art 2(a); for transitional provisions and savings see SI 2013/3204, r 137 and SI 2014/954, art 3.

[32.5A Cancellation of registration of a High Court order by the High Court]

[The Part 19 procedure applies to an application to the High Court under section 24(2) of the 1950 Act.]

NOTES

Amendment
>Inserted by SI 2013/3204, rr 2, 80.
>>Date in force: 22 April 2014 (being the date on which the Crime and Courts Act 2013,
>>s 17(3) is brought fully into force): see SI 2013/3204, r 1 and SI 2014/954, art 2(a);
>>for transitional provisions and savings see SI 2013/3204, r 137 and SI 2014/954, art 3.

32.6 Application of this Chapter to a [family court] order

Rules 32.3 to [32.5A] apply to [a family court order] as if—

(a) references to a High Court order were references to a [family court] order;

[(aa) in rule 32.5A, references to the High Court were to the family court;]

(b) where the order is to be registered in Scotland, references to the Court of Session and the clerk of the Court of Session were references to the sheriff court and the sheriff-clerk of the sheriff court respectively; and

(c) where the order is to be registered in Northern Ireland, references to the Court of Judicature of Northern Ireland and the registrar of Northern Ireland were references to the court of summary jurisdiction and the clerk of the court of summary jurisdiction respectively.

NOTES

Amendment
>Provision heading: words "family court" in square brackets substituted by SI 2013/3204,
>rr 2, 81(a).
>>Date in force: 22 April 2014 (being the date on which the Crime and Courts Act 2013,
>>s 17(3) is brought fully into force): see SI 2013/3204, r 1 and SI 2014/954, art 2(a);
>>for transitional provisions and savings see SI 2013/3204, r 137 and SI 2014/954, art 3.
>Reference to "32.5A" in square brackets substituted by SI 2013/3204, rr 2, 81(b).
>>Date in force: 22 April 2014 (being the date on which the Crime and Courts Act 2013,
>>s 17(3) is brought fully into force): see SI 2013/3204, r 1 and SI 2014/954, art 2(a);
>>for transitional provisions and savings see SI 2013/3204, r 137 and SI 2014/954, art 3.
>Words"a family court order" in square brackets substituted by SI 2013/3204, rr 2, 81(c).
>>Date in force: 22 April 2014 (being the date on which the Crime and Courts Act 2013,
>>s 17(3) is brought fully into force): see SI 2013/3204, r 1 and SI 2014/954, art 2(a);
>>for transitional provisions and savings see SI 2013/3204, r 137 and SI 2014/954, art 3.
>In para (a) words "family court" in square brackets substituted by SI 2013/3204, rr 2, 81(d).
>>Date in force: 22 April 2014 (being the date on which the Crime and Courts Act 2013,
>>s 17(3) is brought fully into force): see SI 2013/3204, r 1 and SI 2014/954, art 2(a);
>>for transitional provisions and savings see SI 2013/3204, r 137 and SI 2014/954, art 3.
>Para (aa) inserted by SI 2013/3204, rr 2, 81(e).
>>Date in force: 22 April 2014 (being the date on which the Crime and Courts Act 2013,
>>s 17(3) is brought fully into force): see SI 2013/3204, r 1 and SI 2014/954, art 2(a);
>>for transitional provisions and savings see SI 2013/3204, r 137 and SI 2014/954, art 3.

[32.6A Variation of a family court order: section 22(1) of the 1950 Act]

[Where a family court order, which is registered in a court in Scotland or Northern Ireland, is varied under section 22(1) of the 1950 Act by the court in which it is registered—

(a) the court officer for the court which made the order will be the prescribed officer to whom notice of the variation must be given under section 23(1) of the 1950 Act; and

(b) on receipt of a notice under section 23(1) of the 1950 Act, the court officer will enter particulars of the notice in the register.]

NOTES

Amendment
>Inserted by SI 2013/3204, rr 2, 82.
>>Date in force: 22 April 2014 (being the date on which the Crime and Courts Act 2013,
>>s 17(3) is brought fully into force): see SI 2013/3204, r 1 and SI 2014/954, art 2(a);
>>for transitional provisions and savings see SI 2013/3204, r 137 and SI 2014/954, art 3.

[32.6B Application to adduce evidence: section 22(5) of the 1950 Act]
[(1) The Part 18 procedure applies to an application under section 22(5) of the 1950 Act where a maintenance order was made by the family court.

(2) The family court will send a transcript or summary of any evidence taken to the clerk of the court in which the order is registered.

(3) The court officer for the court in England and Wales which made the maintenance order will be the prescribed officer to whom any transcript or summary of evidence adduced in the court in Scotland or Northern Ireland must be sent under section 22(5) of the 1950 Act.]

NOTES

Amendment
Inserted by SI 2013/3204, rr 2, 82.
Date in force: 22 April 2014 (being the date on which the Crime and Courts Act 2013, s 17(3) is brought fully into force): see SI 2013/3204, r 1 and SI 2014/954, art 2(a); for transitional provisions and savings see SI 2013/3204, r 137 and SI 2014/954, art 3.

SECTION 3
Registration etc of Scottish and Northern Irish orders

32.7 Registration of Scottish and Northern Irish orders
On receipt of a certified copy of a Scottish order or a Northern Irish order for registration, a court officer in the principal registry (who is the prescribed officer [in the High Court] for the purposes of section 17(2) of the 1950 Act) [or a court officer in the family court (who is the prescribed officer in the family court for the purposes of section 17(2) of the 1950 Act)] will—

(a) enter particulars of the order in . . . the register;

(b) notify the clerk of [the court which made the order] or the registrar in Northern Ireland, as the case may be, that the order has been registered; and

(c) file the certified copy of the order and any statutory declaration, affidavit(GL) or statement as to the amount of any arrears due under the order.

[(Section 17(3) of the 1950 Act makes provision as to the court in England and Wales to which a Northern Irish order or a Scottish order should be sent, which depends on which court originally made the order.)]

NOTES

Amendment
Words "in the High Court" in square brackets inserted by SI 2013/3204, rr 2, 83(a).
Date in force: 22 April 2014 (being the date on which the Crime and Courts Act 2013, s 17(3) is brought fully into force): see SI 2013/3204, r 1 and SI 2014/954, art 2(a); for transitional provisions and savings see SI 2013/3204, r 137 and SI 2014/954, art 3.
Words from "or a court" to "the 1950 Act)" in square brackets inserted by SI 2013/3204, rr 2, 83(b).
Date in force: 22 April 2014 (being the date on which the Crime and Courts Act 2013, s 17(3) is brought fully into force): see SI 2013/3204, r 1 and SI 2014/954, art 2(a); for transitional provisions and savings see SI 2013/3204, r 137 and SI 2014/954, art 3.
In para (a) words omitted revoked by SI 2013/3204, rr 2, 83(c).
Date in force: 22 April 2014 (being the date on which the Crime and Courts Act 2013, s 17(3) is brought fully into force): see SI 2013/3204, r 1 and SI 2014/954, art 2(a); for transitional provisions and savings see SI 2013/3204, r 137 and SI 2014/954, art 3.
In para (b) words "the court which made the order" in square brackets substituted by SI 2013/3204, rr 2, 83(d).
Date in force: 22 April 2014 (being the date on which the Crime and Courts Act 2013, s 17(3) is brought fully into force): see SI 2013/3204, r 1 and SI 2014/954, art 2(a); for transitional provisions and savings see SI 2013/3204, r 137 and SI 2014/954, art 3.
Words in parentheses inserted by SI 2013/3204, rr 2, 83(e).
Date in force: 22 April 2014 (being the date on which the Crime and Courts Act 2013, s 17(3) is brought fully into force): see SI 2013/3204, r 1 and SI 2014/954, art 2(a); for transitional provisions and savings see SI 2013/3204, r 137 and SI 2014/954, art 3.

[32.8 Application to adduce evidence: sections 21(2) and 22(5) of the 1950 Act]
[(1) The Part 18 procedure applies to the applications under these provisions of the 1950 Act—

(a) an application to the High Court to adduce evidence under section 21(2) by a person liable to make payments under a Scottish order registered in the High Court;

(b) an application to the family court to adduce evidence under section 21(2) by a person liable to make payments under a Scottish order registered in the High Court under the 1950 Act and registered in the family court under Part 1 of the 1958 Act; and

(c) an application to the family court to adduce evidence under section 22(5) by a person entitled to payments or a person liable to make payments under a Scottish order or a Northern Irish order registered in the family court under Part 1 of the 1950 Act.

(2) The court officer for the family court (being the court in which the order is registered) will be the prescribed officer under section 22(5) of the 1950 Act to whom any transcript or summary of evidence adduced in the court in Scotland or Northern Ireland by which the order was made must be sent.]

NOTES

Amendment
> Substituted by SI 2013/3204, rr 2, 84.
>> Date in force: 22 April 2014 (being the date on which the Crime and Courts Act 2013, s 17(3) is brought fully into force): see SI 2013/3204, r 1 and SI 2014/954, art 2(a); for transitional provisions and savings see SI 2013/3204, r 137 and SI 2014/954, art 3.

32.9 Notice of variation etc of Scottish and Northern Irish orders
(1) This rule applies where—

(a) a Scottish order or a Northern Irish order, which is registered in the High Court [or the family court], is discharged or varied [by the court in Scotland or Northern Ireland]; and

(b) notice of the discharge or variation is given to [the court officer in the High Court or in the family court, as the case may be] (who is the prescribed officer for the purposes of section 23(1)(a) of the 1950 Act).

(2) On receipt of a notice of discharge or variation, the court officer will enter particulars of the notice in . . . the register.

NOTES

Amendment
> Para (1): in sub-para (a) words "or the family court" in square brackets inserted by SI 2013/3204, rr 2, 85(a)(i).
>> Date in force: 22 April 2014 (being the date on which the Crime and Courts Act 2013, s 17(3) is brought fully into force): see SI 2013/3204, r 1 and SI 2014/954, art 2(a); for transitional provisions and savings see SI 2013/3204, r 137 and SI 2014/954, art 3.
> Para (1): in sub-para (a) words "by the court in Scotland or Northern Ireland" in square brackets inserted by SI 2013/3204, rr 2, 85(a)(ii).
>> Date in force: 22 April 2014 (being the date on which the Crime and Courts Act 2013, s 17(3) is brought fully into force): see SI 2013/3204, r 1 and SI 2014/954, art 2(a); for transitional provisions and savings see SI 2013/3204, r 137 and SI 2014/954, art 3.
> Para (1): in sub-para (b) words "the court officer in the High Court or in the family court, as the case may be" in square brackets substituted by SI 2013/3204, rr 2, 85(b).
>> Date in force: 22 April 2014 (being the date on which the Crime and Courts Act 2013, s 17(3) is brought fully into force): see SI 2013/3204, r 1 and SI 2014/954, art 2(a); for transitional provisions and savings see SI 2013/3204, r 137 and SI 2014/954, art 3.
> Para (2): words omitted revoked by SI 2013/3204, rr 2, 85(c).
>> Date in force: 22 April 2014 (being the date on which the Crime and Courts Act 2013, s 17(3) is brought fully into force): see SI 2013/3204, r 1 and SI 2014/954, art 2(a); for transitional provisions and savings see SI 2013/3204, r 137 and SI 2014/954, art 3.

[32.9A Variation of Scottish and Northern Irish orders by the family court]

[(1) The Part 18 procedure applies to an application to the family court under section 22(1) of the 1950 Act to vary a Scottish order or a Northern Irish order which is registered in the family court.

(2) Where a Scottish order or a Northern Irish order is varied by the family court on an application under section 22(1) of the 1950 Act, the court officer will give notice of the variation to the clerk of the court in Scotland or Northern Ireland which made the order by sending a certified copy of the order of variation.]

NOTES

Amendment
>   Inserted by SI 2013/3204, rr 2, 86.
>>   Date in force: 22 April 2014 (being the date on which the Crime and Courts Act 2013, s 17(3) is brought fully into force): see SI 2013/3204, r 1 and SI 2014/954, art 2(a); for transitional provisions and savings see SI 2013/3204, r 137 and SI 2014/954, art 3.

32.10 Cancellation of registration of Scottish and Northern Irish orders

(1) The Part 18 procedure applies to an application [under section 24(1) of the 1950 Act] for the cancellation of the registration of a Scottish order or a Northern Irish order in the High Court [or the family court].

(2) The application must be made without notice to the person liable to make payments under the order.

(3) If the registration of the order is cancelled, the court officer will—

    (a)   note the cancellation in . . . the register; and

    (b)   send written notice of the cancellation to—

        (i)   the clerk of the [court which made the order] or the registrar in Northern Ireland, as the case may be; and

        (ii)   the court officer [of the family court if the order has been registered in the family court] in accordance with section 2(5) of the 1958 Act.

[(4) Where a maintenance order is registered under the 1950 Act in the family court, the court officer for the family court is the prescribed officer for the purposes of section 24(2) of the 1950 Act, and in paragraphs (5) and (6) references to the court officer are to the court officer of the family court.

(5) If a notice under section 24(2) of the 1950 Act is received, the court officer will—

    (a)   cancel the registration of the order; and

    (b)   send written notice of the cancellation to the clerk of the court which made the order.

(6) Where a maintenance order is registered in the family court under Part 1 of the 1958 Act and the court officer receives a notice of cancellation under section 24(3) of the 1950 Act from the appropriate officer of the High Court, the court officer will—

    (a)   enter the details of the notice in the register;

    (b)   cancel the registration under Part 1 of the 1958 Act; and

    (c)   give notice of the cancellation to the appropriate officer of the court which made the order, being—

        (i)   the Deputy Principal Clerk of Session, in the case of the Court of Session; or

        (ii)   the Chief Registrar of the Queen's Bench Division (Matrimonial), in the case of the High Court of Justice in Northern Ireland.]

NOTES

Amendment
>   Para (1): words "under section 24(1) of the 1950 Act" in square brackets inserted by SI 2013/3204, rr 2, 87(a)(i).

Date in force: 22 April 2014 (being the date on which the Crime and Courts Act 2013, s 17(3) is brought fully into force): see SI 2013/3204, r 1 and SI 2014/954, art 2(a); for transitional provisions and savings see SI 2013/3204, r 137 and SI 2014/954, art 3.

Para (1): words "or the family court" in square brackets inserted by SI 2013/3204, rr 2, 87(a)(ii).

Date in force: 22 April 2014 (being the date on which the Crime and Courts Act 2013, s 17(3) is brought fully into force): see SI 2013/3204, r 1 and SI 2014/954, art 2(a); for transitional provisions and savings see SI 2013/3204, r 137 and SI 2014/954, art 3.

Para (3): in sub-para (a) words omitted revoked by SI 2013/3204, rr 2, 87(b)(i).

Date in force: 22 April 2014 (being the date on which the Crime and Courts Act 2013, s 17(3) is brought fully into force): see SI 2013/3204, r 1 and SI 2014/954, art 2(a); for transitional provisions and savings see SI 2013/3204, r 137 and SI 2014/954, art 3.

Para (3): in sub-para (b)(i) words "court which made the order" in square brackets substituted by SI 2013/3204, rr 2, 87(b)(ii).

Date in force: 22 April 2014 (being the date on which the Crime and Courts Act 2013, s 17(3) is brought fully into force): see SI 2013/3204, r 1 and SI 2014/954, art 2(a); for transitional provisions and savings see SI 2013/3204, r 137 and SI 2014/954, art 3.

Para (3): in sub-para (b)(ii) words "of the family court if the order has been registered in the family court" in square brackets substituted by SI 2013/3204, rr 2, 87(b)(iii).

Date in force: 22 April 2014 (being the date on which the Crime and Courts Act 2013, s 17(3) is brought fully into force): see SI 2013/3204, r 1 and SI 2014/954, art 2(a); for transitional provisions and savings see SI 2013/3204, r 137 and SI 2014/954, art 3.

Paras (4)–(6): inserted by SI 2013/3204, rr 2, 87(c).

Date in force: 22 April 2014 (being the date on which the Crime and Courts Act 2013, s 17(3) is brought fully into force): see SI 2013/3204, r 1 and SI 2014/954, art 2(a); for transitional provisions and savings see SI 2013/3204, r 137 and SI 2014/954, art 3.

[32.10A Payments under a maintenance order registered in the family court]

[(1)   This rule applies where section 22(1A) of the 1950 Act applies and the family court orders that payments under a maintenance order registered in the family court are to be made by a particular means.

(2)   The court officer will record on a copy of the order the means of payment that the court has ordered.

(3)   The court officer will notify, in writing, the person liable to make payments under the order how the payments are to be made.

(4)   Where [under section 1(4A) of the Maintenance Enforcement Act 1991] the family court orders payment to the court by a method of payment specified in [section 1(5) of that Act], the court officer will notify the person liable to make payments under the order of sufficient details of the account into which the payments should be made to enable payments to be made into that account.

(5)   The Part 18 procedure applies to an application under section 1(7) of the Maintenance Enforcement Act 1991 [(application from an interested party to revoke, suspend, revive or vary a means of payment order)].

[(6)   Where the court makes an order under section 1(7) of the Maintenance Enforcement Act 1991 or dismisses an application for such an order, the court officer will, as far as practicable, notify in writing all interested parties of the effect of the order and will take the steps set out in paragraphs (2), (3) and (4), as appropriate.

(7)   In this rule, "interested party" has the meaning given in section 1(10) of the Maintenance Enforcement Act 1991.]]

NOTES

Amendment

Inserted by SI 2013/3204, rr 2, 88.

Date in force: 22 April 2014 (being the date on which the Crime and Courts Act 2013, s 17(3) is brought fully into force): see SI 2013/3204, r 1 and SI 2014/954, art 2(a); for transitional provisions and savings see SI 2013/3204, r 137 and SI 2014/954, art 3.

Para (4): words "under section 1(4A) of the Maintenance Enforcement Act 1991" in square brackets inserted by SI 2014/667, rr 2, 27(a)(i).

Date in force: 22 April 2014: see SI 2014/667, r 1; for transitional and saving provision see r 45.

Para (4): words "section 1(5) of that Act" in square brackets substituted by SI 2014/667, rr 2, 27(a)(ii).

Date in force: 22 April 2014: see SI 2014/667, r 1; for transitional and saving provision see r 45.

Para (5): words "(application from an interested party to revoke, suspend, revive or vary a means of payment order)" in square brackets substituted by SI 2014/667, rr 2, 27(b).

Date in force: 22 April 2014: see SI 2014/667, r 1; for transitional and saving provision see r 45.

Paras (6), (7): substituted, for para (6), by SI 2014/667, rr 2, 27(c).

Date in force: 22 April 2014: see SI 2014/667, r 1; for transitional and saving provision see r 45.

32.11 Enforcement

(1) [Subject to paragraph (2), Part 33] applies to an application for or with respect to the enforcement of a Scottish order or a Northern Irish order registered in the High Court [or the family court].

(2) The application may be made without notice to the person liable to make payments under the order.

NOTES

Amendment

Para (1): words "Subject to paragraph (2), Part 33" in square brackets substituted by SI 2013/3204, rr 2, 89(a).

Date in force: 22 April 2014 (being the date on which the Crime and Courts Act 2013, s 17(3) is brought fully into force): see SI 2013/3204, r 1 and SI 2014/954, art 2(a); for transitional provisions and savings see SI 2013/3204, r 137 and SI 2014/954, art 3.

Para (1): words "or the family court" in square brackets inserted by SI 2013/3204, rr 2, 89(b).

Date in force: 22 April 2014 (being the date on which the Crime and Courts Act 2013, s 17(3) is brought fully into force): see SI 2013/3204, r 1 and SI 2014/954, art 2(a); for transitional provisions and savings see SI 2013/3204, r 137 and SI 2014/954, art 3.

32.12 Inspection of register and copies of order

Any person—

- (a) who is entitled to receive, or liable to make, payments under [a Scottish order or a Northern Irish order registered in the High Court or the family court under the 1950 Act]; or
- (b) with the permission of the court,

may—

- (i) inspect the register; or
- (ii) request a copy of any order registered in the High Court [or the family court] under Part 2 of the 1950 Act and any statutory declaration, affidavit(GL) or statement filed with the order.

NOTES

Amendment

In para (a) words "a Scottish order or a Northern Irish order registered in the High Court or the family court under the 1950 Act" in square brackets substituted by SI 2013/3204, rr 2, 90(a).

Date in force: 22 April 2014 (being the date on which the Crime and Courts Act 2013, s 17(3) is brought fully into force): see SI 2013/3204, r 1 and SI 2014/954, art 2(a); for transitional provisions and savings see SI 2013/3204, r 137 and SI 2014/954, art 3.

In sub-para (ii) words "or the family court" in square brackets inserted by SI 2013/3204, rr 2, 90(b).

Date in force: 22 April 2014 (being the date on which the Crime and Courts Act 2013, s 17(3) is brought fully into force): see SI 2013/3204, r 1 and SI 2014/954, art 2(a); for transitional provisions and savings see SI 2013/3204, r 137 and SI 2014/954, art 3.

[32.12A Notices and certificates: section 19(4), 20(1) and 24(5) and (5A) of the 1950 Act]

[(1) Practice Direction 32A contains the form of—

- (a) a notice under section 19(4) of the 1950 Act that payments under a maintenance order made by a sheriff court in Scotland or a court of summary jurisdiction in Northern Ireland have become payable through or to any officer or person;

(b) a notice under section 19(4) of the 1950 Act that the payments under a maintenance order made by the family court have, on its registration under Part 2 of the 1950 Act in a court in Scotland or Northern Ireland, ceased to be payable to or through the court or any person;

(c) a certificate lodged under section 20(1) of the 1950 Act as to the amount of any arrears due under a maintenance order made by the family court; and

(d) a notice under section 24(5) or (5A) of the 1950 Act of the cancellation of the registration under Part 2 of the 1950 Act of a maintenance order in the family court.

(2) The court officer will send a notice referred to in paragraph (1)(a), (b) or (d) to the person liable to make the payments under the order at that person's last known address.]

NOTES

Amendment
Inserted by SI 2013/3204, rr 2, 91.
Date in force: 22 April 2014 (being the date on which the Crime and Courts Act 2013, s 17(3) is brought fully into force): see SI 2013/3204, r 1 and SI 2014/954, art 2(a); for transitional provisions and savings see SI 2013/3204, r 137 and SI 2014/954, art 3.

CHAPTER 3

REGISTRATION OF MAINTENANCE ORDERS UNDER THE 1958 ACT

32.13 Interpretation
In this Chapter "the register" means the register kept for the purposes of the 1958 Act.

32.14 Registration of orders—prescribed period
The prescribed period for the purpose of section 2(2) of the 1958 Act is 14 days.
(Section 2(2) sets out the period during which an order, which is to be registered in a magistrates' court, may not be enforced)

32.15 Application for registration of a maintenance order in [the family court—procedure in the High Court]
(1) An application under section 2(1) of the 1958 Act may be made by sending to the court officer at the court which made the order—

(a) a certified copy of the maintenance order; and

(b) two copies of the application.

(2) When, on the grant of an application, the court officer sends the certified copy of the maintenance order to the [family court] in accordance with section 2(2), the court officer must—

(a) note on the order that the application for registration has been granted; and

(b) send to the [family court] a copy of the application for registration of the order.

(3) On receiving notice that the [family court] has registered the order, the court officer [of the High Court] must enter particulars of the registration in the court records.

NOTES

Amendment
Provision heading: words "the family court—procedure in the High Court" in square brackets substituted by SI 2013/3204, rr 2, 92(a).

Date in force: 22 April 2014 (being the date on which the Crime and Courts Act 2013, s 17(3) is brought fully into force): see SI 2013/3204, r 1 and SI 2014/954, art 2(a); for transitional provisions and savings see SI 2013/3204, r 137 and SI 2014/954, art 3.
Para (2): words "family court" in square brackets substituted by SI 2013/3204, rr 2, 92(b).
Date in force: 22 April 2014 (being the date on which the Crime and Courts Act 2013, s 17(3) is brought fully into force): see SI 2013/3204, r 1 and SI 2014/954, art 2(a); for transitional provisions and savings see SI 2013/3204, r 137 and SI 2014/954, art 3.
Para (2): in sub-para (b) words "family court" in square brackets substituted by SI 2013/3204, rr 2, 92(b).
Date in force: 22 April 2014 (being the date on which the Crime and Courts Act 2013, s 17(3) is brought fully into force): see SI 2013/3204, r 1 and SI 2014/954, art 2(a); for transitional provisions and savings see SI 2013/3204, r 137 and SI 2014/954, art 3.
Para (3): words "family court" in square brackets substituted by SI 2013/3204, rr 2, 92(b).
Date in force: 22 April 2014 (being the date on which the Crime and Courts Act 2013, s 17(3) is brought fully into force): see SI 2013/3204, r 1 and SI 2014/954, art 2(a); for transitional provisions and savings see SI 2013/3204, r 137 and SI 2014/954, art 3.
Para (3): words "of the High Court" in square brackets inserted by SI 2013/3204, rr 2, 92(c).
Date in force: 22 April 2014 (being the date on which the Crime and Courts Act 2013, s 17(3) is brought fully into force): see SI 2013/3204, r 1 and SI 2014/954, art 2(a); for transitional provisions and savings see SI 2013/3204, r 137 and SI 2014/954, art 3.

[32.15A Application for registration of a maintenance order in the family court—procedure in the family court]

[(1) This rule applies where the court officer for the family court receives from the court officer of the High Court a certified copy of a High Court order, in accordance with section 2(2)(b) of the 1958 Act.

(2) The court officer of the family court will—

    (a)   register the order in the family court by entering particulars in the register; and

    (b)   send notice to the court officer of the High Court that the order has been registered.]

NOTES

Amendment

Inserted by SI 2013/3204, rr 2, 93.
Date in force: 22 April 2014 (being the date on which the Crime and Courts Act 2013, s 17(3) is brought fully into force): see SI 2013/3204, r 1 and SI 2014/954, art 2(a); for transitional provisions and savings see SI 2013/3204, r 137 and SI 2014/954, art 3.

32.16 Registration in [the family court] of an order registered in the High Court[—procedure in the High Court]

(1) This rule applies where—

    (a)   a maintenance order is registered in the High Court in accordance with section 17(4) of the 1950 Act; and

    (b)   the court officer [of the High Court] receives notice that the [family court] has registered the order in accordance with section 2(5) of the 1958 Act.

(2) The court officer [of the High Court] must enter particulars of the registration in . . . the register.

NOTES

Amendment

Provision heading: words "the family court" in square brackets substituted by SI 2013/3204, rr 2, 94(a)(i).
Date in force: 22 April 2014 (being the date on which the Crime and Courts Act 2013, s 17(3) is brought fully into force): see SI 2013/3204, r 1 and SI 2014/954, art 2(a); for transitional provisions and savings see SI 2013/3204, r 137 and SI 2014/954, art 3.
Provision heading: words "—procedure in the High Court" in square brackets inserted by SI 2013/3204, rr 2, 94(a)(ii).
Date in force: 22 April 2014 (being the date on which the Crime and Courts Act 2013, s 17(3) is brought fully into force): see SI 2013/3204, r 1 and SI 2014/954, art 2(a); for transitional provisions and savings see SI 2013/3204, r 137 and SI 2014/954, art 3.

Para (1): in sub-para (b) words "of the High Court" in square brackets inserted by SI 2013/3204, rr 2, 94(b).
> Date in force: 22 April 2014 (being the date on which the Crime and Courts Act 2013, s 17(3) is brought fully into force): see SI 2013/3204, r 1 and SI 2014/954, art 2(a); for transitional provisions and savings see SI 2013/3204, r 137 and SI 2014/954, art 3.

Para (1): in sub-para (b) words "family court" in square brackets substituted by SI 2013/3204, rr 2, 94(c).
> Date in force: 22 April 2014 (being the date on which the Crime and Courts Act 2013, s 17(3) is brought fully into force): see SI 2013/3204, r 1 and SI 2014/954, art 2(a); for transitional provisions and savings see SI 2013/3204, r 137 and SI 2014/954, art 3.

Para (2): words "of the High Court" in square brackets inserted by SI 2013/3204, rr 2, 94(b).
> Date in force: 22 April 2014 (being the date on which the Crime and Courts Act 2013, s 17(3) is brought fully into force): see SI 2013/3204, r 1 and SI 2014/954, art 2(a); for transitional provisions and savings see SI 2013/3204, r 137 and SI 2014/954, art 3.

Para (2): words omitted revoked by SI 2013/3204, rr 2, 94(d).
> Date in force: 22 April 2014 (being the date on which the Crime and Courts Act 2013, s 17(3) is brought fully into force): see SI 2013/3204, r 1 and SI 2014/954, art 2(a); for transitional provisions and savings see SI 2013/3204, r 137 and SI 2014/954, art 3.

[32.16A Registration in the family court of an order registered in the High Court—procedure in the family court]

[(1) This rule applies where—

    (a)   a maintenance order is registered in the High Court in accordance with section 17(4) of the 1950 Act; and

    (b)   the court officer of the family court, in accordance with section 2(2)(b) of the 1958 Act, receives from the appropriate officer of the original court in Scotland or Northern Ireland a certified copy of an order made by the court in Scotland or Northern Ireland.

(2)   The court officer of the family court will—

    (a)   register the order in the family court by entering particulars in the register; and

    (b)   send written notice to the court officer of the High Court and to the appropriate officer of the original court in Scotland or in Northern Ireland that the order has been registered.]

NOTES

Amendment

Inserted by SI 2013/3204, rr 2, 95.
> Date in force: 22 April 2014 (being the date on which the Crime and Courts Act 2013, s 17(3) is brought fully into force): see SI 2013/3204, r 1 and SI 2014/954, art 2(a); for transitional provisions and savings see SI 2013/3204, r 137 and SI 2014/954, art 3.

32.17–32.18 . . .

. . .

NOTES

Amendment

Revoked by SI 2013/3204, rr 2, 96.
> Date in force: 22 April 2014 (being the date on which the Crime and Courts Act 2013, s 17(3) is brought fully into force): see SI 2013/3204, r 1 and SI 2014/954, art 2(a); for transitional provisions and savings see SI 2013/3204, r 137 and SI 2014/954, art 3.

32.19 Variation or discharge of an order registered in [the family court—procedure in the High Court]

(1)   This rule applies where a maintenance order is registered in [the family court] under Part 1 of the 1958 Act.

(2)   If the court which made the order makes an order varying or discharging that order the court officer [of the High Court] must send a certified copy of the order of variation or discharge to [the family court].

(3)   If the court officer [of the High Court] receives from [the family court] a certified copy of an order varying the maintenance order the court officer must—

(a)   file the copy of the order; and

(b)   enter the particulars of the variation in the place where the details required by rule 32.15(3) were entered.

NOTES

Amendment

Provision heading: words "the family court—procedure in the High Court" in square brackets substituted by SI 2013/3204, rr 2, 97(a).

Date in force: 22 April 2014 (being the date on which the Crime and Courts Act 2013, s 17(3) is brought fully into force): see SI 2013/3204, r 1 and SI 2014/954, art 2(a); for transitional provisions and savings see SI 2013/3204, r 137 and SI 2014/954, art 3.

Para (1): words "the family court" in square brackets substituted by SI 2013/3204, rr 2, 97(b).

Date in force: 22 April 2014 (being the date on which the Crime and Courts Act 2013, s 17(3) is brought fully into force): see SI 2013/3204, r 1 and SI 2014/954, art 2(a); for transitional provisions and savings see SI 2013/3204, r 137 and SI 2014/954, art 3.

Para (2): words "of the High Court" in square brackets inserted by SI 2013/3204, rr 2, 97(c)(i).

Date in force: 22 April 2014 (being the date on which the Crime and Courts Act 2013, s 17(3) is brought fully into force): see SI 2013/3204, r 1 and SI 2014/954, art 2(a); for transitional provisions and savings see SI 2013/3204, r 137 and SI 2014/954, art 3.

Para (2): words "the family court" in square brackets substituted by virtue of SI 2013/3204, rr 2, 97(c)(ii).

Date in force: 22 April 2014 (being the date on which the Crime and Courts Act 2013, s 17(3) is brought fully into force): see SI 2013/3204, r 1 and SI 2014/954, art 2(a); for transitional provisions and savings see SI 2013/3204, r 137 and SI 2014/954, art 3.

Para (3): words "of the High Court" in square brackets inserted by SI 2013/3204, rr 2, 97(d)(i).

Date in force: 22 April 2014 (being the date on which the Crime and Courts Act 2013, s 17(3) is brought fully into force): see SI 2013/3204, r 1 and SI 2014/954, art 2(a); for transitional provisions and savings see SI 2013/3204, r 137 and SI 2014/954, art 3.

Para (3): words "the family court" in square brackets substituted by SI 2013/3204, rr 2, 97(d)(ii).

Date in force: 22 April 2014 (being the date on which the Crime and Courts Act 2013, s 17(3) is brought fully into force): see SI 2013/3204, r 1 and SI 2014/954, art 2(a); for transitional provisions and savings see SI 2013/3204, r 137 and SI 2014/954, art 3.

[32.19A Variation, remission, discharge or cancellation of registration of an order registered in the family court—procedure in the family court]

[(1) Where under section 4(2) of the 1958 Act a High Court order registered in the family court is varied by the family court, the court officer for the family court will give notice of the variation to the High Court.

(2) Where under section 4(4) of the 1958 Act an application for the variation of a High Court order registered in the family court is remitted to the High Court by the family court, the court officer for the family court will give notice of its having been remitted to the High Court.

(3) Where under section 5(4) of the 1958 Act the registration of a High Court order in the family court is cancelled by the family court, the court officer for the family court will give notice of cancellation to the High Court, stating (if applicable) that the cancellation is a result of a notice given under section 5(1) of the 1958 Act.

(4) Where under section 5(4) of the 1958 Act the registration in the family court of an order made in Scotland or Northern Ireland is cancelled by the family court, the court officer for the family court will give notice of the cancellation to—

(a)   the appropriate officer of the court which made the order; and

(b)   where the order is registered under Part 2 of the 1950 Act, to the appropriate officer of the High Court.

(5) Where under section 5(4) of the 1958 Act the registration in the family court of an order under Part 2 of the 1950 Act is cancelled by the family court, the court officer for the family court will give notice of the cancellation to the appropriate officer of the original court.

(6) Where under section 5 of the 1958 Act the cancellation of the registration of a High Court order means that any order which requires payment to be made to the

family court is to cease to have effect, the court officer will give notice to the defendant in the form set out in Practice Direction 32A (Form 7).]

NOTES

Amendment
> Inserted by SI 2013/3204, rr 2, 98.
>> Date in force: 22 April 2014 (being the date on which the Crime and Courts Act 2013, s 17(3) is brought fully into force): see SI 2013/3204, r 1 and SI 2014/954, art 2(a); for transitional provisions and savings see SI 2013/3204, r 137 and SI 2014/954, art 3.

32.20–32.21 . . .

. . .

NOTES

Amendment
> Revoked by SI 2013/3204, rr 2, 99.
>> Date in force: 22 April 2014 (being the date on which the Crime and Courts Act 2013, s 17(3) is brought fully into force): see SI 2013/3204, r 1 and SI 2014/954, art 2(a); for transitional provisions and savings see SI 2013/3204, r 137 and SI 2014/954, art 3.

32.22 Cancellation of registration—orders registered in [the family court]
(1)   Where the court gives notice under section 5(2) of the 1958 Act, the court officer must endorse the notice on the certified copy of the order of variation or discharge sent to the [family court] in accordance with rule 32.19(2).
(2)   Where notice is received from [the family court] that registration of an order made by the High Court . . . under Part 1 of the 1958 Act has been cancelled, the court officer must enter particulars of the cancellation in the place where the details required by rule 32.15(3) were entered.

NOTES

Amendment
> Provision heading: words "the family court" in square brackets substituted by SI 2013/3204, rr 2, 100(a).
>> Date in force: 22 April 2014 (being the date on which the Crime and Courts Act 2013, s 17(3) is brought fully into force): see SI 2013/3204, r 1 and SI 2014/954, art 2(a); for transitional provisions and savings see SI 2013/3204, r 137 and SI 2014/954, art 3.
> Para (1): words "the family court" in square brackets substituted by SI 2013/3204, rr 2, 100(b).
>> Date in force: 22 April 2014 (being the date on which the Crime and Courts Act 2013, s 17(3) is brought fully into force): see SI 2013/3204, r 1 and SI 2014/954, art 2(a); for transitional provisions and savings see SI 2013/3204, r 137 and SI 2014/954, art 3.
> Para (2): words "the family court" in square brackets substituted by SI 2013/3204, rr 2, 100(a).
>> Date in force: 22 April 2014 (being the date on which the Crime and Courts Act 2013, s 17(3) is brought fully into force): see SI 2013/3204, r 1 and SI 2014/954, art 2(a); for transitional provisions and savings see SI 2013/3204, r 137 and SI 2014/954, art 3.
> Para (2): words omitted revoked by SI 2013/3204, rr 2, 100(c).
>> Date in force: 22 April 2014 (being the date on which the Crime and Courts Act 2013, s 17(3) is brought fully into force): see SI 2013/3204, r 1 and SI 2014/954, art 2(a); for transitional provisions and savings see SI 2013/3204, r 137 and SI 2014/954, art 3.

[32.22A Notices: payments made through the family court]
[(1)   Paragraph (2) applies where a notice is given under section 2(6ZC) of the 1958 Act that payments under an order registered in the family court are payable to the family court.
(2)   The notice will be in the form set out in Practice Direction 32A (Form 5) and will be given by the court officer of the family court.
(3)   Paragraph (4) applies where a notice is given under section 2(6ZC) of the 1958 Act that payments under an order registered in the family court have ceased to be payable to the family court.
(4)   The notice will be in the form set out in Practice Direction 32A (Form 6) and will be given by the court officer of the family court.]

NOTES

Amendment
>Inserted by SI 2013/3204, rr 2, 101.
>>Date in force: 22 April 2014 (being the date on which the Crime and Courts Act 2013, s 17(3) is brought fully into force): see SI 2013/3204, r 1 and SI 2014/954, art 2(a); for transitional provisions and savings see SI 2013/3204, r 137 and SI 2014/954, art 3.

[32.22B Method of payment]

[(1) This rule applies where the family court exercises its duties or powers under section 4A(2) of the 1958 Act to make, revive or vary any means of payment order within the meaning of section 1(7) of the Maintenance Enforcement Act 1991.

(2) Where the court orders that payments under a registered order are to be made by a particular means—

>(a) the court will record on a copy of the order the means of payment which the court has ordered; and

>(b) the court officer will notify, in writing, the person liable to make payments under the order how the payments are to be made.

(3) Paragraph (4) applies where the court orders that payments be made—

>(a) by the debtor to the creditor; or

>(b) by the debtor to the court;

by a method falling within section 1(5) of the Maintenance Enforcement Act 1991.

(4) The court officer will notify the person liable to make payments under the order of sufficient details of the account into which payments should be made to enable payments to be made into that account.]

NOTES

Amendment
>Inserted by SI 2013/3204, rr 2, 101.
>>Date in force: 22 April 2014 (being the date on which the Crime and Courts Act 2013, s 17(3) is brought fully into force): see SI 2013/3204, r 1 and SI 2014/954, art 2(a); for transitional provisions and savings see SI 2013/3204, r 137 and SI 2014/954, art 3.

[32.22C Variation of method of payment]

[(1) The Part 18 procedure applies to an application under section 1(3)(a) of the Maintenance Enforcement Act 1991 received from an interested party for the method of payment to be varied under section 4A of the 1958 Act.

(2) The court will notify the interested party who made the application and, where practicable, any other interested party, of the result of the application.

(3) The court will record any variation on a copy of the order.]

NOTES

Amendment
>Inserted by SI 2013/3204, rr 2, 101.
>>Date in force: 22 April 2014 (being the date on which the Crime and Courts Act 2013, s 17(3) is brought fully into force): see SI 2013/3204, r 1 and SI 2014/954, art 2(a); for transitional provisions and savings see SI 2013/3204, r 137 and SI 2014/954, art 3.

[32.22D Notices received from another court or from a person entitled to payments]

[(1) This rule applies where any notice is received—

>(a) of the discharge or variation by the High Court of a High Court order registered in the family court;

>(b) of the discharge or variation by a court in Scotland or Northern Ireland of an order made by such a court and registered in the family court; or

>(c) under section 5(1) or (2) of the 1958 Act.

(2) The court officer for the family court will enter details of any such notice in the register.

433

(3)   In the case of a notice under section 5(1) or (2) of the 1958 Act, the court officer for the family court will ensure that the person in possession of any warrant of commitment, issued but not executed, for the enforcement of the order is informed of the giving of that notice.]

NOTES

Amendment
> Inserted by SI 2013/3204, rr 2, 101.
>> Date in force: 22 April 2014 (being the date on which the Crime and Courts Act 2013, s 17(3) is brought fully into force): see SI 2013/3204, r 1 and SI 2014/954, art 2(a); for transitional provisions and savings see SI 2013/3204, r 137 and SI 2014/954, art 3.

CHAPTER 4

REGISTRATION AND ENFORCEMENT OF CUSTODY ORDERS UNDER THE 1986 ACT

32.23 Interpretation
In this Chapter—
  "appropriate court" means, in relation to—
    (a)   Scotland, the Court of Session;
    (b)   Northern Ireland, the High Court in Northern Ireland; and
    (c)   a specified dependent territory, the corresponding court in that territory;
  "appropriate officer" means, in relation to—
    (a)   the Court of Session, the Deputy Principal Clerk of Session;
    (b)   the High Court in Northern Ireland, the Master (Care and Protection) of that court; and
    (c)   the appropriate court in a specified dependent territory, the corresponding officer of that court;
  "Part 1 order" means an order under Part 1 of the 1986 Act;
  "the register" means the register kept for the purposes of Part 1 of the 1986 Act; and
  "specified dependent territory" means a dependent territory specified in column 1 of Schedule 1 to the Family Law Act 1986 (Specified Dependent Territories) Order 1991.

32.24 Prescribed officer and functions of the court
(1)   The prescribed officer for the purposes of sections 27(4) and 28(1) of the 1986 Act is the family proceedings department manager of the principal registry.
(2)   The function of the court under sections 27(3) and 28(1) of the 1986 Act shall be performed by a court officer.

32.25 Application for the registration of an order made by the High Court or [the family court]
(1)   An application under section 27 of the 1986 Act for the registration of an order made in the High Court or [the family court] may be made by sending to a court officer at the court which made the order—
    (a)   a certified copy of the order;
    (b)   a copy of any order which has varied the terms of the original order;
    (c)   a statement which—
        (i)   contains the name and address of the applicant and the applicant's interest under the order;
        (ii)   contains—
            (aa)   the name and date of birth of the child in respect of whom the order was made;

    (bb)   the whereabouts or suspected whereabouts of the child; and

    (cc)   the name of any person with whom the child is alleged to be;

   (iii)   contains the name and address of any other person who has an interest under the order and states whether the order has been served on that person;

   (iv)   states in which of the jurisdictions of Scotland, Northern Ireland or a specified dependent territory the order is to be registered;

   (v)   states that to the best of the applicant's information and belief, the order is in force;

   (vi)   states whether, and if so where, the order is already registered;

   (vii)   gives details of any order known to the applicant which affects the child and is in force in the jurisdiction in which the order is to be registered;

   (viii)   annexes any document relevant to the application; and

   (ix)   is verified by a statement of truth; and

  (d)   a copy of the statement referred to in paragraph (c).

(2)   On receipt of the documents referred to in paragraph (1), the court officer will, subject to paragraph (4)—

  (a)   keep the original statement and send the other documents to the appropriate officer;

  (b)   record in the court records the fact that the documents have been sent to the appropriate officer; and

  (c)   file a copy of the documents.

(3)   On receipt of a notice that the document has been registered in the appropriate court the court officer will record that fact in the court records.

(4)   The court officer will not send the documents to the appropriate officer if it appears to the court officer that—

  (a)   the order is no longer in force; or

  (b)   the child has reached the age of 16.

(5)   Where paragraph (4) applies—

  (a)   the court officer must, within 14 days of the decision, notify the applicant of the decision of the court officer in paragraph (4) and the reasons for it; and

  (b)   the applicant may apply to [the court], in private for an order that the documents be sent to the appropriate court.

NOTES

Amendment

Provision heading: words "the family court" in square brackets substituted by SI 2013/3204, rr 2, 102(a).

    Date in force: 22 April 2014 (being the date on which the Crime and Courts Act 2013, s 17(3) is brought fully into force): see SI 2013/3204, r 1 and SI 2014/954, art 2(a); for transitional provisions and savings see SI 2013/3204, r 137 and SI 2014/954, art 3.

Para (1): words "the family court" in square brackets substituted by SI 2013/3204, rr 2, 102(a); for transitional and saving provision see r 137 thereof.

    Date in force: 22 April 2014 (being the date on which the Crime and Courts Act 2013, s 17(3) is brought fully into force): see SI 2013/3204, r 1 and SI 2014/954, art 2(a); for transitional provisions and savings see SI 2013/3204, r 137 and SI 2014/954, art 3.

Para (5): in sub-para (b) words "the court" in square brackets substituted by SI 2013/3204, rr 2, 102(b).

    Date in force: 22 April 2014 (being the date on which the Crime and Courts Act 2013, s 17(3) is brought fully into force): see SI 2013/3204, r 1 and SI 2014/954, art 2(a); for transitional provisions and savings see SI 2013/3204, r 137 and SI 2014/954, art 3.

32.26 Registration of orders made in Scotland, Northern Ireland or a specified dependent territory

(1)   This rule applies where the prescribed officer receives, for registration, a certified copy of an order made in Scotland, Northern Ireland or a specified dependent territory.

(2)   The prescribed officer will—

    (a)   enter in the register—

        (i)   the name and address of the applicant and the applicant's interest under the order;

        (ii)   the name and date of birth of the child and the date the child will attain the age of 16;

        (iii)   the whereabouts or suspected whereabouts of the child; and

        (iv)   the terms of the order, its date and the court which made it;

    (b)   file the certified copy and accompanying documents; and

    (c)   notify—

        (i)   the court which sent the order; and

        (ii)   the applicant,

that the order has been registered.

32.27 Revocation and variation of an order made in the High Court or [the family court]

(1)   Where a Part 1 order, registered in an appropriate court, is varied or revoked, the court officer of the court making the order of variation or revocation will—

    (a)   send a certified copy of the order of variation or revocation to—

        (i)   the appropriate officer; and

        (ii)   if a different court, the court which made the Part 1 order;

    (b)   record in the court records the fact that a copy of the order has been sent; and

    (c)   file a copy of the order.

(2)   On receipt of notice from the appropriate court that its register has been amended, this fact will be recorded by the court officer of—

    (a)   the court which made the order of variation or revocation; and

    (b)   if different, the court which made the Part 1 order.

NOTES

Amendment

Provision heading: words "the family court" in square brackets substituted by SI 2013/3204, rr 2, 103.

    Date in force: 22 April 2014 (being the date on which the Crime and Courts Act 2013, s 17(3) is brought fully into force): see SI 2013/3204, r 1 and SI 2014/954, art 2(a); for transitional provisions and savings see SI 2013/3204, r 137 and SI 2014/954, art 3.

32.28 Registration of varied, revoked or recalled orders made in Scotland, Northern Ireland or a specified dependent territory

(1)   This rule applies where the prescribed officer receives a certified copy of an order made in Scotland, Northern Ireland or a specified dependent territory which varies, revokes or recalls a registered Part 1 order.

(2)   The prescribed officer shall enter particulars of the variation, revocation or recall in the register and give notice of the entry to—

    (a)   the court which sent the certified copy;

    (b)   if different, the court which made the Part 1 order;

    (c)   the applicant for registration; and

    (d)   if different, the applicant for the variation, revocation of recall of the order.

(3)   An application under section 28(2) of the 1986 Act must be made in accordance with the Part 19 procedure.

(4)   The applicant for the Part 1 order, if not the applicant under section 28(2) of the 1986 Act, must be made a defendant to the application.

(5)   Where the court cancels a registration under section 28(2) of the 1986 Act, the court officer will amend the register and give notice of the amendment to the court which made the Part 1 order.

32.29 Interim directions
The following persons will be made parties to an application for interim directions under section 29 of the 1986 Act—

(a)   the parties to the proceedings for enforcement; and

(b)   if not a party to those proceedings, the applicant for the Part 1 order.

32.30 Staying and dismissal of enforcement proceedings
(1)   The following persons will be made parties to an application under section 30(1) or 31(1) of the 1986 Act—

(a)   the parties to the proceedings for enforcement which are sought to be stayed(GL); and

(b)   if not a party to those proceedings, the applicant for the Part 1 order.

(2)   Where the court makes an order under section 30(2) or (3) or section 31(3) of the 1986 Act, the court officer will amend the register and give notice of the amendment to—

(a)   the court which made the Part 1 order; and

(b)   the applicants for—

(i)   registration;

(ii)   enforcement; and

(iii) stay(GL)or dismissal of the enforcement proceedings.

32.31 Particulars of other proceedings
A party to proceedings for or relating to a Part 1 order who knows of other proceedings which relate to the child concerned (including proceedings out of the jurisdiction and concluded proceedings) must file a witness statement which—

(a)   states in which jurisdiction and court the other proceedings were begun;

(b)   states the nature and current state of the proceedings and the relief claimed or granted;

(c)   sets out the names of the parties to the proceedings and their relationship to the child;

(d)   if applicable and if known, states the reasons why relief claimed in the proceedings for or relating to the Part 1 order was not claimed in the other proceedings; and

(e)   is verified by a statement of truth.

32.32 Inspection of register
The following persons may inspect any entry in the register relating to a Part 1 order and may request copies of the order any document relating to it—

(a)   the applicant for registration of the Part 1 order;

(b)   a person who, to the satisfaction of a district judge, has an interest under the Part 1 order; and

(c)   a person who obtains the permission of a district judge.

[CHAPTER 5

ABILITY OF A COURT OFFICER TO TAKE ENFORCEMENT PROCEEDINGS IN RELATION
TO CERTAIN ORDERS FOR PERIODICAL PAYMENTS]

NOTES

Amendment
> Inserted by SI 2013/3204, rr 2, 104.
>> Date in force: 22 April 2014 (being the date on which the Crime and Courts Act
>> 2013, s 17(3) is brought fully into force): see SI 2013/3204, r 1 and SI 2014/954,
>> art 2(a); for transitional provisions and savings see SI 2013/3204, r 137 and SI
>> 2014/954, art 3.

[32.33 Court officers and enforcement proceedings]
[(1)   In this rule—
"the 1972 Act" means the Maintenance Orders (Reciprocal Enforcement) Act
1972;
"relevant order" means—

(a)   any order made by the family court for periodical payments, other
than an order made by virtue of Part 2 of the 1972 Act;

(b)   any order for periodical payments made by the High Court
(including an order deemed to be made by the High Court by
virtue of section 1(2) of the 1958 Act) and registered under Part 1
of the 1958 Act in the family court; and

(c)   an order made by a court in Scotland or in Northern Ireland
which is registered in the family court under Part 2 of the
1950 Act; and

"the payee" means the person for whose benefit payments under a relevant
order are required to be made.
(2)   Where—

(a)   payments under a relevant order are required to be made periodically to
the family court; and

(b)   any sums payable under the order are in arrears,

a court officer will, if the payee so requests in writing, and unless it appears to the
court officer that it is unreasonable in the circumstances to do so, proceed in the
officer's own name for the recovery of those sums.
(3)   Where payments under a relevant order are required to be made periodically to
the court, the payee may, at any time during the period in which the payments are
required to be so made, give authority in writing to a court officer for the officer to
proceed as mentioned in paragraph (4).
(4)   Where authority is given under paragraph (3) to a court officer, that officer will,
unless it appears unreasonable in the circumstances to do so, proceed in the
officer's own name for the recovery of any sums payable to the court under the
order in question which, on or after the date of the giving of the authority, fall into
arrears.
(5)   In any case where—

(a)   authority under paragraph (3) has been given to a court officer; and

(b)   the payee gives notice in writing to that court officer cancelling the
authority,

the authority will cease to have effect and so the court officer will not continue any
proceedings already commenced by virtue of the authority.
(6)   The payee shall have the same liability for all of the costs properly incurred in, or
in relation to, proceedings taken under paragraph (2) at the payee's request, or under
paragraph (3) by virtue of the payee's authority, including any court fees and any costs
incurred as a result of any proceedings commenced not being continued, as if the
proceedings had been commenced by the payee.

(7)   Nothing in paragraph (2) or (4) shall affect any right of a payee to proceed in his or her own name for the recovery of sums payable under an order of any court.]

NOTES

Amendment
> Inserted by SI 2013/3204, rr 2, 104.
>> Date in force: 22 April 2014 (being the date on which the Crime and Courts Act 2013, s 17(3) is brought fully into force): see SI 2013/3204, r 1 and SI 2014/954, art 2(a); for transitional provisions and savings see SI 2013/3204, r 137 and SI 2014/954, art 3.

PART 33
ENFORCEMENT

CHAPTER 1

GENERAL RULES

33.1 Application
(1)   The rules in this Part apply to an application made in the High Court and [the family court] to enforce an order made in family proceedings.
(2)   [Parts 50, 83 and 84] of, and Schedules 1 and 2 to, the CPR apply, as far as they are relevant and with necessary modification . . ., to an application made in the High Court and [the family court] to enforce an order made in family proceedings.

NOTES

Amendment
> Para (1): words "the family court" in square brackets substituted by SI 2014/667, rr 2, 28(a).
>> Date in force: 22 April 2014: see SI 2014/667, r 1; for transitional and saving provision see r 45.
> Para (2): words "Parts 50, 83 and 84" in square brackets substituted by SI 2014/667, rr 2, 28(b)(i).
>> Date in force: 22 April 2014: see SI 2014/667, r 1; for transitional and saving provision see r 45.
> Para (2): words omitted revoked by SI 2014/667, rr 2, 28(b)(ii).
>> Date in force: 22 April 2014: see SI 2014/667, r 1; for transitional and saving provision see r 45.
> Para (2): words "the family court" in square brackets substituted by SI 2014/667, rr 2, 28(b)(iii).
>> Date in force: 22 April 2014: see SI 2014/667, r 1; for transitional and saving provision see r 45.

SECTION 1
Enforcement of orders for the payment of money

33.2 Application of the Civil Procedure Rules
Part 70 of the CPR applies to proceedings under this Section as if—
(a)   in rule 70.1, in paragraph (2)(d), "but does not include a judgment or order for the payment of money into court" is omitted; . . .
[(a1) in rule 70.3(1), for "County Court" there is substituted "family court"; and]
(b)   rule 70.5 is omitted.

NOTES

Amendment
> In para (a) word omitted revoked by SI 2014/667, rr 2, 29(a).
>> Date in force: 22 April 2014: see SI 2014/667, r 1; for transitional and saving provision see r 45.
> Para (a1) inserted by SI 2014/667, rr 2, 29(b).
>> Date in force: 22 April 2014: see SI 2014/667, r 1; for transitional and saving provision see r 45.

33.3 How to apply

(1)   Except where a rule or practice direction otherwise requires, an application for an order to enforce an order for the payment of money must be made in a notice of application accompanied by a statement which must—

      (a)   state the amount due under the order, showing how that amount is arrived at; and

      (b)   be verified by a statement of truth.

(2)   The notice of application may either—

      (a)   apply for an order specifying the method of enforcement; or

      (b)   apply for an order for such method of enforcement as the court may consider appropriate.

(3)   If an application is made under paragraph (2)(b), an order to attend court will be issued and rule 71.2 (6) and (7) of the CPR will apply as if the application had been made under that rule.

33.4 Transfer of orders

(1)   This rule applies to an application for the transfer—

      (a)   to the High Court of an order made in [the family court]; and

      (b)   to [the family court] of an order made in the High Court.

(2)   The application must be—

      (a)   made without notice; and

      (b)   accompanied by a statement which complies with rule 33.3(1).

(3)   The transfer will have effect upon the filing of the application.

(4)   Where an order is transferred from [the family court] to the High Court—

      (a)   it will have the same force and effect; and

      (b)   the same proceedings may be taken on it,

as if it were an order of the High Court.

(5)   This rule does not apply to the transfer of orders for periodical payments or for the recovery of arrears of periodical payments.

NOTES

Amendment

      Para (1): in sub-paras (a), (b) words "the family court" in square brackets substituted by SI 2014/667, rr 2, 30.

          Date in force: 22 April 2014: see SI 2014/667, r 1; for transitional and saving provision see r 45.

      Para (4): words "the family court" in square brackets substituted by SI 2014/667, rr 2, 30.

          Date in force: 22 April 2014: see SI 2014/667, r 1; for transitional and saving provision see r 45.

SECTION 2

Committal and injunction

[33.5 Enforcement of orders by way of committal]

[Part 37 applies as appropriate for the enforcement by way of committal of an order made in family proceedings.]

NOTES

Amendment

      Rule 33.5 substituted, for rr 33.5–33.8, by SI 2014/667, rr 2, 31.

          Date in force: 22 April 2014: see SI 2014/667, r 1; for transitional and saving provision see r 45.

33.6–33.8 . . .

. . .

NOTES

Amendment

Rule 33.5 substituted, for rr 33.5–33.8, by SI 2014/667, rr 2, 31.

Date in force: 22 April 2014: see SI 2014/667, r 1; for transitional and saving provision see r 45.

CHAPTER 2

COMMITTAL BY WAY OF JUDGMENT SUMMONS

33.9 Interpretation

In this Chapter, unless the context requires otherwise—

"order" means an order made in family proceedings for the payment of money;

"judgment creditor" means a person entitled to enforce an order under section 5 of the Debtors Act 1869;

"debtor" means a person liable under an order; and

"judgment summons" means a summons under section 5 of the [Debtors] Act 1869 requiring a debtor to attend court.

NOTES

Amendment

In definition "judgment summons" word "Debtors" in square brackets substituted by SI 2015/1420, rr 2, 18.

Date in force: 24 August 2015: see SI 2015/1420, r 1(4); for transitional provisions see r 26.

33.10 Application

[(1) An application for the issue of a judgment summons may be made—

    (a)   in the case of an order of the High Court, to—

        (i)   the principal registry;

        (ii)   a district registry; or

        (iii)   the family court,

whichever in the opinion of the judgment creditor is most convenient, and if to the family court, to whichever Designated Family Judge area is in the opinion of the judgment creditor most convenient; and

    (b)   in the case of an order of the family court, to whichever Designated Family Judge area is in the opinion of the judgment creditor most convenient,

having regard (in any case) to the place where the debtor resides or carries on business and irrespective of the location of the court or registry in which the order was made. (For the way in which information will be provided to enable Designated Family Judge areas and Designated Family Courts to be identified, see Practice Direction 34E.)]

(2) An application must be accompanied by a statement which—

    (a)   complies with rule 33.3(1);

    (b)   contains all the evidence on which the judgment creditor intends to rely; and

    (c)   has exhibited to it a copy of the order.

NOTES

Amendment

Para (1): substituted by SI 2014/667, rr 2, 32.

Date in force: 22 April 2014: see SI 2014/667, r 1; for transitional and saving provision see r 45.

33.11 Judgment summons

(1) If the debtor is in default under an order of committal made on a previous judgment summons in respect of the same order, a judgment summons must not be issued without the court's permission.

[(2) A judgment summons must be accompanied by the statement referred to in rule 33.10(2).

(3) A judgment summons must be served on the debtor—

    (a) personally; or

    (b) by the court sending it to the debtor by first class post—

        (i) at the address stated in the application for the issue of a judgment summons; or

        (ii) in a case where a court officer is proceeding for the recovery of a debt in accordance with rule 32.33, at the last known address for the debtor shown on court records.

(4) In a case to which paragraph (3)(b)(i) applies, the judgment creditor must file with the court a certificate for postal service.

(5) A judgment summons must be served on the debtor not less than 14 days before the hearing.

(6) Paragraph (3) is subject to any direction of the court that the judgment summons must be served personally on the debtor.]

NOTES

Amendment

    Paras (2)–(6): substituted, for paras (2), (3) as originally enacted, by SI 2015/1420, rr 2, 19.
        Date in force: 24 August 2015: see SI 2015/1420, r 1(4); for transitional provision see r 26.

33.12 Successive judgment summonses

Subject to rule 33.11(1), successive judgment summonses may be issued even if the debtor has ceased to reside or carry on business at the address stated in the application for the issue of a judgment summons since the issue of the original judgment summons.

[33.13 Order or summons to attend adjourned hearing: requirement for personal service]

[(1) Paragraph (2) applies in proceedings for committal by way of judgment summons where—

    (a) the family court has ordered under section 110(1) of the County Courts Act 1984 that the debtor must attend an adjourned hearing; or

    (b) the High Court has summonsed the debtor to attend an adjourned hearing following the debtor's failure to attend the hearing of the judgment summons.

(2) The following documents must be served personally on the debtor—

    (a) the notice of the date and time fixed for the adjourned hearing; and

    (b) copies of the judgment summons and the documents mentioned in rule 33.10(2).]

NOTES

Amendment

    Substituted by SI 2015/1420, rr 2, 20.
        Date in force: 24 August 2015: see SI 2015/1420, r 1(4); for transitional provisions see r 26.

[33.14 Committal on application for judgment summons]

[(1) Subject to paragraph (2), on a hearing of an application for a judgment summons the debtor may be committed for making default on payment of a debt if the judgment creditor proves that the debtor—

(a)   has, or has had, since the date of the order the means to pay the sum in respect of which the debtor has made default; and

(b)   has refused or neglected, or refuses or neglects, to pay that sum.

(2)   A debtor may not be committed in accordance with paragraph (1) where the judgment summons was served by post, unless the debtor attends the hearing.

(3)   Where the debtor has been ordered or summonsed to attend an adjourned hearing in accordance with rule 33.13, the debtor may be committed—

(a)   for failure to attend the adjourned hearing; or

(b)   for making default on payment of a debt, if the judgment creditor proves that the debtor—

(i)   has, or has had, since the date of the order the means to pay the sum in respect of which the debtor has made default; and

(ii)   has refused or neglected, or refuses or neglects, to pay that sum.

(4)   The debtor may not be compelled to give evidence.]

NOTES

Amendment
Substituted by SI 2015/1420, rr 2, 21.
Date in force: 24 August 2015: see SI 2015/1420, r 1(4); for transitional provisions see r 26.

[33.14A Expenses]

[(1)   A debtor must not be committed to prison under section 110(2) of the County Courts Act 1984 unless the debtor has been paid or offered a sum reasonably sufficient to cover the expenses of travelling to and from the court building at which the debtor is summoned or ordered to appear.

(2)   The sum must be paid or offered at the time of service of—

(a)   the judgment summons; or

(b)   the order to attend under section 110(1) of the County Courts Act 1984.]

NOTES

Amendment
Inserted by SI 2015/1420, rr 2, 22.
Date in force: 24 August 2015: see SI 2015/1420, r 1(4); for transitional provisions see r 26.

33.15 Orders for the benefit of different persons

Where an applicant has obtained one or more orders in the same application but for the benefit of different persons—

(a)   where the judgment creditor is a child, the applicant may apply for the issue of a judgment summons in respect of those orders on behalf of the judgment creditor without seeking permission to act as the child's litigation friend; and

(b)   only one judgment summons need be issued in respect of those orders.

33.16 Hearing of judgment summons

(1)   On the hearing of the judgment summons the court may—

(a)   where the order is for lump sum provision or costs; or

(b)   where the order is an order for maintenance pending suit, an order for maintenance pending outcome of proceedings or an order for other periodical payments and it appears to the court that the order would have been varied or suspended if the debtor had made an application for that purpose,

make a new order for payment of the amount due under the original order, together with the costs of the judgment summons, either at a specified time or by instalments.

(2)   If the court makes an order of committal, it may direct its execution to be suspended on terms that the debtor pays to the judgment creditor—

(a)   the amount due;

(b)   the costs of the judgment summons; and

(c)   any sums accruing due under the original order,

either at a specified time or by instalments.

(3)   All payments under a new order or an order of committal must be made to the judgment creditor unless the court directs otherwise.

(4)   Where an order of committal is suspended on such terms as are mentioned in paragraph (2)—

(a)   all payments made under the suspended order will be deemed to be made—

(i)   first, in or towards the discharge of any sums from time to time accruing due under the original order; and

(ii)   secondly, in or towards the discharge of a debt in respect of which the judgment summons was issued and the costs of the summons; and

(b)   the suspended order must not be executed until the judgment creditor has filed a statement of default on the part of the debtor.

33.17 Special provisions as to judgment summonses in the High Court

(1)   [The High Court] may summons witnesses to give evidence to prove the means of the debtor and may issue a witness summons for that purpose.

(2)   Where the debtor appears at the hearing, [the High Court] may direct that the travelling expenses paid to the debtor be allowed as expenses of a witness.

(3)   Where the debtor appears at the hearing and no order of committal is made, [the High Court] may allow the debtor's proper costs including compensation for any loss of earnings.

(4)   When [the High Court] makes—

(a)   a new order; or

(b)   an order of committal,

a court officer must send notice of the order to the debtor and, if the original order was made in another court, to that court.

(5)   An order of committal must be directed—

(a)   where the order is to be executed by the tipstaff, to the tipstaff; or

(b)   where the order is to be executed by a deputy tipstaff, to the [Designated Family Judge area within] which the debtor is to be found.

NOTES

Amendment

Para (1): words "The High Court" in square brackets substituted by SI 2015/1420, rr 2, 23(a).

Date in force: 24 August 2015: see SI 2015/1420, r 1(4); for transitional provision see r 26.

Para (2): words "the High Court" in square brackets substituted by SI 2015/1420, rr 2, 23(b).

Date in force: 24 August 2015: see SI 2015/1420, r 1(4); for transitional provision see r 26.

Para (3): words "the High Court" in square brackets substituted by SI 2015/1420, rr 2, 23(b).

Date in force: 24 August 2015: see SI 2015/1420, r 1(4); for transitional provision see r 26.

Para (4): words "the High Court" in square brackets substituted by SI 2015/1420, rr 2, 23(b).

Date in force: 24 August 2015: see SI 2015/1420, r 1(4); for transitional provision see r 26.

Para (5): in sub-para (b) words "Designated Family Judge area within" in square brackets substituted by SI 2014/667, rr 2, 35.

Date in force: 22 April 2014: see SI 2014/667, r 1; for transitional and saving provision see r 45.

33.18 . . .

. . .

NOTES

Amendment
Revoked by SI 2014/667, rr 2, 36.
Date in force: 22 April 2014: see SI 2014/667, r 1; for transitional and saving provision see r 45.

CHAPTER 3

ATTACHMENT OF EARNINGS

[33.19 Enforcement by attachment of earnings order]
[Part 39 applies to applications for an attachment of earnings order to secure payments under a maintenance order.]

NOTES

Amendment
Substituted by SI 2016/355, rr 2, 4.
Date in force: 6 April 2016: see SI 2016/355, r 1(2); for transitional provision see r 9.

[33.19A Application of CCR Order 27: enforcement of a maintenance order]
[(1) Order 27 of the CCR applies to proceedings under this Part for the enforcement of a maintenance order as it applies to proceedings for the enforcement of a judgment debt, subject to the following provisions of this rule—

(a) paragraphs (2) and (3) in relation to failure by a debtor under a maintenance order to attend court and the application of section 23 of the Attachment of Earnings Act 1971; and

(b) paragraphs (4) to (11) in relation to applications for an attachment of earnings order to secure payments under a maintenance order, the making of such attachment of earnings orders and their discharge.

(2) An order under section 23(1) of the Attachment of Earnings Act 1971 for the attendance of the debtor at an adjourned hearing for an attachment of earnings order to secure payments under a maintenance order must—

(a) be served on the debtor personally not less than 5 days before the day fixed for the adjourned hearing; and

(b) direct that any payments made thereafter must be paid into the court and not direct to the judgment creditor.

(3) An application by a debtor for the revocation of an order committing the debtor to prison and (if already in custody) for discharge under section 23(7) of the Attachment of Earnings Act 1971 must—

(a) be made to court in writing without notice to any other party, stating the reasons for the debtor's failure to attend the court or refusal to be sworn or to give evidence (as the case may be) and containing an undertaking by the debtor to attend the court or to be sworn or to give evidence when next required to do so; and

(b) if the debtor has already been lodged in prison, be attested by the governor of the prison (or any other officer of the prison not below the rank of principal officer), and in any other case be made in a witness statement or affidavit,

and before dealing with the application the court may, if it thinks fit, cause notice to be given to the judgment creditor that the application has been made and of a date and time when the judgment creditor may attend and be heard.

(4)   An application for an attachment of earnings order to secure payments under a maintenance order must be made to the Designated Family Judge area within which the order was made.

(5)   Any application under section 32 of the 1973 Act for permission to enforce the payment of arrears which became due more than 12 months before the application for an attachment of earnings order must be made in the application for the attachment of earnings order.

(6)   Notice of the application, together with a form of reply in the appropriate form, must be served on the debtor in the manner set out in rule 6.23 and—

    (a)   service of the notice must be effected not less than 21 days before the hearing, but may be effected at any time before the hearing on the applicant satisfying the court by witness statement or affidavit that the respondent is about to move from the address for service; and

    (b)   rule 5(2A) of CCR Order 27 does not apply.

(7)   An application by the debtor for an attachment of earnings order to secure payments under a maintenance order may be made on the making of the maintenance order or of an order varying the maintenance order, and rules 4 and 5 of CCR Order 27 do not apply in such a case.

(8)   Rule 7 of CCR Order 27 has effect as if for paragraphs (1) to (8) of that rule there were substituted the following paragraph—

    "(1)   An application for an attachment of earnings order to secure payments under a maintenance order shall be heard in private.".

(9)   Where an attachment of earnings order made by the High Court designates the court officer of the family court as the collecting officer, that officer shall, on receipt of a certified copy of the order from the court officer of the High Court, send to the person to whom the order is directed a notice as to the mode of payment.

(10)   Where an attachment of earnings order made by the family court to secure payments under a maintenance order ceases to have effect and—

    (a)   the related maintenance order was made by that court; or

    (b)   the related maintenance order was an order of the High Court and—

        (i)   the court officer of the family court has received notice of the cessation from the court officer of the High Court; or

        (ii)   a committal order has been made in the family court for the enforcement of the related maintenance order,

the court officer of the family court shall give notice of the cessation to the person to whom the attachment of earnings order was directed.

(11)   Rule 13 of CCR Order 27 has effect as if for paragraphs (4) to (7) there were substituted the following paragraph—

    "(4)   Where the family court has made an attachment of earnings order and it appears to the court that the related maintenance order has ceased to have effect (whether by virtue of the terms of the maintenance order or under section 238 of the 1973 Act or otherwise), the court may discharge or vary the attachment of earnings order.".]

NOTES

Amendment
    Rules 33.19, 33.19A substituted, for r 33.19, by SI 2014/667, rr 2, 37.
        Date in force: 22 April 2014: see SI 2014/667, r 1; for transitional and saving provision see r 45.

CHAPTER 4

WARRANT OF [CONTROL]

NOTES

Amendment
> Chapter heading: word "Control" in square brackets substituted by SI 2014/667, rr 2, 38.
>> Date in force: 22 April 2014: see SI 2014/667, r 1; for transitional and saving provision see r 45.

33.20 Applications to vary existing orders
Where an application is pending for a variation of—
- (a)   a financial order;
- (b)   an order under section 27 of the 1973 Act; or
- (c)   an order under Part 9 of Schedule 5 to the 2004 Act,

no warrant of [control] may be issued to enforce payment of any sum due under those orders, except with the permission of the [court].

NOTES

Amendment
> Word "control" in square brackets substituted by SI 2014/667, rr 2, 39(a).
>> Date in force: 22 April 2014: see SI 2014/667, r 1; for transitional and saving provision see r 45.
> Word "court" in square brackets substituted by SI 2014/667, rr 2, 39(b).
>> Date in force: 22 April 2014: see SI 2014/667, r 1; for transitional and saving provision see r 45.

33.21 . . .

. . .

NOTES

Amendment
> Revoked by SI 2014/667, rr 2, 40.
>> Date in force: 22 April 2014: see SI 2014/667, r 1; for transitional and saving provision see r 45.

CHAPTER 5

COURT'S POWER TO APPOINT A RECEIVER

33.22 Application of the CPR
Part 69 of the CPR applies to proceedings under this Part.

CHAPTER 6

ORDERS TO OBTAIN INFORMATION FROM JUDGMENT DEBTORS

[33.23 Application of the CPR]
[(1)   Part 71 of the CPR applies to proceedings under this Part with the following modifications.
(2)   In rule 71.2, for sub-paragraph (b) substitute—
>   "(b)   must be—
>> (i)   issued in the High Court if the High Court made the judgment or order which it is sought to enforce; or
>> (ii)   made to the Designated Family Court for the Designated Family Judge area within which the judgment or order was made,

except that if the proceedings have since been transferred to a different court or Designated Family Judge area, it must be issued in that court or made to that area.]

NOTES

Amendment
> Substituted by SI 2014/667, rr 2, 41.
>> Date in force: 22 April 2014: see SI 2014/667, r 1; for transitional and saving provision see r 45.

CHAPTER 7

THIRD PARTY DEBT ORDERS

33.24 Application of the CPR

(1)   Part 72 of the CPR applies to proceedings under this Part with the following modifications.

[(1A)   In rule 72.3, for paragraph (1)(b) there is substituted—

> "(b)   must be issued in the court which made the judgment or order which it is sought to enforce, or made to the Designated Family Judge area within which that judgment or order was made, except that if the proceedings have since been transferred to a different court or Designated Family Judge area, it must be issued in that court or made to that area."]

(2)   In rule 72.4—

    (a)   in paragraph (1), for "a judge" there is substituted "the court"; and

    (b)   in paragraph (2), for "judge" there is substituted "court".

[(3)   In rule 72.7—

    (a)   in paragraph (2)(a), after "the Royal Courts of Justice" there is inserted "or the principal registry"; and

    (b)   in paragraph (2)(b), for "in County Court proceedings, to any County Court hearing centre" there is substituted "in family court proceedings, to any Designated Family Judge area".]

(4)   Rule 72.10 is omitted.

NOTES

Amendment
> Para (1A): substituted by SI 2014/667, rr 2, 42(a).
>> Date in force: 22 April 2014: see SI 2014/667, r 1; for transitional and saving provision see r 45.
> Para (3): substituted by SI 2014/667, rr 2, 42(b).
>> Date in force: 22 April 2014: see SI 2014/667, r 1; for transitional and saving provision see r 45.

CHAPTER 8

CHARGING ORDER, STOP ORDER, STOP NOTICE

[33.25 Application for a charging order, stop order or stop notice]

[Part 40 applies for the enforcement of a judgment or order made in family proceedings by way of a charging order, stop order or stop notice.]

NOTES

Amendment
> Substituted by SI 2016/355, rr 2, 5.
>> Date in force: 6 April 2016: see SI 2016/355, r 1(2); for transitional provision see r 9.

PART 34

RECIPROCAL ENFORCEMENT OF MAINTENANCE ORDERS

34.1 Scope and interpretation of this Part

(1) This Part contains rules about the reciprocal enforcement of maintenance orders.

(2) In this Part—

"the 1920 Act" means the Maintenance Orders (Facilities for Enforcement) Act 1920;

"the 1972 Act" means the Maintenance Orders (Reciprocal Enforcement) Act 1972;

"the 1982 Act" means the Civil Jurisdiction and Judgments Act 1982;

"the 1988 Convention" means the Convention on jurisdiction and the enforcement of judgments in civil and commercial matters done at Lugano on 16th September 1988;

"the Judgments Regulation" means Council Regulation (EC) No 44/2001 of 22nd December 2000 on jurisdiction and the recognition and enforcement of judgments in civil and commercial matters; and

"the Lugano Convention" means the Convention on jurisdiction and the recognition and enforcement of judgments in civil and commercial matters, between the European Community and the Republic of Iceland, the Kingdom of Norway, the Swiss Confederation and the Kingdom of Denmark signed on behalf of the European Community on 30th October 2007.

(3) Chapter 1 of this Part relates to the enforcement of maintenance orders in accordance with the 1920 Act.

(4) Chapter 2 of this Part relates to the enforcement of maintenance orders in accordance with [Parts 1 and 2] of the 1972 Act.

(5) Chapter 3 of this Part relates to the enforcement of maintenance orders in accordance with—

    (a)   the 1982 Act;
    (b)   the Judgments Regulation; . . .
    (c)   the Lugano Convention[; . . .
    (d)   the Maintenance Regulation][; and
    (e)   the 2007 Hague Convention].

NOTES

Amendment

Para (4): words "Parts 1 and 2" in square brackets substituted by SI 2013/3204, rr 2, 105.
    Date in force: 22 April 2014 (being the date on which the Crime and Courts Act 2013, s 17(3) is brought fully into force): see SI 2013/3204, r 1 and SI 2014/954, art 2(a); for transitional provisions and savings see SI 2013/3204, r 137 and SI 2014/954, art 3.
Para (5): in sub-para (b) word omitted revoked by SI 2011/1328, rr 2, 17(a).
    Date in force: 18 June 2011: see SI 2011/1328, r 1.
Para (5): sub-para (d) and word omitted immediately preceding it inserted by SI 2011/1328, rr 2, 17(b), (c).
    Date in force: 18 June 2011: see SI 2011/1328, r 1.
Para (5): in sub-para (c) word omitted revoked by SI 2012/2806, rr 2, 18(a).
    Date in force: 20 December 2012: see SI 2012/2806, r 1.
Para (5): sub-para (e) and word "; and" immediately preceding it inserted by virtue of SI 2012/2806, rr 2, 18(b).
    Date in force: 20 December 2012: see SI 2012/2806, r 1.

34.2 Meaning of prescribed officer in [the family court]

(1) For the purposes of the 1920 Act, the prescribed officer in relation to [the family court is the court officer].

(2) For the purposes of Part 1 of the 1972 Act and section 5(2) of the 1982 Act, the prescribed officer in relation to [the family court is the court officer].

[(3) For the purposes of an application under Article 30 of the Maintenance Regulation for a declaration of enforceability of a maintenance order or under Article

23(2) or (3) of the 2007 Hague Convention for registration of a maintenance order, the prescribed officer in relation to the family court is the court officer.]

NOTES

Amendment
> Provision heading: words "the family court" in square brackets substituted by SI 2013/3204, rr 2, 106(a).
>> Date in force: 22 April 2014 (being the date on which the Crime and Courts Act 2013, s 17(3) is brought fully into force): see SI 2013/3204, r 1 and SI 2014/954, art 2(a); for transitional provisions and savings see SI 2013/3204, r 137 and SI 2014/954, art 3.
> Para (1): words "the family court is the court officer" in square brackets substituted by SI 2013/3204, rr 2, 106(b).
>> Date in force: 22 April 2014 (being the date on which the Crime and Courts Act 2013, s 17(3) is brought fully into force): see SI 2013/3204, r 1 and SI 2014/954, art 2(a); for transitional provisions and savings see SI 2013/3204, r 137 and SI 2014/954, art 3.
> Para (2): words "the family court is the court officer" in square brackets substituted by SI 2013/3204, rr 2, 106(c).
>> Date in force: 22 April 2014 (being the date on which the Crime and Courts Act 2013, s 17(3) is brought fully into force): see SI 2013/3204, r 1 and SI 2014/954, art 2(a); for transitional provisions and savings see SI 2013/3204, r 137 and SI 2014/954, art 3.
> Para (3): inserted by SI 2013/3204, rr 2, 106(d).
>> Date in force: 22 April 2014 (being the date on which the Crime and Courts Act 2013, s 17(3) is brought fully into force): see SI 2013/3204, r 1 and SI 2014/954, art 2(a); for transitional provisions and savings see SI 2013/3204, r 137 and SI 2014/954, art 3.

34.3 Registration of maintenance orders in [the family court]

Where [the family court] is required by any of the enactments referred to in rule 34.1(2) [or by virtue of the Maintenance Regulation] [or the 2007 Hague Convention] to register a foreign order the court officer must—

(a)   enter . . . a memorandum of the order in the register . . .; and

(b)   state on the memorandum the statutory provision [or international instrument] under which the order is registered.

NOTES

Amendment
> Provision heading: words "the family court" in square brackets substituted by SI 2013/3204, rr 2, 107(a).
>> Date in force: 22 April 2014 (being the date on which the Crime and Courts Act 2013, s 17(3) is brought fully into force): see SI 2013/3204, r 1 and SI 2014/954, art 2(a); for transitional provisions and savings see SI 2013/3204, r 137 and SI 2014/954, art 3.
> Words "the family court" in square brackets substituted by SI 2013/3204, rr 2, 107(b).
>> Date in force: 22 April 2014 (being the date on which the Crime and Courts Act 2013, s 17(3) is brought fully into force): see SI 2013/3204, r 1 and SI 2014/954, art 2(a); for transitional provisions and savings see SI 2013/3204, r 137 and SI 2014/954, art 3.
> Words "or by virtue of the Maintenance Regulation" in square brackets inserted by SI 2011/1328, rr 2, 18.
>> Date in force: 18 June 2011: see SI 2011/1328, r 1.
> Words "or the 2007 Hague Convention" in square brackets inserted by SI 2012/2806, rr 2, 19(a).
>> Date in force: 20 December 2012: see SI 2012/2806, r 1.
> In para (a) first words omitted revoked by SI 2012/679, rr 2, 27.
>> Date in force: 6 April 2012: see SI 2012/679, r 1; for transitional provisions and savings see r 30 thereof.
> In para (a) second words omitted revoked by SI 2013/3204, rr 2, 107(c); for transitional and saving provision see r 137 thereof.
>> Date in force: 22 April 2014 (being the date on which the Crime and Courts Act 2013, s 17(3) is brought fully into force): see SI 2013/3204, r 1 and SI 2014/954, art 2(a); for transitional provisions and savings see SI 2013/3204, r 137 and SI 2014/954, art 3.
> In para (b) words "or international instrument" in square brackets inserted by SI 2012/2806, rr 2, 19(b).
>> Date in force: 20 December 2012: see SI 2012/2806, r 1.

CHAPTER 1

ENFORCEMENT OF MAINTENANCE ORDERS UNDER THE MAINTENANCE ORDERS
(FACILITIES FOR ENFORCEMENT) ACT 1920

34.4 Interpretation

(1) In this Chapter—

"payer", in relation to a maintenance order, means the person liable to make the payments for which the order provides; and

"reciprocating country" means a country or territory to which the 1920 Act extends.

(2) In this Chapter, an expression defined in the 1920 Act has the meaning given to it in that Act.

34.5 Confirmation of provisional orders made in a reciprocating country

(1) This rule applies where, in accordance with section 4(1) of the 1920 Act, the court officer receives a provisional maintenance order.

(2) The court must fix the date, time and place for a hearing.

(3) The court officer must register the order in accordance with rule 34.3.

(4) The court officer must serve on the payer—

    (a) certified copies of the provisional order and accompanying documents; and

    (b) a notice—

        (i) specifying the time and date fixed for the hearing; and

        (ii) stating that the payer may attend to show cause why the order should not be confirmed.

(5) The court officer must inform—

    (a) the court which made the provisional order; and

    (b) the Lord Chancellor,

whether the court confirms, with or without modification, or decides not to confirm, the order.

34.6 Payment of sums due under registered orders

Where an order made by a reciprocating country is registered in [the family court under section 1 of the 1920 Act], the court must order payments due to be made to the court . . ..

(Practice Direction 34A contains further provisions relating to the payment of sums due under registered orders.)

NOTES

Amendment

    Words "the family court under section 1 of the 1920 Act" in square brackets substituted by SI 2013/3204, rr 2, 108(a).
        Date in force: 22 April 2014 (being the date on which the Crime and Courts Act 2013, s 17(3) is brought fully into force): see SI 2013/3204, r 1 and SI 2014/954, art 2(a); for transitional provisions and savings see SI 2013/3204, r 137 and SI 2014/954, art 3.
    Word omitted revoked by SI 2013/3204, rr 2, 108(b).
        Date in force: 22 April 2014 (being the date on which the Crime and Courts Act 2013, s 17(3) is brought fully into force): see SI 2013/3204, r 1 and SI 2014/954, art 2(a); for transitional provisions and savings see SI 2013/3204, r 137 and SI 2014/954, art 3.

34.7 [Collection and enforcement] of sums due under registered orders

[(1) This rule applies to—

    (a) an order made in a reciprocating county which is registered in the family court; and

    (b) a provisional order made in a reciprocating country which has been confirmed by the family court,

where the court has ordered that payments due under the order be made to the court.]
(2)   The court officer must—
- (a)   collect the monies due under the order . . .; and
- (b)   send the monies collected to—
  - (i)   the court in the reciprocating country which made the order; or
  - (ii)   such other person or authority as that court or the Lord Chancellor may from time to time direct.

(3)   The court officer may take proceedings in that officer's own name for enforcing payment of monies due under the order.
[(Rule 32.33 makes provision in relation to a court officer taking such proceedings.)]

NOTES

Amendment
   Provision heading: words "Collection and enforcement" in square brackets substituted by SI 2013/3204, rr 2, 109(a).
      Date in force: 22 April 2014 (being the date on which the Crime and Courts Act 2013, s 17(3) is brought fully into force): see SI 2013/3204, r 1 and SI 2014/954, art 2(a); for transitional provisions and savings see SI 2013/3204, r 137 and SI 2014/954, art 3.
   Para (1): substituted by SI 2013/3204, rr 2, 109(b); for transitional and saving provision see r 137 thereof.
      Date in force: 22 April 2014 (being the date on which the Crime and Courts Act 2013, s 17(3) is brought fully into force): see SI 2013/3204, r 1 and SI 2014/954, art 2(a); for transitional provisions and savings see SI 2013/3204, r 137 and SI 2014/954, art 3.
   Para (2): in sub-para (a) words omitted revoked by SI 2013/3204, rr 2, 109(c).
      Date in force: 22 April 2014 (being the date on which the Crime and Courts Act 2013, s 17(3) is brought fully into force): see SI 2013/3204, r 1 and SI 2014/954, art 2(a); for transitional provisions and savings see SI 2013/3204, r 137 and SI 2014/954, art 3.
   Words in parentheses: inserted by SI 2013/3204, rr 2, 109(d).
      Date in force: 22 April 2014 (being the date on which the Crime and Courts Act 2013, s 17(3) is brought fully into force): see SI 2013/3204, r 1 and SI 2014/954, art 2(a); for transitional provisions and savings see SI 2013/3204, r 137 and SI 2014/954, art 3.

34.8 Prescribed notice for the taking of further evidence
(1)   This rule applies where a court in a reciprocating country has sent a provisional order to [the family court] for the purpose of taking further evidence.
(2)   The court officer must send a notice to the person who applied for the provisional order specifying—
- (a)   the further evidence required; and
- (b)   the time and place fixed for taking the evidence.

NOTES

Amendment
   Para (1): words "the family court" in square brackets substituted by SI 2013/3204, rr 2, 110.
      Date in force: 22 April 2014 (being the date on which the Crime and Courts Act 2013, s 17(3) is brought fully into force): see SI 2013/3204, r 1 and SI 2014/954, art 2(a); for transitional provisions and savings see SI 2013/3204, r 137 and SI 2014/954, art 3.

34.9 Transmission of maintenance orders made in a reciprocating country to the High Court
A maintenance order to be sent by the Lord Chancellor to the High Court in accordance with section 1(1) of the 1920 Act will be—
- (a)   sent to the senior district judge who will register it in the register kept for the purpose of the 1920 Act; and
- (b)   filed in the principal registry.

34.10 Transmission of maintenance orders made in the High Court to a reciprocating country
(1)   This rule applies to maintenance orders made in the High Court.
(2)   An application for a maintenance order to be sent to a reciprocating country under section 2 of the 1920 Act must be made in accordance with this rule.

(3)   The application must be made to a district judge in the principal registry unless paragraph (4) applies.

(4)   If the order was made in the course of proceedings in a district registry, the application may be made to a district judge in that district registry.

(5)   The application must be—

    (a)   accompanied by a certified copy of the order; and

    (b)   supported by a record of the sworn written evidence.

(6)   The written evidence must give—

    (a)   the applicant's reason for believing that the payer resides in the reciprocating country;

    (b)   such information as the applicant has as to the whereabouts of the payer; and

    (c)   such other information as may be set out in Practice Direction 34A.

34.11   Inspection of the register in the High Court

(1)   A person may inspect the register and request copies of a registered order and any document filed with it if the district judge is satisfied that that person is entitled to, or liable to make, payments under a maintenance order made in—

    (a)   the High Court; or

    (b)   a court in a reciprocating country.

(2)   The right to inspect the register referred to in paragraph (1) may be exercised by—

    (a)   a solicitor acting on behalf of the person entitled to, or liable to make, the payments referred to in that paragraph; or

    (b)   with the permission of the district judge, any other person.

CHAPTER 2

ENFORCEMENT OF MAINTENANCE ORDERS UNDER PART 1 OF THE 1972 ACT

34.12   Interpretation

(1)   In this Chapter—

    (a)   "reciprocating country" means a country to which Part 1 of the 1972 Act extends; and

    (b)   'relevant court in the reciprocating country' means, as the case may be—

        (i)   the court which made the order which has been sent to England and Wales for confirmation;

        (ii)   the court which made the order which has been registered in a court in England and Wales;

        (iii) the court to which an order made in England and Wales has been sent for registration; or

        (iv)   the court to which a provisional order made in England and Wales has been sent for confirmation.

(2)   In this Chapter, an expression defined in the 1972 Act has the meaning given to it in that Act.

(3)   In this Chapter, "Hague Convention Countries" means the countries listed in Schedule 1 to the Reciprocal Enforcement of Maintenance Orders (Hague Convention Countries) Order [1993].

NOTES

Amendment

    Para (3): reference to "1993" in square brackets substituted by SI 2011/1328, rr 2, 19.

        Date in force: 18 June 2011: see SI 2011/1328, r 1.

34.13 Scope
(1)   Section 1 of this Chapter contains rules relating to the reciprocal enforcement of maintenance orders under Part 1 of the 1972 Act.

(2)   Section 2 of this Chapter modifies the rules contained in Section 1 of this Chapter in their application to—

    (a)   . . .

    (b)   the Hague Convention Countries; and

    (c)   the United States of America.

[(3)   Section 3 of this Chapter contains a rule in relation to notification of proceedings in a Hague Convention Country or the United States of America.

(4)   Section 4 of this Chapter contains rules in relation to proceedings under Part 2 of the 1972 Act (reciprocal enforcement of claims for the recovery of maintenance).]

(Practice Direction 34A sets out in full the rules for . . . the Hague Convention Countries and the United States of America as modified by Section 2 of this Chapter.)

NOTES

Amendment
> Para (2): sub-para (a) revoked by SI 2011/1328, rr 2, 20(a).
>> Date in force: 18 June 2011: see SI 2011/1328, r 1.
> Paras (3), (4): inserted by SI 2013/3204, rr 2, 111.
>> Date in force: 22 April 2014 (being the date on which the Crime and Courts Act 2013, s 17(3) is brought fully into force): see SI 2013/3204, r 1 and SI 2014/954, art 2(a); for transitional provisions and savings see SI 2013/3204, r 137 and SI 2014/954, art 3.
> Words in parentheses: words omitted revoked by SI 2011/1328, rr 2, 20(b).
>> Date in force: 18 June 2011: see SI 2011/1328, r 1.

SECTION 1

Reciprocal enforcement of maintenance orders under Part 1 of the 1972 Act

34.14 Application for transmission of maintenance order to reciprocating country
An application for a maintenance order to be sent to a reciprocating country under section 2 of the 1972 Act must be made in accordance with Practice Direction 34A.

34.15 Certification of evidence given on provisional orders
A document setting out or summarising evidence is authenticated by a court in England and Wales by a certificate signed, [by the judge] before whom that evidence was given.

(Section 3(5)(b), 5(4) and 9(5) of the 1972 Act require a document to be authenticated by the court.)

NOTES

Amendment
> Words "by the judge" in square brackets substituted by SI 2013/3204, rr 2, 112.
>> Date in force: 22 April 2014 (being the date on which the Crime and Courts Act 2013, s 17(3) is brought fully into force): see SI 2013/3204, r 1 and SI 2014/954, art 2(a); for transitional provisions and savings see SI 2013/3204, r 137 and SI 2014/954, art 3.

34.16 Confirmation of a provisional order made in a reciprocating country
(1)   This rule applies to proceedings for the confirmation of a provisional order made in a reciprocating country[, including proceedings in the family court for the confirmation of a provisional order made in a reciprocating country varying a maintenance order to which section 5(5) or 9(6) of the 1972 Act applies].

(2)   Paragraph (3) applies on receipt by the court of—

    (a)   a certified copy of the order; and

    (b)   the documents required by the 1972 Act to accompany the order.

(3)   On receipt of the documents referred to in paragraph (2)—

(a)   the court must fix the date, time and place for a hearing or a directions appointment; and

(b)   the court officer must send to the payer notice of the date, time and place fixed together with a copy of the order and accompanying documents.

(4)   The date fixed for the hearing must be not less than 21 days beginning with the date on which the court officer sent the documents to the payer in accordance with paragraph (2).

(5)   The court officer will send to the relevant court in the reciprocating country a certified copy of any order confirming or refusing to confirm the provisional order.

(6) ...

(Section 5(5) and 7 of the 1972 Act provide for proceedings for the confirmation of a provisional order.)

...

(Rule 34.22 provides for the transmission of documents to a court in a reciprocating country.)

NOTES

Amendment
    Para (1): words from ", including proceedings in" to "1972 Act applies" in square brackets inserted by SI 2013/3204, rr 2, 113(a).
        Date in force: 22 April 2014 (being the date on which the Crime and Courts Act 2013, s 17(3) is brought fully into force): see SI 2013/3204, r 1 and SI 2014/954, art 2(a); for transitional provisions and savings see SI 2013/3204, r 137 and SI 2014/954, art 3.
    Para (6): revoked by SI 2013/3204, rr 2, 113(b).
        Date in force: 22 April 2014 (being the date on which the Crime and Courts Act 2013, s 17(3) is brought fully into force): see SI 2013/3204, r 1 and SI 2014/954, art 2(a); for transitional provisions and savings see SI 2013/3204, r 137 and SI 2014/954, art 3.
    Second words in parentheses (omitted) revoked by SI 2013/3204, rr 2, 113(c).
        Date in force: 22 April 2014 (being the date on which the Crime and Courts Act 2013, s 17(3) is brought fully into force): see SI 2013/3204, r 1 and SI 2014/954, art 2(a); for transitional provisions and savings see SI 2013/3204, r 137 and SI 2014/954, art 3.

34.17 Consideration of revocation of a provisional order made by [the family court]

(1)   This rule applies where—

(a)   [the family court] has made a provisional order by virtue of section 3 of the 1972 Act;

(b)   before the order is confirmed, evidence is taken by the court or received by it as set out in section 5(9) of the 1972 Act; and

(c)   on consideration of the evidence the court considers that the order ought not to have been made.

(Section 5(9) of the 1972 Act provides that [the family court] may revoke a provisional order made by it, before the order has been confirmed in a reciprocating country, if it receives new evidence.)

(2)   The court officer must serve on the person who applied for the provisional order ("the applicant") a notice which must—

(a)   set out the evidence taken or received by the court;

(b)   inform the applicant that the court considers that the order ought not to have been made; and

(c)   inform the applicant that the applicant may—

     (i)   make representations in relation to that evidence either orally or in writing; and

     (ii)   adduce further evidence.

(3)   If an applicant wishes to adduce further evidence—

(a)   the applicant must notify the court officer at the court which made the order;

(b)   the court will fix a date for the hearing of the evidence; and

(c)   the court officer will notify the applicant in writing of the date fixed.

NOTES

Amendment

> Provision heading: words "the family court" in square brackets substituted by SI 2013/3204, rr 2, 114.
>> Date in force: 22 April 2014 (being the date on which the Crime and Courts Act 2013, s 17(3) is brought fully into force): see SI 2013/3204, r 1 and SI 2014/954, art 2(a); for transitional provisions and savings see SI 2013/3204, r 137 and SI 2014/954, art 3.
>
> Para (1): in sub-para (a) words "the family court" in square brackets substituted by SI 2013/3204, rr 2, 114.
>> Date in force: 22 April 2014 (being the date on which the Crime and Courts Act 2013, s 17(3) is brought fully into force): see SI 2013/3204, r 1 and SI 2014/954, art 2(a); for transitional provisions and savings see SI 2013/3204, r 137 and SI 2014/954, art 3.
>
> Words in parentheses below para (1): words "the family court" in square brackets substituted by SI 2013/3204, rr 2, 114.
>> Date in force: 22 April 2014 (being the date on which the Crime and Courts Act 2013, s 17(3) is brought fully into force): see SI 2013/3204, r 1 and SI 2014/954, art 2(a); for transitional provisions and savings see SI 2013/3204, r 137 and SI 2014/954, art 3.

34.18 Notification of variation or revocation of a maintenance order by the High Court or [the family court]

(1) This rule applies where—

    (a)   a maintenance order has been sent to a reciprocating country in pursuance of section 2 of the 1972 Act; and

    (b)   the court makes an order, not being a provisional order, varying or revoking that order.

(2) The court officer must send a certified copy of the order of variation or revocation to the relevant court in the reciprocating country.

(Rule 34.22 provides for the transmission of documents to a court in a reciprocating country.)

NOTES

Amendment

> Provision heading: words "the family court" in square brackets substituted by SI 2013/3204, rr 2, 115.
>> Date in force: 22 April 2014 (being the date on which the Crime and Courts Act 2013, s 17(3) is brought fully into force): see SI 2013/3204, r 1 and SI 2014/954, art 2(a); for transitional provisions and savings see SI 2013/3204, r 137 and SI 2014/954, art 3.

34.19 Notification of confirmation[, variation] or revocation of a maintenance order by [the family court]

(1) This rule applies where [the family court] makes an order—

    (a)   not being a provisional order, revoking [or varying] a maintenance order to which section 5 of the 1972 Act applies;

    (b)   under section 9 of the 1972 Act, revoking [or varying] a registered order; or

    (c)   under section 7(2) of the 1972 Act, confirming an order to which section 7 of that Act applies.

(2) The court officer must send written notice of the making, [variation,] revocation or confirmation of the order, as appropriate, to the relevant court in the reciprocating country.

(3) . . .

(Section 5 of the 1972 Act applies to a provisional order made by [the family court] in accordance with section 3 of that Act which has been confirmed by a court in a reciprocating country.)

. . .

(Rule 34.22 provides for the transmission of documents to a court in a reciprocating country.)

NOTES

Amendment
Provision heading: word ", variation" in square brackets inserted by SI 2013/3204, rr 2, 116(a)(i).
Date in force: 22 April 2014 (being the date on which the Crime and Courts Act 2013, s 17(3) is brought fully into force): see SI 2013/3204, r 1 and SI 2014/954, art 2(a); for transitional provisions and savings see SI 2013/3204, r 137 and SI 2014/954, art 3.
Provision heading: words "the family court" in square brackets substituted by SI 2013/3204, rr 2, 116(a)(ii).
Date in force: 22 April 2014 (being the date on which the Crime and Courts Act 2013, s 17(3) is brought fully into force): see SI 2013/3204, r 1 and SI 2014/954, art 2(a); for transitional provisions and savings see SI 2013/3204, r 137 and SI 2014/954, art 3.
Para (1): words "the family court" in square brackets substituted by SI 2013/3204, rr 2, 116(b)(i).
Date in force: 22 April 2014 (being the date on which the Crime and Courts Act 2013, s 17(3) is brought fully into force): see SI 2013/3204, r 1 and SI 2014/954, art 2(a); for transitional provisions and savings see SI 2013/3204, r 137 and SI 2014/954, art 3.
Para (1): in sub-paras (a), (b) words "or varying" in square brackets inserted by SI 2013/3204, rr 2, 116(b)(ii).
Date in force: 22 April 2014 (being the date on which the Crime and Courts Act 2013, s 17(3) is brought fully into force): see SI 2013/3204, r 1 and SI 2014/954, art 2(a); for transitional provisions and savings see SI 2013/3204, r 137 and SI 2014/954, art 3.
Para (2): word "variation," in square brackets inserted by SI 2013/3204, rr 2, 116(c).
Date in force: 22 April 2014 (being the date on which the Crime and Courts Act 2013, s 17(3) is brought fully into force): see SI 2013/3204, r 1 and SI 2014/954, art 2(a); for transitional provisions and savings see SI 2013/3204, r 137 and SI 2014/954, art 3.
Para (3): revoked by SI 2013/3204, rr 2, 116(d).
Date in force: 22 April 2014 (being the date on which the Crime and Courts Act 2013, s 17(3) is brought fully into force): see SI 2013/3204, r 1 and SI 2014/954, art 2(a); for transitional provisions and savings see SI 2013/3204, r 137 and SI 2014/954, art 3.
Words in parentheses below para (3): words "the family court" in square brackets substituted by SI 2013/3204, rr 2, 116(e)(i).
Date in force: 22 April 2014 (being the date on which the Crime and Courts Act 2013, s 17(3) is brought fully into force): see SI 2013/3204, r 1 and SI 2014/954, art 2(a); for transitional provisions and savings see SI 2013/3204, r 137 and SI 2014/954, art 3.
Final words omitted revoked by SI 2013/3204, rr 2, 116(e)(ii).
Date in force: 22 April 2014 (being the date on which the Crime and Courts Act 2013, s 17(3) is brought fully into force): see SI 2013/3204, r 1 and SI 2014/954, art 2(a); for transitional provisions and savings see SI 2013/3204, r 137 and SI 2014/954, art 3.

34.20 Taking of evidence for court in reciprocating country

(1) This rule applies where a request is made by or on behalf of a court in a reciprocating country for the taking of evidence for the purpose of proceedings relating to a maintenance order to which Part 1 of the 1972 Act applies.
(Section 14 of the 1972 Act makes provision for the taking of evidence needed for the purpose of certain proceedings.)
(2) The High Court has power to take the evidence where—
    (a)   the request for evidence relates to a maintenance order made by a superior court in the United Kingdom; and
    (b)   the witness resides in England and Wales.
[(3) The family court has power to take evidence where—
    (a)   the request for evidence relates to a maintenance order—
        (i)   made by the family court; or
        (ii)   registered in the family court; or
    (b)   the Lord Chancellor sends to the family court a request to take evidence.
(Practice Direction 34E makes further provision on this matter)]
(6) The evidence is to be taken in accordance with Part 22.

NOTES

Amendment
Para (3): substituted, for paras (3)–(5), by SI 2013/3204, rr 2, 117.

Date in force: 22 April 2014 (being the date on which the Crime and Courts Act 2013, s 17(3) is brought fully into force): see SI 2013/3204, r 1 and SI 2014/954, art 2(a); for transitional provisions and savings see SI 2013/3204, r 137 and SI 2014/954, art 3.

34.21 Request for the taking of evidence by a court in a reciprocating country

(1)   This rule applies where a request is made by [the family court] for the taking of evidence in a reciprocating country in accordance with section 14(5) of the 1972 Act.

(2)   The request must be made in writing to the court in the reciprocating country.

(Rule 34.22 provides for the transmission of documents to a court in a reciprocating country.)

NOTES

Amendment

Para (1): words "the family court" in square brackets substituted by SI 2013/3204, rr 2, 118.
Date in force: 22 April 2014 (being the date on which the Crime and Courts Act 2013, s 17(3) is brought fully into force): see SI 2013/3204, r 1 and SI 2014/954, art 2(a); for transitional provisions and savings see SI 2013/3204, r 137 and SI 2014/954, art 3.

34.22 Transmission of documents

(1)   This rule applies to any document, including a notice or request, which is required to be sent to a court in a reciprocating country by—

(a)   Part 1 of the 1972 Act; or

(b)   Section 1 of Chapter 2 of this Part of these rules.

(2)   The document must be sent to the Lord Chancellor for transmission to the court in the reciprocating country.

34.23 Method of payment under registered orders

(1)   Where an order is registered in [the family court] in accordance with section 6(3) of the 1972 Act, the court must order that the payment of sums due under the order be made—

(a)   to the . . . registering court; and

(b)   at such time and place as the court officer directs.

(Section 6(3) of the 1972 Act makes provision for the registration of maintenance orders made in a reciprocating country.)

(2)   Where the court orders payments to be made [to the court], whether in accordance with paragraph (1) or otherwise, the court officer must send the payments—

(a)   by post to either—

(i)   the court which made the order; or

(ii)   such other person or authority as that court, or the Lord Chancellor, directs; or

(b)   if the court which made the order is a country or territory specified in the Practice Direction 34A—

(i)   to the Crown Agents for Overseas Governments and Administrations for transmission to the person to whom they are due; or

(ii)   as the Lord Chancellor directs.

(Practice Direction 34A contains further provisions relating to the payment of sums due under registered orders.)

NOTES

Amendment

Para (1): words "the family court" in square brackets substituted by SI 2013/3204, rr 2, 119(a)(i).
Date in force: 22 April 2014 (being the date on which the Crime and Courts Act 2013, s 17(3) is brought fully into force): see SI 2013/3204, r 1 and SI 2014/954, art 2(a); for transitional provisions and savings see SI 2013/3204, r 137 and SI 2014/954, art 3.
Para (1): in sub-para (a) words omitted revoked by SI 2013/3204, rr 2, 119(a)(ii).

Date in force: 22 April 2014 (being the date on which the Crime and Courts Act 2013, s 17(3) is brought fully into force): see SI 2013/3204, r 1 and SI 2014/954, art 2(a); for transitional provisions and savings see SI 2013/3204, r 137 and SI 2014/954, art 3.
Para (2): words "to the court" in square brackets substituted by SI 2013/3204, rr 2, 119(b).
Date in force: 22 April 2014 (being the date on which the Crime and Courts Act 2013, s 17(3) is brought fully into force): see SI 2013/3204, r 1 and SI 2014/954, art 2(a); for transitional provisions and savings see SI 2013/3204, r 137 and SI 2014/954, art 3.

34.24 Enforcement of payments under registered orders

(1) This rule applies where a court has ordered periodical payments under a registered maintenance order to be made to the court . . ..

(2) The court officer must take reasonable steps to notify the payee of the means of enforcement available.

(3) Paragraph (4) applies where periodical payments due under a registered order are in arrears.

(4) The court officer, on that officer's own initiative—

    (a)   may; or

    (b)   if the sums due are more than 4 weeks in arrears, must,

proceed in that officer's own name for the recovery of the sums due unless of the view that it is unreasonable to do so.

NOTES

Amendment
Para (1): word omitted revoked by SI 2013/3204, rr 2, 120.
Date in force: 22 April 2014 (being the date on which the Crime and Courts Act 2013, s 17(3) is brought fully into force): see SI 2013/3204, r 1 and SI 2014/954, art 2(a); for transitional provisions and savings see SI 2013/3204, r 137 and SI 2014/954, art 3.

34.25 Notification of registration and cancellation

(1) The court officer must send written notice to the Lord Chancellor of the due registration of orders registered in accordance with section 6(3), 7(5), or 10(4) of the 1972 Act.

(2) The court officer must, when registering an order in accordance with section 6(3), 7(5), 9(10), 10(4) or (5) or 23(3) of the 1972 Act, send written notice to the payer stating—

    (a)   that the order has been registered;

    (b)   that payments under the order should be made to the court officer; and

    (c)   the hours during which and the place at which the payments should be made.

(3) The court officer must, when cancelling the registration of an order in accordance with section 10(1) of the 1972 Act, send written notice of the cancellation to the payer.

SECTION 2
Modification of rules in Section 1 of this Chapter

34.26 . . .

. . .

NOTES

Amendment
Revoked by SI 2011/1328, r 22.
Date in force: 18 June 2011: see SI 2011/1328, r 1; for transitional provision see r 38(2) thereof.

Hague Convention Countries

34.27 Application of Section 1 of this Chapter to the Hague Convention Countries
(1)   In relation to the Hague Convention Countries, Section 1 of this Chapter has effect as modified by this rule.
(2)   A reference in this rule, and in any rule which has effect in relation to the Hague Convention Countries by virtue of this rule to—
    (a)   the 1972 Act is a reference to the 1972 Act as modified by Schedule 2 to the Reciprocal Enforcement of Maintenance Orders (Hague Convention Countries) Order 1993; and
    (b)   a section under the 1972 Act is a reference to the section so numbered in the 1972 Act as so modified.
(3)   A reference to a reciprocating country in rule 34.12(1) and Section 1 of this Chapter is a reference to a Hague Convention Country.
(4)   Rules 34.15 (certification of evidence given on provisional orders), 34.16 (confirmation of provisional orders), 34.19 (notification of confirmation[, variation] or revocation of a maintenance order by [the family court]) and 34.21 (request for the taking of evidence by a court in a reciprocating country) do not apply.
(5)   For rule 34.17 (consideration of revocation of a provisional order made by [the family court]) substitute—

"[**34.17 Consideration of variation or revocation of a maintenance order made by the family court**]
(1)   This rule applies where—
    (a)   an application has been made to [the family court by a payee for the variation or revocation] of an order to which section 5 of the 1972 Act applies; and
    (b)   the payer resides in a Hague Convention Country.
(2)   The court officer must serve on the payee, by post, a copy of any representations or evidence adduced by or on behalf of the payer.
. . .".
(6)   For rule 34.18 (notification of variation or revocation of a maintenance order by the High Court or [the family court]) substitute—

"**34.18 Notification of variation or revocation of a maintenance order by the High Court or [the family court]**
(1)   This rule applies if the High Court or [the family court] makes an order varying or revoking a maintenance order to which section 5 of the 1972 Act applies.
(2)   If the time for appealing has expired without an appeal having been entered, the court officer will send to the Lord Chancellor—
    (a)   the documents required by section 5(8) of the 1972 Act; and
    (b)   a certificate signed by [a judge] stating that the order of variation or revocation is enforceable and no longer subject to the ordinary forms of review.
(3)   A party who enters an appeal against the order of variation or revocation must, at the same time, give written notice to the court officer.".
(7)   For rule 34.23(2) (method of payment under registered orders) substitute—
"(2)   Where the court orders payment to be [made to the court], the court officer must send the payments by post to the payee under the order.".
(8)   For rule 34.25 (notification of registration and cancellation) substitute—

"**34.25 Notification of registration and cancellation**
The court officer must send written notice to—

        (a)   the Lord Chancellor, on the due registration of an order under section 10(4) of the 1972 Act; and

        (b)   the payer under the order, on—

            (i)   the registration of an order under section 10(4) of the 1972 Act; or

            (ii)   the cancellation of the registration of an order under section 10(1) of the 1972 Act.".

(9)   After rule 34.25 insert—

"34.25A General provisions as to notices

(1)   A notice to a payer of the registration of an order in [the family court] in accordance with section 6(3) of the 1972 Act must be in the form referred to in a practice direction.

(Section 6(8) of the 1972 Act requires notice of registration to be given to the payer.)

(2)   If the court sets aside the registration of a maintenance order following an appeal under section 6(9) of the 1972 Act, the court officer must send written notice of the decision to the Lord Chancellor.

(3)   A notice to a payee that the court officer has refused to register an order must be in the form referred to in a practice direction.

(Section 6(11) of the 1972 Act requires notice of refusal of registration to be given to the payee.)

(4)   Where, under any provision of Part 1 of the 1972 Act, a court officer serves a notice on a payer who resides in a Hague Convention Country, the court officer must send to the Lord Chancellor a certificate of service.".

NOTES

Amendment

Para (4): word "variation" in square brackets inserted by SI 2013/3204, rr 2, 122(a)(i).
    Date in force: 22 April 2014 (being the date on which the Crime and Courts Act 2013, s 17(3) is brought fully into force): see SI 2013/3204, r 1 and SI 2014/954, art 2(a); for transitional provisions and savings see SI 2013/3204, r 137 and SI 2014/954, art 3.
Para (4): words "the family court" in square brackets substituted by SI 2013/3204, rr 2, 122(a)(ii).
    Date in force: 22 April 2014 (being the date on which the Crime and Courts Act 2013, s 17(3) is brought fully into force): see SI 2013/3204, r 1 and SI 2014/954, art 2(a); for transitional provisions and savings see SI 2013/3204, r 137 and SI 2014/954, art 3.
Para (5): words "the family court" in square brackets substituted by SI 2013/3204, rr 2, 122(b)(i).
    Date in force: 22 April 2014 (being the date on which the Crime and Courts Act 2013, s 17(3) is brought fully into force): see SI 2013/3204, r 1 and SI 2014/954, art 2(a); for transitional provisions and savings see SI 2013/3204, r 137 and SI 2014/954, art 3.
Para (5): in r 34.17 (as set out) heading substituted by SI 2013/3204, rr 2, 122(b)(ii)(aa).
    Date in force: 22 April 2014 (being the date on which the Crime and Courts Act 2013, s 17(3) is brought fully into force): see SI 2013/3204, r 1 and SI 2014/954, art 2(a); for transitional provisions and savings see SI 2013/3204, r 137 and SI 2014/954, art 3.
Para (5): in r 34.17 (as set out) in para (1)(a) words "the family court by a payee for the variation or revocation" in square brackets substituted by SI 2013/3204, rr 2, 122(b)(ii)(bb).
    Date in force: 22 April 2014 (being the date on which the Crime and Courts Act 2013, s 17(3) is brought fully into force): see SI 2013/3204, r 1 and SI 2014/954, art 2(a); for transitional provisions and savings see SI 2013/3204, r 137 and SI 2014/954, art 3.
Para (5): in r 34.17 (as set out) words omitted revoked by SI 2013/3204, rr 2, 122(b)(ii)(cc).
    Date in force: 22 April 2014 (being the date on which the Crime and Courts Act 2013, s 17(3) is brought fully into force): see SI 2013/3204, r 1 and SI 2014/954, art 2(a); for transitional provisions and savings see SI 2013/3204, r 137 and SI 2014/954, art 3.
Para (6): words "the family court" in square brackets substituted by SI 2013/3204, rr 2, 122(c)(i).
    Date in force: 22 April 2014 (being the date on which the Crime and Courts Act 2013, s 17(3) is brought fully into force): see SI 2013/3204, r 1 and SI 2014/954, art 2(a); for transitional provisions and savings see SI 2013/3204, r 137 and SI 2014/954, art 3.
Para (6): in r 34.18 (as set out) in heading words "the family court" in square brackets substituted by SI 2013/3204, rr 2, 122(c)(ii)(aa).

Date in force: 22 April 2014 (being the date on which the Crime and Courts Act 2013, s 17(3) is brought fully into force): see SI 2013/3204, r 1 and SI 2014/954, art 2(a); for transitional provisions and savings see SI 2013/3204, r 137 and SI 2014/954, art 3.

Para (6): in r 34.18 (as set out) in para (1) words "the family court" in square brackets substituted by SI 2013/3204, rr 2, 122(c)(ii)(aa).

Date in force: 22 April 2014 (being the date on which the Crime and Courts Act 2013, s 17(3) is brought fully into force): see SI 2013/3204, r 1 and SI 2014/954, art 2(a); for transitional provisions and savings see SI 2013/3204, r 137 and SI 2014/954, art 3.

Para (6): in r 34.18 (as set out) in para (2)(b) words "a judge" in square brackets substituted by SI 2013/3204, rr 2, 122(c)(ii)(bb).

Date in force: 22 April 2014 (being the date on which the Crime and Courts Act 2013, s 17(3) is brought fully into force): see SI 2013/3204, r 1 and SI 2014/954, art 2(a); for transitional provisions and savings see SI 2013/3204, r 137 and SI 2014/954, art 3.

Para (7): in r 34.23(2) (as set out) words "made to the court" in square brackets substituted by SI 2013/3204, rr 2, 122(d).

Date in force: 22 April 2014 (being the date on which the Crime and Courts Act 2013, s 17(3) is brought fully into force): see SI 2013/3204, r 1 and SI 2014/954, art 2(a); for transitional provisions and savings see SI 2013/3204, r 137 and SI 2014/954, art 3.

Para (9): in r 34.25A (as set out) in para (1) words "the family court" in square brackets substituted by SI 2013/3204, rr 2, 122(e).

Date in force: 22 April 2014 (being the date on which the Crime and Courts Act 2013, s 17(3) is brought fully into force): see SI 2013/3204, r 1 and SI 2014/954, art 2(a); for transitional provisions and savings see SI 2013/3204, r 137 and SI 2014/954, art 3.

United States of America

34.28 Application of Section 1 of this Chapter to the United States of America

(1)   In relation to the United States of America, Section 1 of this Chapter has effect as modified by this rule.

(2)   A reference in this rule and in any rule which has effect in relation to the United States of America by virtue of this rule to—

   (a)   the 1972 Act is a reference to the 1972 Act as modified by Schedule 1 to the Reciprocal Enforcement of Maintenance Orders (United States of America) Order 2007; and

   (b)   a section under the 1972 Act is a reference to the section so numbered in the 1972 Act as so modified.

(3)   A reference to a reciprocating country in rule 34.12(1) and Section 1 of this Chapter is a reference to the United States of America.

(4)   Rules 34.15 (certification of evidence given on provisional orders), 34.16 (confirmation of provisional orders), 34.19 (notification of confirmation[, variation] or revocation of a maintenance order made by [the family court]) and 34.21 (request for the taking of evidence in a reciprocating country) do not apply.

(5)   For rule 34.17 (consideration of revocation of a provisional order made by [the family court]) substitute—

"**[34.17 Consideration of variation or revocation of a maintenance order made by the family court]**

(1)   This rule applies where—

   (a)   an application has been made to [the family court by a payee for the variation or revocation] of an order to which section 5 of the 1972 Act applies; and

   (b)   the payer resides in the United States of America.

(2)   The court officer must serve on the payee by post a copy of any representations or evidence adduced by or on behalf of the payer.
   . . .".

(6)   For rule 34.18 (notification of variation or revocation), substitute—

"34.18 Notification of variation or revocation

If the High Court or [the family court] makes an order varying or revoking a maintenance order to which section 5 of the 1972 Act applies, the court officer will send to the Lord Chancellor the documents required by section 5(7) of that Act.".

(7) For 34.23(2)(method of payment under registered orders) substitute—

"(2) Where the court orders payment to be [made to the court], the court officer must send the payments by post to the payee under the order.".

(8) For rule 34.25 (notification of registration and cancellation) substitute—

"34.25 Notification of registration and cancellation

The court officer must send written notice to—

(a) the Lord Chancellor, on the due registration of an order under section 10(4) of the 1972 Act; or

(b) the payer under the order, on—

(i) the registration of an order under section 10(4) of the 1972 Act; or

(ii) the cancellation of the registration of an order under section 10(1) of that Act."

NOTES

Amendment

Para (4): word ", variation" in square brackets inserted by SI 2013/3204, rr 2, 123(a)(i).
Date in force: 22 April 2014 (being the date on which the Crime and Courts Act 2013, s 17(3) is brought fully into force): see SI 2013/3204, r 1 and SI 2014/954, art 2(a); for transitional provisions and savings see SI 2013/3204, r 137 and SI 2014/954, art 3.
Para (4): words "the family court" in square brackets substituted by SI 2013/3204, rr 2, 123(a)(ii).
Date in force: 22 April 2014 (being the date on which the Crime and Courts Act 2013, s 17(3) is brought fully into force): see SI 2013/3204, r 1 and SI 2014/954, art 2(a); for transitional provisions and savings see SI 2013/3204, r 137 and SI 2014/954, art 3.
Para (5): words "the family court" in square brackets substituted by SI 2013/3204, rr 2, 123(b)(i).
Date in force: 22 April 2014 (being the date on which the Crime and Courts Act 2013, s 17(3) is brought fully into force): see SI 2013/3204, r 1 and SI 2014/954, art 2(a); for transitional provisions and savings see SI 2013/3204, r 137 and SI 2014/954, art 3.
Para (5): in r 34.17 (as set out) heading substituted by SI 2013/3204, rr 2, 123(b)(ii)(aa).
Date in force: 22 April 2014 (being the date on which the Crime and Courts Act 2013, s 17(3) is brought fully into force): see SI 2013/3204, r 1 and SI 2014/954, art 2(a); for transitional provisions and savings see SI 2013/3204, r 137 and SI 2014/954, art 3.
Para (5): in r 34.17 (as set out) in para (1)(a) words "the family court by a payee for the variation or revocation" in square brackets substituted by SI 2013/3204, rr 2, 123(b)(ii)(bb).
Date in force: 22 April 2014 (being the date on which the Crime and Courts Act 2013, s 17(3) is brought fully into force): see SI 2013/3204, r 1 and SI 2014/954, art 2(a); for transitional provisions and savings see SI 2013/3204, r 137 and SI 2014/954, art 3.
Para (5): in r 34.17 (as set out) in para (2) words omitted revoked by SI 2013/3204, rr 2, 123(b)(ii)(cc).
Date in force: 22 April 2014 (being the date on which the Crime and Courts Act 2013, s 17(3) is brought fully into force): see SI 2013/3204, r 1 and SI 2014/954, art 2(a); for transitional provisions and savings see SI 2013/3204, r 137 and SI 2014/954, art 3.
Para (6): in r 34.18 (as set out) words "the family court" in square brackets substituted by SI 2013/3204, rr 2, 123(c).
Date in force: 22 April 2014 (being the date on which the Crime and Courts Act 2013, s 17(3) is brought fully into force): see SI 2013/3204, r 1 and SI 2014/954, art 2(a); for transitional provisions and savings see SI 2013/3204, r 137 and SI 2014/954, art 3.
Para (7): in r 34.23(2) (as set out) words "made to the court" in square brackets substituted by SI 2013/3204, rr 2, 123(d).
Date in force: 22 April 2014 (being the date on which the Crime and Courts Act 2013, s 17(3) is brought fully into force): see SI 2013/3204, r 1 and SI 2014/954, art 2(a); for transitional provisions and savings see SI 2013/3204, r 137 and SI 2014/954, art 3.

[SECTION 3

Proceedings in a Hague Convention Country or in the United States of America]

NOTES

Amendment
> Inserted by SI 2013/3204, rr 2, 124.
>> Date in force: 22 April 2014 (being the date on which the Crime and Courts Act 2013, s 17(3) is brought fully into force): see SI 2013/3204, r 1 and SI 2014/954, art 2(a); for transitional provisions and savings see SI 2013/3204, r 137 and SI 2014/954, art 3.

[34.28ZA Notification of proceedings in a Hague Convention Country or in the United States of America]
[Practice Direction 34E applies where the court officer receives from the Lord Chancellor notice of the institution of proceedings, including notice of the substance of a claim, in a Hague Convention Country or in the United States of America in relation to the making, variation or revocation of a maintenance order.]

NOTES

Amendment
> Inserted by SI 2013/3204, rr 2, 124.
>> Date in force: 22 April 2014 (being the date on which the Crime and Courts Act 2013, s 17(3) is brought fully into force): see SI 2013/3204, r 1 and SI 2014/954, art 2(a); for transitional provisions and savings see SI 2013/3204, r 137 and SI 2014/954, art 3.

[SECTION 4

Reciprocal enforcement of claims for the recovery of maintenance]

NOTES

Amendment
> Inserted by SI 2013/3204, rr 2, 124.
>> Date in force: 22 April 2014 (being the date on which the Crime and Courts Act 2013, s 17(3) is brought fully into force): see SI 2013/3204, r 1 and SI 2014/954, art 2(a); for transitional provisions and savings see SI 2013/3204, r 137 and SI 2014/954, art 3.

[34.28ZB Interpretation]
[In this Section—
> "convention country" means a country or territory specified in an Order in Council made under section 25 of the 1972 Act; and

an expression defined in the 1972 Act has the meaning given to it in that Act.]

NOTES

Amendment
> Inserted by SI 2013/3204, rr 2, 124.
>> Date in force: 22 April 2014 (being the date on which the Crime and Courts Act 2013, s 17(3) is brought fully into force): see SI 2013/3204, r 1 and SI 2014/954, art 2(a); for transitional provisions and savings see SI 2013/3204, r 137 and SI 2014/954, art 3.

[34.28ZC Dismissal of an application under section 27A of the 1972 Act or application for variation]
[(1) Where the family court dismisses an application under—
    (a)   section 27A of the 1972 Act (application for recovery of maintenance); or
    (b)   an application by a person in a convention country for the variation of a registered order,
the court officer will send a written notice of the court's decision to the Lord Chancellor.
(2) The notice will include a statement of the court's reasons for its decision.]

NOTES

Amendment
>Inserted by SI 2013/3204, rr 2, 124.
>>Date in force: 22 April 2014 (being the date on which the Crime and Courts Act 2013, s 17(3) is brought fully into force): see SI 2013/3204, r 1 and SI 2014/954, art 2(a); for transitional provisions and savings see SI 2013/3204, r 137 and SI 2014/954, art 3.

[34.28ZD Application for recovery of maintenance in England and Wales: section 27B of the 1972 Act]

[(1)   Where the family court receives an application for the recovery of maintenance sent from the Lord Chancellor under section 27B of the 1972 Act, the court will—

    (a)   fix the date, time and place for a hearing or directions appointment, allowing sufficient time for service under this rule to be effected at least 21 days before the date fixed; and

    (b)   serve copies of the application and any accompanying documents, together with a notice stating the date, time and place so fixed, on the respondent.

(2)   Within 14 days of service under this rule, the respondent must file an answer to the application in the form referred to in Practice Direction 5A.]

NOTES

Amendment
>Inserted by SI 2013/3204, rr 2, 124.
>>Date in force: 22 April 2014 (being the date on which the Crime and Courts Act 2013, s 17(3) is brought fully into force): see SI 2013/3204, r 1 and SI 2014/954, art 2(a); for transitional provisions and savings see SI 2013/3204, r 137 and SI 2014/954, art 3.

[34.28ZE Application under section 26(1) or (2) of the 1972 Act and certificate under section 26(3A) of the 1972 Act: registration]

[Where—

    (a)   an application under section 26(1) or (2) of the 1972 Act; or

    (b)   a certificate under section 26(3A) of the 1972 Act,

is required to be registered in the family court by virtue of the Recovery of Maintenance (United States of America) Order 2007, the court officer will enter a minute or memorandum of the application or certificate in the register.]

NOTES

Amendment
>Inserted by SI 2013/3204, rr 2, 124.
>>Date in force: 22 April 2014 (being the date on which the Crime and Courts Act 2013, s 17(3) is brought fully into force): see SI 2013/3204, r 1 and SI 2014/954, art 2(a); for transitional provisions and savings see SI 2013/3204, r 137 and SI 2014/954, art 3.

[34.28ZF Registration of an order: sections 27C(7) and 32(3) and (6) of the 1972 Act]

[(1)   Where the family court makes an order which is required under section 27C(7) of the 1972 Act to be registered, the court officer will enter a minute or memorandum of the order in the register.

(2)   Where a court officer receives under section 32(3) of the 1972 Act a certified copy of an order, the court officer will register the order by means of a minute or memorandum in the register.

(3)   Every minute or memorandum entered under paragraph (1) or (2) will specify the section and subsection of the 1972 Act under which the order in question is registered.

(4)   Where a court officer registers an order as required by section 27C(7) or 32(3) of the 1972 Act, the court officer will send written notice to the Lord Chancellor that the order has been registered.

(5)   Where a court officer is required by section 32(6) of the 1972 Act to give notice of the registration of an order, the court officer will do this by sending written notice to the officer specified in that subsection that the order has been registered.]

NOTES

Amendment
>Inserted by SI 2013/3204, rr 2, 124.
>>Date in force: 22 April 2014 (being the date on which the Crime and Courts Act 2013, s 17(3) is brought fully into force): see SI 2013/3204, r 1 and SI 2014/954, art 2(a); for transitional provisions and savings see SI 2013/3204, r 137 and SI 2014/954, art 3.

[34.28ZG Payments made to the family court]

[(1)   Where payments are made to the family court by virtue of section 27C or 34A of the 1972 Act, the court officer will send those payments by post to such person or authority as the Lord Chancellor may from time to time direct.

(2)   Subject to paragraph (3), if it appears to a court officer that any sums payable under a registered order are in arrears, the officer may proceed in the officer's own name for the recovery of those sums.

(3)   Where it appears to the officer that sums payable under the order are in arrears to an amount equal—

>(a)   in the case of payments to be made monthly or less frequently, to twice the sum payable periodically; or

>(b)   in any other case, to four times the sum payable periodically,

the officer will proceed in the officer's own name for the recovery of those sums, unless it appears to the officer that it is unreasonable in the circumstances to do so.]

NOTES

Amendment
>Inserted by SI 2013/3204, rr 2, 124.
>>Date in force: 22 April 2014 (being the date on which the Crime and Courts Act 2013, s 17(3) is brought fully into force): see SI 2013/3204, r 1 and SI 2014/954, art 2(a); for transitional provisions and savings see SI 2013/3204, r 137 and SI 2014/954, art 3.

[34.28ZH Method of payment]

[(1)   This rule applies where the family court exercises its duties or powers under section 27C or 34A of the 1972 Act.

(2)   Where the court orders that payments under the order are to be made by a particular means—

>(a)   the court will record on the copy of the order the means of payment that the court has ordered; and

>(b)   the court officer will, as soon as practicable, notify, in writing, the person liable to make the payments under the order how payments are to be made.

(3)   Paragraph (4) applies where the court orders that payments be made to the court by a method of payment falling within section 1(5) of the Maintenance Enforcement Act 1991.

(4)   The court officer will notify the person liable to make the payments under the order of sufficient details of the account into which the payments should be made to enable payments to be made into that account.]

NOTES

Amendment
>Inserted by SI 2013/3204, rr 2, 124.
>>Date in force: 22 April 2014 (being the date on which the Crime and Courts Act 2013, s 17(3) is brought fully into force): see SI 2013/3204, r 1 and SI 2014/954, art 2(a); for transitional provisions and savings see SI 2013/3204, r 137 and SI 2014/954, art 3.

[34.28ZI Application under section 34 of the 1972 Act: variation or revocation]

[(1) This rule applies in relation to an application under section 34 of the 1972 Act for the variation or revocation of a registered order.

(2) An application which is made directly to the registering court must be filed in the form referred to in Practice Direction 5A.

(3) Where the court receives an application, either filed in accordance with paragraph (2) or sent from the Lord Chancellor under section 34(3) of the 1972 Act—

  (a) the court will set the date, time and place for a hearing or directions appointment; and

  (b) the court officer will notify the applicant of the date, time and place.]

NOTES

Amendment
  Inserted by SI 2013/3204, rr 2, 124.
    Date in force: 22 April 2014 (being the date on which the Crime and Courts Act 2013, s 17(3) is brought fully into force): see SI 2013/3204, r 1 and SI 2014/954, art 2(a); for transitional provisions and savings see SI 2013/3204, r 137 and SI 2014/954, art 3.

[34.28ZJ Application under section 35 of the 1972 Act: variation or revocation]

[(1) This rule applies in relation to an application under section 35 of the 1972 Act for the variation or revocation of a registered order.

(2) Notice under section 35(3)(b) of the 1972 Act of the time and place appointed for the hearing of the application will be in the form specified in Practice Direction 34D.

(3) The court officer will send the notice by post to the Lord Chancellor for onward transmission to the appropriate authority in the convention country in which the respondent is residing.

(4) The time appointed for the hearing of the application will not be less than six weeks later than the date on which the notice is sent to the Lord Chancellor.]

NOTES

Amendment
  Inserted by SI 2013/3204, rr 2, 124.
    Date in force: 22 April 2014 (being the date on which the Crime and Courts Act 2013, s 17(3) is brought fully into force): see SI 2013/3204, r 1 and SI 2014/954, art 2(a); for transitional provisions and savings see SI 2013/3204, r 137 and SI 2014/954, art 3.

[34.28ZK Request under section 38(1) of the 1972 Act to the family court]

[(1) This rule applies where the family court receives from the Lord Chancellor a request under section 38(1) of the 1972 Act (taking evidence at the request of a court in a convention country) to take the evidence of any person.

(2) Subject to paragraph (3)—

  (a) the evidence will be taken in the same manner as if the person concerned were a witness in family proceedings;

  (b) any oral evidence so taken will be put into writing and read to the person who gave it, who must sign the document; and

  (c) the judge who takes any such evidence of any person will certify at the foot of the document setting out the evidence of, or produced in evidence by, that person that such evidence was taken, or document received in evidence, as the case may be, by that judge.

(3) Where the request referred to in section 38(2) of the 1972 Act includes a request that the evidence be taken in a particular manner, the court by which the evidence is taken will, so far as circumstances permit, comply with that request.]

NOTES

Amendment
  Inserted by SI 2013/3204, rr 2, 124.

Date in force: 22 April 2014 (being the date on which the Crime and Courts Act 2013, s 17(3) is brought fully into force): see SI 2013/3204, r 1 and SI 2014/954, art 2(a); for transitional provisions and savings see SI 2013/3204, r 137 and SI 2014/954, art 3.

[34.28ZL Request under section 38(1) of the 1972 Act to the officer of the court]

[(1) This rule applies where an officer of the court receives from the Lord Chancellor a request under section 38(1) of the 1972 Act to take the evidence of any person.

(2) Subject to paragraph (3)—

(a) the person whose evidence is to be taken will be examined on oath by or before a [justices' legal adviser] or any other court officer determined by the Lord Chancellor;

(b) any oral evidence will be put into writing and read to the person who gave it, who must sign the document; and

(c) the [justices' legal adviser] or other officer will certify at the foot of the document setting out the evidence of, or produced by, that person, that such evidence was taken, or document received in evidence, as the case may be, by that justices' clerk or other officer.

(3) Where the request referred to in section 38(1) of the 1972 Act includes a request that the evidence be taken in a particular manner, the [justices' legal adviser] or other officer by whom the evidence is taken will, so far as circumstances permit, comply with that request.

(4) For the purposes of this rule, the [justices' legal adviser] or other officer has the same power to administer oaths as a single justice of the peace.]

NOTES

Amendment

Inserted by SI 2013/3204, rr 2, 124.
Date in force: 22 April 2014 (being the date on which the Crime and Courts Act 2013, s 17(3) is brought fully into force): see SI 2013/3204, r 1 and SI 2014/954, art 2(a); for transitional provisions and savings see SI 2013/3204, r 137 and SI 2014/954, art 3.
Para (2): in sub-paras (a), (c) words "justices' legal adviser" in square brackets in each place they occur substituted by SI 2020/135, rr 2, 29.
Date in force: 6 April 2020: see SI 2020/135, r 1.
Para (3): words "justices' legal adviser" in square brackets substituted by SI 2020/135, rr 2, 29.
Date in force: 6 April 2020: see SI 2020/135, r 1.
Para (4): words "justices' legal adviser" in square brackets substituted by SI 2020/135, rr 2, 29.
Date in force: 6 April 2020: see SI 2020/135, r 1.

[34.28ZM Onward transmission of documents]

[Any document mentioned in rule 34.28ZK(2)(c) or rule 34.28ZL(2)(c) will be sent to the Lord Chancellor for onward transmission to the appropriate authority in the convention country in which the request referred to in section 38(1) of the 1972 Act originated.]

NOTES

Amendment

Inserted by SI 2013/3204, rr 2, 124.
Date in force: 22 April 2014 (being the date on which the Crime and Courts Act 2013, s 17(3) is brought fully into force): see SI 2013/3204, r 1 and SI 2014/954, art 2(a); for transitional provisions and savings see SI 2013/3204, r 137 and SI 2014/954, art 3.

CHAPTER 3

ENFORCEMENT OF MAINTENANCE ORDERS UNDER THE CIVIL JURISDICTION AND
JUDGMENTS ACT 1982, THE JUDGMENTS REGULATION[, THE MAINTENANCE
REGULATION][, THE 2007 HAGUE CONVENTION] AND THE LUGANO CONVENTION

NOTES

Amendment
> Chapter heading: words ", the Maintenance Regulation" in square brackets inserted by SI
> 2011/1328, rr 2, 23.
>> Date in force: 18 June 2011: see SI 2011/1328, r 1.
> Chapter heading: words ", the 2007 Hague Convention" in square brackets inserted by SI
> 2012/2806, rr 2, 20.
>> Date in force: 20 December 2012: see SI 2012/2806, r 1.

[34.28A Application of this Chapter]
[(1) In this Chapter—
   [(a)   references to a maintenance order include—
      (i)   a decision, a court settlement or an authentic instrument within
             the meaning of Article 2 of the Maintenance Regulation where
             that Regulation applies;
      (ii)   a maintenance decision to which Chapter V of the 2007
             Hague Convention applies by virtue of Article 19(1) of
             that Convention;
      (iii) a maintenance arrangement (as defined in Article 3(e) of the 2007
             Hague Convention) which is to be recognised and enforceable in
             the same way as a maintenance decision by virtue of Article 30 of
             that Convention;]
   (b)   references to the Hague Protocol are to the Protocol on the Law
          Applicable to Maintenance Obligations done at The Hague on
          23 November 2007[;
   (c)   "the 1968 Convention" has the meaning given in the 1982 Act].
(2) In relation to the Maintenance Regulation—
   (a)   Section 1 applies to maintenance orders to which Sections 2 and 3 of
          Chapter IV of the Maintenance Regulation apply (decisions given in a
          Member State which does not apply the rules of the Hague Protocol, that
          is, Denmark, and decisions to which Sections 2 and 3 of Chapter IV of
          that Regulation apply by virtue of Article 75(2)(a) or (b));
   (b)   Section 2 applies to all maintenance orders made in a magistrates' court
          in England and Wales for which reciprocal enforcement is sought in any
          Member State of the European Union, including Denmark.
. . .]

NOTES

Amendment
> Inserted by SI 2011/1328, rr 2, 24.
>> Date in force: 18 June 2011: see SI 2011/1328, r 1.
> Para (1): sub-para (a) substituted by SI 2012/2806, rr 2, 21.
>> Date in force: 20 December 2012: see SI 2012/2806, r 1.
> Para (1): sub-para (c) inserted by SI 2012/679, rr 2, 28(a), (b).
>> Date in force: 6 April 2012: see SI 2012/679, r 1; for transitional provisions and
>> savings see r 30 thereof.
> Words omitted revoked by SI 2013/3204, rr 2, 125; for transitional and saving provision see
> r 137 thereof.
>> Date in force: 22 April 2014 (being the date on which the Crime and Courts Act 2013,
>> s 17(3) is brought fully into force): see SI 2013/3204, r 1 and SI 2014/954, art 2(a);
>> for transitional provisions and savings see SI 2013/3204, r 137 and SI 2014/954, art 3.

SECTION 1
Registration and Enforcement in a Magistrates' Court of Maintenance Orders made in a Contracting State to the 1968 Convention, a Contracting State to the 1988 Convention, a Regulation State[, a State bound by the 2007 Hague Convention other than a Member State of the European Union] or a State bound by the Lugano Convention

NOTES

Amendment
> Cross-heading: words from ", a State bound" to "the European Union" in square brackets inserted by SI 2012/2806, rr 2, 22.
>> Date in force: 20 December 2012: see SI 2012/2806, r 1.

34.29 Interpretation
In this Section—

    (a)   an expression defined in the 1982 Act has the meaning given to it in that Act[, subject to paragraph (b)]; and

    [(b)   "Regulation State" means a Member State of the European Union which does not apply the rules of the Hague Protocol, or, where registration is sought for a maintenance order to which Article 75(2)(a) or (b) of the Maintenance Regulation applies, the Member State of the European Union from which the order originated].

NOTES

Amendment
> In para (a) words ", subject to paragraph (b)" in square brackets inserted by SI 2011/1328, rr 2, 25(a).
>> Date in force: 18 June 2011: see SI 2011/1328, r 1.
> Para (b) substituted by SI 2011/1328, rr 2, 25(b).
>> Date in force: 18 June 2011: see SI 2011/1328, r 1.

[34.29A . . .]
[. . .]

NOTES

Amendment
> Inserted by SI 2011/1328, rr 2, 26.
>> Date in force: 18 June 2011: see SI 2011/1328, r 1.
> Revoked by SI 2013/3204, rr 2, 126.
>> Date in force: 22 April 2014 (being the date on which the Crime and Courts Act 2013, s 17(3) is brought fully into force): see SI 2013/3204, r 1 and SI 2014/954, art 2(a); for transitional provisions and savings see SI 2013/3204, r 137 and SI 2014/954, art 3.

34.30 Registration of maintenance orders
(1)   ...

(2)   [This rule and Practice Direction 34E apply where the family court] receives—

    (a)   an application under Article 31 of the 1968 Convention for the enforcement of a maintenance order made in a Contracting State other than the United Kingdom;

    (b)   an application under Article 31 of the 1988 Convention for the enforcement of a maintenance order made in a State bound by the 1988 Convention other than a Member State of the European Union;

    [(c)   an application under Article 26 of the Maintenance Regulation for a declaration of enforceability of a maintenance order made in a Regulation State other than the United Kingdom; . . .]

    (d)   an application under Article 38 of the Lugano Convention for the enforcement of a maintenance order made in a State bound by the Lugano Convention other than a Member State of the European Union[; or

      (e)   an application under Article 23 of the 2007 Hague Convention for registration of a maintenance order made in a State bound by that Convention other than a Member State of the European Union].

(3) . . .

(4) . . .

(5) . . .

(6)   Except where [Practice Direction 34E provides otherwise, the court] must register the order unless—

      (a)   in the case of an application under Article 31 of the 1968 Convention, Articles 27 or 28 of that Convention apply; . . .

      (b)   in the case of an application under Article 31 of the 1988 Convention, Articles 27 or 28 of that Convention apply[; and

      (c)   in the case of an application under Article 23(2) or (3) of the 2007 Hague Convention, Article 22(a) of that Convention applies].

(7)   If the court . . . refuses to register an order to which this rule relates the court officer must notify the applicant.

(8)   If the court . . . registers an order the court officer must send written notice of that fact to—

      (a)   the Lord Chancellor;

      (b)   the payer; and

      (c)   the applicant.

(9) . . .

NOTES

Amendment

    Para (1): revoked by SI 2013/3204, rr 2, 127(a).
        Date in force: 22 April 2014 (being the date on which the Crime and Courts Act 2013, s 17(3) is brought fully into force): see SI 2013/3204, r 1 and SI 2014/954, art 2(a); for transitional provisions and savings see SI 2013/3204, r 137 and SI 2014/954, art 3.
    Para (2): words "This rule and Practice Direction 34E apply where the family court" in square brackets substituted by SI 2013/3204, rr 2, 127(b).
        Date in force: 22 April 2014 (being the date on which the Crime and Courts Act 2013, s 17(3) is brought fully into force): see SI 2013/3204, r 1 and SI 2014/954, art 2(a); for transitional provisions and savings see SI 2013/3204, r 137 and SI 2014/954, art 3.
    Para (2): sub-para (c) substituted by SI 2011/1328, rr 2, 27.
        Date in force: 18 June 2011: see SI 2011/1328, r 1; for transitional provisions see r 38(1)(a), (3) thereof.
    Para (2): in sub-para (c) word omitted revoked by SI 2012/2806, rr 2, 24(a)(i).
        Date in force: 20 December 2012: see SI 2012/2806, r 1.
    Para (2): sub-para (e) and word "; or" immediately preceding it inserted by SI 2012/2806, rr 2, 24(a)(ii).
        Date in force: 20 December 2012: see SI 2012/2806, r 1.
    Paras (3)–(5): revoked by SI 2013/3204, rr 2, 127(c).
        Date in force: 22 April 2014 (being the date on which the Crime and Courts Act 2013, s 17(3) is brought fully into force): see SI 2013/3204, r 1 and SI 2014/954, art 2(a); for transitional provisions and savings see SI 2013/3204, r 137 and SI 2014/954, art 3.
    Para (6): words "Practice Direction 34E provides otherwise, the court" in square brackets substituted by SI 2013/3204, rr 2, 127(d).
        Date in force: 22 April 2014 (being the date on which the Crime and Courts Act 2013, s 17(3) is brought fully into force): see SI 2013/3204, r 1 and SI 2014/954, art 2(a); for transitional provisions and savings see SI 2013/3204, r 137 and SI 2014/954, art 3.
    Para (6): in sub-para (a) word omitted revoked by SI 2012/2806, rr 2, 24(b)(i).
        Date in force: 20 December 2012: see SI 2012/2806, r 1.
    Para (6): sub-para (c) and word "; and" immediately preceding it inserted by SI 2012/2806, rr 2, 24(b)(ii).
        Date in force: 20 December 2012: see SI 2012/2806, r 1.
    Para (7): word omitted revoked by SI 2013/3204, rr 2, 127(e).
        Date in force: 22 April 2014 (being the date on which the Crime and Courts Act 2013, s 17(3) is brought fully into force): see SI 2013/3204, r 1 and SI 2014/954, art 2(a); for transitional provisions and savings see SI 2013/3204, r 137 and SI 2014/954, art 3.
    Para (8): word omitted revoked by SI 2013/3204, rr 2, 127(e).

Date in force: 22 April 2014 (being the date on which the Crime and Courts Act 2013, s 17(3) is brought fully into force): see SI 2013/3204, r 1 and SI 2014/954, art 2(a); for transitional provisions and savings see SI 2013/3204, r 137 and SI 2014/954, art 3.
Para (9): revoked by SI 2013/3204, rr 2, 127(f).
Date in force: 22 April 2014 (being the date on which the Crime and Courts Act 2013, s 17(3) is brought fully into force): see SI 2013/3204, r 1 and SI 2014/954, art 2(a); for transitional provisions and savings see SI 2013/3204, r 137 and SI 2014/954, art 3.

34.31 Appeal from a decision relating to registration

(1)   This rule applies to an appeal under—

(a)   Article 36 or Article 40 of the 1968 Convention;

(b)   Article 36 or Article 40 of the 1988 Convention;

[(c)   Article 32 of the Maintenance Regulation; . . .]

(d)   Article 43 of the Lugano Convention[; or

(e)   Article 23(5) of the 2007 Hague Convention].

[(2)   The appeal must be to the family court.

(Practice Direction 34E makes provision in relation to such cases.)]

NOTES

Amendment
Para (1): sub-para (c) substituted by SI 2011/1328, rr 2, 28.
Date in force: 18 June 2011: see SI 2011/1328, r 1; for transitional provisions see r 38(1)(a), (3) thereof.
Para (1): in sub-para (c) word omitted revoked by SI 2012/2806, rr 2, 25(a).
Date in force: 20 December 2012: see SI 2012/2806, r 1.
Para (1): sub-para (e) and word "; or" immediately preceding it inserted by SI 2012/2806, rr 2, 25(b).
Date in force: 20 December 2012: see SI 2012/2806, r 1.
Para (2) and words in parentheses: substituted, for para (2) as originally enacted, by SI 2013/3204, rr 2, 128.
Date in force: 22 April 2014 (being the date on which the Crime and Courts Act 2013, s 17(3) is brought fully into force): see SI 2013/3204, r 1 and SI 2014/954, art 2(a); for transitional provisions and savings see SI 2013/3204, r 137 and SI 2014/954, art 3.

34.32 Payment of sums due under a registered order

(1)   Where an order is registered in accordance with section 5(3) of the 1982 Act[,] Article 38 of the Judgments Regulation[,] Article 38 of the Lugano Convention [or Article 23 of the 2007 Hague Convention] [or declared enforceable under Article 26 of the Maintenance Regulation by virtue of registration], the court [may] order that payment of sums due under the order be made [to the court, at such time and place as directed].

(2)   Where the court orders payments to be made to the court . . ., whether in accordance with paragraph (1) or otherwise, the court officer must send the payments by post either—

(a)   to the court which made the order; or

(b)   to such other person or authority as that court, or the Lord Chancellor, directs.

(Practice Direction 34A contains further provisions relating to the payment of sums due under registered orders.)

NOTES

Amendment
Para (1): first comma in square brackets substituted by SI 2011/1328, rr 2, 29(a).
Date in force: 18 June 2011: see SI 2011/1328, r 1.
Para (1): final comma in square brackets substituted by SI 2012/2806, rr 2, 26(a).
Date in force: 20 December 2012: see SI 2012/2806, r 1.
Para (1): words "or Article 23 of the 2007 Hague Convention" in square brackets inserted by SI 2012/2806, rr 2, 26(b).
Date in force: 20 December 2012: see SI 2012/2806, r 1.
Para (1): words from "or declared enforceable" to "virtue of registration" in square brackets inserted by SI 2011/1328, rr 2, 29(b).
Date in force: 18 June 2011: see SI 2011/1328, r 1.

Family Procedure Rules 2010 **A1.1**

Para (1): word "may" in square brackets substituted by SI 2013/3204, rr 2, 129(a)(i).
> Date in force: 22 April 2014 (being the date on which the Crime and Courts Act 2013,
> s 17(3) is brought fully into force): see SI 2013/3204, r 1 and SI 2014/954, art 2(a);
> for transitional provisions and savings see SI 2013/3204, r 137 and SI 2014/954, art 3.

Para (1): words "to the court, at such time and place as directed" in square brackets
substituted by SI 2013/3204, rr 2, 129(a)(ii).
> Date in force: 22 April 2014 (being the date on which the Crime and Courts Act 2013,
> s 17(3) is brought fully into force): see SI 2013/3204, r 1 and SI 2014/954, art 2(a);
> for transitional provisions and savings see SI 2013/3204, r 137 and SI 2014/954, art 3.

Para (2): word omitted revoked by SI 2013/3204, rr 2, 129(b).
> Date in force: 22 April 2014 (being the date on which the Crime and Courts Act 2013,
> s 17(3) is brought fully into force): see SI 2013/3204, r 1 and SI 2014/954, art 2(a);
> for transitional provisions and savings see SI 2013/3204, r 137 and SI 2014/954, art 3.

34.33 Enforcement of payments under registered orders

(1)   This rule applies where a court has ordered periodical payments under a registered maintenance order to be made to the [the family court].

(2)   The court officer must take reasonable steps to notify the payee of the means of enforcement available.

(3)   Paragraph (4) applies where periodical payments due under a registered order are in arrears.

(4)   The court officer, on that officer's own initiative—

> (a)   may; or
> (b)   if the sums due are more than 4 weeks in arrears, must,

proceed in that officer's own name for the recovery of the sums due unless of the view that it is unreasonable to do so.

NOTES

Amendment
> Para (1): words "the family court" in square brackets substituted by SI 2013/3204, rr 2, 130.
>> Date in force: 22 April 2014 (being the date on which the Crime and Courts Act 2013,
>> s 17(3) is brought fully into force): see SI 2013/3204, r 1 and SI 2014/954, art 2(a);
>> for transitional provisions and savings see SI 2013/3204, r 137 and SI 2014/954, art 3.

34.34 Variation and revocation of registered orders

(1)   This rule applies where the court officer for a registering court receives notice that a registered maintenance order has been varied or revoked by a competent court in a Contracting State to the 1968 Convention, a Contracting State to the 1988 Convention (other than a Member State of the European Union), a Regulation State or a State bound by the Lugano Convention [or by the 2007 Hague Convention], other than a Member State of the European Union.

(2)   The court officer for the registering court must—

> (a)   register the order of variation or revocation; and
> (b)   send notice of the registration by post to the payer and payee under the order.

[(3)   Where the court officer for a registering court receives notice that a maintenance order registered in that court by virtue of the provisions of the Judgments Regulation has been varied or revoked by a competent court in another Member State of the European Union, the court officer must—

> (a)   note against the entry in the register that the original order so registered has been varied or revoked, as the case may be; and
> (b)   send notice of the noting of the variation or revocation, as the case may be, by post to the payer and payee under the order.]

NOTES

Amendment
> Para (1): words "or by the 2007 Hague Convention" in square brackets inserted by SI 2012/2806, rr 2, 27.
>> Date in force: 20 December 2012: see SI 2012/2806, r 1.
> Para (3): inserted by SI 2011/1328, rr 2, 30.

Date in force: 18 June 2011: see SI 2011/1328, r 1.

[34.35 Registered order: payer residing in an area covered by a different Maintenance Enforcement Business Centre]

[Practice Direction 34E makes provision for cases where a court officer in the Maintenance Enforcement Business Centre for the Designated Family Judge area where an order is registered considers that the payer is residing in a Designated Family Judge area covered by a different Maintenance Enforcement Business Centre.

(For the way in which information will be provided to enable Maintenance Enforcement Business Centres to be identified, see Practice Direction 34E.)]

NOTES

Amendment
Substituted by SI 2015/1420, rr 2, 24.
Date in force: 31 July 2015: see SI 2015/1420, r 1(3).

34.36 Cancellation of registered orders

[(1) Where the court officer for the registering court—

(a)   has no reason to send papers to another Maintenance Enforcement Business Centre under Practice Direction 34E; and

(b)   considers that the payer under the registered order is not residing within the area covered by the Maintenance Enforcement Business Centre for the Designated Family Judge area where the order is registered and has no assets in England and Wales,

the court officer must cancel the registration.]

(2)   The court officer must—

(a)   give notice of cancellation to the payee; and

[(b)   send to the Lord Chancellor—

(i)   the information and documents relating to the registration;

(ii)   a certificate of arrears, if applicable, signed by the court officer;

(iii)   a statement giving such information as the court officer possesses as to the whereabouts of the payer and the nature and location of the payer's assets; and

(iv)   any other relevant documents which the court officer has relating to the case].

[(Practice Direction 34E makes further provision on this matter.)]

NOTES

Amendment
Para (1): substituted by SI 2015/1420, rr 2, 25.
Date in force: 31 July 2015: see SI 2015/1420, r 1(3).
Para (2): sub-para (b) substituted and parenthesis inserted by SI 2015/913, rr 2, 13.
Date in force: 1 July 2015: see SI 2015/913, r 1; for transitional provision see r 14.

[34.36A Directions as to stays, documents and translations]

[At any stage in proceedings for registration of a maintenance order under this Section of this Chapter, the court may give directions about the conduct of the proceedings, including—

(a)   staying of proceedings in accordance with—

(i)   Article 30 or 38 of the 1968 Convention,

(ii)   Article 30 or 38 of the 1988 Convention,

(iii)   Article 37 or 46 of the Lugano Convention, . . .

(iv)   Article 25 or 35 of the Maintenance Regulation[, or

(v)   Article 30(6) of the 2007 Hague Convention];

(b)   the provision of documents in accordance with—

(i)   Article 48 of the 1968 Convention,

> (ii) Article 48 of the 1988 Convention,
> (iii) Article 55 of the Lugano Convention, . . .
> (iv) Article 29 of the Maintenance Regulation[, or
> (v) Article 25 or 30 of the 2007 Hague Convention];
>
> (c) the provision of translations in accordance with—
>> (i) Article 48 of the 1968 Convention,
>> (ii) Article 48 of the 1988 Convention,
>> (iii) Article 55 of the Lugano Convention, . . .
>> (iv) Article 28 of the Maintenance Regulation[, or
>> (v) in relation to an application under this Section relating to the 2007 Hague Convention, without prejudice to Article 44 of that Convention].]

NOTES

Amendment
Inserted by SI 2011/1328, rr 2, 32.
 Date in force: 18 June 2011: see SI 2011/1328, r 1; for transitional provisions see r 38(1)(b), (3) thereof.
In para (a)(iii) word omitted revoked by SI 2012/2806, rr 2, 29(a)(i).
 Date in force: 20 December 2012: see SI 2012/2806, r 1.
Para (a)(v) and word ", or" immediately preceding it inserted by SI 2012/2806, rr 2, 29(a)(ii).
 Date in force: 20 December 2012: see SI 2012/2806, r 1.
In para (b)(iii) word omitted revoked by SI 2012/2806, rr 2, 29(b)(i).
 Date in force: 20 December 2012: see SI 2012/2806, r 1.
Para (b)(v) and word ", or" in square brackets inserted by SI 2012/2806, rr 2, 29(b)(ii).
 Date in force: 20 December 2012: see SI 2012/2806, r 1.
In para (c)(iii) word omitted revoked by SI 2012/2806, rr 2, 29(c)(i).
 Date in force: 20 December 2012: see SI 2012/2806, r 1.
Para (c)(v) and word ", or" immediately preceding it inserted by SI 2012/2806, rr 2, 29(c)(ii).
 Date in force: 20 December 2012: see SI 2012/2806, r 1.

[34.36B International Maintenance Obligations; Communication with the Central Authority for England and Wales]
[(1) Where the Lord Chancellor requests information or a document from the court officer for the relevant court for the purposes of Article 58 of the Maintenance Regulation, or Article 12 or 25(2) of the 2007 Hague Convention, the court officer shall provide the requested information or document to the Lord Chancellor forthwith.

(2) In this rule, "relevant court" means the court at which an application under Article 56 of the Maintenance Regulation or Article 10 of the 2007 Hague Convention has been filed.

[The Lord Chancellor is the Central Authority for the 2007 Hague Convention and the Maintenance Regulation]]

NOTES

Amendment
Inserted by SI 2012/2806, rr 2, 30.
 Date in force: 20 December 2012: see SI 2012/2806, r 1.

[34.36C The Maintenance Regulation: applications for enforcement or for refusal or suspension of enforcement]
[Practice Direction 34E makes provision regarding—
 (a) an application for enforcement of a maintenance decision to which section 1 of Chapter IV of the Maintenance Regulation applies; and
 (b) an application by a debtor under Article 21 of the Maintenance Regulation for refusal or suspension of enforcement.]

NOTES

Amendment
> Inserted by SI 2013/3204, rr 2, 133.
>> Date in force: 22 April 2014 (being the date on which the Crime and Courts Act 2013, s 17(3) is brought fully into force): see SI 2013/3204, r 1 and SI 2014/954, art 2(a); for transitional provisions and savings see SI 2013/3204, r 137 and SI 2014/954, art 3.

SECTION 2
Reciprocal enforcement in a Contracting State or [a Member State of the European Union] of Orders of a court in England and Wales

NOTES

Amendment
> Cross-heading: words "a Member State of the European Union" in square brackets substituted by SI 2011/1328, rr 2, 33.
>> Date in force: 18 June 2011: see SI 2011/1328, r 1.

34.37 ...

...

NOTES

Amendment
> Revoked by SI 2011/1328, rr 2, 34.
>> Date in force: 18 June 2011: see SI 2011/1328, r 1.

34.38 Admissibility of Documents

(1)   This rule applies to a document, referred to in paragraph (2) and authenticated in accordance with paragraph (3), which comprises, records or summarises evidence given in, or information relating to, proceedings in a court in another part of the UK , another Contracting State to the 1968 Convention or the 1988 Convention, [Member State of the European Union] or State bound by the Lugano Convention, [or by the 2007 Hague Convention,] and any reference in this rule to "the court", without more, is a reference to that court.

(2)   The documents referred to at paragraph (1) are documents which purport to—

    (a)   set out or summarise evidence given [to] the court;

    (b)   have been received in evidence [to] the court;

    (c)   set out or summarise evidence taken in the court for the purpose of proceedings in a court in England and Wales to which the 1982 Act[, the Judgments Regulation[,] the Maintenance Regulation] [or the 2007 Hague Convention] applies; or

    (d)   record information relating to payments made under an order of the court.

(3)   A document to which paragraph (1) applies shall, in any proceedings in [the family court] relating to a maintenance order to which the 1982 Act[, the Judgments Regulation[,] the Maintenance Regulation] [or the 2007 Hague Convention] applies, be admissible as evidence of any fact stated in it to the same extent as oral evidence of that fact is admissible in those proceedings.

(4)   A document to which paragraph (1) applies shall be deemed to be authenticated—

    (a)   in relation to the documents listed at paragraph 2(a) or (c), if the document purports to be—

        (i)   certified by the judge or official before whom the evidence was given or taken; or

        (ii)   the original document recording or summarising the evidence, or a true copy of that document;

(b)   in relation to a document listed at paragraph (2)(b), if the document purports to be certified by a judge or official of the court to be, or to be a true copy of, the document received in evidence; and

(c)   in relation to the document listed at paragraph (2)(d), if the document purports to be certified by a judge or official of the court as a true record of the payments made under the order.

(5)   It shall not be necessary in any proceedings in which evidence is to be received under this rule to prove the signature or official position of the person appearing to have given the certificate referred to in paragraph (4).

(6)   Nothing in this rule shall prejudice the admission in evidence of any document which is admissible in evidence apart from this rule.

[(7)   Any request by [the family court] for the taking or providing of evidence by a court in a State listed in paragraph (8) for the purposes of proceedings to which an instrument listed in that paragraph applies, or by a court in another part of the United Kingdom, shall be communicated in writing to the court in question.

(8)   The States and instruments referred to in paragraph (7) are—

(a)   a Contracting State to the 1968 Convention;

(b)   a Contracting State to the 1988 Convention;

(c)   a State bound by the Lugano Convention;

(d)   Denmark, in relation to proceedings to which the Maintenance Regulation applies;

(e)   a State bound by the 2007 Hague Convention,

but this paragraph and paragraph (7) do not apply where the State in question is a Member State of the European Union to which the Taking of Evidence Regulation (as defined in rule 24.15) applies.]

(Chapter 2 of Part 24 makes provision for taking of evidence by a court in another [Member State of the European Union]).

NOTES

Amendment

Para (1): words "Member State of the European Union" in square brackets substituted by SI 2011/1328, rr 2, 35(a).
    Date in force: 18 June 2011: see SI 2011/1328, r 1.
Para (1): words "or by the 2007 Hague Convention," in square brackets inserted by SI 2012/2806, rr 2, 31(a).
    Date in force: 20 December 2012: see SI 2012/2806, r 1.
Para (2): in sub-para (a) word "to" in square brackets substituted by SI 2011/1328, rr 2, 35(b)(i).
    Date in force: 18 June 2011: see SI 2011/1328, r 1.
Para (2): in sub-para (b) word "to" in square brackets inserted by SI 2011/1328, rr 2, 35(b)(ii).
    Date in force: 18 June 2011: see SI 2011/1328, r 1.
Para (2): in sub-para (c) words ", the Judgments Regulation or the Maintenance Regulation" in square brackets inserted by SI 2011/1328, rr 2, 35(b)(iii).
    Date in force: 18 June 2011: see SI 2011/1328, r 1.
Para (2): in sub-para (c) comma in square brackets substituted by SI 2012/2806, rr 2, 31(b)(i).
    Date in force: 20 December 2012: see SI 2012/2806, r 1.
Para (2): in sub-para (c) words "or the 2007 Hague Convention" in square brackets inserted by SI 2012/2806, rr 2, 31(b)(ii).
    Date in force: 20 December 2012: see SI 2012/2806, r 1.
Para (3): words "the family court" in square brackets substituted by SI 2013/3204, rr 2, 134.
    Date in force: 22 April 2014 (being the date on which the Crime and Courts Act 2013, s 17(3) is brought fully into force): see SI 2013/3204, r 1 and SI 2014/954, art 2(a); for transitional provisions and savings see SI 2013/3204, r 137 and SI 2014/954, art 3.
Para (3): words ", the Judgments Regulation or the Maintenance Regulation" in square brackets inserted by SI 2011/1328, rr 2, 35(c).
    Date in force: 18 June 2011: see SI 2011/1328, r 1.
Para (3): comma in square brackets substituted by SI 2012/2806, rr 2, 31(c)(i).
    Date in force: 20 December 2012: see SI 2012/2806, r 1.

Para (3): words "or the 2007 Hague Convention" in square brackets inserted by SI 2012/2806, rr 2, 31(c)(ii).
> Date in force: 20 December 2012: see SI 2012/2806, r 1.

Paras (7), (8): substituted, for para (7) as originally enacted, by SI 2012/2806, rr 2, 31(d).
> Date in force: 20 December 2012: see SI 2012/2806, r 1.

Para (7): words "the family court" in square brackets substituted by SI 2013/3204, rr 2, 134.
> Date in force: 22 April 2014 (being the date on which the Crime and Courts Act 2013, s 17(3) is brought fully into force): see SI 2013/3204, r 1 and SI 2014/954, art 2(a); for transitional provisions and savings see SI 2013/3204, r 137 and SI 2014/954, art 3.

Words in parentheses: words "Member State of the European Union" in square brackets substituted by SI 2011/1328, rr 2, 35(e).
> Date in force: 18 June 2011: see SI 2011/1328, r 1.

34.39 Enforcement of orders of [the family court]

[(1)   A person who wishes to enforce a maintenance order obtained in [the family court] in a State to which paragraph (2) applies must apply for a certified copy of the order and, where required by Practice Direction 34A, a certificate giving particulars relating to the judgment and proceedings in which it was given.

(2)   The States referred to in paragraph (1) are—

- (a)   a Contracting State to the 1968 Convention;
- (b)   a Contracting State to the 1988 Convention (other than a Member State of the European Union);
- (c)   a Member State of the European Union;
- (d)   a State bound by the Lugano Convention (other than a Member State of the European Union); or
- (e)   a State bound by the 2007 Hague Convention (other than a Member State of the European Union).]

(3)   An application under this rule must be made in writing to the court officer and must specify—

- (a)   the names of the parties to the proceedings;
- (b)   the date, or approximate date, of the proceedings in which the maintenance order was made and the nature of those proceedings;
- (c)   the [State] in which the application for recognition or enforcement has been made or is to be made; and
- (d)   the postal address of the applicant.

(4)   The court officer must, on receipt of the application, send a copy of the order to the applicant certified in accordance with . . . practice direction [34A][, together with a copy of any certificate required by that practice direction].

(5)   Paragraph (6) applies where—

- (a)   a maintenance order is registered in [the family court]; and
- (b)   a person wishes to obtain a certificate giving details of any payments made or arrears accrued under the order while it has been registered, for the purposes of an application made or to be made in connection with that order in—
  - (i)   another Contracting State to the 1968 Convention;
  - (ii)   another Contracting State to the 1988 Convention (other than a Member State of the European Union);
  - (iii)   another [Member State of the European Union];
  - (iv)   another State bound by the Lugano Convention (other than a Member State of the European Union); . . .
  - (v)   another part of the United Kingdom[; or
  - (vi)   another State bound by the 2007 Hague Convention (other than a Member State of the European Union)].

(6)   The person wishing to obtain the certificate referred to in paragraph (5) may make a written application to the court officer for the registering court.

(7) On receipt of an application under paragraph (6) the court officer must send to the applicant a certificate giving the information requested.

(Rule 74.12 (application for certified copy of a judgment) and 74.13 (evidence in support) of the CPR apply in relation to the application for a certified copy of a judgment obtained in the High Court or a county court.)

NOTES

Amendment

Provision heading: words "the family court" in square brackets substituted by SI 2013/3204, rr 2, 135(a).

Date in force: 22 April 2014 (being the date on which the Crime and Courts Act 2013, s 17(3) is brought fully into force): see SI 2013/3204, r 1 and SI 2014/954, art 2(a); for transitional provisions and savings see SI 2013/3204, r 137 and SI 2014/954, art 3.

Paras (1), (2): substituted by SI 2012/2806, rr 2, 32(a).

Date in force: 20 December 2012: see SI 2012/2806, r 1.

Para (1): words "the family court" in square brackets substituted by SI 2013/3204, rr 2, 135(a).

Date in force: 22 April 2014 (being the date on which the Crime and Courts Act 2013, s 17(3) is brought fully into force): see SI 2013/3204, r 1 and SI 2014/954, art 2(a); for transitional provisions and savings see SI 2013/3204, r 137 and SI 2014/954, art 3.

Para (3): in sub-para (c) word "State" substituted by SI 2012/679, rr 2, 29.

Date in force: 6 April 2012: see SI 2012/679, r 1; for transitional provisions and savings see r 30 thereof.

Para (4): word omitted revoked by SI 2012/2806, rr 2, 32(b)(i).

Date in force: 20 December 2012: see SI 2012/2806, r 1.

Para (4): reference to "34A" in square brackets inserted by SI 2012/2806, rr 2, 32(b)(ii).

Date in force: 20 December 2012: see SI 2012/2806, r 1.

Para (4): words from ", together with a" to "that practice direction" in square brackets substituted by SI 2012/2806, rr 2, 32(b)(iii).

Date in force: 20 December 2012: see SI 2012/2806, r 1.

Para (5): in sub-para (a) words "the family court" in square brackets substituted by SI 2013/3204, rr 2, 135(b).

Date in force: 22 April 2014 (being the date on which the Crime and Courts Act 2013, s 17(3) is brought fully into force): see SI 2013/3204, r 1 and SI 2014/954, art 2(a); for transitional provisions and savings see SI 2013/3204, r 137 and SI 2014/954, art 3.

Para (5): in sub-para (b)(iii) words "Member State of the European Union" in square brackets substituted by SI 2011/1328, rr 2, 36(e).

Date in force: 18 June 2011: see SI 2011/1328, r 1.

Para (5): in sub-para (b)(iv) word omitted revoked by SI 2012/2806, rr 2, 32(c)(i).

Date in force: 20 December 2012: see SI 2012/2806, r 1.

Para (5): sub-para (b)(vi) and word "; or" immediately preceding it inserted by SI 2012/2806, rr 2, 32(c)(ii).

Date in force: 20 December 2012: see SI 2012/2806, r 1.

[34.40 Enforcement of orders of the High Court or [the family court]]

[(1) This rule applies where a person wishes to enforce a maintenance order obtained in the High Court or [the family court] in a Member State of the European Union or a State bound by the 2007 Hague Convention (other than a Member State of the European Union).

(2) Subject to the requirements of Practice Direction 34A, rules 74.12 (application for a certified copy of a judgment) and 74.13 (evidence in support) of the CPR apply in relation to—

  (a)   an application under Article 40(2) of the Maintenance Regulation for a certified copy of a judgment and an extract relating to that judgment in the form of Annex II to that Regulation;

  (b)   an application for a certified copy of a judgment and a certificate giving particulars relating to the judgment and the proceedings in which it was given.]

NOTES

Amendment

Substituted by SI 2012/2806, rr 2, 33.

Date in force: 20 December 2012: see SI 2012/2806, r 1.

Provision heading: words "the family court" in square brackets substituted by SI 2013/3204, rr 2, 136(a).

    Date in force: 22 April 2014 (being the date on which the Crime and Courts Act 2013, s 17(3) is brought fully into force): see SI 2013/3204, r 1 and SI 2014/954, art 2(a); for transitional provisions and savings see SI 2013/3204, r 137 and SI 2014/954, art 3.

Para (1): words "the family court" in square brackets substituted by SI 2013/3204, rr 2, 136(b).

    Date in force: 22 April 2014 (being the date on which the Crime and Courts Act 2013, s 17(3) is brought fully into force): see SI 2013/3204, r 1 and SI 2014/954, art 2(a); for transitional provisions and savings see SI 2013/3204, r 137 and SI 2014/954, art 3.

PART 35
MEDIATION DIRECTIVE

35.1 Scope and Interpretation

(1)   This Part applies to mediated cross-border disputes that are subject to Directive 2008/52/EC of the European Parliament and of the Council of 21 May 2008 on certain aspects of mediation in civil and commercial matters ("the Mediation Directive").

(2)   In this Part—

    "cross-border dispute" has the meaning given by article 2 of the Mediation Directive;

    "mediation" has the meaning given by article 3(a) of the Mediation Directive;

    "mediation administrator" means a person involved in the administration of the mediation process;

    "mediation evidence" means evidence regarding information arising out of or in connection with a mediation process;

    "mediator" has the meaning given by article 3(b) of the Mediation Directive; and

    "relevant dispute" means a cross-border dispute that is subject to the Mediation Directive.

35.2 Relevant disputes: applications for consent orders in respect of financial remedies

(1)   This rule applies in relation to proceedings for a financial remedy where the applicant, with the explicit consent of the respondent, wishes to make an application that the content of a written agreement resulting from mediation of a relevant dispute be made enforceable by being made the subject of a consent order.

(2)   The court will not include in a consent order any matter which is contrary to the law of England and Wales or which is not enforceable under that law.

(3)   The applicant must file two copies of a draft of the order in the terms sought.

(4)   Subject to paragraph (5), the application must be supported by evidence of the explicit consent of the respondent.

(5)   Where the respondent has written to the court consenting to the making of the order sought, the respondent is deemed to have given explicit consent to the order and paragraph (4) does not apply.

(6)   Paragraphs (1)(b) and (2) to (6) of rule 9.26 apply to an application to which this rule applies.

35.3 Mediation evidence: disclosure and inspection

(1)   Where a party to proceedings seeks disclosure or inspection of mediation evidence that is in the control of a mediator or mediation administrator, that party must first obtain the court's permission to seek the disclosure or inspection, by an application made in accordance with Part 18.

(2)   The mediator or mediation administrator who has control of the mediation evidence must be named as a respondent to the application and must be served with a copy of the application notice.

(3)   Evidence in support of the application must include evidence that—

(a)   all parties to the mediation agree to the disclosure or inspection of the mediation evidence;

(b)   disclosure or inspection of the mediation evidence is necessary for overriding considerations of public policy, in accordance with article 7(1)(a) of the Mediation Directive; or

(c)   the disclosure of the content of an agreement resulting from mediation is necessary to implement or enforce that agreement.

(4)   Where this rule applies, Parts 21 to 24 apply to the extent they are consistent with this rule.

35.4 Mediation evidence: witnesses and depositions

(1)   This rule applies where a party wishes to obtain mediation evidence from a mediator or mediation administrator by—

(a)   a witness summons;

(b)   cross-examination with permission of the court under rule 22.8 or 23.4;

(c)   an order under rule 24.7 (evidence by deposition);

(d)   an order under rule 24.9 (enforcing attendance of witness);

(e)   an order under rule 24.10(4) (deponent's evidence to be given orally); or

(f)   an order under rule 24.12 (order for the issue of a letter of request).

(2)   When applying for a witness summons, permission under rule 22.8 or 23.4 or order under rule24.7, 24.9, 24.10(4) or24.12, the party must provide the court with evidence that-

(a)   all parties to the mediation agree to the obtaining of the mediation evidence;

(b)   obtaining the mediation evidence is necessary for overriding considerations of public policy in accordance with article 7(1)(a) of the Mediation Directive; or

(c)   the disclosure of the content of an agreement resulting from mediation is necessary to implement or enforce that agreement.

(3)   When considering a request for a witness summons, permission under rule 22.8 or 23.4 or order under rule 24.7, 24.9, 24.10(4) or 24.12, the court may invite any person, whether or not a party, to make representations.

(4)   Where this rule applies, Parts 21 to 24 apply to the extent they are consistent with this rule.

PRACTICE DIRECTION 5A – FORMS

This Practice Direction supplements FPR Part 5, rule 5.1 (Forms)

SCOPE AND INTERPRETATION

1.1 This Practice Direction lists the forms to be used in family proceedings on or after 6 April 2011. Table 1 lists the forms against the part of the FPR to which they are relevant, and Table 2 lists the forms individually with their description.

1.2 The forms may be—

(a) modified as the circumstances require, provided that all essential information, especially information or guidance which the form gives to the recipient, is included;

(b) expanded to include additional pages where that may be necessary, provided that any additional pages are also verified by a statement of truth.

1.3 Any reference in family proceedings forms to a Part, rule or Practice Direction is to be read as a reference to the equivalent Part, rule or Practice Direction in the FPR and any reference to a Practice Direction in any CPR form used in family proceedings is to be read as a reference to the equivalent Practice Direction in the FPR.

. . .

APPLICATION NOTICES

2.2 Where an application under the Part 18 procedure is to be made by application notice, the forms to be used are:

(i) Form C2 where the application is made in the course of or in connection with proceedings under Part 12;

(ii) Subject to sub-paragraphs (iii) and (iv), Form D11 where the application is made in the course of or in connection with proceedings under Parts 7, 8 or 9;

(iii) Form D650 where the application is to vary or set aside a financial order where a Form E calculator error has been identified in an online HMCTS FormFinder Form E and the applicant asserts that this has materially or significantly affected the order;

(iv) Form D651 where the application is to vary or set aside an order made in financial remedy proceedings where a Form E1 calculator error has been identified in an online HMCTS FormFinder Form E1 and the applicant asserts that this has materially or significantly affected the order;

(v) Form N244 where the application is made in the course of or in connection with appeal proceedings in the family court;

(vi) Form FP244 where the application is made in the course of or in connection with appeal proceedings in the High Court;

(vii) Form FP2 in any other case.

OTHER FORMS

3.1 Other forms may be authorised by practice directions.

FPR Part	Forms
Part 3 Alternative Dispute Resolution (Family Mediation)	FM1
Part 6 Service	C9, D5, D89, FL415, FP6

FPR Part	Forms
Part 7 Matrimonial and Civil Partnership Proceedings	D6, D8, D8 Notes, D8A, D8B, D8D, D8D Notes, D8N, D8N Notes, D9B, D11, D13B, D20, D36, D80A, D80B, D80C, D80D, D80E, D80F, D80G, D81, D84,
Part 8 Miscellaneous Applications	D50, D50A, D50B, D50C, D50D, D50E, D50F, D50G, D50H, D50J, D50K
Part 8 Chapter 5 Applications for declarations	C63, C64, C65, D70
Part 9 Applications for a Financial Remedy	Form A, Form A1, Form B, Form E, Form E Notes, Form E1, Form E2, Form F, Form I, Form P, Form P1, Form P2, Form PPF, Form PPF1, Form PPF2
Part 10 Applications under Part 4 of the Family Law Act 1996	FL401, FL403, FL407, FL415
Part 11 Applications under Part 4A of the Family Law Act 1996 or Part 1 of Schedule 2 to the Female Genital Mutilation Act 2003	FGM001, FGM003, FGM005, FGM006, FGM007, FL401A, FL403A, FL407A, FL430, FL431
Part 12 Applications in respect of children	C1, C1A, C2, C3, C4, C5, C8, C9, C12, C13A, C14, C15, C16, C18, C19, C20, C66, C67, C68, C78, C79, C100, C110A, C(PRA1), C(PRA2) C(PRA3), PLO8, PLO9, PLP10 (PLO8 and PLO9 do not apply to Part 4 proceedings)
Part 13 Applications under section 54 of Human Fertilisation and Embryology Act 2008	C51, C52, A64A, A101A
Part 14 Adoption	A4, A5, A50, A51, A52, A53, A54, A55, A56, A57, A58, A59, A60, A61, A62, A63, A50 Notes, A51 Notes, A52 Notes, A53 Notes, A54 Notes, A55 Notes, A56 Notes, A57 Notes, A58 Notes, A59 Notes, A60 Notes, A61 Notes, A62 Notes, A63 Notes, A64, A65, A100, A101, A102, A103, A104, A105, A106, A107
Part 15 Representation of Protected Parties	FP9
Part 16 Representation of children	FP9
Part 18 Applications in proceedings	C2, D11, D650, D651, FP2
Part 19 Alternative Procedure for applications	FP1, FP1A, FP1B, FP3, FP5
Part 22 Evidence	N285
Part 24 Witnesses	FP25
Part 26 Notification of change of solicitor	FP8
Part 28 Costs	D252, D254, D258, D258A, D258B, D258C, D259, Form H, Form H1, N260
Part 30 Appeals	FP161, FP161A, FP162, FP162A, N161, N161A, N161B, N161D, N162, N162A, N162, N164

FPR Part	Forms
Part 31 Registration of Orders under the Hague Convention 1996	C69
Part 32 Registration and Enforcement of Orders	D151
Part 33 Enforcement	D62, N323, N349
Part 34 Reciprocal Enforcement of Maintenance Orders	REMO 1, REMO 2
Part 37	Form No. 67
Part 39	FE15, FE16, FE17
Part 40	FE6, FE7

Number	Name
A4	Application for Revocation of an Order Freeing a Child for Adoption
A5	Application for Substitution of One Adoption Agency for Another
A50	Application for a placement order Section 22 Adoption and Children Act 2002
A51	Application for variation of a placement order Section 23 Adoption and Children Act 2002
A52	Application for revocation of a placement order Section 24 Adoption and Children Act 2002
A53	Application for a contact order Section 26 of the Adoption and Children Act 2002 or an order for contact or prohibiting contact under section 51A of the Adoption and Children Act 2002
A54	Application for variation or revocation of a contact order Section 27(1)(b) or Section 51B(1)(c) Adoption and Children Act 2002
A55	Application for permission to change a child's surname Section 28 Adoption and Children Act 2002
A56	Application for permission to remove a child from the United Kingdom Section 28 Adoption and Children Act 2002
A57	Application for a recovery order Section 41 Adoption and Children Act 2002
A58	Application for an adoption order Section 46 Adoption and Children Act 2002
A59	Application for a Convention adoption order Section 46 Adoption and Children Act 2002
A60	Application for an adoption order (excluding a Convention adoption order) where the child is habitually resident outside the British Islands and is brought into the United Kingdom for the purposes of adoption Section 46 Adoption and Children Act 2002
A61	Application for an order for parental responsibility prior to adoption abroad Section 84 Adoption and Children Act 2002
A62	Application for a direction under section 88(1) of the Adoption and Children Act 2002
A63	Application for an order to annul a Convention adoption or Convention adoption order or for an overseas adoption or determination under section 91 to cease to be valid Section 89 Adoption and Children Act 2002
A50 Notes	Application for a placement order Section 22 Adoption and Children Act 2002 – Notes on completing the form

Number	Name
A51 Notes	Application for variation of a placement order Section 23 Adoption and Children Act 2002 – Notes on completing the form
A52 Notes	Application for revocation of a placement order Section 24 Adoption and Children Act 2002 – Notes on completing the form
A53 Notes	Application for a contact order Section 26 Adoption and Children Act 2002 or an order under section 51A of the Act – Notes on completing the form
A54 Notes	Application for variation or revocation of a contact order Section 27(1)(b) or section 51B(1)(c) Adoption and Children Act 2002 – Notes on completing the form
A55 Notes	Application for permission to change a child's surname Section 28 Adoption and Children Act 2002 – Notes on completing the form
A56 Notes	Application for permission to remove a child from the United Kingdom Section 28 Adoption and Children Act 2002 – Notes on completing the form
A57 Notes	Application for a recovery order Section 41 Adoption and Children Act 2002 – Notes on completing the form
A58 Notes	Application for an adoption order Section 46 Adoption and Children Act 2002 – Notes on completing the form
A59 Notes	Application for a Convention adoption order Section 46 Adoption and Children Act 2002 – Notes on completing the form
A60 Notes	Application for an adoption order (excluding a Convention adoption order) where the child is habitually resident outside the British Islands and is brought into the United Kingdom for the purposes of adoption Section 46 Adoption and Children Act 2002 – Notes on completing the form
A61 Notes	Application for an order for parental responsibility prior to adoption abroad Section 84 Adoption and Children Act 2002 – Notes on completing the form
A62 Notes	Application for a direction under section 88(1) of the Adoption and Children Act 2002 – Notes on completing the form
A63 Notes	Application for an order to annul a Convention adoption or Convention adoption order or for an overseas adoption or determination under section 91 to cease to be valid Section 89 Adoption and Children Act 2002 – Notes on completing the form
A64	Application to receive information from court records Section 60(4) Adoption and Children Act 2002
A64A	Application to receive information from court records about a parental order Section 60(4) Adoption and Children Act 2002
A65	Confidential information
A100	Consent to the placement of my child for adoption with any prospective adopters chosen by the Adoption Agency Section 19 of the Adoption and Children Act 2002
A101	Consent to the placement of my child for adoption with identified prospective adopters Section 19 of the Adoption and Children Act 2002
A101A	Agreement to the making of a parental order in respect of my child Section 54 of the Human Fertilisation and Embryology Act 2008
A102	Consent to the placement of my child for adoption with identified prospective adopter(s) and, if the placement breaks down, with any prospective adopter(s) chosen by the adoption agency Section 19 of the Adoption and Children Act 2002

Number	Name
A103	Advance Consent to Adoption Section 20 of the Adoption and Children Act 2002
A104	Consent to Adoption. The Adoption and Children Act 2002
A105	Consent to the making of an Order under Section 84 of the Adoption and Children Act 2002
A106	Withdrawal of Consent Sections 19 and 20 of the Adoption and Children Act 2002
A107	Consent by the child's parent to adoption by their partner The Adoption and Children Act 2002
C1	Application for an Order
C1A	Allegations of harm and domestic violence (Supplemental information form)
C2	Application For permission to start proceedings For an order or directions in existing proceedings To be joined as, or cease to be, a party in existing family proceedings under the Children Act 1989
C3	Application for an order authorising search for, taking charge of and delivery of child
C4	Application for an order for disclosure of a child's whereabouts
C5	Local Authority application concerning the registration of a childminder or a provider of day care
C8	Confidential contact details
C9	Statement of service
C12	Supplement for an application for a warrant to assist a person authorised by an Emergency Protection Order
C13A	Supplement for an application for a Special Guardianship Order Section 14A Children Act 1989
C14	Supplement for an application for authority to refuse contact with a child in care
C15	Supplement for an application for contact with a child in care
C16	Supplement for an application for a Child Assessment Order
C18	Supplement for an application for a Recovery Order
C19	Application for a warrant of assistance
C20	Supplement for an application for an order to hold a child in Secure Accommodation
C51	Application for a Parental Order Section 54 Human Fertilisation and Embryology Act 2008
C52	Acknowledgement of an application for a Parental Order
C63	Application for declaration of parentage under section 55A of the Family Law Act 1986
C64	Application for declaration of legitimacy or legitimation under section 56(1)(b) and (2) of the Family Law Act 1986
C65	Application for declaration as to adoption effected overseas under section 57 of the Family Law Act 1986
C66	Application for inherent jurisdiction order in relation to children
C67	Application under the Child Abduction and Custody Act 1985
C68	Application for international transfer of jurisdiction to or from England and Wales

Number	Name
C69	Application for registration, recognition or non-recognition of a judgment under the 1996 Hague Convention
C78	Application for attachment of a warning notice to a child arrangements order
C79	Application related to enforcement of a child arrangements order
C100	Application under the Children Act 1989 for a child arrangements, prohibited steps or specific issue section 8 order or to vary or discharge a section 8 order
C110A	Application for a Care or Supervision Order and other orders under Part 4 of the Children Act 1989 or an Emergency Protection Order under section 44 of the Children Act 1989
C(PRA1)	Parental Responsibility Agreement
C(PRA2)	Step Parent Parental Responsibility Agreement
C(PRA3)	Parental Responsibility Agreement Section 4ZA Children Act 1989 (Acquisition of parental responsibility by second female parent)
D5	Notice to be indorsed on documents served in accordance with rule 6.14
D6	Statement of Reconciliation
D8	Divorce/dissolution/(judicial) separation petition
D8 Notes	Supporting notes for guidance on completing a divorce/dissolution/(judicial) separation petition
D8A	Statement of arrangements for children
D8B	Answer to a divorce/dissolution/(judicial) separation or nullity petition
D8D	Petition for a presumption of death order and dissolution of a civil partnership
D8D Notes	Supporting notes for guidance on completing a petition for a presumption of death order and dissolution of a civil partnership
D8N	Nullity petition
D8N Notes	Supporting notes for guidance on completing a nullity petition
D9B	Particulars of person whose address is being sought where details are unknown
D11	Application Notice
D13B	Statement in support of a request to dispense with service of the divorce/dissolution/nullity/(judicial) separation petition on the Respondent
D20	Medical Examination: statement of parties & examiner
D36	Notice of Application for Decree Nisi to be made Absolute or Conditional Order to be made final
D50	Notice of application under section 17 of the Married Women's Property Act 1882/section 66 of the Civil Partnership Act 2004
D50A	Statement in support of divorce/ (judicial) separation – adultery
D50B	Statement in support of divorce/ dissolution/ (judicial) separation – unreasonable behaviour
D50C	Statement in support of divorce/ dissolution/ (judicial) separation – desertion
D50D	Statement in support of divorce/ dissolution/ (judicial) separation – 2 years consent

Number	Name
D50E	Statement in support of divorce/ dissolution/ (judicial) separation – 5 years separation
D50F	Statement in support of annulment – void marriage/ civil partnership
D50G	Statement in support of annulment – voidable marriage/ civil partnership
D81	Statement of information for a Consent Order in relation to a financial remedy
D84	Application for a decree nisi/conditional order or (judicial) separation decree/order
D89	Request for personal service by a court bailiff
D151	Application for registration of maintenance order in the family court
D252	Notice of commencement of assessment of bill of costs.
D254	Request for a default costs certificate
D258	Request for a detailed assessment of hearing
D258A	Request for detailed assessment (legal aid only)
D258B	Request for detailed assessment (Costs payable out of a fund other than the Community Legal Service Fund)
D258C	Request for detailed assessment hearing pursuant to an order under Part III of the Solicitors Act 1974
D259	Notice of appeal against a detailed assessment (divorce)
D650	Notice of application to vary or set aside a financial order (Form E calculator error)
D651	Notice of application to vary or set aside a financial remedy (Form E1 calculator error)
FE6	Application for a charging order on land or property
FE7	Application for a charging order on securities
FE15	Request for attachment of earnings order
FE16	Request and result of search in the attachment of earnings index
FE17	Form for replying to an attachment of earnings application (statement of means)
FGM001	Application for a Female Genital Mutilation (FGM) Protection Order
FGM003	Application to vary, extend or discharge a Female Genital Mutilation (FGM) Protection Order
FGM005	Application for a warrant of arrest – Female Genital Mutilation Protection Order
FGM006	Application for leave to apply for a Female Genital Mutilation (FGM) Protection Order
FGM007	Application to be joined as, or cease to be, a party to a Female Genital Mutilation (FGM) Protection Order
FL401	Application for a non-molestation order/an occupation order
FL401A	Application for a Forced Marriage Protection Order
FL403	Application to vary, extend or discharge
FL403A	Application to vary, extend or discharge Forced Marriage Protection Orders
FL407	Applications for warrant of Arrest
FL407A	Application for warrant of arrest for a Forced Marriage Protection Order

Number	Name
FL415	Statement of service
FL430	Application for leave to apply for a Forced Marriage Protection Order
FL431	Application to join / cease as a party to Forced Marriage Protection Proceedings
FM1	Family Mediation Information and Assessment Form FM1
Form A	Notice of [intention to proceed with] an application for a financial order (NOTE: This form should be used whether the applicant is proceeding with an application in the petition or making a freestanding application)
Form A1	Notice of [intention to proceed with] an application for a financial remedy (other than a financial order) in the family or high court
Form B	Notice of an application to consider the financial position of the Respondent after the divorce/dissolution
Form E	Financial statement – For a financial order (other than a variation order) under the Matrimonial Causes Act 1973/Civil Partnership Act 2004 – For financial relief after an overseas divorce etc under Part 3 of the Matrimonial and Family Proceedings Act 1984/Schedule 7 to the Civil Partnership Act 2004
Form E Notes	Form E (Financial Statement for a financial order (other than a variation order) or for financial relief after an overseas divorce or dissolution etc) Notes for guidance
Form E1	Financial Statement for a financial remedy (other than a financial order or financial relief after an overseas divorce/dissolution etc) in the family or high court
Form E2	Financial Statement for a variation of an order for a financial remedy
Form F	Notice of allegation in proceedings for financial remedy
Form H	Estimate of costs (financial remedy)
Form H1	Statement of Costs (financial remedy)
Form I	Notice of request for periodical payments order at the same rate as order for interim maintenance pending outcome of proceeding
Form P	Pension inquiry form
Form P1	Pension sharing annex
Form P2	Pension attachment annex
Form PPF	Pension Protection Fund Inquiry Form
Form No 67	Writ of sequestration (rule 37.26)
Form PPF1	Pension Protection Fund sharing annex
Form PPF2	Pension Protection Fund attachment annex
FP1	Application under Part 19 of the Family Procedure Rules 2010
FP1A	Application under Part 19 of the Family Procedure Rules 2010 Notes for applicant on completing the application (Form FP1)
FP1B	Application under Part 19 of the Family Procedure Rules 2010 Notes for respondent
FP2	Application notice Part 18 of the Family Procedure Rules 2010
FP3	Application for injunction (General form)
FP5	Acknowledgment of service Application under Part 19 of the Family Procedure Rules 2010

Number	Name
FP6	Certificate of service
FP8	Notice of change of solicitor
FP9	Certificate of suitability of litigation friend
FP25	Witness Summons
FP161	Appellant's Notice
FP161A	Guidance Notes on completing the FP161 – Appellant's Notice
FP162	Respondent's Notice
FP162A	Guidance Notes on completing the FP162 – Respondent's Notice
FP244	Application Notice
FP244A	Application Notice (FP244) – Notes for Guidance
N161	Appellant's Notice
N161A	Guidance Notes on Completing the Appellant's Notice
N161B	Important Notes for Respondents
N161D	Guidance Notes on completing the form N161 – Appellant's notice (all family proceedings appeals in the Court of Appeal (Civil Division) and the family court)
N162	Respondent's Notice
N162A	Guidance Notes for Completing the Respondent's Notice
N163	Skeleton Argument
N164	Appellant's Notice
N244	Application Notice
N260	Statement of costs (summary assessment)
N285	General Affidavit
N323	Request for Warrant of Execution
N349	Application for a third party debt order
PLO8	Standard Directions on Issue
PLO9	Standard Directions at First Appointment
PLP10	Order Menu – Directions Revised Private Law Programme
REMO 1	Notice of Registration
REMO 2	Notice of Refusal of Registration.

PRACTICE DIRECTION 7C – POLYGAMOUS MARRIAGES

This Practice Direction supplements FPR Part 7 (procedure for applications in matrimonial and civil partnership proceedings), Part 9 (applications for a financial remedy) and Part 18 (procedure for other applications in proceedings)

SCOPE OF THIS PRACTICE DIRECTION

1.1   This practice direction applies where an application is made for—

(a)   a matrimonial order;
(b)   an order under section 27 of the 1973 Act;
(c)   an order under section 35 of the 1973 Act;
(d)   an order under the 1973 Act which is made in connection with, or with proceedings for any of the above orders; or
(e)   an order under Part 3 of the 1984 Act,

and either party to the marriage is, or has during the course of the marriage, been married to more than one person (a polygamous marriage).

POLYGAMOUS MARRIAGES

2.1   Where this practice direction applies the application must state—

(a)   that the marriage is polygamous;
(b)   whether, as far as the party to the marriage is aware, any other spouse (that is, a spouse other than the spouse to whom the application relates) of that party is still living (the 'additional spouse'); and
(c)   if there is such an additional spouse—
      (i)   the additional spouse's name and address;
      (ii)   the date and place of the marriage to the additional spouse.

2.2   A respondent who believes that the marriage is polygamous must include the details referred to in paragraph 2.1 above in the acknowledgment of service if they are not included in the application.

2.3   The applicant in any proceedings to which this practice direction applies must apply to the court for directions as soon as possible after the filing of the application or the receipt of an acknowledgment of service mentioning an additional spouse.

2.4   On such an application or of its own initiative the court may—

(a)   give the additional spouse notice of any of the proceedings to which this practice direction applies; and
(b)   make the additional spouse a party to such proceedings.

2.5   In any case where the application or acknowledgment of service states that the marriage is polygamous (whether or not there is an additional spouse) a court officer must clearly mark the file with the words 'Polygamous Marriage'. The court officer must also check whether an application under paragraph 2.4 has been made in the case and, where no application has been made, refer the file to the court for consideration.

REFERENCES IN DECREES TO SECTION 47 OF THE 1973 ACT

3.1   Every decree nisi and decree absolute which is made in respect of a polygamous marriage must refer to the fact that the order is made with reference to section 47 of the 1973 Act.

PRACTICE DIRECTION 9A – APPLICATION FOR A FINANCIAL REMEDY

This Practice Direction supplements FPR Part 9

INTRODUCTION

1.1 Part 9 of the Family Procedure Rules sets out the procedure applicable to the financial proceedings that are included in the definition of a 'financial remedy'.

1.2 The fast-track procedure set out in Chapter 5 of Part 9 of the Family Procedure Rules applies to—

(a)   any application where the financial remedy sought is only for an order for periodical payments (as defined in rule 9.9B(1));

(b)   any application made under—
    (i)   the Domestic Proceedings and Magistrates' Courts Act 1978;
    (ii)   Schedule 6 to the Civil Partnership Act, 2004;
    (iii)   (omitted)
    (iv)   Article 10 of the 2007 Hague Convention;

(c)   any application for the variation of an order for periodical payments, except where the appli-cant seeks the dismissal (immediate or otherwise) of the periodical payments order and its substitution with one or more of a lump sum order, a property adjustment order, a pension sharing order or a pension compensation sharing order

1.2A The standard procedure set out in Chapter 4 of Part 9 applies in respect of all other applications for a financial remedy. In a case to which the fast-track procedure applies any party may seek a direction from the court that the standard procedure should apply to the application. An applicant who seeks such a direction must include a request in the application for a financial remedy and give reasons; any such request by a respondent, or any representations about a request by the applicant, must be made, giving reasons, within 7 days after service of the application for a financial remedy. At any stage in the proceedings the court may order that an application proceeding under the fast-track procedure must proceed under the standard procedure.

1.3 Where an application for a financial remedy includes an application relating to land, details of any mortgagee must be included in the application.

PRE-APPLICATION PROTOCOL

2.1 The 'pre-application protocol' annexed to this Direction outlines the steps parties should take to seek and provide information from and to each other prior to the commencement of any application for a financial remedy. The court will expect the parties to comply with the terms of the protocol.

COSTS

3.1 Rule 9.27(1) requires each party to file with the court, and serve on each other party, not less than one day before a hearing or appointment, an estimate of the costs incurred by that party up to the date of that hearing or appointment. Rule 9.27(2) and (3) make provision for the filing and service of estimates of specified future costs not less than one day before a first appointment and a FDR appointment. The rule also makes provision for the filing and service of particulars of costs not less than 14 days before a final hearing of an application for a financial remedy. The rule makes provision to ensure that all parties are aware of all incurred and estimated future costs (including their own) and for the court to give directions as to compliance if these requirements are not satisfied.

3.1A References in rule 9.27 (and any other rule) to a time period of a day or a number of days must be read by reference to rule 2.9 (computation of time).

3.2 The purpose of this rule is to enable the court to take account of the impact of each party's costs liability on their financial situations. Parties should ensure that the information contained in the estimate is as full and accurate as possible and that any sums already paid in respect of a party's financial remedy costs are clearly set out. Where relevant, any liability arising from the costs of other proceedings between the parties should continue to be referred to in the appropriate section of a party's financial statement; any such costs should not be included in the estimates under rule 9.27.

3.2A   An estimate of costs which is to be filed and served in accordance with rule 9.27(1), (2) or (3), and particu-lars of costs which are to be filed and served in accordance with rule 9.27(4) must be verified by a statement of truth.

3.2B   Where an estimate of costs or particulars of costs are to be filed by a party who is not legally represented, the statement of truth should be as follows—

'I confirm that:

- (a)   to the best of my knowledge and belief, the contents of [this estimate of costs/ these particulars of costs] are true and accurate; and
- (b)   [this estimate of costs/ these particulars of costs] will be filed with the court and served on each other party, in accordance with rule 9.27 of the Family Procedure Rules 2010.'

3.2C   Where an estimate of costs or particulars of costs are to be filed by a party's legal representative, the statement of truth should be as follows—

'I confirm that:

- (a)   to the best of my knowledge and belief, the contents of this [estimate of costs/ these particulars of costs] are true and accurate;
- (b)   I have discussed the contents of [this estimate of costs/ these particulars of costs] with my client (the [applicant/ respondent] in these proceedings);
- (c)   [this estimate of costs/ these particulars of costs] will be filed with the court and served on each other party, in accordance with rule 9.27 of the Family Procedure Rules 2010.'

3.3   Rule 28.3 provides that the general rule in financial remedy proceedings is that the court will not make an order requiring one party to pay the costs of another party. However the court may make such an order at any stage of the proceedings where it considers it appropriate to do so because of the conduct of a party in relation to the proceedings.

3.4   Any breach of this practice direction or the pre-application protocol annexed to it will be taken into account by the court when deciding whether to depart from the general rule as to costs.

PROCEDURE BEFORE THE FIRST APPOINTMENT

4.1   In addition to the matters listed at rule 9.14(5), the parties should, if possible, with a view to identifying and narrowing any issues between the parties, exchange and file with the court—

- (a)   a summary of the case agreed between the parties;
- (b)   a schedule of assets agreed between the parties; and
- (c)   details of any directions that they seek, including, where appropriate, the name of any expert they wish to be appointed.

4.2   Where a party is prevented from sending the details referred to in (c) above, the party should make that information available at the first appointment.

FINANCIAL STATEMENTS AND OTHER DOCUMENTS

5.1   Practice Direction 22A (Written Evidence) applies to any financial statement filed in accordance with rules 9.14 or 9.19 and to any exhibits to a financial statement. In preparing a bundle of documents to be exhibited to or attached to a financial statement, regard must be had in particular to paragraphs 11.1 to 11.3 and 13.1 to 13.4 of that

Direction. Where on account of their bulk, it is impracticable for the exhibits to a financial statement to be retained on the court file after the First Appointment, the court may give directions as to their custody pending further hearings.

5.2 Where the court directs a party to provide information or documents by way of reply to a questionnaire or request by another party, the reply must be verified by a statement of truth. Unless otherwise directed, a reply to a questionnaire or request for information and documents shall not be filed with the court.

(Part 17 and Practice Direction 17A make further provision about statements of truth)

Financial Dispute Resolution (FDR) Appointment

6.1 A key element in the procedure is the Financial Dispute Resolution (FDR) appointment. Rule 9.17 provides that the FDR appointment is to be treated as a meeting held for the purposes of discussion and negotiation. Such meetings have been developed as a means of reducing the tension which inevitably arises in family disputes and facilitating settlement of those disputes.

6.2 In order for the FDR to be effective, parties must approach the occasion openly and without reserve. Non-disclosure of the content of such meetings is vital and is an essential prerequisite for fruitful discussion directed to the settlement of the dispute between the parties. The FDR appointment is an important part of the settlement process. As a consequence of *Re D (Minors) (Conciliation: Disclosure of Information)* [1993] Fam 231, evidence of anything said or of any admission made in the course of an FDR appointment will not be admissible in evidence, except at the trial of a person for an offence committed at the appointment or in the very exceptional circumstances indicated in *Re D*.

6.3 Courts will therefore expect—

(a) parties to make offers and proposals;
(b) recipients of offers and proposals to give them proper consideration; and
(c) (subject to paragraph 6.4), that parties, whether separately or together, will not seek to exclude from consideration at the appointment any such offer or proposal.

6.4 paragraph 6.3(c) does not apply to an offer or proposal made during non-court dispute resolution.

6.5 In order to make the most effective use of the first appointment and the FDR appointment, the legal representatives attending those appointments will be expected to have full knowledge of the case.

6.5A Where at a FDR appointment a settlement is not reached, the parties have an obligation to make open proposals for settlement in accordance with rule 9.27A. The normal direction would be that each party must file and serve their open proposals within 21 days of the FDR appointment. The court must consider whether it is appropriate to give any further directions about the filing and service of open proposals.

6.6 (*omitted*)

(Provision relating to experts in financial remedy proceedings is contained in Practice Direction 25D (Financial Remedy Proceedings and Other Family Proceedings (Except Children Proceedings) – The Use of Single Joint Experts and the Process Leading to Expert Evidence Being Put Before The Court).)

CONSENT ORDERS

7.1 Rule 9.26(1)(a) requires an application for a consent order to be accompanied by two copies of the draft order in the terms sought, one of which must be endorsed with a statement signed by the respondent to the application signifying the respondent's agreement. The rule is considered to have been properly complied with if the endorsed statement is signed by solicitors on record as acting for the respondent; but where the consent order applied for contains undertakings, it should be signed by the party giving the undertakings as well as by that party's solicitor.

(Provision relating to the enforcement of undertakings is contained in the Practice Direction 33A supplementing Part 33 of the FPR)

7.2 Rule 9.26(1)(b) requires each party to file with the court and serve on the other party a statement of information. Where this is contained in one form, both parties must sign the statement to certify that each has read the contents of the other's statement.

7.3 Rule 35.2 deals with applications for a consent order in respect of a financial remedy where the parties wish to have the content of a written mediation agreement to which the Mediation Directive applies made the subject of a consent order.

SECTION 10(2) OF THE MATRIMONIAL CAUSES ACT 1973 AND SECTION 48(2) OF THE CIVIL PARTNERSHIP ACT 2004

8.1 Where a respondent who has applied under section 10(2) of the Matrimonial Causes Act 1973, or section 48(2) of the Civil Partnership Act 2004, for the court to consider his or her financial position after a divorce or dissolution elects not to proceed with the application, a notice of withdrawal of the application signed by the respondent or by the respondent's solicitor may be filed without leave of the court. In this event a formal order dismissing or striking out the application is unnecessary. Notice of withdrawal should also be given to the applicant's solicitor.

8.2 An application under section 10(2) or section 48(2) which has been withdrawn is not a bar to making in matrimonial proceedings, the decree absolute and in civil partnership proceedings, the final order.

MAINTENANCE ORDERS – REGISTRATION IN THE FAMILY COURT

9.1 Where periodical payments are required to be made to a child under an order registered in the family court, section 31L(3) and (4) of the 1984 Act permits the payments to be made instead to the person with whom the child has his home. That person may proceed in his own name for variation, revival or revocation of the order and may enforce payment in his own name.

9.2 The registration in the family court of an order made direct to a child entails a considerable amount of work. Accordingly, when the High Court is considering the form of an order where there are children, care should be taken not to make orders for payment direct where such orders would be of no benefit to the parties.

PENSIONS

10.1 The phrase 'party with pension rights' is used in FPR Part 9, Chapter 8. For matrimonial proceedings, this phrase has the meaning given to it by section 25D(3) of the Matrimonial Causes Act 1973 and means 'the party to the marriage who has or is likely to have benefits under a pension arrangement'. There is a definition of 'civil partner with pension rights' in paragraph 29 of Schedule 5 to the Civil Partnership Act 2004 which mirrors the definition of 'party with pension rights' in section 25D(3) of the 1973 Act. The phrase 'is likely to have benefits' in these definitions refers to accrued rights to pension benefits which are not yet in payment.

PPF COMPENSATION

11.1 The phrase 'party with compensation rights' is used in FPR Part 9, Chapter 9. For matrimonial proceedings, the phrase has the meaning given to it by section 25G(5) of the Matrimonial Causes Act 1973 and means the party to the marriage who is or is likely to be entitled to PPF compensation. There is a definition of 'civil partner with compensation rights' in paragraph 37(1) of Schedule 5 to the Civil Partnership Act 2004 which mirrors the definition of 'party with compensation rights' in section 25G(5). The phrase 'is likely to be entitled to PPF Compensation' in those definitions refers to statutory entitlement to PPF Compensation which is not yet in payment.

ORDERS FOR PAYMENT IN RESPECT OF LEGAL SERVICES

12.1 An application for an order for payment in respect of legal services under section 22ZA of the 1973 Act or paragraph 38A of Part 8 of Schedule 5 to the 2004 Act must be made in accordance with FPR 9.7 using the Part 18 procedure. Where the application is made at the same time as an application for an order for maintenance pending suit or maintenance pending outcome, the applications may be included in one application notice, and evidence in support of or in response to the applications may be contained in one witness statement.

(Where an application is made for an order under FPR 9.7, a copy of the application notice must be served in accordance with the provisions of FPR Part 6 at least 14 days before the court is to deal with the application: FPR 18.8(1)(b).)

12.2   The evidence filed in support of an application for an order for payment in respect of legal services must, in addition to the matters referred to in rule 9.7(3), include a concise statement of the applicant's case on—

(a)   the criteria set out in section 22ZA(3) and (4) of the 1974 Act or paragraph 38A(3) and (4) of Part 8 of Schedule 5 to the 2004 Act as applicable; and

(b)   the matters set out in section 22ZB(1) of the 1973 Act or paragraph 38B(1) of Part 8 of Schedule 5 to the 2004 Act as applicable.

APPLICATIONS TO SET ASIDE A FINANCIAL REMEDY

13.1   As set out in rule 9.9A(4), the Part 18 procedure applies to applications to set aside a financial remedy. Where such an application was made before rule 9.9A came into force, the Part 18 procedure will still apply subject to any directions that the court might make for the purpose of ensuring the proceedings are dealt with fairly (see the Family Procedure (Amendment No 2) Rules 2016, rule 5).

13.2   If the financial remedy order was made before 22 April 2014, by any court, an application to set it aside under rule 9.9A is to be made to the family court. This is the combined effect of rule 9.9A(3), which provides that the application is made within the original proceedings, and the Crime and Courts Act 2013 (Family Court: Transitional and Savings Provision) Order 2014, which provides that any such proceedings became family court proceedings as of 22 April 2014.

13.3   If the financial remedy order was made on or after 22 April 2014, an application to set it aside under rule 9.9A is to be made to the court that made the order.

13.4   An application under rule 9.9A is to be dealt with by the same level of judge that dealt with the original application, by virtue of rule 17 of the Family Court (Composition and Distribution of Business) Rules 2014. Where reasonably possible, the application will be dealt with by the same judge that dealt with the original application.

13.5   An application to set aside a financial remedy order should only be made where no error of the court is alleged. If an error of the court is alleged, an application for permission to appeal under Part 30 should be considered. The grounds on which a financial remedy order may be set aside are and will remain a matter for decisions by judges. The grounds include (i) fraud; (ii) material non-disclosure; (iii) certain limited types of mistake; (iv) a subsequent event, unforeseen and unforeseeable at the time the order was made, which invalidates the basis on which the order was made.

13.6   The effect of rules 9.9A(1)(a) and (2) is that an application may be made to set aside all or only part of a financial remedy order, including a financial remedy order that has been made by consent.

13.7   The family court has the power under section 31F(6) of the Matrimonial and Family Proceedings Act 1984 to vary or set aside a financial remedy order. The High Court has the power under rule 9.9A and section 17(2) of the Senior Courts Act 1981 to set aside a financial remedy order. The difference in the wording of the legislative provisions is the reason that "set aside" has been defined as it has in rule 9.9A(1)(b).

13.8   In applications under rule 9.9A, the starting point is that the order which one party is seeking to have set aside was properly made. A mere allegation that it was obtained by, eg, non-disclosure, is not sufficient for the court to set aside the order. Only once the ground for setting aside the order has been established (or admitted) can the court set aside the order and rehear the original application for a financial remedy. The court has a full range of case management powers and considerable discretion as to how to determine an application to set aside a financial remedy order, including where appropriate the power to strike out or summarily dispose of an application to set aside. If and when a ground for setting aside has been established, the court may decide to set aside the whole or part of the order there and then, or may delay doing so, especially if there are third party claims to the parties' assets. Ordinarily, once the court has decided to set aside a financial remedy order, the court would give directions for a full rehearing to re-determine the original application. However, if the court is satisfied that it has sufficient information to do so, it may proceed to re-determine the original application at the same time as setting aside the financial remedy order.

13.9 The effect of rule 28.3(9) is that the Part 28 rules relating to costs do not apply to applications under rule 9.9A.

ANNEX – PRE-APPLICATION PROTOCOL

Notes of guidance

Scope of the Protocol

1 This protocol is intended to apply to all applications for a financial remedy as defined by rule 2.3. It is designed to cover all classes of case, ranging from a simple application for periodical payments to an application for a substantial lump sum and property adjustment order. The protocol is designed to facilitate the operation of the procedure for financial remedy applications.

2 In considering the options of pre-application disclosure and negotiation, solicitors should bear in mind the advantage of having a court timetable and court managed process. There is sometimes an advantage in preparing disclosure before proceedings are commenced. However, solicitors should bear in mind the objective of controlling costs and in particular the costs of discovery and that the option of pre-application disclosure and negotiation has risks of excessive and uncontrolled expenditure and delay. This option should only be encouraged where both parties agree to follow this route and disclosure is not likely to be an issue or has been adequately dealt with in mediation or otherwise.

3 Solicitors should consider at an early stage and keep under review whether it would be appropriate to suggest mediation and/or collaborative law to the clients as an alternative to solicitor negotiation or court based litigation.

4 Making an application to the court should not be regarded as a hostile step or a last resort, rather as a way of starting the court timetable, controlling disclosure and endeavouring to avoid the costly final hearing and the preparation for it.

First letter

5 The circumstances of parties to an application for a financial remedy are so various that it would be difficult to prepare a specimen first letter. The request for information will be different in every case. However, the tone of the initial letter is important and the guidelines in paragraphs 14 and 15 should be followed. It should be approved in advance by the client. Solicitors writing to an unrepresented party should always recommend that he seeks independent legal advice and enclose a second copy of the letter to be passed to any solicitor instructed. A reasonable time limit for an answer may be 14 days.

Negotiation and settlement

6 In the event of pre-application disclosure and negotiation, as envisaged in paragraph 12 an application should not be issued when a settlement is a reasonable prospect.

Disclosure

7   The protocol underlines the obligation of parties to make full and frank disclosure of all material facts, documents and other information relevant to the issues. Solicitors owe their clients a duty to tell them in clear terms of this duty and of the possible consequences of breach of the duty, which may include criminal sanctions under the Fraud Act 2006. This duty of disclosure is an ongoing obligation and includes the duty to disclose any material changes after initial disclosure has been given. Solicitors are referred to the Good Practice Guides available to Resolution members at www.resolut ion.org.uk and can also contact the Law Society's Practice Advice Service on 0870 606 2522.

The Protocol

General principles

8   All parties must always bear in mind the overriding objective set out at rules 1.1 to 1.4 and try to ensure that applications should be resolved and a just outcome achieved as speedily as possible without costs being unreasonably incurred. The needs of any children should be addressed and safeguarded. The procedures which it is appropriate to follow should be conducted with minimum distress to the parties and in a manner designed to promote as good a continuing relationship between the parties and any children affected as is possible in the circumstances.

9   The principle of proportionality must be borne in mind at all times. It is unacceptable for the costs of any case to be disproportionate to the financial value of the subject matter of the dispute.

10   Parties should be informed that where a court is considering whether to make an order requiring one party to pay the costs of another party, it will take into account pre-application offers to settle and conduct of disclosure.

Identifying the issues

11   Parties must seek to clarify their claims and identify the issues between them as soon as possible. So that this can be achieved, they must provide full, frank and clear disclosure of facts, information and documents, which are material and sufficiently accurate to enable proper negotiations to take place to settle their differences. Openness in all dealings is essential.

Disclosure

12   If parties carry out voluntary disclosure before the issue of proceedings the parties should exchange schedules of assets, income, liabilities and other material facts, using the financial statement as a guide to the format of the disclosure. Documents should only be disclosed to the extent that they are required by the financial statement. Excessive or disproportionate costs should not be incurred.

Correspondence

13   Any first letter and subsequent correspondence must focus on the clarification of claims and identification of issues and their resolution. Protracted and unnecessary correspondence and 'trial by correspondence' must be avoided.

14   The impact of any correspondence upon the reader and in particular the parties must always be considered. Any correspondence which raises irrelevant issues or which might cause the other party to adopt an entrenched, polarised or hostile position is to be discouraged.

Summary

15 The aim of all pre-application proceedings steps must be to assist the parties to resolve their differences speedily and fairly or at least narrow the issues and, should that not be possible, to assist the court to do so.

PENSIONS ON DIVORCE ETC (PROVISION OF INFORMATION) REGULATIONS 2000

SI 2000/1048

1 Citation, commencement and interpretation

(1)   These Regulations may be cited as the Pensions on Divorce etc (Provision of Information) Regulations 2000 and shall come into force on 1st December 2000.

(2)   In these Regulations—

"the 1993 Act" means the Pension Schemes Act 1993;

"the 1995 Act" means the Pensions Act 1995;

"the 1999 Act" means the Welfare Reform and Pensions Act 1999;

[. . .]

"the Charging Regulations" means the Pensions on Divorce etc (Charging) Regulations 2000;

"the Implementation and Discharge of Liability Regulations" means the Pension Sharing (Implementation and Discharge of Liability) Regulations 2000;

"the Valuation Regulations" means the Pension Sharing (Valuation) Regulations 2000;

"active member" has the meaning given by section 124(1) of the 1995 Act;

"day" means any day other than—

(a)   Christmas Day or Good Friday; or

(b)   a bank holiday, that is to say, a day which is, or is to be observed as, a bank holiday or a holiday under Schedule 1 to the Banking and Financial Dealings Act 1971;

"deferred member" has the meaning given by section 124(1) of the 1995 Act;

"implementation period" has the meaning given by section 34(1) of the 1999 Act;

"member" means a person who has rights to future benefits, or has rights to benefits payable, under a pension arrangement;

"money purchase benefits" has the meaning given by section 181(1) of the 1993 Act;

"normal benefit age" has the meaning given by section 101B of the 1993 Act;

["normal pension age" has the meaning given in section 180 of the 1993 Act (normal pension age);]

"notice of discharge of liability" means a notice issued to the member and his former spouse [or former civil partner] by the person responsible for a pension arrangement when that person has discharged his liability in respect of a pension credit in accordance with Schedule 5 to the 1999 Act;

"notice of implementation" means a notice issued by the person responsible for a pension arrangement to the member and his former spouse [or former civil partner] at the beginning of the implementation period notifying them of the day on which the implementation period for the pension credit begins;

"occupational pension scheme" has the meaning given by section 1 of the 1993 Act;

"the party with pension rights" and "the other party" have the meanings given by section 25D(3) of the [Matrimonial Causes Act 1973];

"pension arrangement" has the meaning given in section 46(1) of the 1999 Act;

"pension credit" means a credit under section 29(1)(b) of the 1999 Act;

"pension credit benefit" means the benefits payable under a pension arrangement or a qualifying arrangement to or in respect of a person by virtue of rights under the arrangement in question which are attributable (directly or indirectly) to a pension credit;

"pension credit rights" means rights to future benefits under a pension arrangement or a qualifying arrangement which are attributable (directly or indirectly) to a pension credit;

"pension sharing order or provision" means an order or provision which is mentioned in section 28(1) of the 1999 Act;

"pensionable service" has the meaning given by section 124(1) of the 1995 Act;

["pensioner member" has the meaning given by section 124(1) of the 1995 Act;]

"person responsible for a pension arrangement" has the meaning given by section 46(2) of the 1999 Act;

"personal pension scheme" has the meaning given by section 1 of the 1993 Act;

"qualifying arrangement" has the meaning given by paragraph 6 of Schedule 5 to the 1999 Act;

. . .

"retirement annuity contract" means a contract or scheme [which is to be treated as becoming a registered pension scheme under 153(9) of the Finance Act 2004 in accordance with paragraph 1(1)(f) of Schedule 36 to that Act];

["salary related occupational pension scheme" has the meaning given by regulation 1A of the Transfer Values Regulations;]

. . .

"transfer day" has the meaning given by section 29(8) of the 1999 Act;

["the Transfer Values Regulations" means the Occupational Pension Schemes (Transfer Values) Regulations 1996;]

"transferee" has the meaning given by section 29(8) of the 1999 Act;

"transferor" has the meaning given by section 29(8) of the 1999 Act;

"trustees or managers" has the meaning given by section 46(1) of the 1999 Act.

NOTES

Amendment
Para (2): definition "the Board for Actuarial Standards" (omitted) inserted by SI 2007/60, reg 2, Schedule, para 9(a).
    Date in force: 6 April 2007: see SI 2007/60, reg 1.
Para (2): definition "the Board for Actuarial Standards" (omitted) revoked by SI 2008/1050, reg 8, Sch 2, para 3(a)(iii).
    Date in force: 1 October 2008: see SI 2008/1050, reg 1(1).
Para (2): definition "normal pension age" inserted by SI 2008/1050, reg 8, Sch 2, para 3(a)(i).
    Date in force: 1 October 2008: see SI 2008/1050, reg 1(1).
Para (2): in definition "notice of discharge of liability" words "or former civil partner" in square brackets inserted by SI 2005/2877, art 2(1), Sch 1, para 1(1), (2)(a).
    Date in force: 5 December 2005: see SI 2005/2877, art 1.
Para (2): in definition "notice of implementation" words "or former civil partner" in square brackets inserted by SI 2005/2877, art 2(1), Sch 1, para 1(1), (2)(b).
    Date in force: 5 December 2005: see SI 2005/2877, art 1.
Para (2): in definition ""the party with pension rights" and "the other party"" words "Matrimonial Causes Act 1973" in square brackets substituted by SI 2016/289, reg 2(1), (2)(b).
    Date in force: 6 April 2016: see SI 2016/289, reg 1(2).
Para (2): definition "pensioner member" inserted by SI 2016/289, reg 2(1), (2)(a).
    Date in force: 6 April 2016: see SI 2016/289, reg 1(2).
Para (2): definition "relevant date" (omitted) revoked by SI 2000/2691, reg 8(1), (2).
    Date in force: 1 December 2000: see SI 2000/2691, reg 1(1).
Para (2): in definition "retirement annuity contract" words from "which is to be" to "Schedule 36 to that Act" in square brackets substituted by SI 2006/744, art 15.
    Date in force: 6 April 2006: see SI 2006/744, art 1.
Para (2): definition "salary related occupational pension scheme" substituted by SI 2008/1050, reg 8, Sch 2, para 3(a)(ii).
    Date in force: 1 October 2008: see SI 2008/1050, reg 1(1).
Para (2): definition "the Regulatory Authority" (omitted) revoked by SI 2009/615, reg 12(1), (2).
    Date in force: 6 April 2009: see SI 2009/615, reg 1(2).
Para (2): definition "the Transfer Values Regulations" inserted by SI 2008/1050, reg 8, Sch 2, para 3(a)(i).

Date in force: 1 October 2008: see SI 2008/1050, reg 1(1).

2 Basic information about pensions and divorce [or dissolution of a civil partnership]
(1)   The requirements imposed on a person responsible for a pension arrangement for the purposes of section 23(1)(a) of the 1999 Act (supply of pension information in connection with divorce etc) are that he shall furnish—

(a)   on request from a member, the information referred to in paragraphs (2) and (3)(b) to (f);

(b)   on request from the spouse [or civil partner] of a member, the information referred to in paragraph (3); or

(c)   pursuant to an order of the court, the information referred to in paragraph (2), (3) or (4),

to the member, the spouse [or civil partner] of the member, or, as the case may be, to the court.
(2)   The information in this paragraph is a valuation of pension rights or benefits accrued under that member's pension arrangement.
(3)   The information in this paragraph is—

(a)   a statement that on request from the member, or pursuant to an order of the court, a valuation of pension rights or benefits accrued under that member's pension arrangement, will be provided to the member, or, as the case may be, to the court;

(b)   a statement summarising the way in which the valuation referred to in paragraph (2) and sub-paragraph (a) is calculated;

(c)   the pension benefits which are included in a valuation referred to in paragraph (2) and sub-paragraph (a);

(d)   whether the person responsible for the pension arrangement offers membership to a person entitled to a pension credit, and if so, the types of benefits available to pension credit members under that arrangement;

(e)   whether the person responsible for the pension arrangements intends to discharge his liability for a pension credit other than by offering membership to a person entitled to a pension credit; and

(f)   the schedule of charges which the person responsible for the pension arrangement will levy in accordance with regulation 2(2) of the Charging Regulations (general requirements as to charges).

(4)   The information in this paragraph is any other information relevant to any power with respect to the matters specified in section 23(1)(a) of the 1999 Act and which is not specified in [Schedules 2 to 5 (basic information; information to be given on request; summary funding statements; statements of benefits: non money purchase benefits) and Schedule 6 (statements of benefits: money purchase benefits and cash balance benefits) or 7 (information to be given by schemes that relates to accessing benefits) (whichever is relevant) to the Occupational and Personal Pension Schemes (Disclosure of Information) Regulations 2013, in a case where those Regulations apply].
(5)   Where the member's request for, or the court order for the provision of, information includes a request for, or an order for the provision of, a valuation under paragraph (2), the person responsible for the pension arrangement shall furnish all the information requested, or ordered, to the member—

(a)   within 3 months beginning with the date the person responsible for the pension arrangement receives that request or order for the provision of the information;

(b)   within 6 weeks beginning with the date the person responsible for the pension arrangement receives the request, or order, for the provision of the information, if the member has notified that person on the date of the request or order that the information is needed in connection with proceedings commenced under any of the provisions referred to in section 23(1)(a) of the 1999 Act; or

    (c)   within such shorter period specified by the court in an order requiring the person responsible for the pension arrangement to provide a valuation in accordance with paragraph (2).

(6)   Where—

    (a)   the member's request for, or the court order for the provision of, information does not include a request or an order for a valuation under paragraph (2); or

    (b)   the member's spouse [or civil partner] requests the information specified in paragraph (3),

the person responsible for the pension arrangement shall furnish that information to the member, his spouse, [civil partner,] or the court, as the case may be, within one month beginning with the date that person responsible for the pension arrangement receives the request for, or the court order for the provision of, the information.

(7)   At the same time as furnishing the information referred to in paragraph (1), the person responsible for a pension arrangement may furnish the information specified in regulation 4(2) (provision of information in response to a notification that a pension sharing order or provision may be made).

NOTES

Amendment

    Provision heading: words "or dissolution of a civil partnership" in square brackets inserted by SI 2005/2877, art 2(1), Sch 1, para 1(1), (3)(a).
        Date in force: 5 December 2005: see SI 2005/2877, art 1.
    Para (1): words "or civil partner" in square brackets in both places they occur inserted by SI 2005/2877, art 2(1), Sch 1, para 1(1), (3)(b).
        Date in force: 5 December 2005: see SI 2005/2877, art 1.
    Para (4): words from "Schedules 2 to" to "those Regulations apply" in square brackets substituted by SI 2016/289, reg 2(1), (3).
        Date in force: 6 April 2016: see SI 2016/289, reg 1(2).
    Para (6): in sub-para (b) words "or civil partner" in square brackets inserted by SI 2005/2877, art 2(1), Sch 1, para 1(1), (3)(c)(i).
        Date in force: 5 December 2005: see SI 2005/2877, art 1.
    Para (6): words "civil partner," in square brackets inserted by SI 2005/2877, art 2(1), Sch 1, para 1(1), (3)(c)(ii).
        Date in force: 5 December 2005: see SI 2005/2877, art 1.

3 Information about pensions and divorce [and dissolution of a civil partnership]: valuation of pension benefits

(1)   Where an application for financial relief under any of the provisions referred to in [section 23(a)(i), (ia), (iii) or (iv)] of the 1999 Act (supply of pension information in connection with domestic and overseas divorce etc in England and Wales and corresponding Northern Ireland powers) has been made or is in contemplation, the valuation of benefits under a pension arrangement shall be calculated and verified for the purposes of regulation 2 of these Regulations in accordance with—

    [(a)   paragraphs (3) and (4), if the person with pension rights is an active member, a deferred member or a pensioner member of an occupational pension scheme;]

    (b)   . . .

    (c)   paragraphs (5) and (6), if—

        (i)   the person with pension rights is a member of a personal pension scheme; or

        (ii)   those pension rights are contained in a retirement annuity contract; or

    (d)   [paragraphs (7) and (8)], if—

        (i)   the pension of the person with pension rights is in payment;

[(ii)   the rights of the person with pension rights are contained in an insurance policy or annuity contract other than a retirement annuity contract;]

(iii)   the rights of the person with pension rights are contained in a deferred annuity contract other than a retirement annuity contract[; or

(iv)   the pension of the person with pension rights is not in payment and the person has attained normal pension age].

(2)   Where an application for financial provision under any of the provisions referred to in section 23(1)(a)(ii) of the 1999 Act (corresponding Scottish powers) has been made, or is in contemplation, the valuation of benefits under a pension arrangement shall be calculated and verified for the purposes of regulation 2 of these Regulations in accordance with regulation 3 of the Divorce etc (Pensions) (Scotland) Regulations 2000 (valuation).

[(3)   Where a person with pension rights is an active member, a deferred member or a pensioner member of an occupational pension scheme, the value of those rights in relation to a category of benefits referred to in section 93(6) of the 1993 Act (category of benefits) must be calculated and verified in accordance with regulations 7 to 7C and 7E(1) to (3) of the Transfer Values Regulations (calculation and verification of cash equivalent), as if—

(a)   in the case of benefits other than money purchase benefits, the member has made an application for a statement of entitlement under section 93A of the 1993 Act (right to statement of entitlement: benefits other than money purchase) on the date that the request for the valuation was received; or

(b)   in the case of money purchase benefits, the member has made an application under section 95 of the 1993 Act (ways of taking right to cash equivalent) to take the cash equivalent of those benefits on the date that the request for the valuation was received.

(4)   Where the person with pension rights is continuing to accrue rights to benefits in the category of benefits to be valued, paragraph (3) applies as if the person had ceased to accrue rights in that category of benefits on the date that the request for the valuation was received.]

(5)   Where the person with pension rights is a member of a personal pension scheme, or those rights are contained in a retirement annuity contract, the value of the benefits which he has under that scheme or contract shall be taken to be the cash equivalent to which he would have acquired a right under [section 94 of the 1993 Act (right to cash equivalent)], if he had made an application under section 95(1) of that Act on the date on which the request for the valuation was received.

(6)   In relation to a personal pension scheme which is comprised in a retirement annuity contract made before 4th January 1988, paragraph (5) shall apply as if such a scheme were not excluded from the scope of [Chapter 1 of Part 4ZA of the 1993 Act by section 93(5)(b) of that Act (scope of Chapter 1)].

[(7)   Cash equivalents are to be calculated and verified in accordance with regulations 7 to 7C and 7E(1) to (3) of the Transfer Values Regulations as appropriate.]

[(8)   When calculating and verifying a cash equivalent, regulations 7 to 7C and 7E(1) to (3) of the Transfer Values Regulations are to be read as if—

(a)   in regulation 7—

(i)   in paragraph (1)(a), the words "and then making any reductions in accordance with regulation 7D" do not appear;

(ii)   in paragraph (1)(b), the words "regulation 7E" are replaced with "regulation 7E(1) to (3)";

(iii)   in paragraphs (2) and (4), the word "trustees" is replaced with "person responsible for the pension arrangement";

        (iv)   in paragraph (3), the words "trustees are" are replaced with "person responsible for the pension arrangement is";

        (v)   in paragraph (5), the words "trustees of the scheme in question have" are replaced with "person responsible for the pension arrangement has";

  (b)   in regulations 7A and 7B, in each place where it appears, the word "trustees" is replaced with "person responsible for the pension arrangement";

  (c)   in regulation 7C—

        (i)   in paragraph (3), in both places where it appears, the word "trustees" is replaced with "person responsible for the pension arrangement";

        (ii)   in paragraph (4)(b)(iv), the words "trustees determine" are replaced with "person responsible for the pension arrangement determines";

  (d)   in regulation 7E—

        (i)   in paragraph (1), the words "trustees have" are replaced with "person responsible for the pension arrangement has";

        (ii)   in paragraph (2), the word "trustees" is replaced with "person responsible for the pension arrangement".]

NOTES

Amendment

Provision heading: words "and dissolution of a civil partnership" in square brackets inserted by SI 2005/2877, art 2(1), Sch 1, para 1(1), (4)(a).
    Date in force: 5 December 2005: see SI 2005/2877, art 1.
Para (1): words "section 23(a)(i), (ia), (iii) or (iv)" in square brackets substituted by SI 2005/2877, art 2(1), Sch 1, para 1(1), (4)(b).
    Date in force: 5 December 2005: see SI 2005/2877, art 1.
Para (1): sub-para (a) substituted by SI 2016/289, reg 2(1), (4)(a)(i).
    Date in force: 6 April 2016: see SI 2016/289, reg 1(2).
Para (1): sub-para (b) revoked by SI 2016/289, reg 2(1), (4)(a)(ii).
    Date in force: 6 April 2016: see SI 2016/289, reg 1(2).
Para (1): in sub-para (d) words "paragraphs (7) and (8)" in square brackets substituted by SI 2008/1050, reg 8, Sch 2, para 3(b)(i)(aa).
    Date in force: 1 October 2008: see SI 2008/1050, reg 1(1).
Para (1): sub-para (d)(ii) substituted by SI 2016/289, reg 2(1), (4)(a)(iii).
    Date in force: 6 April 2016: see SI 2016/289, reg 1(2).
Para (1): sub-para (d)(iv) and word "; or" immediately preceding it inserted by SI 2008/1050, reg 8, Sch 2, para 3(b)(i)(bb).
    Date in force: 1 October 2008: see SI 2008/1050, reg 1(1).
Paras (3), (4): substituted by SI 2016/289, reg 2(1), (4)(b).
    Date in force: 6 April 2016: see SI 2016/289, reg 1(2).
Para (5): words "section 94 of the 1993 Act (right to cash equivalent)" in square brackets substituted by SI 2016/289, reg 2(1), (4)(c).
    Date in force: 6 April 2016: see SI 2016/289, reg 1(2).
Para (6): words from "Chapter 1 of" to "of Chapter 1)" in square brackets substituted by SI 2016/289, reg 2(1), (4)(d).
    Date in force: 6 April 2016: see SI 2016/289, reg 1(2).
Paras (7), (8): substituted, for paras (7)–(9) as originally enacted, by SI 2008/1050, reg 8, Sch 2, para 3(b)(iii).
    Date in force: 1 October 2008: see SI 2008/1050, reg 1(1).
Para (8): substituted, for paras (8), (10), by SI 2016/289, reg 2(1), (4)(e).
    Date in force: 6 April 2016: see SI 2016/289, reg 1(2).

4 Provision of information in response to a notification that a pension sharing order or provision may be made

(1) A person responsible for a pension arrangement shall furnish the information specified in paragraph (2) to the member or to the court, as the case may be—

  (a)   within 21 days beginning with the date that the person responsible for the pension arrangement received the notification that a pension sharing order or provision may be made; or

(b) if the court has specified a date which is outside the 21 days referred to in sub-paragraph (a), by that date.

(2) The information referred to in paragraph (1) is—

    (a) the full name of the pension arrangement and address to which any order or provision referred to in section 28(1) of the 1999 Act (activation of pension sharing) should be sent;

    (b) in the case of an occupational pension scheme, whether the scheme is winding up, and, if so,—

        (i) the date on which the winding up commenced; . . .

        (ii) the name and address of the trustees who are dealing with the winding up; [and

        (iii) whether the member's rights to benefit are to be or are likely to be reduced in accordance with sections 73 to 74 of the 1995 Act (winding up provisions);]

    (c) in the case of an occupational pension scheme, whether a cash equivalent of the member's pension rights, if calculated on the date the notification referred to in paragraph (1)(a) was received by the trustees or managers of that scheme, would be reduced in accordance with the provisions of [paragraphs 2, 3 and 12 of Schedule 1A to the Transfer Values Regulations (reductions in initial cash equivalents)] [if the member were to transfer the cash equivalent of those rights out of the scheme];

    (d) whether the person responsible for the pension arrangement is aware that the member's rights under the pension arrangement are subject to any, and if so, to specify which, of the following—

        (i) any order or provision specified in section 28(1) of the 1999 Act;

        (ii) an order under section 23 of the Matrimonial Causes Act 1973 (financial provision orders in connection with divorce etc), so far as it includes provision made by virtue of section 25B or 25C of that Act (powers to include provisions about pensions);

        (iii) an order under section 12A(2) or (3) of the Family Law (Scotland) Act 1985 (powers in relation to pensions lump sums when making a capital sum order) which relates to benefits or future benefits to which the member is entitled under the pension arrangement;

        (iv) an order under Article 25 of the Matrimonial Causes (Northern Ireland) Order 1978, so far as it includes provision made by virtue of Article 27B or 27C of that Order (Northern Ireland powers corresponding to those mentioned in paragraph (2)(d)(ii));

        (v) a forfeiture order;

        (vi) a bankruptcy order;

        (vii) an award of sequestration on a member's estate or the making of the appointment on his estate of a judicial factor under section 41 of the Solicitors (Scotland) Act 1980 (appointment of judicial factor);

    (e) whether the member's rights under the pension arrangement include rights specified in regulation 2 of the Valuation Regulations (rights under a pension arrangement which are not shareable);

    (f) if the person responsible for the pension arrangement has not at an earlier stage provided the following information, whether that person requires the charges specified in regulation 3 (charges recoverable in respect of the provision of basic information), 5 (charges in respect of pension sharing activity), or 6 (additional amounts recoverable in respect of pension sharing activity) of the Charging Regulations to be paid before the commencement of the implementation period, and if so,—

        (i) whether that person requires those charges to be paid in full; or

        (ii)   the proportion of those charges which he requires to be paid;

(g)   whether the person responsible for the pension arrangement may levy additional charges specified in regulation 6 of the Charging Regulations, and if so, the scale of the additional charges which are likely to be made;

(h)   whether the member is a trustee of the pension arrangement;

(i)   whether the person responsible for the pension arrangement may request information about the member's state of health from the member if a pension sharing order or provision were to be made;

(j)   . . .

(k)   whether the person responsible for the pension arrangement requires information additional to that specified in regulation 5 (information required by the person responsible for the pension arrangement before the implementation period may begin) in order to implement the pension sharing order or provision.

NOTES

Amendment

Para (2): in sub-para (b)(i) word omitted revoked by SI 2016/289, reg 2(1), (5)(a).
    Date in force: 6 April 2016: see SI 2016/289, reg 1(2).
Para (2): sub-para (b)(iii) and word "and" immediately preceding it inserted by SI 2016/289, reg 2(1), (5)(b).
    Date in force: 6 April 2016: see SI 2016/289, reg 1(2).
Para (2): in sub-para (c) words from "paragraphs 2, 3" to "initial cash equivalents)" in square brackets substituted by SI 2008/1050, reg 8, Sch 2, para 3(c).
    Date in force: 1 October 2008: see SI 2008/1050, reg 1(1).
Para (2): in sub-para (c) words from "if the member" to "of the scheme" in square brackets inserted by SI 2016/289, reg 2(1), (5)(c).
    Date in force: 6 April 2016: see SI 2016/289, reg 1(2).
Para (2): sub-para (j) revoked by SI 2000/2691, reg 8(1), (3).
    Date in force: 1 December 2000: see SI 2000/2691, reg 1(1).

5 Information required by the person responsible for the pension arrangement before the implementation period may begin

The information prescribed for the purposes of section 34(1)(b) of the 1999 Act (information relating to the transferor and the transferee which the person responsible for the pension arrangement must receive) is—

(a)   in relation to the transferor—
    (i)   all names by which the transferor has been known;
    (ii)   date of birth;
    (iii)   address;
    (iv)   National Insurance number;
    (v)   the name of the pension arrangement to which the pension sharing order or provision relates; and
    (vi)   the transferor's membership or policy number in that pension arrangement;

(b)   in relation to the transferee—
    (i)   all names by which the transferee has been known;
    (ii)   date of birth;
    (iii)   address;
    (iv)   National Insurance number; and
    (v)   if the transferee is a member of the pension arrangement from which the pension credit is derived, his membership or policy number in that pension arrangement;

(c)   where the transferee has given his consent in accordance with paragraph 1(3)(c), 3(3)(c) or 4(2)(c) of Schedule 5 to the 1999 Act (mode of discharge of liability for a pension credit) to the payment of the pension credit to the person responsible for a qualifying arrangement—

       (i)   the full name of that qualifying arrangement;

       (ii)   its address;

       (iii) if known, the transferee's membership number or policy number in that arrangement; and

       (iv) the name or title, business address, business telephone number, and, where available, the business facsimile number and electronic mail address of a person who may be contacted in respect of the discharge of liability for the pension credit;

  (d)   where the rights from which the pension credit is derived are held in an occupational pension scheme which is being wound up, whether the transferee has given an indication whether he wishes to transfer his pension credit rights which may have been reduced in accordance with the provisions of regulation 16(1) of the Implementation and Discharge of Liability Regulations (adjustments to the amount of the pension credit—occupational pension schemes which are underfunded on the valuation day) to a qualifying arrangement; and

  (e)   any information requested by the person responsible for the pension arrangement in accordance with regulation 4(2)(i) or (k).

6 Provision of information after the death of the person entitled to the pension credit before liability in respect of the pension credit has been discharged

[(1) Where the person entitled to the pension credit dies before the person responsible for the pension arrangement has discharged his liability in respect of the pension credit, the person responsible for the pension arrangement shall, within 21 days of the date of receipt of the notification of the death of the person entitled to the pension credit, notify in writing any person whom the person responsible for the pension arrangement considers should be notified of the matters specified in paragraph (2).]

(2)   The matters specified in this paragraph are—

  (a)   how the person responsible for the pension arrangement intends to discharge his liability in respect of the pension credit;

  (b)   whether the person responsible for the pension arrangement intends to recover charges from the person nominated to receive pension credit benefits, in accordance with regulations 2 to 9 of the Charging Regulations, and if so, a copy of the schedule of charges issued to the parties to pension sharing in accordance with regulation 2(2)(b) of the Charging Regulations (general requirements as to charges); and

  (c)   a list of any further information which the person responsible for the pension arrangement requires in order to discharge his liability in respect of the pension credit.

NOTES

Amendment

Para (1): substituted by SI 2000/2691, reg 8(1), (4).
Date in force: 1 December 2000: see SI 2000/2691, reg 1(1).

7 Provision of information after receiving a pension sharing order or provision

(1) A person responsible for a pension arrangement who is in receipt of a pension sharing order or provision relating to that arrangement shall provide in writing to the transferor and transferee, or, where regulation 6(1) applies, to the person other than the person entitled to the pension credit referred to in regulation 6 of the Implementation and Discharge of Liability Regulations (discharge of liability in respect of a pension credit following the death of the person entitled to the pension credit), as the case may be,—

(a) a notice in accordance with the provisions of regulation 7(1) of the Charging Regulations (charges in respect of pension sharing activity—postponement of implementation period);

(b) a list of information relating to the transferor or the transferee, or, where regulation 6(1) applies, the person other than the person entitled to the pension credit referred to in regulation 6 of the Implementation and Discharge of Liability Regulations, as the case may be, which—

   (i) has been requested in accordance with regulation 4(2)(i) and (k), or, where appropriate, 6(2)(c), or should have been provided in accordance with regulation 5;

   (ii) the person responsible for the pension arrangement considers he needs in order to begin to implement the pension sharing order or provision; and

   (iii) remains outstanding;

(c) a notice of implementation; or

(d) a statement by the person responsible for the pension arrangement explaining why he is unable to implement the pension sharing order or agreement.

(2) The information specified in paragraph (1) shall be furnished in accordance with that paragraph within 21 days beginning with—

(a) in the case of sub-paragraph (a), (b) or (d) of that paragraph, the day on which the person responsible for the pension arrangement receives the pension sharing order or provision; or

(b) in the case of sub-paragraph (c) of that paragraph, the later of the days specified in section 34(1)(a) and (b) of the 1999 Act (implementation period).

8 Provision of information after the implementation of a pension sharing order or provision

(1) The person responsible for the pension arrangement shall issue a notice of discharge of liability to the transferor and the transferee, or, as the case may be, the person entitled to the pension credit by virtue of regulation 6 of the Implementation and Discharge of Liability Regulations no later than the end of the period of 21 days beginning with the day on which the discharge of liability in respect of the pension credit is completed.

(2) In the case of a transferor whose pension is not in payment, the notice of discharge of liability shall include the following details—

(a) the value of the transferor's accrued rights as determined by reference to the cash equivalent value of those rights calculated and verified in accordance with regulation 3 of the Valuation Regulations (calculation and verification of cash equivalents for the purposes of the creation of pension debits and credits);

(b) the value of the pension debit;

(c) any amount deducted from the value of the pension rights in accordance with regulation 9(2)(c) of the Charging Regulations (charges in respect of pension sharing activity—method of recovery);

(d) the value of the transferor's rights after the amounts referred to in sub-paragraphs (b) and (c) have been deducted; and

(e) the transfer day.

(3) in the case of a transferor whose pension is in payment, the notice of discharge of liability shall include the following details—

(a) the value of the transferor's benefits under the pension arrangement as determined by reference to the cash equivalent value of those rights calculated and verified in accordance with regulation 3 of the Valuation Regulations;

(b)   the value of the pension debit;

(c)   the amount of the pension which was in payment before liability in respect of the pension credit was discharged;

(d)   the amount of pension which is payable following the deduction of the pension debit from the transferor's pension benefits;

(e)   the transfer day;

(f)   if the person responsible for the pension arrangement intends to recover charges, the amount of any unpaid charges—

    (i)   not prohibited by regulation 2 of the Charging Regulations (general requirements as to charges); and

    (ii)   specified in regulations 3 and 6 of those Regulations;

(g)   how the person responsible for the pension arrangement will recover the charges referred to in sub-paragraph (f), including—

    (i)   whether the method of recovery specified in regulation 9(2)(d) of the Charging Regulations will be used;

    (ii)   the date when payment of those charges in whole or in part is required; and

    (iii)   the sum which will be payable by the transferor, or which will be deducted from his pension benefits, on that date.

(4)   In the case of a transferee—

(a)   whose pension is not in payment; and

(b)   who will become a member of the pension arrangement from which the pension credit rights were derived,

the notice of discharge of liability to the transferee shall include the following details—

    (i)   the value of the pension credit;

    (ii)   any amount deducted from the value of the pension credit in accordance with regulation 9(2)(b) of the Charging Regulations;

    (iii)   the value of the pension credit after the amount referred to in sub-paragraph (b)(ii) has been deducted;

    (iv)   the transfer day;

    (v)   any periodical charges the person responsible for the pension arrangement intends to make, including how and when those charges will be recovered from the transferee; and

    (vi)   information concerning membership of the pension arrangement which is relevant to the transferee as a pension credit member.

(5)   In the case of a transferee who is transferring his pension credit rights out of the pension arrangement from which those rights were derived, the notice of discharge of liability to the transferee shall include the following details—

(a)   the value of the pension credit;

(b)   any amount deducted from the value of the pension credit in accordance with regulation 9(2)(b) of the Charging Regulations;

(c)   the value of the pension credit after the amount referred to in sub-paragraph (b) has been deducted;

(d)   the transfer day; and

(e)   details of the pension arrangement, including its name, address, reference number, telephone number, and, where available, the business facsimile number and electronic mail address, to which the pension credit has been transferred.

(6)   In the case of a transferee, who has reached normal benefit age on the transfer day, and in respect of whose pension credit liability has been discharged in accordance with paragraph 1(2), 2(2), 3(2) or 4(4) of Schedule 5 to the 1999 Act (pension credits: mode of discharge— funded pension schemes, unfunded public service pension

schemes, other unfunded pension schemes, or other pension arrangements), the notice of discharge of liability to the transferee shall include the following details—

- (a) the amount of pension credit benefit which is to be paid to the transferee;
- (b) the date when the pension credit benefit is to be paid to the transferee;
- (c) the transfer day;
- (d) if the person responsible for the pension arrangement intends to recover charges, the amount of any unpaid charges—
  - (i) not prohibited by regulation 2 of the Charging Regulations; and
  - (ii) specified in regulations 3 and 6 of those Regulations; and
- (e) how the person responsible for the pension arrangement will recover the charges referred to in sub-paragraph (d), including—
  - (i) whether the method of recovery specified in regulation 9(2)(e) of the Charging Regulations will be used;
  - (ii) the date when payment of those charges in whole or in part is required; and
  - (iii) the sum which will be payable by the transferee, or which will be deducted from his pension credit benefits, on that date.

(7) In the case of a person entitled to the pension credit by virtue of regulation 6 of the Implementation and Discharge of Liability Regulations, the notice of discharge of liability shall include the following details(i)whether the method of recovery specified in regulation 9(2)(e) of the —

- (a) the value of the pension credit rights as determined in accordance with regulation 10 of the Implementation and Discharge of Liability Regulations (calculation of the value of appropriate rights);
- (b) any amount deducted from the value of the pension credit in accordance with regulation 9(2)(b) of the Charging Regulations;
- (c) the value of the pension credit;
- (d) the transfer day; and
- (e) any periodical charges the person responsible for the pension arrangement intends to make, including how and when those charges will be recovered from the payments made to the person entitled to the pension credit by virtue of regulation 6 of the Implementation and Discharge of Liability Regulations.

9 Penalties

Where any trustee or manager of an occupational pension scheme fails, without reasonable excuse, to comply with any requirement imposed under regulation 6, 7 or 8, the Regulatory Authority may [by notice in writing] require that trustee or manager to pay within 28 days from the date of its imposition, a penalty which shall not exceed—

- (a) £200 in the case of an individual, and
- (b) £1,000 in any other case.

NOTES

Amendment
  Words "by notice in writing" in square brackets inserted by SI 2009/615, reg 12(1), (3).
   Date in force: 6 April 2009: see SI 2009/615, reg 1(2).

10 Provision of information after receipt of an earmarking order

(1) The person responsible for the pension arrangement shall, within 21 days beginning with the day that he receives—

- (a) an order under section 23 of the Matrimonial Causes Act 1973, so far as it includes provision made by virtue of section 25B or 25C of that Act (powers to include provision about pensions);

(b)   an order under section 12A(2) or (3) of the Family Law (Scotland) Act 1985; or

(c)   an order under Article 25 of the Matrimonial Causes (Northern Ireland) Order 1978, so far as it includes provision made by virtue of Article 27B or 27C of that Order (Northern Ireland powers corresponding to those mentioned in sub-paragraph (a)),

issue to the party with pension rights and the other party a notice which includes the information specified in paragraphs (2) and (5), or (3), (4) and (5), as the case may be.

(2)   Where an order referred to in paragraph (1)(a), (b) or (c) is made in respect of the pension rights or benefits of a party with pension rights whose pension is not in payment, the notice issued by the person responsible for a pension arrangement to the party with pension rights and the other party shall include a list of the circumstances in respect of any changes of which the party with pension rights or the other party must notify the person responsible for the pension arrangement.

(3)   Where an order referred to in paragraph (1)(a) or (c) is made in respect of the pension rights or benefits of a party with pension rights whose pension is in payment, the notice issued by the person responsible for a pension arrangement to the party with pension rights and the other party shall include—

(a)   the value of the pension rights or benefits of the party with pension rights;

(b)   the amount of the pension of the party with pension rights after the order has been implemented;

(c)   the first date when a payment pursuant to the order is to be made; and

(d)   a list of the circumstances, in respect of any changes of which the party with pension rights or the other party must notify the person responsible for the pension arrangement.

(4)   Where an order referred to in paragraph (1)(a) or (c) is made in respect of the pension rights of a party with pension rights whose pension is in payment, the notice issued by the person responsible for a pension arrangement to the party with pension rights shall, in addition to the items specified in paragraph (3), include—

(a)   the amount of the pension of the party with pension rights which is currently in payment; and

(b)   the amount of pension which will be payable to the party with pension rights after the order has been implemented.

(5)   Where an order referred to in paragraph (1)(a), (b) or (c) is made the notice issued by the person responsible for a pension arrangement to the party with pension rights and the other party shall include—

(a)   the amount of any charges which remain unpaid by—

    (i)   the party with pension rights; or

    (ii)   the other party,

in respect of the provision by the person responsible for the pension arrangement of information about pensions and divorce [or dissolution of a civil partnership] pursuant to regulation 3 of the Charging Regulations, and in respect of complying with an order referred to in paragraph (1)(a), (b) or (c); and

(b)   information as to the manner in which the person responsible for the pension arrangement will recover the charges referred to in sub-paragraph (a), including—

    (i)   the date when payment of those charges in whole or in part is required;

    (ii)   the sum which will be payable by the party with pension rights or the other party, as the case may be; and

    (iii)   whether the sum will be deducted from payments of pension to the party with pension rights, or, as the case may be, from payments to be made to the other party pursuant to an order referred to in paragraph (1)(a), (b) or (c).

NOTES

Amendment
Para (5): in sub-para (a) words "or dissolution of a civil partnership" in square brackets inserted by SI 2005/2877, art 2(1), Sch 1, para 1(1), (5).
Date in force: 5 December 2005: see SI 2005/2877, art 1.

[11 Provision of information]

[(1) Subject to paragraph (2) a person required to provide information under regulation 2, 4, 6, 7, 8 or 10 must provide that information in accordance with regulations 26 to 28 of the Occupational and Personal Pension Schemes (Disclosure of Information) Regulations 2013 (giving information and documents).

(2) Information may be provided to the court by means of an electronic communication only where the court has given its permission.

(3) In this regulation "electronic communication" has the meaning given by the Electronic Communications Act 2000.]

NOTES

Amendment
Inserted by SI 2013/2734, reg 1(4), Sch 9, para 7.
Date in force: 6 April 2014: see SI 2013/2734, reg 1(1).

PENSION SHARING (VALUATION) REGULATIONS 2000

SI 2000/1052

1 Citation, commencement and interpretation

(1)   These Regulations may be cited as the Pension Sharing (Valuation) Regulations 2000 and shall come into force on 1st December 2000.

(2)   In these Regulations—

"the 1993 Act" means the Pension Schemes Act 1993;

"the 1995 Act" means the Pensions Act 1995;

"the 1999 Act" means the Welfare Reform and Pensions Act 1999;

["the 2004 Act" means the Pensions Act 2004;]

[. . .]

[. . .]

"employer" has the meaning given by section 181(1) of the 1993 Act;

[. . .]

"occupational pension scheme" has the meaning given by section 1 of the 1993 Act;

"pension arrangement" has the meaning given by section 46(1) of the 1999 Act;

"relevant arrangement" has the meaning given by section 29(8) of the 1999 Act;

. . .

"scheme" means an occupational pension scheme;

. . .

"transfer credits" has the meaning given by section 181(1) of the 1993 Act;

["transfer day" has the meaning given by section 29(8) of the 1999 Act;]

"transferor" has the meaning given by section 29(8) of the 1999 Act;

["the Transfer Values Regulations" means the Occupational Pension Schemes (Transfer Values) Regulations 1996;]

"trustees or managers" has the meaning given by section 46(1) of the 1999 Act;

"valuation day" has the meaning given by section 29(7) of the 1999 Act.

NOTES

Amendment

Para (2): definition "the 2004 Act" inserted by SI 2005/3377, reg 20(1), Sch 3, para 9(1), (2).
Date in force: 30 December 2005: see SI 2005/3377, reg 1.
Para (2): definition "the Board for Actuarial Standards" (omitted) inserted by SI 2007/60, reg 2, Schedule, para 10(a).
Date in force: 6 April 2007: see SI 2007/60, reg 1.
Para (2): definition "the Board for Actuarial Standards" (omitted) revoked by SI 2008/1050, reg 8, Sch 2, para 5(a)(ii).
Date in force: 1 October 2008: see SI 2008/1050, reg 1(1).
Para (2): definition "effective date" (omitted) inserted by SI 2003/1727, reg 4(1), (2).
Date in force: 4 August 2003: see SI 2003/1727, reg 1.
Para (2): definition "effective date" (omitted) revoked by SI 2008/1050, reg 8, Sch 2, para 5(a)(ii).
Date in force: 1 October 2008: see SI 2008/1050, reg 1(1).
Para (2): definition "initial cash equivalent" (omitted) inserted by SI 2008/1050, reg 8, Sch 2, para 5(a)(i).
Date in force: 1 October 2008: see SI 2008/1050, reg 1(1).
Para (2): definition "initial cash equivalent" (omitted) revoked by SI 2016/289, reg 4(1), (2).
Date in force: 6 April 2016: see SI 2016/289, reg 1(2).
Para (2): definition "relevant benefits" (omitted) revoked by SI 2006/744, art 16(1), (2).
Date in force: 6 April 2006: see SI 2006/744, art 1.
Para (2): definition "scheme actuary" (omitted) revoked by SI 2008/1050, reg 8, Sch 2, para 5(a)(ii).
Date in force: 1 October 2008: see SI 2008/1050, reg 1(1).

Para (2): definition "transfer day" inserted by SI 2000/2691, reg 10(1), (2).
    Date in force: 1 December 2000: see SI 2000/2691, reg 1(1).
Para (2): definition "the Transfer Values Regulations" inserted by SI 2008/1050, reg 8, Sch 2, para 5(a)(i).
    Date in force: 1 October 2008: see SI 2008/1050, reg 1(1).

2 Rights under a pension arrangement which are not shareable

(1) Rights under a pension arrangement which are not shareable are—

  (a) subject to paragraph (2), any rights accrued between 1961 and 1975 which relate to contracted-out equivalent pension benefit within the meaning of section 57 of the National Insurance Act 1965 (equivalent pension benefits, etc);

  (b) any rights in respect of which a person is in receipt of—

    (i) a pension;

    (ii) an annuity; [or]

    (iii) . . .

    [(iv) dependants', nominees' or successors' income withdrawal within the meaning of, as the case may be, paragraph 21 (dependants' income withdrawal), 27D (nominees' income withdrawal) or 27J (successors' income withdrawal) of Schedule 28 to the Finance Act 2004,]

by virtue of being the widow, widower[, surviving civil partner][, nominee, successor] or other dependant of a deceased person with pension rights under a pension arrangement; . . .

  [(ba) any rights relating to sums and assets held for the purposes of—

    (i) a dependant's drawdown pension fund or flexi-access drawdown fund within the meaning of, as the case may be, paragraph 22 (dependant's drawdown pension fund) or 22A (dependant's flexi-access drawdown fund) of Schedule 28 to the Finance Act 2004;

    (ii) a nominee's or successor's flexi-access drawdown fund within the meaning of, as the case may be, paragraph 27E (nominee's flexi-access drawdown fund) or 27K (successor's flexi-access drawdown fund) of Schedule 28 to the Finance Act 2004;]

  [(c) any rights which will result in the payment of a benefit which is to be provided solely by reason of the—

    (i) disablement, or

    (ii) death,

due to an accident suffered by a person occurring during his pensionable service][; and

  (d) any rights in respect of a cash transfer sum or contribution refund that the member would be entitled to under section 101AB of the 1993 Act (right to cash transfer sum and contribution refund) if pensionable service were to be terminated].

(2) Paragraph (1)(a) applies only when those rights are the only rights held by a person under a pension arrangement.

NOTES

Amendment
Para (1): in sub-para (b)(ii) word "or" in square brackets inserted by SI 2011/1245, reg 12(a).
    Date in force: 6 April 2012: see SI 2011/1245, reg 1(2)(a).
Para (1): sub-para (b)(iii) revoked by SI 2011/1245, reg 12(b).
    Date in force: 6 April 2012: see SI 2011/1245, reg 1(2)(a).
Para (1): sub-para (b)(iv) substituted by SI 2016/289, reg 4(1), (3)(a)(i).
    Date in force: 6 April 2016: see SI 2016/289, reg 1(2).
Para (1): in sub-para (b) words ", surviving civil partner" in square brackets inserted by SI 2005/2877, art 2(1), Sch 1, para 3.
    Date in force: 5 December 2005: see SI 2005/2877, art 1.

Para (1): in sub-para (b) words ", nominee, successor" in square brackets inserted by SI 2016/289, reg 4(1), (3)(a)(ii).
> Date in force: 6 April 2016: see SI 2016/289, reg 1(2).

Para (1): in sub-para (b) word omitted revoked by SI 2016/289, reg 4(1), (3)(a)(iii).
> Date in force: 6 April 2016: see SI 2016/289, reg 1(2).

Para (1): sub-para (ba) inserted by SI 2016/289, reg 4(1), (3)(b).
> Date in force: 6 April 2016: see SI 2016/289, reg 1(2).

Para (1): sub-para (c) substituted by SI 2006/744, art 16(1), (3)(b).
> Date in force: 6 April 2006: see SI 2006/744, art 1.

Para (1): sub-para (d) and word "; and" immediately preceding it inserted by SI 2016/289, reg 4(1), (3)(c).
> Date in force: 6 April 2016: see SI 2016/289, reg 1(2).

3 Calculation and verification of cash equivalents for the purposes of the creation of pension debits and credits

For the purposes of section 29 of the 1999 Act (creation of pension debits and credits), cash equivalents may be calculated and verified—

(a) where the relevant arrangement is an occupational pension scheme in accordance with [regulation 4]; or

(b) in any other case, in accordance with [regulations 5 and 7].

NOTES

Amendment

In para (a) words "regulation 4" in square brackets substituted by SI 2010/499, reg 5(1), (2)(a).
> Date in force: 6 April 2010: see SI 2010/499, reg 1.

In para (b) words "regulations 5 and 7" in square brackets substituted by SI 2010/499, reg 5(1), (2)(b).
> Date in force: 6 April 2010: see SI 2010/499, reg 1.

[4 Manner of calculation and verification of cash equivalents: occupational pension schemes]

[(1) Subject to this regulation, where a person with pension rights is, for the purposes of Part I of the 1995 Act, an active member, a deferred member or a pensioner member of an occupational pension scheme, or where a person with pension rights attains, or is over, normal pension age and is not in receipt of the pension, the value of rights in relation to a category of benefits referred to in section 93(6) of the 1993 Act (category of benefits) must be calculated and verified in accordance with regulations 7 to 7C and 7E(1) to (3) of the Transfer Values Regulations (calculation and verification of cash equivalents), as if—

(a) in the case of benefits other than money purchase benefits, the member has made an application for a statement of entitlement under section 93A of the 1993 Act (right to statement of entitlement: benefits other than money purchase); or

(b) in the case of money purchase benefits, the member has made an application under section 95 of the 1993 Act (ways of taking right to cash equivalent) to use the cash equivalent of those benefits.

(2) Where a person with pension rights is continuing to accrue rights to benefits in the category of benefits to be valued, paragraph (1) applies as if the person had ceased to accrue rights in that category of benefits on the valuation day.

(3) Where a person with pension rights is entitled to present payment of the pension, but the pension is not yet in payment, the cash equivalent must be calculated and verified on the assumption that the pension comes into payment on the transfer day.

(4) When calculating and verifying the cash equivalent, regulations 7 to 7C and 7E(1) to (3) of the Transfer Values Regulations are to be read as if—

(a) in regulation 7—

(i) in paragraph (1)(a), the words "and then making any reductions in accordance with regulation 7D" do not appear;

(ii) in paragraph (1)(b), the words "regulation 7E" are replaced with "regulation 7E(1) to (3)";

(b) in regulation 7A(2), the words "guarantee date" are replaced with "valuation day";

(c) in regulation 7C(2), the words "at the date of calculation" are replaced with "on the valuation day"; and

(d) "valuation day" has the meaning given by section 29(7) of the 1999 Act (meaning of valuation day).]

NOTES

Amendment
Substituted by SI 2016/289, reg 4(1), (4).
Date in force: 6 April 2016: see SI 2016/289, reg 1(2).

[5 Manner of calculation and verification of cash equivalents: other relevant arrangements]

[(1) Subject to this regulation, cash equivalents for members of a relevant arrangement other than an occupational pension scheme are to be calculated and verified in accordance with regulations [7 to 7C and 7E(1) to (3) of the Transfer Values Regulations, as if the person with the pension rights had made a valid application under section 95 of the 1993 Act to use the cash equivalent of the rights to benefits].

(2) When calculating and verifying the cash equivalent, the Transfer Value Regulations are to be read as if—

[(za) in regulation 7(1)(a), the words "and then making any reductions in accordance with regulation 7D" do not appear;

(zb) in regulation 7(1)(b), the words "regulation 7E" are replaced with "regulation 7E(1) to (3)";]

(a) in regulation 1(2)—

(i) for the definition of "trustees" there were substituted—
""trustees" means the person responsible for the relevant arrangement;"; and

(ii) there were inserted at the appropriate alphabetical places—
""personal pension scheme" has the meaning given by section 1 of the 1993 Act (categories of pension scheme);";
""transfer day" has the meaning given by section 29(8) of the Welfare Reform and Pensions Act 1999 (creation of pension debits and credits);";

(b) in regulation 7(1) (manner of calculation and verification of cash equivalents – general provisions), for "paragraphs (4) and (7)" there were substituted "paragraphs (4), (7) and (8)"; and

(c) after regulation 7(7), there were inserted—

"(8) Where the person with pension rights is a member of a personal pension scheme, or those rights are contained in a retirement annuity contract, the value of the benefits which he has accrued under that scheme or contract on the transfer day must be taken to be the cash equivalent to which he would have acquired a right under section 94(1)(b) of the 1993 Act (right to cash equivalent), if he had made an application under section 95(1) of that Act (ways of taking right to cash equivalent) on the date on which the request for the valuation was received.".

(3) In relation to a personal pension scheme which is comprised in a retirement annuity contract made before 4th January 1988, this regulation applies as if such a scheme were not excluded from the scope of [Chapter 1 of Part 4ZA of the 1993 Act by section 93(5)(b) of that Act (scope of Chapter 1)].";

(c) regulation 7 (other relevant arrangements: reduction of cash equivalents) becomes paragraph (1) of regulation 7; and

(d) in regulation 7, after paragraph (1) insert—

"(2) This regulation does not apply to occupational pension schemes.".]

NOTES

Amendment
>Substituted, together with reg 4, for this regulation and regs 4, 6 as originally enacted, by SI 2008/1050, reg 8, Sch 2, para 5(b).
>>Date in force: 1 October 2008: see SI 2008/1050, reg 1(1).
>Para (1): words from "7 to 7C" to "rights to benefits" in square brackets substituted by SI 2016/289, reg 4(1), (5)(a).
>>Date in force: 6 April 2016: see SI 2016/289, reg 1(2).
>Para (2): sub-paras (za), (zb) inserted by SI 2016/289, reg 4(1), (5)(b).
>>Date in force: 6 April 2016: see SI 2016/289, reg 1(2).
>Para (3): words from "Chapter 1 of" to "of Chapter 1)" in square brackets substituted by SI 2016/289, reg 4(1), (5)(c).
>>Date in force: 6 April 2016: see SI 2016/289, reg 1(2).

6 . . .

. . .

NOTES

Amendment
>Substituted, together with regs 4, 5, by new regs 4, 5, by SI 2008/1050, reg 8, Sch 2, para 5(b).
>>Date in force: 1 October 2008: see SI 2008/1050, reg 1(1).

7 Other relevant arrangements: reduction of cash equivalents

[(1)]   Where all or any of the benefits to which a cash equivalent relates have been surrendered, commuted or forfeited before the date on which the person responsible for the relevant arrangement discharges his liability for the pension credit in accordance with the provisions of Schedule 5 to the 1999 Act, the cash equivalent of the benefits so surrendered, commuted or forfeited shall be reduced in proportion to the reduction in the total value of the benefits.

[(2)   This regulation does not apply to occupational pension schemes.]

NOTES

Amendment
>Para (1): numbered as such by SI 2008/1050, reg 8, Sch 2, para 5(c).
>>Date in force: 1 October 2008: see SI 2008/1050, reg 1(1).
>Para (2): inserted by SI 2008/1050, reg 8, Sch 2, para 5(d).
>>Date in force: 1 October 2008: see SI 2008/1050, reg 1(1).

DIVORCE ETC (PENSIONS) REGULATIONS 2000

SI 2000/1123

1 Citation, commencement and transitional provisions

(1)   These Regulations may be cited as the Divorce etc (Pensions) Regulations 2000 and shall come into force on 1st December 2000.

(2)   These Regulations shall apply to any proceedings for divorce, judicial separation or nullity of marriage commenced on or after 1st December 2000, and any such proceedings commenced before that date shall be treated as if these Regulations had not come into force.

2 Interpretation

In these Regulations:

(a)   a reference to a section by number alone means the section so numbered in the Matrimonial Causes Act 1973;

(b)   "the 1984 Act" means the Matrimonial and Family Proceedings Act 1984;

(c)   expressions defined in sections 21A and 25D(3) have the meanings assigned by those sections;

(d)   every reference to a rule by number alone means the rule so numbered in the [Family Procedure Rules 2010].

NOTES

Amendment

In para (d) words "Family Procedure Rules 2010" in square brackets substituted by SI 2011/1045, arts 26, 27.

   Date in force: 6 April 2011: see SI 2011/1045, art 1; for transitional provision see art 39 thereof.

3 Valuation

(1)   For the purposes of the court's functions in connection with the exercise of any of its powers under Part II of the Matrimonial Causes Act 1973, benefits under a pension arrangement shall be calculated and verified in the manner set out in regulation 3 of the Pensions on Divorce etc (Provision of Information) Regulations 2000, and—

(a)   the benefits shall be valued as at a date to be specified by the court (being not earlier than one year before the date of the petition and not later than the date on which the court is exercising its power);

(b)   in determining that value the court may have regard to information furnished by the person responsible for the pension arrangement pursuant to any of the provisions set out in paragraph (2); and

(c)   in specifying a date under sub-paragraph (a) above the court may have regard to the date specified in any information furnished as mentioned in sub-paragraph (b) above.

(2)   The relevant provisions for the purposes of paragraph (1)(b) above are:

(a)   the Pensions on Divorce etc (Provision of Information) Regulations 2000;

(b)   regulation 5 of and Schedule 2 to the Occupational Pension Schemes (Disclosure of Information) Regulations 1996 and regulation 11 of and Schedule 1 to the Occupational Pension Schemes (Transfer Value) Regulations 1996;

(c)   [sections 93A and 94(1)] of the Pension Schemes Act 1993;

(d)   [section 94(2)] of the Pension Schemes Act 1993 or paragraph 2(a) (or, where applicable, 2(b)) of Schedule 2 to the Personal Pension Schemes (Disclosure of Information) Regulations 1987.

Amendment

> Para (2): in sub-para (c) words "sections 93A and 94(1)" in square brackets substituted by SI 2016/289, reg 6(a).
>> Date in force: 6 April 2016: see SI 2016/289, reg 1(2).
> Para (2): in sub-para (d) words "section 94(2)" in square brackets substituted by SI 2016/289, reg 6(b).
>> Date in force: 6 April 2016: see SI 2016/289, reg 1(2).

4 Pension attachment: notices

(1)   This regulation applies in the circumstances set out in section 25D(1)(a) (transfers of pension rights).

(2)   Where this regulation applies, the person responsible for the first arrangement shall give notice in accordance with the following paragraphs of this regulation to

    (a)   the person responsible for the new arrangement, and

    (b)   the other party.

(3)   The notice to the person responsible for the new arrangement shall include copies of the following documents:

    (a)   every order made under section 23 imposing any requirement on the person responsible for the first arrangement in relation to the rights transferred;

    (b)   any order varying such an order;

    (c)   all information or particulars which the other party has been required to supply under any provision of [rule 9.33 or 9.34] for the purpose of enabling the person responsible for the first arrangement:—

        (i)   to provide information, documents or representations to the court to enable it to decide what if any requirement should be imposed on that person; or

        (ii)   to comply with any order imposing such a requirement;

    (d)   any notice given by the other party to the person responsible for the first arrangement under regulation 6;

    (e)   where the pension rights under the first arrangement were derived wholly or partly from rights held under a previous pension arrangement, any notice given to the person responsible for the previous arrangement under paragraph (2) of this regulation on the occasion of that acquisition of rights.

(4)   The notice to the other party shall contain the following particulars:

    (a)   the fact that the pension rights have been transferred;

    (b)   the date on which the transfer takes effect;

    (c)   the name and address of the person responsible for the new arrangement;

    (d)   the fact that the order made under section 23 is to have effect as if it had been made in respect of the person responsible for the new arrangement.

(5)   Both notices shall be given:

    (a)   within the period provided by section 99 of the Pension Schemes Act 1993 for the person responsible for the first arrangement to carry out what the member requires; and

    (b)   before the expiry of 21 days after the person responsible for the first arrangement has made all required payments to the person responsible for the new arrangement.

Amendment

> Para (3): in sub-para (c) words "rule 9.33 or 9.34" in square brackets substituted by SI 2011/1045, arts 26, 28.
>> Date in force: 6 April 2011: see SI 2011/1045, art 1; for transitional provision see art 39 thereof.

5 Pension attachment: reduction in benefits

(1)   This regulation applies where:

- (a)   an order under section 23 or under section 17 of the 1984 Act has been made by virtue of section 25B or 25C imposing any requirement on the person responsible for a pension arrangement;
- (b)   an event has occurred which is likely to result in a significant reduction in the benefits payable under the arrangement, other than:
    - (i)   the transfer from the arrangement of all the rights of the party with pension rights in the circumstances set out in section 25D(1)(a), or
    - (ii)   a reduction in the value of assets held for the purposes of the arrangement by reason of a change in interest rates or other market conditions.

(2)   Where this regulation applies, the person responsible for the arrangement shall, within 14 days of the occurrence of the event mentioned in paragraph (1)(b), give notice to the other party of:

- (a)   that event;
- (b)   the likely extent of the reduction in the benefits payable under the arrangement.

(3)   Where the event mentioned in paragraph (1)(b) consists of a transfer of some but not all of the rights of the party with pension rights from the arrangement, the person responsible for the first arrangement shall, within 14 days of the transfer, give notice to the other party of the name and address of the person responsible for any pension arrangement under which the party with pension rights has acquired rights as a result of that event.

6 Pension attachment: change of circumstances

(1)   This regulation applies where:

- (a)   an order under section 23 or under section 17 of the 1984 Act has been made by virtue of section 25B or 25C imposing any requirement on the person responsible for a pension arrangement; and
- (b)   any of the events set out in paragraph (2) has occurred.

(2)   Those events are:

- (a)   any of the particulars supplied by the other party under [rule 9.33 or 9.34] for any purpose mentioned in regulation 4(3)(c) has ceased to be accurate; or
- (b)   by reason of the remarriage of the other party[, or his having formed a subsequent civil partnership,] or otherwise, the order has ceased to have effect.

(3)   Where this regulation applies, the other party shall, within 14 days of the event, give notice of it to the person responsible for the pension arrangement.

(4)   Where, because of the inaccuracy of the particulars supplied by the other party under [rule 9.33 or 9.34] or because the other party has failed to give notice of their having ceased to be accurate, it is not reasonably practicable for the person responsible for the pension arrangement to make a payment to the other party as required by the order:

- (a)   it may instead make that payment to the party with pension rights, and
- (b)   it shall then be discharged of liability to the other party to the extent of that payment.

(5)   Where an event set out in paragraph (2)(b) has occurred and, because the other party has failed to give notice in accordance with paragraph (3), the person responsible for the pension arrangement makes a payment to the other party as required by the order:

(a)   its liability to the party with pension rights shall be discharged to the extent of that payment, and

(b)   the other party shall, within 14 days of the payment being made, make a payment to the party with pension rights to the extent of that payment.

NOTES

Amendment

Para (2): in sub-para (a) words "rule 9.33 or 9.34" in square brackets substituted by SI 2011/1045, arts 26, 28.

Date in force: 6 April 2011: see SI 2011/1045, art 1; for transitional provision see art 39 thereof.

Para (2): in sub-para (b) words ", or his having formed a subsequent civil partnership," in square brackets inserted by SI 2005/2114, art 2(1), Sch 1, para 8.

Date in force: 5 December 2005: see SI 2005/2114, art 1.

Para (4): words "rule 9.33 or 9.34" in square brackets substituted by SI 2011/1045, arts 26, 28.

Date in force: 6 April 2011: see SI 2011/1045, art 1; for transitional provision see art 39 thereof.

7 Pension attachment: transfer of rights

(1) This regulation applies where:

(a)   a transfer of rights has taken place in the circumstances set out in section 25D(1)(a);

(b)   notice has been given in accordance with regulation 4(2)(a) and (b);

(c)   any of the events set out in regulation 6(2) has occurred; and

(d)   the other party has not, before receiving notice under regulation 4(2)(b), given notice of that event to the person responsible for the first arrangement under regulation 6(3).

(2) Where this regulation applies, the other party shall, within 14 days of the event, give notice of it to the person responsible for the new arrangement.

(3) Where, because of the inaccuracy of the particulars supplied by the other party under [rule 9.33 or 9.34] for any purpose mentioned in regulation 4(3)(c) or because the other party has failed to give notice of their having ceased to be accurate, it is not reasonably practicable for the person responsible for the new arrangement to make a payment to the other party as required by the order:

(a)   it may instead make that payment to the party with pension rights, and

(b)   it shall then be discharged of liability to the other party to the extent of that payment.

(4) Subject to paragraph (5), where this regulation applies and the other party, within one year from the transfer, gives to the person responsible for the first arrangement notice of the event set out in regulation 6(2) in purported compliance with regulation 7(2), the person responsible for the first arrangement shall:

(a)   send that notice to the person responsible for the new arrangement, and

(b)   give the other party a second notice under regulation 4(2)(b);

and the other party shall be deemed to have given notice under regulation 7(2) to the person responsible for the new arrangement.

(5) Upon complying with paragraph (4) above, the person responsible for the first arrangement shall be discharged from any further obligation under regulation 4 or 7(4), whether in relation to the event in question or any further event set out in regulation 6(2) which may be notified to it by the other party.

NOTES

Amendment

Para (3): words "rule 9.33 or 9.34" in square brackets substituted by SI 2011/1045, arts 26, 28.

Date in force: 6 April 2011: see SI 2011/1045, art 1; for transitional provision see art 39 thereof.

8 Service
A notice under regulation 4, 5, 6 or 7 may be sent by fax or by ordinary first class post to the last known address of the intended recipient and shall be deemed to have been received on the seventh day after the day on which it was sent.

9 Pension sharing order not to take effect pending appeal
(1)   No pension sharing order under section 24B or variation of a pension sharing order under section 31 shall take effect earlier than 7 days after the end of the period for filing notice of appeal against the order.
(2)   The filing of a notice of appeal within the time allowed for doing so prevents the order taking effect before the appeal has been dealt with.

10 Revocation
The Divorce etc (Pensions) Regulations 1996 and the Divorce etc (Pensions) (Amendment) Regulations 1997 are revoked.

Index

A

Accountants
lump sum orders
valuation of businesses 4.41
Age
child support 11.27–11.31
parties 1.108, 1.109
Agreements of parties
case law 1.216–1.233, 1.235
compromising litigation 1.236–1.240
consideration by court of 1.199–1.206
fairness in court handling of 1.212–1.215
foreign element 1.211
general approach to 1.207–1.208
order for alteration of
introduction 14.1
jurisdiction 14.22
procedure 14.23
statutory provisions 14.19–14.21
vitiating factors 1.209–1.210
All circumstances 1.48–1.51
Alteration of agreements, order for
introduction 14.1
jurisdiction 14.22
procedure 14.23
statutory provisions 14.19–14.21
Ancillary orders
avoidance of dispositions 8.9–8.11
Ancillary provisions
sale of property orders 7.7–7.9
Appeals
costs 17.41–17.42
introduction 18.1
material omissions 18.21
notice
contents 18.14
permission 18.3–18.9
powers of appellate court 18.15–18.20
procedure 18.2, 18.23
routes 18.13
setting aside or 18.67–18.68
time limits 18.10–18.12
Applicants
issue of proceedings 16.4–16.6

Arbitration
arbitrator's award
challenging 22.13–22.18
availability 22.8
generally 22.8–22.11
judicial approval 22.10
stay, proceedings in 22.11
use 22.18
Attachment of earnings orders
enforcement 19.8–19.13
Avoidance of disposition orders
applicants 8.12
court powers 8.1–8.3
discretion of court 8.26–8.29
disposition, meaning of 8.13
draft orders 8.36
foreign property 8.30
inherent jurisdiction 8.37–8.41
intention of defeating claim 8.14–8.18
procedure 8.31–8.32
setting aside dispositions
consequential directions 8.25
distinction from prevention of disposition 8.19
presumption of intention to defeat claim 8.23–8.24
reviewable dispositions 8.20–8.22
statutory provision
ancillary nature of 8.9–8.11
generally 8.4–8.6
types of remedy 8.7–8.8

B

Bankruptcy
financial relief order, effect on 12.13–12.15
lump sum orders 12.24–12.31
periodical payments orders 12.32–12.34
pensions, and 10.99
property adjustment orders 12.16–12.23
Big money cases
financial needs 1.103
lump sum orders 4.19–4.30

C

Capital orders
child support
applications to court **11.21**
variation **13.7–13.8**
Case preparation
practical hints **24.14**
Change of circumstances
variation applications
discretion of court **13.28–13.34**
Charging orders
creditors' rights **12.37–12.39**
enforcement **19.17–19.20**
Children
child support
age limits **11.27–11.31**
applications to court **11.17–11.33**
calculation of **11.3, 11.4, 11.6–11.15**
capital support **11.40–11.45**
duration **11.23**
generally **11.2**
interim applications **11.48–11.50**
jurisdiction **11.18, 11.26, 11.32, 11.33**
periodic orders **11.34–11.39**
school fees **11.46–11.47**
summary of provisions **11.3–11.4**
variation **11.23**
introduction **11.1**
lump sum orders **11.40–11.45**
orders for
guidelines **1.244**
property adjustment orders **11.40–11.45**
school fees **11.46, 11.47**
welfare of **11.1, 24.4**
first consideration of court **1.52–1.54**
sale of matrimonial home **12.5, 12.12**
Clean break 2.70
consent orders **9.31**
immediate
compensation **2.93**
earning capacity **2.94**
generally **2.79–2.92, 2.96–2.98**
presumption **2.95**
Inheritance (Provision for Family and Dependants) Act1975, and **2.100–2.102**
meaning **2.71**
self-sufficiency **1.241–1.243, 24.12**
statutory provisions **2.72–2.74, 2.76**
variation applications
discretion of court **13.26–13.27**
variation, on **2.99**
when appropriate **2.77–2.78**

Cohabitation
consent orders
setting aside **18.53–18.55**
periodical payments
effect on application **2.13–2.18**
Collaborative law 22.7
Compensation 1.44–1.47
Compromising litigation
agreement of parties **1.236–1.240**
Conduct of parties
effect of **1.175**
financial conduct **1.176–1.180**
non-course of proceedings, in **1.187–1.190, 1.192**
non-financial conduct **1.181–1.186**
periodical payments, effect on **2.19**
Confiscation orders 21.12–21.22
Consent orders
child support
applications to court **11.20**
definition **9.2**
drafting
clean break **9.31**
common faults **9.32–9.33**
dismissal of claims **9.31**
generally **9.16–9.19**
recitals of agreement **9.21–9.23**
recitals of fact **9.20**
undertakings **9.24–9.30**
duty and role of court **9.4–9.8**
forms **9.34**
information required by court
exceptions **9.13–9.15**
generally **9.9–9.12**
introduction **9.1–9.3**
setting aside **18.24–18.28, 18.36–18.43**
asset valuation, dispute over **18.47–18.52**
cohabitation **18.53–18.55**
death **18.56–18.60**
fraud **18.29–18.34**
misrepresentation **18.29–18.34**
new or supervening circumstances **18.44–18.46**
non-disclosure **18.29–18.35**
other matters **18.61–18.66**
remarriage **18.53–18.55**
Contributions of parties
consideration of **1.132**
exceptional contributions **1.141–1.146**
financial contributions **1.133–1.140**
future contributions **1.173, 1.174**
non-financial contributions **1.166–1.172**
non-marital contributions **1.148–1.156**

Costs
appeals **17.41–17.42**
application of CPR **17.5**
assessment basis **17.28**
both parties, against **17.16**
capping **17.37**
claims for **17.24–17.25**
clean sheet principle **17.17–17.20**
client care **17.31–17.33**
court discretion **17.5, 17.16**
detailed assessment **17.27, 17.30**
failure to comply with rules **17.9**
financial effect of order on parties **17.9**
funding **17.43–17.49**
future developments **17.34–17.37**
general principles **17.5**
general rule **17.6–17.16**
information about **17.21–17.23**
introduction **17.1–17.4**
legal aid **17.43**
litigation misconduct **17.13**
matters to guide the court **17.9**
non-parties, against **17.38–17.40**
open offers **17.32–17.33**
orders, types of **17.15**
payment of **17.29–17.30**
proportionality **17.11**
quantifying **17.26–17.28**
solicitors' expenses **17.44–17.49**
summary assessment **17.26–17.27**
Creditors' rights
generally **12.35–12.42**
introduction **12.1**
Criminal property
confiscation/restraint orders **21.12–21.22**
Crypto-assets
enforcement **19.57**

D

Death
consent orders
setting aside **18.56–18.60**
Defined benefit scheme
features of **10.12**
private sector, in **10.14**
public service pensions **10.13**
Defined contribution scheme
features of **10.12**
occupational schemes **10.15**
personal pensions, as **10.16**
Deferred orders
variation **13.4**
Delivery up
sale of property orders **7.14–7.15**

Disability
Consideration of **1.131**
Disclosure
financial resources **1.67–1.70**
Discretion
All circumstances **1.48–1.51**
avoidance of disposition orders **8.26–8.29**
child support orders **11.24–11.25**
exercise of, principles for **1.8–1.12, 1.55–1.60**
variation of orders
change of circumstances **13.28–13.34**
clean break **13.26–13.27**
generally **13.22–13.25**
Dismissal of claims
consent orders **9.31**
Disposition
meaning **8.13**
Dissipated assets
financial resources, establishment of **1.88–1.89**
Dispute resolution
generally **22.1**
Dividend yield
business valuation
lump sum orders **4.44**
Division of assets
ability to provide **24.8**
clean break **24.12**
housing needs **24.9**
pensions **24.13**
reasonable needs **24.8**
redistribution of capital **24.10**
starting point **24.7**
yardstick of equality **24.11**
Divorce
overseas divorce
financial relief after **15.1–15.4, 15.6–15.21**
pension attachment orders **10.7**
pensions on, background to **10.6–10.10**
separation grounds
financial provision on **14.10–14.18**
Drafting
consent orders
clean break **9.31**
common faults **9.32, 9.33**
dismissal of claims **9.31**
generally **9.16–9.19**
recitals of agreement **9.21–9.23**
recitals of fact **9.20**
undertakings **9.24–9.30**
Duration
child support orders **11.23**
Duration of marriage
short marriages **1.110–1.130**

Duxbury order
big money cases **4.24–4.30**
generally **4.2**

E

Enforcement
adjustment of orders **19.45**
attachment of earnings **19.8–19.13**
bankruptcy, effect of **19.48–19.49**
burden of proof **19.29–19.30**
charging orders **19.17–19.20**
committal for contempt of court **19.39–
19.40**
CPR, application of **19.24**
crypto-assets, against **19.57**
execution of documents by third
party **17.36, 19.38**
freezing injunction **19.51**
'Hadkinson' orders **19.42–19.44**
introduction **19.1–19.2**
judgment summons **19.25–19.31**
orders available **19.31**
passport, surrender of **19.41**
payments, means of **19.46**
pension sharing orders **10.96–10.97**
property, sale of **19.32–19.36**
receiver, appointment of **19.50**
reciprocal **19.56**
reform **19.58**
registration of order **19.52**
third party debt orders **19.14–19.16**
types **19.3–19.7**
undertakings **19.47**
variation, and **19.53–19.55**
warrants of control **19.21–19.23**
Equality of spouses
all circumstances **1.48–1.51**
case-law **1.17–1.24**
Charman v Charman **1.32–1.33**
case-law since **1.34–1.42**
emphasis on **24.4**
generally **1.13–1.16**
legitimate expectations **1.25–1.26**
lump sum orders
big money cases **4.19–4.30**
smaller money cases **1.27–1.31**
standard of living **1.25–1.26**
yardstick **24.11**
Evidence
documents required **16.22**
expert evidence **16.32–16.35**
filing of **16.19–16.21**
Ex parte orders
search orders **8.49–8.50**

Execution of documents
third party, by **17.36–19.38**
Expert evidence
pension sharing cases, in
procedure for instruction **10.38–10.40**
type of expert **10.36–10.37**
when to instruct **10.32–10.35**
procedure **16.32–16.35**

F

Facts
importance of findings **24.5–24.6**
Fair trial, right to 20.8–20.12
Fairness
agreements of parties **1.212–1.215**
all the circumstances **1.48–1.51**
case-law **1.17–1.24**
Charman v Charman **1.32–1.33**
case-law since **1.34–1.42**
generally **1.13–1.16**
legitimate expectations **1.25–1.26**
smaller money cases **1.27–1.31**
standard of living **1.25, 1.26**
Family Justice Review
reforms, and **23.15**
Family life, right to 20.13–20.16
FDR hearing
evidence, filing of **16.21**
private **22.19–22.20**
procedure **16.36–16.43**
Final hearing
procedure **16.44–16.45**
**Financial needs, obligations and
responsibilities**
big money cases **1.103**
consideration of **1.98–1.100**
meaning **1.101, 1.102**
Financial order
definition **1.5–1.7**
Financial provision
clean break, and **2.100–2.102**
Financial relief
meaning **8.5–8.6**
Financial remedies
definitions **1.5–1.7**
introduction **1.1–1.4**
Financial resources
application for consideration of
introduction **14.1, 14.10–14.18**
court duty to establish **1.61–1.66**
disclosure, duty of **1.67–1.70**
dissipated assets **1.88, 1.89**
expectations **1.90–1.97**

Financial resources – *cont.*
income and earnings
'earning potential' **1.73**
generally **1.71–1.72**
pension, as **10.4**
property **1.74–1.87**
First appointment
evidence, filing of **16.21**
procedure **16.27–16.31**
Foreign property
avoidance of disposition orders **8.30**
Fraud
consent orders
setting aside **18.29–18.34**
Freezing injunctions
court powers **8.2**
origins **8.42–8.43**
Practice Direction **8.46–8.47**
purpose of **8.42–8.43**
statutory basis for **8.44**
transfer to High Court **8.44**

G

Grave financial hardship
third party creditors' rights **12.40–12.42**

H

High Court
transfer to
freezing injunctions **8.44**
search orders **8.51**
Housing needs
importance of **24.9**
transfer of property orders **5.3, 5.11–5.16**
Human rights
1998 Act, effect in practice of **20.7–20.16**
introduction **20.1, 20.2**
overview **20.3–20.6**
public authorities, acts of **20.5**
right to fair trial **20.8–20.12**
right to private and family
life **20.13–20.16**

I

Inherent jurisdiction
avoidance of dispositions **8.2, 8.37–8.41**
Injunctions
avoidance of dispositions **8.2**

Insolvency
bankruptcy order
financial relief order, effect on **12.13–12.15**
introduction **12.1**
lump sum orders **12.24–12.31**
matrimonial home, and **12.2–12.12**
periodical payments orders **12.32–12.34**
property adjustment orders, and **12.16–12.23**
third-party creditors' rights **12.35–12.42**
Interim orders
child support **11.48–11.50**
procedure **16.53–16.55**
sale of property orders **7.13**
Interim sale of property
sale of property orders **7.15**
Issue of application
procedure **16.8–16.12**
Issue of proceedings
procedure **16.4–16.6**

J

Joint property
sale of property orders **7.10, 7.11**
Judgment summons
enforcement **19.25–19.31**
Judicial separation
pension attachment orders **10.7**
Jurisdiction
child support **11.18, 11.26, 11.32–11.33**
generally **1.247–1.253**
neglect to maintain
financial provision in cases of **14.4, 14.5**
sale of property orders **7.12**
search orders **8.51**

L

Legal aid
abolition **17.47**
Legal services order 2.61–2.65
Legitimate expectation
equality and fairness **1.25, 1.26**
Litigation loan 17.45–17.46
Lost benefits, effect of 1.193–1.198
Lump sum orders
assets not exceeding needs **4.18**
bankruptcy, effect of **12.24–12.31**
big money cases **4.3, 4.19–4.30**

Index

Lump sum orders – *cont.*
business cases
valuation **4.31–4.52**
calculation of **4.14–4.18**
child support **11.40–11.45**
instalments
variation **13.15**
introduction **4.1–4.3**
number of **4.5–4.11**
statutory provisions **4.4**
tax **4.53–4.55**
variation **13.4**

M

Magistrates' court
registration of order in **19.52**
Maintenance pending suit 2.55–2.60
form of order **2.67, 2.68**
variation **13.4, 13.9–13.13**
Martin orders
settlement of property **6.5–6.6**
transfer of property **5.37, 5.38**
Matrimonial home
insolvency, and **12.2–12.12**
order for sale of **12.3–12.12**
Matrimonial property
establishing extent of **1.74–1.87**
meaning **24.6**
**Mediation Information and Assessment
Meetings**
requirement **16.8, 22.2–22.6**
Mesher orders
settlement of property **6.5–6.6**
transfer of property **5.29–5.36**
Misrepresentation
consent orders
setting aside **18.29–18.34**
Money laundering
proceeds of crime **21.3–21.5**

N

National Crime Agency
proceeds of crime **21.6**
Needs
division of assets, and **24.8**
Neglect to maintain
financial provision in cases of **14.1–14.9**
Non-disclosure
consent orders
setting aside **18.29–18.43**
Nullity
pension attachment orders **10.7**

Nullity – *cont.*
pension sharing **10.8**

O

Occupational pensions
defined contribution scheme, as **10.16**
Open offers
costs, and **17.32–17.33**
Orders
combination of **1.4, 4.2**
jurisdiction **1.247–1.253**
timing of **1.245, 1.246**
Overriding objective 16.7
Overseas divorce
financial relief after **15.1**
jurisdiction **15.2–15.5**
permission, applications for **15.6–15.13**
types of order **15.14–15.24**

P

Parties
age **1.108–1.109**
joinders **16.15–16.16**
Pension attachment orders
death benefits, securing, by **10.67**
disadvantages of **10.64–10.65**
features of **10.61–10.63**
generally **10.7, 10.10**
implementation **10.69**
'income-gap' cases, in **10.66**
restrictions **10.68**
variation **10.94–10.95**
Pension Protection Fund
compensation
cap **10.86**
orders available **10.88**
defined benefit pension schemes,
and **10.89–10.90**
establishment **10.86**
Financial Assistance Scheme, and **10.89**
procedural issues **10.87**
Pension sharing orders
arrangements under **10.41–10.43**
disadvantages **10.48–10.51**
enforcement **10.96, 10.97**
implementation **10.52–10.58**
legislation affecting **10.8, 10.10**
pension freedoms, and **10.56, 10.59–10.60**
restrictions **10.47**
state pension rights **10.44–10.46**
variation **10.94–10.95, 13.4**
Pensions
asset, as **10.1**

530

Pensions – *cont.*
    bankruptcy, and **10.99**
    defined benefit scheme **10.12–10.14**
    defined contribution scheme **10.12, 10.15**
    divorce on, background to **10.6–10.10**
    entitlement to **24.13**
    'freedoms', Taxation of Pensions Act 2014
        under **10.1, 10.9–10.10, 10.56,**
        10.59–10.60
    guidance **10.21–10.25**
    income or capital **10.5**
    needs, MCA 1973, s 25 under **10.81**
        discounting
            post-marital pension contribu-
                tions **10.83**
            pre-marital pension contribu-
                tions **10.82**
        health issues **10.84–10.85**
    orders available **10.11**
    overseas pensions **10.91–10.93**
    pension attachment orders **10.7, 10.10,**
        10.61–10.69
    pension offsetting **10.70–10.80**
    pension sharing **10.8, 10.10, 10.41–10.60**
    procedure **16.18**
    rights, variation **13.16–13.18**
    same sex couple **10.98**
    state pension **10.17–10.20**
    types of **10.12–10.20**
    valuation **10.21–10.25**
        expert evidence, for **10.31–10.40**
        needs, assessment **10.26–10.30**
Pension Advisory Group (PAG)
    formation **10.3**
    guidance **10.33**
Periodic orders
    child support **11.34–11.39**
Periodical payments order
    amount **2.21–2.52**
    applicant **2.5**
    bankruptcy, and **12.32–12.34**
    clean break **2.10, 2.11, 2.70, 2.94, 2.95**
        immediate **2.79–2.92, 2.95–2.98**
        meaning **2.71**
        statutory provisions **2.72–2.74, 2.76**
        when appropriate **2.77–2.78**
    compensation **2.93**
    definitions **2.3–2.4**
    duration, limit **2.53–2.54**
    extension of terms **2.103**
    factors for court **2.9**
        cohabitation **2.13–2.18**
        conduct **2.19**
        earning capacity/potential **2.12**
        length of marriage **2.20**
        need for order **2.10–2.11**

Periodical payments order – *cont.*
    form of order **2.67–2.68**
    general principles **2.7–2.8**
    introduction **2.1–2.2**
    pension funding **10.6**
    procedure for application **2.6**
    remarriage **2.10–2.11**
    secured periodical payments
        circumstances for **3.15–3.17**
        introduction **3.1–3.2**
        nature of **3.5–3.14**
        statutory provisions **3.3–3.4**
        variation **3.18**
    tax considerations **2.69**
    variation **13.4, 13.9–13.13**
Permission to appeal 18.3–18.9
Post-separation accruals 1.157–1.165
Practice Direction
    consent orders
        information required by court **9.9–9.12**
    freezing injunctions **8.46, 8.47**
Pre-emptive remedies
    prevention of disposition **8.7–8.8**
Personal pensions
    defined contribution scheme, as **10.16**
Private life, right to 20.13–20.16
Procedure
    appeals **18.23**
    arbitration **22.13–22.18**
    communications with court **16.61**
    court bundles **16.59**
    costs, application of CPR **17.5**
    disclosure orders **16.50–16.52**
    documents **16.22**
    evidence, filing of **16.19–16.21**
    expert evidence **16.32–16.35**
    'fast-track' procedure **16.56, 16.57**
    FDR hearing **16.36–16.43**
    final hearing **16.44, 16.45**
        transparency **16.49**
    first appointment **16.27–16.31**
    interim orders **16.53–16.55**
    introduction **16.1–16.3**
    issue of application **16.8–16.12**
        delay **16.10–16.12**
        Form A **16.9**
    issue of proceedings **16.4–16.6**
    litigants in person **16.60**
    Mediation Information and Assessment
        Meetings **16.8**
    order
        drafting and submission **16.46–16.48**
    overriding objective **16.7**
    parties
        joinder of **16.15–16.16**
    pensions **16.18**

Procedure – *cont.*
  protocols, use of 16.58
  questionnaires 16.25–16.26
  requests for documents 16.25–16.26
  sanctions, relief from 16.62
  service 16.13–16.17
  skeleton arguments 16.59
  statement of apparent issues 16.23–16.24
Proceeds of crime
  anti-money laundering regulations 21.3–21.5
  criminal property, confiscation of 21.12–21.22
  introduction 21.1–21.2
  Money Laundering Reporting Officer, appointment 21.5
  offences 21.6–21.11
  purpose of POCA 2002 21.9–21.11
  tax fraud 21.7–21.8
Property adjustment orders
  children 11.40–11.45
  insolvency, and 12.16–12.23
Property
  criminal, confiscation of 21.12–21.22
Protocols
  use of 16.58
Public authorities, acts of
  human rights 20.5
Public sector pensions
  defined benefit scheme, as 10.16

Q

Questionnaires
  procedure 16.25–16.26

R

Receiver
  appointment of 19.50
Reciprocal enforcement 19.56
Recitals of agreement
  consent orders 9.21–9.23
Recitals of fact
  consent orders 9.20
Redistribution of capital
  purpose of 24.10
Reforms
  Family Justice Review 23.15
  generally 23.2–23.11
  introduction 23.1
Registration of order
  magistrates' court, in 19.52

Remarriage
  consent orders
    setting aside 18.53–18.55
  periodical payments
    effect on application 2.10–2.11
Requests for documents
  procedure 16.25–16.26
Restraint orders 21.12–21.22
Right to fair trial 20.8–20.12

S

Sale of property orders
  ancillary provisions 7.7–7.9
  delivery up 7.14–7.15
  interim orders 7.13
  introduction 7.1
  joint property 7.10–7.11
  jurisdiction, exercise of 7.12
  matrimonial home 12.3–12.12
  statutory provision
    ancillary nature of 7.3–7.6
    ancillary provisions 7.7–7.9
    generally 7.2
  term 7.3–7.6
  trusts of land 7.16–7.19
  variation 13.4
Same sex couple
  pension rights 10.98
School fees
  children 11.46–11.47
Search orders
  Court powers 8.2
  ex parte orders 8.49–8.50
  generally 8.48
  rarity of 8.49–8.50
  transfer to High Court 8.51
Secured creditors
  rights of 12.35–12.36
Secured periodical payments
  circumstances for 3.15–3.17
  introduction 3.1–3.2
  nature of
    amount 3.9
    generally 3.5
    lodging with paying party 3.13–3.14
    security 3.6, 3.10–3.12
    term 3.7–3.8
  statutory provisions 3.3–3.4
  variation 3.18, 13.4, 13.14
Separation
  divorce on grounds of
    financial provision on 14.10–14.18
Service
  procedure 16.13–16.17

Setting aside
  appeals or **18.67–18.68**
  avoidance of dispositions
    consequential direction **8.25**
    distinction from prevention of disposition **8.19**
    presumption of intention to defeat claim **8.23–8.24**
    reviewable dispositions **8.20–8.22**
  consent orders **18.24–18.28, 18.36–18.43**
    asset valuation, dispute over **18.47–18.52**
    cohabitation **18.53–18.55**
    death **18.56–18.60**
    fraud **18.29–18.34**
    misrepresentation **18.29–18.34**
    new or supervening circumstances **18.44–18.46**
    non-disclosure **18.29–18.35**
    other matters **18.61–18.66**
    remarriage **18.53–18.55**
  introduction **18.1–18.2**
  rehearing, following **18.70–18.71**
Settlement
  meaning **6.4**
Settlement of property orders
  introduction **6.1**
  power to settle **6.6**
  rarity of **6.5**
  settlement, meaning of **6.4**
  statutory provisions **6.2–6.3**
  variation **13.4, 13.19, 13.20**
    approach of court **6.8**
    court powers **6.20–6.23**
    generally **6.7**
    proof of settlement **6.9–6.19**
Short marriage
  duration, effect of **1.110–1.130**
  periodical payments, effect on **2.20**
Skeleton arguments
  length of **16.59**
Smaller money cases
  equality and fairness **1.27–1.31**
Standard of living
  equality and fairness **1.25, 1.26**
  generally **1.104–1.107**
State pension
  Old State Pension **10.18**
  New State Pension **10.19**
  sharing of rights **10.44–10.46**
  State Pension Credit **10.19**
Statement of apparent issues
  requirements **16.23–16.24**
Statutory provisions
  primacy of **24.3–24.4**

T

Tax
  lump sum orders **4.53–4.55**
Tenancies
  fraud **21.7–21.8**
  transfer of property orders **5.4, 5.41–5.49**
Third party debt orders
  enforcement **19.14–19.16**
Transactions at an undervalue
  property adjustment orders **12.16–12.23**
Transfer of property orders
  basis for **5.11–5.16**
  housing needs **5.3**
  introduction **5.1–5.4**
  rules **5.10**
  statutory provisions **5.5–5.9**
  tenancies **5.41–5.49**
  types of
    generally **5.17–5.18**
    Martin orders **5.37–5.38**
    Mesher orders **5.29–5.36**
    other orders **5.39, 5.40**
    outright transfer **5.19–5.24**
    transfer subject to charge **5.25–5.28**
Trusts of land
  sale of property orders **7.16–7.19**

U

Undertakings
  consent orders **9.24–9.30**
  variation **13.21**
Urgent ex parte applications
  consent orders **9.15**

V

Valuation
  businesses
    dividend yield **4.44**
    lump sum orders **4.31–4.52**
  consent orders
    disputed **18.47–18.52**
Variation
  capital orders **13.7–13.8**
  child support orders **11.23**
  conditions, subject to **13.37–13.39**
  court powers **13.5**
  discretion of court
    change of circumstances **13.28–13.34**
    clean break **13.26–13.27**
    generally **13.22–13.25**
  factors for court to consider **13.6**
  introduction **13.1–13.2**

Variation – *cont.*
  lump sum orders by instalments 13.15
  maintenance pending suit 13.9–13.13
  orders capable of 13.3–13.6
  pension rights 13.16–13.18
  periodical payments order 13.9–13.13
  procedure 13.35
  secured periodical payments 3.18–13.14
  settlement of property orders 13.19–13.20
    approach of court 6.8
    court powers 6.20–6.23
    generally 6.7

Variation – *cont.*
  settlement of property orders – *cont.*
    proof of settlement 6.9–6.19
  statutory provisions 13.3–13.6

W

Welfare of child
  first consideration of court 1.52–1.54,
    11.1